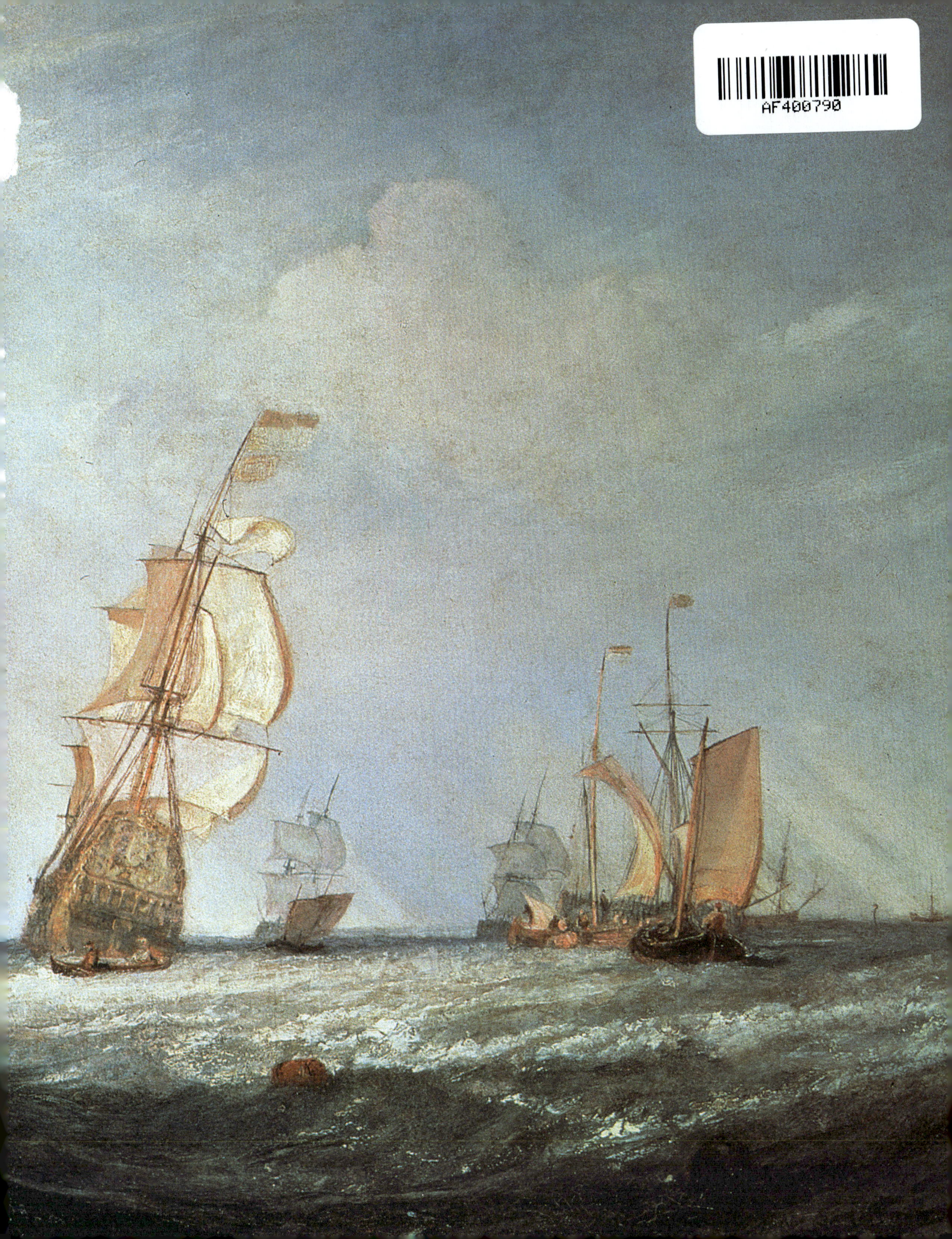

AF400790

TURNER

HIS LIFE AND WORKS IN 500 IMAGES

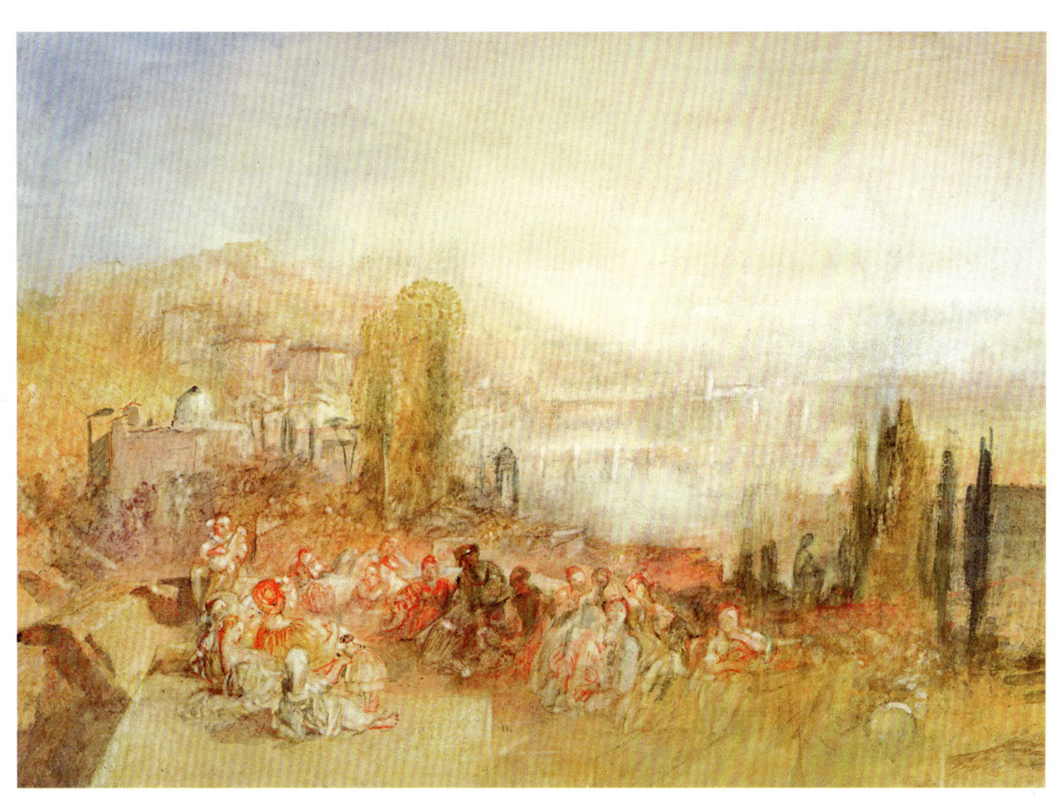

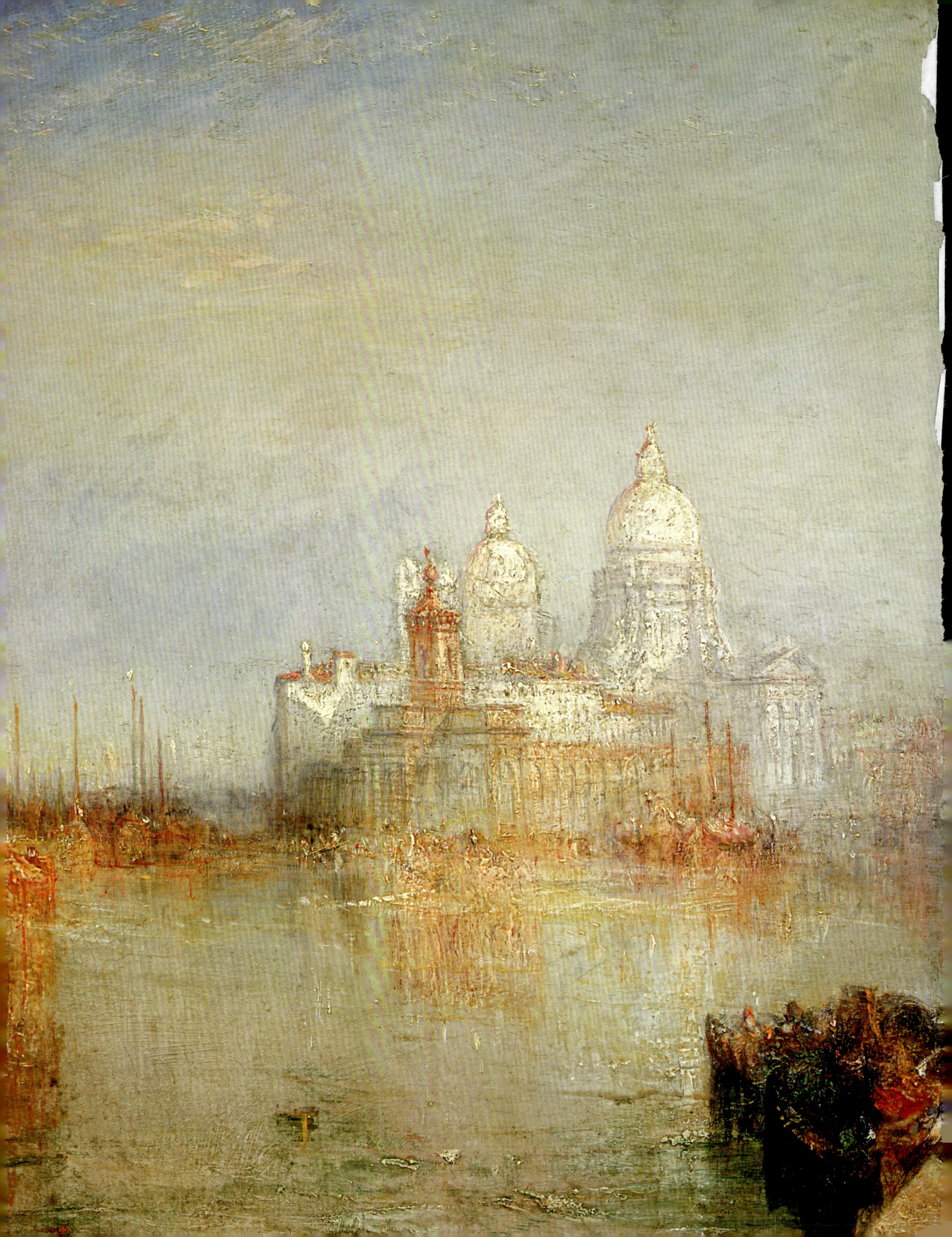

TURNER

HIS LIFE AND WORKS IN 500 IMAGES

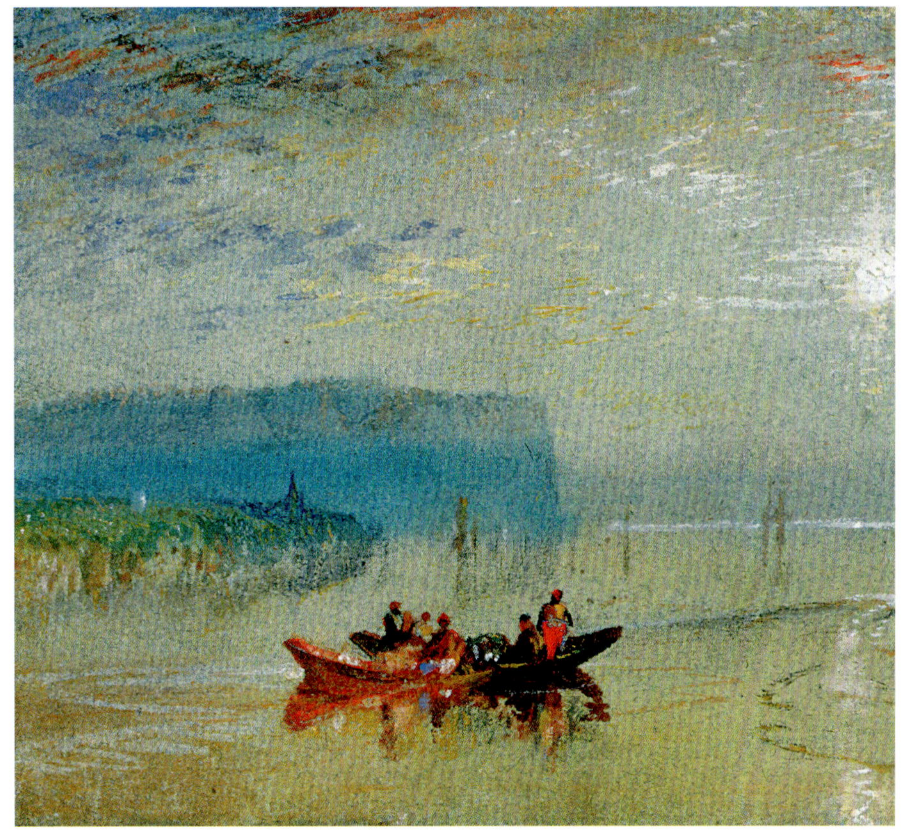

AN ILLUSTRATED EXPLORATION OF THE ARTIST, HIS LIFE AND
CONTEXT, WITH A GALLERY OF 300 OF HIS FINEST PAINTINGS

MICHAEL ROBINSON

LORENZ BOOKS

This edition is published by Lorenz Books, an imprint of Anness Publishing Ltd, 108 Great Russell Street, London WC1B 3NA; info@anness.com

www.lorenzbooks.com;
www.annesspublishing.com;
twitter: @Anness_Books

Anness Publishing has a new picture agency outlet for images for publishing, promotions or advertising. Please visit our website www.practicalpictures.com for more information.

Publisher: Joanna Lorenz
Project Editor: Anne Hildyard
Designer: Sarah Rock
Production Controller: Stephanie Moe

PUBLISHER'S NOTE
Although the information in this book is believed to be accurate and true at the time of going to press, neither the authors nor the publisher can accept any legal responsibility or liability for any errors or omissions that may have been made.

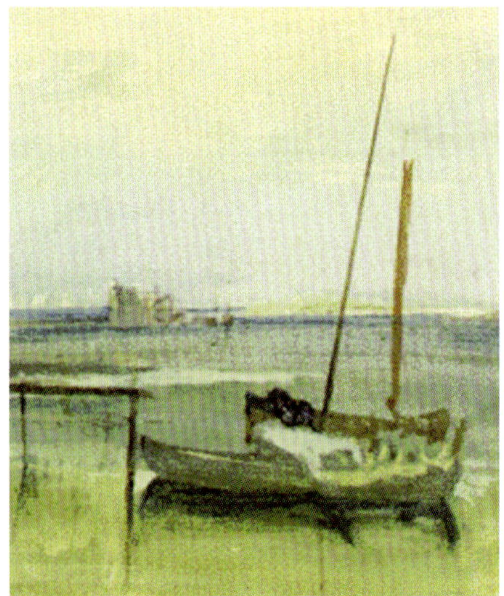

PICTURE ACKNOWLEDGEMENTS
Art Archive: British Museum: 5c, 7r, 24t, 71tr, 129t; Tate Britain: 5c, 20t, 58l, 61tl, 93t, 96b, 114b, 128t, 134c, 148b, 178b, 181, 206c, 209b, 216, 223 (both), 229b, 234, 243b, 244b, 248c, 249t; Gulbenkian Foundation, Lisbon: 126t; Private Collection: 141t; Victoria & Albert Museum, London, UK: 248c;
Bridgeman Art Library: Abbot Hall Art Gallery, UK: 6l, 178t; Allen Memorial Art Museum, Ohio, USA: 237t; Anglesey Abbey, UK: 24b; The Argory, County Armagh, Northern Ireland: 36b; Art Gallery and Museum, Kelvingrove, Scotland, UK: 227b; Art Gallery of New South Wales, Australia: 51; Art Gallery of South Australia: 138b; Ashmolean Museum, Oxford, UK: 3, 38b, 56t, 73t, 90l, 95tr, 95b, 173, 193b, 195c; The Barber Institute of Fine Arts, Birmingham, UK: 30, 56b, 136t; The Berger Collection at the Denver Art Museum, UK: 76r; Birmingham Museums and Art Gallery, UK: 7t, 169t; Blackburn Museum and Art Gallery, UK: 161, 198c, 221; Bolton Museum and Art Gallery, UK: 44b, 59t, 174b; The Bowes Museum, UK: 55t, 164t; British Library, London, UK: 214t; British Museum: 7b, 13b, 27tr, 48 (both), 67t, 68tr, 75br, 83t, 113t, 136b, 139t, 160c, 179b, 180c, 182t, 185b, 189, 206t, 215b, 219b, 230b, 233t, 244t; Bury Art Gallery, UK: 193t; Carisbrooke Castle Museum, Isle of Wight, UK: 72b; Cecil Higgins Art Gallery, Bedford, UK: 15t, 20b, 35t, 117t, 167b, 170t, 179t, 227t; Corpus Christi College, Oxford, UK: 91b; Courtauld Institute, UK: 49t, 167t, 238t; Fitzwilliam Museum, Cambridge, UK: 17t, 28t, 31b, 42 (both), 43t, 52t, 63t, 64 (both), 68br, 71br, 87, 104b, 127, 131t, 132b, 133b, 140t, 141t, 142, 144, 146, 147 (both), 148t, 149b, 150b, 155b, 156, 157c, 162b, 165b, 168t, 169b, 183b, 185t, 186t, 202b, 207b, 213t, 225t, 232, 236c, 241c, 243t, 247t, 251t; Fogg Art Museum, Harvard, USA: 184, 188c; Getty Museum, LA, USA: 247c; Goethe National Museum, Germany: 89b; Guildhall Art Gallery, London, UK: 13t, 41bl, 180t; Guildhall Library, London, UK: 14t, 18, 31tl, 57t, 76tl, 92t, 94; Hamburger Kunsthalle, Germany: 43b, 66t; Harrogate Museum, UK: 175b; Hunterian Art Gallery, Glasgow, UK: 97b; Indianapolis Museum of Art, USA: 17t, 19bl, 19br, 63b, 82b, 98, 102t, 105b, 120, 121, 159t, 165t, 176, 187t, 202c, 211b, 237b, 238b; The Israel Museum, Jerusalem: 217b; The Iveagh Bequest, Kenwood House, London, UK: 126b; Kimbell Art Museum, Fort Worth, USA: 239t; Lady Lever Art Gallery, Liverpool, UK: 208t, 239b; Leeds Art Gallery, UK: 20t, 22b, 29t, 53t, 58r, 104t, 110b, 118b, 119b, 123t, 152c, 152b, 155t, 162t, 170b, 220b, 229t, 236l; Lloyds, London, UK: 80l; Louvre, Paris, France: 36b, 218b; Maidstone Museum and Art Gallery, UK: 78bl; Manchester Art Gallery, UK: 70, 92b, 218t, 250b; Musée des Beaux-Arts, Arras, France: 32t; Musée Marmottan, Paris, France: 96t; Museu Calouste Gulbenkian, Lisbon, Portugal: 55b; National Gallery, London, UK: 27b, 34t, 57b, 77, 122b, 130, 151b, 190t, 226b, 228c, 246; National Gallery of Art, Washington, USA: 2, 245t; National Gallery of Victoria, Australia: 117c, 242b; National Museum and Gallery of Wales, UK: 22t, 215b, 219t, 231t, 248b, 251c; Nationalmuseum, Stockholm, Sweden: 251b; New Walk Museum, Leicester, UK: 100; Noortman, Maastricht, Netherlands: 61tr; Nottingham Castle, UK: 205t; Petworth House, Sussex, UK: 37t, 39t, 40. 44t, 46bl, 47t, 73b, 79t, 122t, 128b, 131c, 133t, 134t, 134b, 143, 147, 150t, 177b, 188t, 188b; Philadelphia Museum of Art: 6r; Private Collection: 1; 15b, 16b, 19t, 26, 27tl, 28b, 31tr, 34b, 38t, 39b, 41t, 46br, 52b, 60, 62b, 66b, 67b, 72t, 75bl, 79b, 80r, 81t, 84 (both), 85t, 86tl, 88t, 90r, 91t, 95tl, 101, 107c, 116, 124b, 125t, 126c, 137 (both), 145, 149t, 152t, 157b, 158b, 160b, 163b, 170c, 171, 177c, 183t, 185c, 187b, 195t, 196b, 199, 200, 203, 204t, 206b, 211t, 212, 213c, 213b, 214b, 217c, 220t, 220c, 222b, 224, 226b, 228b, 230t, 236b, 245b, 247b; Reading University, UK: 11; The Royal Institution, London, UK: 59t, 76bl; Roy Miles Fine Paintings: 68tl, 78br; Schloss Charlottenburg, Berlin, Germany: 32b; Sheffield Galleries and Museums Trust, UK: 5, 222t; Sir John Soane's Museum, London, UK: 45 (both), 117b, 204b; Southampton City Art Gallery, UK: 54l, 123b; Tabley House Collection, University of Manchester, UK: 47b, 65 (both); Tate Britain: 20t, 249t; UCL Art Collections, London, UK: 241b; University of Liverpool Art Gallery & Collections, UK: 115b, 135, 152c, 154t, 158t, 225c; Tokyo Fuji Art Museum, Japan: 210b; Usher Gallery, Lincoln, UK: 37b, 186b; Victoria & Albert Museum, London, UK: 74, 102b, 118t, 164b, 182b, 191 (both), 198t, 202t, 233c, 233b, 235, 248c; Victoria Art Gallery, Bath, UK: 113c; Walker Art Gallery, Liverpool, UK: 88b, 138t, 240b; Walters Art Museum, Baltimore, USA: 61l; Whitworth Art Gallery, University of Manchester, UK: 10, 12, 83b, 85b, 105t, 107t, 108b, 140b, 141b, 163t, 205b, 225b, 242t, 178b; Wolverhampton Art Gallery, UK: 16t; Worcester Art Museum, USA: 190b; Yale Center for British Art, USA: 4, 5, 8, 20b, 23b, 25t, 25b, 29b, 32 (both), 35b, 41br, 48b, 50, 53b, 54r, 62t, 68, 71tl, 71bl, 75t, 81b, 82t, 86bl, 86r, 93b, 97t, 102c, 103, 106, 107b, 108t, 109 (both), 110t, 111t, 111b, 112, 113b, 114t, 115t, 119t, 125b, 129b, 131b, 132t, 139t, 145b, 146 (both), 151t, 153, 154b, 157t, 159b, 160t, 166, 167c, 168b, 174t, 175t, 177t, 180b, 192 (both), 194, 195b, 196t, 197 (both), 198b, 201, 207t, 209t, 210t, 217t, 228t, 241t, 248t, 249b, 250t, 250c; York Art Gallery, UK: 23t, 240t; **Corbis**: Burstein Collection: 89t, 231b; The Gallery Collection: 124t; Philadelphia Museum of Art, USA: 6r; Value Art: 172, 209b.

Page 1: Florence, *1851*.

Page 2: The Dogana and Santa Maria della Salute, Venice, *1843*.

Page 3: Scene on the Loire, near the Côteaux de Mauves, c.*1830*.

Page 4: Coast Scene with White Cliffs and Boats on Shore, c.*19C*.

Page 5: Portrait of JMW Turner, *Cornelius Varley, 19C*; Angel Standing in the Sun, c.*1846*; The Fighting Temeraire, Tugged to Her Last Berth to Be Broken Up, *1838*.

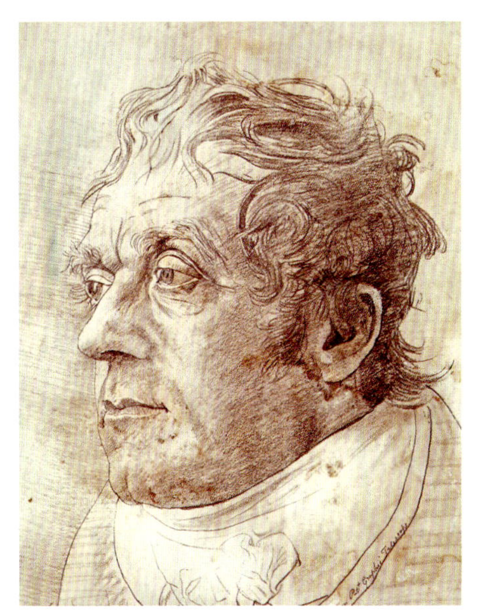 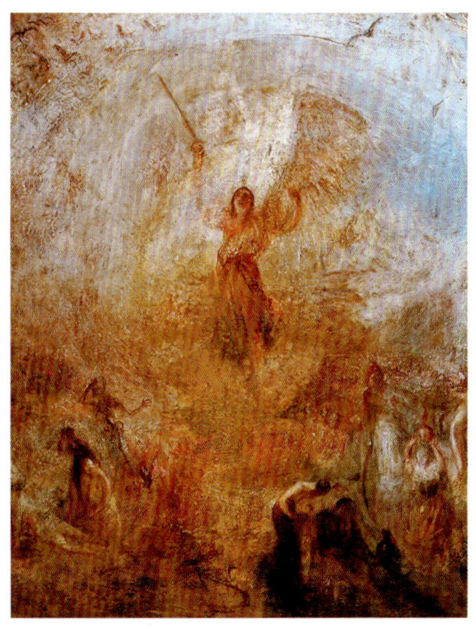 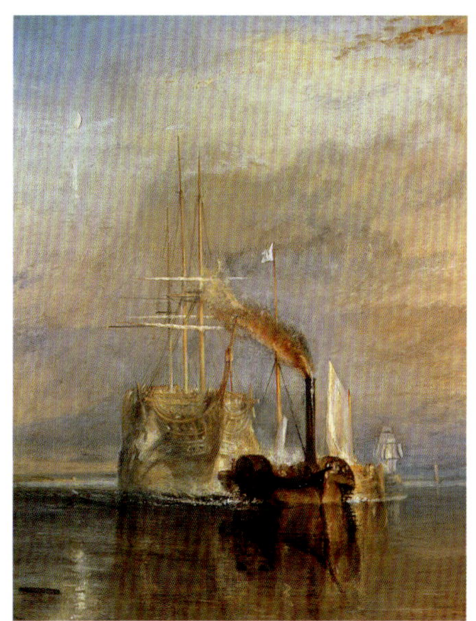

CONTENTS

INTRODUCTION

Turner was a wealth of contradictions: a flamboyant showman, a recluse, a shrewd businessman and, above all, a genius. He had a lengthy career that spanned massive social change; the influence of his body of work would take even longer to be fully appreciated.

Joseph Mallord William Turner and his art are quintessentially English. He was born on St George's Day, an auspicious day in itself, but one that was possibly also shared with another artistic genius of a previous age, William Shakespeare. Turner's early passion was for landscape painting in watercolour, a particularly English tradition, but Turner's interest in painting was no genteel pastime. He was effectively a proto-Modernist. Many of his later paintings, experiments in abstraction, colour and paint techniques, were not made for public consumption, at least in his lifetime – they anticipate Impressionism and even Expressionism by several decades.

It was not until the mid-1960s, more than 100 years after his death, that an exhibition at the Museum of Modern Art, New York, made links between Turner's aesthetic and Modernist abstraction. The scholarship was further expanded in 2004 with the exhibition Turner, Whistler, Monet, showing the influence of the former on the latter two by comparing not only the ethereal effects of light in their landscapes, but also their aspirations to depict modern life. Many of the abuses hurled at Whistler and Monet about 'lack of finish' had already been thrown at Turner 50 years before. However, both Whistler and Monet rejected the Academy conventions of their day, whereas Turner, having achieved the status of Royal Academician at an early age, supported the institution his whole life. His paintings were rooted in tradition, but his long career spanned a transitional period in art, during which he became one of the main protagonists.

In the late 18th century, landscape painting was considered inferior to its history or portrait counterparts. Landscape pictures were usually represented by topographical views, or as a backdrop to a portrait or history painting. Turner began his career as a topographical artist, but after seeing the paintings of Claude Lorrain (c.1600–82), and visiting Italy, became a 'painter of light', embracing the cultural shift toward Romanticism, which eschewed the Enlightenment rationale of nature in favour of expressions of human experience. Turner's paintings also anticipated avant-gardism, a movement characterized by artists using innovative ways to question art's status quo and challenge social inequalities and injustice.

Turner was an artist of conflicting and contradictory dualisms. He wished for and then enjoyed his status as an Academician and yet, at least in the early days, he was seen as a rather

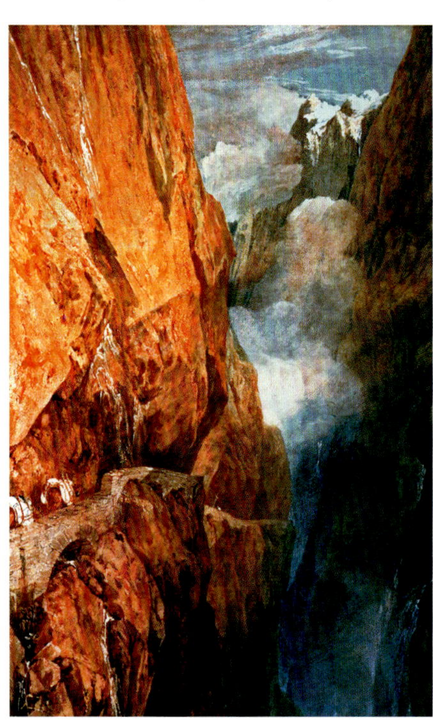

Below: The Passage of Mount St Gotthard, *watercolour, 1804. Executed after his first trip to Switzerland in 1802, defining an aesthetic shift toward Romantic notions of the landscape.*

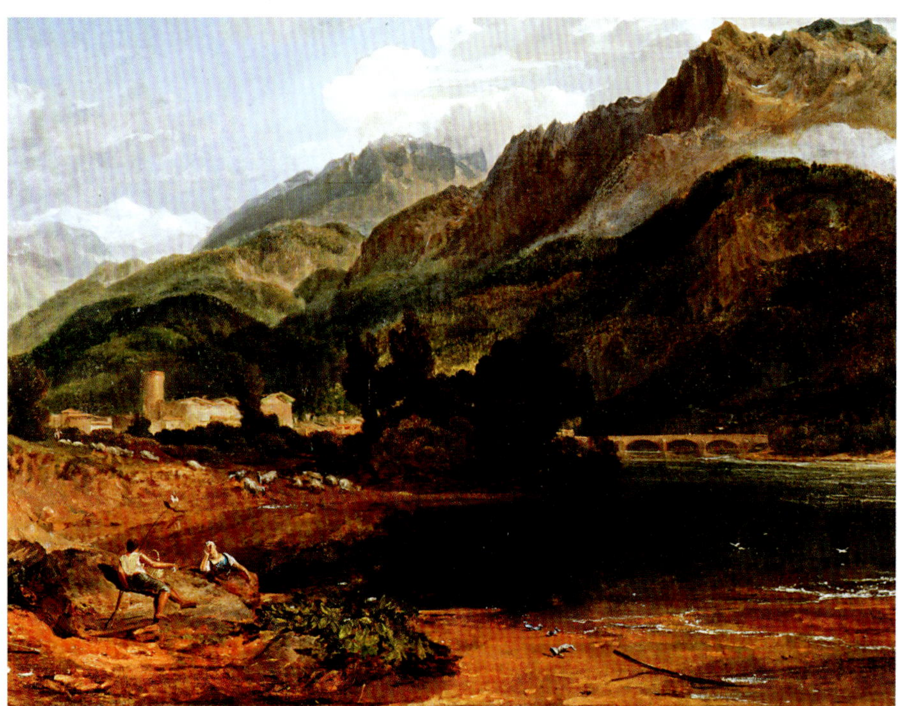

Below: A View of the Castle of St Michael, near Bonneville, Savoy, *oil on canvas, 1802. This is one of the versions that Turner painted of this view.*

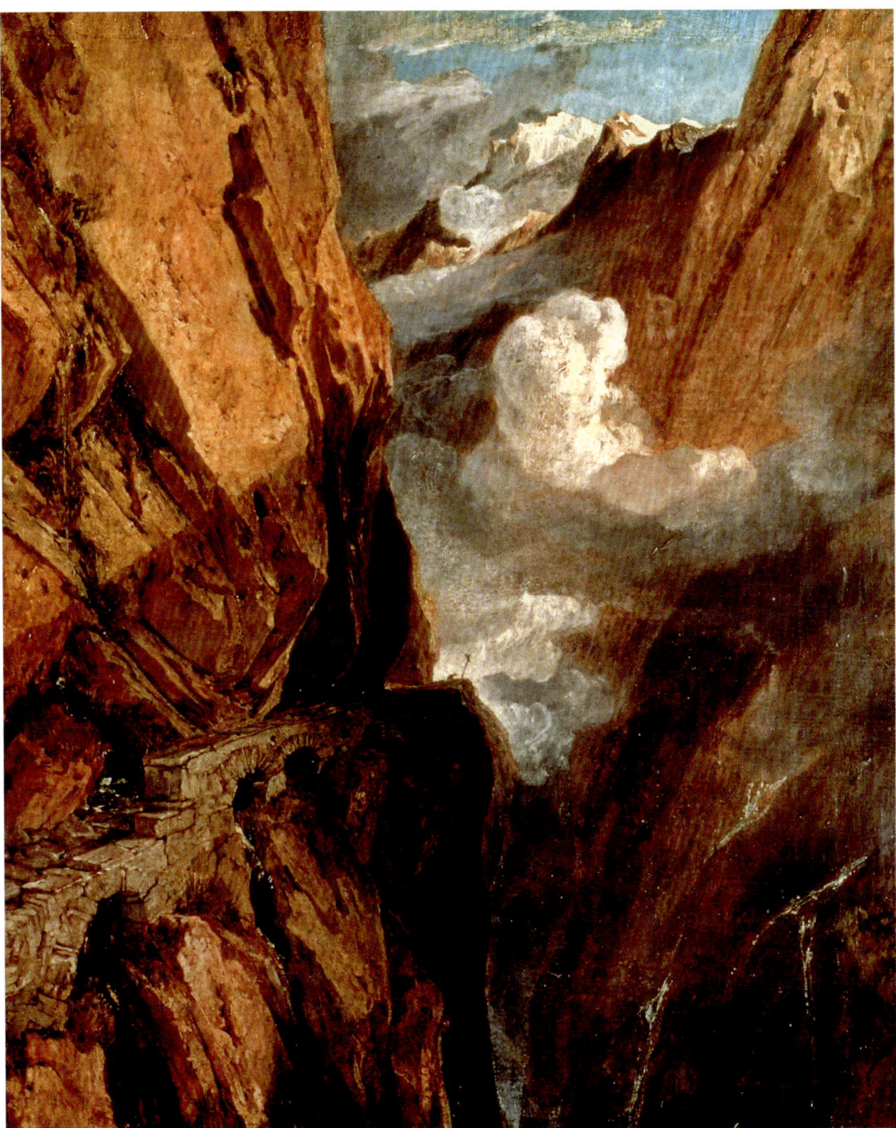

Left: The Pass of St Gotthard, *oil on canvas, 1804. An oil painting of the same subject at St Gotthard, demonstrating Turner's ability to utilize his watercolour techniques in an alternative medium.*

The first part of this book examines Turner's personal life against the backdrop of the society and political climate of his times. As the Industrial Revolution started to impact on the old agrarian order, roads were built, canals dug, factories erected and townscapes established by an increasingly peripatetic population. As a result, Turner saw a shift in artistic patronage from one that was dominated by the aristocracy, to one prevalent among the industrialists and entrepreneurs of the Industrial Age.

The second part surveys Turner's key works over his 60-year career, examining the execution, exhibition and patronage of the paintings.

The aim of this book is to provide an insight into Turner and his work, creating a springboard for further examination of this extraordinary genius and his paintings. As the writer John Ruskin said, "through his paintings the world can be seen in new ways".

Below: Swiss Figures, *watercolour, 1802. This was one of the more intimate watercolours from Turner's sketchbook.*

vulgar and offensive upstart by many fellow professionals, and was often ridiculed for his deviation from the Academic norm. His very public persona at the Academy in his later years, particularly his artistic flamboyance on Varnishing Days (the days before an exhibition when artists were able to come in and varnish their paintings or make final adjustments), contrasted with the reticence he showed concerning his private life. Turner was never married, and seemed happier in the company of his fellow Academicians or his patrons rather than the intimacy of a family. He had a sense of his own artistic genius, but this was always tempered with a pragmatism that he had inherited from his father, which ensured an appreciation of the commercial potential of his art.

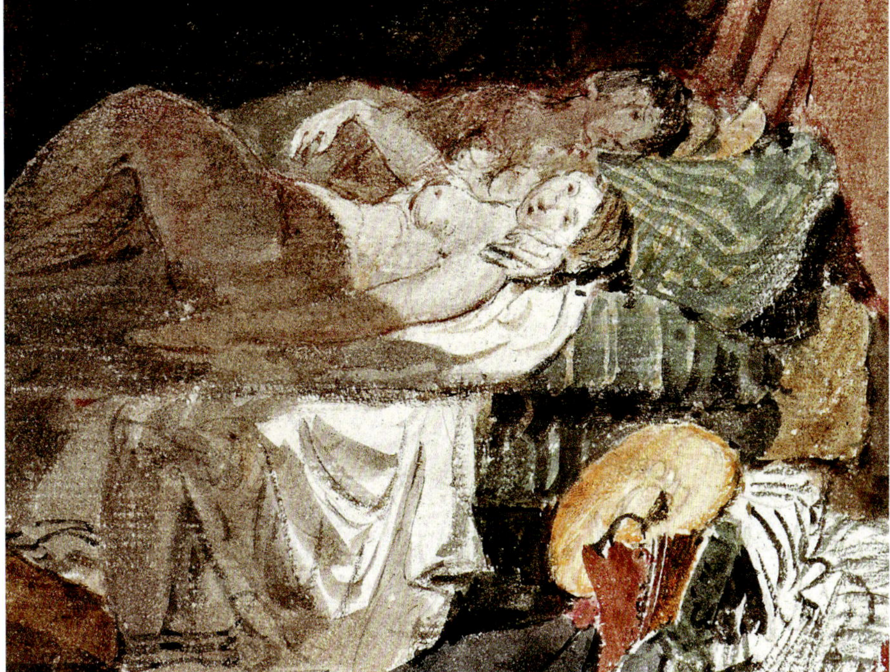

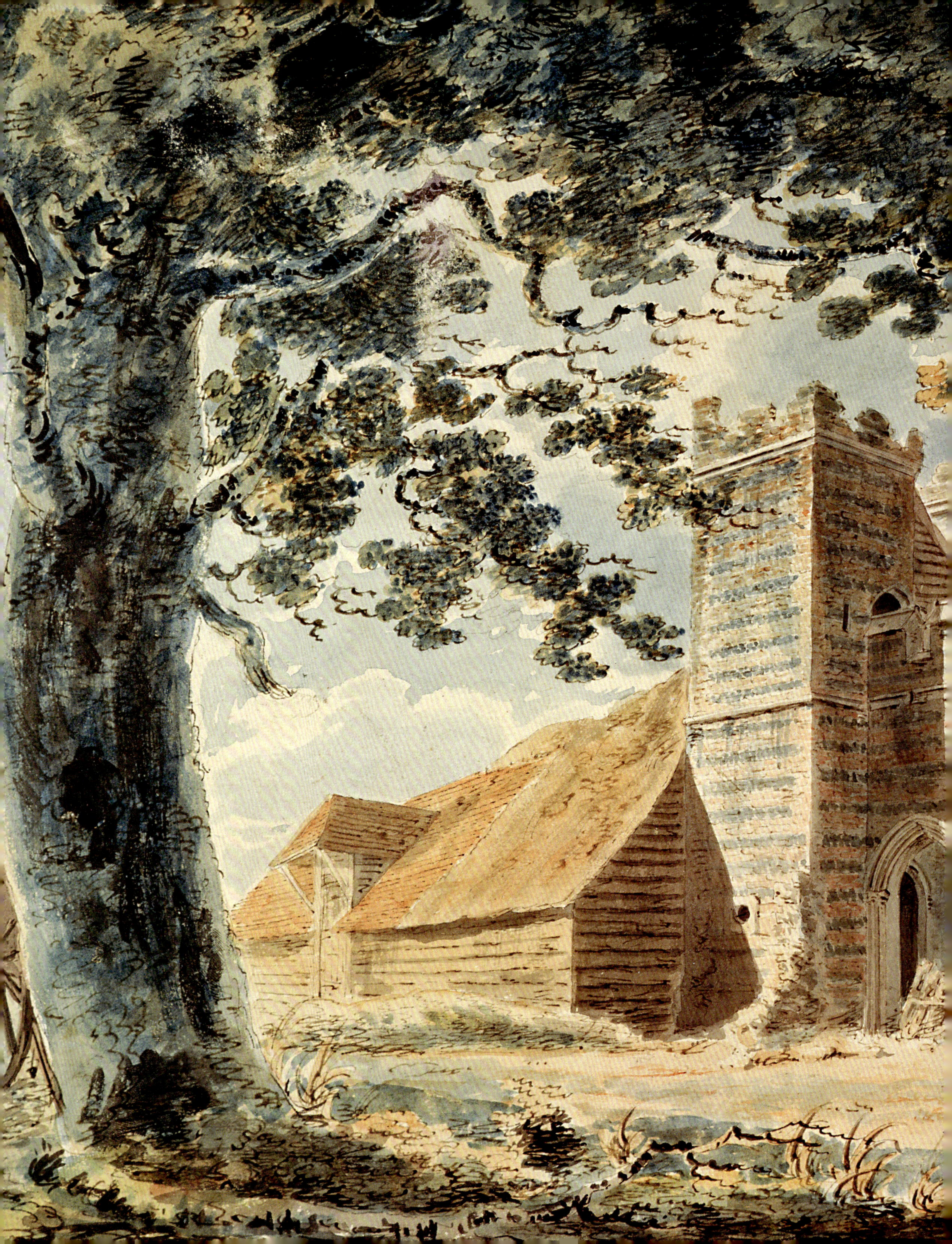

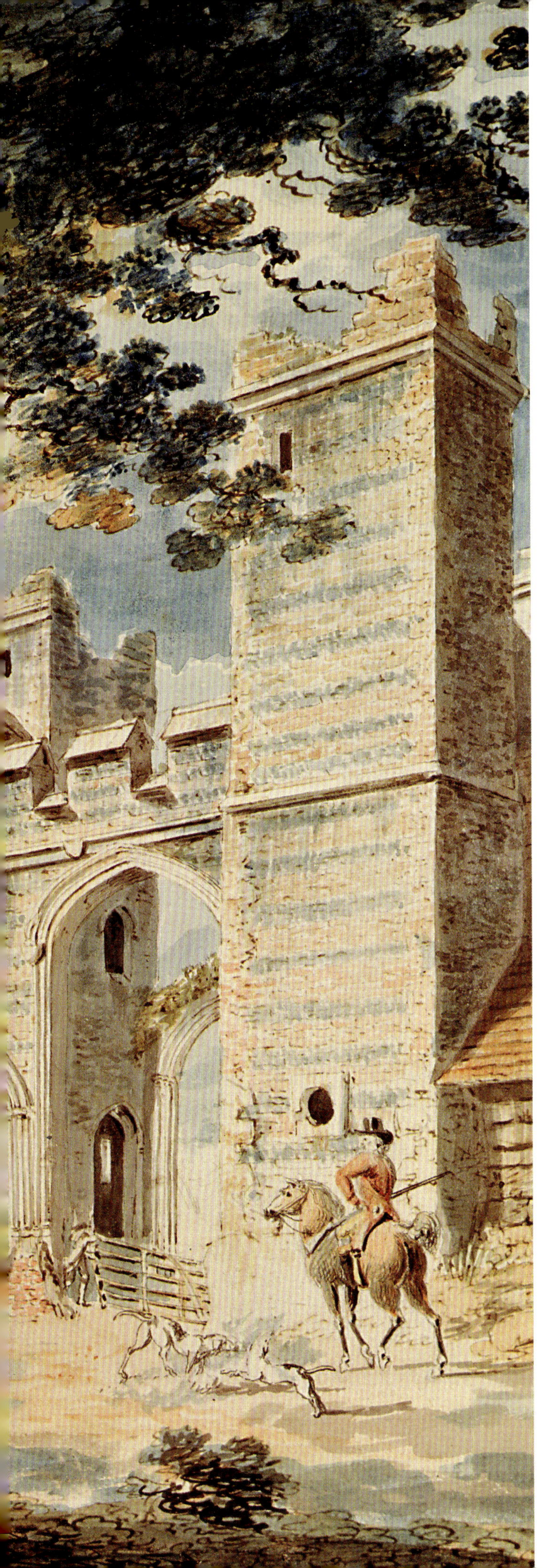

TURNER, HIS LIFE AND TIMES

In an extraordinary career of more than 60 years, Turner achieved his first success at only 24 years of age by being accepted as an Associate of the Royal Academy. As a watercolour painter he achieved early recognition as a topographical illustrator, with many commissions from book publishers. His development as an artist involved adapting the skill he acquired as a watercolour painter to oil painting. He used this medium and his observations of the effects of light to create ethereal and vaporous effects – a technique that reached its apogee after his first visit to Venice in 1819. Turner was devoted to his art and to the Academy, and appeared indifferent to family matters. His story is told within the context of his society, a time of political and social reform in an Industrial Age.

Left: Dent de Lion, Margate, *1791, watercolour, graphite and ink. One of Turner's first paintings executed when he was just 16 years old. Margate became one of his most visited towns.

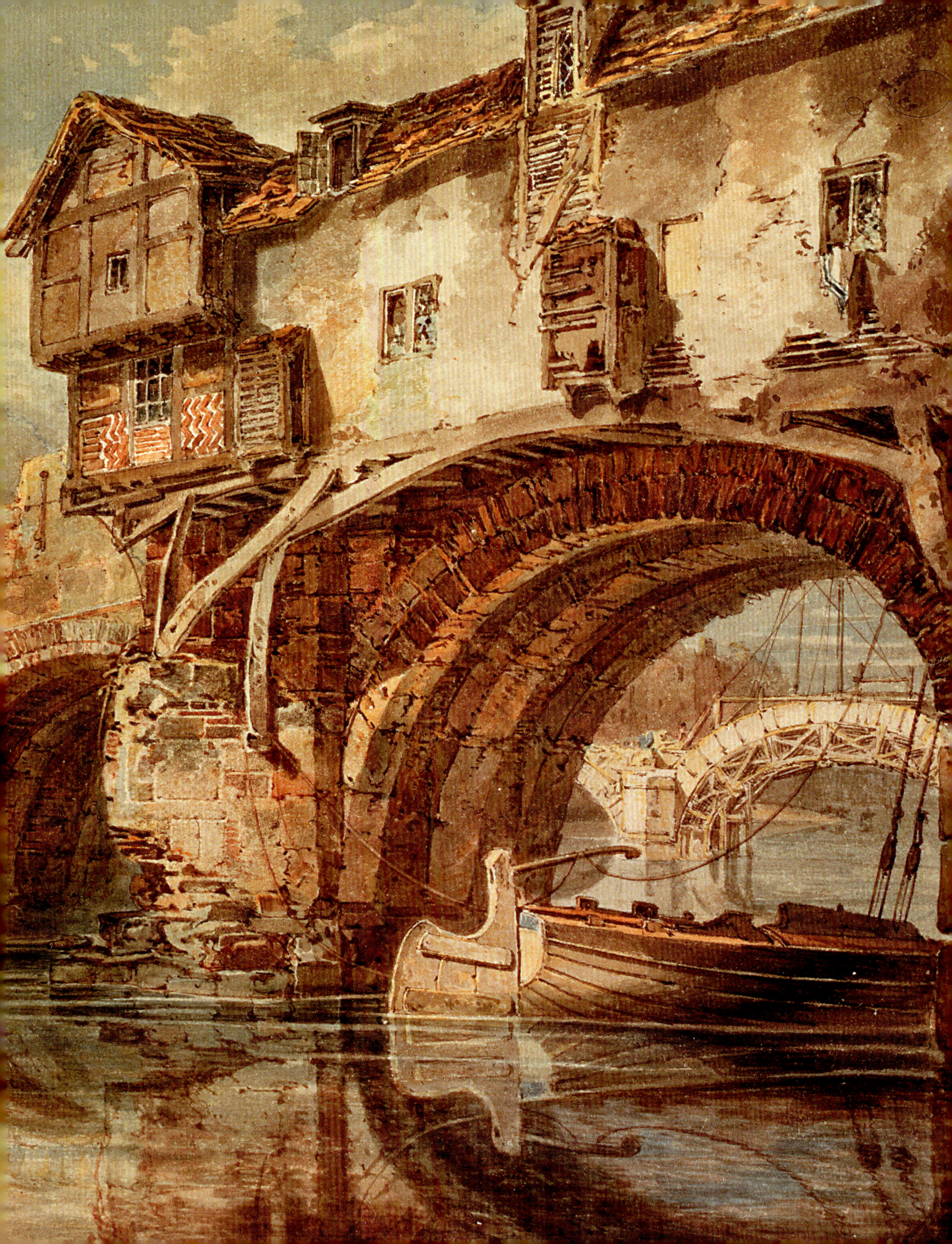

TOWARD THE ROYAL ACADEMY

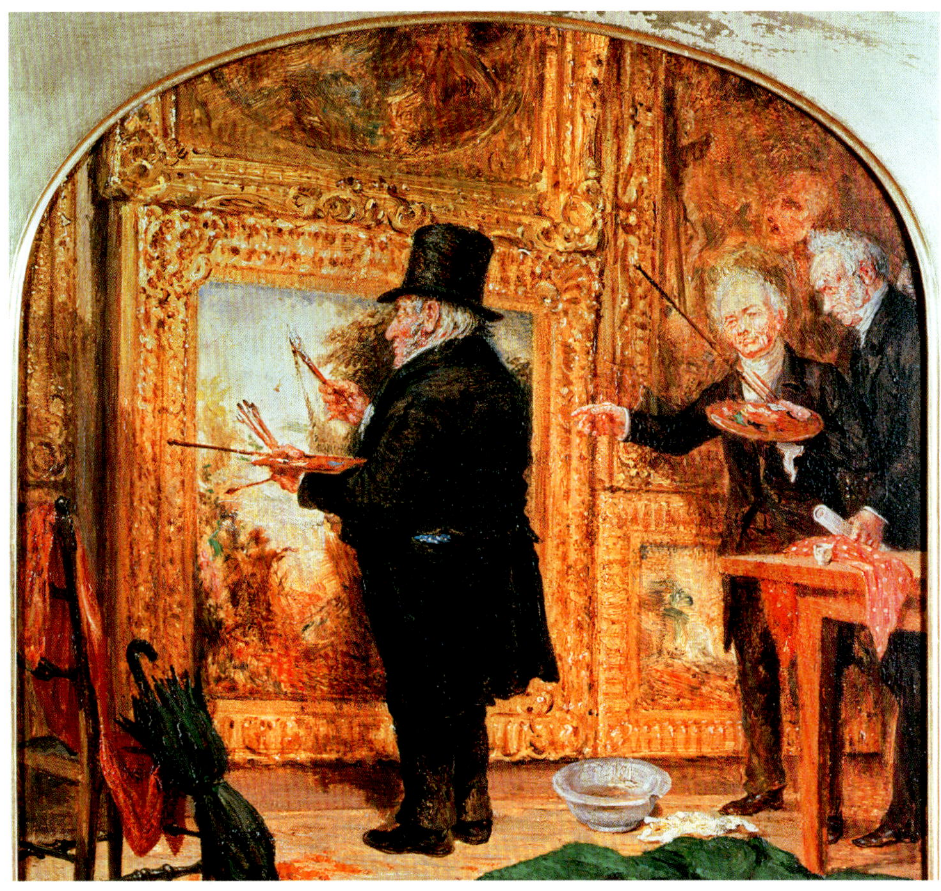

Turner's life began in Covent Garden, London. From an early age he showed a prodigious talent for copying landscapes by Old Masters and an older generation of watercolour artists such as John Cozens, which he displayed in his father's shop. He was admitted to the Royal Academy schools at 14 years of age and exhibited his first work at their annual exhibition the following year. By the time he was 26, he had been elected a full member of the Royal Academy, and was enjoying critical acclaim and wide patronage.

Above: JMW Turner at the Royal Academy on Varnishing Day, *William Parrott, oil, 1846. By the time this picture was painted, Turner had achieved mastery of his craft, often to the envy of his contemporaries.*
Left: Old Welsh Bridge, Shrewsbury, *watercolour, 1794. This early topographical watercolour already begins to show the potential for the artist's ethereal effects.*

FROM BIRTH TO CHILD PRODIGY

Born in the centre of a teeming, foggy, foul-smelling city, Turner was the son of a humble
but proud West End barber. His talent was recognized from a young age, propelling him
from architect's draughtsman toward the Royal Academy.

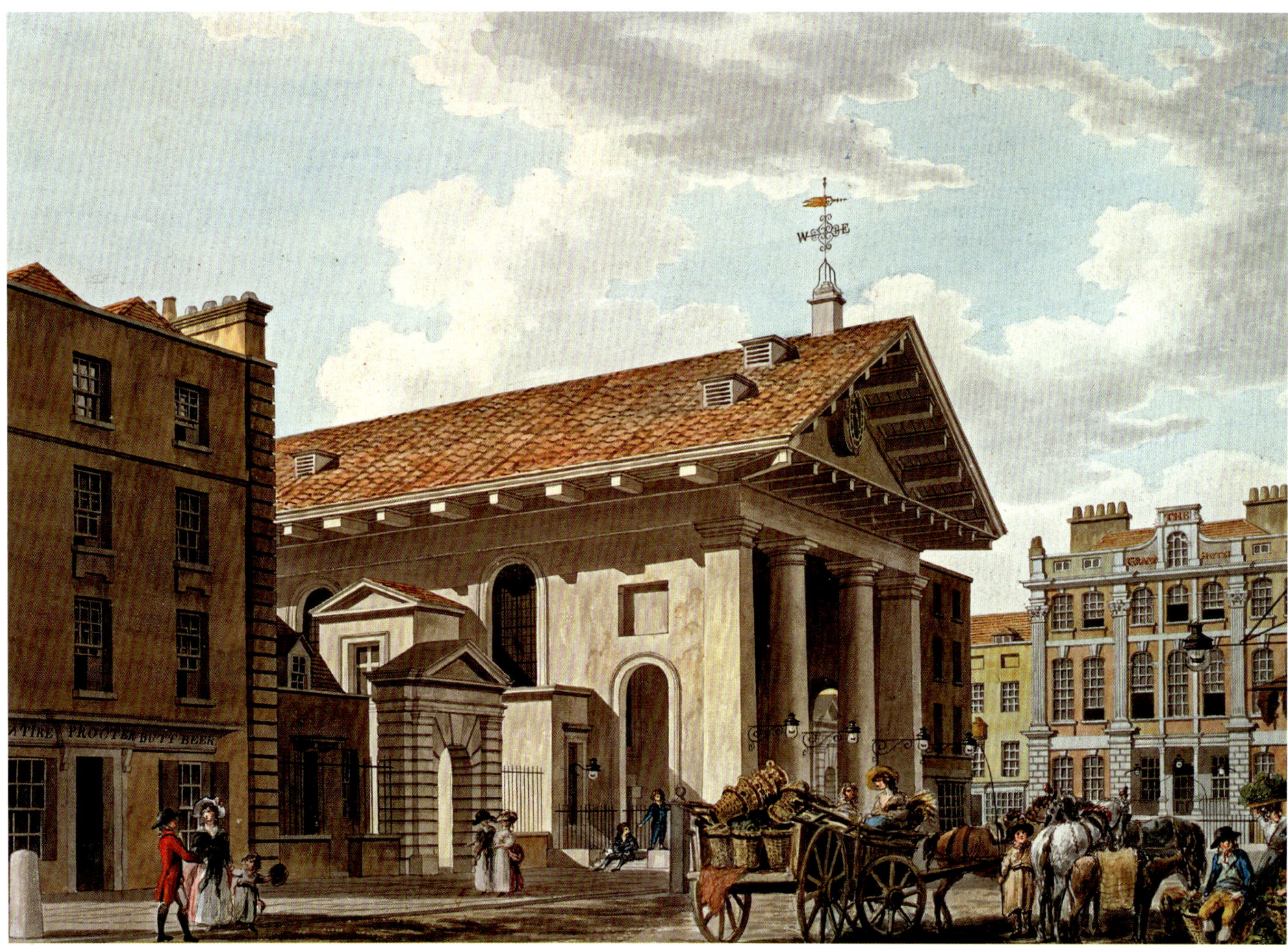

Above: St Paul's Church, Covent Garden, *Thomas Malton Jr, 18th century. A view of the church in which Turner was baptized, typical of late 18th-century idealized topography.*

Joseph Mallord William Turner was christened on 14 May 1775 at St Paul's Church in Covent Garden, London. The exact date and place of his birth are less certain, but the accepted record is 23 April 1775 at Maiden Lane, a narrow street running between Covent Garden market and the Strand, with its direct shoreline access to the River Thames.

COVENT GARDEN

Because of its location, Maiden Lane was a noisy, dark, bustling thoroughfare that would have been subjected to many unpleasant odours. The Thames, probably the busiest river in the world at the time, was also subject to hazy fogs and early morning mists that were to be so influential to the vaporous effects Turner used in his later paintings. The artist's parents were William Turner (1745–1829), a wig-maker and barber, originally from Devon, and Mary (née Marshall, 1738–1804), who was from London. They were married at St Paul's Church, Covent Garden, in August 1773. Their son was also to be known as William, his other names chosen in deference to his maternal ancestors. Turner was effectively an only child after his sister Mary Ann (1778–85) died aged seven. This may well have been the catalyst for sending the young Turner, then aged ten, to stay with his uncle Joseph (Mallord William) Marshall (?1735–1820), a successful butcher living and working in New Brentford, about 15km (9 miles) west of Covent Garden.

THE FIRST ARTISTIC JOURNEYS

During his stay in New Brentford in 1785, the young Turner was fortunate to be able to attend a free day school

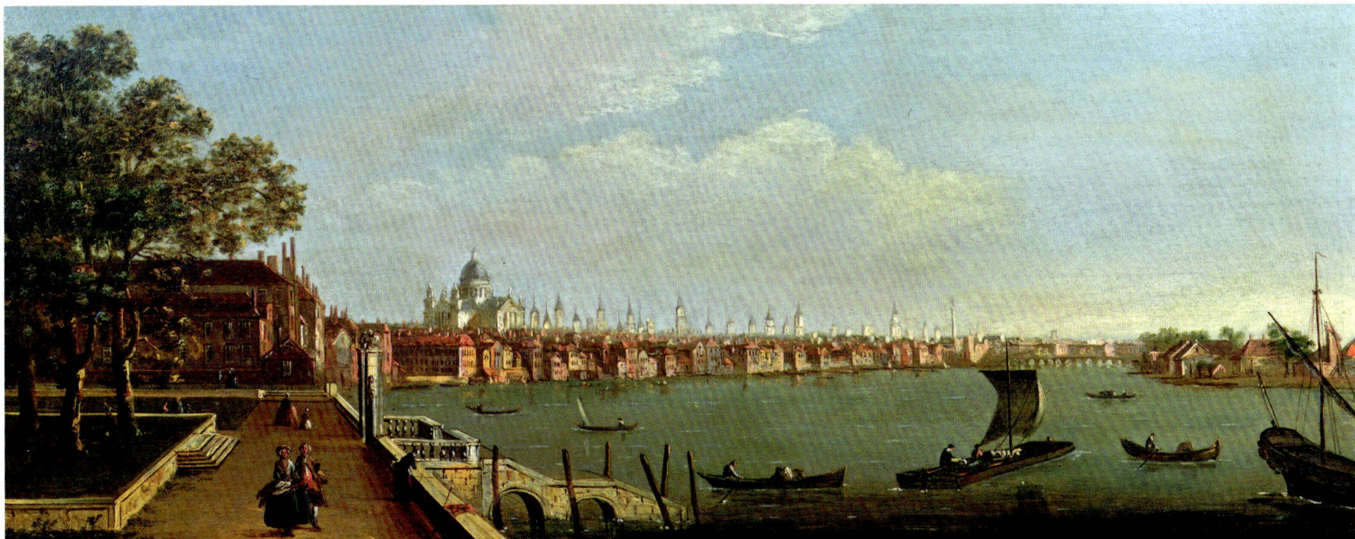

Above: London Bridge and the City from Somerset House, *Francis Smith, c.1770. An idealized view of the Thames at the time of Turner's birth. In reality the river would have been much busier than this picture depicts.*

run by John White. There he met two brothers, John and Henry Scott Trimmer. The latter was to become a lifelong friend. Their mother Sarah was in touch with various artistic circles in London and later introduced Turner to artists such as Henry Howard (1769–1847). In 1786, Turner travelled with Sarah and some of her children to Margate in Kent, staying with another relative, and drawing a series of topographical views, the first of his prodigious output. These and subsequent early drawings were displayed in his father's barber shop in Covent Garden, for sale to his many hairdressing clients. Turner continued to draw topographical views of London, becoming extremely competent at architectural detail and perspective. These brought him to the attention of a number of architects, including Thomas Hardwick (1752–1829), who in 1789 began using his services as a draughtsman. At the time Hardwick was working on the new St Mary the Virgin Church in Wanstead for which Turner contributed

Right: Christ Church, Oxford, 1794. *An early watercolour, one of several made in and around Oxford, after Turner's visits in 1789 and 1792.*

a number of watercolour views of the old and new churches. In the following year Hardwick went on to refurbish St Paul's Church in Covent Garden where Turner had been baptized.

TO THE ACADEMY SCHOOLS

In the summer of 1789, Turner went to stay again with his uncle, but this time in Oxford, Joseph having moved there from Brentford. There he continued his topographical views, completing his first Oxford Sketchbook. By the autumn he was apprenticed to Thomas Malton Jr (1748–1804), a leading topographer whose London views were well known and sought-after. Turner very quickly

mastered 'the Malton style' and later in life was to refer to him as "my real master". Turner was fortunate to gain this apprenticeship through a bequest of £100 (about £10,000 today) made to his father by a customer after seeing some of the young Turner's paintings for sale in the barber shop. In December, Turner, after a month's probationary period, was accepted as a pupil at the Royal Academy Schools. His acceptance, with five others, was based on a number of drawings he had produced from studies in the Royal Academy's so-called Plaster Academy, drawing from casts of antique sculpture. Turner remained a pupil at the schools until 1793.

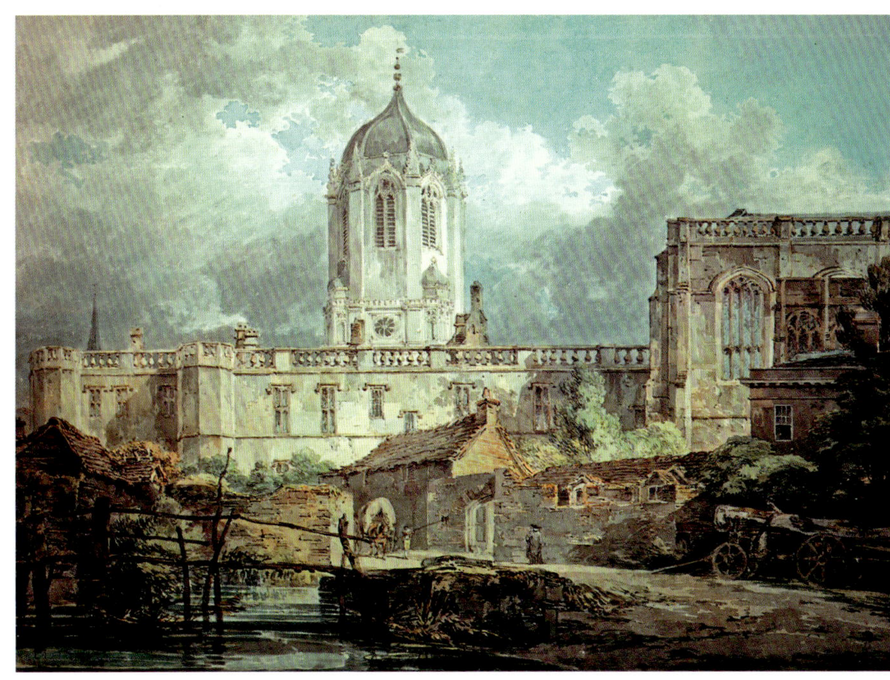

THE ROYAL ACADEMY

The Royal Academy was the dominant artistic institution of its day, espousing the Classical ideas of beauty. Turner was single-minded in pursuing his approach to these ideas, and applying them to his early work. He was close to Joshua Reynolds, the President at the time.

Having been a respected student at the Royal Academy Schools, Turner's first painting was accepted for exhibition at the Royal Academy.

THE ROYAL ACADEMY AS INSTITUTION

The Academy was set up originally as a rival to the Society of Artists after some of its members, including Sir William Chambers (1723–96), who was later to design the new Somerset House, disputed issues concerning its leadership. Chambers had influential connections with King George III (1738–1820) who signed the Academy's charter in December 1768. Its first president was Sir Joshua Reynolds (1723–92), another disaffected member of the Society of Artists. Reynolds was responsible for creating the 15 Discourses (written and published lectures) on art, which were delivered over a 20-year period and designed as didactic rules for all artists. At a time of European Enlightenment, these Discourses provided a rationalist ideal of beauty at an intellectual level based on Classical tradition. Reynolds suggested a subject hierarchy for pictures with history painting at the top and landscapes at the other end of the scale. However, by way of contrast, he also singled out the dominant landscape artist of the time, Thomas

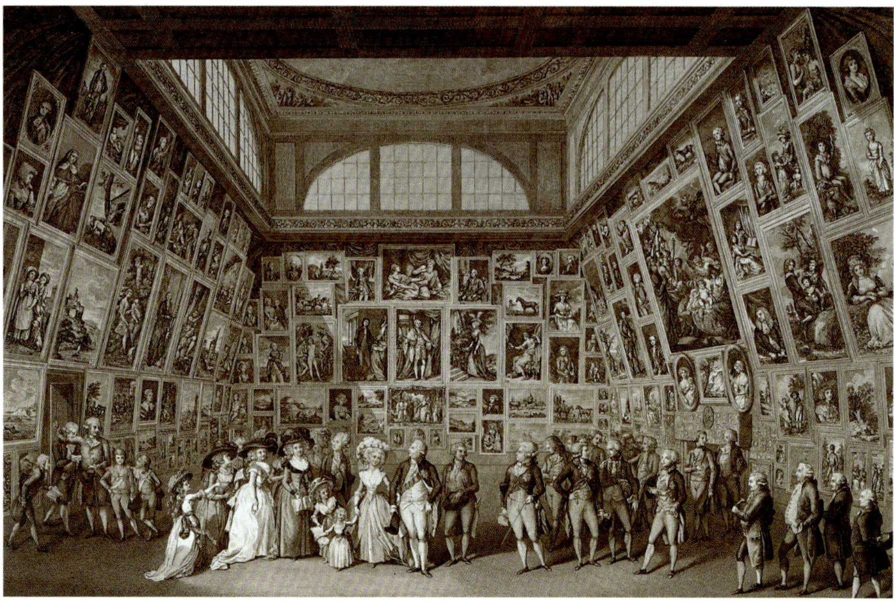

Above: Interior view of Somerset House showing George III at the Royal Academy Exhibition, *Johann Ramberg, etching, 1788.*

Gainsborough (1727–88), for the "powerful impression of nature in his *landskips*". This lecture was delivered in 1788, the year Gainsborough died, and was intended as a tribute to his fellow Academician. In his early career, Turner was in awe of Reynolds, but his later paintings are an example of the new and burgeoning Romanticism that was to dominate the 19th century.

A DEVELOPING STYLE

A scene depicting the Archbishop's Palace at Lambeth was the first of Turner's paintings to be exhibited at the Royal Academy; a watercolour that is imbued with the architectural detail synonymous with this period in the artist's oeuvre, and clearly indebted to

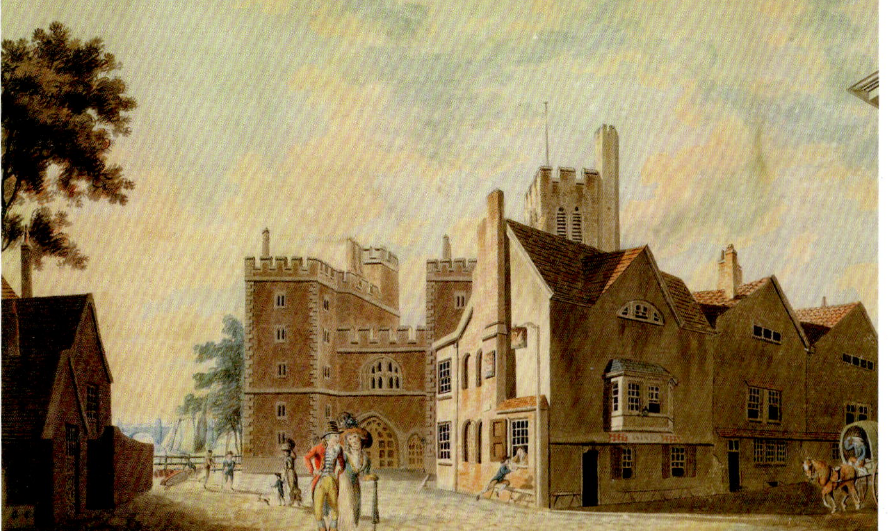

Left: A View of the Archbishop's Palace, Lambeth, *pencil and watercolour, 1790. This was Turner's first work accepted for exhibition at the Royal Academy.*

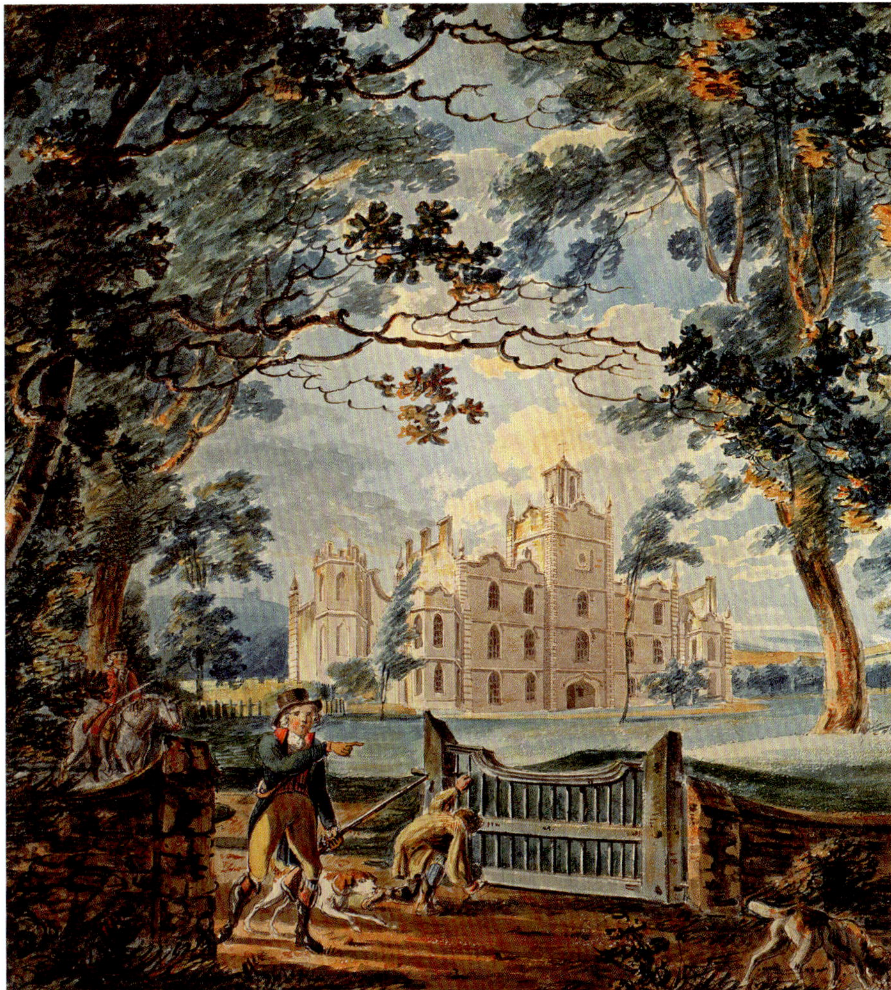

Right: Cote House, Bristol, *watercolour, 1792. A watercolour worked up from the Bristol and Malmesbury Sketchbook.*

Thomas Malton. Turner was, however, developing his painting style by exploring a number of different approaches. Apart from his architectural studies at Malton's studio and at the Academy, the artist was avidly copying the landscape styles and colorations of Gainsborough, Richard Wilson (1714–82) and the Dutch landscape artists, particularly Jacob van Ruisdael (1628–82). Turner was also learning the arts of etching and engraving.

In September 1791, he made his longest journey to date, staying with John Narraway, a friend of his father's, in Bristol. There he explored the Avon Gorge at Clifton (prior to the building of the suspension bridge), travelling also to Malmesbury and Bath. His hosts, the Narraways, referred to Turner as the 'Prince of Rocks' after his habit of climbing along the Avon Gorge in search of 'the view'. According to them, Turner was a solitary and even reclusive figure, often leaving the house before breakfast and again after the evening meal to capture the variations of light on those views. All contemporary accounts of Turner suggest that he was very single-minded, earnest and diligent regarding his work. He was not, however, an ungrateful guest and he painted a miniature self-portrait as a gift to the Narraways in appreciation of their hospitality.

THE LIFE CLASS

On 25 June 1792, Turner joined the Life Class at the Royal Academy Schools, staying there until 1799 – an unusually long time for a student of the human form. The effect of his attendance can be summarized by the self-portraits executed at either end of the period: the previously mentioned 'Narraway' miniature self-portrait, compared to the confident, self-assured artist on the cusp of Royal Academy membership as depicted in his *Self-Portrait of 1799*. However, Turner was not, nor wanted to be, a portrait painter. His figures were to become the supporting cast rather than the focus of his landscapes, but they often reflected qualities of humanity, creating pathos in the pictures and demanding that his viewers reflect on contemporary social issues.

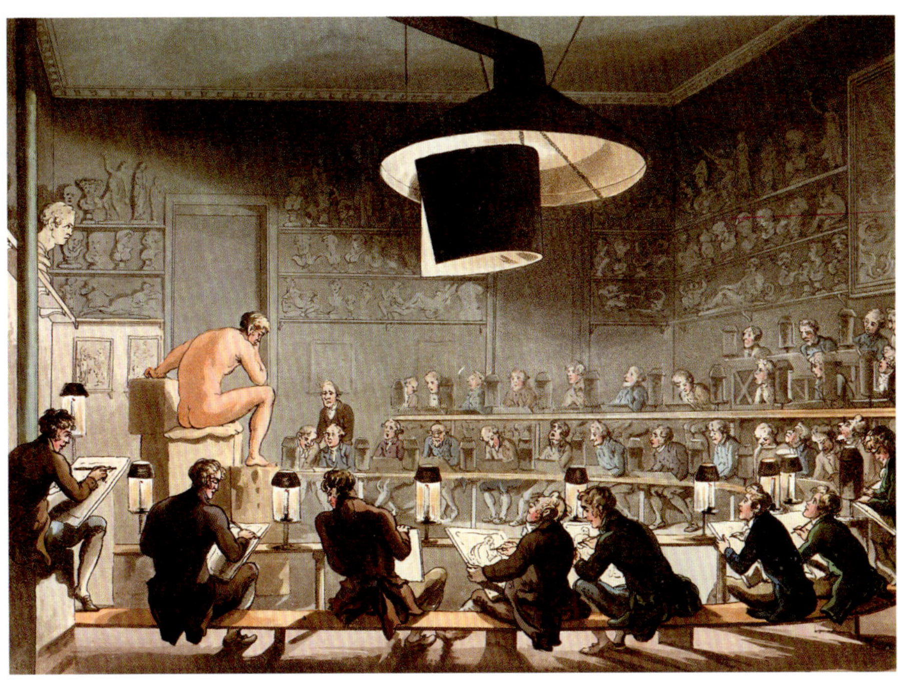

Left: Drawing from Life at the Royal Academy, *Rowlandson and Pugin, (after) coloured engraving, 19th century.*

FIRST SKETCHING TOUR

After showing at the Royal Academy exhibition of 1792, Turner embarked on his first
full sketching tour, a journey he was to replicate most years for the rest of his life.
He was also to receive the first, and only, official award for his art.

For his first tour in 1792, many of Turner's pictures were of buildings such as abbeys and cathedrals, and bridges and towns. He sought subjects all around Britain, in towns and rural areas.

In the same year, he submitted two pictures to the Royal Academy exhibition, one of which was *The Pantheon, the Morning after the Fire*.

THE PANTHEON FIRE

The Pantheon was a place of entertainment in Oxford Street, London, with a coffered-style rotunda based on the Pantheon in Rome dominating its central space. It had opened in 1772 and, in the year before the fire, Turner had been employed there as a scene painter. Working there from March to July 1791, he earned about four guineas a week (equivalent to £400 today) and also provided himself with some valuable experience in painting on a large scale.

On 14 January 1792, the Pantheon burnt to the ground. Turner made a detailed sketch of the building the day after the fire, working up the finished watercolour for exhibition later that year. From the watercolour detail, it is possible to see the huge icicles at the top of the building, a testament to the extreme cold that Turner endured in order to make the sketch.

THE FIRST TOURS OF WALES, HEREFORD AND WORCESTER

In the summer of 1792, Turner made his first tour of South Wales and north into the Black Mountains before he re-crossed the border into England at Hereford. Using the Narraway house in Bristol as his base, he travelled to Wales, which he had viewed the previous year from the top of the Avon Gorge. The tour became the pattern for all subsequent ones in his life, which involved making careful plans about the

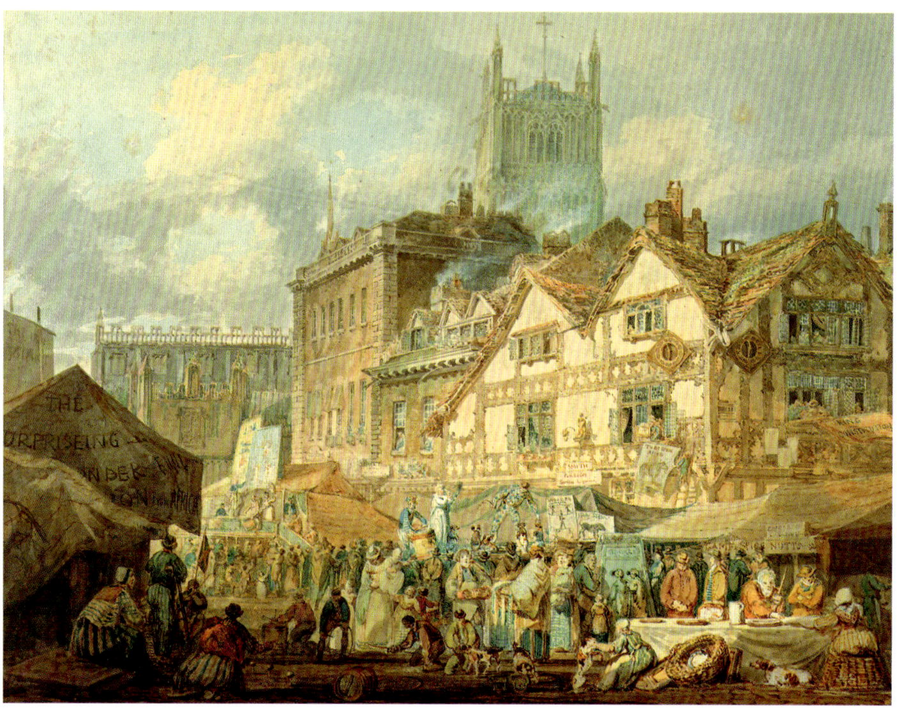

Above: High Green, Queen Square, Wolverhampton, *watercolour, 1795.*

Below: Pantheon Masquerade, *John Bluck, engraving, 1800.*

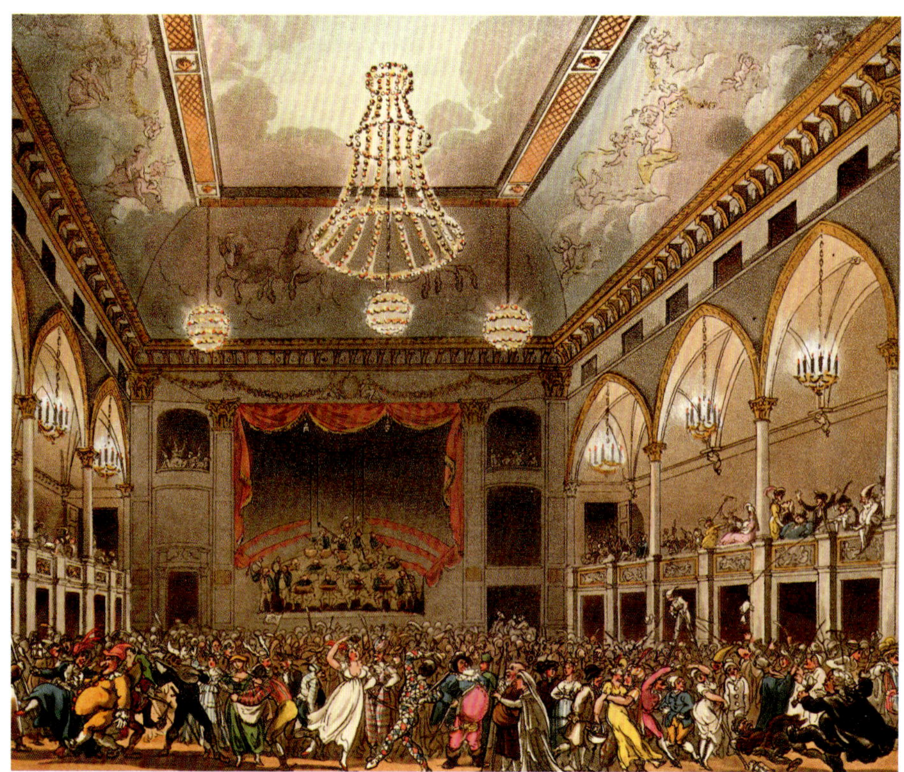

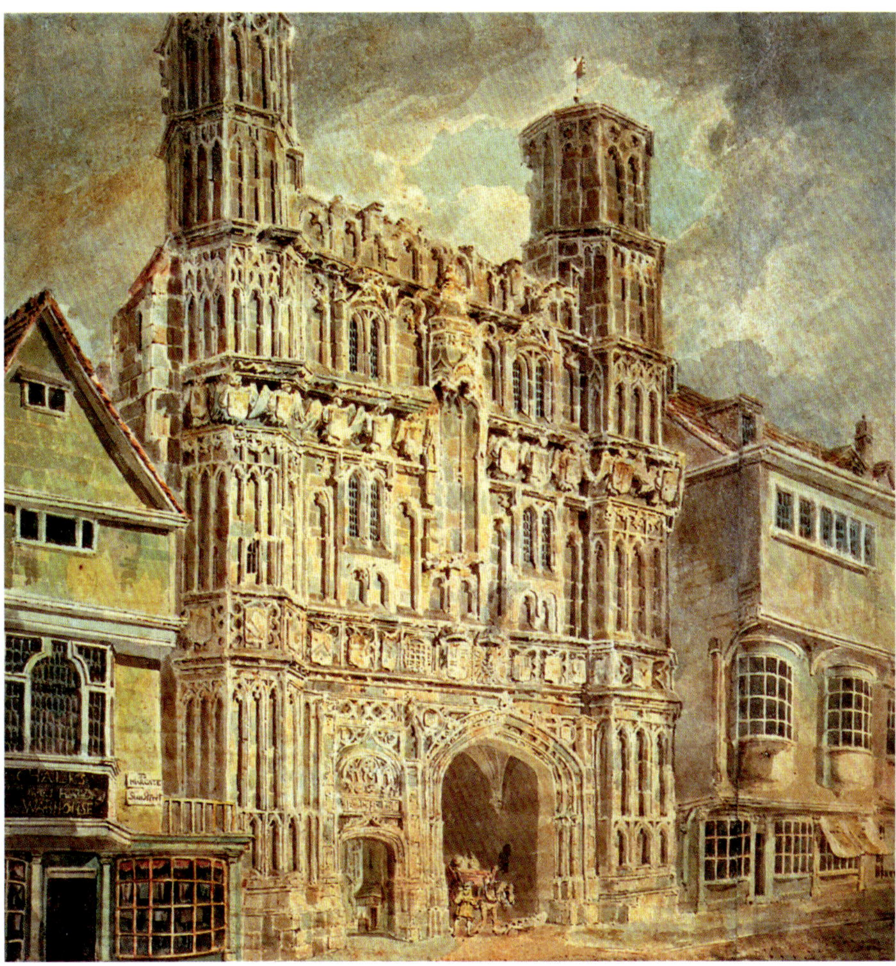

Above: Christchurch Gate, Canterbury, *watercolour, 1792–3.*

Royal Society of Arts after 1847), for his landscape drawing *Lodge Farm near Hambleton, Surrey,* submitted by the artist the previous year. The Society was founded in 1754 to "embolden enterprise, to enlarge science, to refine art, to improve manufacture and to extend our commerce". By "our", the Society was referring to British commerce, an important aspect of the increasingly prosperous and burgeoning bourgeois society of Britain, many of whose members would become Turner's patrons and clients. It seems likely that the artist submitted the work as recognition of the commercial potential for topographical views. The Society was, after all, a pragmatically based organization that recognized and rewarded arts with a practical skill, such as drawing and etching. Thus Turner may have had one eye on commercial opportunities, particularly those that had a connection to a patron.

In the autumn of 1793, Turner toured Kent and Sussex, possibly responding to a commercial opportunity for topographical views for the *Copperplate Magazine,* run by the engraver John Walker. At this time, Turner was working with a number of engravers and publishers, producing commercially viable views for publication.

places to see and where to stay. Turner was able to cover 40km (25 miles) in a day, sketching and making notes before working up watercolours back at his studio. On the longer distances, he carefully planned the coach journeys in every detail possible. He also budgeted very well and adequately projected his earnings from the work he would produce. Thus in every sense he was a commercially minded artist from the beginning. Turner continued this journey in 1793, beginning in Hereford again and then travelling to Great Malvern, Tewkesbury and Worcester.

OFFICIAL RECOGNITION

Prior to sending in his two watercolour paintings of Bristol and the Avon Gorge to the Royal Academy in 1793, Turner received an early accolade. He was awarded the prestigious 'Greater Silver Palette' by the Society of Arts (the

Right: King Edgar's Gate, Worcester, *watercolour, 1794.*

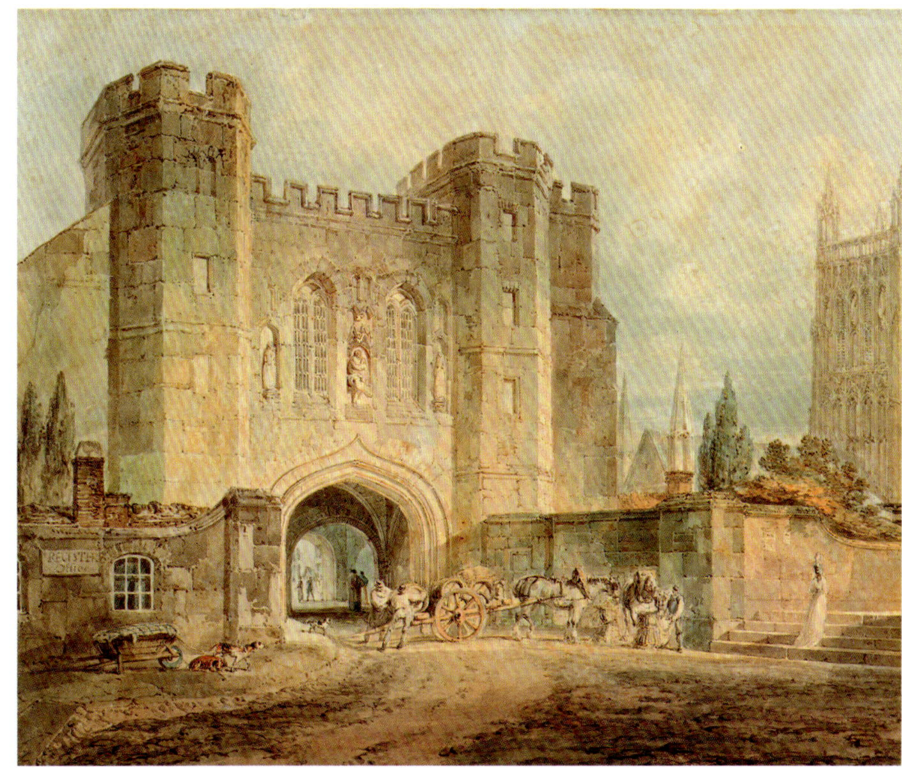

EARLY PATRONS

Following his 'apprenticeship' and the continuous sales of topographical views in his father's barber shop, Turner became known to a number of influential and wealthy people who would eventually support him by buying his work.

After meeting the physician Dr Thomas Monro (1759–1833) in 1793, Turner engaged with other protégés such as Thomas Girtin (1775–1802). Between them they produced many topographical scenes that stimulated further patronage.

Essentially, Dr Monro's protégés copied both the contemporary and Old Masters' drawings and paintings that were in Monro's extensive collection at his London home. The Royal Academician Joseph Farington (1747–1821) stated, somewhat disparagingly, in his diary that "Dr Monro's house is like an Academy in an evening". Turner's own account of these Friday evenings was more simplistic, stating that "Girtin drew in outlines and I washed in the effects". Although Turner and Girtin did not need tuition from Monro, who was a competent amateur draughtsman himself, what they gained was experience in dealing with, and satisfying, influential and wealthy clients. Working with Girtin, every bit his equal, Turner was also gaining experience in creating more atmospheric renditions of topographical views. The artists were also rewarded for their efforts, being paid about three shillings (equivalent to about £12 today) for an evening's efforts.

RICHARD COLT HOARE

In 1794, Turner came to the notice of the larger public when his submissions to the Royal Academy that year were reported in the newspapers. The *Morning Post* commented on the "first rate ability" of "a very young artist" whose productions are "tinctured with truth and fidelity". Dr Monro subsequently purchased one of these pictures, *St Anselm's Chapel*.

Turner's fame was becoming widespread, and this resulted in a number of commissions from other influential and wealthy patrons, including the banker Sir Richard Colt Hoare (1758–1838). Hoare had inherited the successful banking business of Hoare & Co. established in the 17th century, and with it the baronetcy and property at Stourhead, in Wiltshire. His grandfather, Henry Hoare II, had designed the gardens at Stourhead in the mid-18th century, inspired by the landscape paintings of Claude Lorrain (c.1600–82) and Nicolas Poussin (1594–1665), two artists who were to play a significant inspirational role in Turner's own aesthetic. After visiting Stourhead in

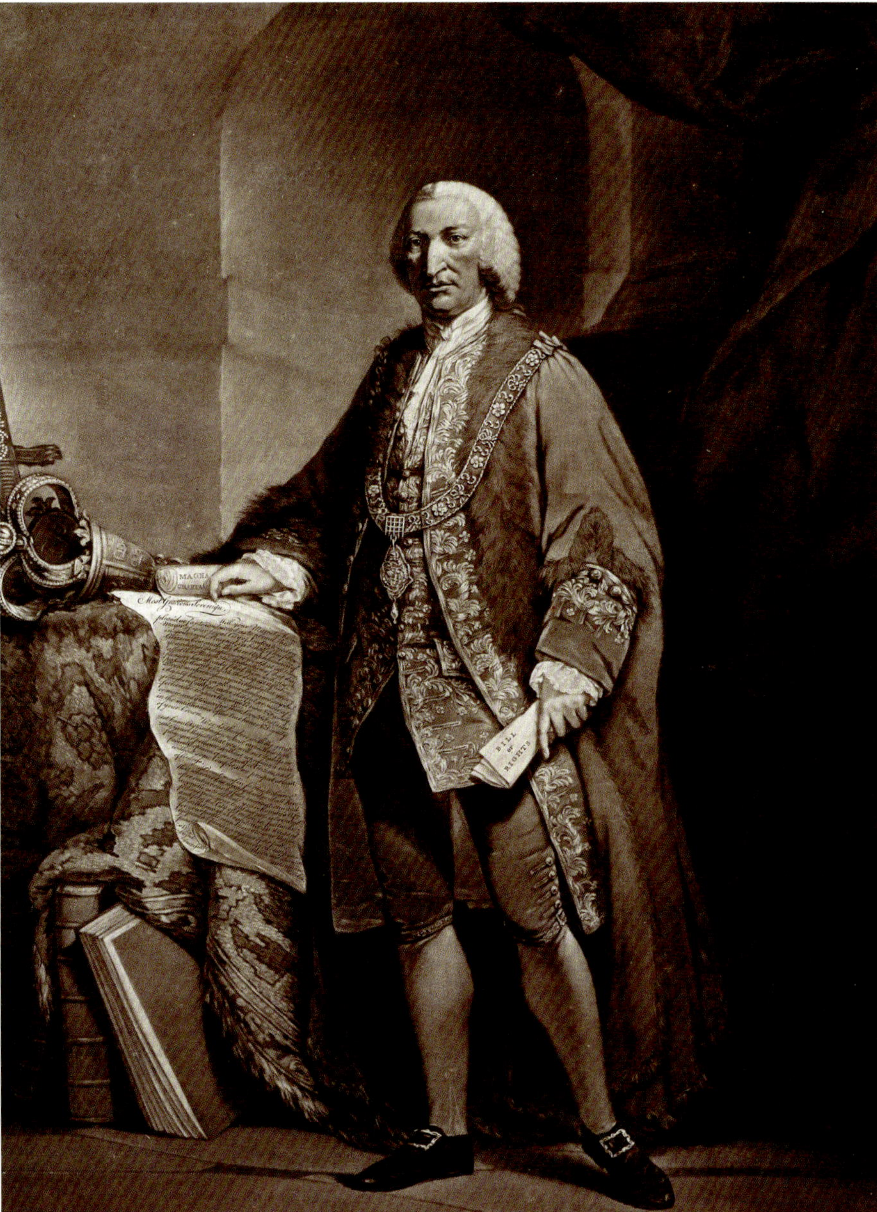

Left: The Right Honourable William Beckford Esquire, *John Dixon (1720–1804), engraving, c.1790s.*

WILLIAM BECKFORD

Through Hoare, Turner was introduced to another wealthy Wiltshire landowner, William Beckford (1760–1844). Beckford's house, Fonthill Abbey, was being built by the architect James Wyatt, who was also refurbishing Salisbury Cathedral at the time. Beckford was something of a reclusive figure, having endured a scandal a decade before and been forced to live in exile in Switzerland before returning to England in 1796. At that time he was one of the wealthiest men in England and spent a large portion of his fortune on the construction of the Gothic Abbey.

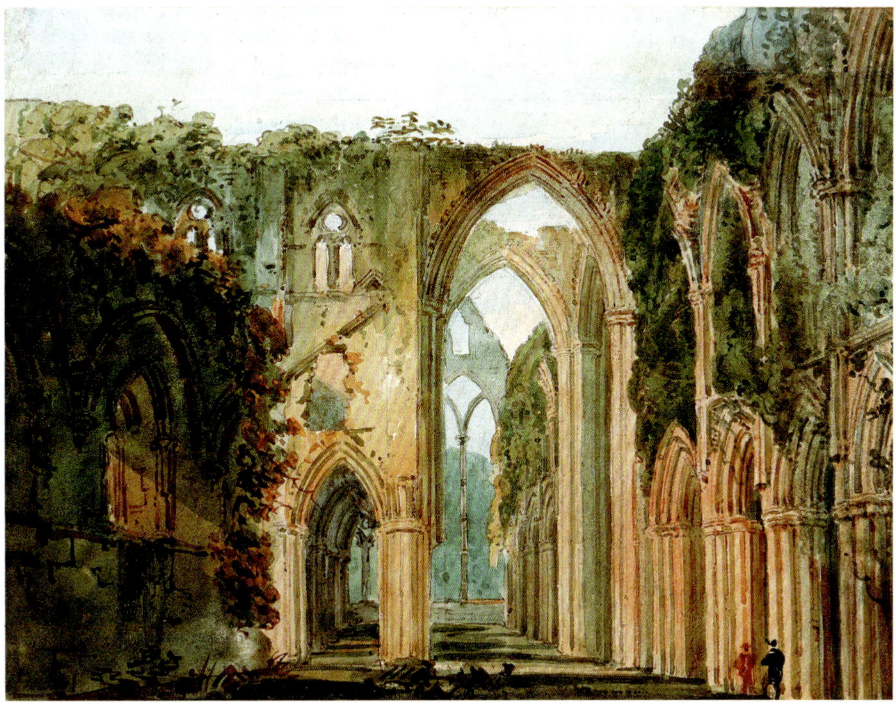

1795, where he saw some influential architectural prints by Giovanni Battista Piranesi (1720–78), Turner was commissioned by Hoare to paint a series of watercolours of Salisbury town and cathedral. Altogether Turner produced 17 finished paintings of Salisbury between 1796 and 1805.

Below: View of Fonthill from a Stone Quarry, *watercolour, pen and ink, 1799. One of many studies for William Beckford; a view of the 'abbey' from the east.*

Owing to his association with William Beckford, Turner was commissioned to paint views of Fonthill Abbey. He chose to depict the abbey in different lights to experiment with the various effects light has on architecture.

Importantly for Turner, Beckford was a great art collector and had recently acquired two Claude Lorrain paintings from the Altieri Collection in Rome. Turner viewed these at Beckford's London home in 1799, and as before when he had seen Claude's paintings

Above: Interior of Tintern Abbey, *Thomas Girtin (1775–1802), watercolour, 1798. The picture reveals a skill that is comparable to Turner's.*

as a young boy, he was considerably moved by their serenity and the artist's interpretations of the reflective qualities of light on water.

Below: Portrait of JMW Turner, *Thomas Monro (1759–1833), pencil, 1795, focusing on Turner's earnestness.*

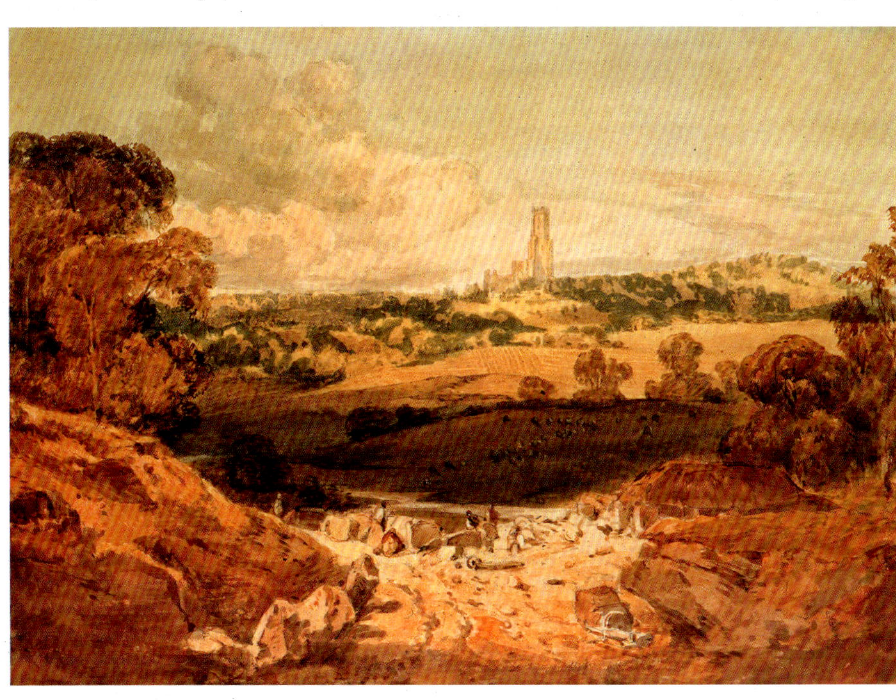

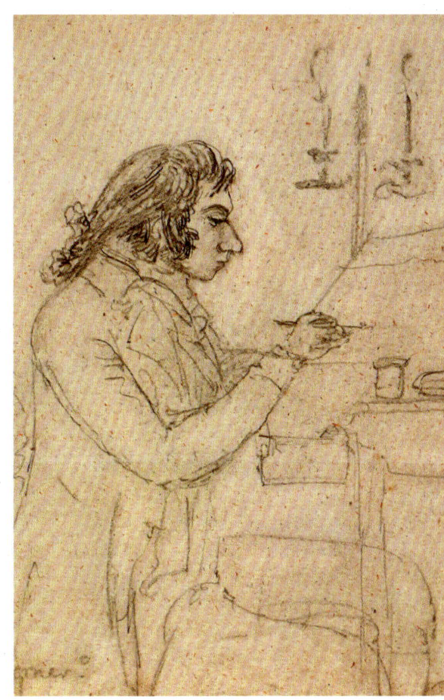

FIRST OIL PAINTINGS

A relative latecomer to oil painting, Turner quickly rose to master the techniques required, and was soon receiving commissions for his oil works. Turner's first experiments in oil in the mid-1790s were surprisingly competent and belied his inexperience of the medium.

Together with ten watercolours shown at the Royal Academy exhibition of 1796, Turner included an oil painting called *Fishermen at Sea*, a picture that was well received by the press. He had been experimenting with oil for two or three years, having no formal training in the medium other than studying the Old Masters in the possession of his patrons, and making visits to the studios of, for example, Sir Joshua Reynolds. His *Fishermen at Sea* is a competent exercise in paint handling to an Academic standard. By the time Turner had become an Academician in 1802, he had mastered a technique of using the medium that became distinctly his.

TRAVELS TO THE NORTH

At this time, Turner also began to travel farther afield. Probably due to a combination of overwork and the stress at home caused by his mother's mental illness and violent temper, Turner became ill in the summer of 1796 and sought rest and recuperation in

Below: The Bishop's Palace, Salisbury, *watercolour, c.1795. One of many executed for Turner's patron Richard Colt Hoare.*

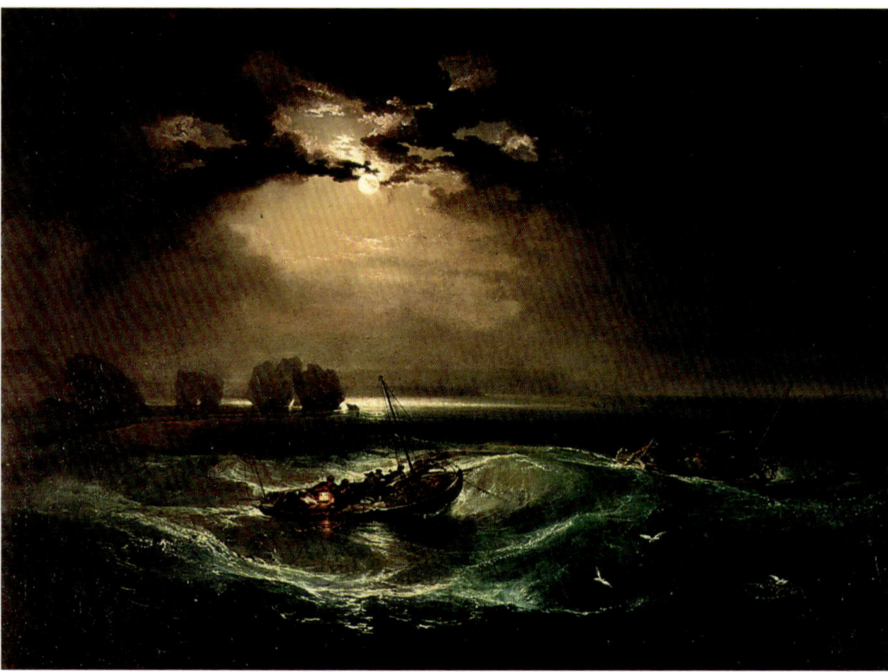

Above: Fishermen at Sea, *oil on canvas, 1796, was a creditable work in a relatively unfamiliar medium for Turner.*

Brighton. His Studies in Brighton Sketchbook indicates that he managed to create only about a hundred drawings, a very small number compared to his normally prodigious output, an indication perhaps of how unwell he was at the time. After the Royal Academy exhibition in the spring of the following year, to which he

submitted two oil paintings and five watercolours, Turner had sufficiently recovered to begin another of his arduous trips, this time to the very north of England. Initially he would have travelled by stagecoach from London, probably disembarking at York, a journey of around 300km (200 miles) that would have taken several days to complete. It has been recorded that Turner often walked up to 40km (25 miles) in a day while searching out the most suitable view for a particular motif. On this trip, he travelled to many parts of Yorkshire, the Lake District and the Northumberland coast, sketching in particular Norham Castle, a leitmotif he used for the rest of his career. The North of England and Tweed and Lakes Sketchbooks made on the trip provided core material for Turner's paintings that was to last right up until the 1830s.

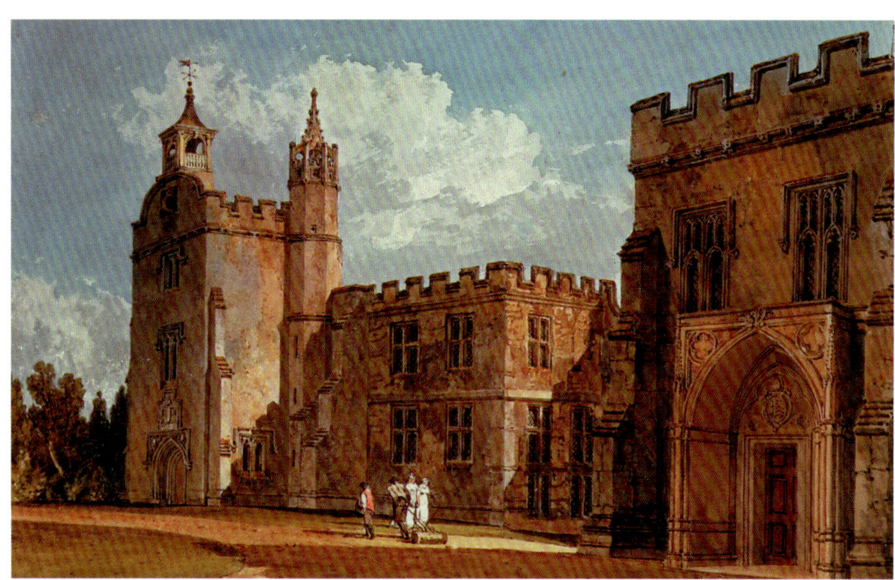

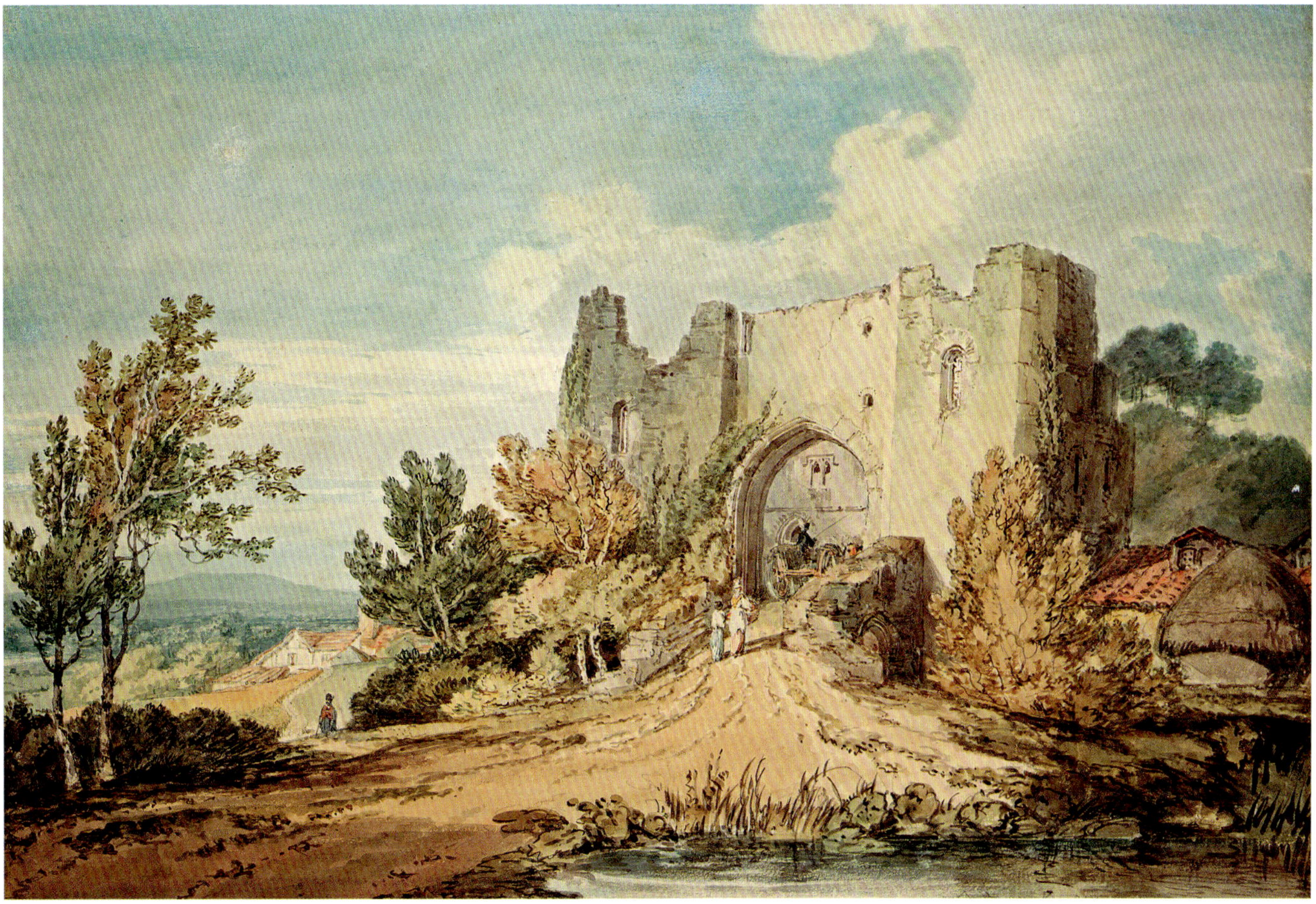

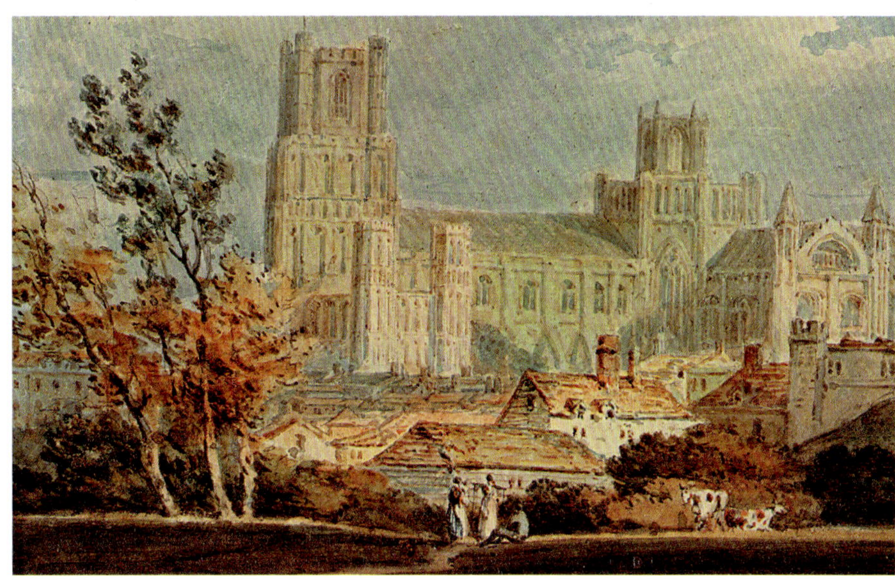

TWO NEW COMMISSIONS

As Turner left the North, he stayed at the home of Edward Lascelles (1740–1820), the first Earl of Harewood. He owned a magnificent stately home called Harewood House, designed by Robert Adam and set in grounds designed by the famous Lancelot 'Capability' Brown. Lascelles, whose family had made a fortune in the West Indies, mainly through the exploitation of the slave trade, had been the main patron of Thomas Girtin, but had commissioned Turner to execute two oil paintings of Plompton Rocks near Harrogate in North Yorkshire. This was the first commission he received for an oil painting, which was completed in 1798.

Charles Anderson-Pelham (1781–1846) also figures in Turner's life at this time. The artist visited him sometime in the early autumn of

Right: View of Ely Cathedral, *pencil and watercolour, 1796. A panoramic view of Ely Cathedral, Cambridgeshire, one of the oldest and largest of its kind in England.*

1797 at Brocklesby Park, his estate in Lincolnshire, to make drawings of his mausoleum. Like Lascelles, Anderson-Pelham had recently been a Member of Parliament and was later to be raised to the peerage as the first Earl of Yarborough. Turner made sketches of the mausoleum, producing one significant painting of the interior

Above: Llanblethian Castle Gateway, *pen and ink and watercolour, 1797, painted during one of Turner's journeys to Wales. Once part of the ancient town wall, this gate was demolished in the 19th century.*

that he was to use later in his perspective lectures at the Royal Academy after 1811.

TOWARD A NEW AESTHETIC

The landscape painters Claude-Joseph Vernet, Richard Wilson and William Gilpin were a great influence on the young Turner with respect to his painting, but it was the death of his friend John Danby that was to have a significant impact on Turner's personal life.

As Turner aspired toward Royal Academician status, he began to study other landscape paintings in more detail and to adopt a new aesthetic beyond topography. In 1796, he began studying the works of Richard Wilson (1714–82), a founder member of the Academy who challenged the idea that English landscape painting was merely topographical.

THE WILSON AND VERNET SERIES

After visiting Italy in the 1750s, Wilson became captivated by the landscape paintings of Claude Lorrain, who had worked just outside Rome. Turner recognized that Wilson had reinterpreted Claude's poetic and emotive paintings, applying the same aesthetic considerations to his English and Welsh landscapes. Turner eagerly made studies of Wilson's paintings, creating a sketchbook of more than 100 watercolour references for future use. Another artist Turner studied was Wilson's exact contemporary Claude-Joseph Vernet (1714–89).

ANOTHER AESTHETIC CONCEPT

The notion of the 'Picturesque' is an aesthetic ideal first mooted by the Reverend William Gilpin (1724–1804) in 1782. It required travellers to study their surroundings as part of the challenge to Enlightenment theories of rationality, and to consider notions of beauty in terms of experience and instinct. This was particularly relevant to the emerging leisured class in Britain, many of whom were Turner's potential clients. They were encouraged to participate in a 'Grand Tour' of Britain – a complete antithesis to the European Grand Tour. Aesthetic considerations on a British tour would be irregular ruins, gnarled

Right: Rome: after Richard Wilson, *pencil and watercolour, 1797. This landscape shows a bridge over the Tiber.*

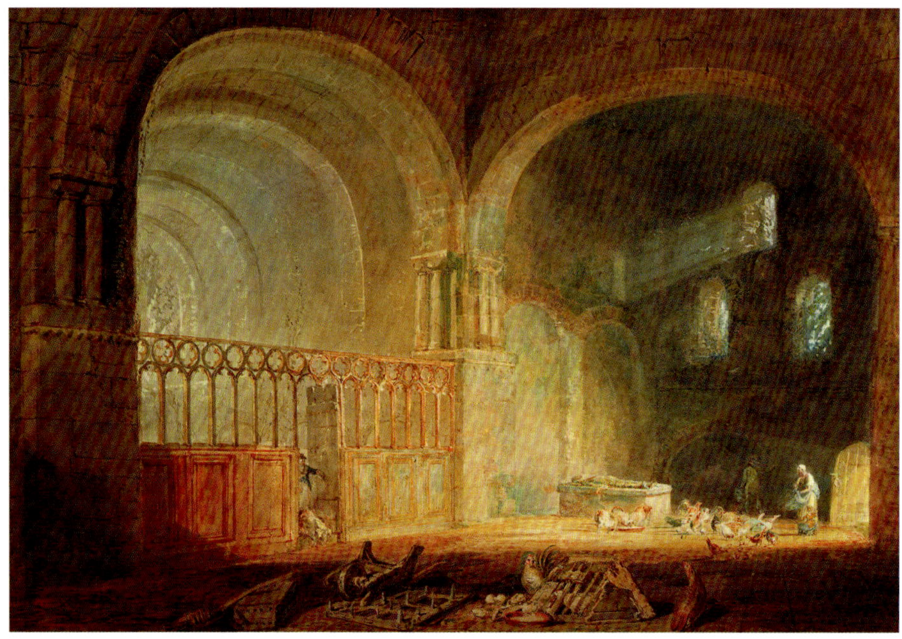

Above: Transept of Ewenny Priory, Glamorganshire, *watercolour over pencil, 1797.*

trees and even unkempt people. Ruined monasteries provided this ideal, their Gothic irregular features reclaimed by nature. *The Dormitory and Transept at Fountains Abbey* ably demonstrates this.

AN APPLICATION TO THE ACADEMY

William Gilpin's brother was the artist Sawrey Gilpin (1733–1807), who supported Turner's first application for Associate Academician. Turner's subsequent rejection was probably as a consequence of his own ineligibility, since he was a year younger than the required entry age of 24, and the fact

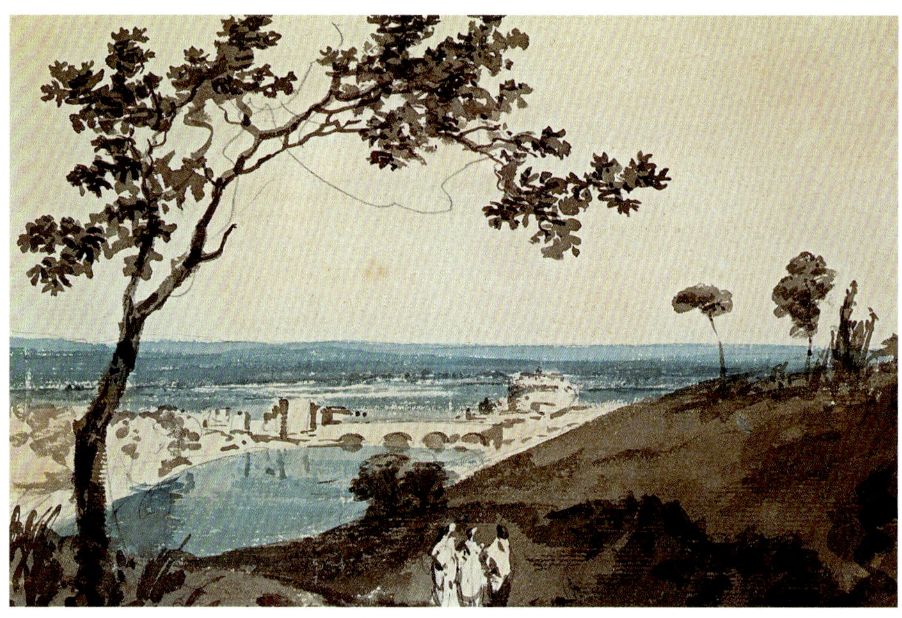

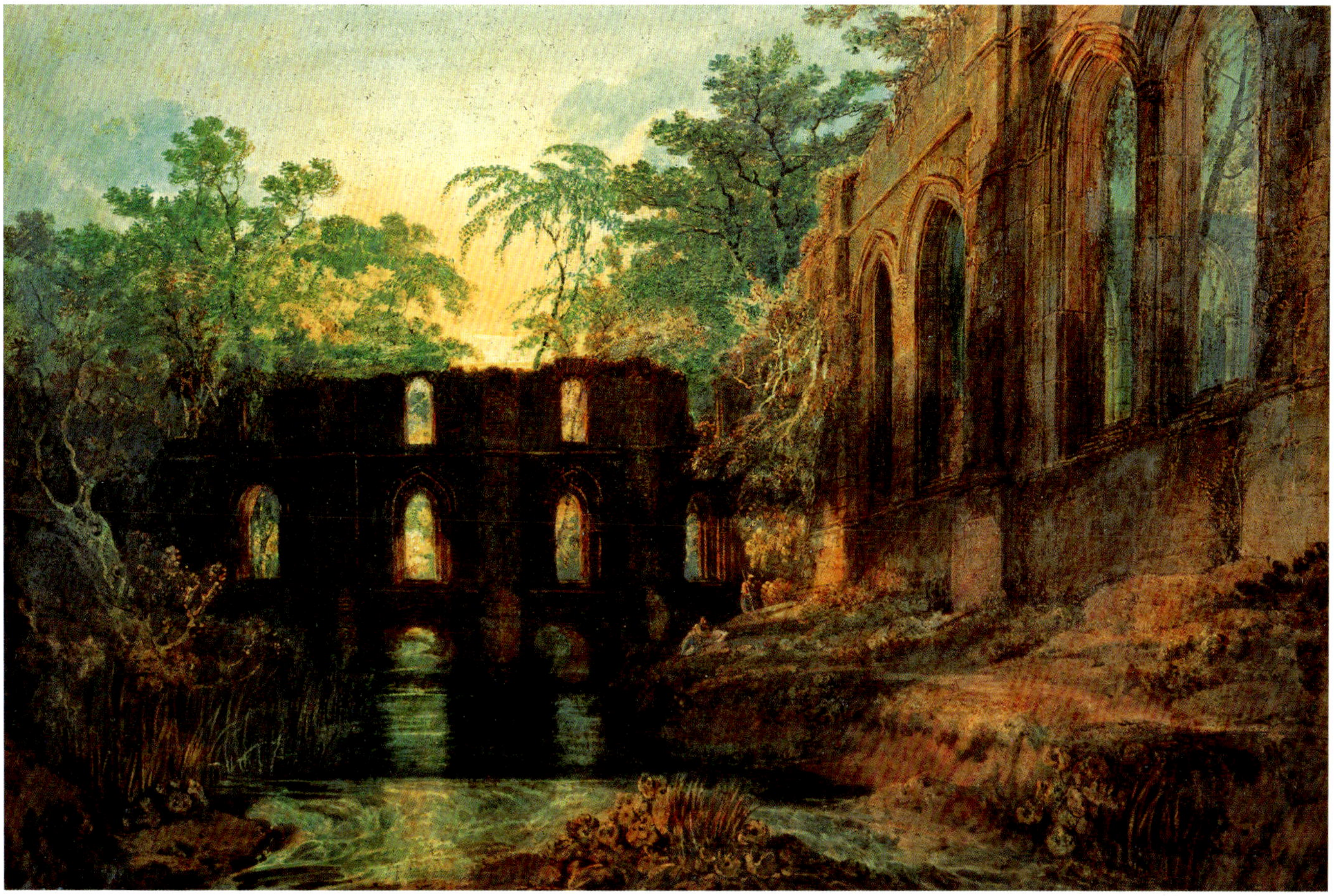

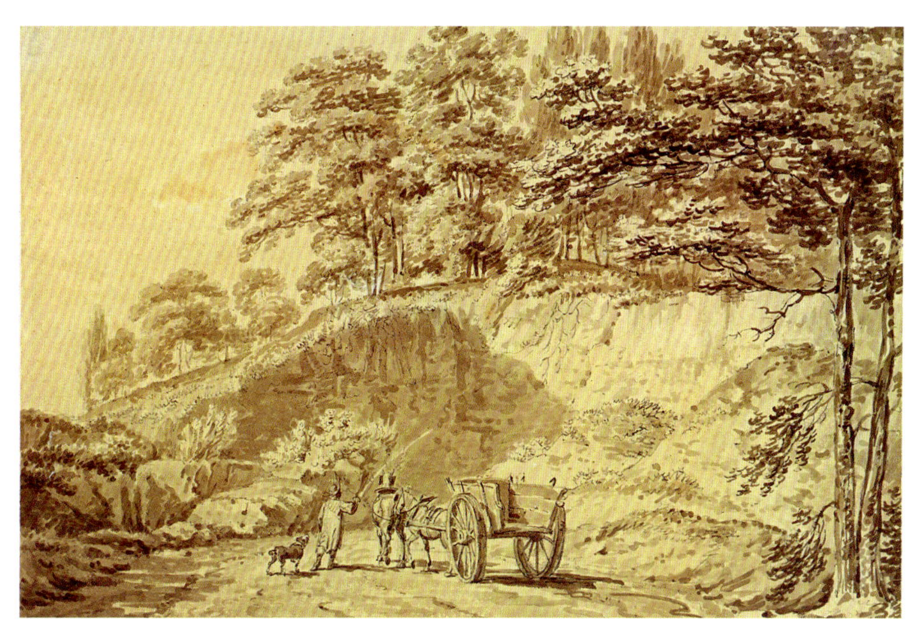

Above: The Dormitory and Transept of Fountains Abbey, Yorkshire, *watercolour, 1798, typifies the picturesque aesthetic.*

that Gilpin had himself only been made a full member two years previously and lacked any real influence. Nevertheless, one can notice a change in Turner's palette, albeit for a short time, since he was clearly influenced by Gilpin's 'Letter on Landscape Painting', which advocated using a more sombre watercolour palette.

In May 1798, Turner's close friend the musician John Danby (1757–98) died, leaving behind his pregnant widow Sarah, and their three children. Turner had a great love of music, and as a close neighbour, he was drawn into the Danby family circle. John had been a very accomplished musician and composer of sacred music and had suffered a short illness, possibly a stroke, before dying. Within a few months, Sarah became Turner's mistress.

Right: Man with Horse and Cart Entering a Quarry, *graphite and grey wash, 1797.*

Staying again with his friends the Narraways in Bristol in the summer of 1798, Turner borrowed a pony to ride through Wales, from South to North, before returning through Hereford, completing more than 500 drawings and small watercolours in five separate sketchbooks along the way. Many of these were worked up into watercolour and oil paintings and submitted to the Royal Academy exhibition the following year, including *Harlech Castle from Twgwyn Ferry, Summer's Evening Twilight* and *Abergavenny Bridge, Monmouthshire.*

In his sketchbooks of the time, Turner wrote down the words to a number of songs, a tribute possibly to his late friend, Danby.

ROMANTICISM

Artistic endeavour never exists in a cultural vacuum and Turner, like every other great artist, created an aesthetic that was akin to his own era – his was the Romantic period. The artist did for painting what Walter Scott and Lord Byron were doing for literature.

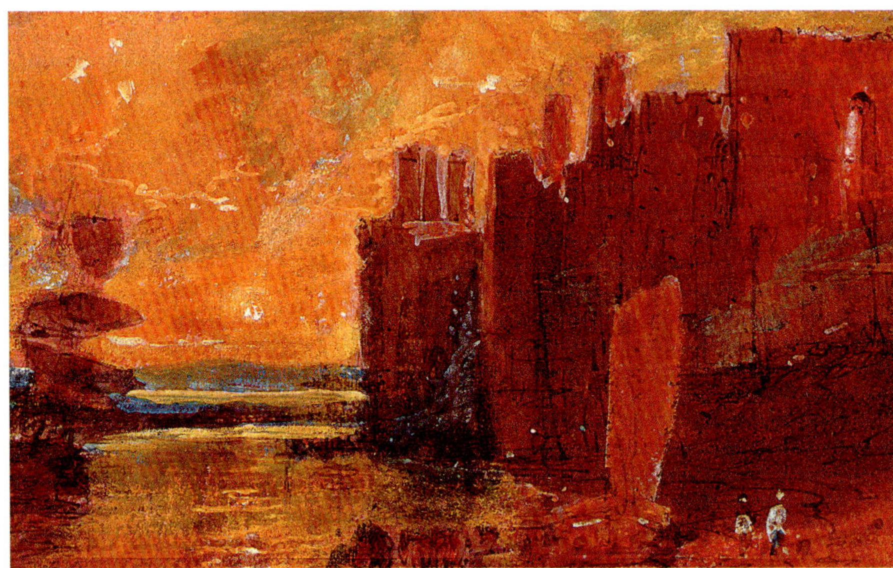

Above: Caernarvon Castle at Sunset, *watercolour, 1798. The painting was shown the same year at the Royal Academy.*

Romanticism was a complex artistic movement at the end of the 18th century, offering ideas that continued through and beyond the 19th century. The 'Picturesque' aesthetic was a part of the same anti-rational movement that favoured human emotion over rational Enlightenment.

ROMANTICISM AS AN AESTHETIC

Set against the background of a burgeoning Industrial Revolution, in which the agricultural land was being depleted to make way for urbanization, Romanticism offered escapism from the problems that were associated with progress, a regression to a previous era that embraced notions of medievalism and the embrace of an imaginative, often exotic 'otherness'. These ideas were most strongly realized in the paintings of Phillip James de Loutherbourg (1740–1812),

the music of Ludwig van Beethoven (1770–1827) and the poetry of George Gordon, Lord Byron (1788–1824), and were to provide an important source of influence and inspiration for Turner's own aesthetic.

EXHIBITIONS OF 1798 AND 1799

New rules at the Royal Academy allowed Turner to append citations to work submitted to its annual exhibition after 1798, thereby enhancing his reputation as a Romantic artist. His submission for that year included an oil painting, *Coniston Fells*, to which he attached a quotation from Milton's *Paradise Lost*. He also included some lines from James Thomson's 'Seasons' poems to four of the six watercolours he submitted. At the end of the year Turner had been offered a commission by Richard Colt Hoare to depict the story of *Aeneas and the Sybil*, which was to be a complementary work to one by Richard Wilson. The painting became Turner's first exercise in classical landscape painting, akin to that of Claude, Poussin and Wilson. The following year Turner exhibited a painting called *Battle of the Nile*, a ferocious contemporary naval battle scene depicting the exact moment when the French flagship *L'Orient* was destroyed in August 1798, giving victory to Lord Nelson. Such a display of

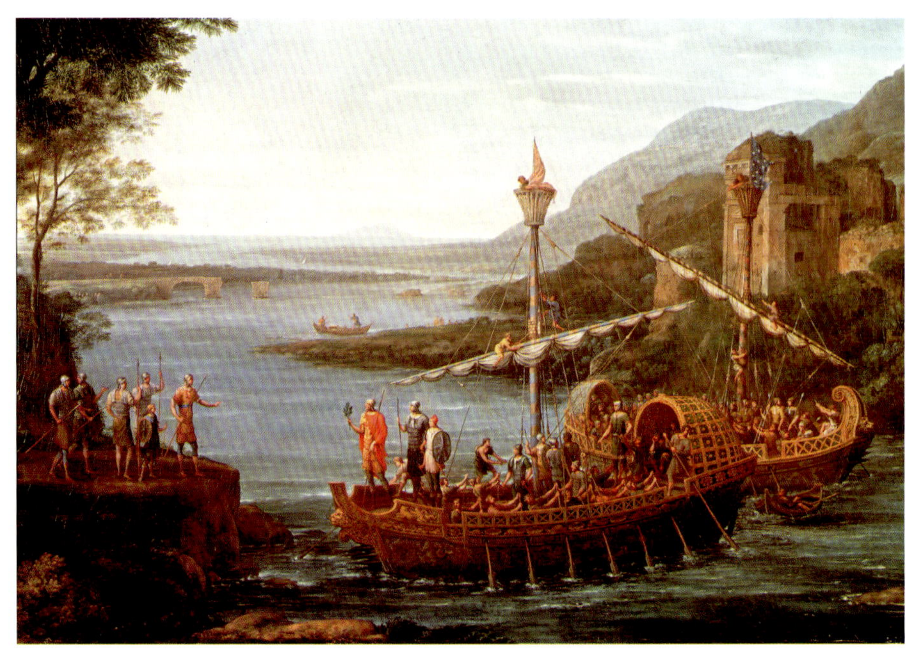

Right: Arrival of Aeneas at Pallanteum *(detail), Claude, oil on canvas, 1675. This picture was typical of the classical landscape tradition, and Claude's style became a source of inspiration for Turner.*

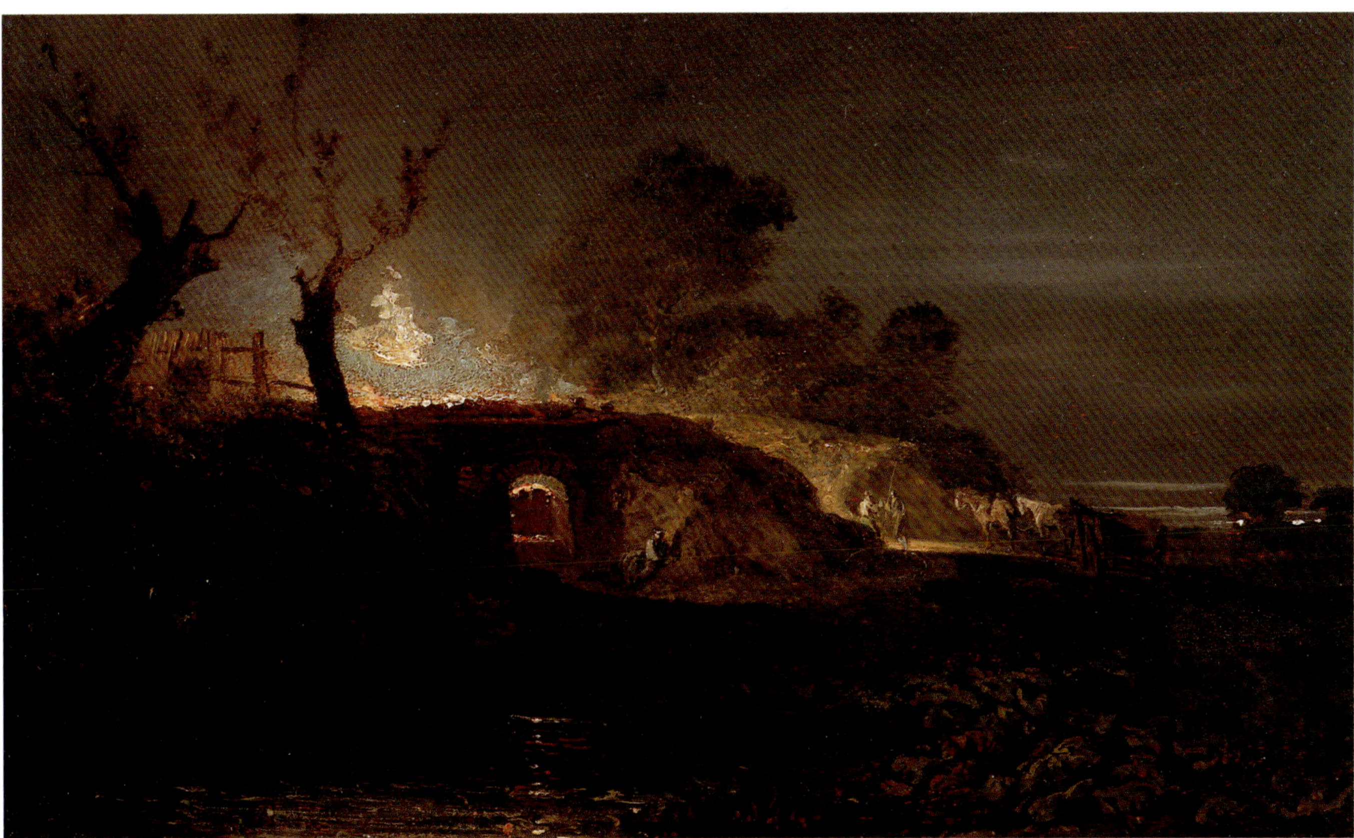

obvious patriotism must have been in the back of Turner's mind as he sought election again to the Royal Academy. Again he appended lines from Milton's *Paradise Lost* to the painting.

PUBLISHING

Turner saw another way of creating an awareness of his talent among a greater public and making extra money – by publishing his images as engraved prints. In 1798, he was commissioned by the Clarendon Press to create a painting for use in the yearly *Oxford Almanack*, distributed to every college from 1799 until 1811. He was also commissioned to paint a series of ten watercolours for the Lancastrian vicar and antiquarian Dr Thomas Dunham Whitaker (1759–1821), who was writing a *History*

Above: A Limekiln at Coalbrookdale, *oil on panel, 1797, demonstrates Turner's fascination with the Romanticism of the Industrial Revolution and its effects on the landscape.*

of the Parish of Whalley; typical of rural parishes in Lancashire that had become surrounded by the urban sprawl of industrialization. Turner had been invited to Townley Hall in Burnley, about 12km (8 miles) from Whalley, by the antiquarian collector Charles Townley (1737–1805) to carry out this small commission. However, he met Thomas Lister Parker (1779–1858), whose large estate, Browsholme Hall, was included in the schema. It was Parker who later introduced Turner to two of his most important patrons, Walter Ramsden Fawkes and Sir John Fleming Leicester. Meanwhile, Turner was entering the world of printmaking, which was to become a major part of his future artistic output and income.

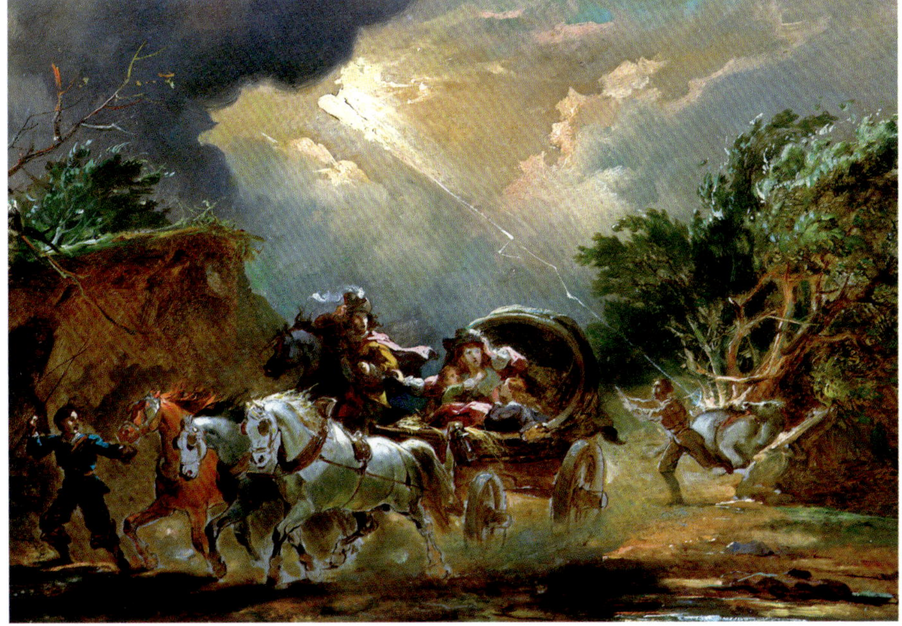

Left: Coach in a Thunderstorm, *Phillip James de Loutherbourg, oil on millboard, 1799. The artist was at the forefront of Romantic painting.*

ASSOCIATE ACADEMICIAN

Although the year 1799 began badly – with a rejection of Turner's financial terms for a commission – it was to end on a high note. Ten years after being accepted as a student at the Royal Academy, he was elected to Associate membership, at the earliest permitted age.

Having been rejected the previous year for membership of the Royal Academy as an associate, Turner may well have judged that the proposal by Thomas Bruce, 7th Earl of Elgin (1766–1841), to accompany him to Greece and then on to Turkey, where Lord Elgin was to take up the post of British Ambassador to the Ottoman Empire, was inopportune. Elgin wanted to commission Turner to

Below: Francis Egerton, 3rd Duke of Bridgewater, E. Scriven (1775–1841), lithograph, c.1835. The Duke of Bridgewater was responsible for building the Manchester Ship Canal, which was an important mode of transport during the Industrial Revolution.

create a series of landscape paintings en route, but he refused to meet Turner's £400 fee, which did not include the pictures themselves. Subsequently, Lord Elgin employed the Italian artist, Giovanni Lusieri.

SECOND APPLICATION TO THE ACADEMY

Having lost the election in the previous year, Turner was determined to put his best foot forward for his application in 1799. Apart from his submissions to the Academy exhibition, which would of course be his best work, he decided to court two established Academicians for support: the painter Joseph Farington (1747–1821) and the architect Robert

Smirke (1780–1867), who later designed the British Museum. Turner also knew that he had the support of some of the old guard such as George Dance the younger (1741–1825). To add to the support, *The Times* reported favourably on Turner's submissions to the exhibition referring to his "excellent pieces (that) continue to support the reputation he has acquired".

MOVING HOME

At the end of 1799, Turner had officially been elected to membership of the Royal Academy as an Associate. At the same time he was concerned about his existing accommodation in Maiden Lane. First, if he wanted to pursue a painting career as an Academician that included large-scale history paintings, then his existing studio space was inadequate; second, the address itself was not prestigious enough for an aspirant artist. After consulting fellow Academician Joseph Farington, he secured rooms at 64 Harley Street, a newly formed row of large town houses that were occupied by the wealthy and influential. This proved to be a shrewd move by Turner who now had premises in an affluent area and a studio that was clean, modern and had ample daylight, a contrast to his dimly lit studio in Maiden Lane. Turner also installed his mistress Sarah Danby, with her now four children, in Upper John Sreet, close to his new premises.

Turner's mother had been suffering from mental illness for some time, and in the last month of the 18th century, she was committed to a private lunatic asylum. A year later, she was transferred to Bethlem Hospital, where she died in April 1804. Turner's father also left Maiden Lane sometime in 1800, moving to Harley Sreet with his son, where he acted as general factotum and manager in the house and studio.

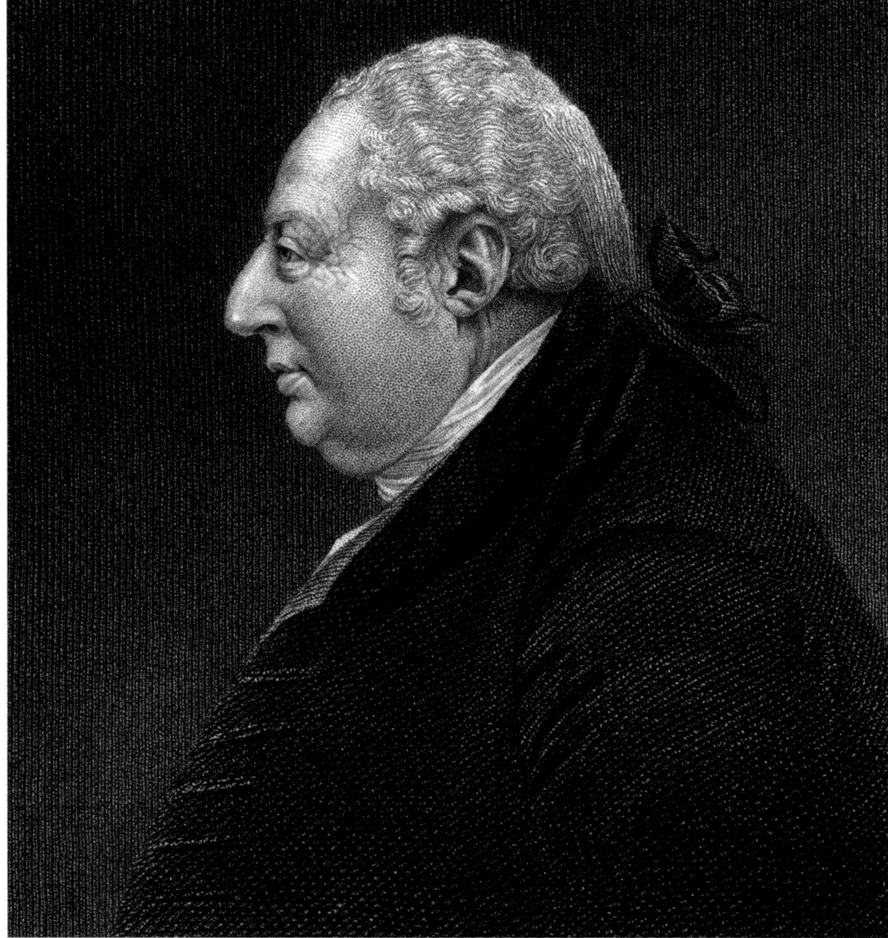

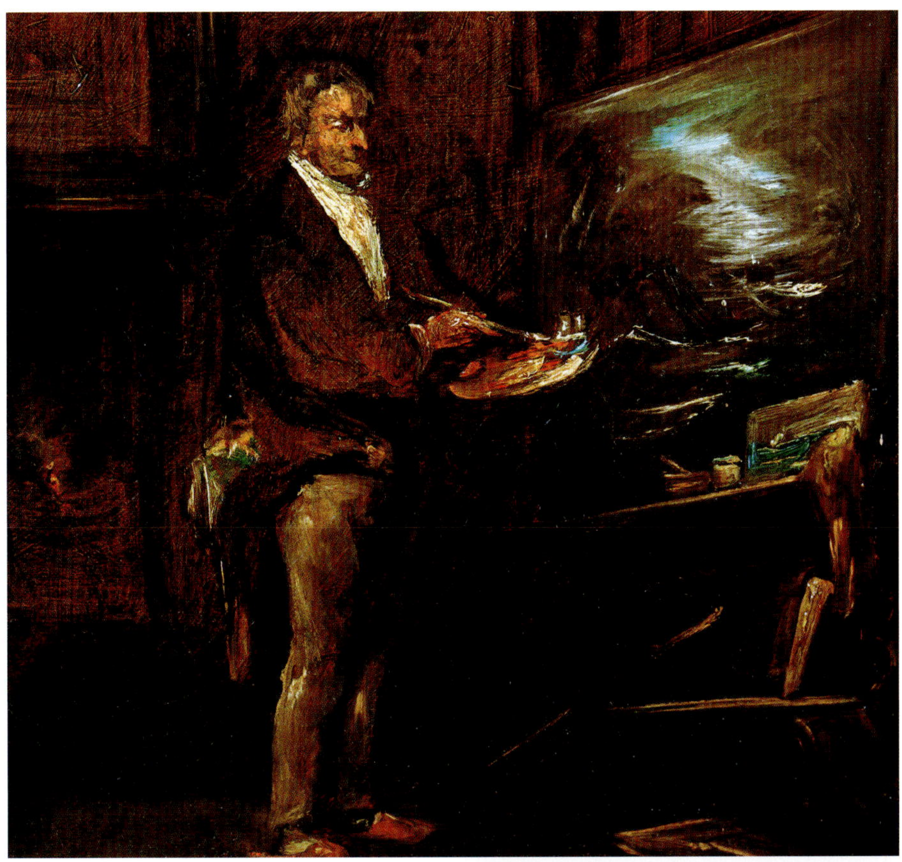

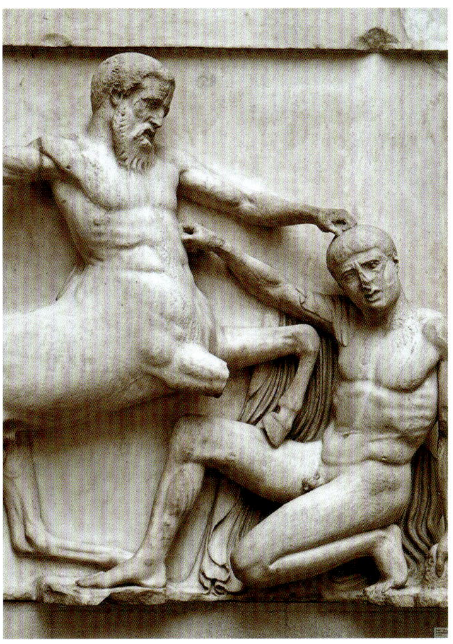

Above: Part of the Elgin Marbles, *British Museum, photograph.*

Left: Portrait of Joseph Mallord William Turner, *Sir John Gilbert (1817–97), oil on canvas, c.1845. This was Gilbert's second study of Turner.*

THE TURN OF THE CENTURY

Turner began the 19th century as an Associate Academician. In his first year, he was commissioned by the Duke of Bridgewater to paint a companion piece to a work by a Dutch painter. The fee for the painting was 250 guineas, the largest payment he had commanded to date for a single painting. The result was *Dutch Boats in a Gale.* The painting, which was completed in 1801, depicts fishermen endeavouring to haul their catch of fish on board.

These elaborate titles became a hallmark of many of Turner's paintings from this time. In conjunction with the citations he often appended to his Royal Academy exhibition submissions, they give an indication of his earnest endeavours toward Classical painting in the mould of Claude Lorrain.

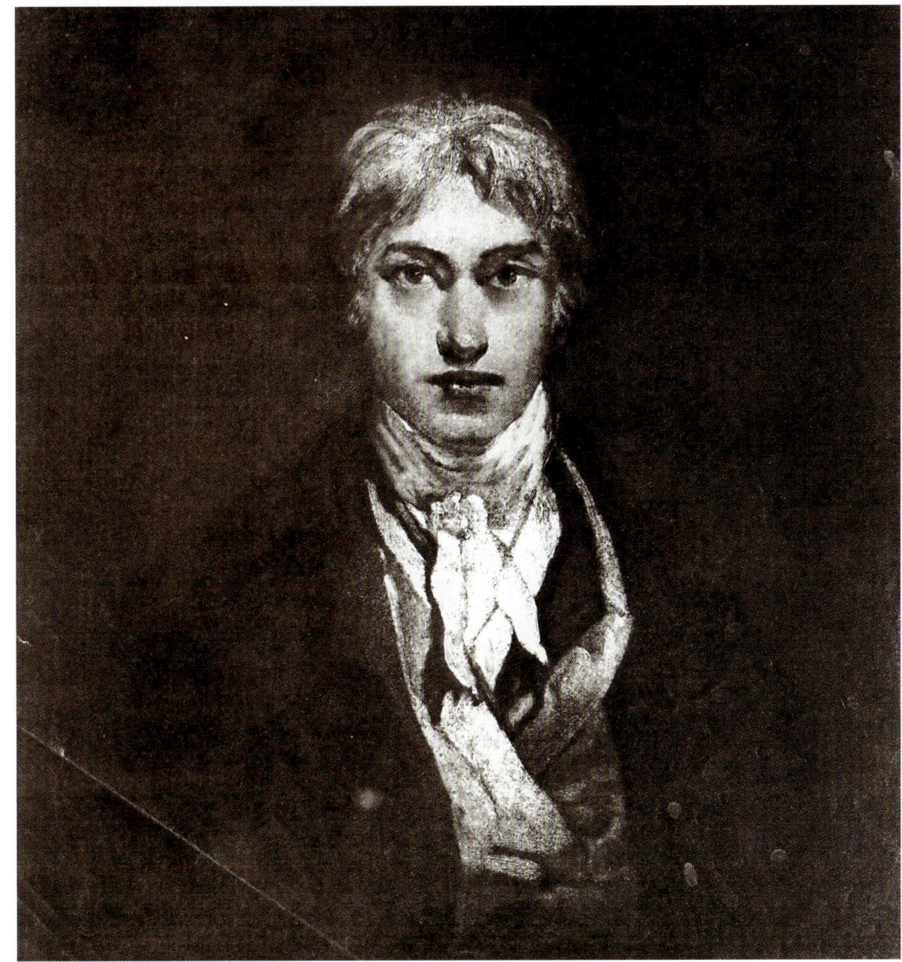

Right: Portrait of the Artist Aged about Twenty-three *(self-portrait), oil on canvas, 1799. The elaborate clothing befitting a gentleman symbolizes Turner's ambition at this time to mix in important social circles in order to attract patrons.*

THE SUBLIME IN LANDSCAPE

Moving farther from the Classical, rational, Enlightenment aesthetic, toward a non-rational, Romantic 'Sublime', Turner was drawn to the landscapes of Scotland, though his diligence and career pragmatism were never left behind.

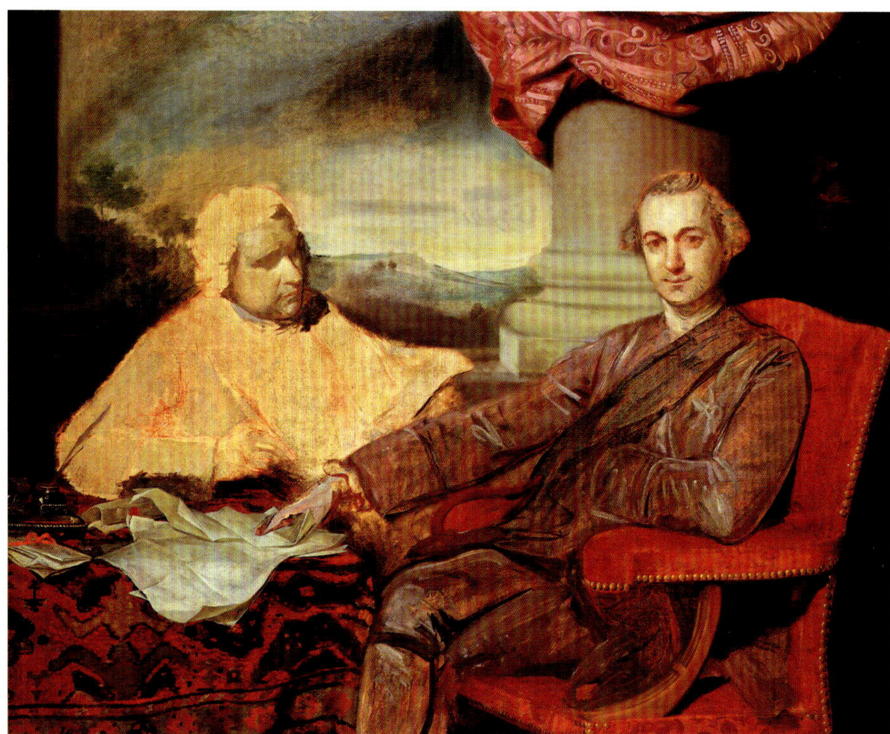

Left: Portrait of Lord Rockingham and Edmund Burke, *Sir Joshua Reynolds, oil on canvas, c.1766. This unfinished portrait reflects the precarious nature of the then Prime Minister Lord Rockingham, seen on the left, and the ascension of Edmund Burke as a philosophical thinker.*

Turner's journey to Scotland in 1801 was to embrace those aspects of the 'Sublime' aesthetic that he had first encountered on his trips to Wales. As part of the Romantic ideal, Turner began to shift the emphasis of his painting from mere topography to one that embraced the more ethereal aspects of a landscape.

AN AESTHETIC CONCEPT

As a new Academician, Turner sought to embrace the Sublime aesthetic and Classical landscape painting in his range of work at the start of the new century. Although one can see aspects of the Sublime in the work of for example Phillip James de Loutherbourg, his figures always appear at a safe distance from the impending disaster, whereas

Right: Loch Lomond, *watercolour, 1803. One of the best known and loved of the Scottish lochs, it is the largest lake in Great Britain.*

Turner's figures seem to actually be an inherent part of the 'terror'. The concept of the Sublime was the delight invoked by a frightening sight that would not harm the viewer. Turner's embrace of the Sublime began with his painting *The Fifth Plague of Egypt*, exhibited in

1800, and reached its apogee in the painting *Snow Storm: Steam Boat off a Harbour's Mouth* in 1842. His journey to seek out the Sublime began in 1801 with his trip to Scotland.

SCOTTISH LANDSCAPE

When Turner travelled to Scotland in June 1801, his mistress Sarah Danby had given birth to their daughter Evelina. Turner travelled to York and through Berwick-upon-Tweed on to Edinburgh, arriving there in the first week of July. Before his arrival in Edinburgh, Turner made more than three hundred drawings and sketches around Kirkstall, Helmsley and the Guisborough shoreline. In the city, he completed over one hundred more and began a sketchbook that was entitled 'Scotch figures' that he wished to use in future paintings. These figures would of

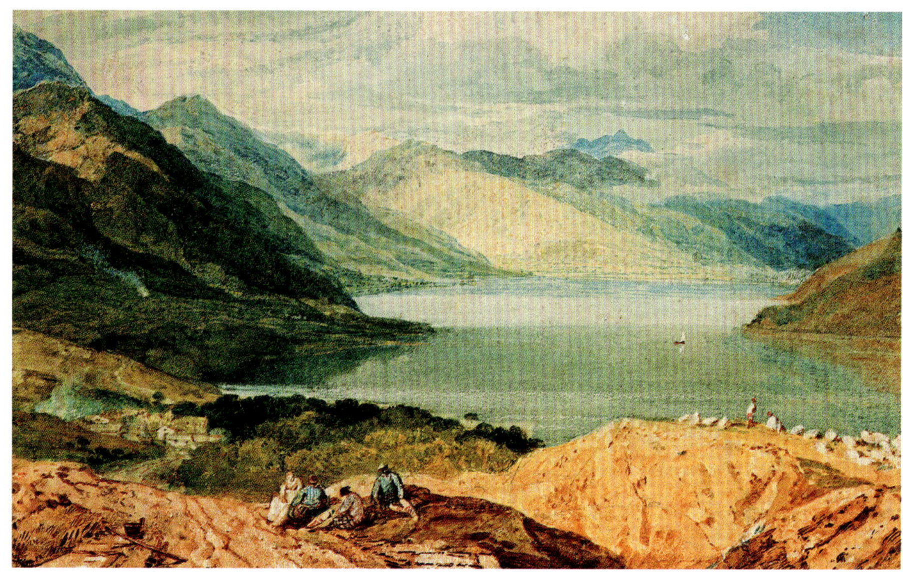

WHAT IS THE SUBLIME?

The concept of the Sublime was originally a 17th-century notion that sought to explain nature's magnificence in a non-rational or scientific way. A treatise by Edmund Burke (1729–97) called *A Philosophical Inquiry into the Origin of Our Ideas of the Sublime and Beautiful* (1756) was being discussed in terms of focusing on the physiological effects of the Sublime, in particular how humans deal with the dual emotions of fear and awe when confronted with an aspect of nature, such as thunderstorms, avalanches and large waterfalls. By encountering the Sublime object, according to Burke, we derive 'delight' since 'the mind is so entirely filled with its object, that it cannot entertain any other'. The notion of the Sublime is antithetical to those of Classical landscape painting, which is ordered and usually tranquil.

course have differed from their English counterparts because of their attire. Turner also created a series of drawings that were later termed the 'Scottish pencils', a series of larger sketches that he referred to many times in his studio as they included a great deal of information on the topographical and physical features of particular landscape views. From Edinburgh, he travelled north-west to Loch Lomond, Inverary and finally to Tummel Bridge in the Highlands. Turner's journey would have been particularly difficult owing to the terrain and absence of any road infrastructure. He had first discussed the journey with Joseph Farington, who advised on the route, and in particular the best vantage points for 'Picturesque views'. Despite the arduousness of the journey, Turner managed to make over five hundred drawings en route, the most notable being the 'Scotch Lakes' Sketchbook.

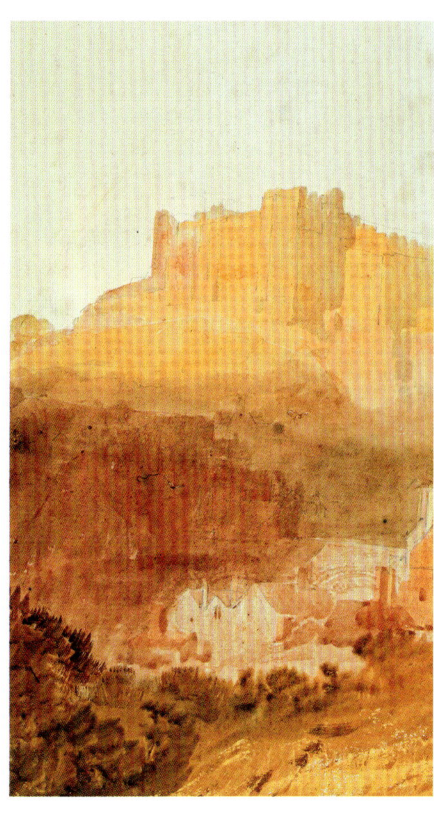

Above: Durham Castle, watercolour, 1801. This Norman castle was built in the 11th century and used as a defensive fortress.

Below: Tummel Bridge, Perthshire, oil on panel, c.1801–3. Tummel is a village in the central Highlands of Scotland.

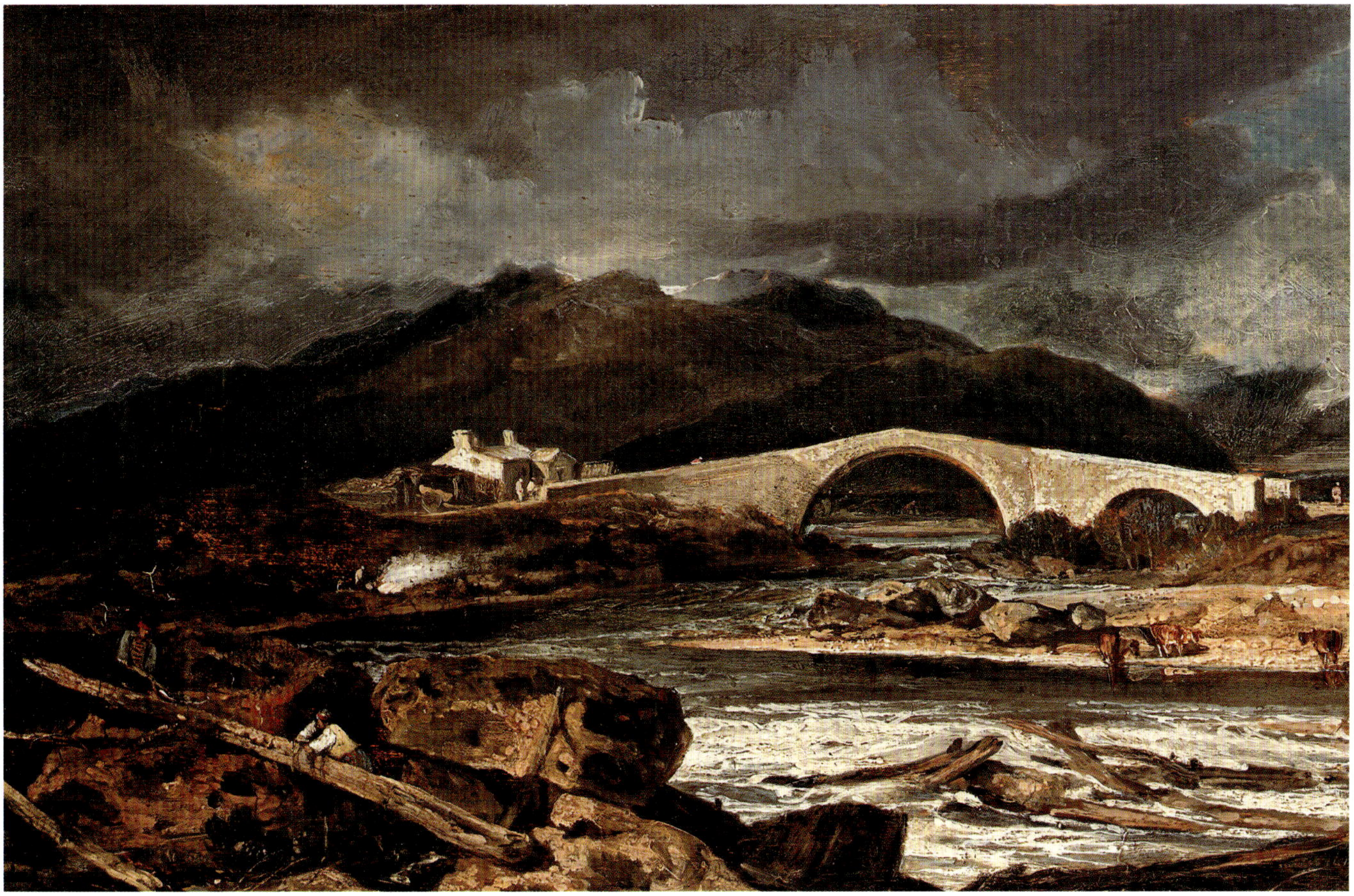

ELECTED TO THE ACADEMY

Turner's long-held ambition to join the Royal Academy was in sight. High praise from influential members, combined with luck and good timing, assured his entry, but his advancement was to come at one of the Academy's most turbulent periods.

Having been an Associate of the Royal Academy for only two years, Turner returned to London in the autumn of 1801, determined to become a full member.

THE ELECTION

Traditionally there were 80 members of the Academy, of whom a certain number had to be architects and sculptors, with the remainder being either painters or printmakers. In effect, the election by the existing membership, held in February, depended on the number of vacancies and candidates. Before the election in 1802, two other Academicians had also died, making Turner's electability less doubtful. In any event he was elected along with the architect John Soane (1753–1837), and the sculptor Charles Rossi (1762–1839). Joseph Farington, Turner's main supporter at the time, was keen to include a young artist who in many ways represented the future of the English school of painting, an acknowledgment of the high esteem that Turner's reputation already commanded.

TROUBLE AT THE ROYAL ACADEMY

The president of the Royal Academy at the time of Turner's elevation to Academician was an Anglo-American founder member, Benjamin West (1738–1820). It was in fact West, together with Sir William Chambers, who first mooted the idea of an Academy with a royal charter to King George III. The Academy was started in 1768 and enjoyed royal patronage in its early years. After the death of its first president Sir Joshua Reynolds in 1792, the Academy elected West as his successor. West was a court painter and seemed unable to separate his loyalties to the king and to the Academy. In consequence, the king was deemed to be interfering in the affairs of the Academy, and this was causing divisions in the rank and file membership.

Turner became a member of the Council in 1803 and, having sided with West, was by May of 1804 unable to attend the meetings any longer because of the acrimonious atmosphere.

Below: Ludlow Castle, *watercolour on paper, 1800, painted on a trip to the Midlands. A subsequent version made in 1829 was reproduced as an engraving.*

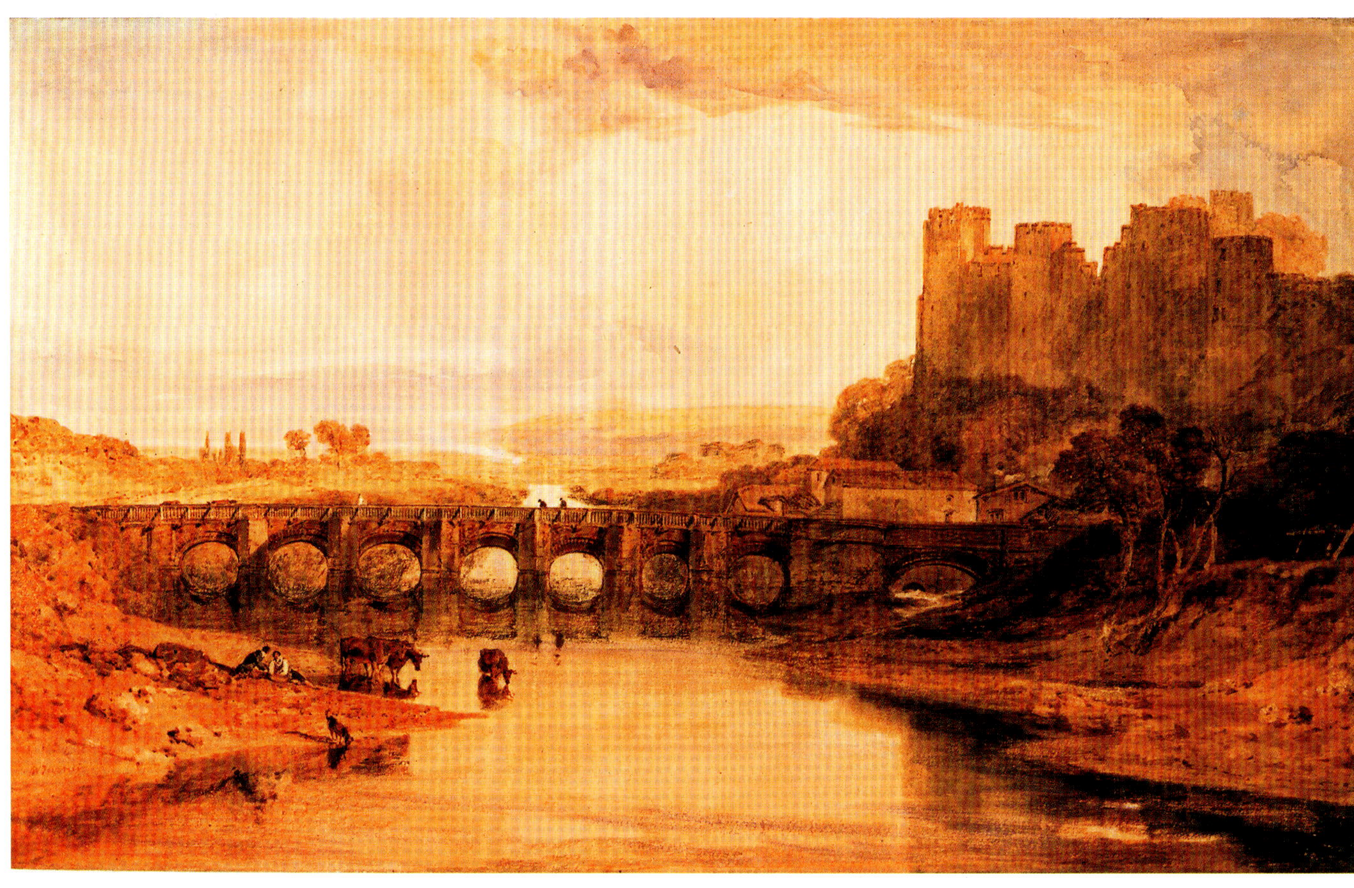

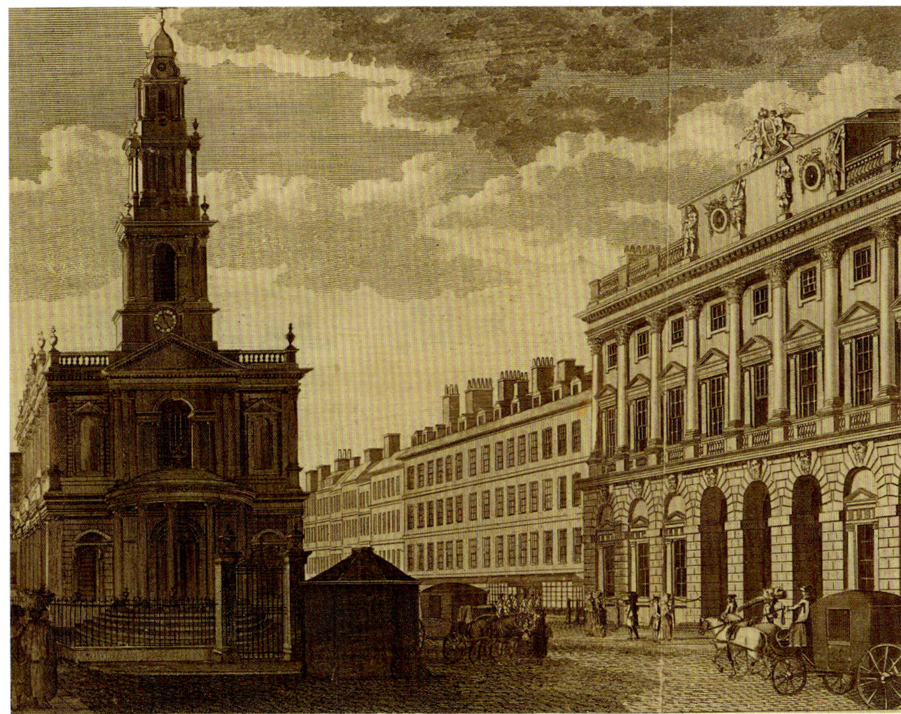

Above: Perspective View of the Royal Academy of Arts, *Paul Sandby, engraving, 1795.*

West had been kind to Turner in his early career, and others such as John Constable (1776–1837) had occasionally acted as a mentor. By 1805, West's career was in decline and he stepped

Below: Portrait of Benjamin West (1738–1820), President of the Royal Academy, *Josi Christian (d. 1828), engraving, 1794.*

down from the presidency. In the following year, however, his colleagues pleaded with him to accept the presidency once again, and he went on to hold the title until his death in 1820. Calm had been restored at the Academy.

A STUDIO ASSISTANT

With a now immense workload, it was necessary for Turner to have a studio assistant to stretch his large canvases, which also needed to be primed and prepared. Until now the artist had been outsourcing the work to Sebastian

Turner always considered the commercial aspects of painting first and foremost, since to him painting was a business. By allowing his father to make and prepare the canvases he could save both time and money. These canvases would be those on which his first paintings as a Royal Academician would be executed and then displayed at the annual exhibition. Included in this show was the enormous canvas *The Tenth Plague of Egypt*, which enjoyed great critical acclaim.

Grandi, an artists' colourman who had prepared grounds for Sir Joshua Reynolds. Grandi's workshop was in Long Acre, close to Maiden Lane in Covent Garden. Turner's painting surfaces were extremely absorbent and required much preparation. Turner's father, who acted as his manager, watched Grandi's techniques very carefully before attempting the process himself and becoming his son's assistant.

Below: The Tenth Plague of Egypt *(from the* Liber Studorium, *engraved by William Say), etching, 1816. This etching is taken from the enormous historical painting that Turner executed and exhibited at the Royal Academy in 1802.*

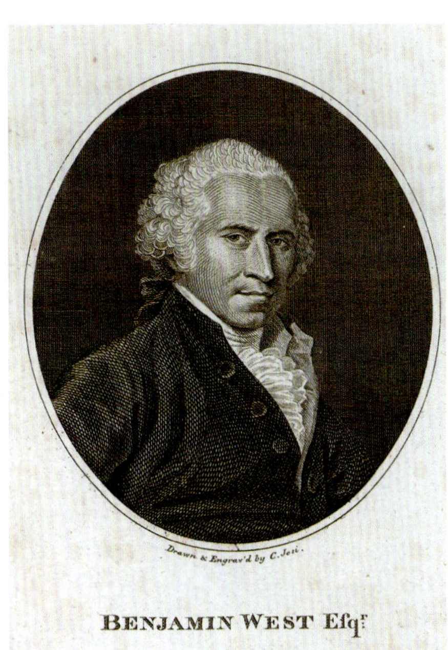

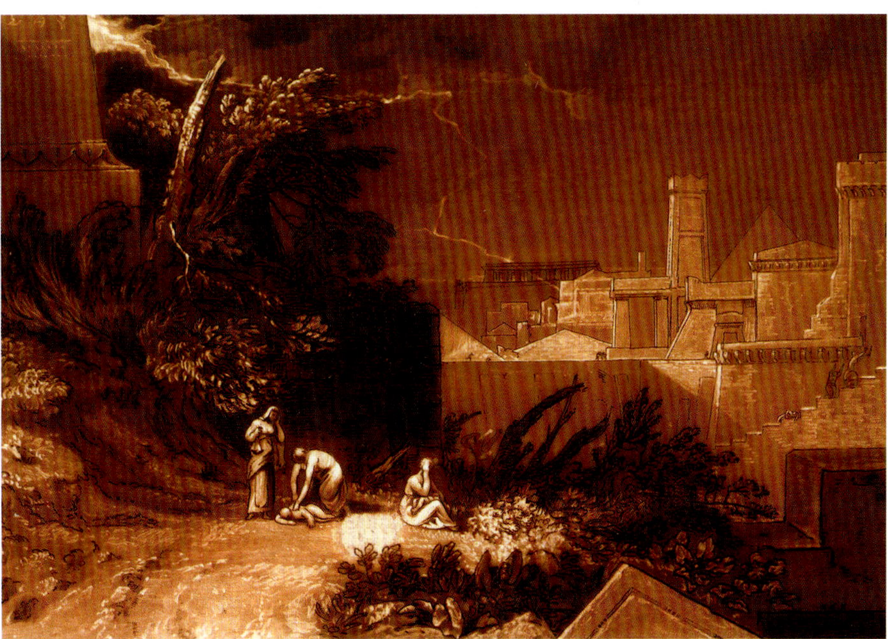

THE FIRST CONTINENTAL TOUR

Following the Treaty of Amiens, Britons were able to visit the Continent once more and Turner took full advantage of this by travelling to France and Switzerland. His return journey took him to Paris where he was able to see the art collection at the Louvre.

In the month following Turner's election to the Academy, the Treaty of Amiens was signed, effectively bringing to an end the hostilities between France and Britain, which were known as the French Revolutionary Wars.

THE TREATY OF AMIENS

During the Wars, Britons had been unable to travel through France. This break in hostilities provided the opportunity for a number of affluent British citizens to flock to Paris. Turner had other ideas, wanting to enjoy the Sublime aspects of the Alpine region. The treaty was short lived and a little over a year later hostilities were resumed with many Britons unable to escape until after the Battle of Waterloo in 1815. Turner was more fortunate and returned to England via Paris in October 1802.

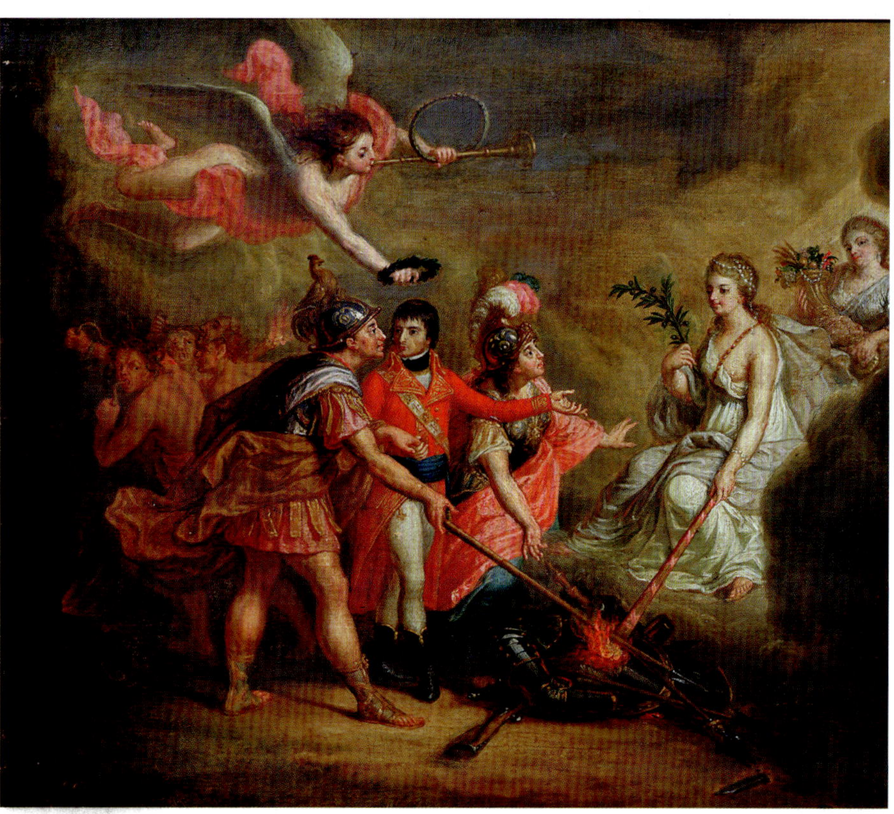

Above: The Peace of Amiens, 25th March 1802, *Dominique Doncre, oil on canvas, 19th century.*

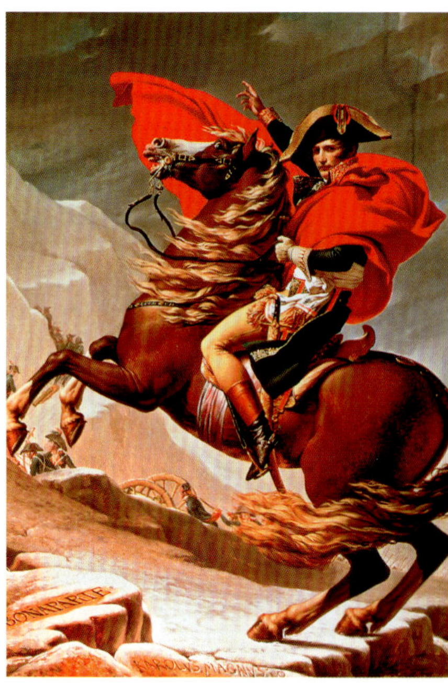

Above: Napoleon Crossing the Alps, *Jacques-Louis David, oil on canvas, 1800. Turner met this revolutionary political painter during his visit to Paris.*

THE ALPS

In July 1802, Turner set sail for France on what would be a three-month journey 'to study on the Continent the works of the great masters'. He was sponsored on this trip by three patrons including Lord Yarborough and was accompanied by a country gentleman named Newby Lowson (1773–1853). The weather was atrocious on the cross channel trip and was recorded in Turner's Small Calais Pier Sketchbook. One of these was annotated with the comment 'Our landing at Calais. Nearly swamped'. From these sketches he worked up one of his major oil paintings, *Calais Pier, with French Poissards Preparing for Sea: An English Packet Arriving*, exhibited the following year at the Royal Academy. From here Turner and his companion travelled by carriage to Paris before proceeding on a four-day journey to Lyons. Around

Grenoble, another day's journey south, Turner encountered the largest and most awesome Sublime object he had seen so far, La Grande Chartreuse, a mountain range also known as the Prealps. From here he went on to Chamonix and saw the massive Mont Blanc as well as the infamous Mer de Glace on its northern side. Turner was always well prepared for these trips and on this occasion brought a Swiss guide with him, whom he had hired in Paris. As on his previous expeditions he made copious notes and drawings, amassing some four hundred reference sketches. In addition he recorded a series of some eighty 'Swiss figures' drawings, some coloured, that he would use as reference material.

LONDON, 1802

Back in London and armed with a vast array of reference material, Turner set about using it to create some of his most ambitious works to date. He created a series of large-format Swiss-themed watercolours, including *St Huges Denouncing Vengeance on the Shepherd of Cormayer, in the Valley of d'Aoust*, exhibited in 1803 at the Royal Academy. He also painted a large oil entitled *The Festival upon the Opening of the Vintage at Macon*, emulating the style of Claude Lorrain. Turner also attended the funeral of his friend Thomas Girtin, whom he had known since youth, and who had died, probably from asthma, when he was aged only 27. Later in life, Turner remarked that "Had Tom Girtin lived, I should have starved".

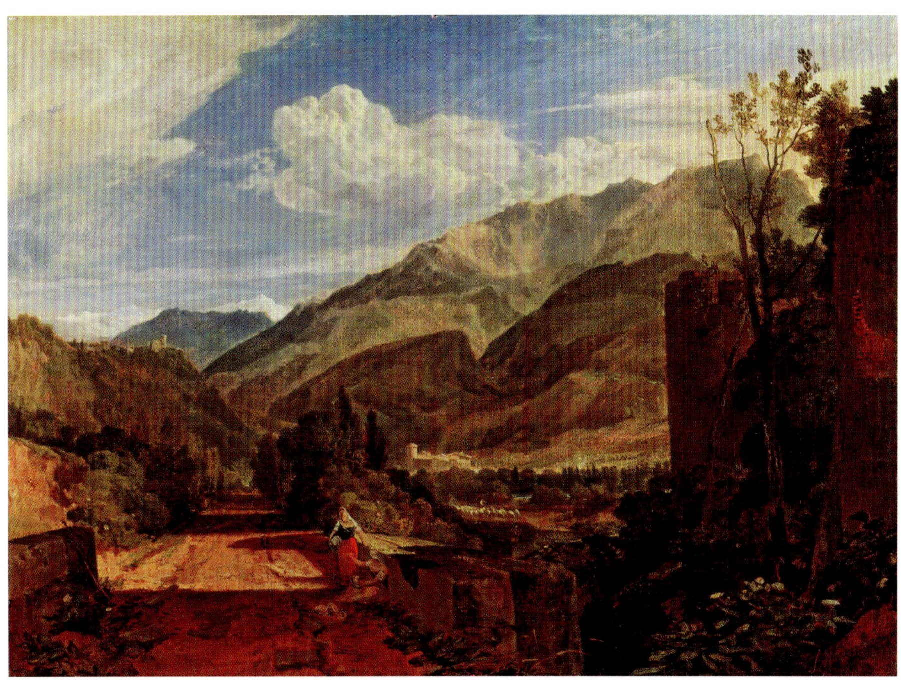

Above right: Château de St Michael, Bonneville, Savoy, *oil on canvas, 1803 is one of two oil paintings of the subject.*

THE LOUVRE, PARIS

Turner made his return journey along the Rhine before crossing France to his final destination, Paris. He met Farington (and several other Royal Academicians) at the Louvre Museum, which had only been open to the public for ten years, after the French Revolution. Significantly the Louvre contained a number of artworks that had been looted by Napoleon from collections in Italy, including works by Titian (Tiziano Vecellio) and Paolo Veronese. Turner spent over two weeks in Paris, creating his studies in the Louvre Sketchbook containing more than 100 careful sketches of the Old Masters. He paid particular attention to the use of colour that was so vibrant in the Venetian school. The Louvre housed a number of Poussin paintings that Turner also studied, as well as some Claude Lorrain pictures.

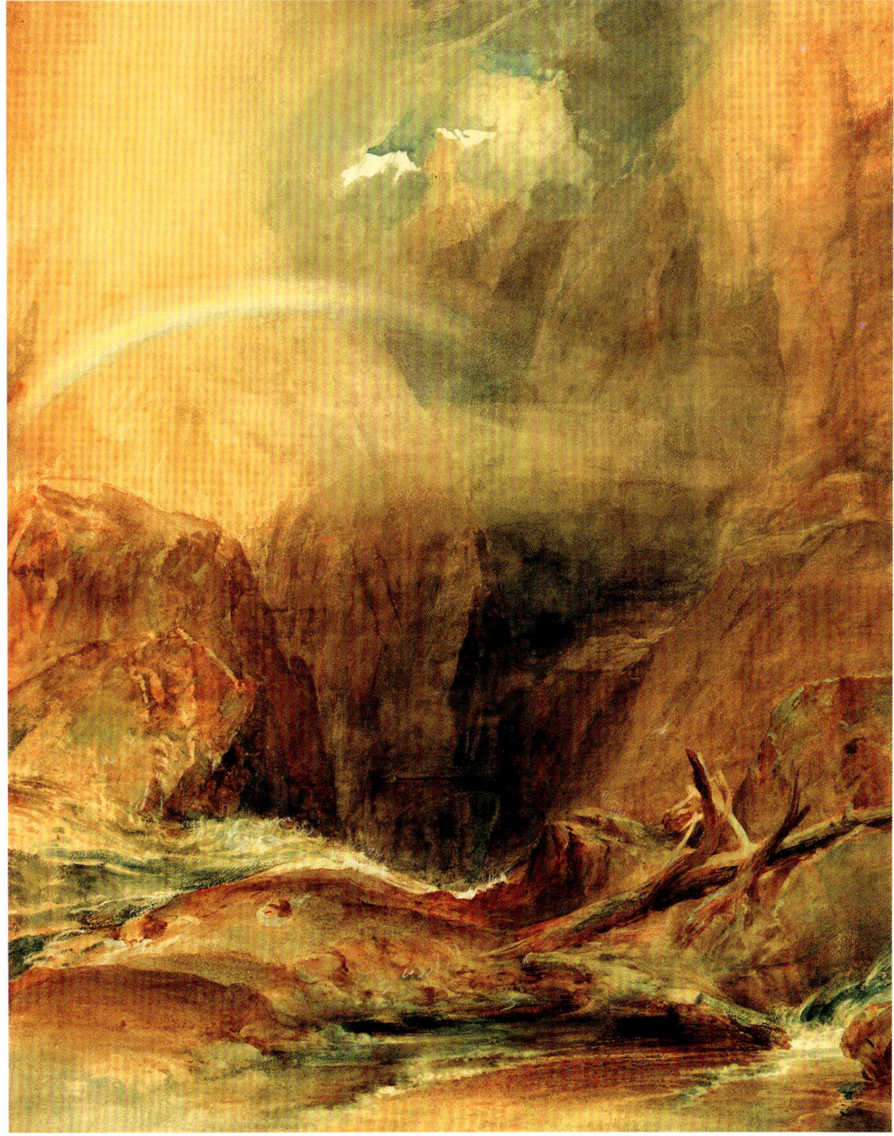

Right: The Devil's Bridge, Passage of St Gotthard, *watercolour and white wax, 1804.*

ARTIST OR TOPOGRAPHER?

Turner was singled out for unfavourable comment from the more conservative members of the Academy and press. His paintings were criticized, in particular by the influential George Beaumont, for his use of colour and their lack of 'finish'.

Sir George Beaumont (1753–1827) was an amateur artist and self-styled arbiter of good taste based on his experiences of a Grand Tour in 1782. On his return to England he built a collection of Old Master paintings such as Claude Lorrain's *A Landscape with Hagar and the Angel*, which was his favourite picture.

Of contemporary culture, Beaumont had a passion for the Picturesque aesthetic and enjoyed the friendship of the poet William Wordsworth. By the early 19th century, he had earned the epithet 'supreme dictator on works of art' – such was his dogmatic view of how paintings should be executed in an Academic manner. He was a supporter of Reynolds and certain artists who followed that tradition, such as the young John Constable, of whom he became a patron. Much of Beaumont's collection was given to the new National Gallery, which had opened in 1824, including four Claude paintings and two by Canaletto (Giovanni Antonio Canal).

CRITIC OF TURNER

The conservatively minded Beaumont was critical of many of Turner's paintings, beginning with *The Festival upon the Opening of the Vintage at Macon* of 1803, stating that "its subject was borrowed from Claude, but the colouring forgotten". He was also critical of the "finish" in Turner's work, claiming that his foregrounds were "comparatively blots".

By 1809, it was all-out war on Turner, whom he had singled out as doing "more harm in misleading the taste than any other artist". He was suggesting that other young artists had become tainted by Turner's painting methods – adopting a watercolour technique to provide washes in his oil paintings and thus eliminating "finish" in certain areas of the picture. Turner retaliated by refusing to sell one of his pictures, *Fishing upon*

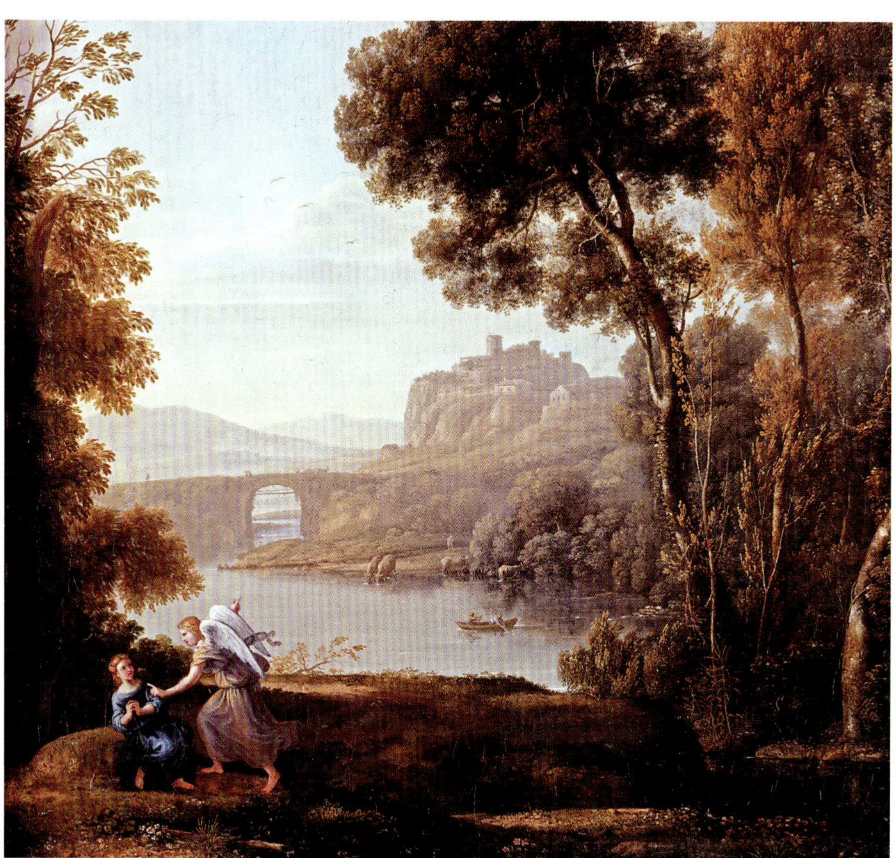

Top: Landscape with Hagar and the Angel, *Claude Lorrain (c.1600–82), oil on canvas, 1646. This painting was first owned by Sir George Beaumont.*

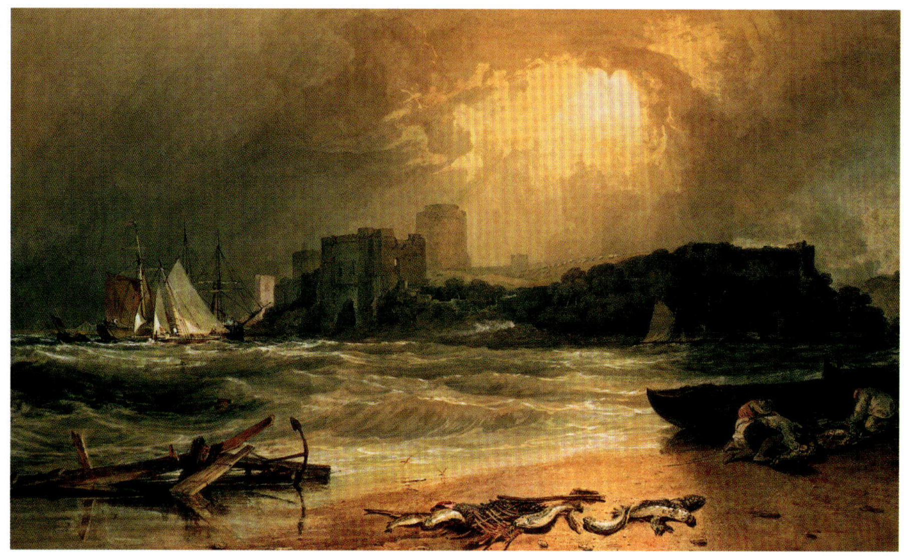

Above: Pembroke Castle, Clearing up after a Thunderstorm, *watercolour, 1806. This scene shows Turner's use of the Claudian motif of looking into the light source.*

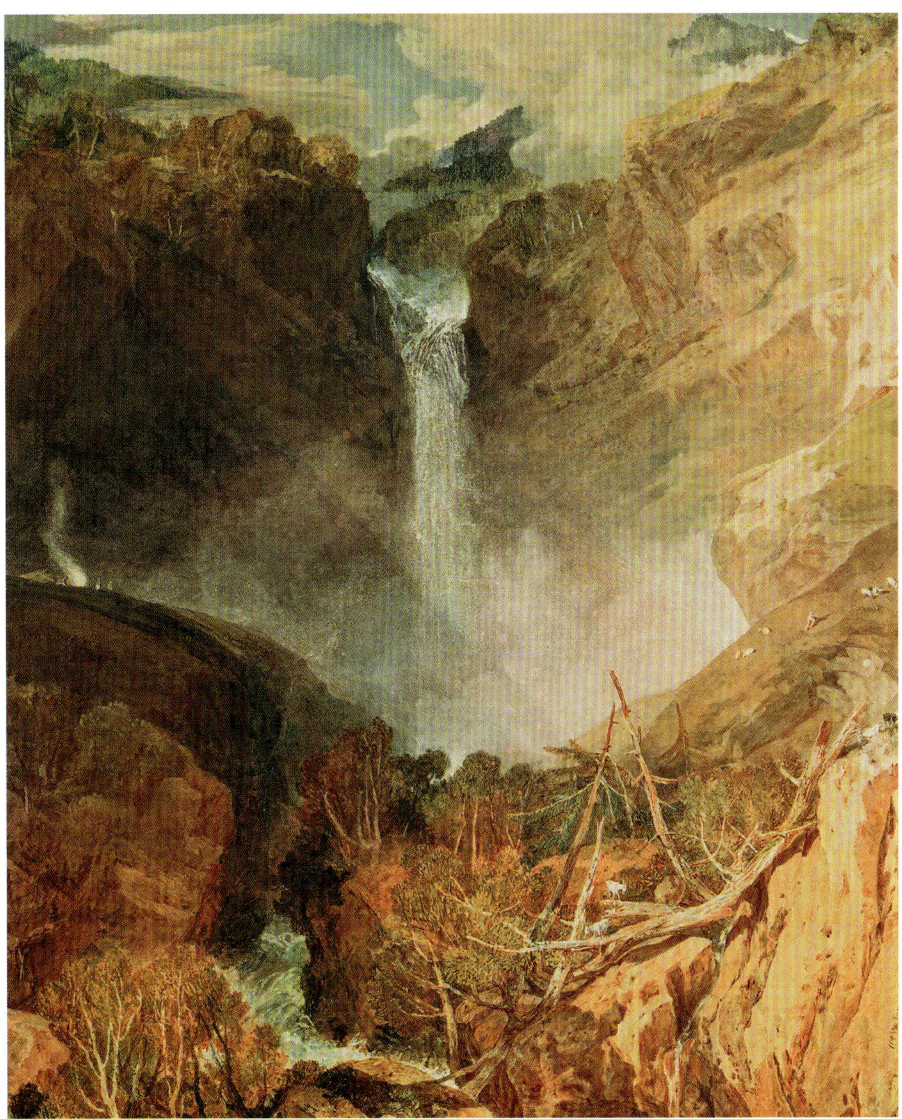

Above: The Great Falls of the Reichenbach, *watercolour, 1804. The large scale of this watercolour suggests that Turner considered this medium as important as oil.*

the *Blythe Sand*, when Beaumont tried to purchase it in 1810, instead using the picture in his own studio as a catflap!

THE KEY DEBATES

One aspect of Beaumont's criticism was that Turner was sensationalizing rather than portraying nature's realism. This criticism had also been levelled at Turner from others in the more

Right: Evening Landscape with Castle and Bridge in Yorkshire, *watercolour, 1799. Here, the mood is more important than the topography.*

conservative sections of the Academy, artists such as John Hoppner (1758–1810) and Joseph Farington. The press joined in the vitriol, suggesting in his *Calais Pier* picture that the sea "looks like soap and chalk" and that his sky "is a heap of marble mountains".

Turner had begun to experiment with colour and form before becoming an Academician, seeking to depict nature's spirit rather than just its geographical features. He realized that for landscape painting to be effectual and to have some purpose beyond topography, nature needed to be expressed as a force. The debates had therefore widened. Was a painting merely a topographical view of a landscape or could it express its mood and spirit? Should the new century herald new forms of patronage, in which artistic integrity took precedence?

TURNER'S RESPONSES

Turner's background precluded him from the social graces normally associated with his aristocratic clientele. His tone with clients was arrogant and often rude, and this worsened after his appointment as an Academician. Joseph Farington remarked that "his manners, so presumptive and arrogant were spoken of with great disgust." Turner responded in paint.

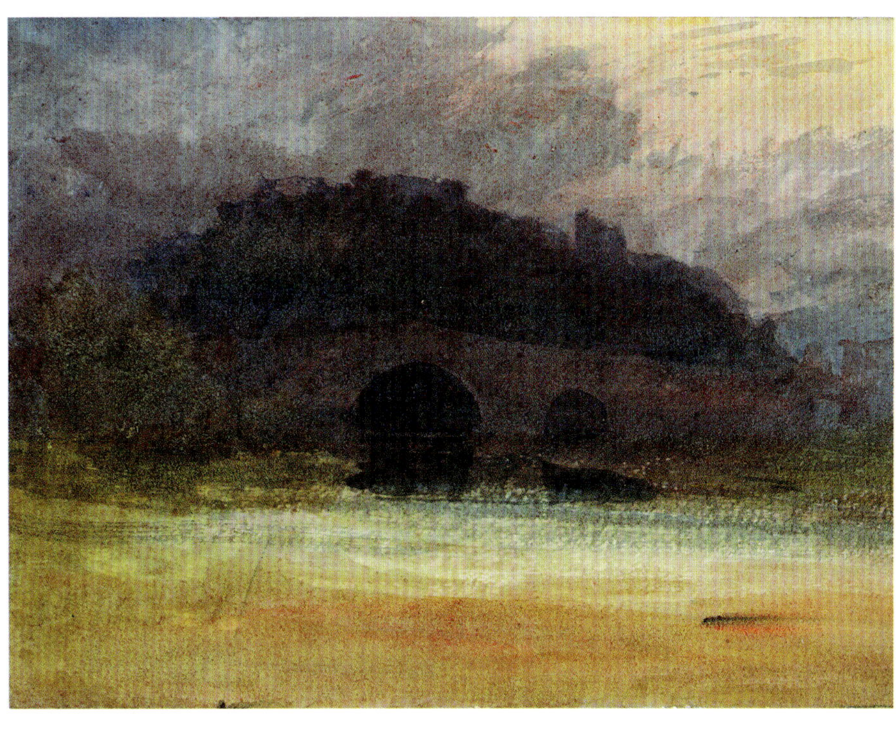

MYTH AND GENRE

With the appointment of a new, more socially aware, president at the Academy, genre painting, making social comment, came into vogue. Turner reacted to his critics by showing that he could execute accomplished genre paintings as well as classical grand works.

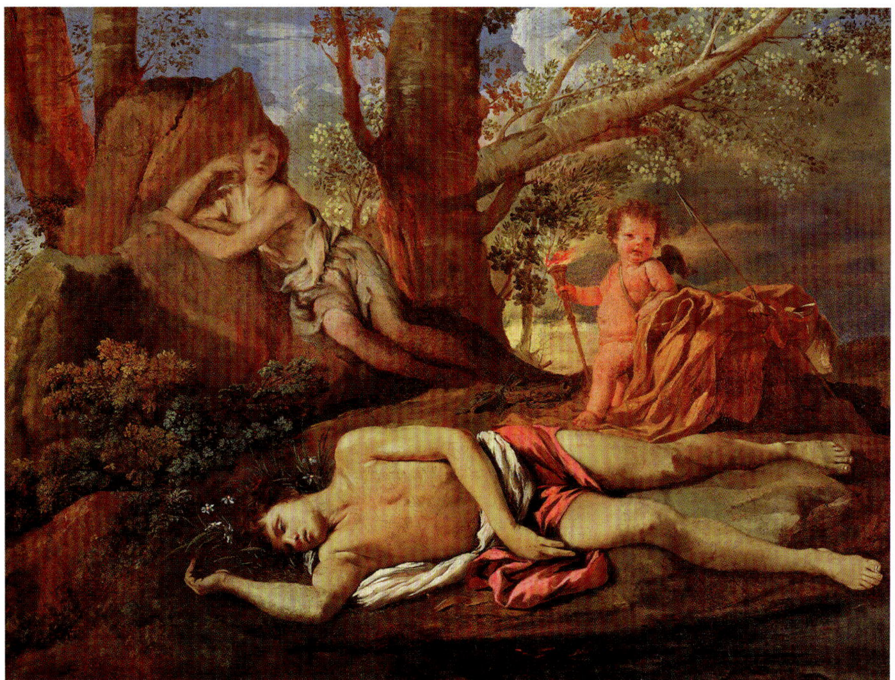

Left: Echo and Narcissus, *oil on canvas, Nicolas Poussin, 17th century. Probably seen by Turner on his visit to Paris in 1802, and the inspiration for his own work of a similar title.*

THE INDUSTRIAL REVOLUTION

By the beginning of the 19th century, the Industrial and Agricultural Revolutions were under way in England. The Enclosure Act of 1801 was part of a gradual process that sought to deprive the poor of using so-called common land to graze animals and grow crops at a subsistence level. The enclosures now belonged to wealthy landowners who had developed organized farming and were employing the once-free subsistence farmers, usually at an exploitative rate. The alternative for the disenfranchised workers was to look for work in the towns, where numerous factories were now opening to cater for the boom in manufactured goods. Needless to say, the rich landowners and factory owners were often one and the same.

As a response to Beaumont and others who were critical of his style, Turner embarked on a series of oil paintings of mythological and historical subjects in the grand manner.

he sought to rebuff Beaumont's criticism by proving that he could execute paintings in an Academic manner, if he chose to, and show his knowledge – albeit limited – of classical prose.

FENDING OFF THE CRITICS

Although Turner had already painted pictures based on historical or mythological subjects before 1804, *Narcissus and Echo* was probably the first oil painting to be executed after seeing the collection at the Louvre. Turner's picture is redolent of Poussin in style and subject matter, since a version of it is at the Louvre, but it could well be that Turner saw Claude's version of the subject before his Continental visit.

Turner chose to paint this subject in a 'finished' way, and append verses from Ovid's *Metamorphoses* at the Royal Academy exhibition. This suggests that

Right: Village Politicians, *David Wilkie, engraving, 19th century, explores the theme of parliamentary reform.*

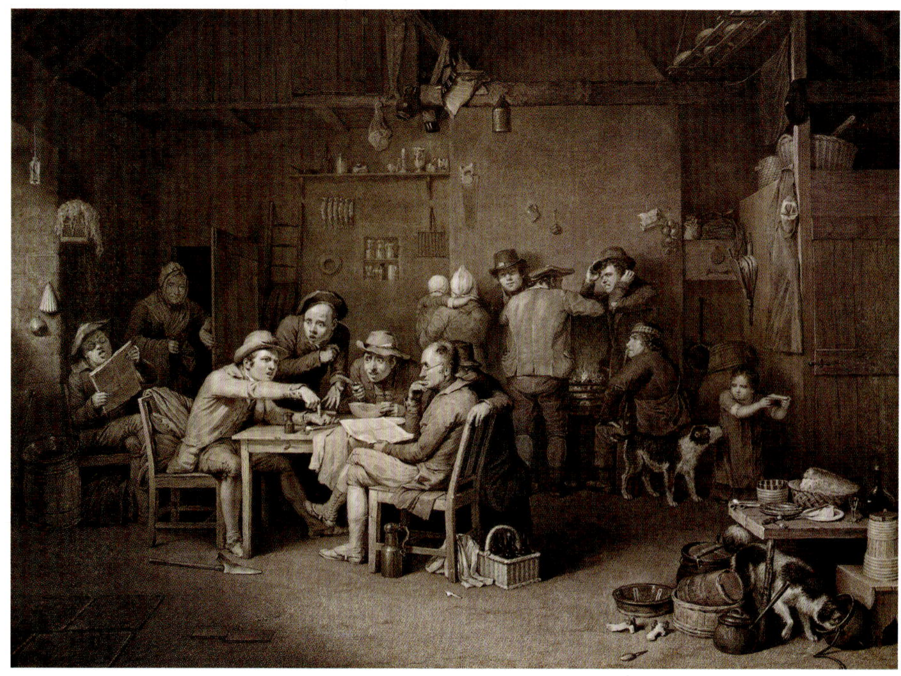

Right: Narcissus and Echo, *oil on canvas, 1804. Purchased by Lord Egremont.*

A number of artists, including Turner, reflected this and other social concerns in their paintings, one example being the ironical recreation of an Arcadian landscape such as that depicted in *Narcissus and Echo*. Another was genre painting, often openly commenting on topical concerns of the time, which came into its own after the death in 1792 of the disapproving Sir Joshua Reynolds, and the appointment of his more socially aware successor, Benjamin West.

One of the brightest rising stars of genre painting was David Wilkie (1785–1841). Like Turner, Wilkie came to prominence at an early age, studying first in Edinburgh and then at the Royal Academy Schools. In 1806, at his first Royal Academy exhibition, he showed *Village Politicians*, an anecdotal genre painting par excellence. It was the star of the show and overshadowed Turner's

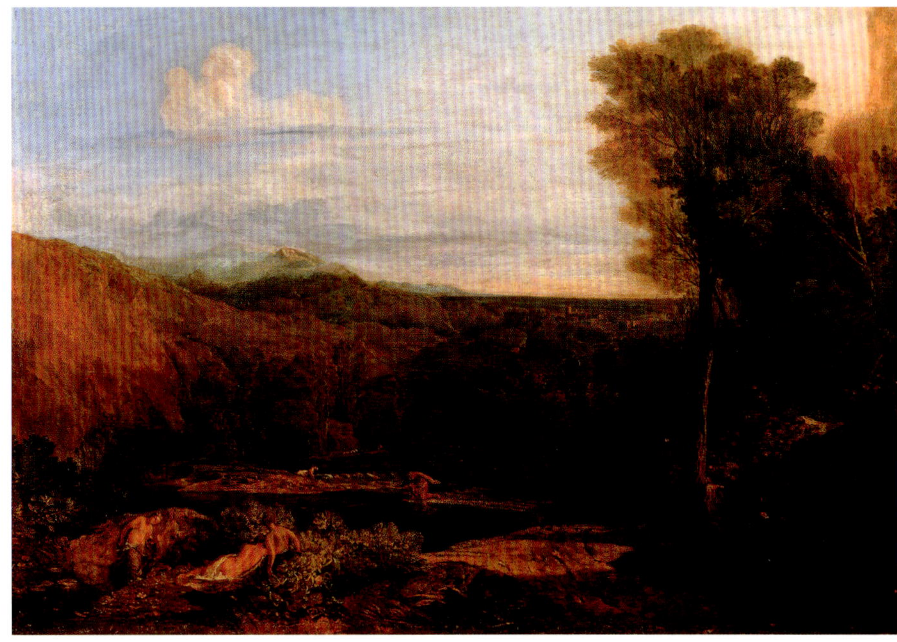

Below: Lincoln Cathedral from the Holmes, *pencil and watercolour, 1802–3. A panoramic view of the cathedral and castle, which houses one of only four copies of the Magna Carta.*

lacklustre offerings of only one oil painting and one watercolour that year. Beaumont singled out Wilkie's highly "finished" work and commissioned him to paint *The Blind Fiddler*, which was exhibited at the Royal Academy the following year.

Turner responded in a spectacular way, painting *A Country Blacksmith Disputing upon the Price of Iron, and the Price Charged to the Butcher for Shoeing His Pony*. The painting was well received

and demonstrated that Turner could paint anything, highly finished or not. It also showed that, unlike Wilkie, who had painted a rather general anecdotal scene, Turner could make political and social comment in his pictures by dealing specifically with key issues of his day. The fact that he then returned to depicting ethereal landscapes rather than continuing with genre painting showed single-mindedness concerning subject matter.

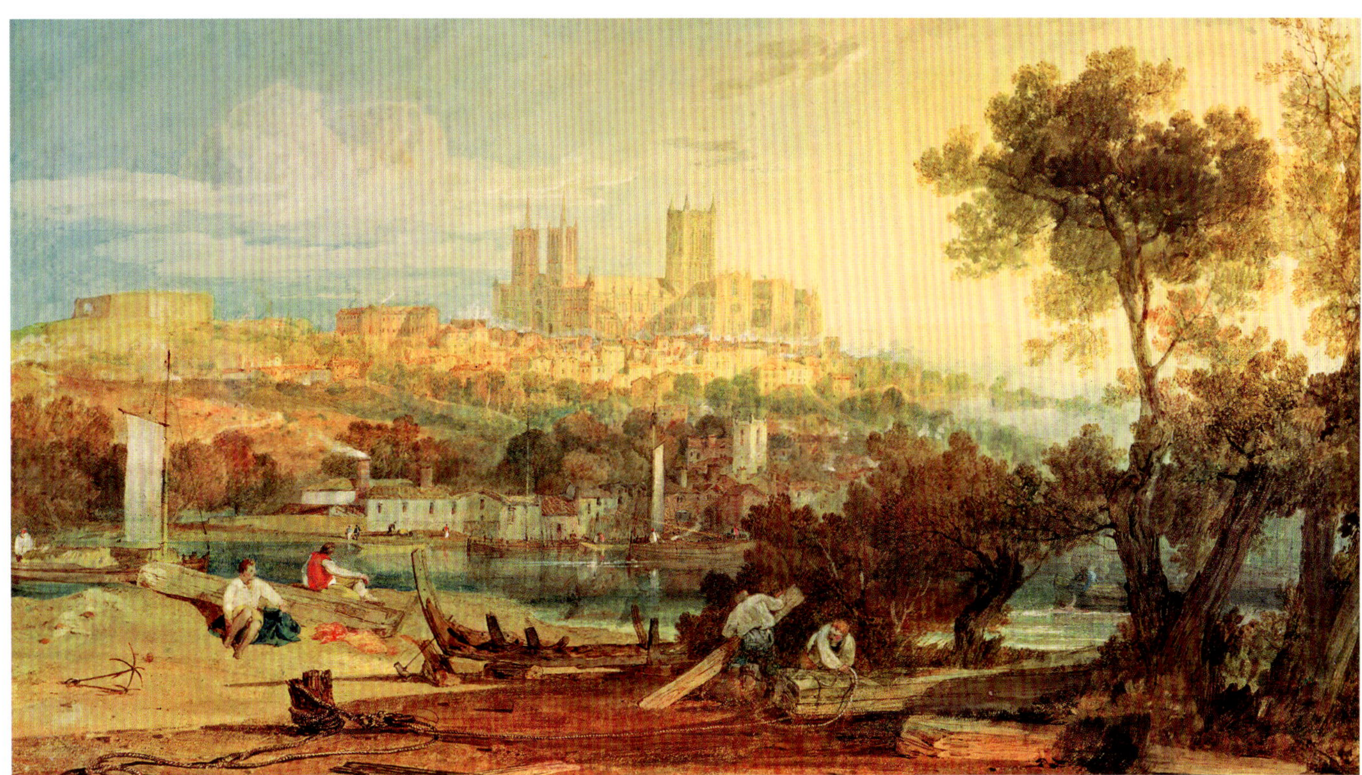

THE EXHIBITION SCENE

Although Turner had many critics and detractors, he also had supporters who recognized his outstanding artistic ability. At this time, owing to the war in Europe, he stayed in England and became drawn to the River Thames, where he enjoyed a period of reflection.

As opportunities for exhibiting paintings increased, and in an attempt to further promote his work, Turner decided to take an extraordinary step.

THE TURNER GALLERY

Perhaps following the internal disputes and animosity felt at the Royal Academy, Turner decided not to exhibit at the annual exhibition of 1805 and showed only two paintings there in the following year. In an unusual move for a new Academician, Turner decided to carry out an idea he had had as early as 1803: to create his own gallery. He built an extension to his house in Harley Street, to create a gallery space of around 55.74sq m (600sq ft). The gallery opened for its first exhibition in April 1804, and Turner showed the large Swiss watercolours he had executed in 1803. The following year, 1805, he exhibited *The Shipwreck*, which was purchased by his new patron Sir John Fleming Leicester (1762–1827).

Although Turner resumed exhibiting at the Academy after 1806, he also continued to exhibit at his own gallery up to 1815, when it was closed for enlargement and some refurbishments.

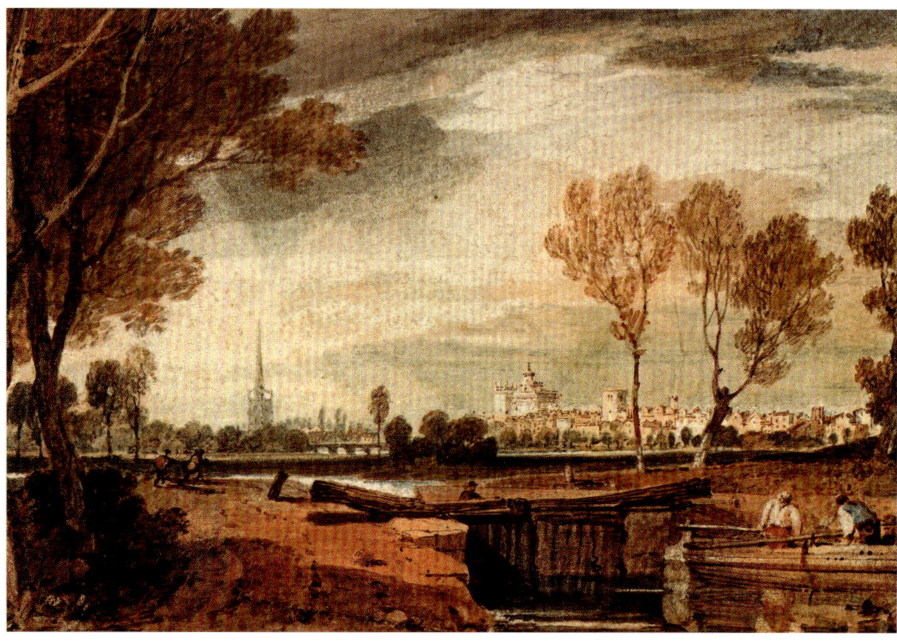

Above: Abingdon, Oxfordshire, *watercolour, 1805. A delightful watercolour showing the small town of Abingdon, the origins of which date back to before the Roman occupation.*

OTHER EXHIBITIONS

The Society of Painters in Watercolours was founded in 1804 and opened its first exhibition in 1805. Although Turner was precluded from membership of the Society by virtue of his status as an Academician (a rule that stayed in force until 1870), he had a number of friends who were founder members. Among them were William Wells (1762–1836), with whom he had enjoyed sketching trips, and at whose house at Knockholt in Kent Turner often stayed. The first president of the Society was William Gilpin, the nephew of the Reverend William Gilpin, whose advocacy of the Picturesque aesthetic had been such a motivation for Turner.

Another new society that held its first exhibition in 1806 was the British Institution for Promoting the Fine Arts. This august body was set up by connoisseurs who wished to establish a National Gallery, and promote the British school of painting. Many Academicians, including Turner, contributed to this and subsequent

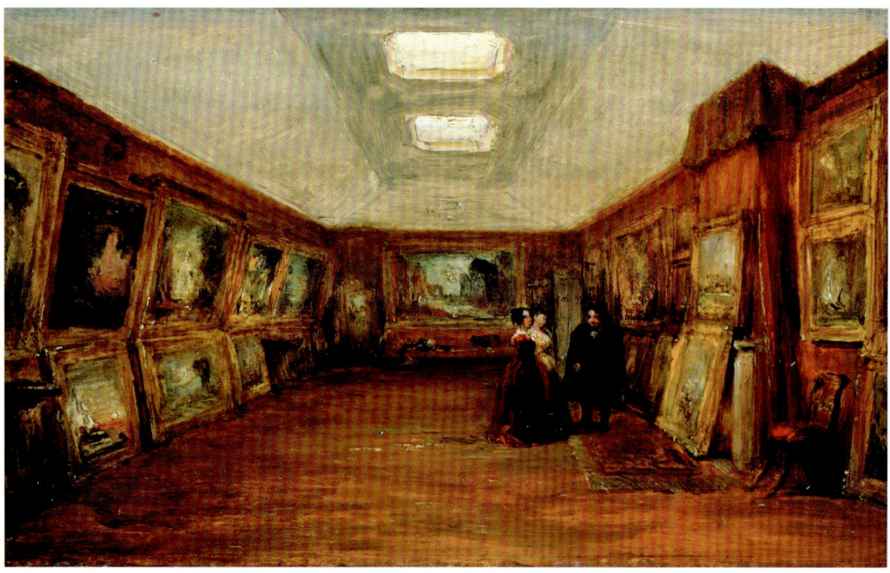

Left: Turner's Gallery: The Artist Showing his Work, *George Jones, oil, c.1852. Note Turner's major work,* Dido Building Carthage, *on the far wall.*

Right: The Thames at Weybridge, *oil on canvas, c.1807–10. This oil painting was possibly exhibited at Turner's gallery in 1806 and purchased by Lord Egremont.*

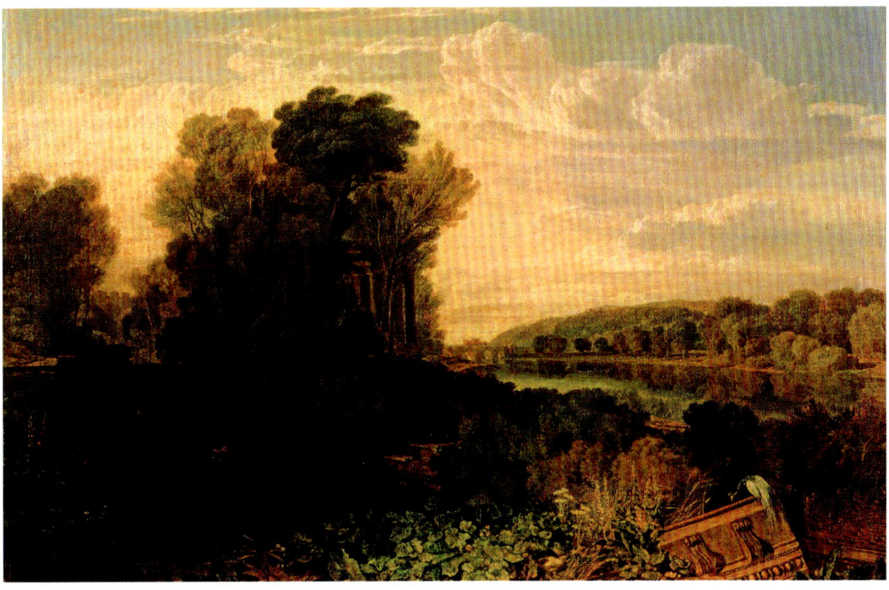

exhibitions until it was realized that the so-called connoisseurs, who included Sir George Beaumont, only wished to promote artists who accorded with their own taste. As one artist, Augustus Wall Callcott (1779–1844), said, "they are not patrons of artists, but breeders of artists – of the kind *they* wanted."

THE FIRST THAMES SERIES

Between 1803 (the end of the Treaty of Amiens) and 1815 (the final defeat of Napoleon), Britons were again unable to travel in Continental Europe so Turner was forced to content himself with the British landscape. He selected the English landscape, thus avoiding extensive, and often hectic, travel. As Turner's biographer James Hamilton has suggested, the artist needed a period of

Below: Society of Painters in Watercolour, *Thomas Rowlandson, aquatint, 1808.*

reflection rather than discovery at this time. He found it beside the quieter parts of the River Thames.

In 1805, Turner acquired a short lease on Sion Ferry House in Isleworth. He purchased a boat, using it to create some water-level pictures such as *The Thames Near Walton Bridges.* The house was ideally situated at the water's edge, with a few houses and a

church in the background, providing a perfect aesthetic setting. This was an experimental time, as suggested by canvases he left unfinished from this period. Turner was smitten by the Thames as a motif and moved to another house at Hammersmith in late 1806 before acquiring land the next year and building a riverside villa to his own design at Twickenham in 1812.

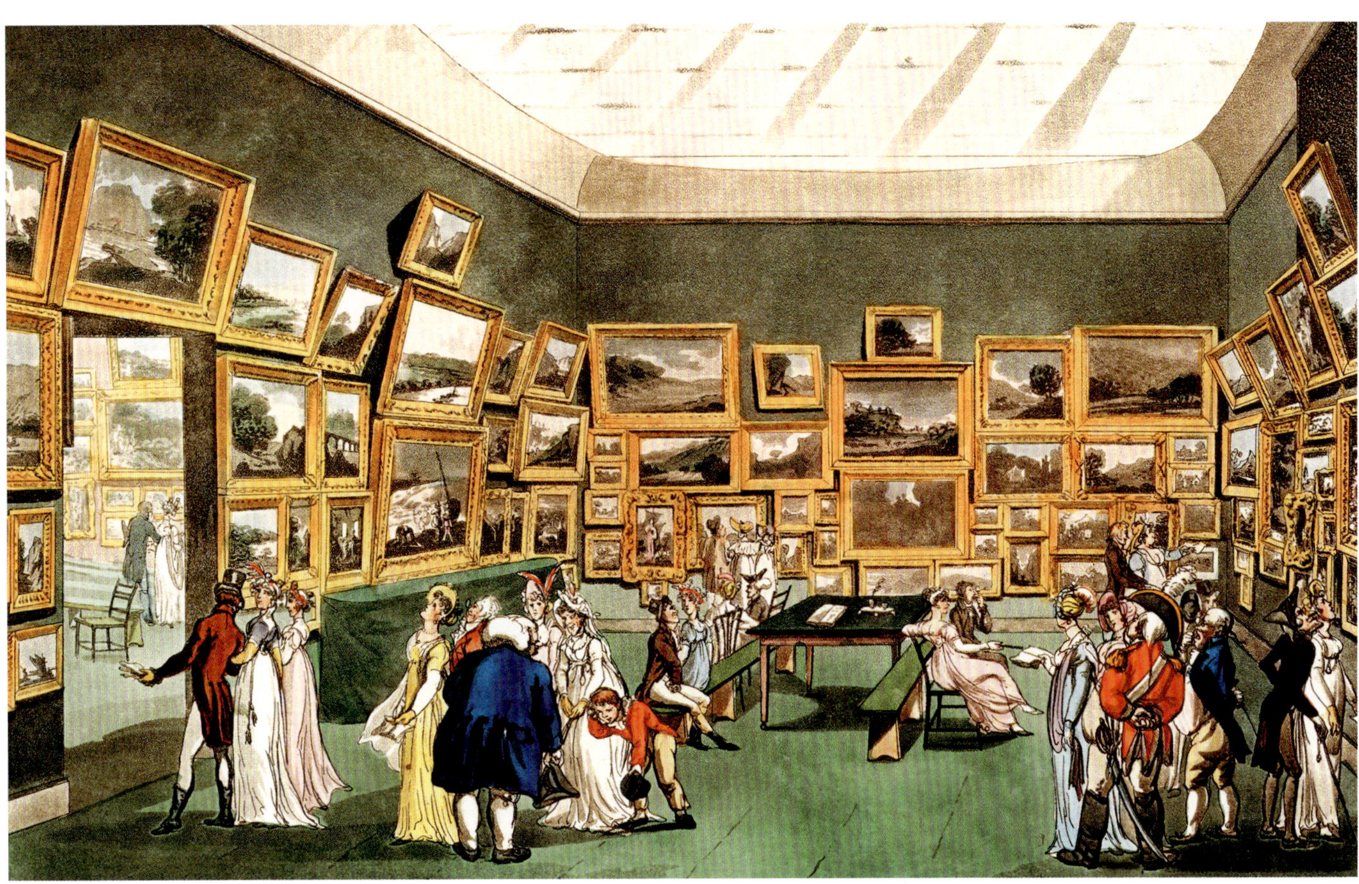

TRAFALGAR AND AFTERWARD

Turner visited HMS *Victory* after her arrival at Sheerness, interviewing some of the crew before painting *The Battle of Trafalgar*, which commemorates the triumphant victory achieved by the British fleet, and an important milestone in history.

After the failure of the Treaty of Amiens, Napoleon prepared for an invasion of England. To achieve this he needed command of the seas and formulated a complex plan that resulted in an engagement of the British fleet off the Spanish coast at Cape Trafalgar in 1805. The British fleet routed the combined fleets of France and Spain, its enforced ally, destroying 22 of their ships, without incurring any losses. However, while commanding the fleet, the hero of the engagement, Vice-Admiral Horatio, Viscount Nelson (1758–1805), was shot and killed by a French sniper. His body was returned to England aboard the flagship HMS *Victory*, which anchored at Sheerness, a town at the estuaries of the rivers Thames and Medway, before its journey to London where Nelson was accorded a heroic state funeral.

VISIT TO HMS *VICTORY*

While it was still anchored at Sheerness, Turner visited the ship and made copious notes and sketches in his Nelson Sketchbook of the uniforms, characters and ship's details. For example, against a drawing of a marine, Turner noted "undress a red jacket; sometimes a fancy red shirt". These were important notes since Turner included a detailed account of the battle when he exhibited the painting *The Battle of Trafalgar, as Seen from the Mizzen Starboard Shrouds of the* Victory, at his own gallery in 1806. The detail included some of the main protagonists such as Captain Adair the marine commander. Unfortunately the painting was first shown in an unfinished state, which attracted much criticism until two years later when it was finished and shown at the Royal Academy.

Below: A Windy Day, oil on canvas, 19th century, is typical of Turner's seascape oeuvre with a large swell.

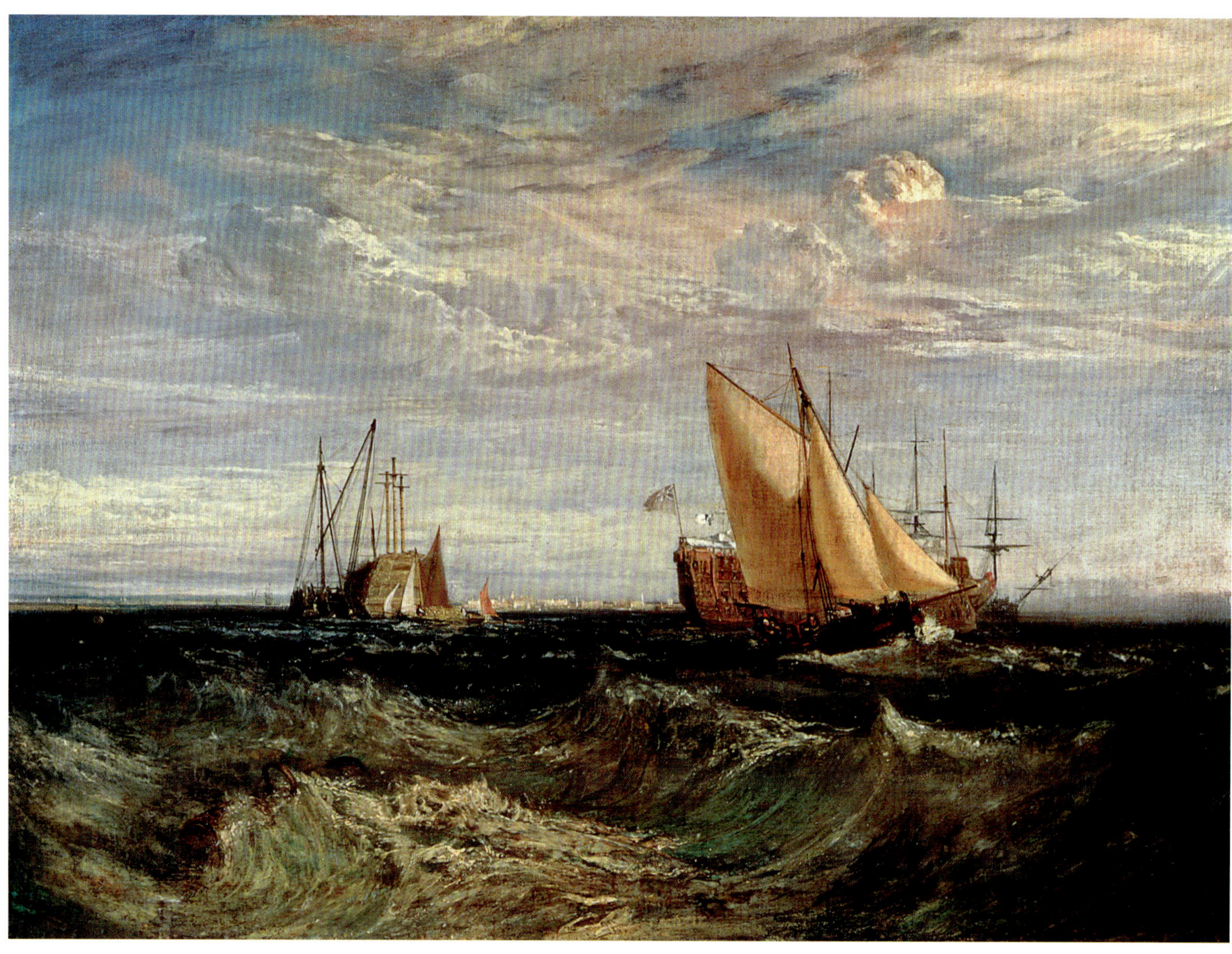

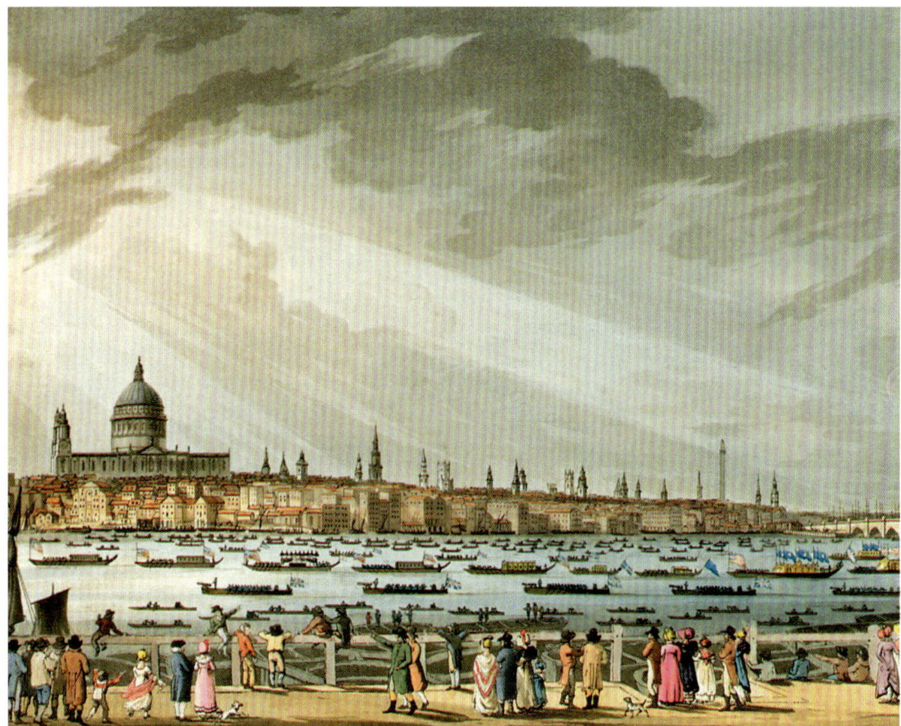

Left: Lord Nelson's Funeral Procession by Water from Greenwich, *coloured engraving by J Clark and H Marke, 1806.*

The picture celebrated Nelson's heroism, since it depicted the moment when he had been fatally wounded. Turner had sought to capitalize on patriotic fervour, celebrating a victory against a background of the continued threat of Napoleon. Turner returned to the theme of victory in 1822, when he was commissioned to paint a version of the Battle of Trafalgar for George IV, to hang at St James's Palace in London.

Below: Horatio, Viscount Nelson, *William Beechey, oil on canvas, 1801.*

OTHER MARINE PICTURES

At this time, Turner completed a number of other action-packed sea pictures, beginning with *The Shipwreck,* of 1805; *The Deluge,* also of 1805, and *Sheerness and the Isle of Sheppey, with the Junction of the Thames and Medway from the Nore,* of 1807. The artist realized the significance of the perilous seas to an island nation threatened by an invasion across the channel. These marine pictures were to play an important part in Turner's oeuvre. His earlier sea pictures, such as *Fishermen upon a Lee Shore in Squally Weather,* had expressed a mood and atmosphere, but *The Shipwreck* gave Turner the opportunity to convey a sense of dynamism by creating a compositional vortex that draws the viewer into the centre of the picture. The circular composition includes the waves and the tilt of the main vessel to enhance the sense of movement. The painting was popular and was engraved as a mezzotint in 1806 by Charles Turner (not related), who became one of the artist's main engravers. The image created a broader awareness of Turner's pictures and set a precedent for further engravings of paintings that had not been specifically commissioned as book illustrations. At a price of two guineas each this was an additional income to the original painting that could only be sold once by the artist. Turner felt the time was ripe for publishing his images on a grander scale.

Below: The *Victory* Returning from Trafalgar, *oil on canvas, 1806. Turner sketched* Victory *as she was entering the mouth of the Medway at Sheerness, and yet has transposed the ship on to a background of the Isle of Wight, perhaps utilizing the white cliffs in the distance for dramatic effect.*

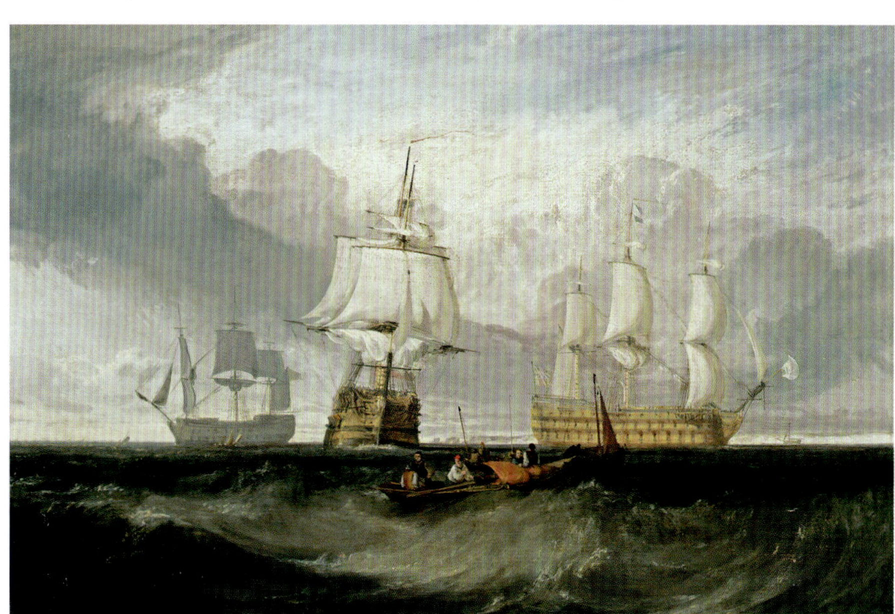

LIBER STUDIORUM

As Turner sought to explore the different modes of a landscape style, and to promote his work at the same time, he developed his *Liber Studiorum*, a series of engraved prints intended as "illustrative of landscape compositions".

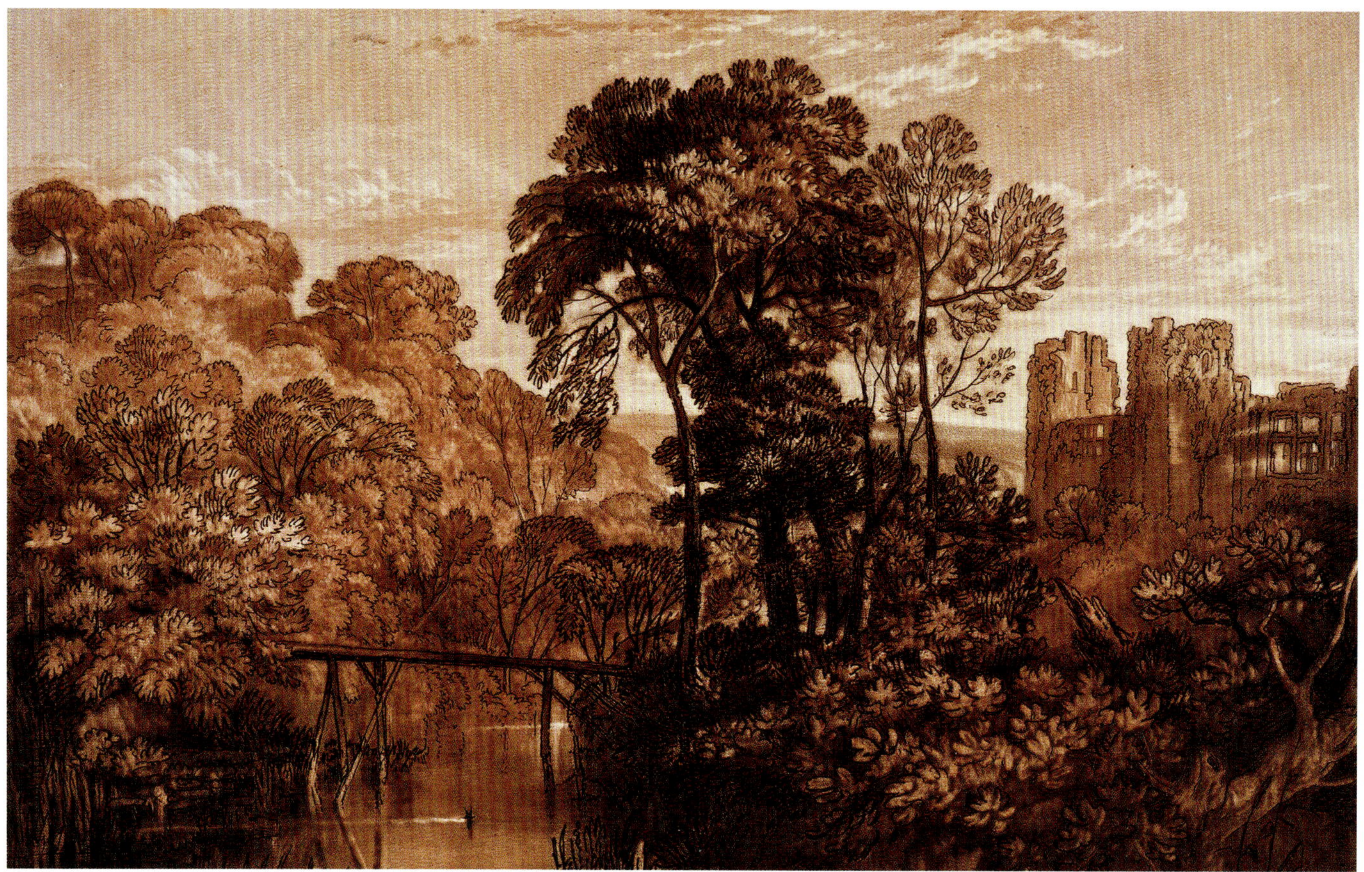

At the time of *The Shipwreck*, Turner appears to have discussed the idea of a treatise on landscape painting with his friend William Wells, resulting in the *Liber Studiorum*, based on the engravings by Richard Earlom of Claude Lorrain's *Liber Veritatis*, or 'Book of truths'.

FIRST DRAFT

That Turner equated his work to that of Claude, an artist held in such high esteem in 18th- and early 19th-century

Above: Liber Studiorum – Berry Pomeroy Castle, engraving, 1816. Also known as Raglan Castle, this image was included in Part 12 issued in 1816.

Right: Liber Studiorum – Frontispiece, etching, 1812. This is Turner's own design for the frontispiece to the Liber.

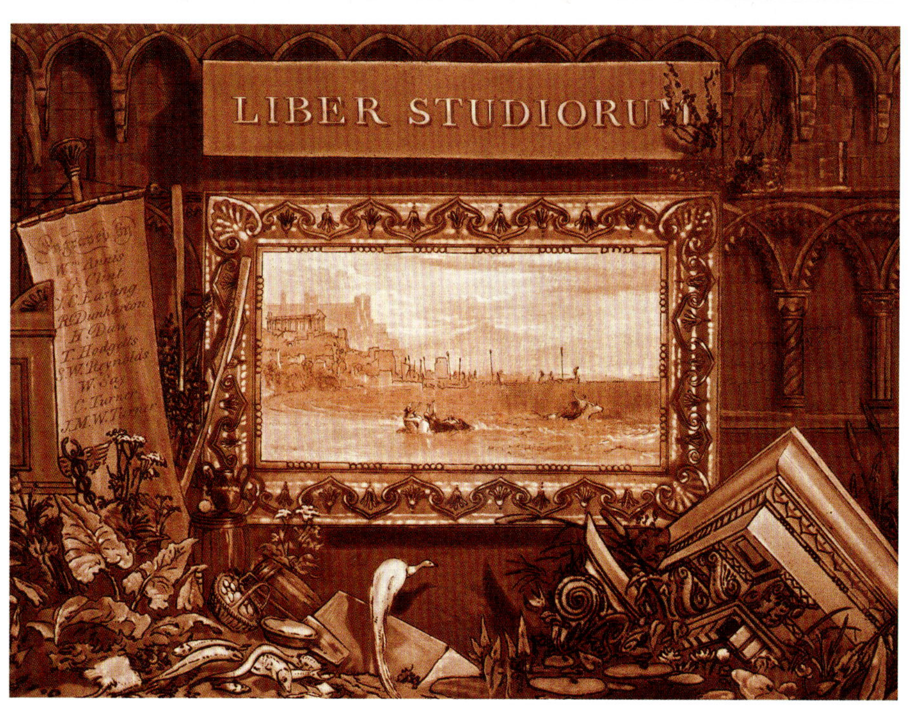

advertise the first series, which were only available through the artist or from the engraver. After the second volume was published in February 1808, the *Review of Publications in Art* promoted the mezzotints, but that appears to be the total publicity for the project beyond word of mouth. Originally, Turner had intended issuing 100 different images, making up the *Liber Studiorum*, but the project ended in 1819 with the publication of Part Fourteen.

CONCLUSION

Although only 70 images were actually included in the project, a number of others were made and not used. Turner also recreated the project as *Little Liber Studiorum* in 1826, producing the original images and engraving his own 12 mezzotint plates. The original *Liber Studiorum* project had mixed fortunes.

On the plus side, Turner's identity and style had been established with the public and the content would be useful when he became Professor of Perspective at the Royal Academy.

On the negative side, he had created a bad reputation with collectors and the project lost money, his estate having to dispose of more than 5,000 unsold prints upon his death.

Above: Liber Studorium: Engraving of a Scene on the French Coast, *engraving, 1807. This view is also known as 'French Coastal Scene' and was incorporated into the first part of the* Liber, *issued in 1807, representing Marine subjects.*

society, is a testament to his self-belief as an artistic genius. A testimony to Wells' involvement in the *Liber Studiorum* is in the form of a letter written in 1853 by his daughter Clara in which she refers to her father's constant haranguing of Turner until he agreed to undertake the project. At the time, October 1806, Turner was staying with the family at Knockholt, and worked on the first draft of the subjects, as discussed with Wells, before he returned home. The plates, and thus the landscape treatise, were to be divided into broad themes — Pastoral, Architectural, Historical, Marine and Mountainous — and printed in sepia, akin to those of Claude's *Liber Veritatis*. Although this was a treatise, there was no accompanying text. It was intended for art students to examine subject matter, composition, line and tone.

MAKING THE ETCHINGS

Having decided on the format of five prints per volume, Turner produced Part One of his *Liber Studiorum*. Having

Right: Landscape with Mercury and Apollo, *Claude Lorrain, pen and wash, 1673. Turner's* Liber Studiorum *is based on works such as this.*

first made a brown ink and wash drawing of the subject, he then created an etching before delivering them to Charles Turner for making mezzotint copies. Prior to the *Liber Studiorum* the mezzotint process had not been used for landscape, but such was Turner's understanding of etching and engraving that he was able to work easily with his namesake to create the prints. In later volumes the etching was dispensed with.

Part One was published in June 1807 priced at 15 shillings (about £50 today). Turner relied on a hand-written prospectus in his own gallery to

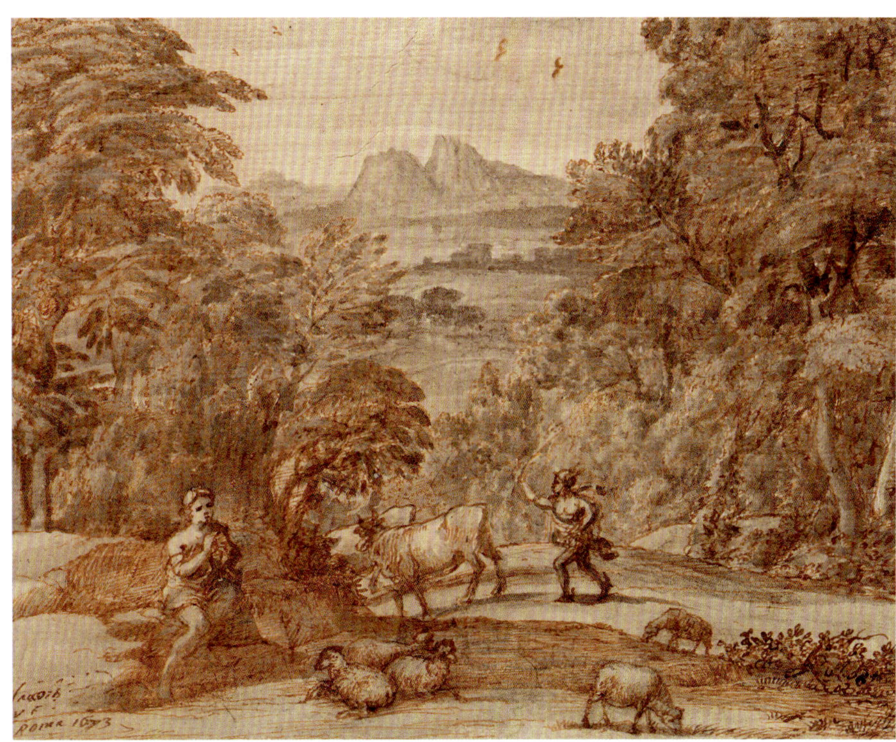

PROFESSOR OF PERSPECTIVE

In November 1807, Turner was made Professor of Perspective at the Royal Academy.
This was an ideal platform for disseminating some of the ideas he had begun to express
in other forums such as the *Liber Studiorum*.

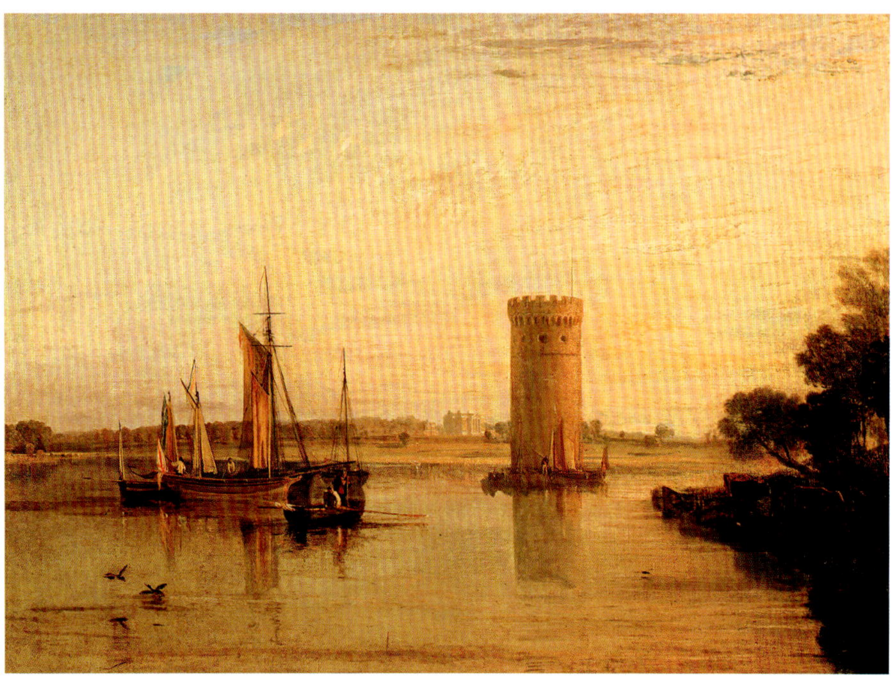

Turner was not naturally didactic and knew that he had difficulty communicating his ideas effectively. He decided, therefore, on a plan of action.

ADVANCE PREPARATION

First, Turner's plan involved copious amounts of reading on perspective, from the Renaissance theorists such as Leon Baptista Alberti (1404–72) and his treatise *Della Pittura* (translated into English in 1755) to the more recent *Dr Brook Taylor's Perspective Made Easy, Both in Theory and Practice*, the standard textbook of the time for students of perspective, written in 1755 by Joshua Kirby (1716–74).

Turner also wrote to the Academy in October 1809 advising them that he would not be ready to begin his lecture

Right: Perspective View of Fonthill Abbey from the South West, *watercolour and bodycolour, 1799. As the new professor of perspective, Turner wanted to explore complex architectural motifs to demonstrate his skills.*

series on perspective until the facilities had been improved, putting forward a proposal with the architect John Soane. At the time, Turner suggested an initial series of 6 lectures lasting on average 40 minutes, that would begin the following January. However, the series was postponed for a year, to allow him more time to prepare his lectures.

Left: Tabley, the Seat of Sir JF Leicester, Bart: Calm Morning, *oil on canvas, 1809.*

THE LECTURE SERIES

After the necessary refurbishment of the Academy facilities, Turner gave his first lectures in January and February 1811. The tickets cost £10 per lecture (about £500 today) and were clearly aimed at wealthy connoisseurs as well as the Academy students. The series was generally well received, Turner having researched it well, but his audience numbers dwindled after each lecture due to his rather awkward style of lecturing. This did not improve over time and he was criticized and, sometimes, ridiculed. Although the lectures were intermittent, Turner continued the series at the same time each year until 1828, but held the Professorship until 1837.

TWO NEW PATRONS

Having purchased *The Shipwreck* in 1805, Sir John Fleming Leicester commissioned Turner to create two views of his home Tabley House near Knutsford, Cheshire, in oil paint. In the summer of 1808, Turner went

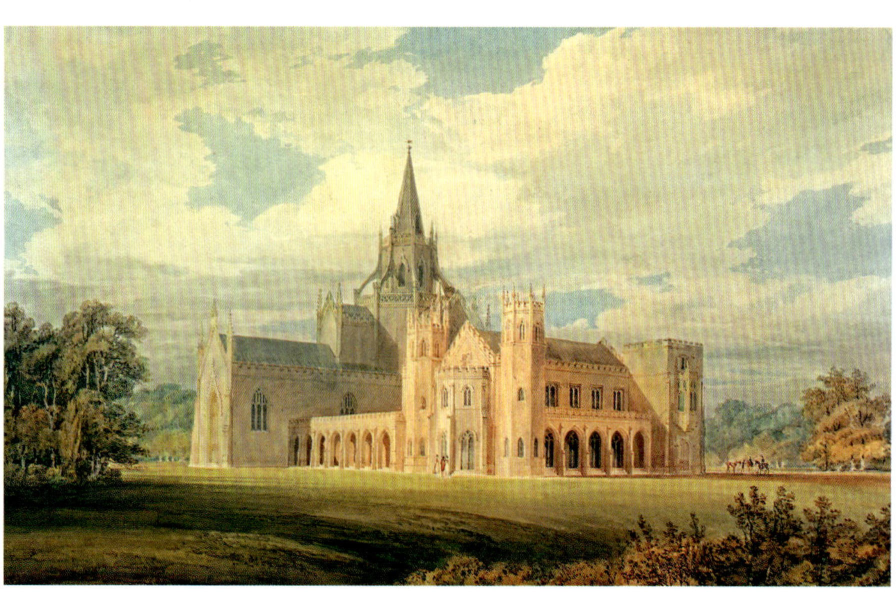

SIR JOHN SOANE

Soane had been elected a Royal Academician at the same time as Turner, 1802. He had already come to prominence much earlier when, in 1788, he was made Surveyor at the Bank of England, substantially remodelling the building between 1792 and 1796 in the Neoclassical style. Soane had studied at the Royal Academy Schools, winning its gold medal in 1776 before journeying to Italy, the result of a scholarship.

Soane's architectural work is marked by its clean and uncomplicated Classical forms, and in particular his use of natural light in a building. His Dulwich Picture Gallery, which was opened in 1817, is still considered to be the *tour de force* benchmark of modern galleries. Although his style is Neoclassical, many of his ideas have a Picturesque aesthetic to them, thus making him a naturally kindred spirit for Turner. Sir John Soane was made Professor of Architecture at the Royal Academy in 1806.

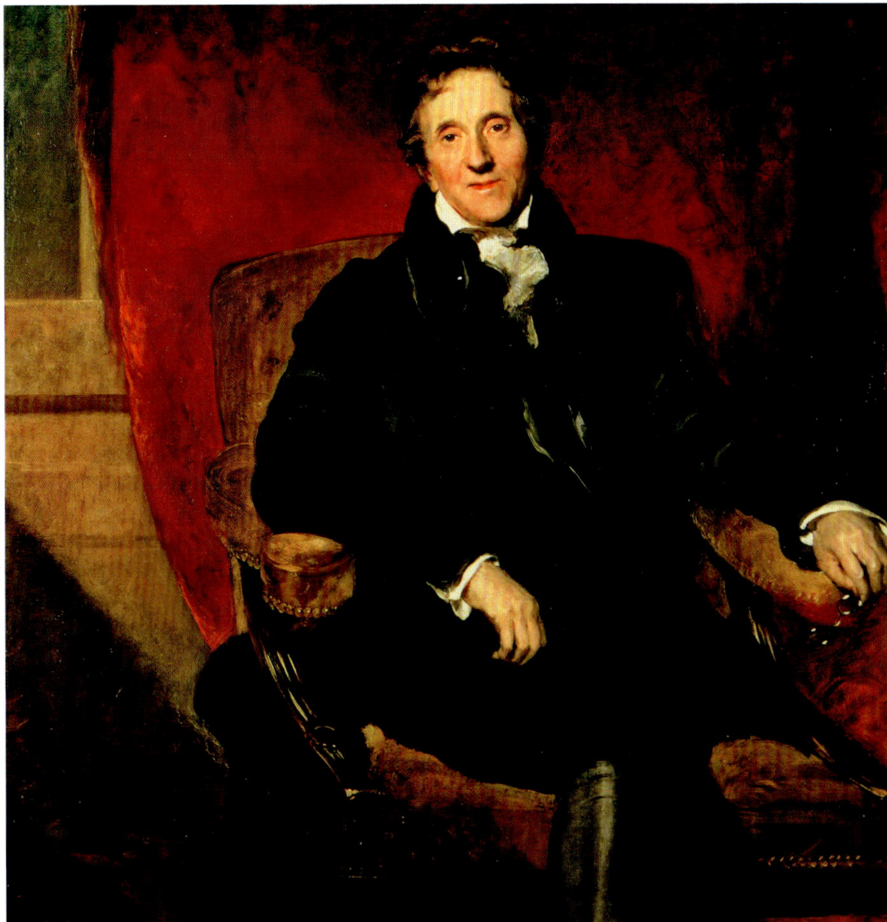

to stay at Tabley House, to make preliminary sketches, completing the commission in time for the Royal Academy exhibition of 1809. Another important patron, who arrived in 1808, was Walter Ramsden Fawkes, in whose home at Farnley Hall in Leeds Turner was a guest that same summer. The artist stayed at Farnley Hall for many summers, creating a number of important paintings of the surrounding area, and nurturing a strong and enduring friendship until Fawkes' death in 1825.

Above: Portrait of Sir John Soane, *Thomas Lawrence, oil on canvas, 1829. Soane was a fellow Academician.*

Below left: St Hughes Denouncing Vengeance on the Shepherd of Cormayer, *watercolour, 1803. This was shown at the Royal Academy exhibition of 1803 and was acquired by Sir John Soane.*

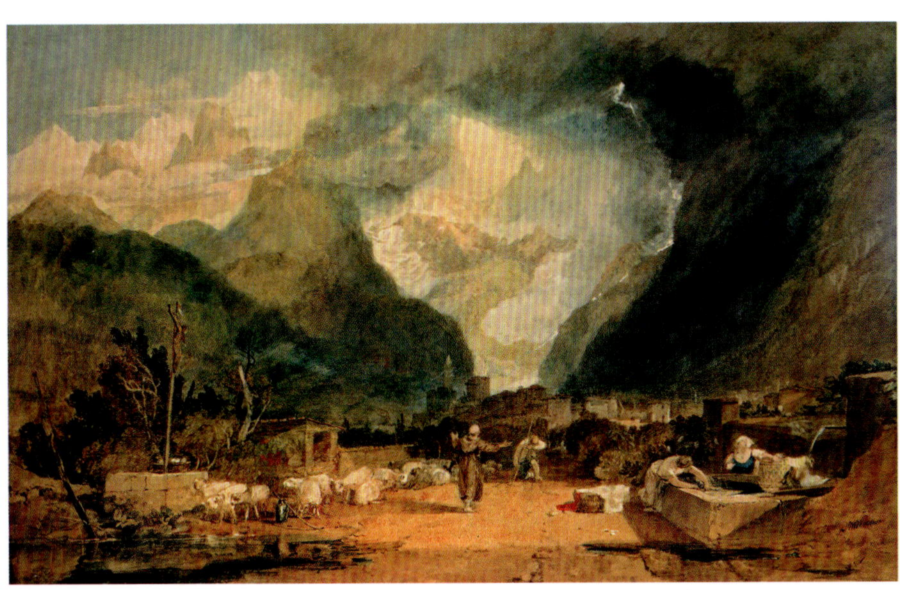

PERSPECTIVE

The notion of creating an illusionary space on a flat surface was developed in the 15th century in Italy and became one of the main tenets of High Renaissance painting. The apogee of this illusionary perspective was the Italian artist Raffaello Santi (Raphael), who became the benchmark for emulation in the Academic tradition in Britain and the Continent up until the mid-19th century. Such conventions were challenged by the Pre-Raphaelite Brotherhood just three years before Turner's death.

A TIME OF CONSOLIDATION

Turner had become a wealthy man from the sale of his paintings and shrewd property deals. At the end of 1810, he was concerned with consolidating his position, both personally and in a professional capacity.

There was no doubting Turner's immense talents as a painter, and as he matured as an artist, he also began expressing himself in the written word.

A PENCHANT FOR POETRY

Since 1798, Turner appended a poetic citation to many of his paintings exhibited at the Academy. Initially he had used lines from Milton or his favourite poet James Thomson. After 1809, he began to use poems that he had written, reflecting his melancholic mood of the time, and derived from his creative frustrations. This leaning toward poetry began during Turner's visit to Tabley, jotting lines down while fishing. His painting *Thomson's Aeolian Harp*, which was exhibited in his gallery in 1809, was accompanied by his own line, showing his homage to Thomson.

A NEW STUDIO

Turner had been purchasing property since 1806, first a freehold cottage and land at Great Missenden, Buckinghamshire, then the land at Twickenham where he intended to build a villa for himself and his 'Daddy'. Turner's own gallery at the rear of Harley Street had proved successful and in May 1810 he acquired the property at 47 Queen Anne St West. This would enable him to create a larger gallery with a more accessible entrance, since the existing gallery backed on to this new property. He then sublet the main premises at Harley Street to a dentist, Benjamin Young, while he continued to live at Hammersmith. The alterations to his new gallery (and home) at Queen Anne Street took place between autumn 1810 and May 1812 when the gallery re-opened. At this time, according to Turner's records, he estimated that he was worth between £12,000 and £13,000 (equivalent to about £700,000 today). Such a large sum would have been the result of a combination of continued picture sales

and shrewd investments in property. Ten years later, Turner acquired other houses in Harley Street, around which he negotiated further developments to his London home and gallery.

In the summer of 1809, Turner made his first visit to Petworth in Sussex, home of Lord Egremont, who had already bought many of his paintings and become one of his most important patrons. Egremont commissioned him to make studies of Petworth and also his home at Cockermouth Castle in Cumbria, which Turner visited in late summer. While there he was also commissioned to make two other paintings by the Earl of Lonsdale.

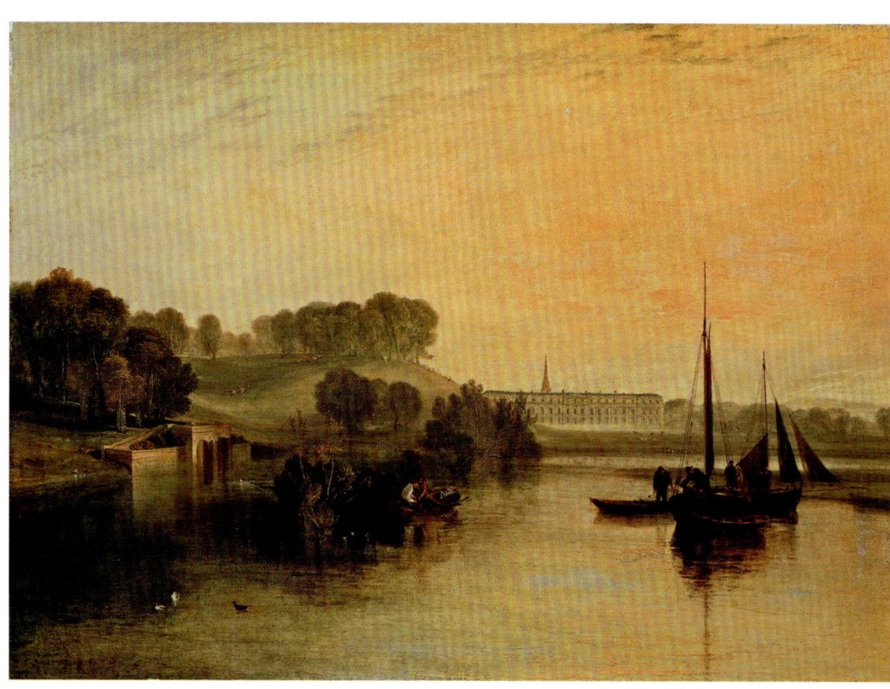

Below: Petworth, Sussex, Seat of the Earl of Egremont: Dewy Morning, *oil on canvas, 1810.*

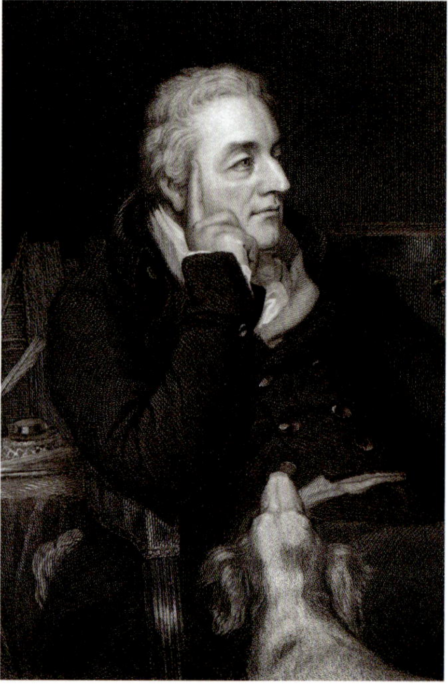

Below: Portrait of George Wyndham, 3rd Earl of Egremont, *Thomas Phillips, engraving, 1835.*

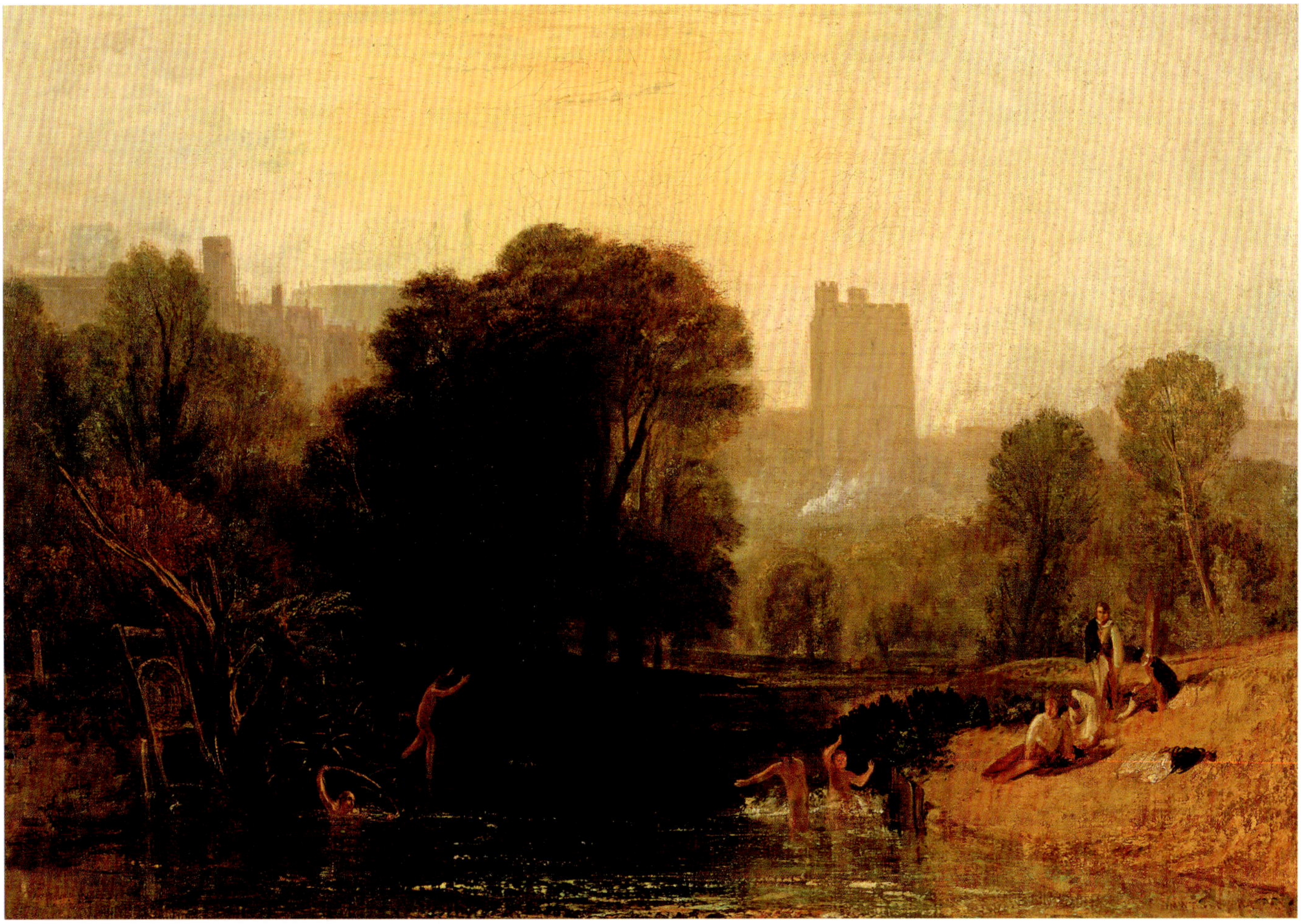

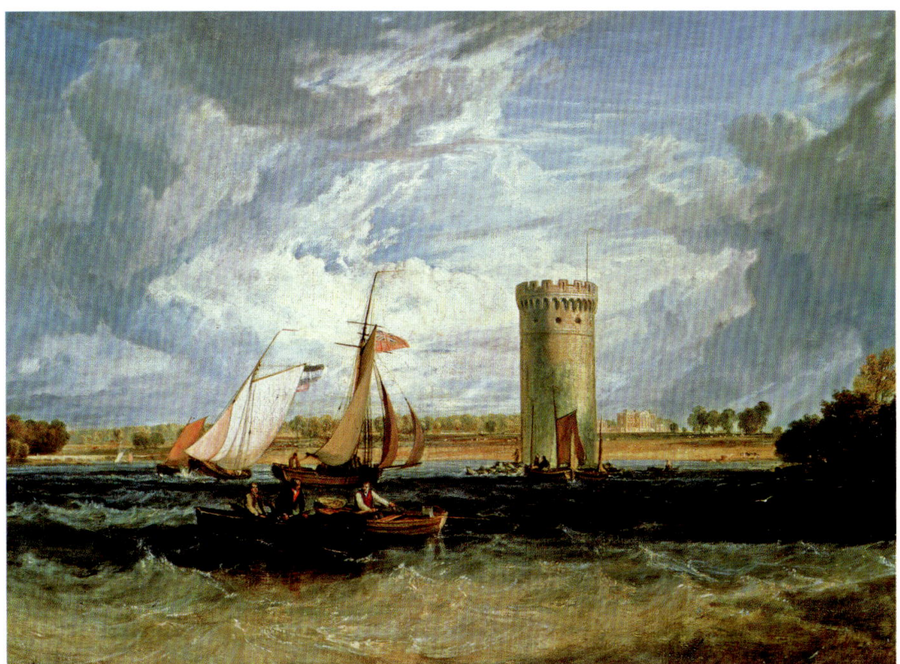

ARRANGEMENTS AT HOME

Sometime in early 1809, Turner sold the house in Norton Street in which his mistress, Sarah Danby, was living with her daughters, including Turner's daughter Evelina. According to a diary entry by Joseph Farington, "Mrs Danby, widow of a musician, now lives with him (Turner)", supposedly at the artist's main residence in Harley Street. It is not known whether she actually lived with Turner, or if she just lived nearby after they both left Harley Street, when their second daughter Georgiana was born.

Turner was very secretive about his personal life, but it does appear that he never settled down with Sarah Danby, and that relations between them were not harmonious. Hannah Danby, Sarah's niece, probably moved into Turner's house in Queen Anne Street at around the same time, where she remained as Turner's housekeeper until his death in 1851.

Above: Near the Thames Lock at Windsor, *oil on canvas, 1809. After seeing this work, Thomas Lawrence wrote to a friend referring to Turner as a 'genius', who is 'undisputably the first landscape painter in Europe'.*

Left: Tabley, the Seat of Sir JF Leicester, Bart: Windy Day, *oil on canvas, 1809, demonstrates Turner's virtuoso handling of light, clouds and sea in his paintings.*

PICTURESQUE VIEWS

In 1811, Turner was approached by a new publishing enterprise to create a range of Picturesque views of the southern coast of England, the first of several grand schemes that the artist was involved in.

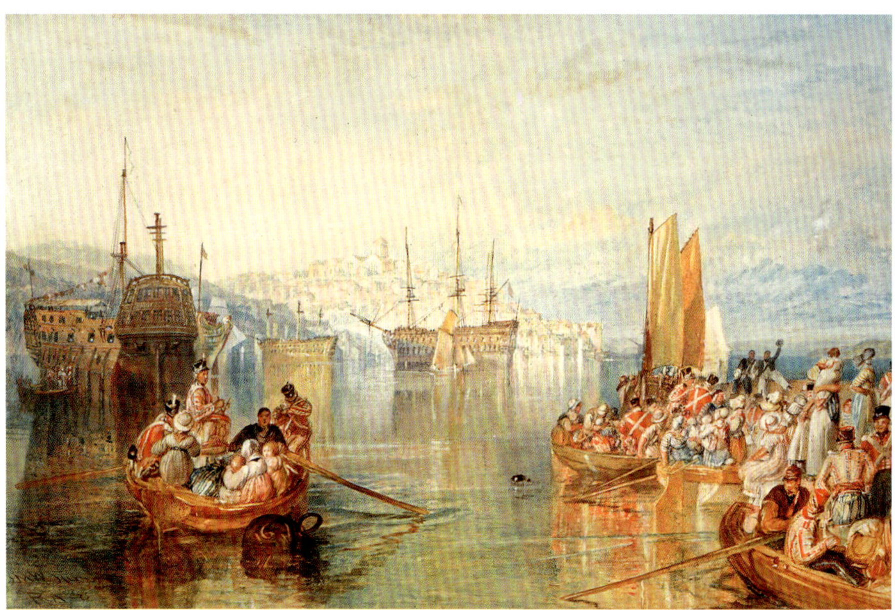

Left: Saltash, *watercolour and bodycolour, 1825. Used in the final version of the* Southern Coast *series, 1826.*

England had improved with some 30,000km (20,000 miles) of turnpike roads. For the trip, Turner purchased a copy of *The British Itinerary* that listed coach times and journey lengths.

On the tour, he completed more than 600 sketches and drawings (some coloured), including the Devonshire Coast Sketchbook, containing 450 alone. Some of the watercolours worked up from these sketches were exhibited in Turner's newly re-opened gallery at Queen Anne Street West in May of the following year.

Turner resumed his touring, again in the West Country, in the summer of 1813, responding to another commission from the Cooke brothers, *Rivers of Devon* (a project that remained largely unfulfilled). The journalist Cyrus Redding (1785–1870) accompanied Turner on the tour that was centred round Plymouth. Turner made nearly 700 drawings and sketches on the trip

One of the problems that Turner had encountered in the *Liber Studiorum* project was the limited number of impressions that etchings and mezzotints could reproduce. New techniques of line engraving were now being made available by a number of skilled engravers such as the Cooke brothers, William and George.

were cleaner and tighter than the warm, soft edges in etching and mezzotint.

THE TOURS

In the summer of 1811, Turner set off on a tour of Devon and the West Country retuning via Stonehenge and Salisbury. By this time, touring in

THE PROPOSAL

In 1811, the two brothers approached Turner with a scheme for a series of topographical prints called *Picturesque Views of the Southern Coast of England* that would include reproductions by a number of artists including him. For this Turner was to be paid £7 10s per drawing (equivalent to £400 today), a sum that would rise to 10 guineas after the first four issues. Aside from the fee, Turner was keen to become involved, because the new technique of line engraving allowed much more architectural detail; engraved lines

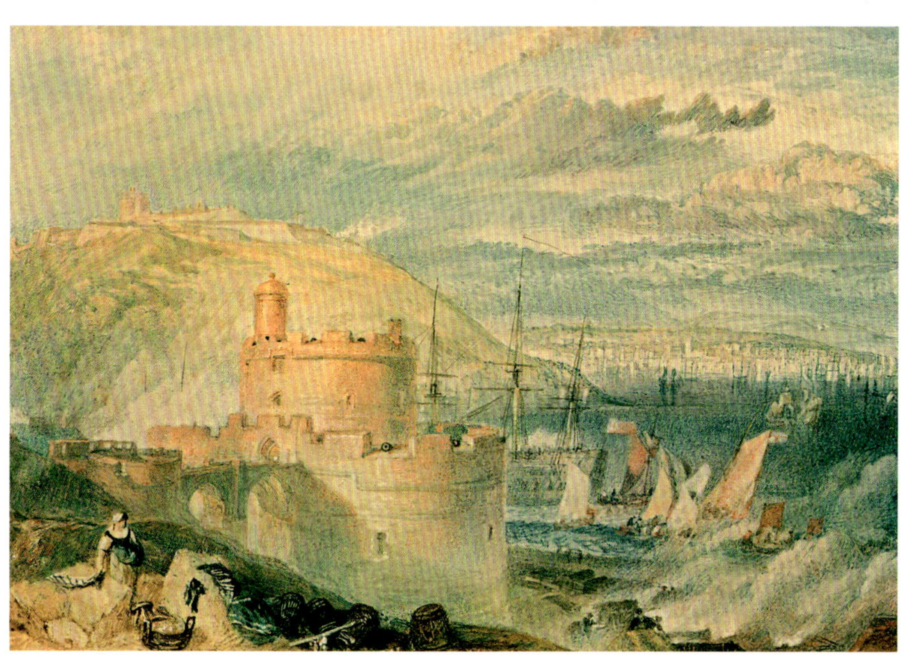

Right: Falmouth, *watercolour and scraping out, 1825. This was part of* The Harbours of England *series, published in 1856.*

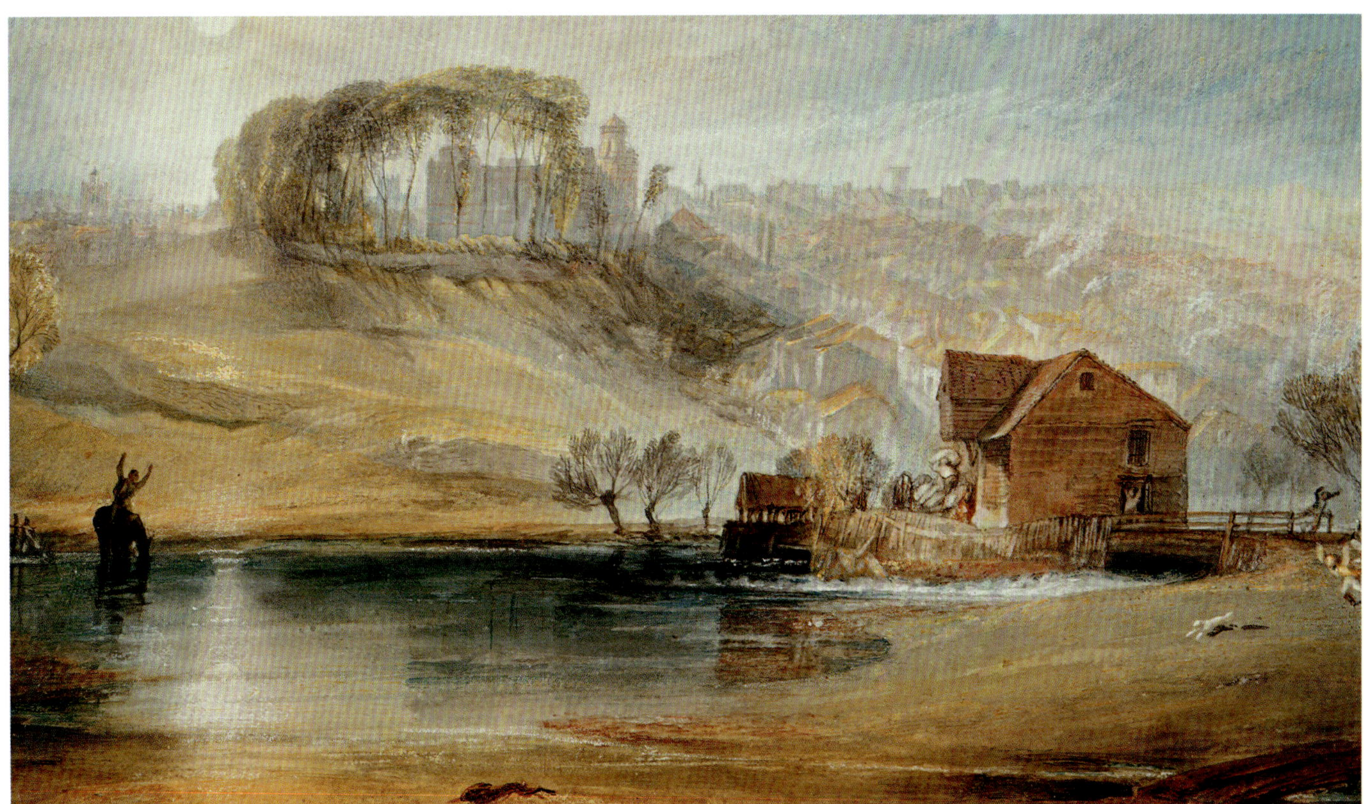

Above: Colchester, Essex, *watercolour and bodycolour, 1826. Despite being able to see Colchester Castle in the distance, Turner's limited palette suggests tonal value rather than pure topography.*

and produced a number of oil sketches, a working practice that he had begun several years earlier on his first Thames series. Redding recalled that on one occasion, when others had joined Turner and him for a picnic, the artist displayed his sketches for all to see. This was a departure from the norm for Turner, and also an indication of his growing confidence.

TURNER VERSUS THE ENGRAVERS

The first four parts of the *Southern Coast* series, which included seven plates by Turner, were published in 1814, and the series continued to be published intermittently until 1826. The series was promoted by the Cooke brothers at an exhibition of paintings in 1822, but by this time Turner was frustrated by the mismanagement of the enterprise. Realizing the importance of getting these images correctly reproduced, he was often at odds with his publishers, and made endless notes

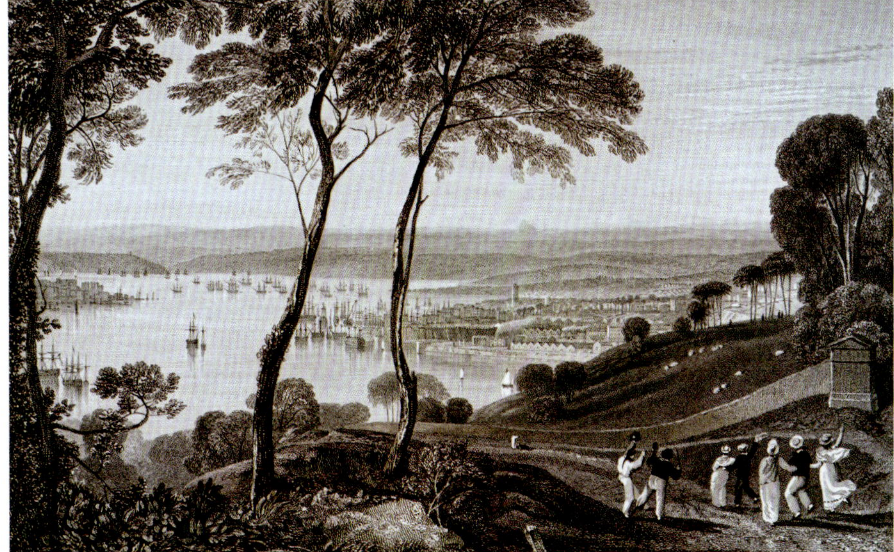

Above: Plymouth Dock from Mount Edgcumbe, *engraving, 1814. The area was renamed Devonport in 1824 to distinguish it from Plymouth.*

on the proof copies and sometimes added his own engraving lines himself. As he said, "engraving is no more an art of copying painting than the English language is an art of copying Greek or Latin." By 1826, Turner had had enough of the Cooke brothers and asked the publishers John and Arthur Arch to complete the project. Using some of the Cooke engravings, they brought in different engravers to complete the series of 48 plates, of which 39 were by Turner.

AFTERMATH

Before parting company with the Cooke brothers, Turner dealt with other publishers on more rewarding projects. Turner saw that the different medium, in the hands of a gifted engraver, offered new creative opportunities for his work.

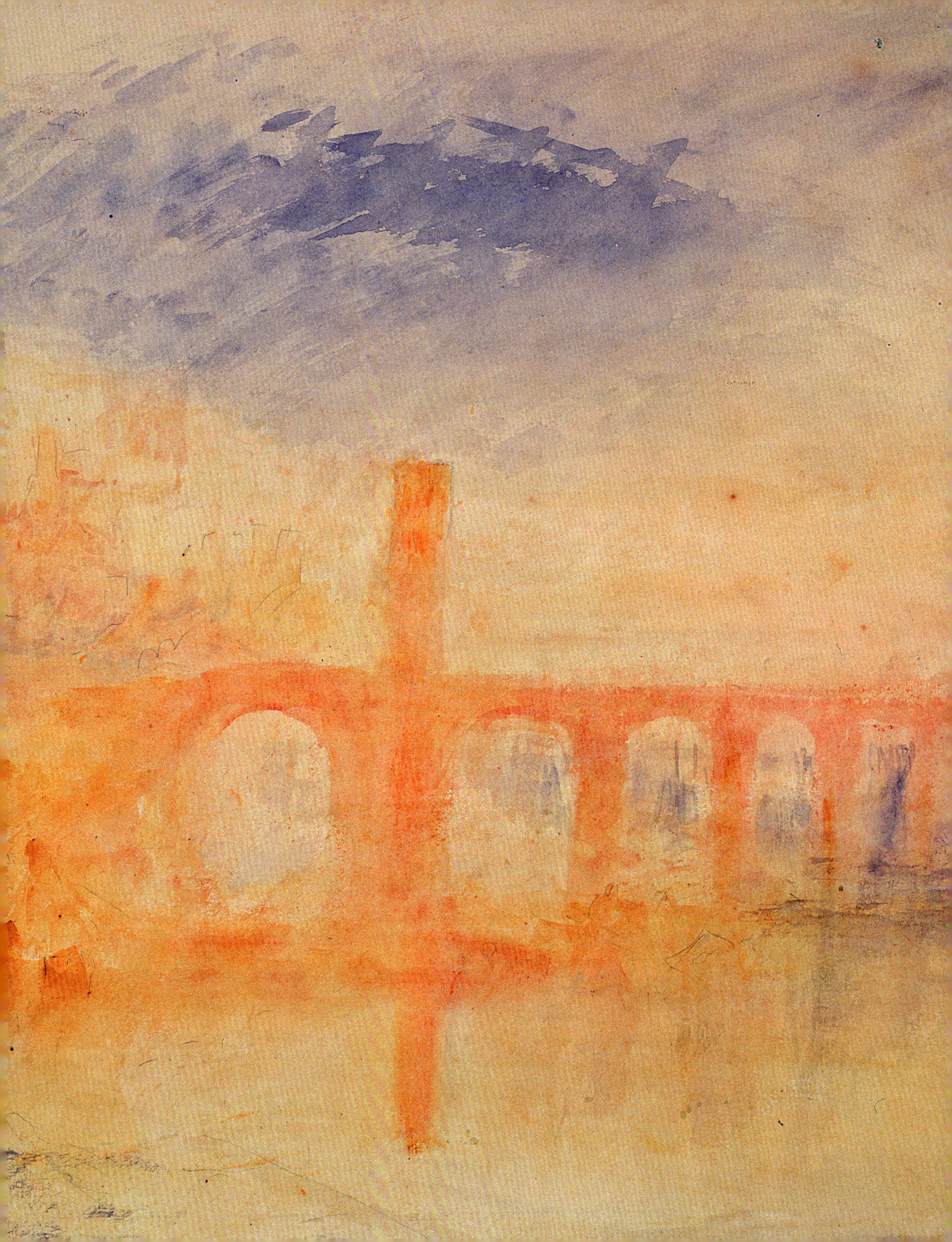

TOWARD A MODERN AESTHETIC

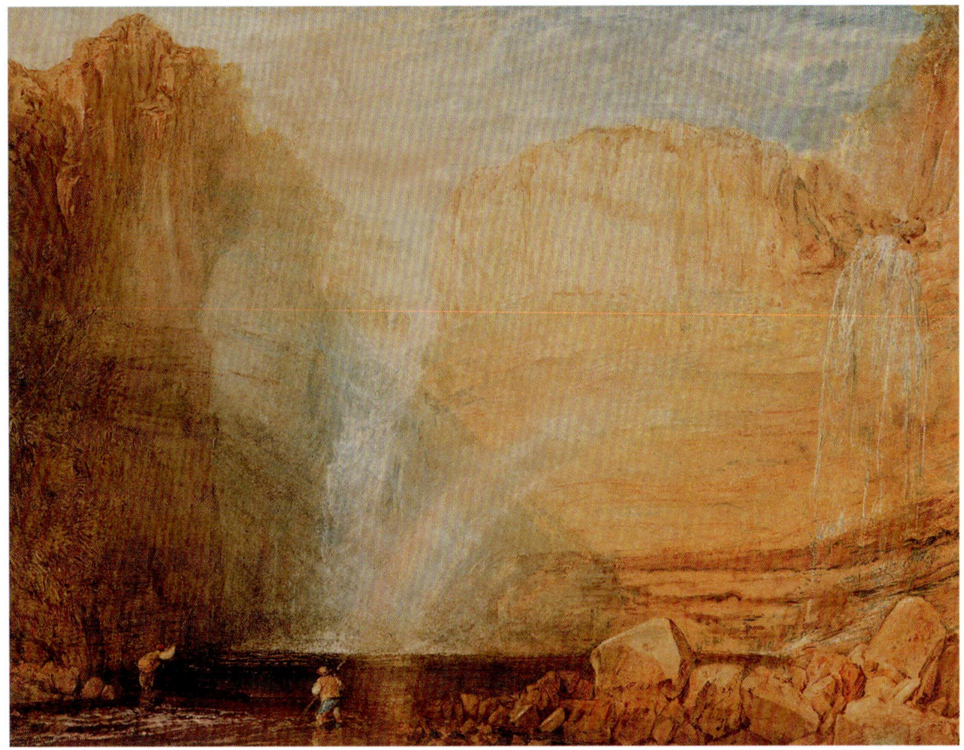

At a time of political upheaval and reform, Turner embraced genre painting, expressing his contempt for social inequality. Paradoxically, he became more involved with the Academy, and sought royal patronage from the new Prince Regent. After his first visit to Italy in 1819, his style changed as he began to explore the effects of light and express them in new modes of the Sublime aesthetic. His painting technique changed as he explored the use of new colours and lighter grounds to become 'the painter of light'.

Above: High Force, Fall of the Trees. Yorkshire, *watercolour, 1816.*
Left: The Moselle Bridge, Coblenz, *graphite and watercolour, c.1842.*

WALTER RAMSDEN FAWKES

A collector since 1803, Fawkes became one of Turner's main patrons. In 1808, Turner
was invited to stay at his home, an exercise that was to be repeated for many summers,
the two establishing and maintaining a strong friendship.

The one time Whig MP and later High Sheriff of Yorkshire Walter Ramsden Fawkes (1769–1825) was in every sense the country gentleman and wealthy landowner. His main home and country seat was at Farnley Hall near Leeds in Yorkshire. Fawkes was also a political radical, supportive of the abolition of the slave trade, and of a parliamentary reform that widened the voting franchise. As an MP for Yorkshire, he empathized with Sir Thomas Fairfax, the Parliamentarian who had held the same post and who had fought alongside Oliver Cromwell in the English Civil War for parliamentary reform in the 17th century.

Fawkes was a collector and had amassed a large number of artefacts belonging to Fairfax and proudly displayed them at Farnley Hall. Apart from his substantial estate in Yorkshire, Fawkes owned a large Regency house in London. Despite his wealth and influence, Fawkes endured a tragic family life. His eldest son and heir, also called Walter, committed suicide in 1811, aged only 16, his first wife Maria died in 1813, and in 1816 his youngest son Richard was killed in a shooting accident. Fawkes was nevertheless a genial man, good company and a kindred spirit for Turner.

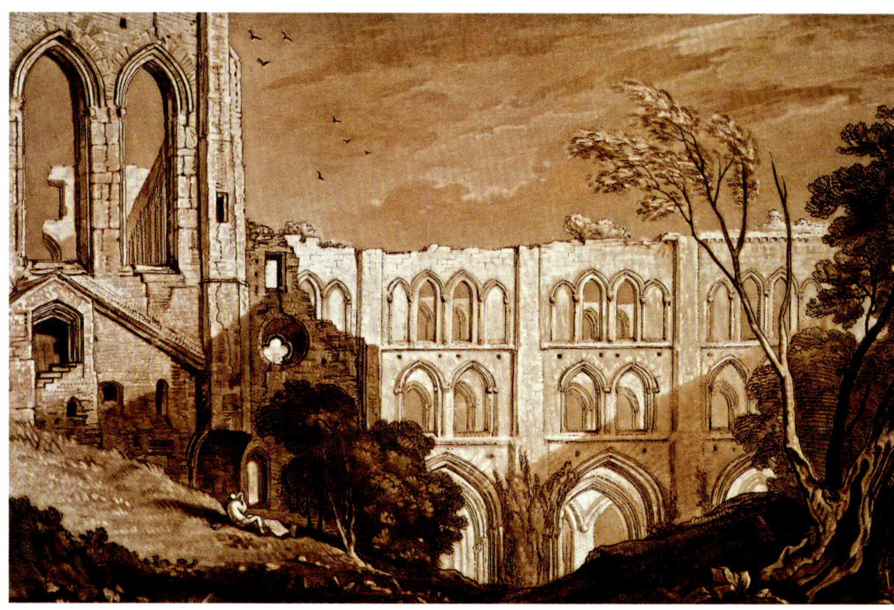

Above: Rivaulx Abbey, *from the* Liber Studorium, *etching, 1812. Turner continued to develop his* Liber Studiorum, *using motifs from everywhere he travelled to, including this scene in North Yorkshire.*

TURNER AND THE FAWKES FAMILY

At the time of his visit to Farnley in 1812, Turner was restless and suffering from what he called 'Maltese Plague' (Malta Fever), with biliousness, feverishness and headache. This was essentially down to his diet and stress caused by overwork. Farnley Hall provided a respite if not a cure. Fawkes and Turner became firm friends from the beginning, the former recognizing

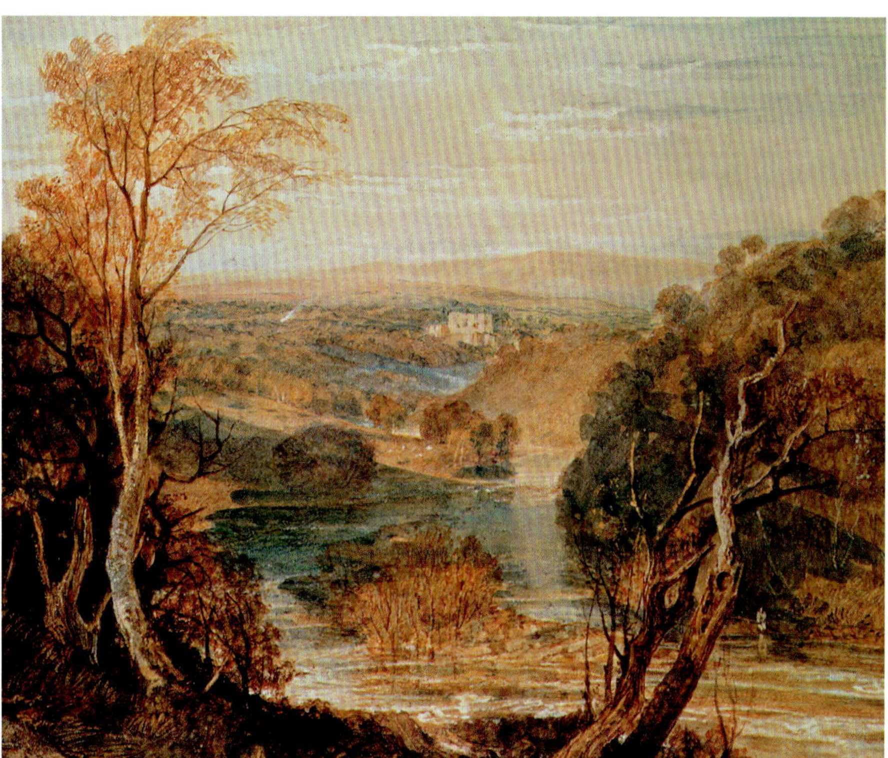

Left: The River Wharfe with a Distant View of Barden Tower, *watercolour, c.1815. One of many watercolours that Turner made of the countryside around the Yorkshire Dales, while he was staying with Walter Fawkes.*

FAWKES' INFLUENCE

Turner produced a number of paintings of the interior of Farnley Hall. A series of 20 studies of birds was also created by Turner for Walter Fawkes' work *The Farnley Book of Birds*. It was, however, Turner's political paintings that had the mark and influence of Fawkes' ideas and agenda. Turner had already begun to make political statements in his genre paintings from about 1806. From 1810 the intent was implied, such as in *Snow Storm: Hannibal and His Army Crossing the Alps*. After 1813 the political intent was more overt as in *Frosty Morning* and later *Northampton* (1830).

Below: Turner and Fawkes at Farnley Hall, *JR Wildman, watercolour, c.1820. A little-known artist, Wildman has managed to differentiate between artist and patron.*

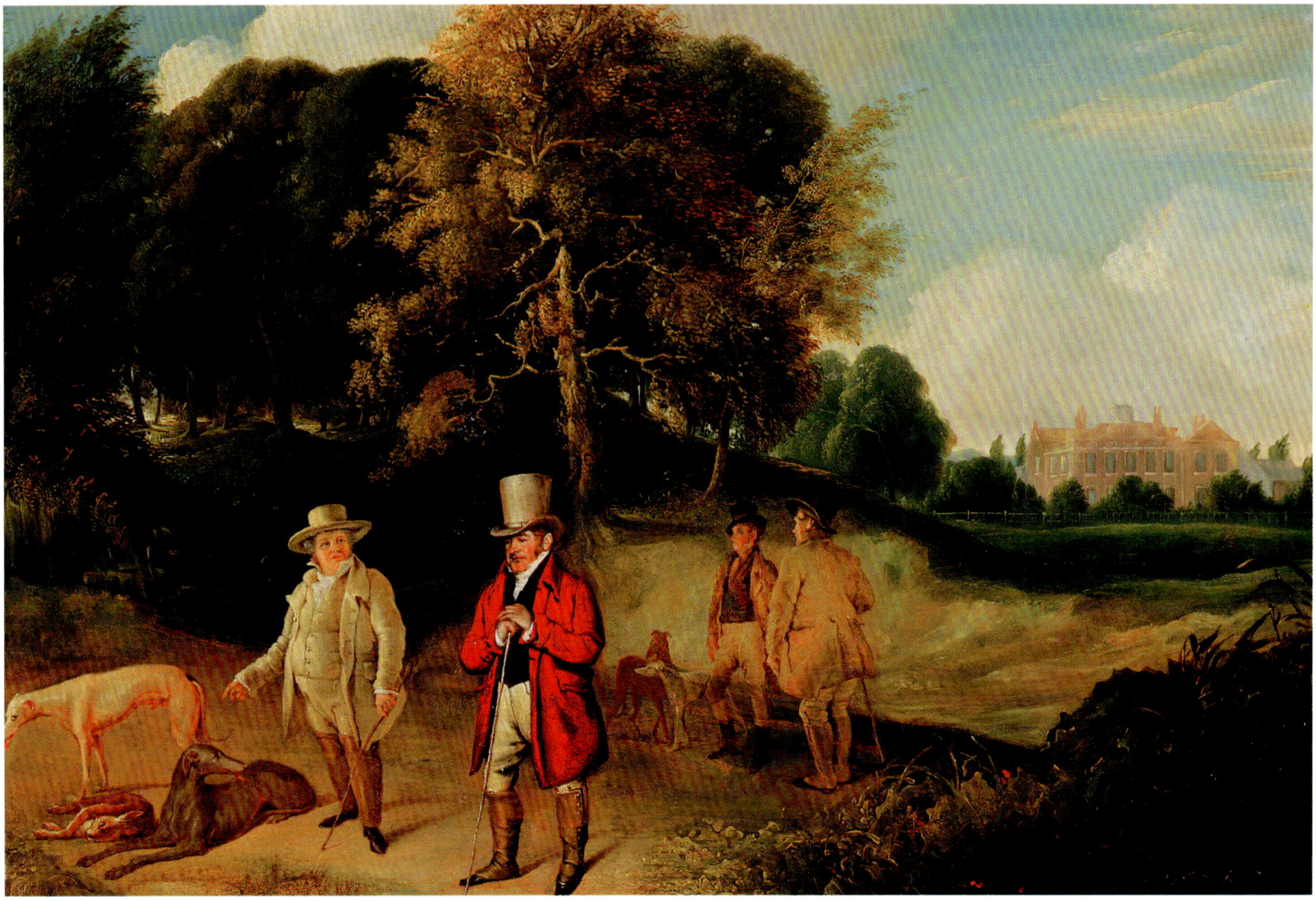

the artist's genius, and affording him a hospitality that ignored his social shortcomings. Their friendship was built on a mutual understanding of social injustices and the need for reform. Turner loved Yorkshire, and particularly the area around Farnley Hall, which looked out over the Dales. Apart from using the area as a painting motif, Turner also indulged his love of fishing, and even tried his hand at grouse shooting on Fawkes' estate.

While a guest at the house, Turner was given a sitting room where he could paint. He also became friends with Hawksworth, one of the sons, whom he affectionately called 'Hawkey'. One evening he called 'Hawkey' to his side to witness a thunderstorm, telling him that the next time he would see these effects would be in a painting that he had decided to execute, *Snow Storm: Hannibal and His Army Crossing the Alps*. For his younger brother Richard, who had an interest in natural history, Turner began a series of ornithological studies.

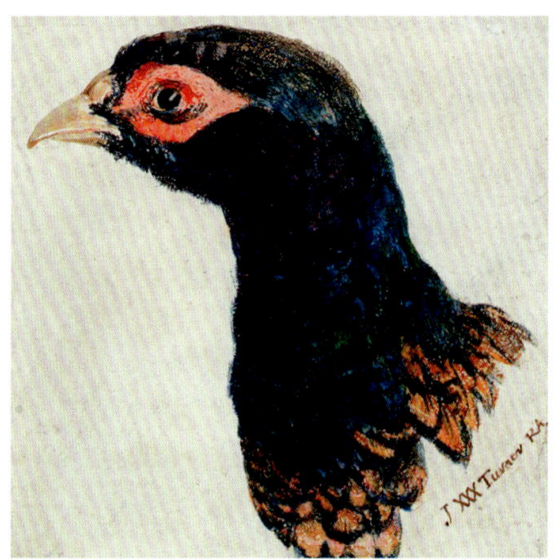

Above: Cock Pheasant *from* The Farnley Book of Birds, *pen and ink and watercolour, 1815. One of many bird studies that Turner made for Fawkes.*

THE WHARFEDALES

Turner produced many watercolours of the area around Farnley that Fawkes referred to as his 'Wharfedales', a reference to the inclusion of the Dales and River Wharfe, which were visible from the front of the house.

EXPLOITING THE SUBLIME

Against a backdrop of war with France and the political upheavals at home, Turner exploited the potential of the Sublime aesthetic for comment as well as in an attempt to raise the profile of landscape painting.

Within his *Liber Studiorum* treatise, Turner created a subdivision of 'Pastoral' that he referred to as 'Elevated Pastoral', intended for his subliminal grand-scale landscape paintings, the first of which had been *The Fifth Plague of Egypt*. He wanted to raise the profile of landscape painting to that of history painting, something that neither Richard Wilson nor Thomas Gainsborough achieved while the Royal Academy was dominated by Sir Joshua Reynolds. At the turn of the 18th into the 19th century, the Sublime, a subject that had been endlessly discussed as an aesthetic consideration, now took its place in the compendium of cultural ideas as having a moral dimension. England at this time was still at war with France, and on the home front parliamentary reform was high on the political agenda.

The Napoleonic war had created a harsh economic climate in England, a factor that led to civil disorder among groups such as the Luddites, who were subsequently sentenced to penal transportation, and in some cases execution. The Sublime aesthetic has inherent power – power to terrorize, enthral and, by implication, control. Since power is associated with both political and social control, the potential was there for Turner to exploit its aesthetic for comment.

USING THE AESTHETIC

An early example of Turner's use of the Sublime in a political context was *Apollo and the Python* in which the artist contrasted light and dark areas of the picture, symbolic of the forces of a good England and an evil Napoleonic France. This simplified form was soon superseded by more subtle forms, the first of which was *Snow Storm: Hannibal and his Army Crossing the Alps*, a historical painting with a contemporary analogy. Turner adopted what was to be a hallmark of his Sublime paintings, the vortex, analogous to the political, military and social upheavals of his time. In *Wreck of a Transport Ship*, Turner was again able to use this distinctive feature of his work to suggest the pain and suffering endured during penal transportation. Since the Sublime had

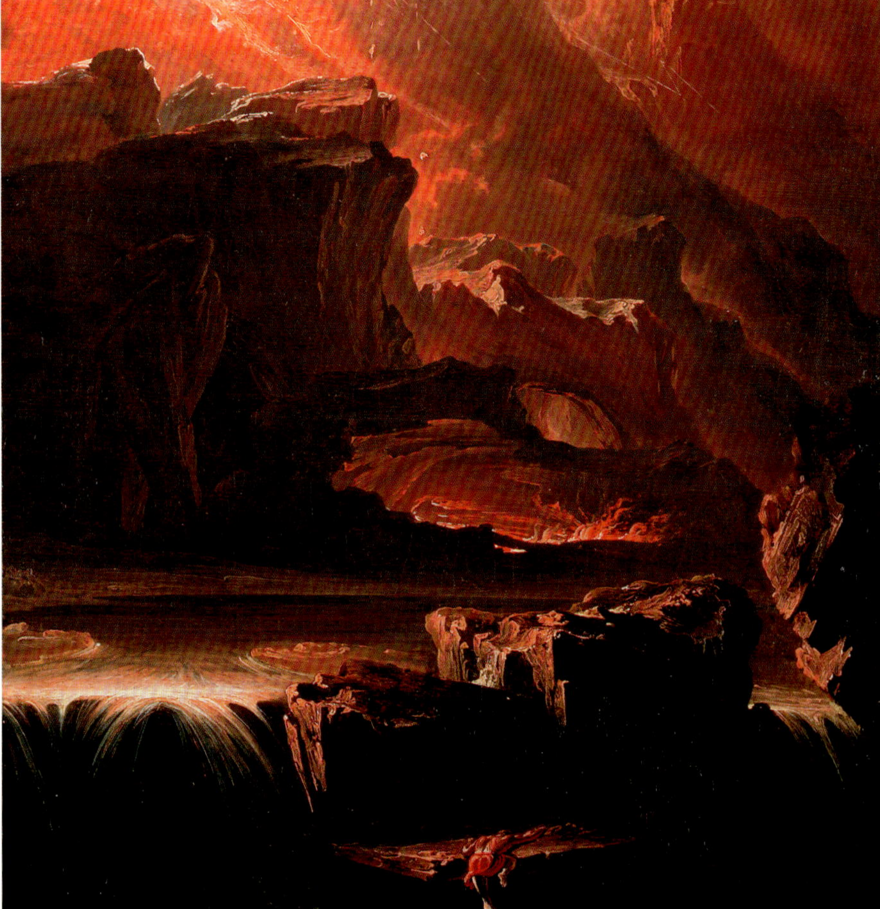

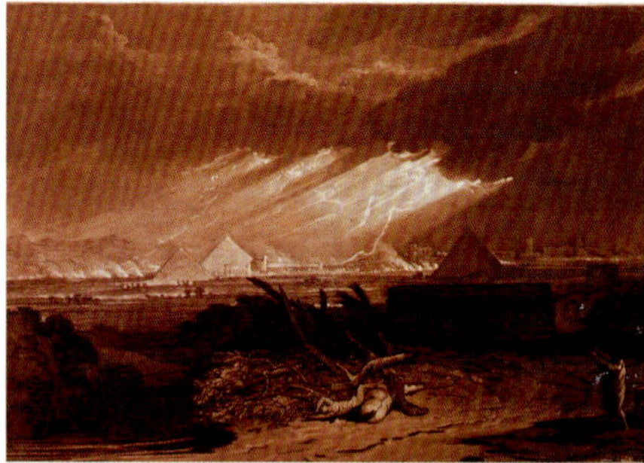

Above: The Fifth Plague of Egypt, *etching and mezzotint, 1808. Part of the* Liber Studiorum *series in which the mezzotint shows a strong contrast of tones, to retain the dynamism of the original painting.*

Left: Sadak in Search of the Waters of Oblivion, *John Martin, oil on canvas, 1812. Many artists, including Martin, exploited the Sublime aesthetic.*

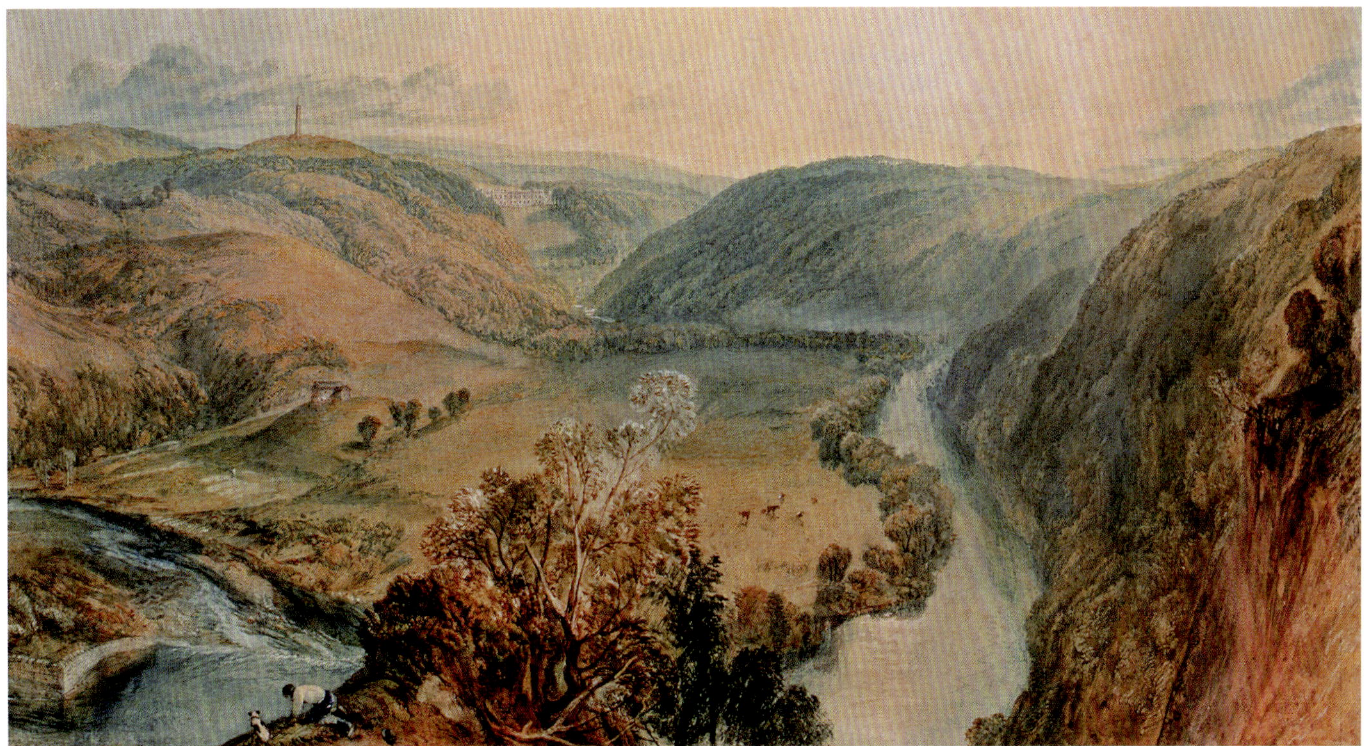

Above: Gibside, County Durham from the North, *watercolour, 1817. The Sublime aesthetic was not always overtly dramatic and could be achieved using an exaggerated viewpoint, as in this painting.*

already been adopted as an aesthetic of moral rectitude, Turner was able to utilize it in contemporary issues to prick society's conscience. He was also able, by this route, to elevate the role of landscape painting, by making it analogous to those contemporary issues. Turner continued to use the Sublime aesthetic in most of his 'political' paintings right up until his death, the most obvious examples being *The Burning of the Houses of Parliament* (1834) and *War: The Exile and the Rock Limpet* (1842).

SUBLIME POETRY

The pictorial representation of a cultural shift is never in a creative vacuum, and is always analogous to other outpourings. An ancient notion that had increasingly gained credibility in the 18th century was that of *ut pictura poesis* or 'as in painting, so in poetry', meaning that poetry deserved the same scholarly approach as painting was already given. Thus for Turner, as with Horace, they were 'sister arts'.

When *Hannibal* was exhibited in 1812, Turner appended poetic lines to the work taken from what he called the 'Fallacies of Hope', a poem that he had written himself, and used on many works:

> *While the fierce archer of the*
> *downward year*
> *Stains Italy's blanch'd barriers with storms*
> *In vain each pass, ensanguin'd deep*
> *with dead*
> *Or rocky fragments, wide*
> *destruction roll'd.*

Little is known about the poem, but it appears to be inspired by the poetry of John Langhorne (1735–79). In later paintings, such as *War: The Exile and the Rock Limpet*, Turner's aesthetic is analogous to Lord Byron's poem *'Ode to Napoleon'*: "who would soar the solar height, to set in such a starless night".

Below: The Wreck of a Transport Ship, *oil on canvas, 1810. A powerful work that comments on the abuses of prisoners being sent to penal colonies.*

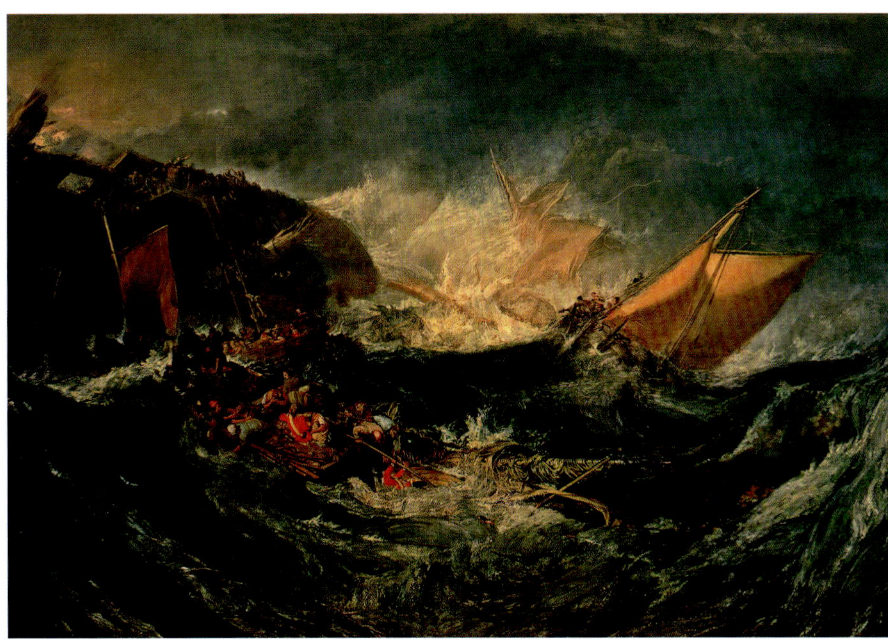

INFLUENTIAL MOTIFS

In the period approaching the Battle of Waterloo and the freedom of Europe, two seemingly incongruous subjects – Carthaginian legends and the river that was his muse – combined to inspire Turner to produce what was perhaps his greatest single work.

Having acquired the plot of land at Twickenham in 1807, Turner began in 1812 to build a villa for himself and his father, completing it in July 1813. Originally the villa was named Solus Lodge, suggesting that Turner wanted a place of solitude in which to paint. However accurate this may be, records show that Turner also entertained there.

SANDYCOMBE LODGE

The name Solus Lodge appears to have been used only once by Turner, at the Royal Academy exhibition of 1813, then the name changed to Sandycombe Lodge. The house was designed using classical proportions redolent of those used by Turner's Academy colleague John Soane, who may well have acted as consultant. At the time of building, Alexander Pope's nearby villa was being demolished, causing widespread anger. Sandycombe Lodge is a scaled down and more modest version of Pope's villa.

Turner's ground floor studio enjoyed the best of the morning light, but from his spacious first floor bedroom window he was able to see the sun

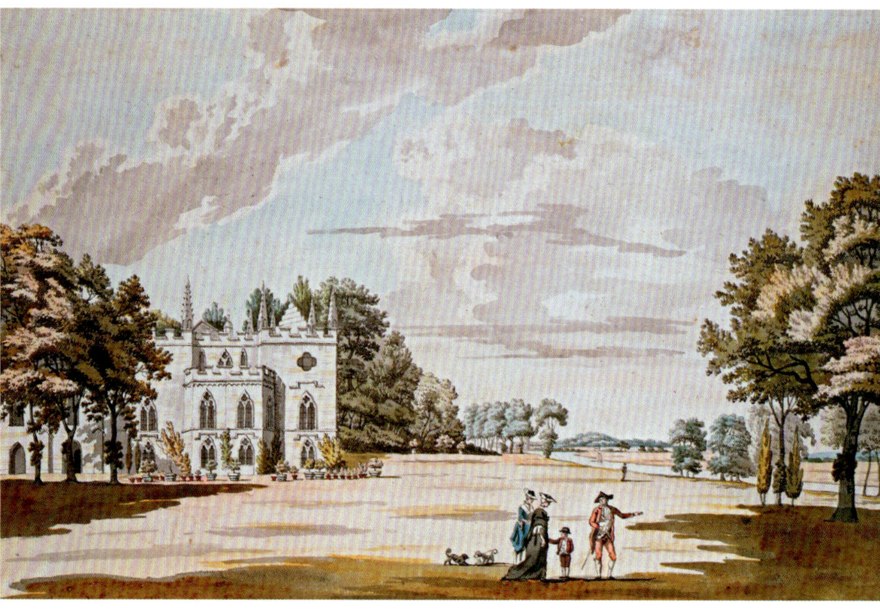

rise, a motif he was to use continuously from this time on. Despite its close proximity to the river, and high vantage point, Turner would not have had a view of the Thames from the villa. However, from this date, copying of the motif ceased to be a key consideration for Turner; he preferred instead remembered aspects rather than actual.

Above: The South Front of Strawberry Hill, *Paul Sandby, pen, ink and watercolour, 18th century. The elegant 'gothick' Strawberry Hill House was built for the writer Horace Walpole.*

THE CARTHAGINIAN LEGENDS

While Turner was living by the Thames, he read stories about the ancient world including the Trojan and Punic Wars. He avidly read Virgil's *Aeneid* and became fascinated by the Carthaginian legends, perhaps because of the British determination to fend off Napoleon. In 1814, he created one of his best known, and perhaps even his greatest picture, *Dido Building Carthage*.

Dido was the legendary queen who built the city, a seaport off the coast of north-west Africa (Tunisia). Probably the largest and most prosperous port in the Mediterranean, its wealth developed through trading, until the

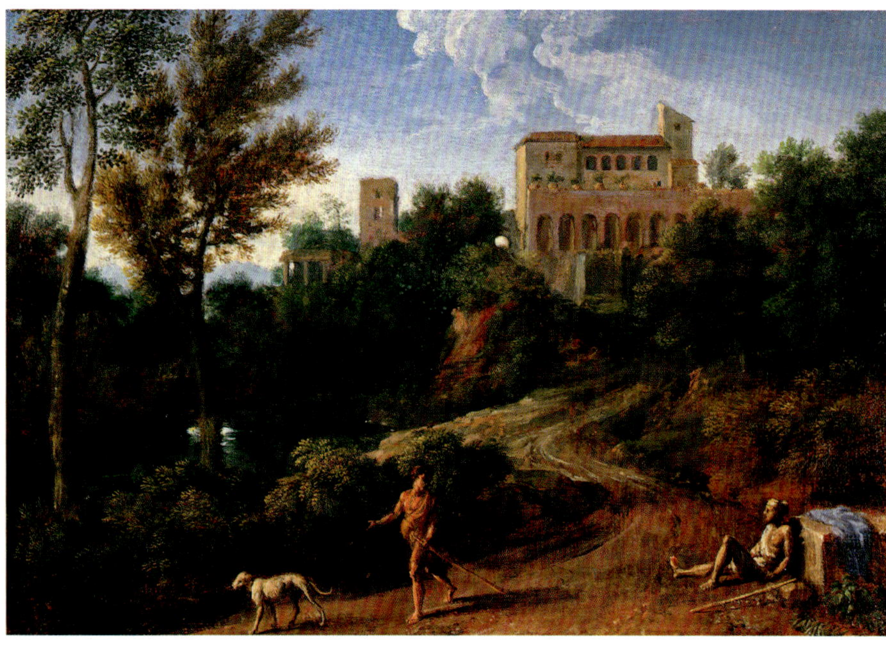

Left: Classical Landscape with Figures, *Gaspard Poussin Dughet, oil on canvas, c.1672–75. A French Arcadian landscape that anticipates the English Picturesque aesthetic of the 18th century.*

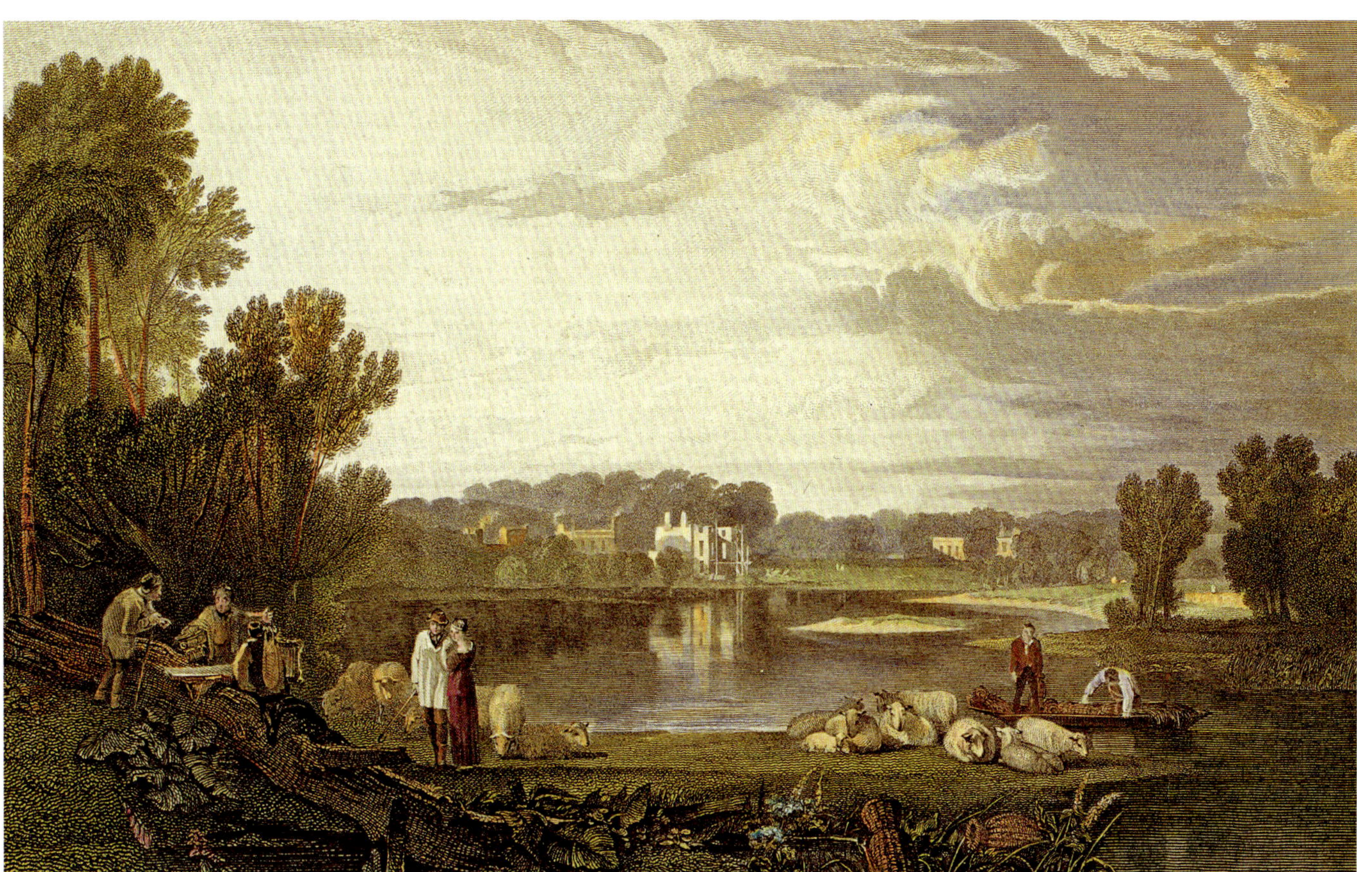

Romans destroyed it in the Punic War of 146BCE. Carthage was viewed by Classical literature as representing a civilization built on democratic co-operation rather than oppression. 'The Shining City', as it came to be known, was homogenous, peaceful and above all optimistic, factors that were influential for Turner. In this masterpiece, the artist selected a motif taken from Claude's *Seaport with the Embarkation of the Queen of Sheba* – the bright sunlight that creates an aura to the work. When Turner exhibited *Dido* at the Royal Academy in 1815, it was well received. The yellow background dominated, and Turner, after criticism by fellow Academicians, used his Varnishing Days to tone it down.

Above: Alexander Pope's Villa at Twickenham, *engraving after Turner, 1811.*

THE RIVER THAMES

This part of the Thames had been popular with the well heeled since the late 17th century and was still a fashionable place to live in Turner's time. The court painter Sir Godfrey Kneller (1646–1723) had lived in Twickenham; Horace Walpole (1717–97) built his 'gothick' lodge close by 50 years before Turner came; and Turner's neighbours included the Duke of Northumberland and the exiled French King Louis-Philippe. A popular feature of this area was its aspiration as a Claude or Poussin landscape, a rural idyll in which residents could escape the hustle and bustle of the metropolis.

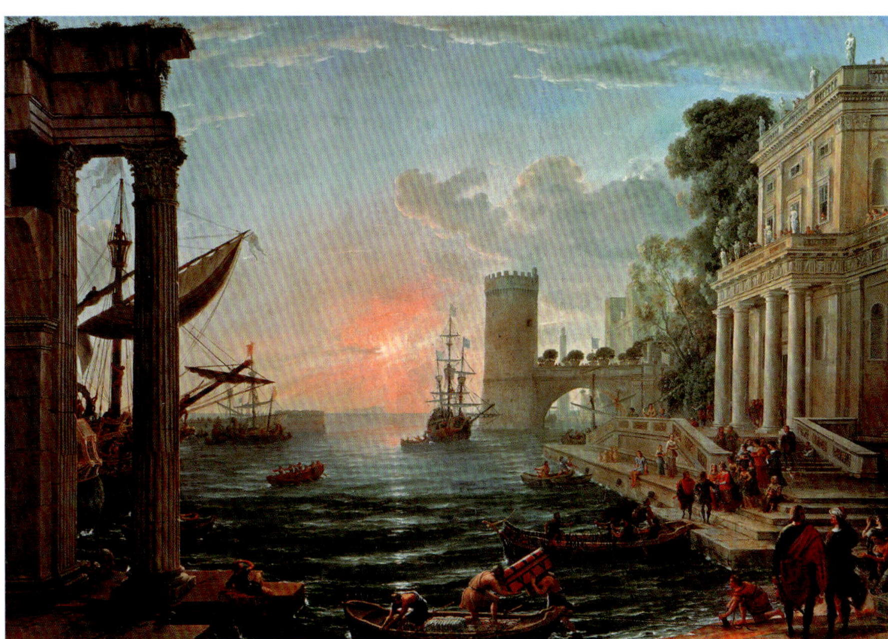

Left: Seaport with the Embarkation of the Queen of Sheba, *Claude Lorrain, oil on canvas, 1648. This masterpiece greatly influenced Turner's appreciation of light.*

MORE VIEWS OF ENGLAND

Turner began two new publishing commissions, one of which was sadly cut short.
His commitments increased, and he was elected a 'Visitor' to the newly created School of Painting
at the Royal Academy, as well as making great efforts to establish a new benevolent institution.

In the summer of 1815, shortly after the Battle of Waterloo, Turner began a series of Views in Sussex commissioned by John 'Mad Jack' Fuller (1757–1834), the former Member of Parliament for Sussex. Fuller was a wealthy but eccentric character; forced to resign his parliamentary seat after a fracas at the House of Commons. He sponsored the Royal Institution and was an early supporter of Michael Faraday's work, founding the Fullerian Professorship of Chemistry in 1833. He also built an observatory at Brightling, near Heathfield in East Sussex. More importantly from Turner's perspective he was a patron of the arts, purchasing some 13 watercolours and 2 oil paintings from him between 1810 and 1818. Among those were commissions for his house and estate Rose Hill, at Brightling. Fuller also wished to create a series of prints of Sussex, including his own Rose Hill, which Turner started in

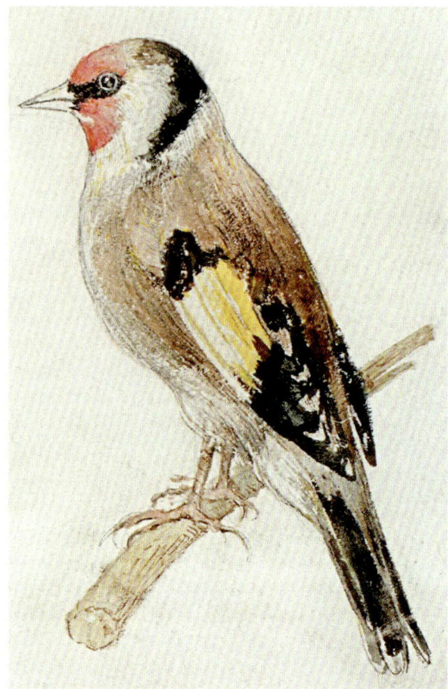

earnest in 1815. From over 300 sketchbook drawings, he completed 13 watercolours in November of the following year. Of these only seven were engraved including the one of Rose Hill Park.

FARNLEY 1815–16

During August 1815, Turner visited Walter Fawkes at Farnley, arriving in time for the annual grouse shoot and then returning there the following year when he stayed for much of the summer. Apart from working on the 'Wharfedale' series for Fawkes, he also made a short trip with him to gather material for a new commission, *A History of Yorkshire*, for the Reverend Doctor Thomas Whitaker, with the publisher Longman. Turner was

Above: Goldfinch, *from* The Farnley Book of Birds, *watercolour, 1816. Another of the 'Bird' series Turner made at Farnley Hall.*

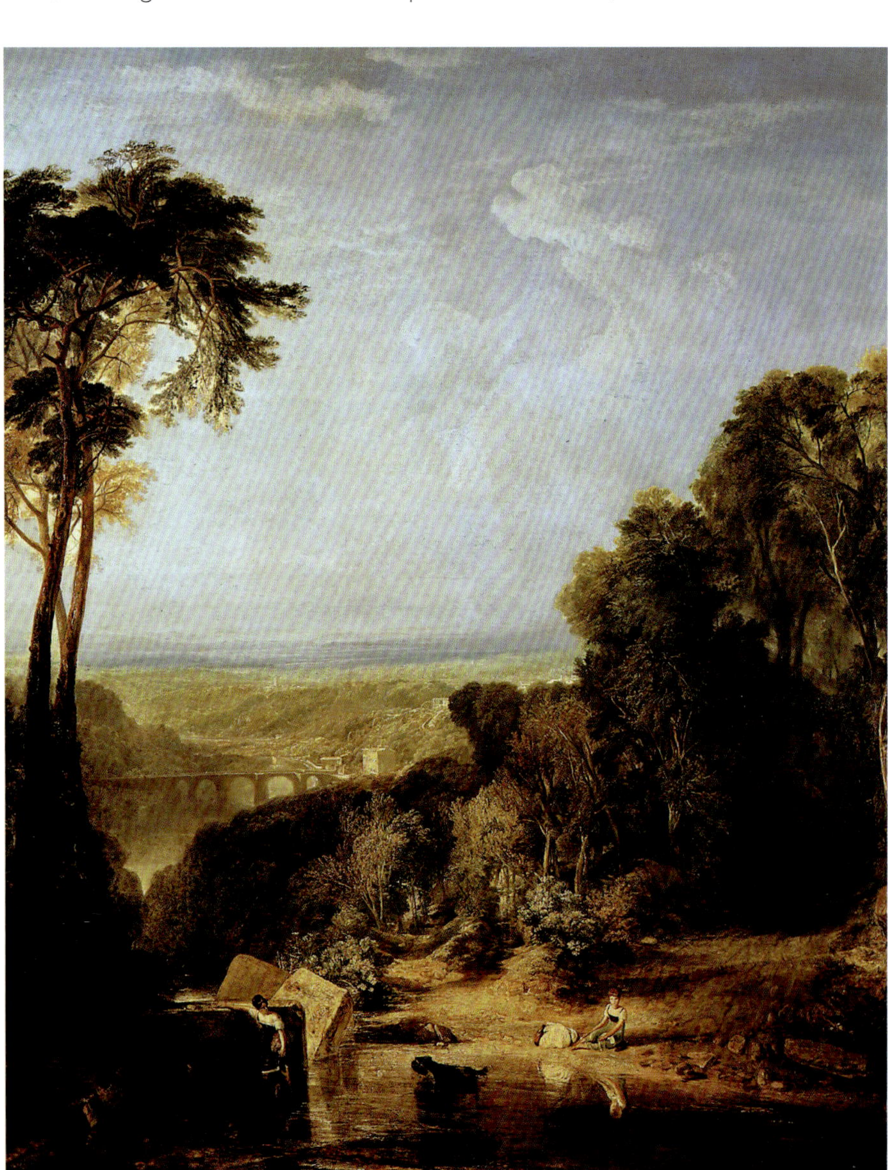

Left: Crossing the Brook, *watercolour, 1815, a view in Devon.*

commissioned to make 120 drawings, for which he was to be paid 3,000 guineas (nearly £200,000 today). Despite the appalling summer weather in 1816, he produced more than 1,000 sketches and drawings for this project, using Farnley Hall as his base. He was staying there in August again for the grouse shoot when Fawkes' youngest son Richard was accidentally shot and killed. Leaving the family to grieve, Turner again endured poor weather on another sketching trip before returning to Farnley in September. Despite the huge number of sketches and drawings made, only the first part of 20 engravings were completed, making up the first volume, *The History of Richmondshire*. This was due mainly to Whitaker dying in 1821.

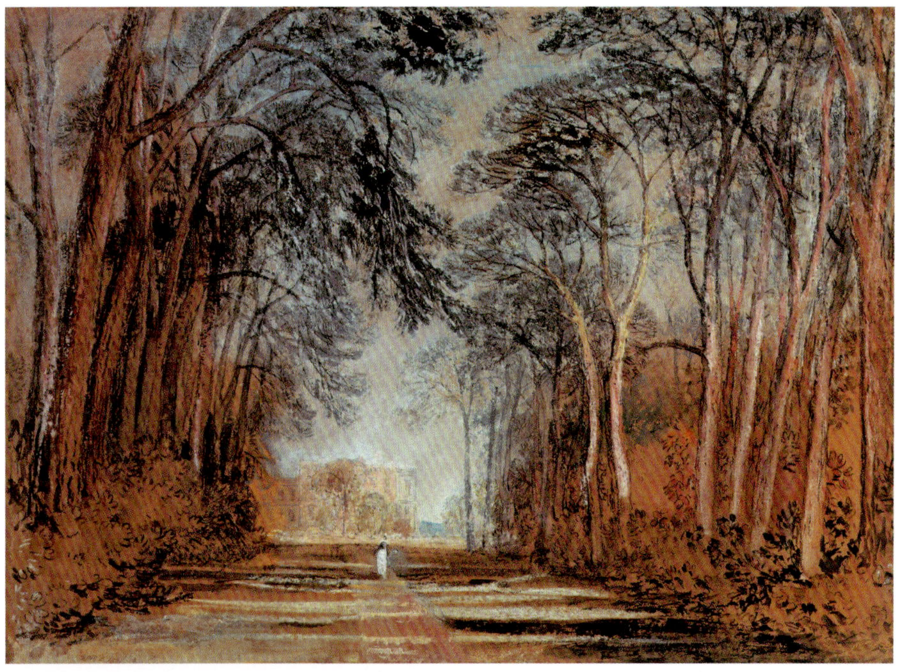

Above: Farnley Avenue, Farnley Hall, *chalk, watercolour and bodycolour, 1815. Here Turner adopted mixed media.*

VISITOR AT THE ACADEMY

The last exhibition took place at Turner's own gallery in 1815, until repairs were made during 1819 and 1820. In 1815, Turner was elected to the position of Visitor to the newly formed School of Painting at the Royal Academy. The emphasis at the schools had been on draughtsmanship, but there was now a recognition that the potential of painting had to be more developed as a discipline. Turner, who could work up a discernible painting within one lecture session, was the ideal candidate to teach by example. Turner had also been a founder member of the Artists' General Benevolent Institution, established in 1810 for the relief of struggling artists and their families. By 1818, he was made chairman. Turner took the role seriously, donating many hours and money. He served as chairman until disagreeing with the committee over the distribution of funds in 1830. However, he left provision for the institution in his will.

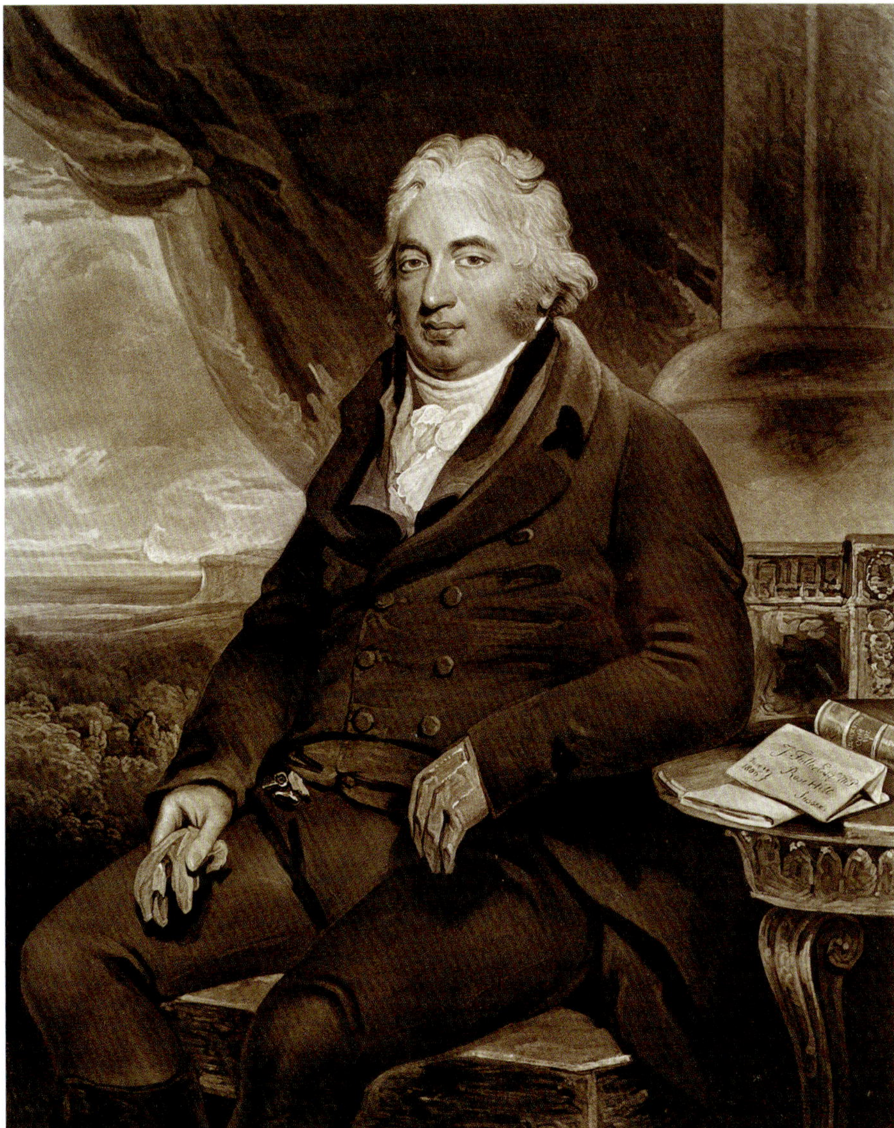

Left: J Fuller Esq, MP, *Henry Singleton, mezzotint, 1808. Engraved by Charles Turner, this formal portrait belies the eccentricity of John 'Mad Jack' Fuller.*

TOURING EUROPE AGAIN

The gates to Europe were opened once again. Turner travelled to Waterloo then back to Durham. His daughter married a diplomat and though he claimed to bless the partnership, plans made later in his will suggest a less than warm relationship.

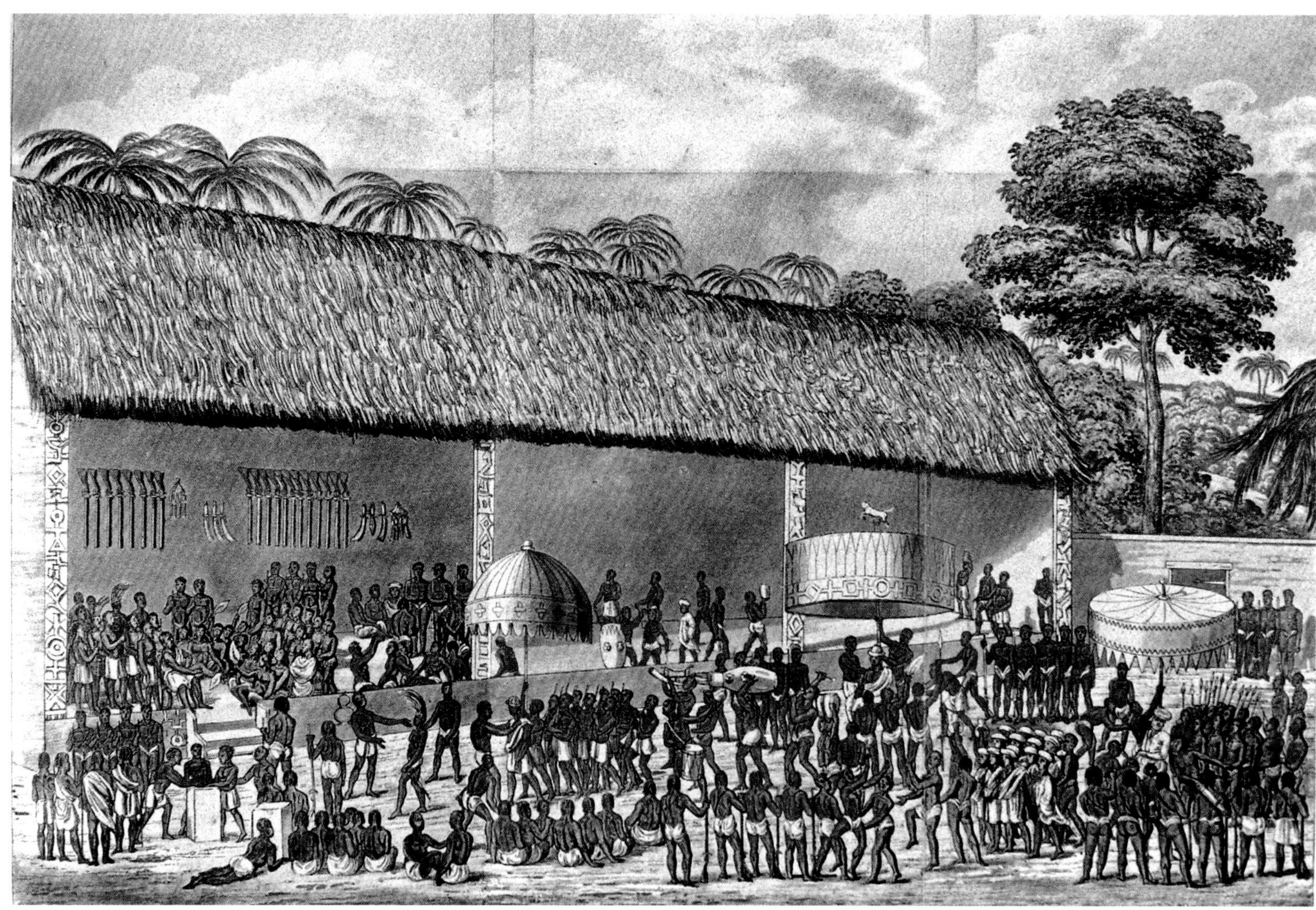

In 1815, having now finally defeated Napoleon and banishing him to the island of St Helena, England was in a state of patriotic euphoria. Apart from a brief respite in 1802, England and France had been at war since 1793, preventing the English from Continental travel. Deprived access to Europe for 13 years, Turner visited the battle site at Waterloo in the summer of 1817.

WATERLOO

The artist set sail from Margate on 10 August 1817. He crossed the channel to Ostend, arriving at the village of Waterloo on the 16th, two years after the battle that was to decide the fate of Europe. It would probably have been unnecessary to interview anyone there about the battle, since during the intervening period it had been well reported in England. In fact, Turner only spent a short time at the site, making about fifty sketches of the field and battle lines. The resultant oil painting was exhibited the following year to a generally favourable response. Lines from Byron's newly published poem *Childe Harold* accompanied the painting, the poem also receiving critical acclaim and establishing the young Romantic poet's reputation.

DURHAM

In the autumn of 1817, Turner visited Raby, home of the Earl of Darlington, to make sketches for a painting of the

Above: Adai Religious Festival at the Court of the King of Ashanti, *Joseph Dupuis, lithograph, 1824. Dupuis, Turner's son-in-law, was an accomplished artist himself and this consular event was reproduced in* Journal of a Residence in Ashantee.

castle there. The castle dates back to the 14th century, its residents being the powerful and influential Nevill family, residing there until they took the side of Mary Queen of Scots in her failed claim to the English throne. After the English Civil War, the Vane family purchased the castle, and it was Henry Vane who was created the first Earl of Darlington in 1754. William Vane (1766–1842), the third Earl and later

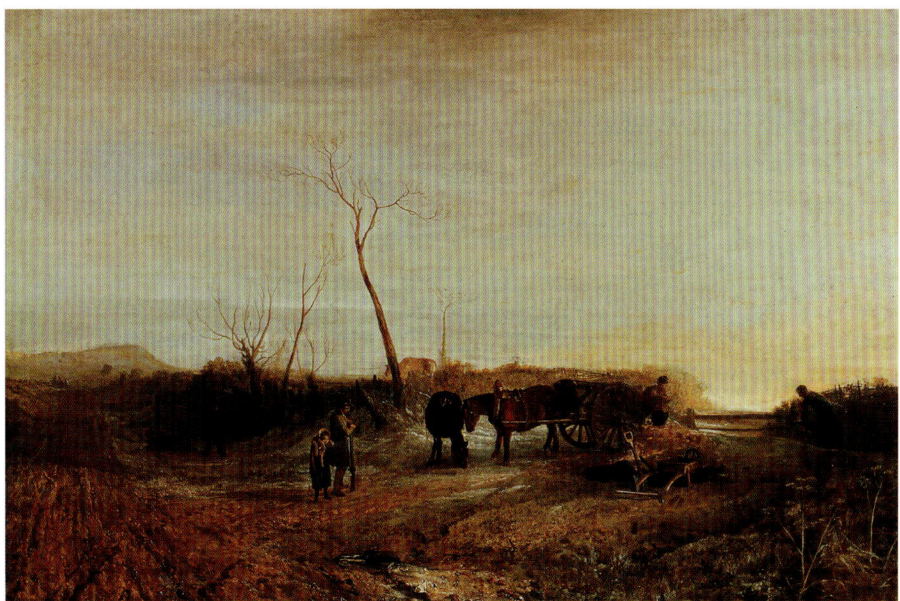

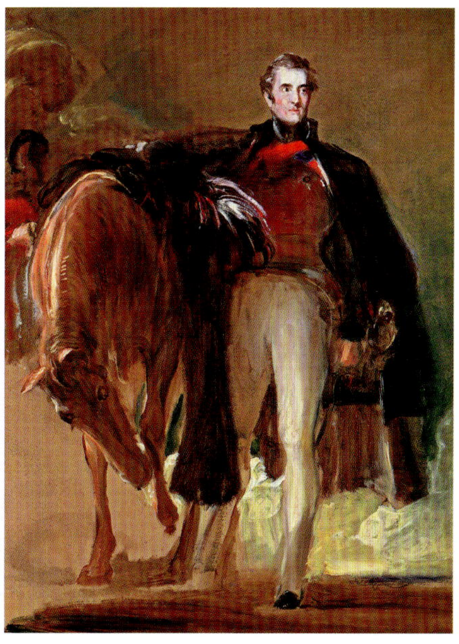

Above: Frosty Morning, *oil on canvas, 1813 – one of Turner's favourite paintings, which he did not want to sell.*

Above right: The Duke of Wellington and His Charger 'Copenhagen', *David Wilkie, oil on canvas, c.1815.*

first Duke of Cleveland, commissioned Turner's painting. The resultant work, exhibited the following year at the Royal Academy, shows the influence of Peter Paul Rubens (1577–1640), whose work Turner must have seen in the summer tour of northern Europe.

Turner was collected from Raby Castle by Lord Strathmore (1773–1846) who took him to Durham and then on to Newcastle to fulfil another commission, a four-volume *History of Durham* commissioned by the antiquary Robert Surtees (1779–1834). Some of the finished drawings and watercolours for this commission were also later used for the publishing venture *Picturesque Views in England and Wales*, beginning in 1827.

A BENEFACTOR

Aside from his work for the Artists' General Benevolent Institution, Turner had always wanted to increase his benevolence toward artists who were less fortunate than himself and so decided to set up alms-houses for "decayed male artists". To that end, in

Right: Raby Castle, the Seat of the Earl of Darlington, *oil on canvas, 1818. When Turner visited Raby he witnessed and recorded a fox-hunting meet.*

August 1818, he purchased some additional land that was situated about 3km (2 miles) from Sandycombe Lodge. His will, which was made some time later, stipulated that the alms-houses were to be occupied only by artists who were English landscape painters, and who were both male and legitimate. This action appears to be a deliberate affront to his daughters, neither of whom benefited under the terms of his will, and who challenged its content in the law courts after Turner's death.

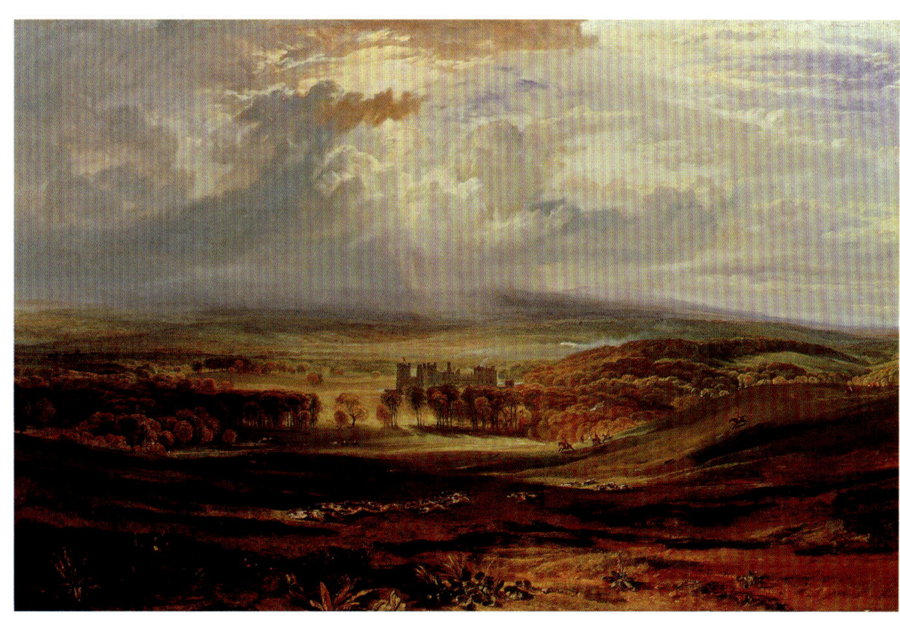

A FATHER-IN-LAW

Evelina, Turner's eldest daughter, was married at St James's Church, Piccadilly, London in the autumn of 1817 to a diplomat, Joseph Dupuis, who was to become the British Consul in Ashanti from 1820. Although the marriage apparently took place with the "consent and approbation of her father", there seems to have been no close contact between Turner and his daughter at this time, particularly since it is likely that his relationship with Sarah Danby had already come to an end.

THE RHINE AND SCOTLAND

A trip along the Rhine provided abundant creative material for Turner. But a departure from his established ways of working, a grand collaborative work, brought out his undesirable side, his colleagues finding him obnoxious and driven only by money.

In August 1817, after his visit to Waterloo, Turner travelled by coach to Cologne to begin an exploration of the Rhine gorge.

THE RHINE
Turner travelled up the River Rhine from Cologne to Mainz, visiting the beautiful towns of Remagen, Sankt Goar and Coblenz. This was perfect Sublime and Picturesque scenery for Turner with its steep escarpments and hilltop castles, which provided him with endless reference material for the rest of his career.

In all, he completed nearly 500 sketches and drawings on this trip, including his return journey through Antwerp and then Amsterdam. This also provided him with an opportunity to see the paintings of Peter Paul Rubens and Rembrandt.

Before returning home, Turner visited the port of Dordrecht, making a number of sketches of a packet boat in harbour that he later worked up into an oil painting, *Dort or Dordrecht: The Dort Packet-Boat from Rotterdam Becalmed*; an obvious homage to the Dutch artist Aelbert Cuyp (1620–91), who was a native of the town.

On his return to England, and after his visit to Durham, Turner stayed with Walter Fawkes at Farnley Hall, making more than 50 colour studies of the Rhine that were then sold to his friend for £500. Turner signed an agreement in February 1819 to create 36 views on the Rhine to be engraved by WB Cooke and JC Allen. He was to be paid 17 guineas for each drawing, but the project failed to materialize in print form.

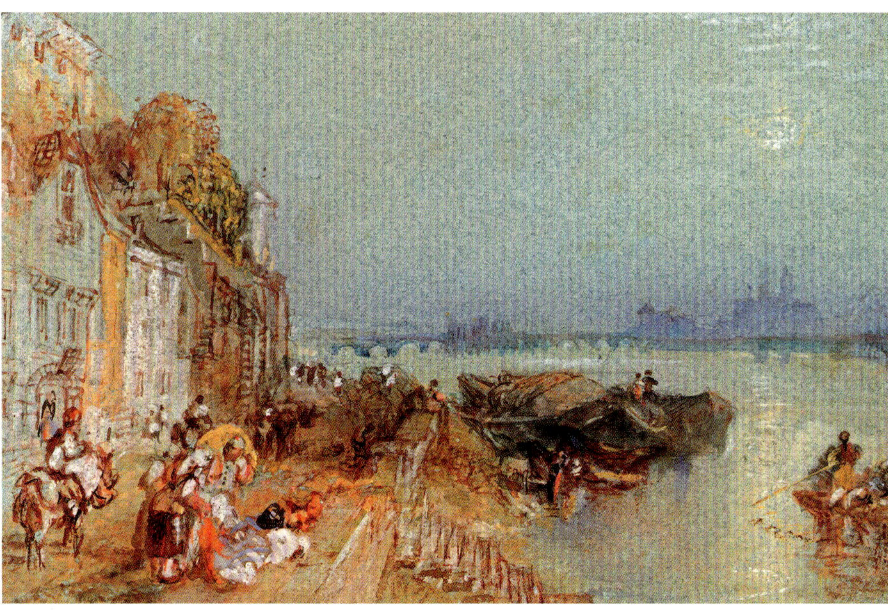

Above: Andernach, *watercolour and ink, 1817. One of the oldest towns in Germany, it was founded by the Romans together with its larger neighbour, Coblenz.*

AN UNUSUAL COMMISSION
In a departure from his usual *modus operandi*, Turner was commissioned to make ten watercolour views of Italy from outlines made by James Hakewill (1778–1843) using a camera lucida (an optical drawing aid). Hakewill was an artist and writer on architecture. Work was completed in 1818 and published in 1820 by John Murray who paid Turner 20 guineas for each watercolour.

SCOTLAND
Turner did not make a Continental visit in the summer of 1818, but in October of that year he travelled to Scotland to collect reference material for the *Provincial Antiquities of Scotland*, a collection of writings on the history of Scotland and the Borders written by Sir

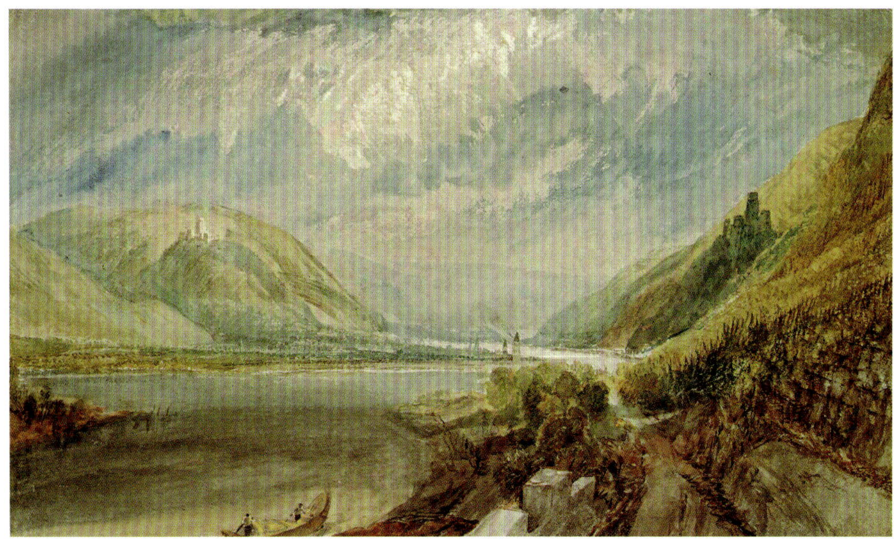

Left: The Junction of the Rhine and the Lahn, *watercolour, 1817. This tributary meets the Rhine near Coblenz.*

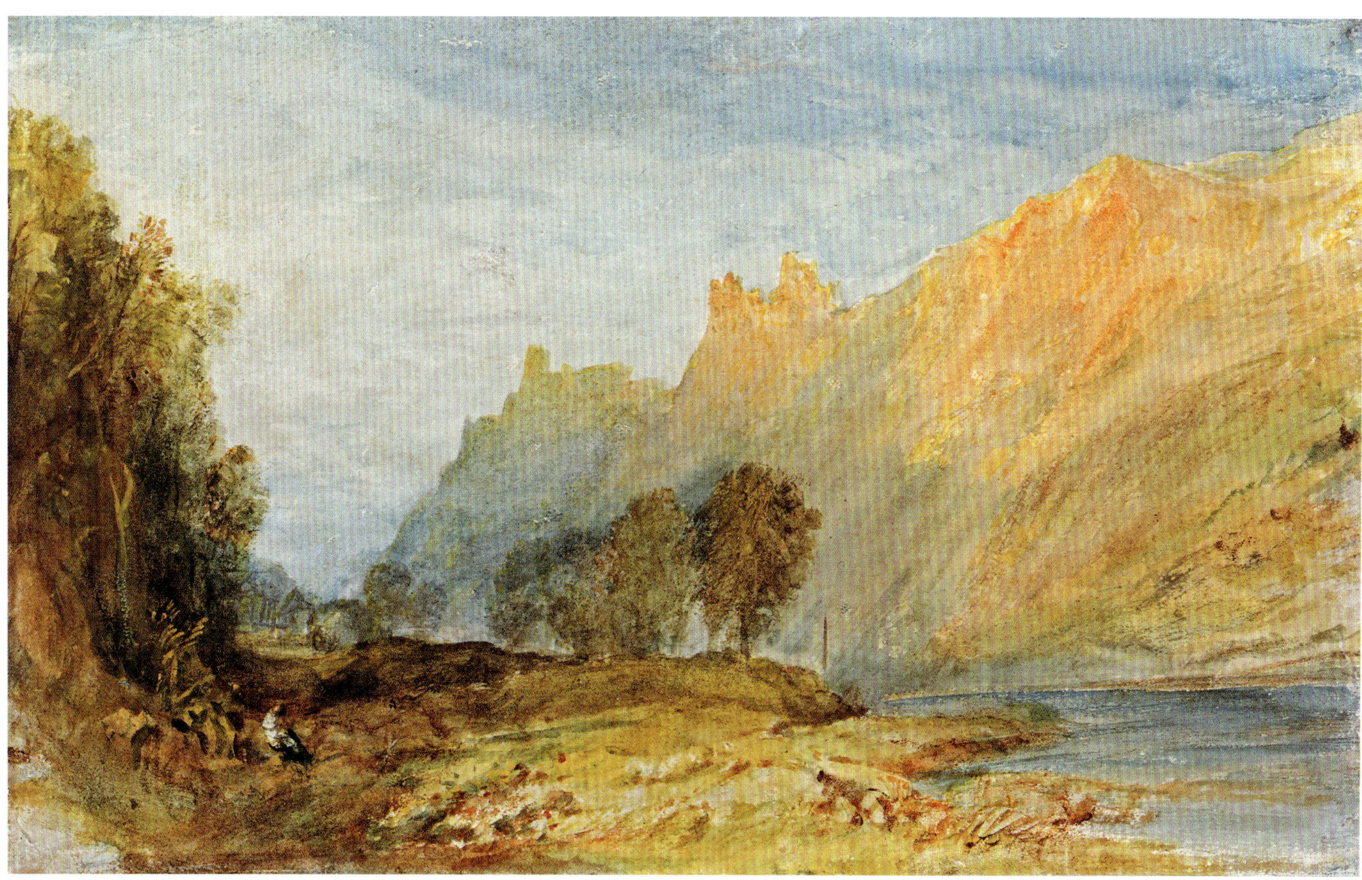

Above: Bruderburgen on the Rhine, *watercolour, 1817. One of a series of Rhineland watercolours executed by Turner during his tour in 1817.*

Walter Scott (1771–1832). Turner was one of a number of prominent artists commissioned to contribute to the work. Scott and Turner, together with the publisher and the artists, all agreed to participate in a shareholding for the venture to spread the risk. The prints came out in several volumes from 1819 to 1826. Turner was paid 25 guineas for each image, twice the rate of the other artists, an indication of the saleability of the Turner name. His tour was centred round Edinburgh, with relatively short journeys to Bass Rock, Dunbar, Roslin and Linlithgow.

Other artists working on the project joined him on these journeys. but they were critical of Turner's secrecy as to his sketches and working methods. To his several hosts, he was at best diffident and at worst rude: "finding him such a *stick*, we did not think the pleasure of showing him to our friends would be adequate to the trouble and expense". The meeting between Scott and Turner was also at best cordial, the poet later writing, "Turner's palm is as itchy as his fingers are ingenious and he will, take my word for it, do nothing without cash and anything for it. He is almost the only man of genius I ever knew who is sordid in these matters."

ROYAL ACADEMY COUNCIL

On 10 December 1818, Turner was elected to serve again on the Royal Academy Council. A newly elected Academician, Francis Chantrey (1781–1841), joined him on the Council.

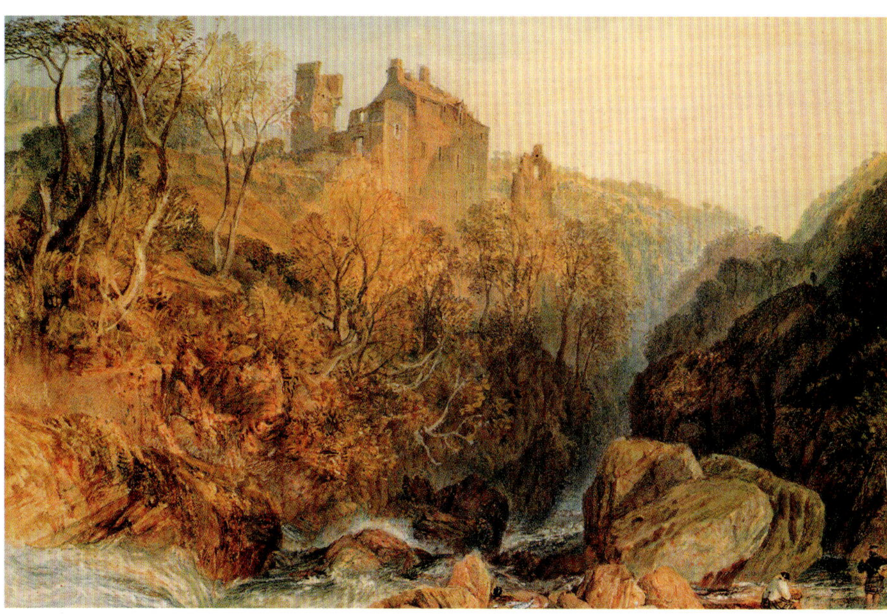

Left: Roslin Castle, *watercolour and bodycolour, 1820. This picturesque ruined castle provided inspiration for both Turner and Sir Walter Scott.*

PATRONS AND EXHIBITIONS

In 1819, before Turner set off for Italy, two of Turner's most important patrons, Sir John Fleming Leicester and Walter Fawkes, put on exhibitions at their London home galleries of 'modern British pictures', that included several of his paintings.

At this time Turner was planning a first major trip to Italy. In the meantime, however, he had also decided to acquire some more property in London, which would enable him to expand his gallery.

TURNER'S GALLERY

During 1818, Turner secured the lease of 47 Queen Anne Street West, the property that he had been renting, and also the leases of 65 and 66 Harley Street. In effect he had surrounded his tenant Benjamin Young, who was renting number 64 from him. Turner entered an agreement with the freeholders, Portland Estates, to demolish the existing buildings and rebuild a new one before Michaelmas 1821. Turner wanted a new and enlarged gallery, which he proposed to open in 1822. He left instructions for the demolition of the old buildings and construction of the foundations to be carried out while he was in Italy.

SIR JOHN FLEMING LEICESTER

In March 1819, Sir John Fleming Leicester exhibited his collection of British art at his London home in Mayfair. He was described by his obituarist as "the greatest patron of the native school of painting that our Island ever possessed". Whether accurate or not, he was certainly a major patron of artists that included Turner, and Leicester placed his acquisitions in specially constructed galleries at his residences in London and Cheshire.

The opening of town houses to the public, rather than just friends, for an admission fee, began in the early 19th century. Aside from the annual Royal Academy exhibition and those of two other societies, the raft of British school talent was not available to view.

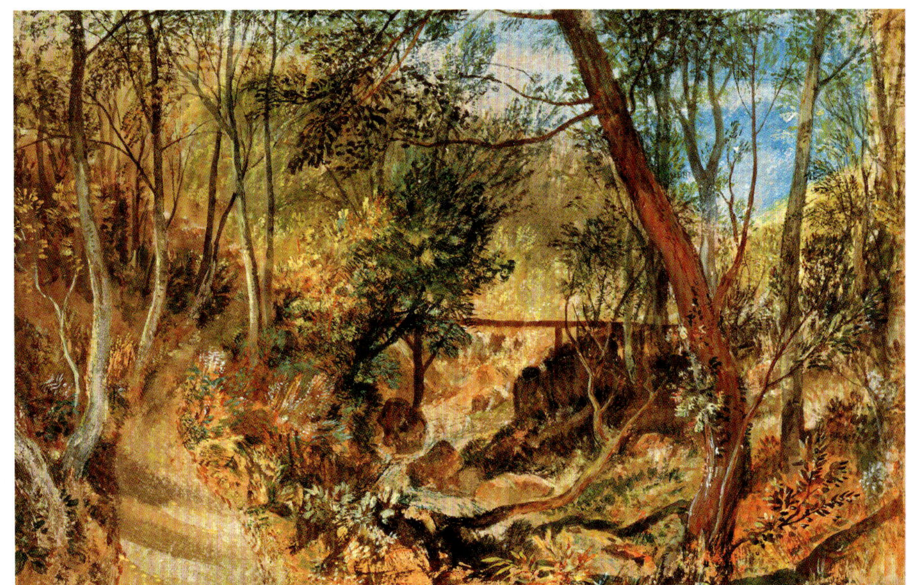

Above: The Woodwalk, Farnley Hall, *graphite and watercolour, 1818. Farnley Hall in Yorkshire belonged to Fawkes.*

Below: Isis, *from Liber Studiorum, etching, 1819. This was the last of the series published in 1819.*

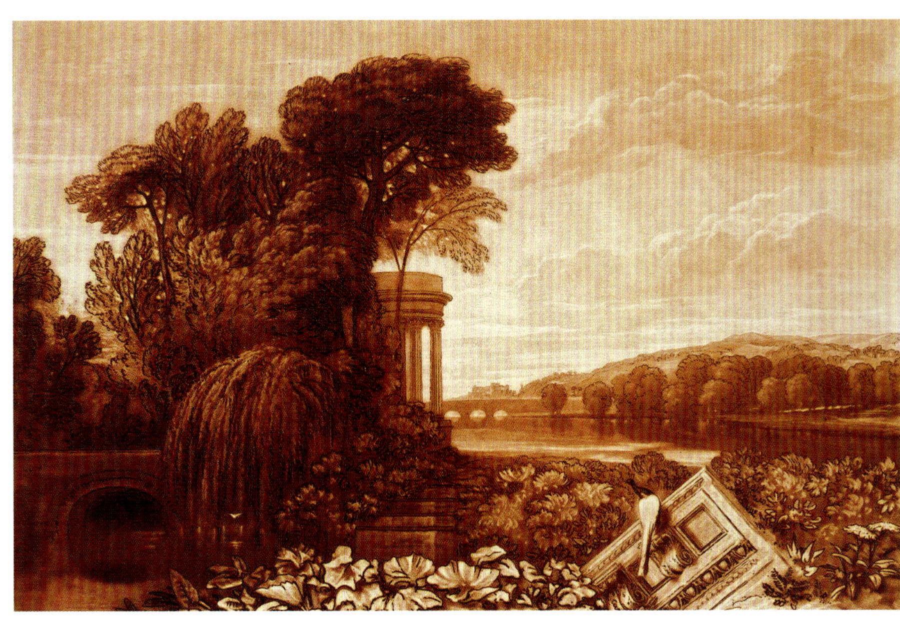

A LARGE CANVAS

During Fawkes' exhibition, Turner submitted one of the largest canvases he ever painted, *England: Richmond Hill on the Prince Regent's Birthday*, to the Royal Academy. Clearly the scale and subject matter was intended to woo royal patronage and to secure a knighthood, succeeding in the first and failing in the second, even when the Prince Regent was made king the following year.

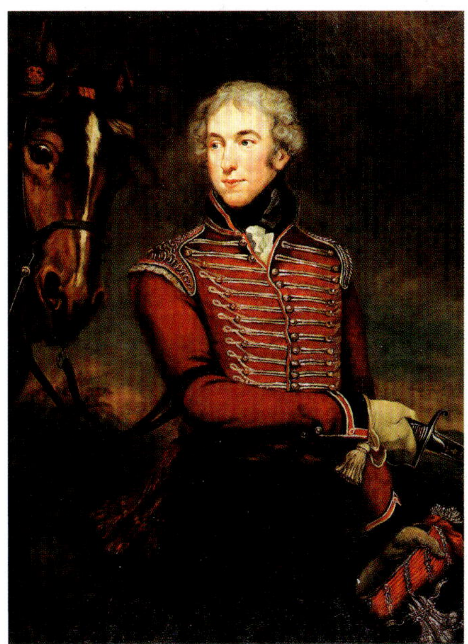

Above: Portrait of Sir John Fleming Leicester, *James Northcote, oil on canvas, 1802. The picture remains at Tabley House.*

Leicester's exhibition was successful, one critic writing that the paintings were "the finest productions of the respective masters. The exhibition displays the genius of British art to the highest advantage". Among the works displayed was Leicester's most recent acquisition, Turner's *The Sun Rising through Vapour*, purchased at the Royal Academy the previous year.

ANOTHER EXHIBITION

Perhaps inspired by Leicester's exhibition, Turner's other main patron of the time, Walter Fawkes, also opened his London house gallery between April and June of the same year. Fawkes, however, chose to exhibit watercolours, including about 70 by Turner. The display of such a large number of watercolours was somewhat unusual for this time. The Royal Academy was dominated by oil paintings. The establishment of the Society of Painters in Water Colours (now the Royal Watercolour Society) at the beginning of the century had highlighted the significance of the medium, but of course Turner, its master, was precluded as an Academician from showing there and chose to emphasize his oils at the Academy because of their prestige and sale value.

At Fawkes's exhibition, paintings by members of the society were hung together, while Turner's works, including the 'Wharfedale' series, were exhibited together. To emphasize the importance that Fawkes attached to the exhibition, and his involvement as one of Turner's main patrons, he had a catalogue printed with a cover designed by the artist. At the close of the exhibition, Fawkes gave a specially printed catalogue to Turner, complete with very favourable newspaper extracts and his own dedication "as an offering of friendship". He wrote of "feeling the delight I have experienced during the greater part of my life from the exertion of your talent, and the pleasure of your society".

Below: Sketch of Sir John Leicester's Gallery, *John Buckler, pencil and wash, 1806. The style of hanging is known as the Picturesque: a central focal point picture has pairs of pictures arranged alongside it symmetrically. The style was adopted in the 18th century and continued to be used in the 19th century in town houses.*

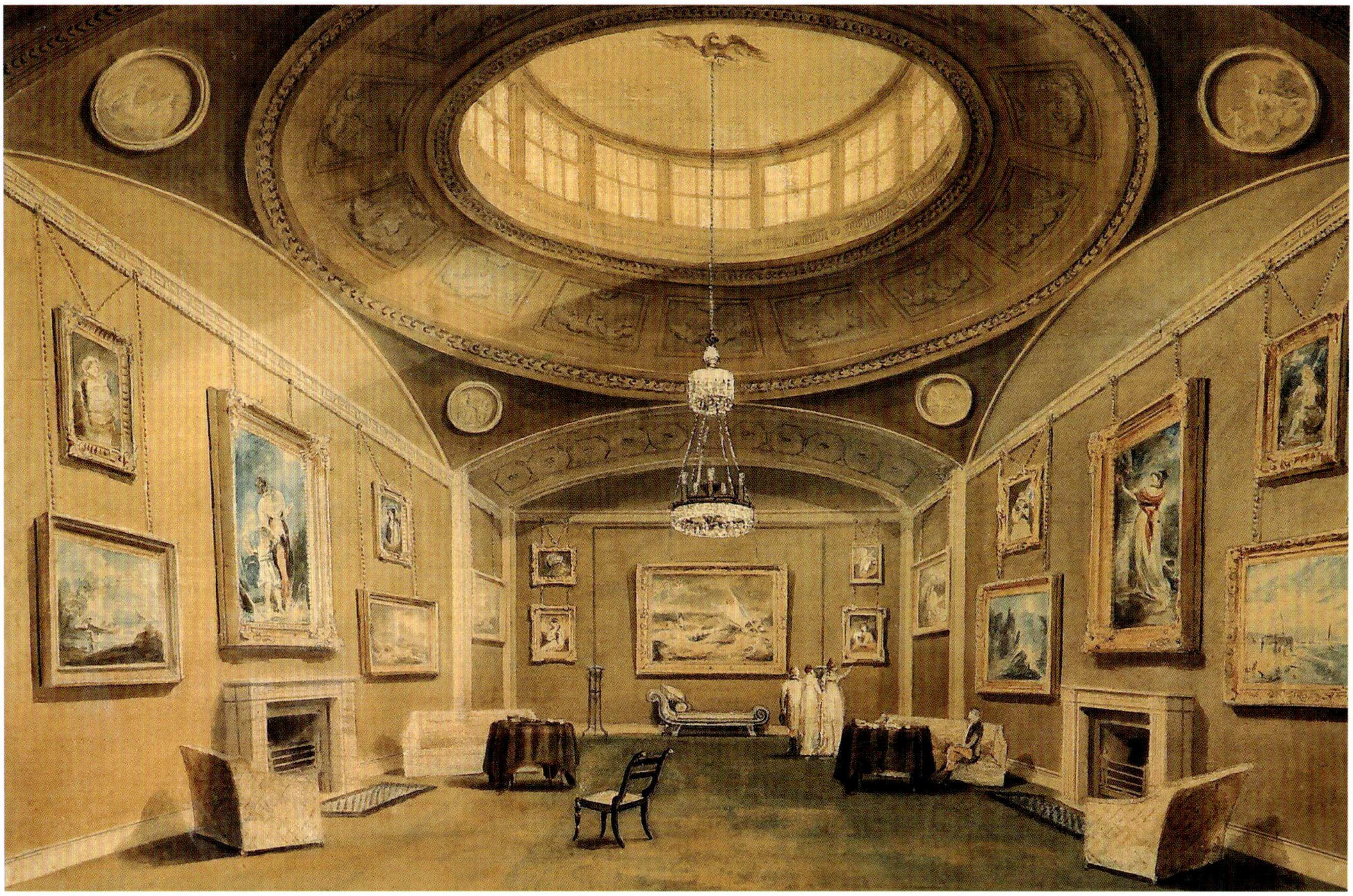

FIRST TRIP TO ITALY

In 1819, Turner departed for an extensive tour of Italy, which he had arranged a long time in advance. His plan was to take in the major cities of Venice, Florence and Rome. The tour lasted six months.

At the close of the Royal Academy exhibition in 1819, Turner had completed his outstanding publishing commissions and was ready to embark on his most ambitious adventure to date, a comprehensive tour of Italy, a trip he had planned for some time. It lasted from August until January of the following year, and during the six months, Turner made nearly 3,000 sketches and drawings that would sustain him in the studio until his next visit to Italy in 1829.

After crossing from Dover to Calais, Turner made his way to Paris and then down to Lyons, Grenoble and through the Alpine pass at Mont Cenis. After visiting Turin and Como he travelled onward to Verona and then Venice, where he stayed for about two weeks. Turner then went to Rome where he met other expatriates, including Chantry, and the recently knighted Sir Thomas Lawrence (1769–1830). He enjoyed these social gatherings, which included others outside the artistic world such as the scientist Sir Humphrey Davy (1778–1829), who had come to view the Raphael paintings.

After leaving Rome, Turner went to Naples to view Mount Vesuvius, which

had erupted as recently as 1794. Sketching in Naples was particularly dangerous due to the high levels of crime and Turner was armed with an umbrella that concealed a sword in its handle. He visited Pompeii and Paestum before arriving in Sorrento to sketch the Bay of Naples from the other side, offering the best view of Vesuvius. The return journey was via Florence, where he probably spent Christmas.

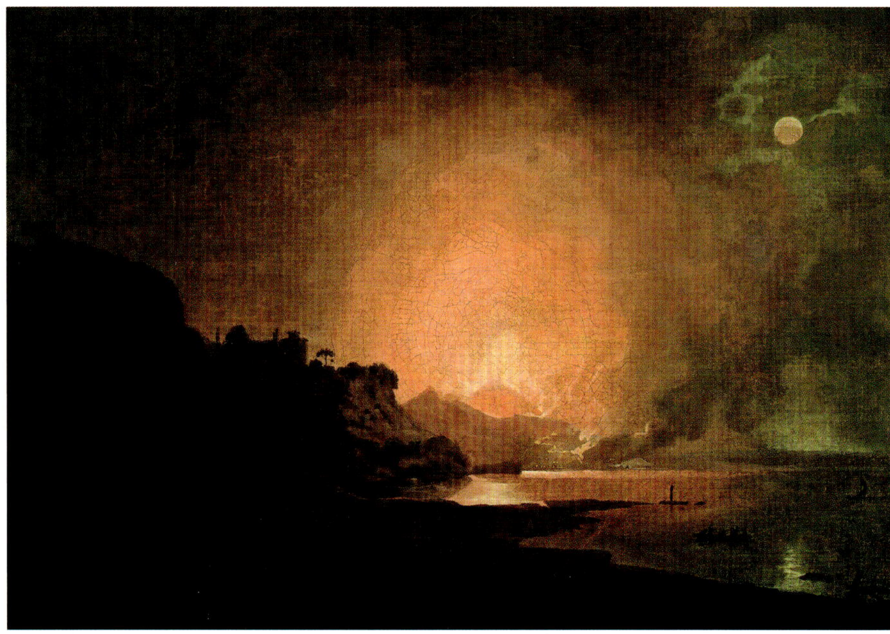

Above: The Eruption of Mount Vesuvius, *Joseph Wright, oil on canvas, c.1774–6. The motif in this Sublime work greatly influenced Turner.*

TURNER'S RESPONSES

Turner's own knowledge of Italian scenes had been gleaned from other artists' pictures, including of course Claude Lorrain. In fact when he was in Loreto, in the Umbrian Hills, he made a note in the sketchbook next to his own drawing, "the first bit of Claude". However, what struck Turner most of all was the quality and strength of light, particularly in Venice, and its impact on colour. In his sketchbook, he jotted notes concerning the colours and the "mass of light". He sketched gondolas and made specific notes on how they worked. His subsequent watercolours began to play with abstract forms due to the colours and strength of light he encountered, that at times bleached out the motif. Turner also responded to the

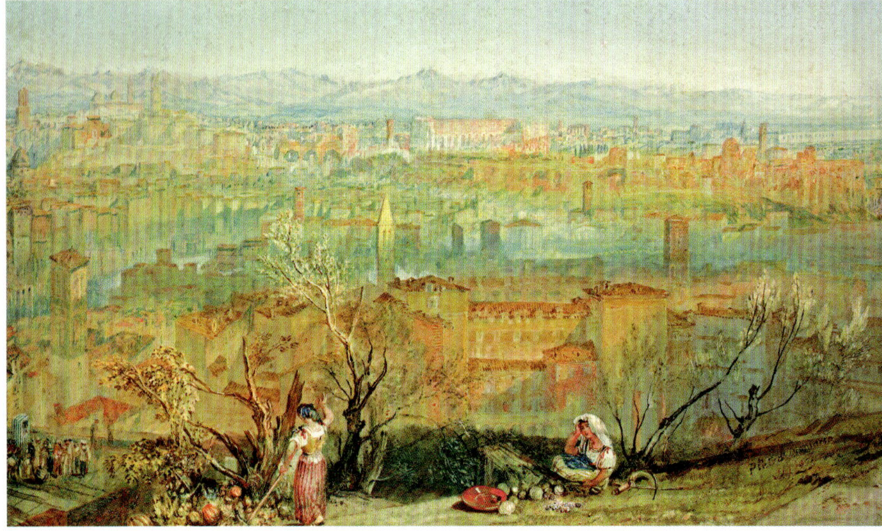

Left: Rome from San Pietro, *watercolour on paper, 1820.*

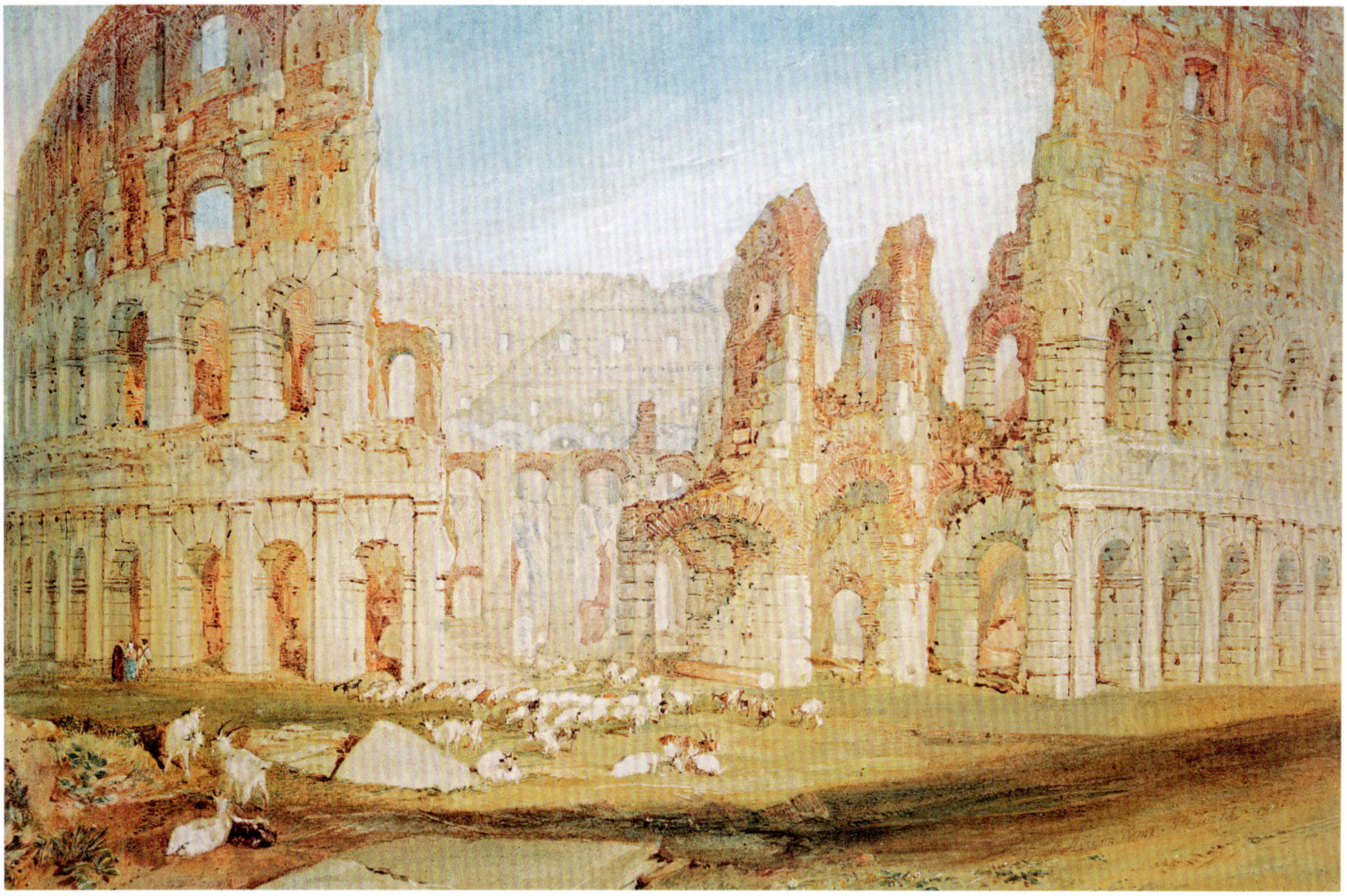

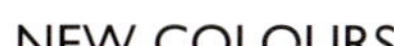

mists, visible across the lagoon, especially in the morning, conjuring up wonderfully ethereal effects even in his sketchbooks.

When he reached Rome at the end of October, Turner had an additional agenda – to study the work of Raphael, having referred to him frequently in his lectures as a master of picture structure. One consequence of this study was the large oil, *Rome from the Vatican: Raphael Accompanied by La Fornarina, Preparing his Pictures for the Decoration of the Loggia*, executed immediately on his return home. In Naples, Turner was captivated by the Bay of Baiae, which he saw as representative of Carthage and other ancient civilizations epitomized in Claude's landscapes. The Bay was a mecca for the Romantics at this time including Percy Bysshe Shelley, writing of it in *Ode to the West Wind* in 1820.

Above: Colosseum, Rome, *watercolour on paper, 1820. As professor of perspective at the Royal Academy, Turner may well have used this watercolour as an exemplary lesson in draughtsmanship.*

It was, however, the unusual quality of Italian light and its effect on colour that became the catalyst for a new direction in Turner's paintings. After 1820, his art changed to express these newfound experiences.

NEW COLOURS

New colour pigments from the 1820s facilitated the changes in Turner's art. Although he had used the new chrome yellow once it was available in 1814, he found it had a particular resonance with the intensity of light in Italy, and after 1820 used it more vividly. By 1826, according to one critic, he had become "the author of gamboge light".

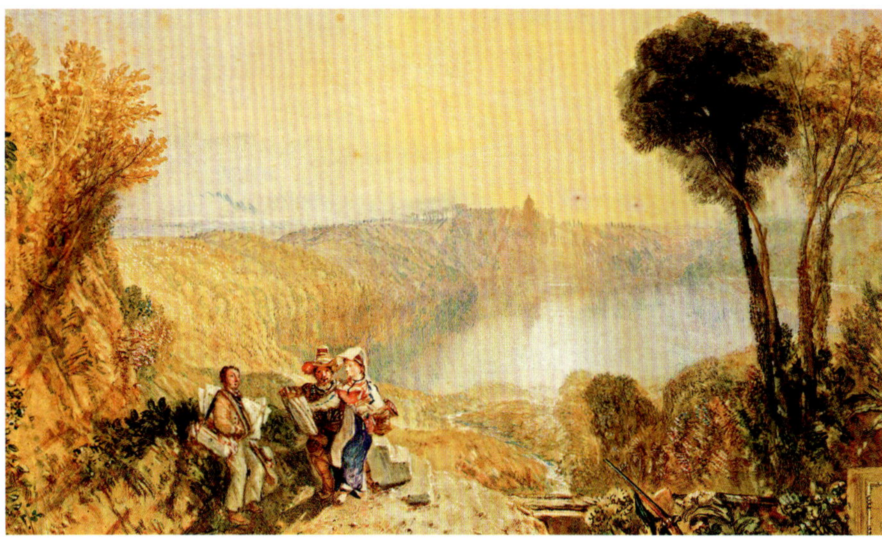

Left: Lake Albano, *watercolour, 1828. The paintings and sketches made on Turner's first trip to Italy continued to inspire him for the rest of his life.*

NEW COMMISSIONS

Back in England it was business as usual, with new publishing opportunities, and the re-opening of his own gallery. Turner was also given new status at the Royal Academy and a commission from King George IV.

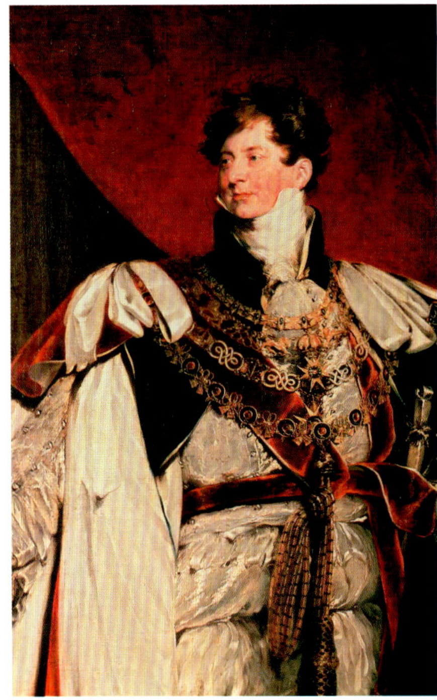

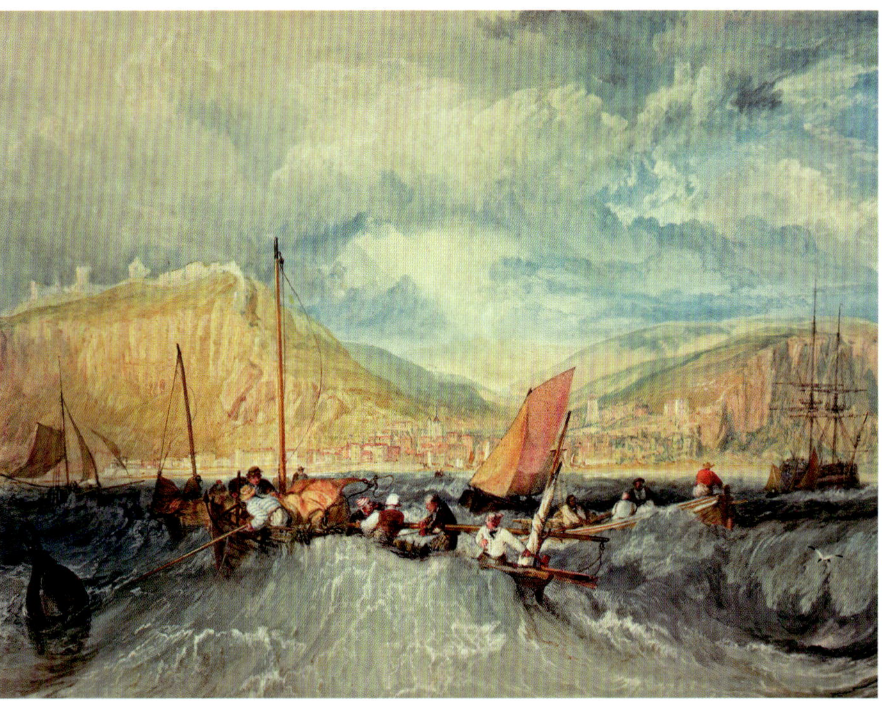

Three days before Turner returned from Italy, the old king had died and the Prince Regent had become King George IV. Under the old regime, Turner had been passed over for royal patronage, but now hoped for recognition of his talents.

THE KING
In the summer of 1822, Turner travelled to Scotland to witness the state visit of the new king to Edinburgh, stage-managed by Sir Walter Scott. This was also an opportunity for Turner to protect his investment in the *Provincial Antiquities of Scotland* series. The artist produced tiny thumbnail sketches of the ceremonies and banquets that the king attended, in order to work up large oil paintings to gain royal favour.

On his return to London, Turner produced four paintings from his sketches but none were completed. However, later that year Turner was commissioned to paint *The Battle of Trafalgar*, for St James's Palace. The

Above left: Portrait of King George IV, Thomas Lawrence, oil on canvas, 1822. Lawrence became the principal court painter to George III and painted many crowned heads of Europe.

Above: Hastings from the Sea, watercolour, 1822. Exhibited by the Cooke brothers in 1822 and published posthumously, along with many other of Turner's images.

painting took over a year to complete because of its size and complexity. It was hung at the palace, but later it was removed to Greenwich, where it remains today. Turner argued with the king's younger brother, who criticized the picture for inaccuracy of detail, which probably cost him future royal patronage and a knighthood.

THE ROYAL ACADEMY
Despite a very limited showing at the Academy exhibitions during 1821–3, recognition of another kind came

Below: The Harbours of England, ink and wash, 1825. This study was executed by Turner as the design for the title page of the book.

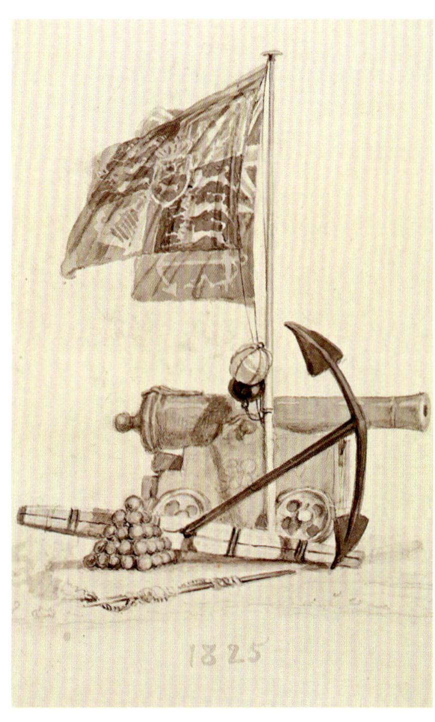

to Turner in 1823 when he, Francis Chantrey and John Soane were elected Auditors to the Academy. Sir Thomas Lawrence as President of the Royal Academy had replaced the late Benjamin West in 1820. Lawrence recognized Turner's extraordinary talents, and was probably responsible for recommending him to the king for the *Trafalgar* picture. The role of Auditor, which Turner held for the next 22 years, was a particularly suitable role for a man who was naturally fastidious in his own affairs.

THE RIVERS AND PORTS SERIES

Despite Turner's irritation at the ineptitude shown by the Cooke brothers in the *Picturesque Views on the Southern Coast of England* series, the artist agreed to embark on a new set of images for them, *The Rivers of England*, in 1822.

He travelled around the Thames and Medway in the autumn, but most of the drawings that he subsequently used were from existing material. In fact Turner was increasingly using memory for much of his watercolour work now, paying less attention to topographical detail and more on creating mood.

The series was published between 1823 and 1827, and included 12 plates made after Turner. For another publisher, Thomas Lupton, Turner produced 15 watercolours for a series to be known as *The Harbours of England*. As with so many of his publishers, Turner quarrelled with Lupton over money, and only 6 of the 12 plates that were subsequently engraved were issued, between 1826 and 1828. The remainder were not published until after Turner's death.

Below: Dartmoor, the Source of the Tamar and Torridge, *watercolour and bodycolour over graphite on paper, 1813. Although not used in the* Rivers of England *series, WB Cooke engraved this image as a tiny reproduction.*

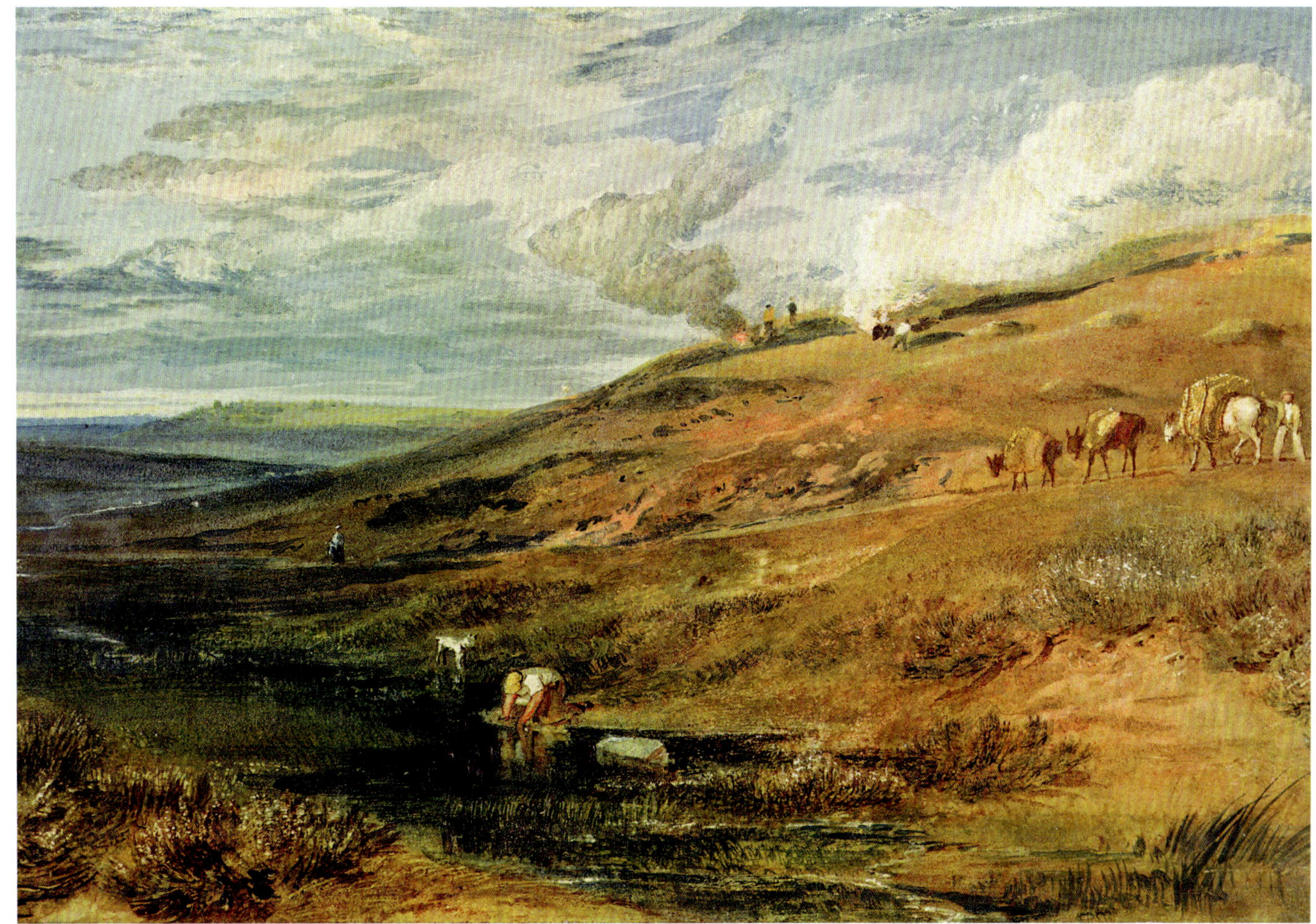

A TIME OF CHANGE

Turner gained a new patron, shortly after losing another, Walter Fawkes, who was probably his closest friend. He also agreed to an ambitious new publishing venture, made a trip to the Low Countries, and moved house.

By 1825, Walter Fawkes had become terminally ill and was to die in October. He had been living in London, and to add to his problems he was seriously in debt to the tune of about £70,000 (around £3 million today). Included in that figure were some personal loans made to him, including one made by Turner £3,000.

Turner appears to have never made any effort to recall the loan and in fact wrote the debt off on Fawkes's death, such was the esteem in which the artist held him and his family. Walter's son Hawksworth, who was by now married, took over the running of Farnley Hall and although Turner kept up a correspondence with him, he never again visited the house.

HUGH MUNRO OF NOVAR

Although none were to be as intimate an acquaintance of Turner as Fawkes, the artist had several friends who enjoyed a mutual companionship within his artistic circle, John Soane, Francis Chantrey and George Jones. Sometime in 1826, Turner met Hugh Andrew Johnstone Munro of Novar (1797–1864).

Munro had inherited the family estates in Scotland in 1809, and became an amateur artist and connoisseur, collecting many of Turner's paintings in his lifetime, as well as Old Masters, and contemporary works by, among others, John Constable and David Wilkie. Like Turner he was diffident and sometimes morose in temperament, but

Below: Exeter, *watercolour and gum arabic on paper, 1827.*

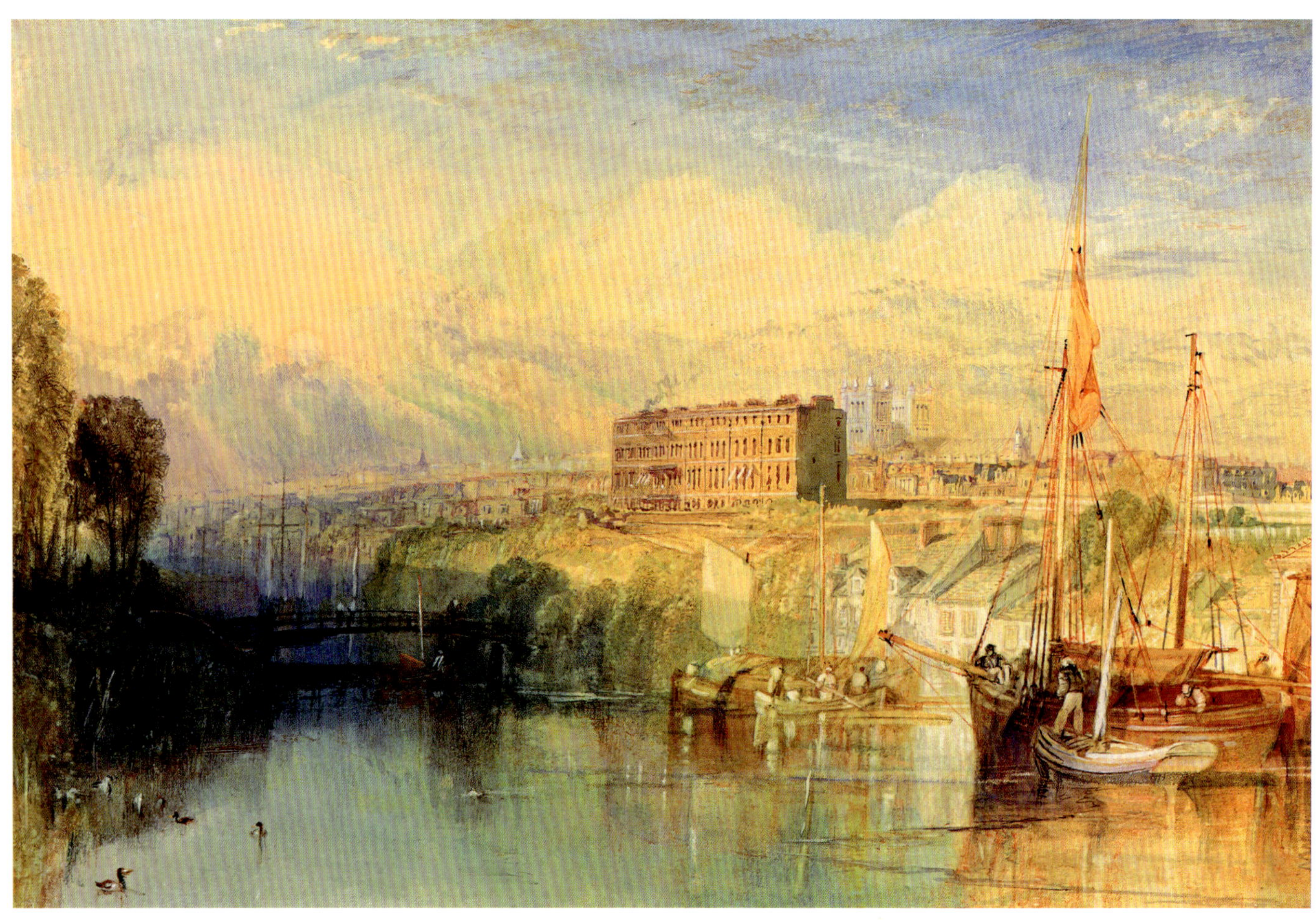

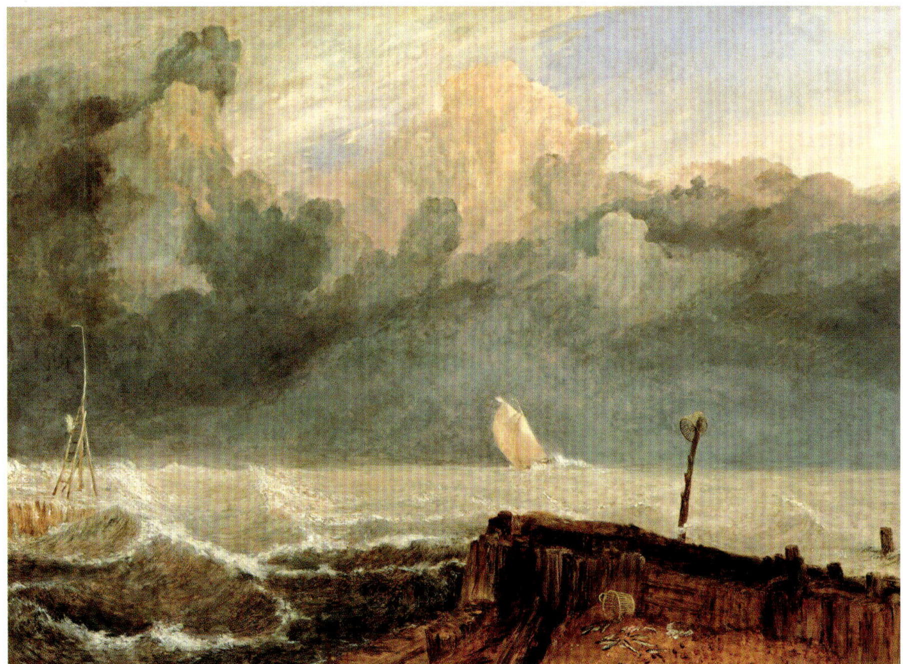

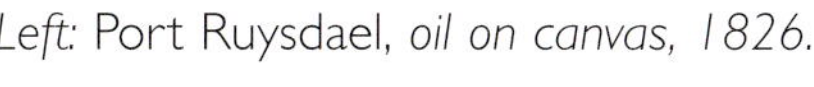

Left: Port Ruysdael, *oil on canvas, 1826.*

Below: Petworth Park, *gouache, 1827.*

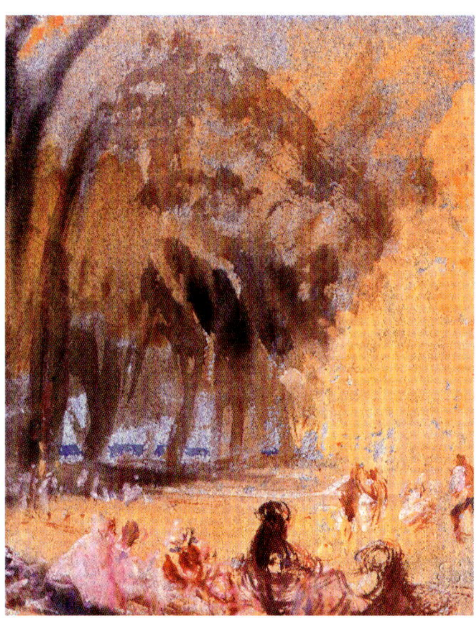

accompanied him on several of his sketching trips; the two becoming good friends. He also financed Turner's visits to Venice in 1833 and 1844, became a trustee for his artist's charity, and one of the executors of his will. His first purchase of a Turner painting was in 1830.

VIEWS IN ENGLAND AND WALES
During 1825, Turner was commissioned by the engraver and publisher Charles Heath to make 120 watercolours for the series *Picturesque Views in England and Wales.* This was his most ambitious publishing project to date, and the

creation of the first 12 works for engraving within a year was proof of the artist's huge enthusiasm for the work. The first engravings were issued in March 1827, and by the time the venture ended in 1838, 96 of his paintings had already been reproduced for the series.

As with all his reproduced work, Turner was particularly fastidious but helpful in their execution, ensuring that the colours of the original watercolours were correctly interpreted as tonal values in the engravings.

THE LOW COUNTRIES AND HOME
Having not travelled abroad for six years, Turner embarked on a tour of the Low Countries in the summer of 1825, travelling to Delft, Amsterdam, Utrecht, Cologne, Antwerp and Ghent, before returning via Bruges and Ostend, a month later. On his return to England he decided to permanently vacate Sandycombe Lodge and move into his newly refurbished accommodation at Queen Anne Street, with his father, who was now 80 years old and in poor health. Turner sold the Lodge the following year.

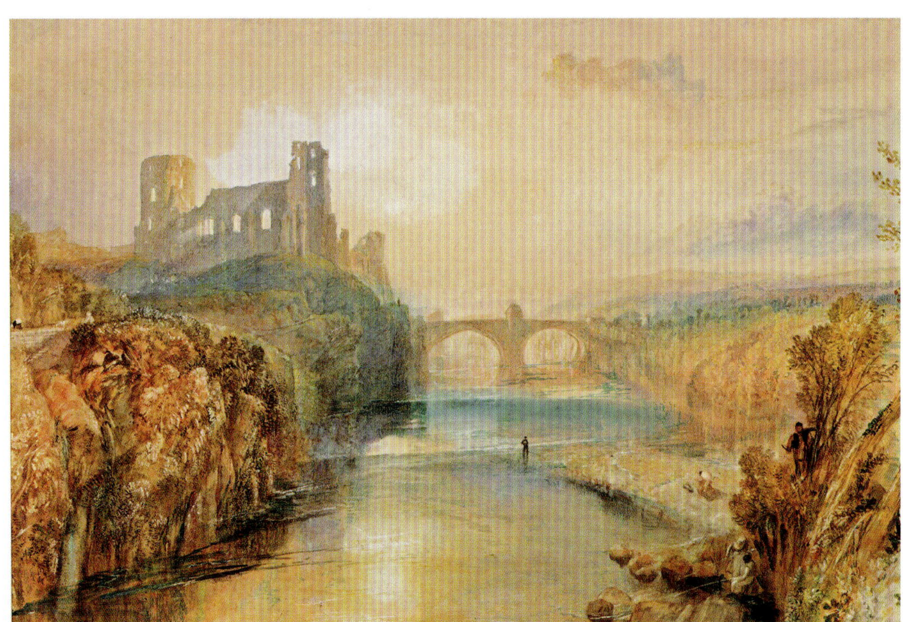

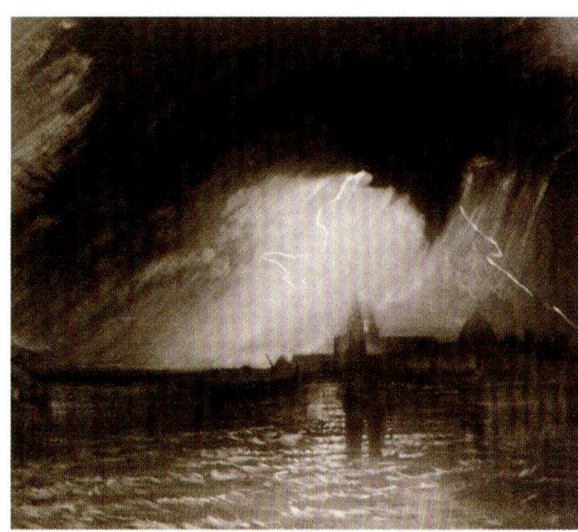

Above: Catania, Sicily, *mezzotint, 1826. From the* Little Liber.

Left: Barnard Castle, *watercolour, 1825. Used in* Picturesque Views in England and Wales.

THE 1826–27 TOURS

Now came a very creative period for Turner. He benefited from well-heeled patrons keen to see him experiment with evocative styles and techniques, and from his friendship with one of the era's most influential architects.

After submitting four paintings to the 1826 Academy exhibition, the most submitted for 11 years, Turner set off again on his European travels.

EUROPEAN RIVERS TOUR

The first of Turner's tours was in pursuit of material for a speculative new series – the Rivers of Europe project, of which only one part materialized under a different guise, *Turner's Annual Tours* in 1833. After landing at Calais Turner explored the north coast of France, before touring the Meuse, Moselle and Loire rivers. He also revisited the Rhine Valley, returning through Paris. On this trip, Turner used a sketchbook that had a soft cover, making it easier to transport, and therefore suitable for his future Continental journeys.

PETWORTH

The following year, again after making a significant contribution to the Academy exhibition, Turner visited Lord Egremont at Petworth, en route to the Isle of Wight, where he intended spending the summer. He had had very little to do with Egremont in the preceding years, since his patron had purchased nothing from him since 1813.

What transpired from this meeting was a commission to create a series of narrow oil-painting panels to decorate the dining room at Petworth. Turner would return in the spring of 1828, when he was made a house guest with

Below: Carisbrooke Castle, Isle of Wight, *watercolour, 1828. This was used in* Picturesque Views, *published in 1830.*

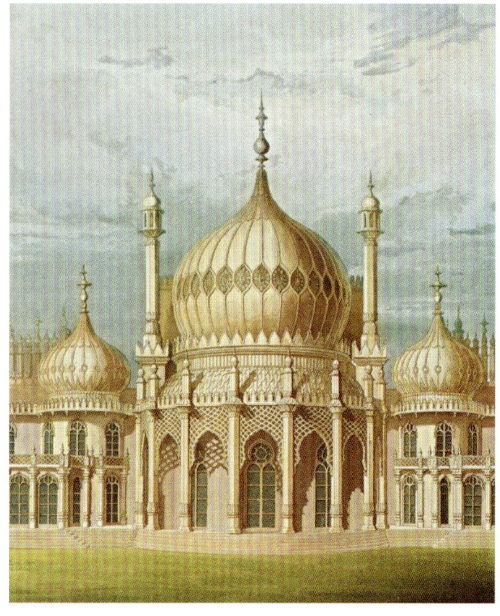

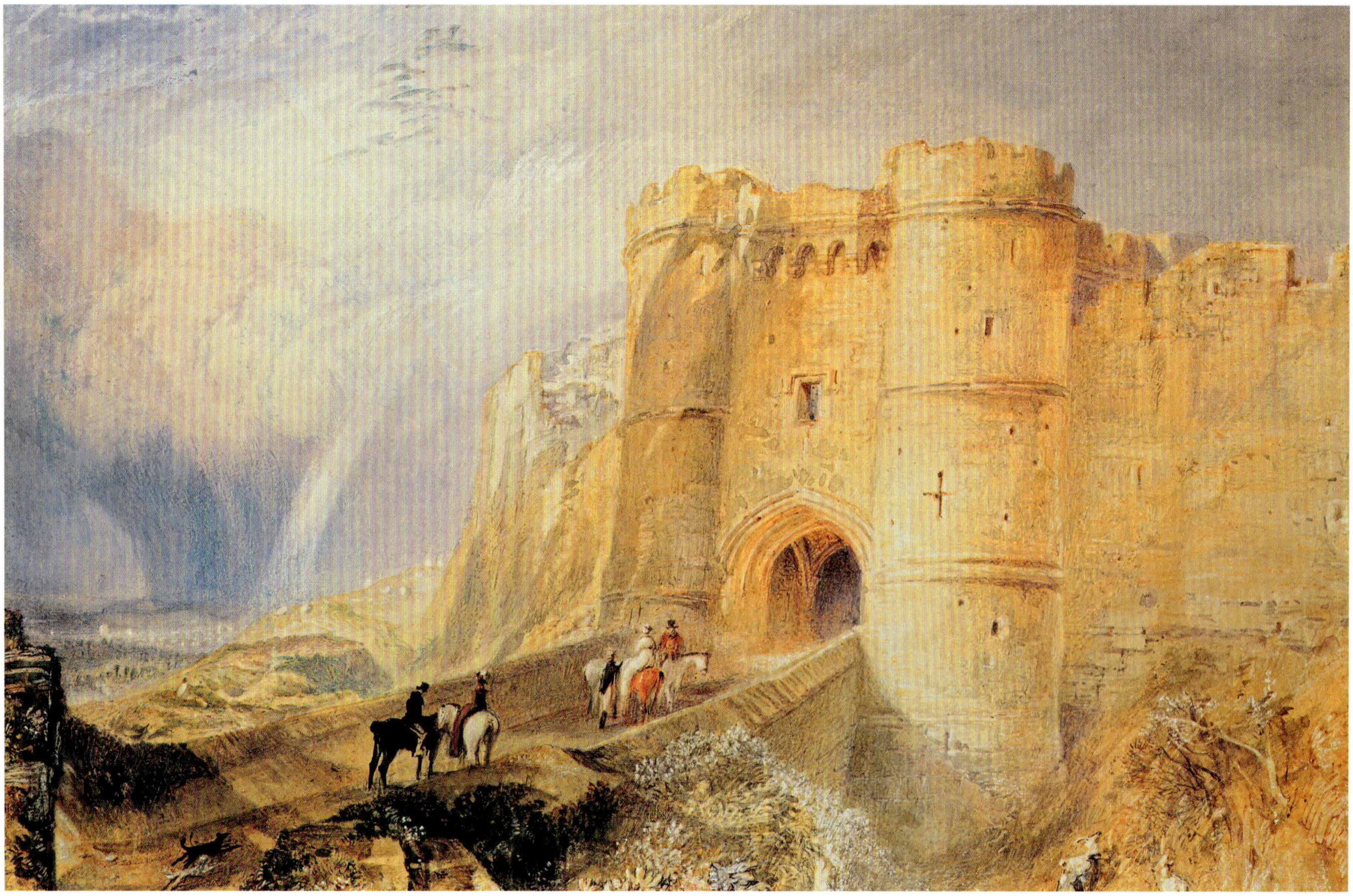

Above: Exterior of the Saloon from Views of the Royal Pavilion, Brighton, *John Nash, print, 1826.*

his own studio to execute the work on site. The resultant pictures are among the most evocative paintings that Turner ever produced and include *Chichester Canal*, *Brighton from the Sea* and the two views of *The Lake, Petworth*.

JOHN NASH

The master of Picturesque architecture, John Nash (1752–1835), was the first English architect to introduce a form of urban planning into London.

His main patron was the Prince Regent (later King George IV), for whom he created the Royal Pavilion in Brighton, and in London, the Regent's Park that included the Regency mansions of Cumberland Terrace, and the Picturesque layout of St James's Park. He also designed his own home, East Cowes Castle, in a Gothic style, beginning the construction in 1789. The castle was demolished in the 1960s.

Nash commissioned Turner to paint two pictures of the Cowes Regatta and invited him to stay for the event at his house in the summer of 1827. At this time, Turner began to use grey and blue paper as a background for his drawings, often executed in ink and

Below: The Lake, Petworth, Sunset, Fighting Bucks, *oil on canvas, 1829. This painting is one of those commissioned by Lord Egremont for the 'carved' dining room at Petworth House, where it still resides.*

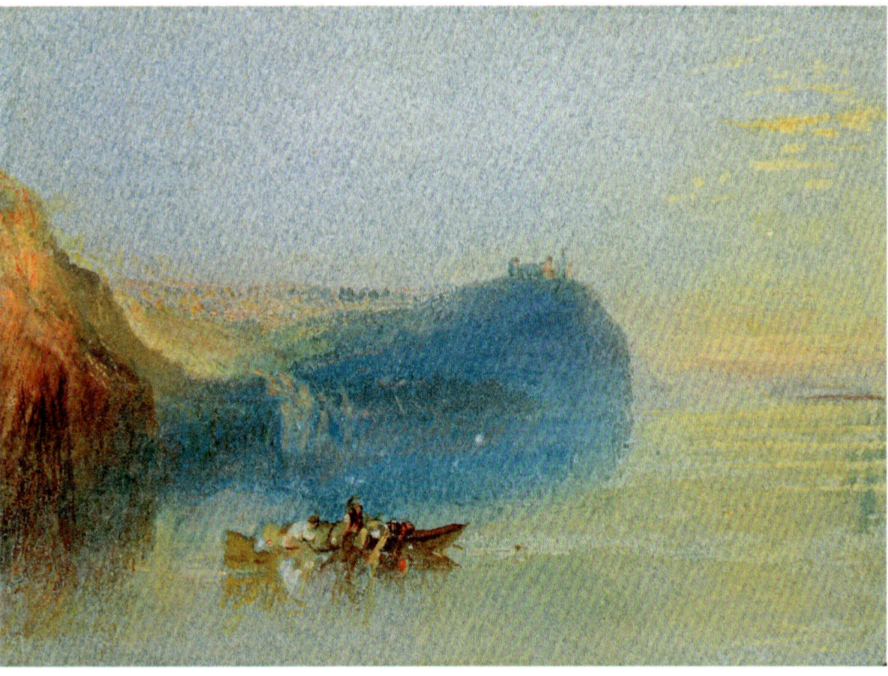

Above: Scene on the Loire, *watercolour, 1830. Recognized by John Ruskin as 'the best of the Loire series', this watercolour is of a sunrise rather than as he had stated, a sunset.*

white chalk. As at Petworth, Turner was allowed to work undisturbed, Nash providing a studio for him to work in at the castle. The artist also took the opportunity to paint some of the members of Nash's family and other house guests at leisure, usually in the garden or music room.

THE ISLE OF WIGHT

Turner's first visit to the Isle of Wight was in 1795. His subsequent picture of Carisbrooke Castle of 1796 is a perfectly executed topographical study in earth colours. By contrast, his 1828 version of the same motif is imbued with the brilliant yellows

he was now using, which make the castle appear to glow from an internal light source. That same 'internal' light source was used again in his *Boccaccio, Relating the Tale of the Birdcage*, painted using East Cowes Castle as a backdrop. The painting is something of a pastiche after Watteau, depicting a group of hedonists at leisure. He exhibited the painting the following year at the Royal Academy.

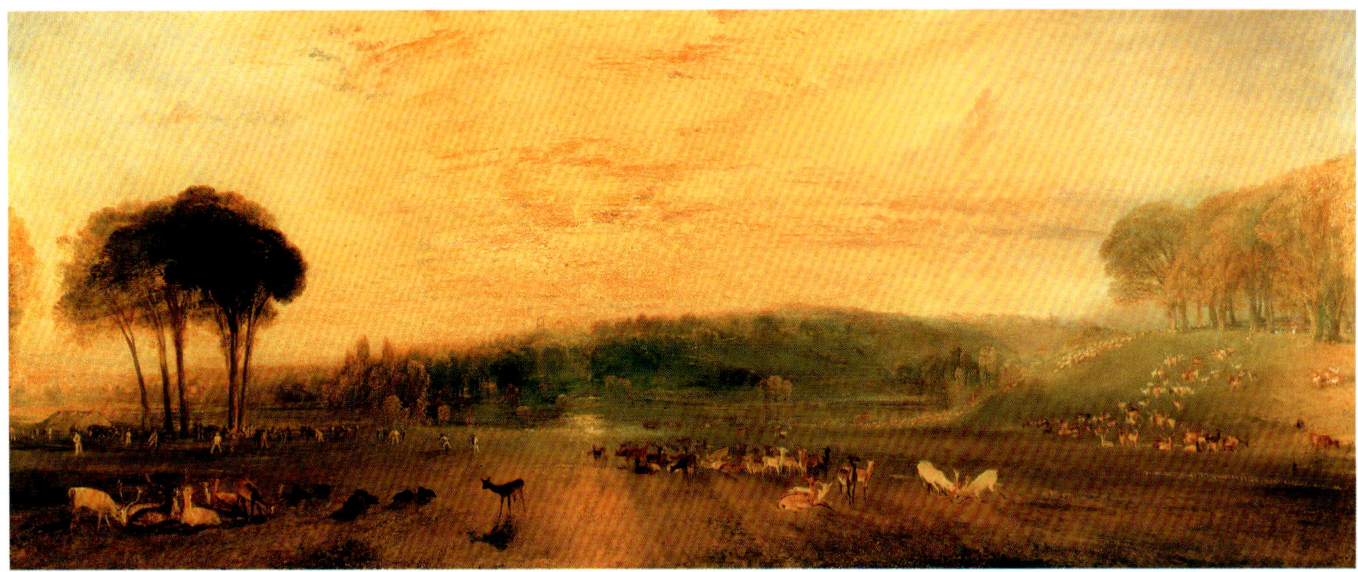

SECOND TOUR OF ITALY

In 1827, Turner and his father were both suffering from ill health, and the artist confined
himself to affairs at home. In the summer of 1828, he left for the Continent, returning
to England during the winter of the following year.

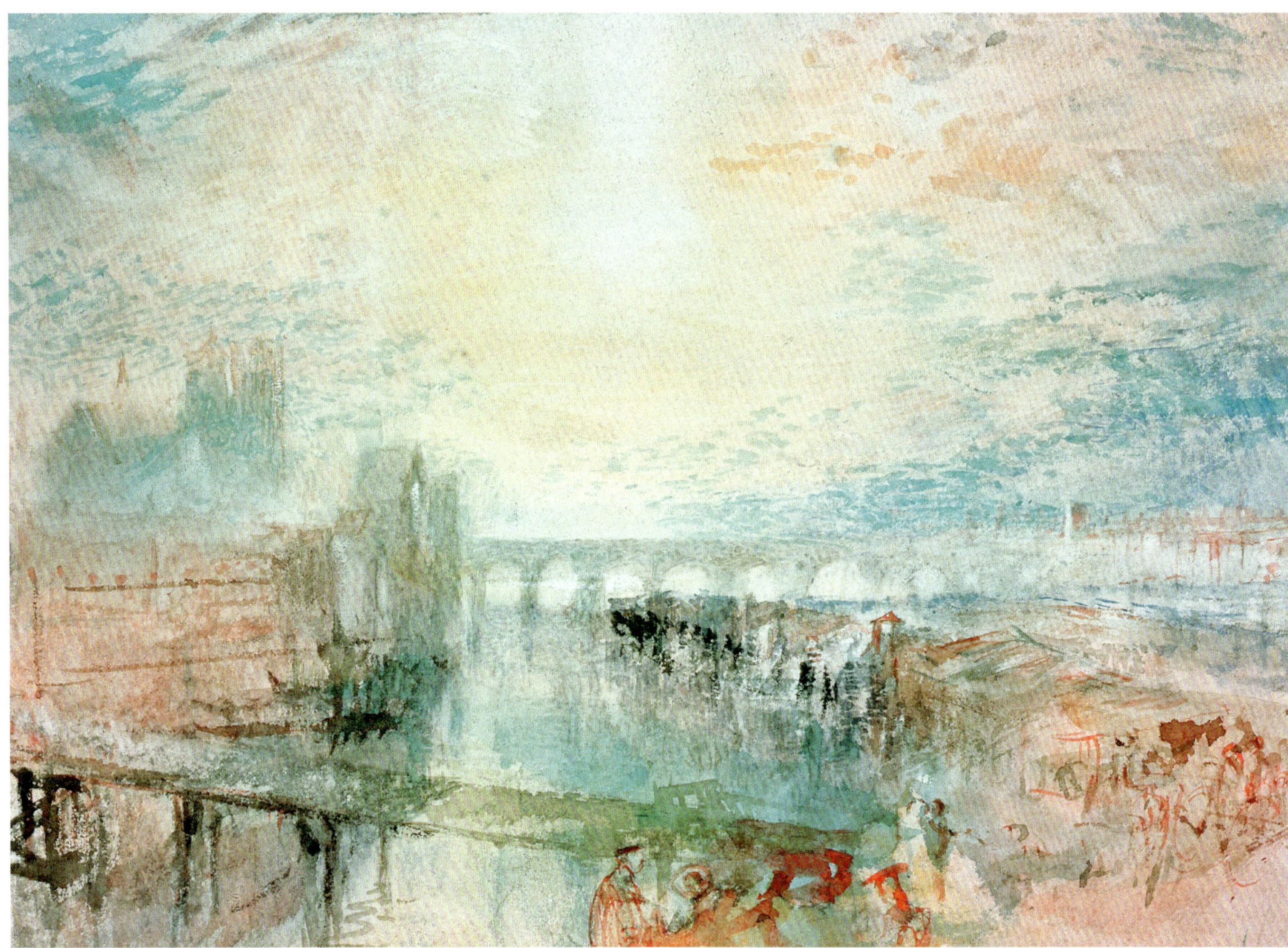

In January of 1827, Turner gave the
penultimate series of his lectures as
Professor of Perspective at the Royal
Academy. The series was cut short to
four because of his own poor health
and more especially his father's, who
was now retired as his general manager
and factotum.

ILLNESS
That winter was particularly severe as
Turner wrote, "poor Daddy never felt
cold so much". In the same letter to the
artist James Holsworthy, he continued,
"I begin to think of being truly alone in
the world, but I believe the bitterness is
past. But he is very much shaken and I

am not the better for wear." Turner
himself was unwell at this time, the
result of overwork and stress about
his father's condition. He had lost a lot
of weight, and it has been suggested
that he may have been suffering from
a heart condition. His illness may well
have been exacerbated by the
continuing vitriol in the press about
his paintings, suggesting that his use
of unnatural colour was the work of
a madman. Given his father's condition,
this must have seemed particularly
spiteful to Turner.

Meanwhile, in July, one of Turner's
most important patrons, Lord Tabley
(formerly Sir JF Leicester), died

Above: View of Lyons, *watercolour on
paper, ? c.1846. The precise date of this
watercolour is unknown, but it is clearly
from his mature period when topography
has given way to ethereal effects of light.*

and at a subsequent auction of his
estate Turner managed to purchase
some of his own paintings.

TOUR OF ITALY
Having completed his annual quota for
the *Picturesque* series, Turner set off
for the Continent once again in August
1828, his destination this time Italy,
which he referred to as his *Terra Pictura*
(the land of all beauty). Turner was to

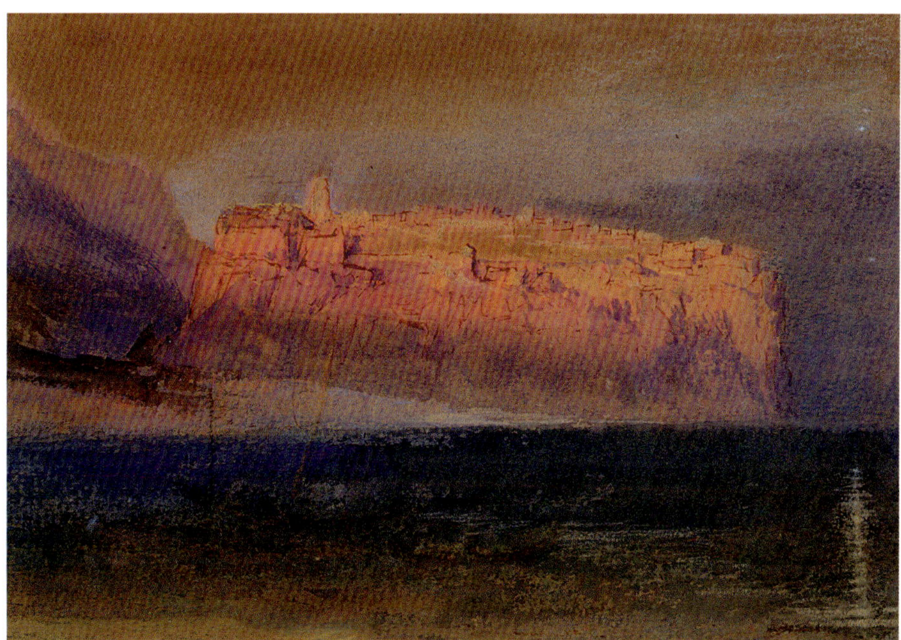

stay with Charles Eastlake (1793–1865), at his house in Rome, where a studio would be available to him. Eastlake had been in Rome since 1816, where he had established himself as a Classical and Picturesque landscape painter, British expatriates, including poets, writers and artists, often peopling his paintings. Turner arrived in Paris, and wrote to Eastlake and asked him to prepare some canvases. His sketchbooks indicate that he travelled from Paris to

Above: Corsica, *watercolour on brown paper, 1828. Perhaps with a hint of irony, Turner has chosen to depict the island of Corsica, where Napoleon was born.*

Orleans and then on to Lyons and Nice via Avignon and Marseilles. Turner travelled to Genoa, La Spezia, Florence and Siena before arriving in Rome in early October. On his outward and return journeys he made more than 1,000 sketches and drawings.

Below: Portrait of Sir Charles Locke Eastlake, *John Jabez Edwin Paisley Mayall, engraving, 1860.*

Below: Florence from near San Miniato, *watercolour and bodycolour, 1828. One of several watercolours of this motif.*

EXHIBITION IN ROME

Turner spent about two months in Eastlake's house, working on between 10 and 12 pictures. He completed three large canvases, *View of Orvieto*, *Medea* and *Regulus*. In December, the artist then took rooms at Quattro Fontane, where he exhibited the three paintings. There was a mixed reception to the pictures, which were seen by over 1,000 people. The foreign artists "could make nothing of them", and the British visitors, perhaps more used to seeing Eastlake's Classical paintings, were generally severe in their judgements. However, as Eastlake wrote, "many were fain to admire what they confessed they dared not imitate". The paintings were eventually packed up and sent to England, with Eastlake suggesting that they be covered in wax cloth to avoid dampness seeping in on the sea voyage. The fact that Turner responded "if any wet gets to them, they will be destroyed", suggests that the paintings were unfinished and therefore unstable at this exhibition. Their late arrival in England meant that Turner was unable to finish the work in time for the Academy exhibition that year.

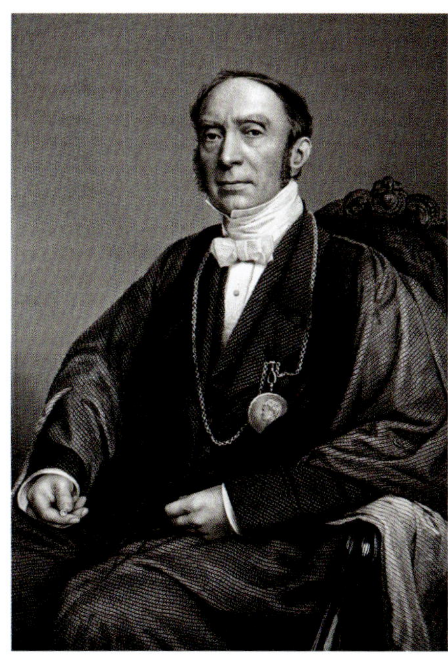

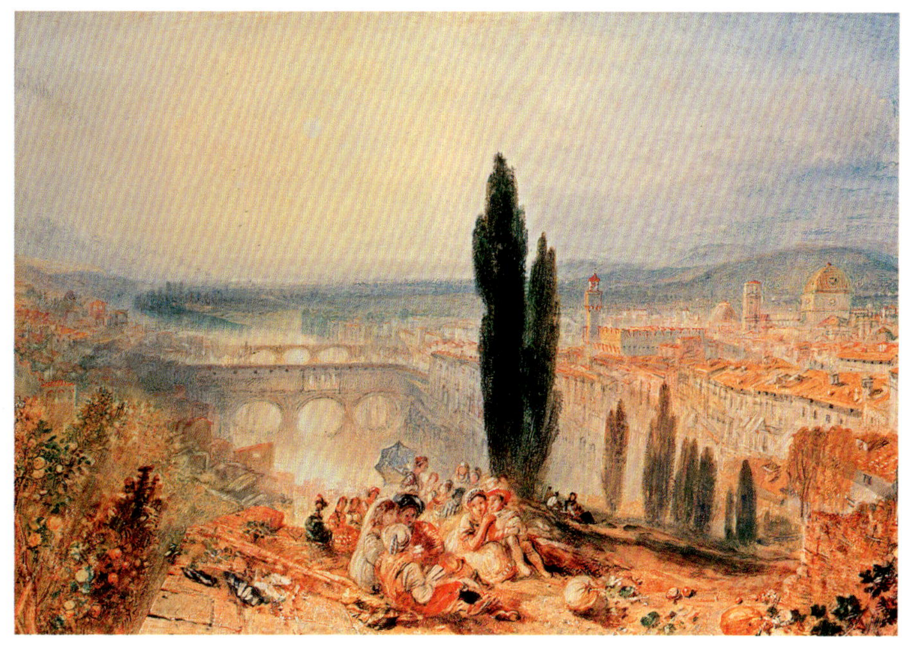

FOR THE SAKE OF POSTERITY

A will made in the aftermath of his father's death showed both Turner's generosity and his cold-hearted pragmatism. Meanwhile, political frustrations ensued at the Academy, and Turner continued to receive lucrative commissions for illustrations.

After giving loyal service to his son as a studio assistant and all-round helper, Turner's father died on 21 September 1829 and was buried in St Paul's Church, Covent Garden on the 29th. He was 84 years old and had been in poor health for some time.

Throughout his life he had supported his son, firstly by showing his early works in his barber shop, and then moving in with him to act as his assistant. As a former barber he was also responsible for keeping his son well groomed, and making sure that he maintained the look that was befitting to a leading Academician.

TURNER'S FIRST WILL

The day after his father's funeral, Turner signed his own will. Such bereavement was bound to focus the artist's mind on his own mortality, and with it, his artistic legacy. Turner had a real sense of his own genius and decided to offer two works to the nation, *Dido Building Carthage* and *The Decline of the Carthaginian Empire* (later changed to *The Sun Rising through Vapour*), providing that they were hung at the National Gallery alongside two of Claude's paintings, *Seaport: The Embarkation of the Queen of Sheba* and *Landscape: The Marriage of Isaac and Rebecca*. Turner made only limited bequests to Sarah and Hannah Danby, and his daughters.

Below: Self Portrait, Thomas Lawrence, oil on canvas, 1787–8. The confident pose resembles Turner's in his self-portrait.

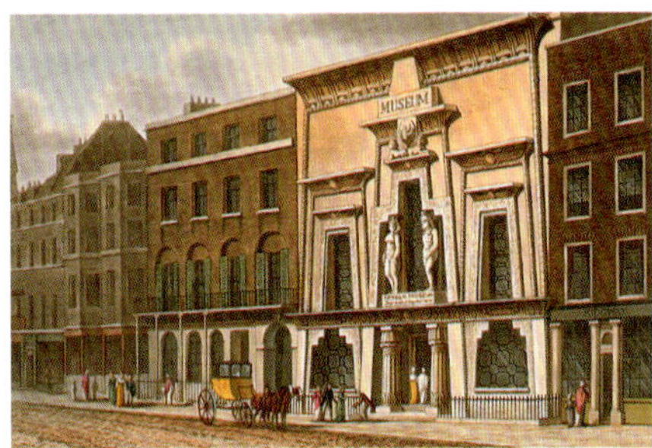

Top: View of the Egyptian Hall, Piccadilly, *Thomas Ackerman, engraving, 1815. The hall was also called 'Bullock's Museum'.*

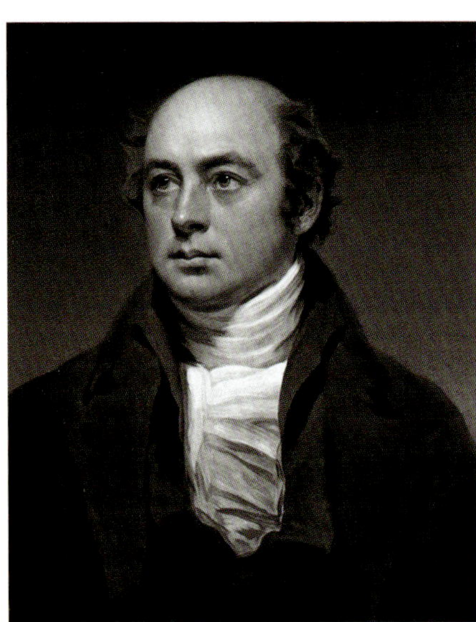

Above: Portrait of Sir Francis Chantrey, *Sir Henry Raeburn, mezzotint, 1843. Chantrey was an executor to Turner's will.*

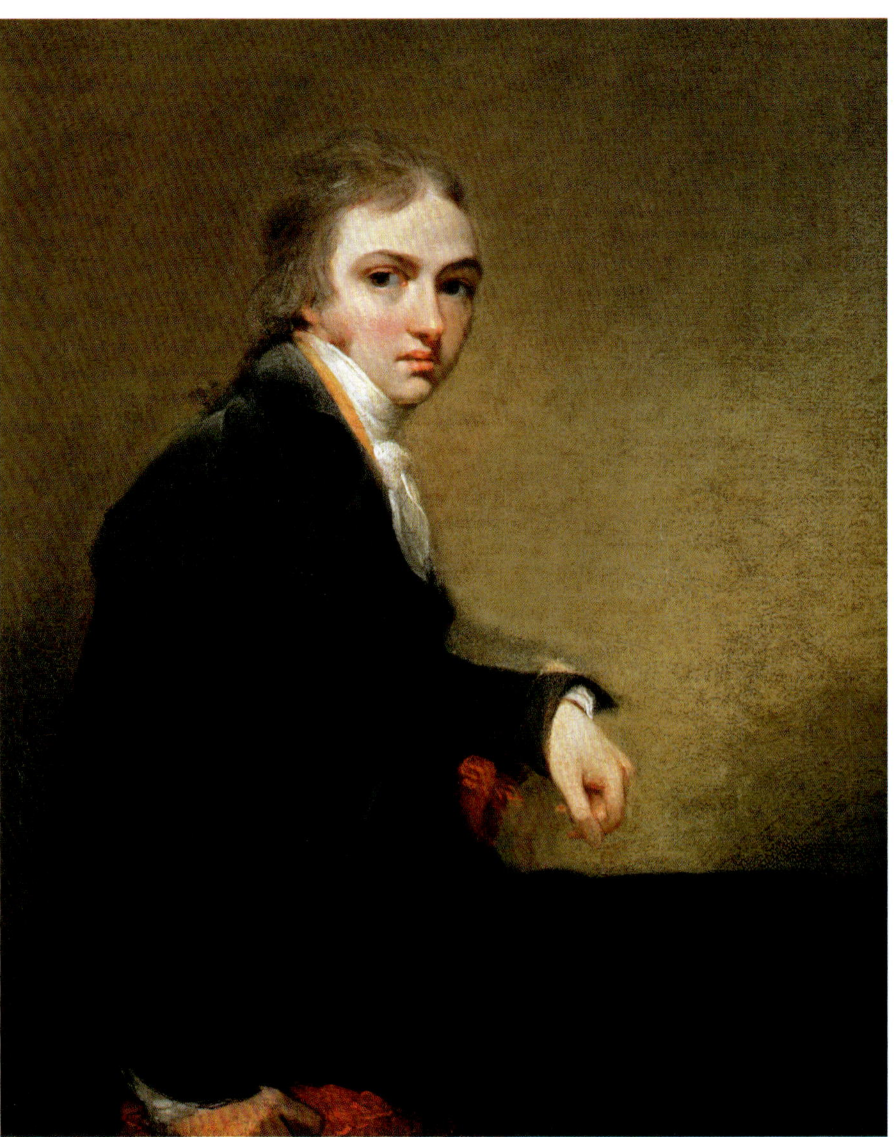

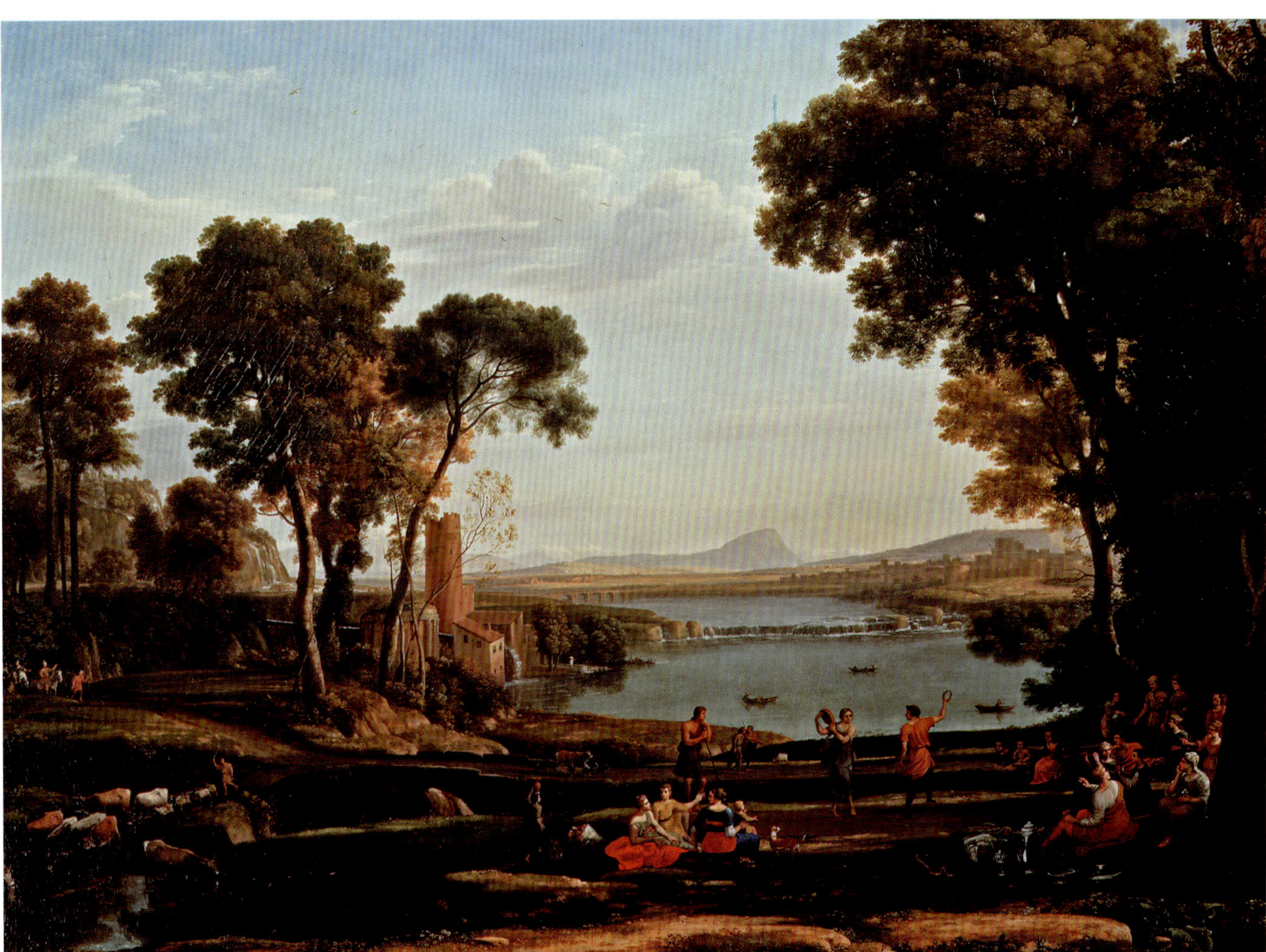

There were, however, bequests made to the Royal Academy for the establishment of a Professorship of Landscape Painting, and a Turner Gold Medal for the subject to be awarded every two years. He proposed also to set up a number of alms-houses at Twickenham for destitute artists.

ROYAL ACADEMY COLLEAGUES

On 10 February 1829, the landscape painter John Constable, a near contemporary of Turner, was elected a full Academician, having waited ten years since being made an Associate. Turner and George Jones celebrated with Constable that evening.

The following October, a fellow Academician called George Dawe (1781–1829) died. He was a portrait painter who worked mainly in Russia during the Napoleonic Wars. Turner acted as a pallbearer at his funeral in St Paul's Cathedral. In January 1830, the president of the Academy, Sir Thomas

Lawrence, died. Turner witnessed the service and painted a large watercolour "sketch from memory". Turner may well have considered applying for the vacant post himself. However, knowing that King George IV was very ill and that his successor would be his younger brother William, with whom Turner had quarrelled, he probably considered it inappropriate given that the Academy still relied on royal patronage. In the event, Sir Martin Archer Shee (1769–1850), the Irish portrait painter, was elected to succeed Lawrence in January 1830. At his first council meeting in February, he presided over the election of Eastlake's appointment as an Academician.

NEW PUBLISHING COMMISSIONS

During June and July 1829, an exhibition of Turner's watercolours used in the *Picturesque Views in England and Wales* series was held at the Egyptian Hall in London. The exhibition was put on by

Above: Landscape: The Marriage of Isaac and Rebekah, *Claude Lorrain, oil on canvas, 1648. Under the terms of Turner's will, this painting was to hang at the National Gallery alongside another by Claude and two of his own for posterity.*

Charles Heath to promote the ongoing programme. Samuel Rogers' poem *Italy* was republished in 1830, with 25 vignettes by Turner illustrating the work. The first edition had been a failure, but Rogers' tenacity reaped huge rewards in the revision, demonstrating the saleability of Turner's images. In 1834, Turner accepted a further commission to illustrate a volume of Rogers' *Poems*. Turner also secured two other commissions for illustrations in 1831. The first was a new edition of Sir Walter Scott's *Poetical Works* and the other was for a series of drawings to illustrate Lord Byron's *Works*, which were to be published the following year.

SCOTLAND AND PETWORTH

Travelling in Europe during 1830–1 was hazardous due to the political turmoil there.
In the summer of 1831, Turner travelled instead to Scotland, and made his first trips
to the west coast and the north of the country.

Turner's mission in Scotland was to collect material for a new edition of Sir Walter Scott's *Poetical Works*. He also made the first of his extended visits to Petworth, in Sussex, as a house guest.

SCOTLAND

On some of his sketching trips, Scott's biographer, John Gibson Lockhart (1794–1854), accompanied him. Turner began his tour at Abbotsford, Scott's home in the Border area. At this time Scott was in poor health but made the journey with Turner around his local area, explaining the texts of his poems for the artist to interpret in painting. While he was at Abbotsford, he was entertained well, particularly at the Lockharts'. One of Scott's most famous poetical locations was Fingal's Cave on

Below: Portrait Bust of Sir Walter Scott, Francis Chantrey, marble, c.1820. Chantrey achieved fame as a sculptor and carved portraits of distinguished persons such as Lord Nelson, the Duke of Wellington and King George III.

the west coast. Turner was determined to make the visit despite Scott being too ill to accompany him. He also visited Fort William, Inverness and Elgin. It also seems likely that he visited Hugh Munro of Novar on his return journey.

Scott was born in Edinburgh, the son of a solicitor. From an early age he enjoyed exploring the city and surrounding countryside. Showing a precocious talent for reading, he began studying classics at the University of Edinburgh, at just 12 years of age, where he met the poet Robert Burns. Scott decided to follow his father and pursue a career in law, but by the time he was 25 he had begun writing.

In 1797, Scott married a French woman, Margaret Charpentier, and they had five children. During the next ten years he published many poems that brought him fame, but it was his Romantic novels, such as *Ivanhoe*, that made him a literary hero. Scott died in September 1832, a year after working with Turner on the new edition of his *Poetical Works*.

A CODICIL TO TURNER'S WILL

Scott's illness and imminent mortality prompted Turner to add a codicil to his will that allowed for funds to be channelled into preserving his own house and gallery at Queen Anne Street, to be saved for posterity in much the same way as his friend Sir John Soane was proposing with his house at Lincoln's Inn.

PETWORTH ONCE MORE

Between 1830 and 1837, Turner spent several Christmases at Petworth as a house guest. Turner was one of a number of guests at the house including John Constable (1776–1837), Francis Chantrey (1781–1841) and the genre painter Charles Leslie (c.1835–90). It was, however, Turner who seems to

Below: Children Playing at Coach and Horses, Charles Robert Leslie, oil on canvas, c.1830. A fellow visiting artist to Petworth and a beneficiary of Lord Egremont's patronage, Leslie was a genre painter who may have influenced Turner.

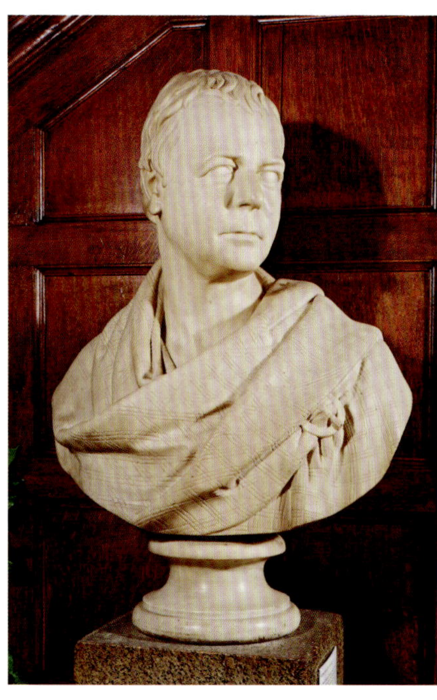

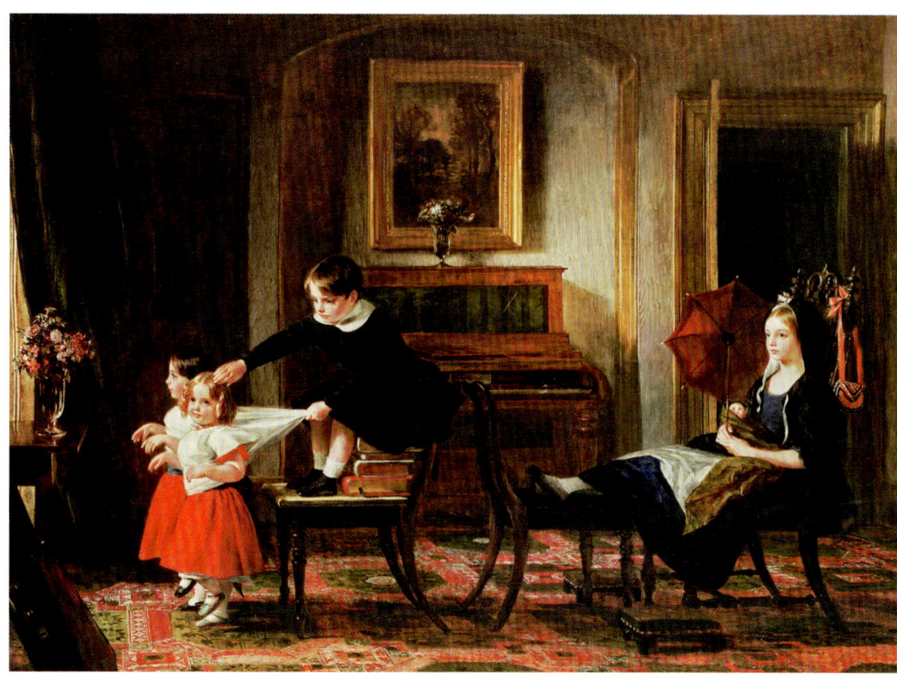

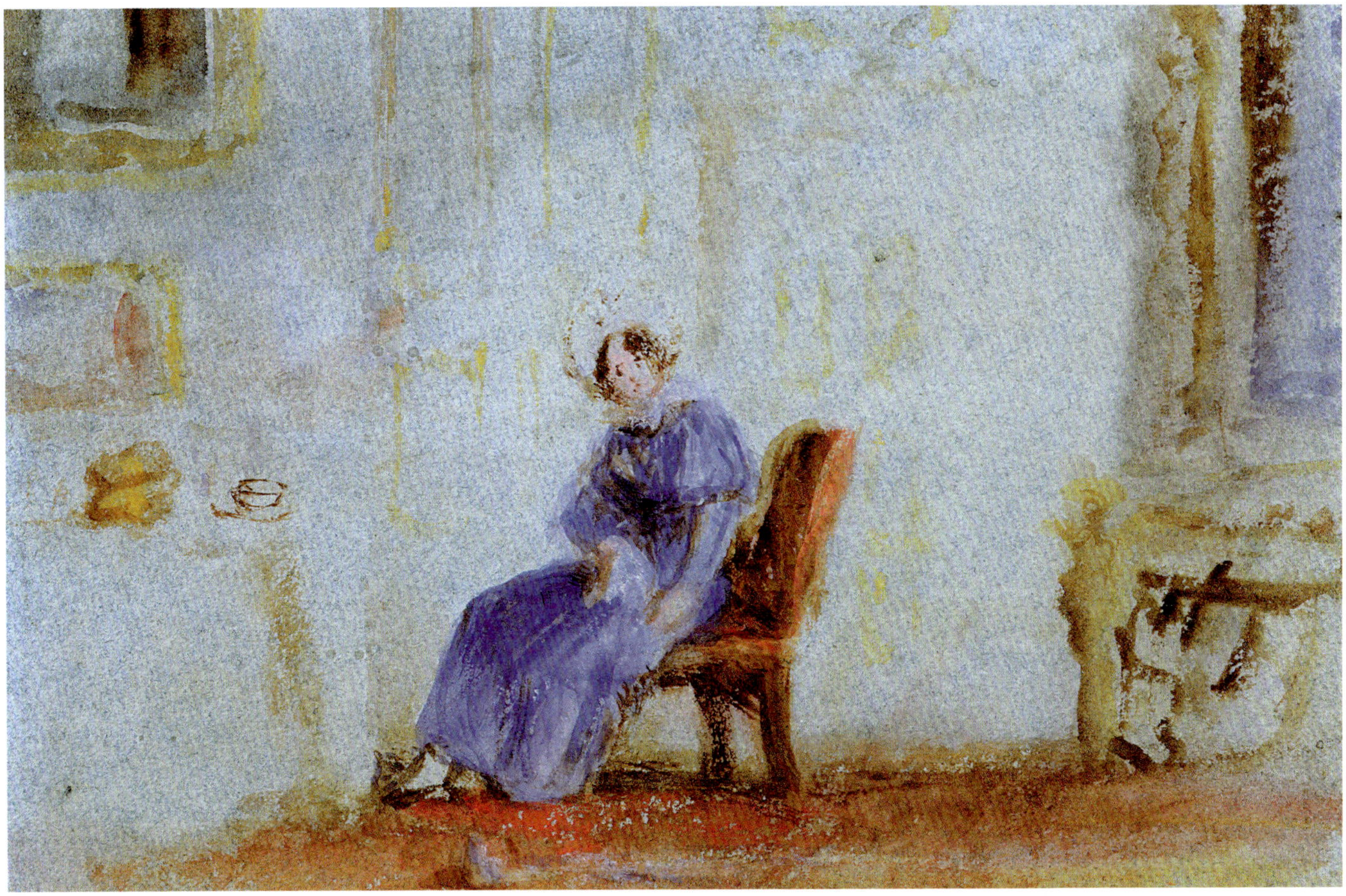

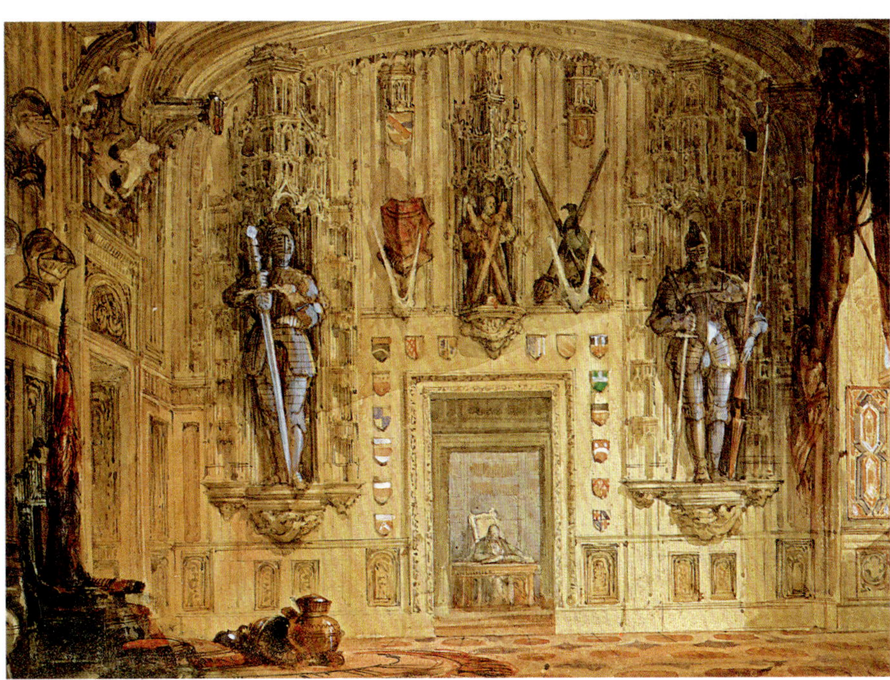

have been most at ease in this large, unorthodox family, moving comfortably around the house and sketching them at leisure and in off-guard moments. He made about 100 coloured sketches on grey paper during his visits to Petworth, at least two of which are of the Old Library, the room above the chapel that Turner used as his studio.

Lord Egremont himself was now in his 80s, "as fresh as may be, with a most incomparable and acute understanding". He was very wealthy, and benevolent to all his guests, particularly if they possessed an artistic temperament.

Although often ill himself, Turner responded well to the ambience at Petworth, which made him, too, convivial and benevolent. On one occasion, George Jones, another house guest, had hurt himself in an accident at Petworth and recalled that "Turner's anxiety to procure for me every attendance and convenience was like the attention of a parent to a child…(his) tenderness toward his friends was almost womanly".

When Lord Egremont died in 1837, Turner attended his funeral in Sussex and walked in the procession with a group of other artists, many of whom had been patronized by him and who had also stayed at Petworth as Egremont's house guests.

Above: Spilt Milk, Petworth, *watercolour and gouache, 1828. A rare example of a genre subject by Turner.*

Below: Abbotsford, the Hall, *David Roberts, watercolour, 1834. The frontispiece for Scott's* Poetical Works.

THE NATIONAL GALLERY

Discussions were under way in 1832 for a new National Gallery, and a new building for the Royal Academy, with Turner on its committee. He had also found refuge at a boarding house in Margate, well away from his problems in London.

In April 1824, Parliament agreed to purchase the collection of John Julius Angerstein (1735–1823) as the foundation for a national gallery to be opened in Pall Mall at the former home of the late collector. Two years later, Sir George Beaumont agreed to donate his collection to the gallery provided that new premises were sought.

The newly transformed Trafalgar Square was chosen as the most appropriate site since its location afforded access to all social classes. Designed by William Wilkins (1778–1839), another Academician,

Below: Portrait of John Julius Angerstein, *Thomas Lawrence, oil on canvas, c.1820.*

work began on the building in 1832 and the gallery was opened to the public six years later. The gallery received a number of paintings from other benefactors, but until the 1850s the collection remained very conservative, largely comprising Renaissance pictures. In 1851, Eastlake (then Sir Charles, and president of the Royal Academy) was appointed director of the gallery, and he was able to broaden the collection.

THE ROYAL ACADEMY BUILDING

Somerset House had been the home of the Royal Academy since 1771, three years after its foundation. In 1832, it was proposed to move the Academy to

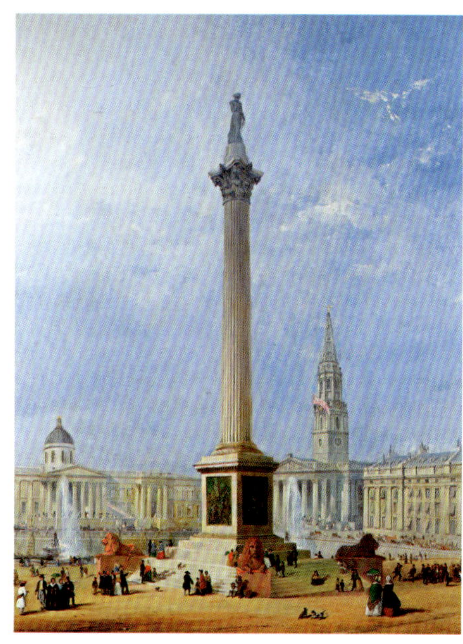

Above: Projected View of Trafalgar Square, *George Andrews, oil on panel, 1844.*

share the accommodation at the new National Gallery. Turner travelled on the Continent in the summer of 1833, as much to look at the buildings housing art collections as the paintings themselves. He travelled to Germany, where he probably met the director of the Berlin Museum, and then Vienna and Prague, reporting back to the committee on the prevalent classicism used for their galleries and museums.

The first Academy exhibition in the new premises took place in April 1837 and was opened by King William IV, who was to die two months later. Turner exhibited traditional paintings only at this exhibition, avoiding the harsh criticism that had befallen him in recent years. With the imminent demise of the king, Turner was perhaps looking forward to royal patronage from the new sovereign. The Royal Academy moved once again into its own building, Burlington House, in 1868, where it still remains today.

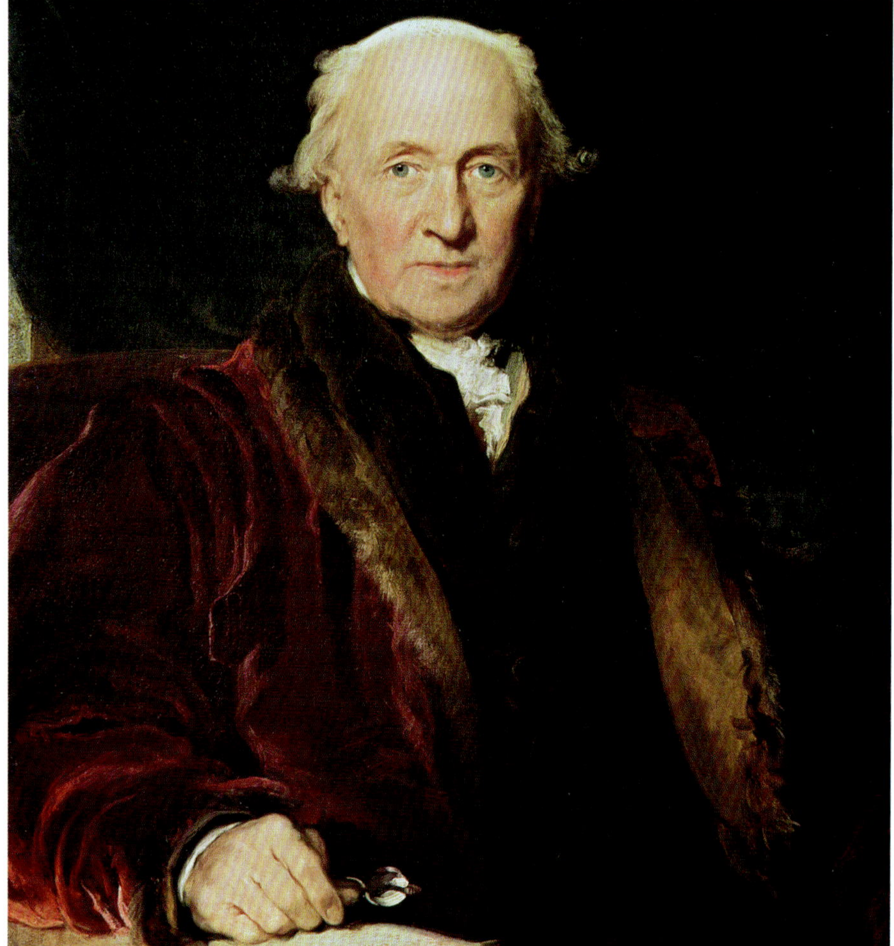

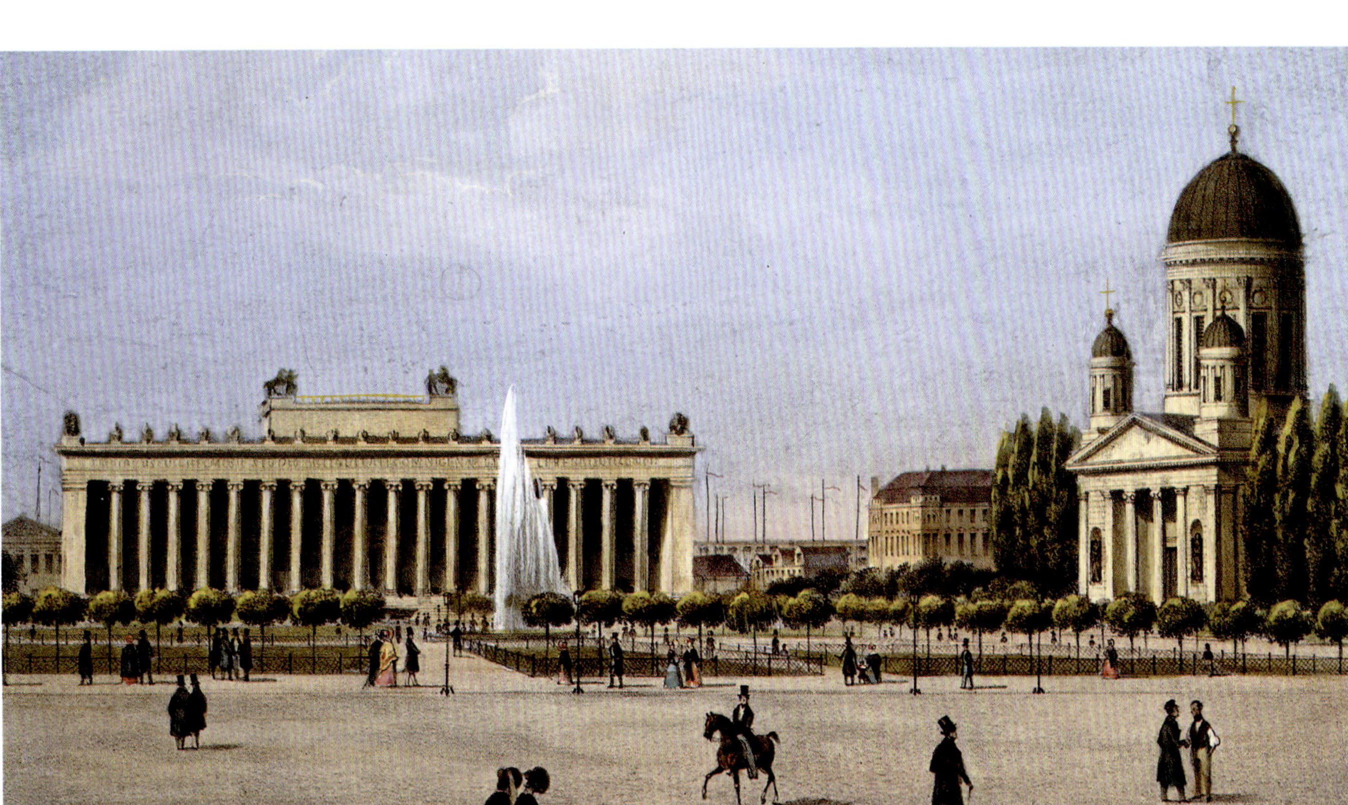

Above: Altes Museum and Berliner Dom, *LE Luetke, lithograph, 1845. Turner visited art museums in Berlin in 1833. He then conveyed his ideas to the committee for the building of the National Gallery.*

MRS BOOTH

Sometime in the early 1830s, Turner began to spend a week or two each year in Margate, out of season at the lodging house of John and Sophia Caroline Booth. Turner was attracted to the house because of its location, a view over both piers and the sea. The house was also a refuge for Turner, a place that he had always enjoyed, and far enough away from the stress of London. He had also no longer to worry about his sick father, and may well have found solace in the Booths' company, outside of his mainstream artistic circle. John Booth died in 1833 and Turner increased the frequency of his visits. He was not in good health and may well have benefited from the sea air, away from the pollution of London. But Margate was also a wonderful motif for Turner who produced a number of magnificent oil paintings such as *Waves Breaking on a Lee-shore* (1835), when he must have been standing on the beach in a gale. However, Turner was equally in his element with calm beach scenes that contain characters reflecting everyday life, such as *The New Moon; or, 'I've lost My Boat, You shan't have Your Hoop'*, exhibited in 1840. Although Turner continued his visits to Margate for some years after, by 1846, Mrs Booth had

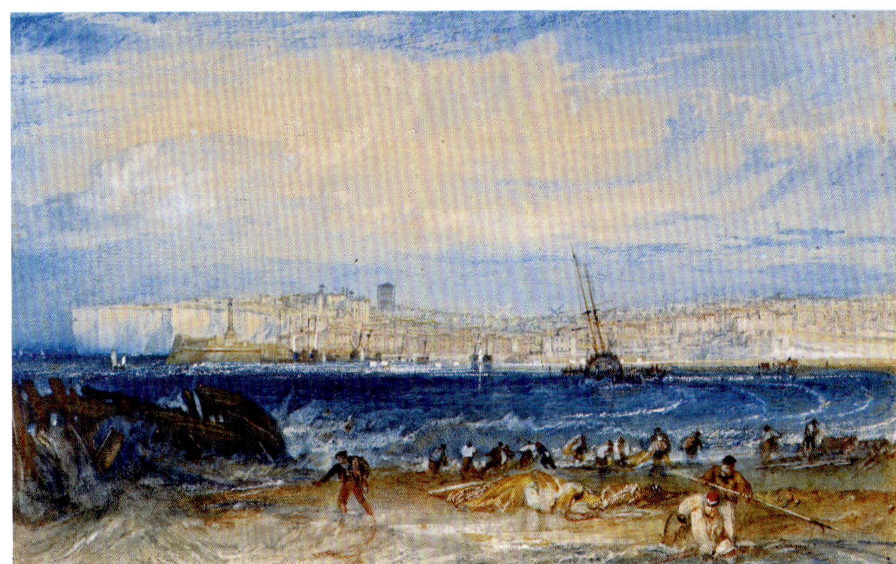

Above: Margate, *watercolour, 1822. Turner found solace at Margate.*

taken the lease on a property in Chelsea, London. She and Turner were often seen out together and for the sake of propriety he was introduced as Mr Booth, and sometimes even Admiral Booth. As he had done before in his life, Turner kept his relationship with Mrs Booth secret from everyone.

EXHIBITIONS AND AN AUCTION

Critical acclaim and increasing esteem from across the establishment did not prevent
Turner from producing the odd financial flop, as was seen with one grand project.
Undaunted, Turner continued to demand the highest prices for his paintings.

At the 1833 Royal Academy exhibition, Turner showed his Venetian oil paintings for the first time.

THE ROYAL ACADEMY 1833

Turner exhibited six oil paintings at the exhibition of which two were Venetian scenes. The oils were smaller than in previous years and yet he elected to charge more for them, stating that "if they will have such scraps instead of important pictures they must pay for them". One of these paintings, *Ducal Palace and Custom House, Venice: Canaletti Painting* was sold to Robert Vernon, a collector of British paintings, who intended bequeathing his collection to the National Gallery. Later that year, Turner was given one of the four 'Visitor to the Life Academy' posts at the Royal Academy Schools.

A SUBSEQUENT EXHIBITION

In June and July of the same year, Moon, Boys and Graves held a 'Private Exhibition' of Turner's work in Pall Mall, London. This gallery had taken over

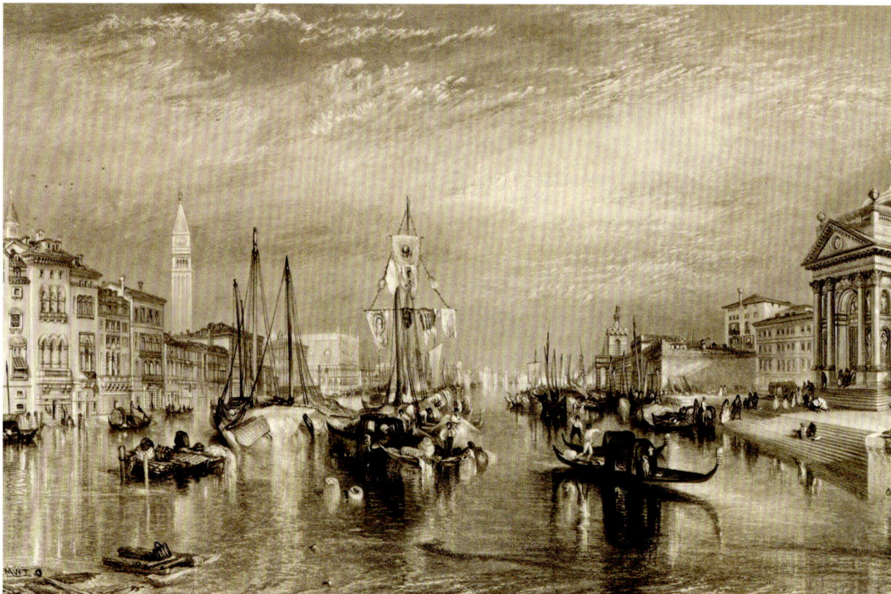

Above: The Grand Canal, Venice, William Miller, engraving, 1838. Large scale Venetian prints such as this proved very popular and facilitated a wider appreciation of Turner's work.

responsibility for the *Picturesque Views in England and Wales* series from Charles Heath who by 1830 was in financial difficulties. The principal partner in the new publishing venture was Francis Moon.

In 1832, Moon published 60 plates of the series in book form with an accompanying text by Hannibal Evans Lloyd. To promote the series, the gallery held an exhibition of 65 of the watercolours used during the making of the *Picturesque Views* series, together with some others used in Scott's *Poetical Works*, making a total of more than 90 exhibits. The gallery borrowed a number of works for the exhibition from Thomas Griffith who had purchased them earlier and started to deal in Turner's work at this time.

A subscription book was available at the exhibition for purchase of the engravings, but despite more than 100 names being listed, most of them failed to honour their obligation. In all the

Picturesque series failed to live up to expectations and proved a financial disaster, despite favourable reviews of the exhibition.

AN AUCTION

Shortly before the exhibition at Moon, Boys and Graves, Dr Monro, Turner's early mentor and physician to his sick mother, had died. In July, an auction was held to dispose of his assets, including many drawings by Turner, some of which had been executed in collaboration with Thomas Girtin. Of these, Turner purchased 13 of his own pictures, together with other works owned by Monro that included paintings by de Loutherbourg and two ascribed to Rembrandt.

At this time a favourable review of Turner was published in Arnold's *Magazine of the Fine Arts* stating that the artist had "emerged as a meteor in

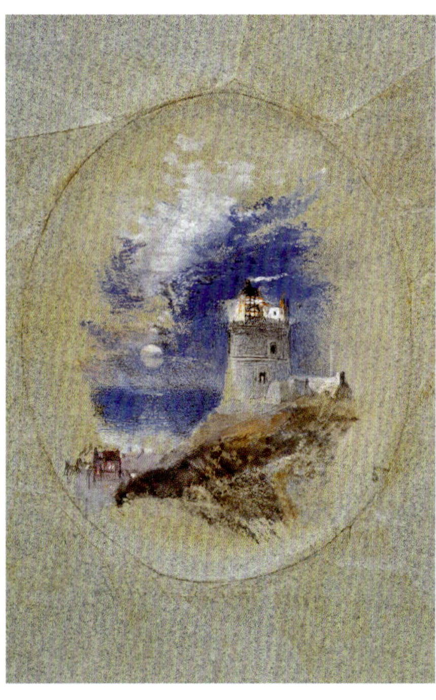

Left: Lowestoffe Lighthouse, *gouache on blue paper, 1832. This vignette was published in 1834 as an illustration to George Crabbe's Poems.*

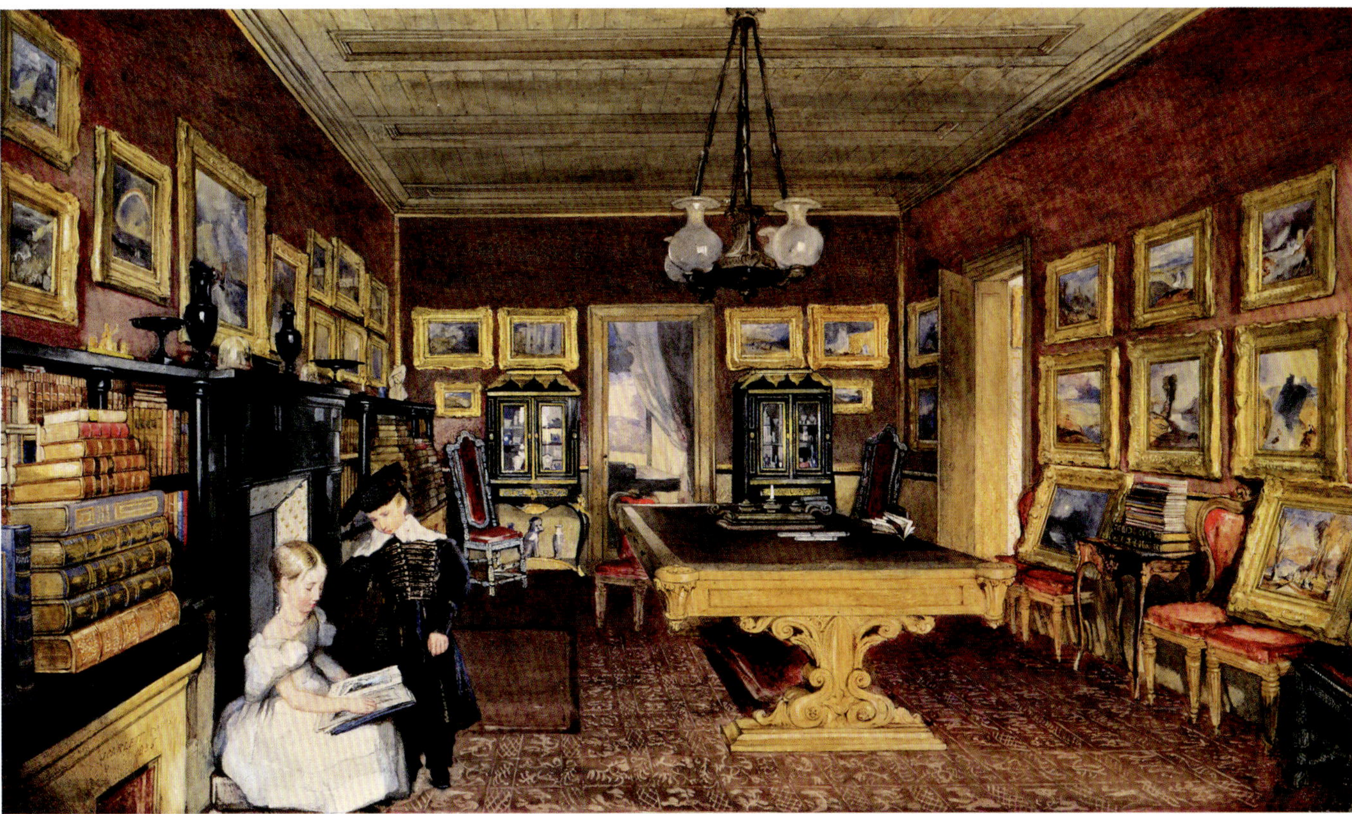

Above: The Library at Tottenham of Benjamin Windus, *John Davis, watercolour, 1835. Benjamin Windus was one of Turner's later patrons amassing over 200 of his works, some of which are shown in this watercolour.*

colouring''. The article was anonymous, but it seemed that Turner's critics were starting to understand where his talent was leading.

ANOTHER EXHIBITION

In the autumn of 1833, the second exhibition of the Society of British Artists was held in Suffolk Street, London. Turner was represented by two watercolours loaned by Sir Watkyn Williams Wynn and by one oil painting, *Margate Cliffs from the Sea* loaned by a Mr Carpenter. The following year, he was represented by two of Lord Egremont's pictures. The Society was formed in 1823 as an alternative venue to the Academy. As an Academician, Turner could not exhibit his own work at the Society, hence the loan pictures.

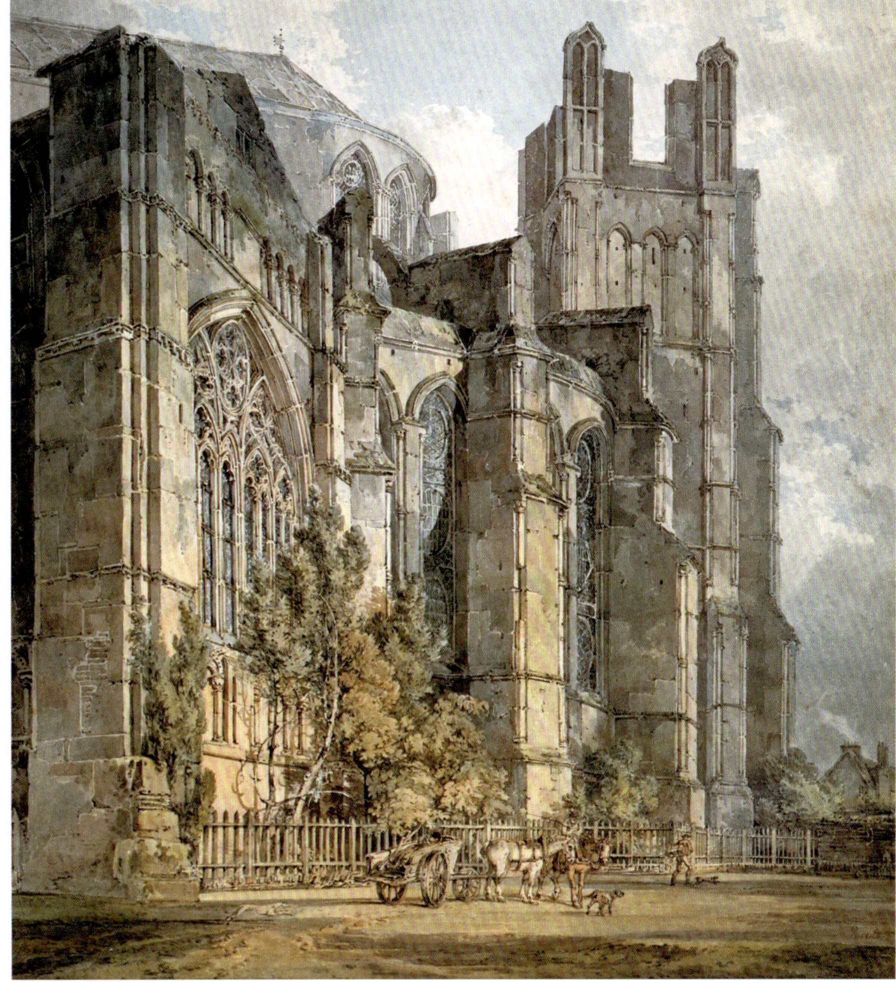

Right: St Anselm's Chapel, Canterbury Cathedral, *watercolour, 1794.*

A SUBLIME EXPERIENCE

Turner was witness to a devastating fire at the heart of the British political establishment, which became, in his hands, an ideal metaphor for political statement. Meanwhile, further attacks from the art establishment only fanned the flames of his popular support.

In London, on 16 October 1834, a fire caused by the burning of wood in a furnace in the cellars of the House of Lords destroyed most of the Houses of Parliament, also known as the Palace of Westminster.

THE HOUSES OF PARLIAMENT

The site of the Palace had been home to the kings of England from the reign of Edward the Confessor in the 11th century. In 1547, St Stephen's Chapel, within the precincts of the Palace grounds, was secularized and made available to the House of Commons, the Lords meeting in the Old Palace itself. After the fire, virtually all that remained was the medieval Westminster Hall, which still stands today in front of the rebuilt Houses of Parliament.

It has been suggested that the fire was a physical cleansing of the old and corrupt system that Walter Fawkes and others had admonished before the Reform Act of 1830, establishing a "Parliament full, free and frequent". Turner may well have seen the fire in much the same way.

Turner's subsequent paintings are evocative of the intense heat generated by the fire, epitomizing the scene's sublimity. Turner made some 60 rapid sketches of the blaze from the shoreline of the Thames and also from a boat. The following year he submitted two oil paintings of the event to the British Institution exhibition. The fact that he had not submitted work to the Institution for 18 years suggests that he wanted to make a political point that the old order was now defunct. A different version of the painting was shown at the Royal Academy in 1835.

Below: The Burning of the Houses of Parliament *(A sketch), watercolour, 1834. This is a vignette that appeared in the pocket book* The Keepsake.

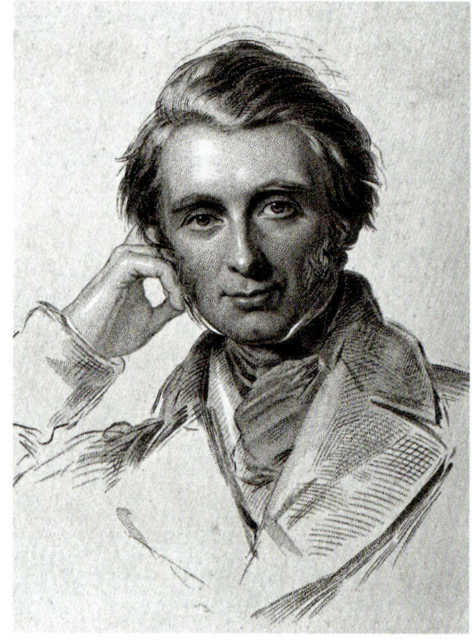

Above: Portrait of John Ruskin, *Francis Holl, engraving, c.1840. Writing one of his earliest pieces of art criticism, John Ruskin was just 17 when he responded to John Eagles' vitriolic attack.*

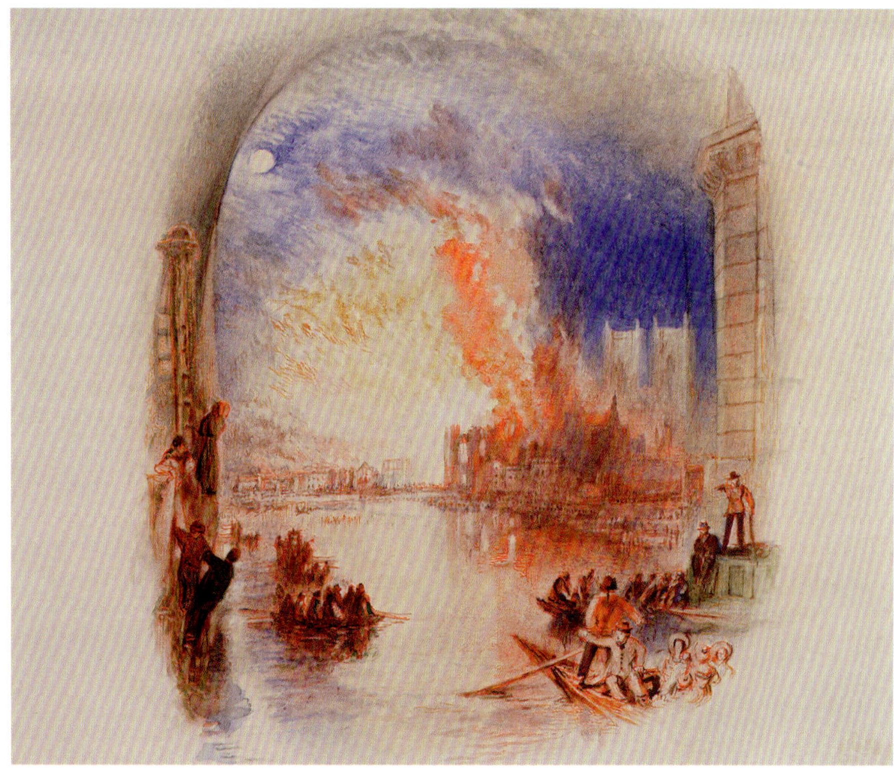

VIGNETTES

During the 1830s, steel plates had become the preferred medium for illustrating books since they could reproduce more copies than copper. Turner also realized that the plate, being harder, could accommodate more distinct lines, and therefore reproduce more detail from his drawings. In this same decade, Turner produced 150 highly detailed vignette watercolours on commissions from literary publishers. Among the commissions he worked on were for Scott's *Poetical Works* (1833–4) and John Macron's edition of Milton's *Poetical Works* (1835). His final work in vignette was in 1839 for Thomas Moore's *The Epicurean*.

CONTINENTAL TOURS

In successive summers between 1834 and 1836, Turner travelled around the Continent. The first trip, in July of 1834,

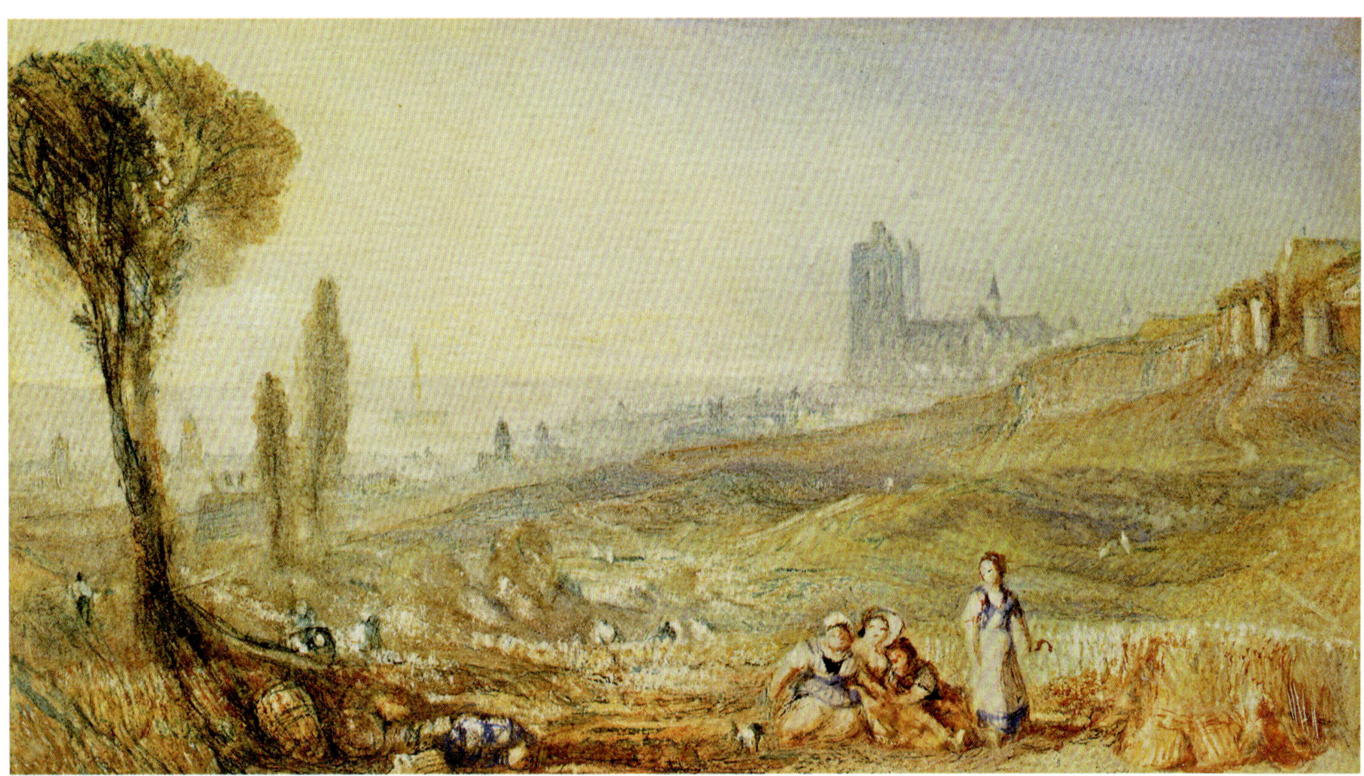

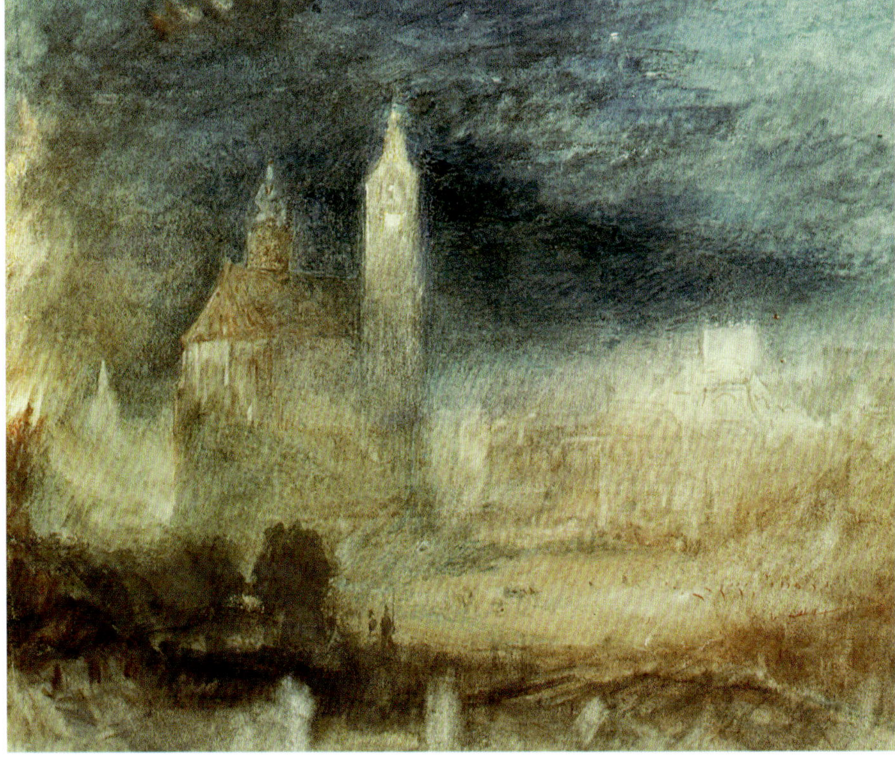

essentially repeated the one he had made in 1826, beginning in Belgium, following the Meuse and Moselle rivers and returning along the Rhine. It seems likely that Turner was still looking for material for the ill-fated 'Rivers of Europe' project. Nevertheless some beautiful and ethereal watercolours began to emerge at this time.

In the summer of 1836, Hugh Munro of Novar accompanied Turner on a sketching tour of Switzerland, taking in Chamonix and Val d'Aosta. Such was the value of his friendship that Turner gave Munro a gift – the sketchbook that he had used on his last visit to Farnley Hall in 1824. Munro had bought several of Turner's paintings, including two from the 1836 Royal Academy exhibition.

In the autumn, a vitriolic attack appeared in a popular conservative journal called *Blackwood's Edinburgh Magazine*, which was aimed at the "false English School of Art". The author was the Reverend John Eagles, who singled out Turner for ridicule – in particular for his Academy submission *Juliet and her Nurse*.

The writer John Ruskin, then aged only 17, was so incensed at the article that he began his great campaign to enlighten Turner's critics and the greater public. Ruskin became Turner's most fervent admirer and he loyally defended his work and his freedom from convention in painting. He was to remain faithful to Turner until the painter died.

Above: Brussels: A Distant View, *watercolour, 1833. This tiny watercolour was executed before his tour of 1834.*

Left: A Conflagration, Lausanne, *watercolour, 1835, possibly recalling the Battle of Ratisbon in 1809.*

THE VICTORIAN AGE BEGINS

The newly rich of the industrial boom, with their liberal modern tastes, brought fresh patronage and wealth to Turner, and with a new queen on the throne, even greater honours seemed to be in view, but frustratingly, they were not to be forthcoming.

Several deaths of friends occurred in the year 1837, marking new beginnings for Turner and others in the forthcoming age.

CHANGES IN PATRONAGE

At the end of the previous decade, changes in patronage for Turner and other artists were already in process. In place of the aristocrats and landed gentry such as Lord Tabley and Sir Richard Colt Hoare were self-made men of the Industrial age such as the manufacturer John Sheepshanks (1787–1863), who had started buying Turner's work in the early 1830s. The last of the great aristocratic patrons of Turner, Lord Egremont, died in 1837. Egremont had a liberal attitude to aesthetic considerations, particularly where Turner was concerned, that ran counter to most other aristocrats who had, by and large, very conservative tastes. Turner's experiments in colour at this time were now being appreciated

QUEEN VICTORIA

The niece of King William IV and George IV, Victoria was not expected to inherit the throne. However, when neither king produced a living heir, she was proclaimed queen shortly after her 18th birthday, and ruled for a record-breaking 63 years, which was arguably the most prosperous period in Britain's long history.

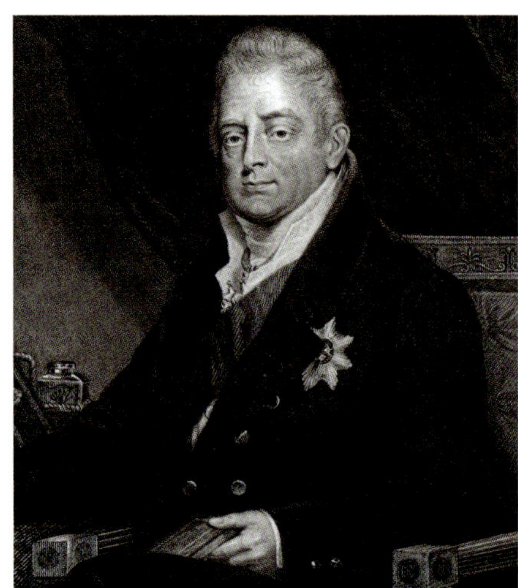

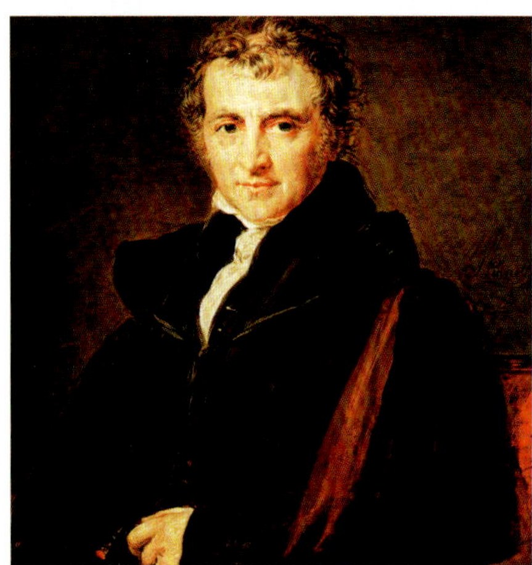

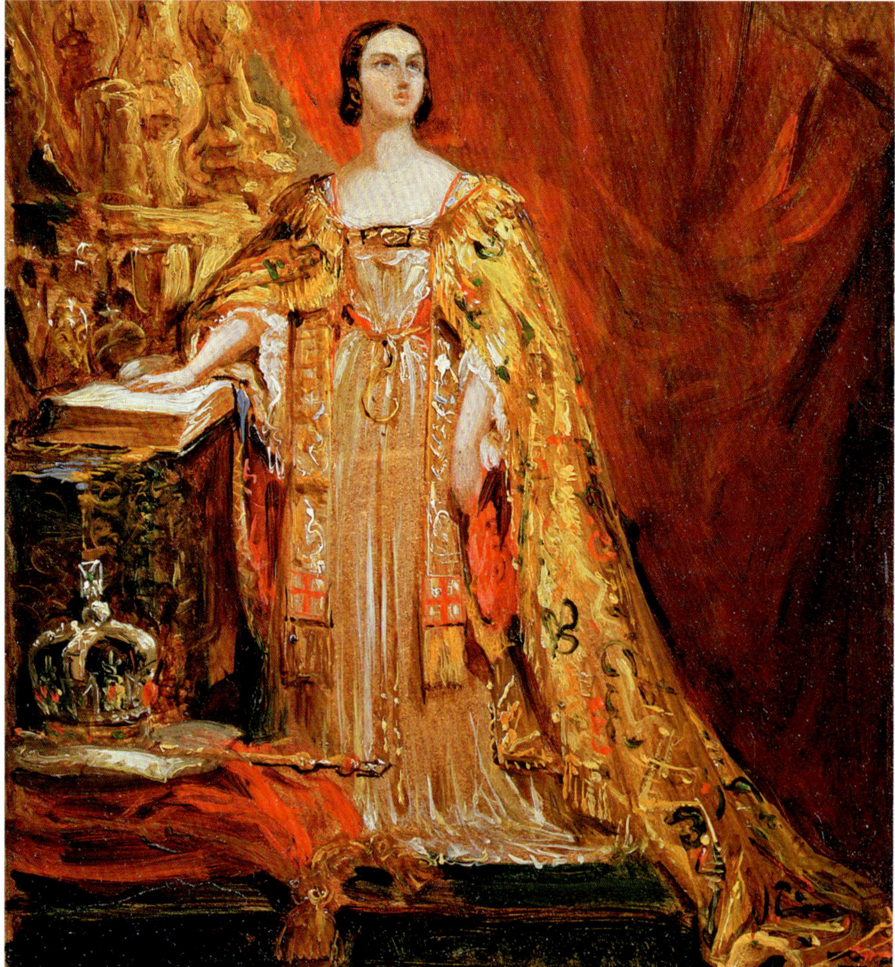

Top left: Portrait of King William IV, *Henry Dawe, lithograph, 1835. William had no children, so his niece, Victoria, became monarch on his death in 1837.*

Above left: Sir Augustus Wall Callcott, *John Linnell, oil on panel, 1847. Callcott received a knighthood when Queen Victoria came to the throne in 1837.*

Above: The Coronation of Queen Victoria, *George Hayter, oil on panel, 1838. Hayter was principal portrait and history painter to the new Queen Victoria.*

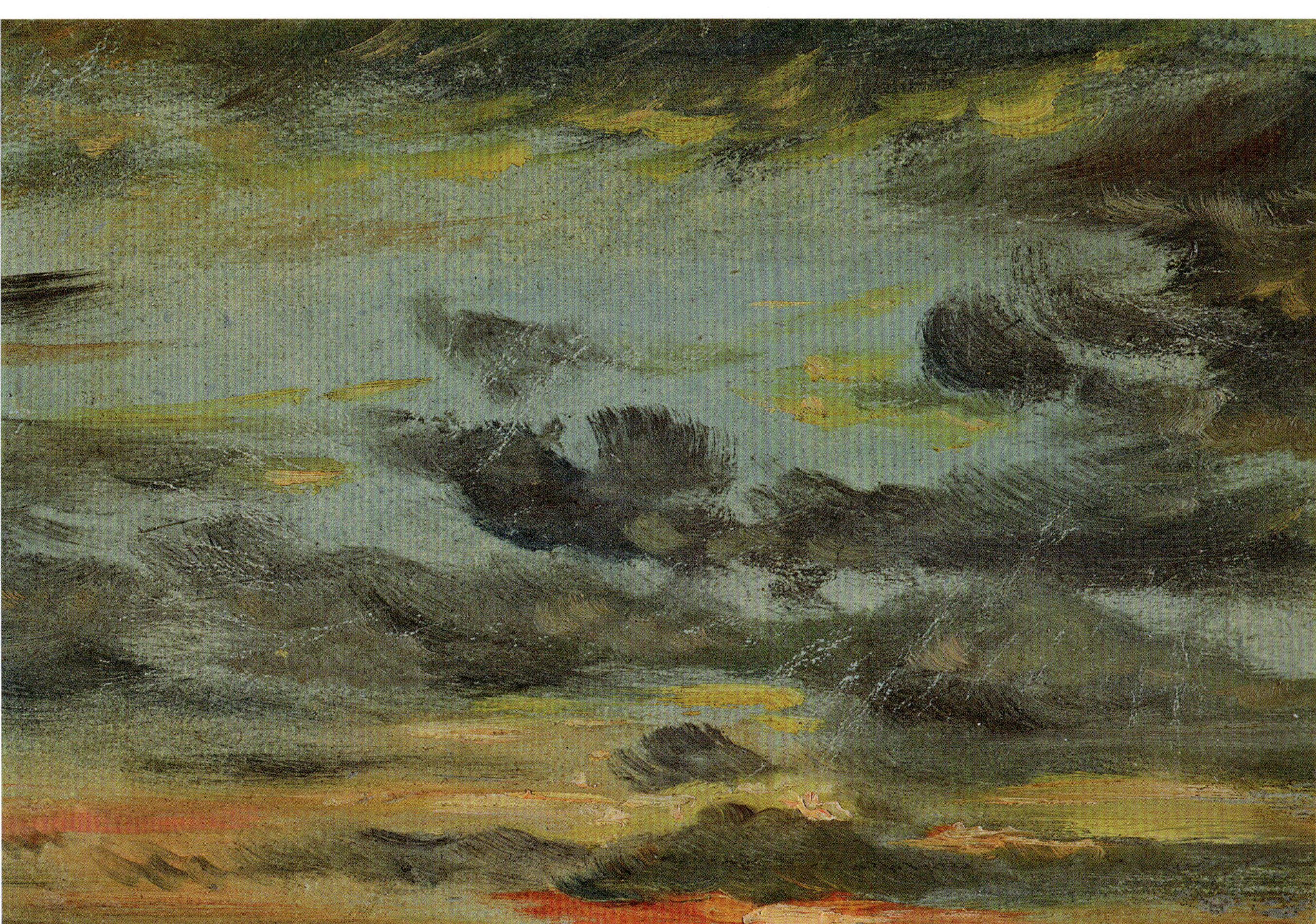

by a merchant class who had none of the aesthetic baggage of their forebears to adhere to.

A PICTURE DEALER

By 1837, Turner was already in his 60s and had not enjoyed the best of health in recent years. At this time, he came into contact with a picture dealer, Thomas Griffith of Norwood. Turner was commercially minded and realized that at his age he was unable to represent his work to prospective clients on all occasions. Turner was also now an established 'Old Master' in his own right, his paintings often coming on to the market for resale. Griffith purchased many of these paintings for resale, and as he gained the artist's trust took preparatory drawings to Turner's clients to gain commissions on his behalf. During the 1840s, Griffith was to become as much a friend as his picture dealer.

The year 1837 also saw the passing of some of Turner's friends, the architect Sir John Soane and the landscape painter John Constable, his near contemporary. In June, King William IV died, heralding the dawn of a new epoch – the ascension to the throne of the king's niece Victoria. She became the new monarch in 1837 and the long Victorian age began.

NO KNIGHTHOOD

It is customary for a new monarch to create new knights, but Turner was to be disappointed, since many other artists around him had already been rewarded, including Sir Francis Chantrey (1835) and Sir David Wilkie (1836), who was ten years his junior. To rub salt in the wound, the new Queen bestowed knighthoods on the painter Augustus Wall Callcott and Turner's exact contemporary the sculptor Richard Westmacott, both of whom were also Royal Academicians.

THE ROYAL ACADEMY 1837

Turner was on the hanging committee for the first Academy exhibition at its new premises in Trafalgar Square. At

Above: Sky Study – Sunset, *John Constable, oil on paper, 1821. Unlike Turner, Constable preferred to paint in England. He liked to paint the sky, with its changing light and atmospheric effects.*

the exhibition he showed four oil paintings of subjects that demonstrated his adherence to the Classical tradition, a return to Claudian subjects, albeit with an air of Turnerian translucence. His return to a more traditional mode, with appended prose to his paintings, suggested that he was courting royal favour in anticipation of a knighthood.

At the end of the year, and with no knighthood, he resigned his position as Professor of Perspective. He had already been the subject of heavy criticism the previous year from Benjamin Haydon (1786–1846), an embittered artist and writer who had brought about a government enquiry into the affairs of the Academy. One complaint against Turner was that he had not provided any lectures on perspective for nearly a decade.

NEW IDEAS IN PAINTING

Late into his life, Turner remained restlessly creative, developing new ways of working, tackling new political issues and visual subjects with his paintings, and exploring new aesthetic and philosophical ideas.

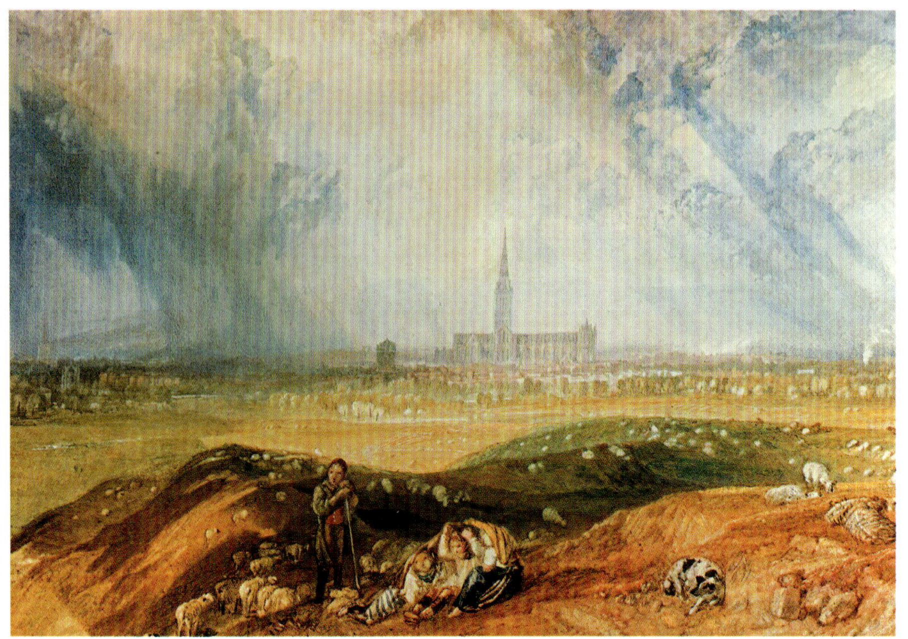

Left: Salisbury Cathedral, *watercolour, 1828. This depicts the rural idyll with a shepherd and his family in the foreground and the cathedral in the distance.*

harmony. Further, he was the first to suggest that colour actually had therapeutic value and that, for example, red and yellow had a positive effect on a viewer, whereas blue had the opposite effect. These ideas were taken up by a number of artists later in the century, particularly the Impressionists and Post-Impressionists. Goethe developed a colour wheel and a colour triangle to demonstrate his ideas, which showed the relationship between primary, secondary and tertiary colours.

At some point in Turner's late career, he began many paintings that remained unfinished when he died. At the time of his death these numbered nearly two hundred. He worked on a number of canvases at the same time, some of which were on a large scale. More and more, Turner used the five Varnishing Days to work canvases up to a finished state from almost nothing, to the amazement of colleagues who dubbed him the 'Grand Old Man' at the Academy.

GOETHE'S COLOUR THEORY

A scientist, writer and poet, Johann Wolfgang von Goethe (1749–1832) published his treatise *Zur Farbenlehre* in 1810. Turner's fellow Academician Charles Eastlake translated it in 1840 as *Theory of Colours*. Broadly speaking, Goethe challenged Newton's purely scientific theories and suggested that colour, as perceived by the eye, was in fact a dynamic reciprocity between dark and light. Although less analytical than Newton, Goethe suggested that colour had a psychological dimension, and that opposing colours could be used in

TURNER'S RESPONSE

An annotated copy of *Theory of Colours* was owned by Turner, and notes suggest that he merely used Goethe's theory to underpin his own: that is, that

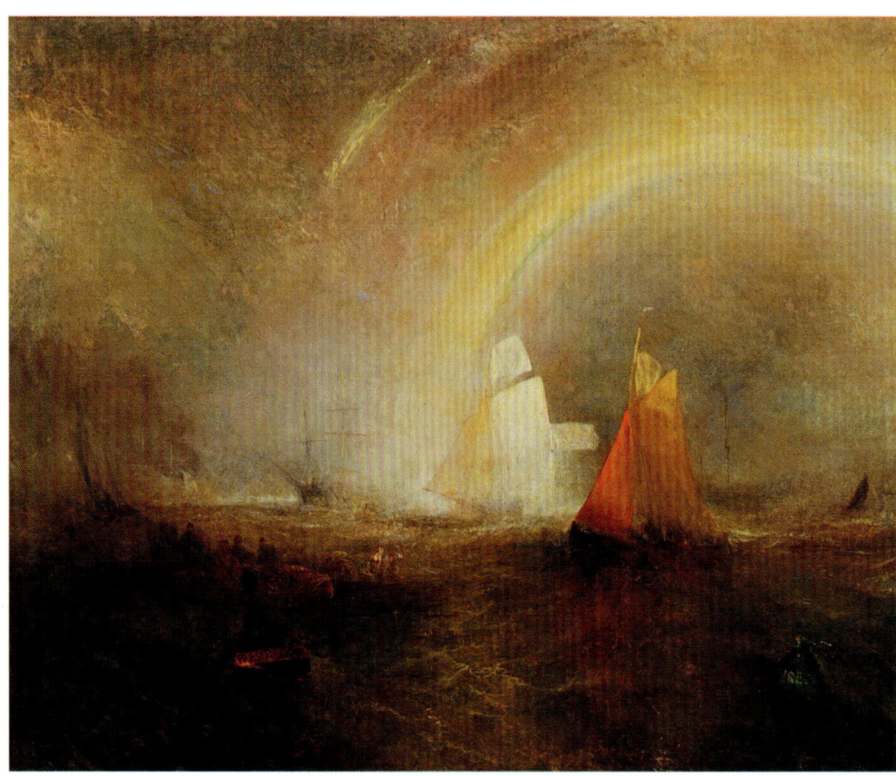

Right: The Wreck Buoy, *oil on canvas, 1807–49 was reworked from an original painting made in 1807.*

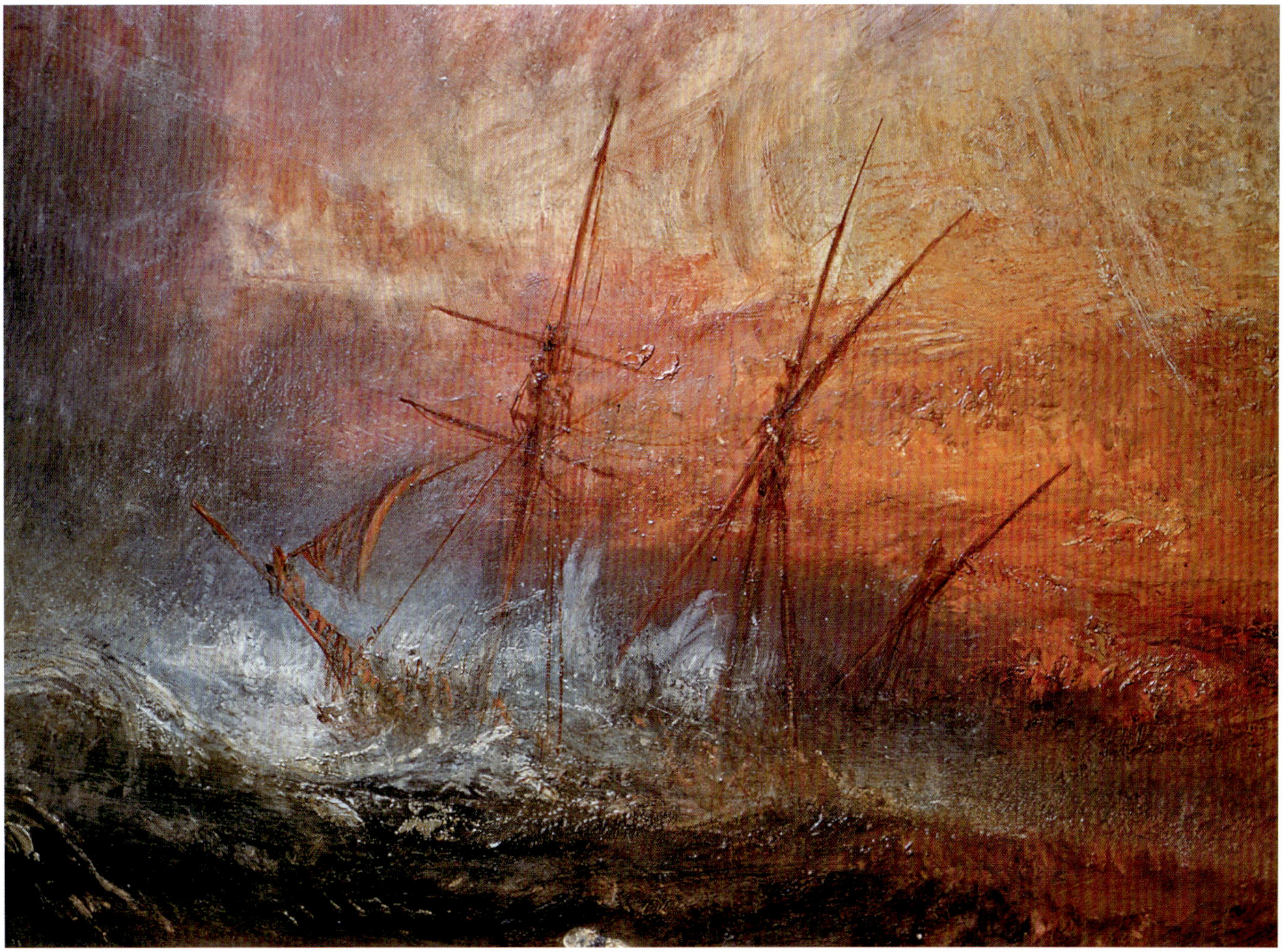

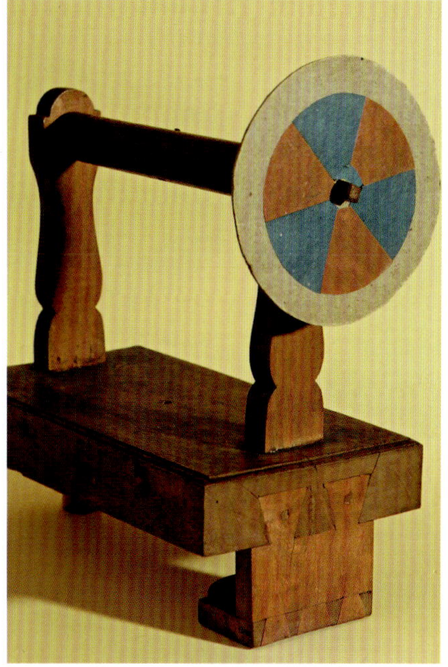

Above: Slavers Throwing Overboard the Dead and Dying *(detail), oil on canvas, 1840. The use of colour to depict the sublimity of nature and man's inhumanity reaches its height in this painting.*

light has an active as well as a passive effect on the eye. In the summer of 1840, Turner travelled for the last time to Venice, and in many of the resultant works there is a hazy, bright sun in the centre of the picture radiating light outward. Turner referred to this as a "wide concave of the circumambient air". Turner showed his affinity with Goethe's ideas most fully in two pictures shown in an exhibition of 1843, *Shade and Darkness – the Evening of the Deluge*, and, *Light and Colour (Goethe's Theory) – The Morning after the Deluge.*

LATE SEASCAPES

Although Turner had always had an affinity with the sea, his frequent visits to Margate from the late 1830s seem to have evoked a pessimistic view, possibly resulting from a sense of his own mortality that found expression in many of his seascapes after 1840. The most evocative of all was *Slavers Throwing Overboard the Dead and Dying – Typhoon Coming on ('The Slave Ship')*, a dismal portrayal of the terrible abuses suffered by transported slaves, exhibited by Turner in 1840, that he painted to coincide with an anti-slavery conference in London. The picture was one of contrasts set against a brilliant red and yellow sky. By way of contrast at the same exhibition, *Rockets and Blue Lights (close at hand) to Warn Steam Boats of Shoal Water*, a seascape set against a brilliant blue backdrop, was shown.

Among Turner's later patrons was Elhanan Bicknell (1788–1861), a wealthy whaling entrepreneur who purchased many of his pictures, and during the 1840s, the artist created a series of seascapes that included whaling vessels.

Above: Equipment for Demonstrating the Theory of Colours, *Johann Wolfgang von Goethe, wood and cardboard, date unknown.*

JOHN RUSKIN

Perhaps the most eloquent writer on art in the 19th century, and enjoying a close relationship with the artist, John Ruskin became Turner's apologist at the age of 24, and in 1843 published *Modern Painters*, in which he extolled the painter's virtues.

Following a period of study at Oxford University between 1837 and 1840, Ruskin toured the Continent, returning to England in June 1841. In those formative years, he had already written on architecture and won a prize for poetry.

JOHN RUSKIN (1819–1900)

Prior to meeting Turner, Ruskin was well aware of the artist's work at the Academy exhibitions and also from studying the collection of Benjamin Windus, one of Turner's new breed of mercantile patrons.

Ruskin's almost obsessive adoration of Turner's paintings led him inexorably to a career as a critic, becoming the most influential writer on art and architecture in the 19th century. His first major work was *Modern Painters* published anonymously in 1843, in which he defended Turner from the increasingly vitriolic criticism that he was being subjected to in the popular press.

Ruskin continued to champion Turner's work long after the artist's death, but was also a significant defender of Pre-Raphaelitism in the second half of the century. He was also an advocate of the Venetian Gothic style, which had a profound effect on subsequent British architecture, and was instrumental in the introduction of the Arts and Crafts

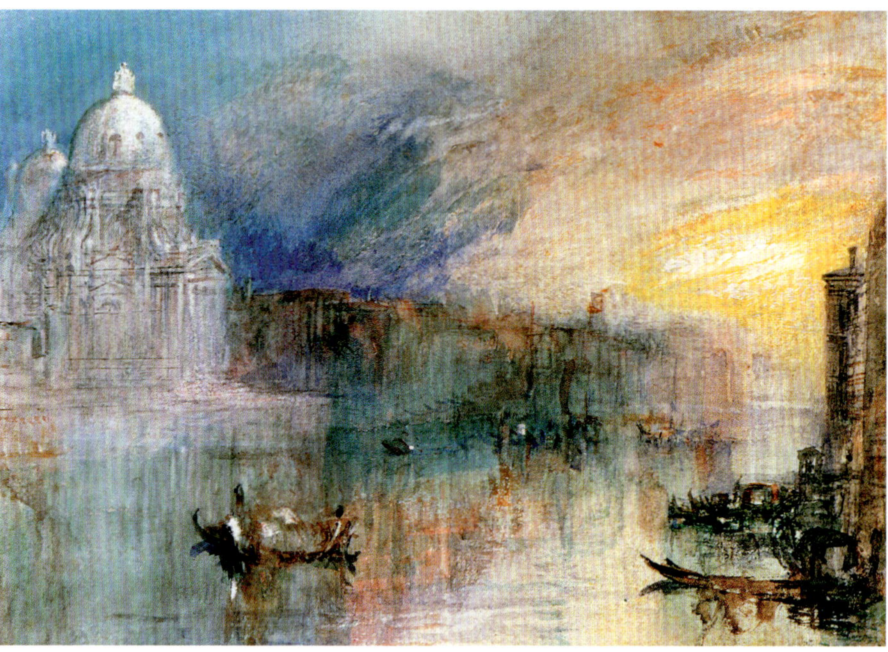

Above: Venice: The Grand Canal with Santa Maria della Salute, *pencil and watercolour, 1840. Venice provided the inspirational setting for Turner's exploration of light and Ruskin's love affair with the city's Gothic style of architecture.*

movement that characterized Ruskin's socialist principles as well as his aesthetic sensibilities.

TURNER AND RUSKIN

Ruskin met Turner in June 1840 at the home of the artist's agent Thomas Griffith. On that occasion Ruskin wrote in his diary of meeting "the greatest (man) of the age". Turner did not make the link with the young man who four years earlier had written as "JR esq", to defend the artist against Reverend Eagles' vitriol. Ruskin persuaded his father to purchase *The Slave Ship*, the painting he enthused about in the first

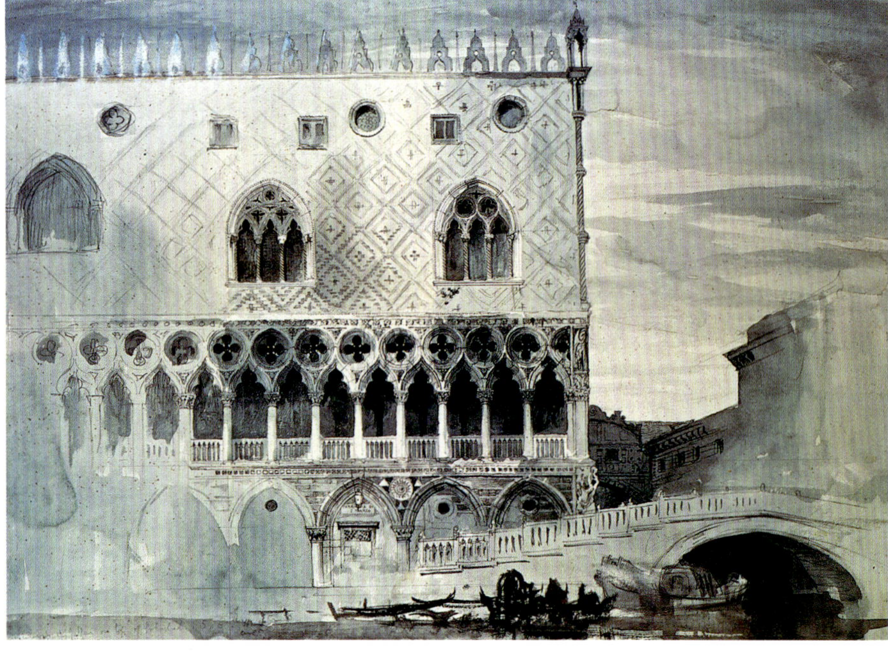

Left: Exterior of Ducal Palace, Venice, *John Ruskin, pen, ink and wash on paper, date unknown. Ruskin was obsessed with Venetian Gothic.*

volume of his book *Modern Painters*, referring to it as "the noblest sea that Turner ever painted". Prior to the publication, Ruskin visited Turner at Queen Anne Street on a regular basis and may well have been invited into the artist's inner sanctum, his studio. Due deference was always paid by Ruskin to the artist who later remarked that "he sees more in my pictures than I ever painted". Ruskin repaid Turner's hospitality by inviting him to his home.

MODERN PAINTERS

Ruskin's first major piece of art criticism, *Modern Painters*, was published anonymously, the author referred to as "a graduate of Oxford". The first volume, dedicated almost entirely to Turner, was innovative in its approach, based on the spiritual aspects of painting rooted in the Romanticism of his age. For Ruskin, Turner's work was its apogee. His analysis examined the formal qualities of the paintings themselves, viewing him as the "greatest of his age" because of his adherence to a "truth to nature". Ruskin was to advocate this doctrine in the next decade and in many aspects of his later writing career.

The text of *Modern Painters* can be difficult to comprehend in terms of its subject matter, since the art criticism is bound up in his observations on nature. For Ruskin, landscape paintings made during the Romantic age, particularly those by Turner, were superior to their predecessors since they were imbued with a spiritual dimension, and therefore wholesome. Separated from that dimension, they would become trivial.

Ruskin published four more volumes of *Modern Painters*, the last published in 1860. The subsequent volumes do not show the same evangelical fervour and are more concerned with European art in the round, Ruskin having travelled more widely by that time.

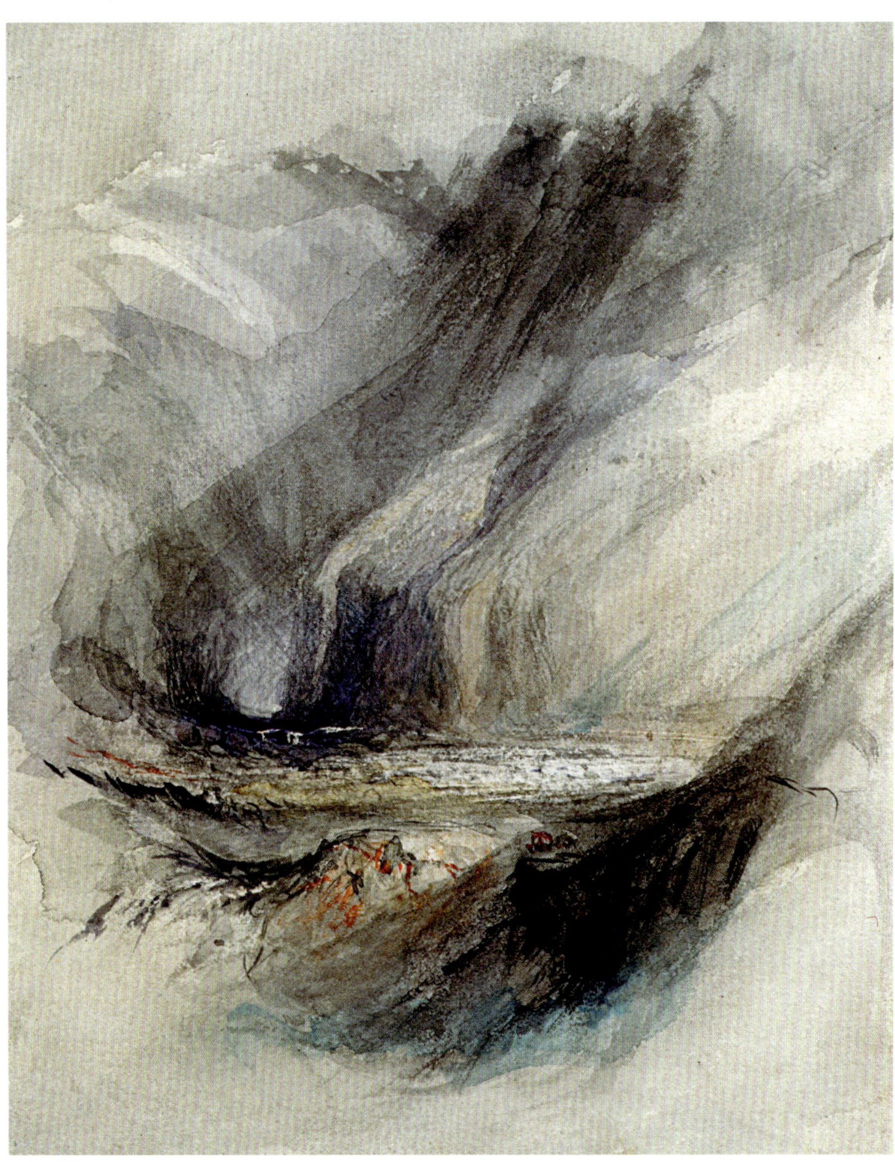

Above: The Gates of the Hills, *John Ruskin, pencil and watercolour, 1843. From volume four of* Modern Painters.

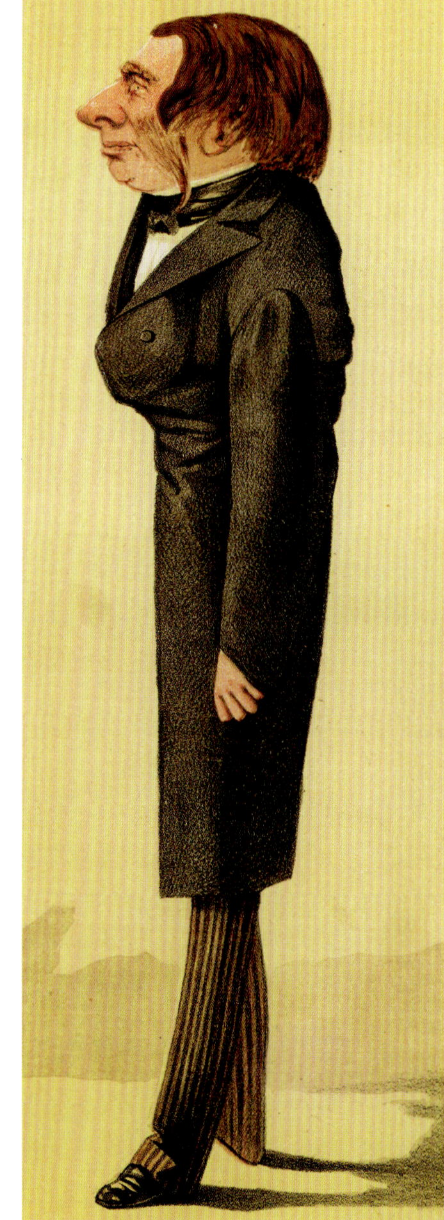

Right: Caricature of John Ruskin, *Cecioni, print, 1872. An image of John Ruskin as he appeared in* Vanity Fair *in 1872.*

THE LAST EUROPEAN TOURS

Not age, nor poor health, nor the loss of close friends could quell Turner's relentless creative quests. He travelled repeatedly to Switzerland, but it was most likely at home in Twickenham where he first made the acquaintance of a king.

In 1841, Turner made the first of four consecutive summer tours of Switzerland, even though at the start of these long and sometimes hazardous journeys, he was already in his sixth decade and in poor health.

SWITZERLAND

On these tours, which took in travel along the Rhine, Turner amassed a further 600 drawings and sketches in his sketchbooks, demonstrating that he still maintained the same *modus operandi* he had always used. He also took some of his roll sketchbooks, which were subsequently broken up, containing about 150 exquisite small watercolours that he executed in the evenings wherever he was staying.

Before embarking on his second trip in 1842, Turner asked his agent, Thomas Griffith, to take 15 of these small watercolours as samples to gain commissions for ten larger versions for which he was to charge 80 guineas. In the event Griffith secured orders for nine. The buyers were Hugh Munro of Novar who took five, and John Ruskin

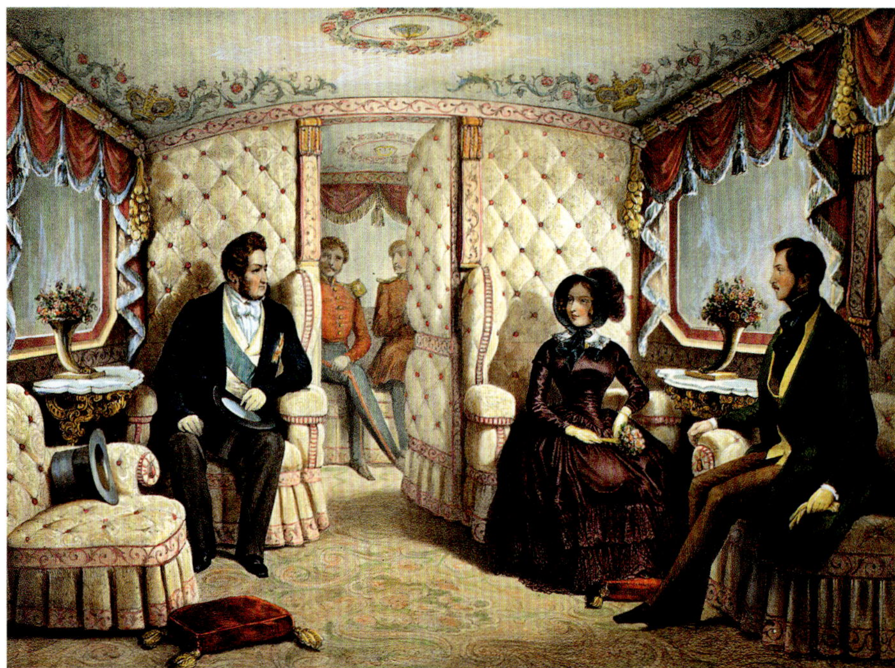

Above: Interior of the Queen's Railway Carriage, *Edouard Pingret, lithograph, 1844. This image was engraved by Jules David and shows the meeting between Queen Victoria and Prince Albert, and King Louis-Philippe.*

and Elhanan Bicknell who each purchased two. In 1843 Turner repeated the same exercise with less success, selling only six, four to Munro and two to Ruskin, who remarked that they represented the apogee of his watercolours.

By the time of Turner's final tour of Switzerland in 1844, *Modern Painters* was beginning to have an effect on sales of the artist's work, with new patrons such as the pen manufacturer Joseph Gillott (1799–1872), and Bicknell buying *Palestrina – Composition*, which had remained unsold since its first showing at the Academy in 1830.

MEETING LOUIS-PHILIPPE

King of the French, Louis-Philippe (1773–1850) spent two periods of exile in England, the first during the

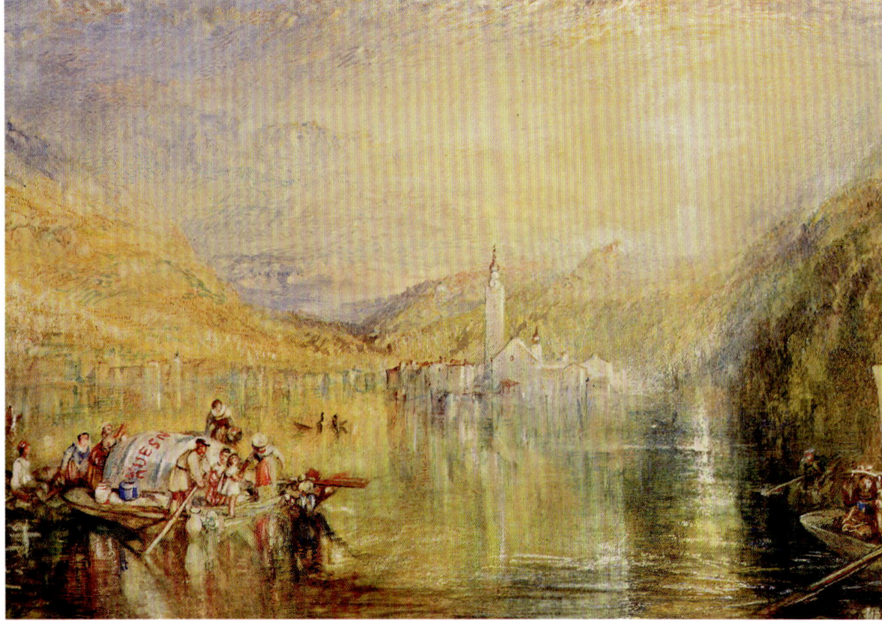

Left: Kussnacht, Lake of Lucerne, Switzerland, *watercolour and bodycolour, 1843. This small village is where, in 1307, William Tell killed Gessler, the enforcer of the brutal Habsburg regime.*

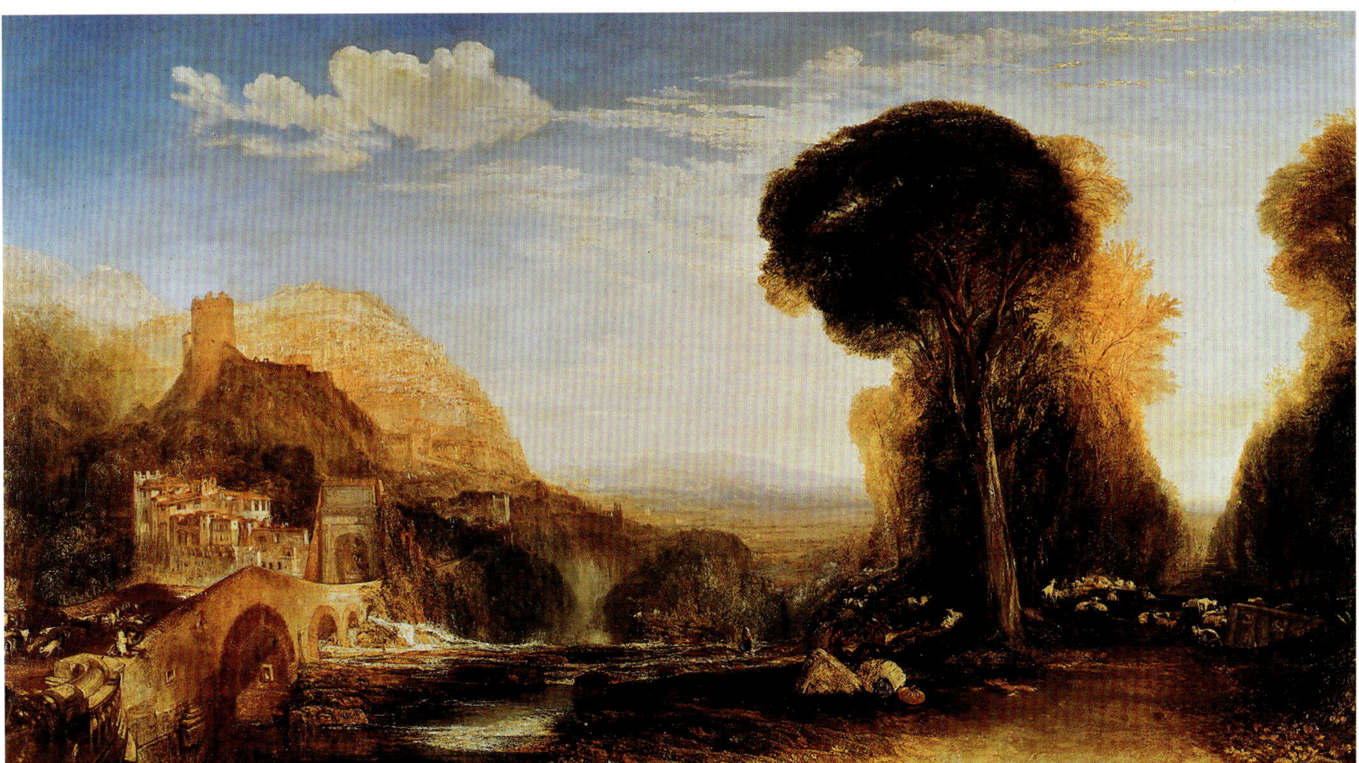

Above: Palestrina – Composition, *oil on canvas, 1830. Turner did not use 'view' in the title, as this is an imaginary landscape.*

THE DEATH OF TWO FRIENDS

Sir David Wilkie contracted malaria during a trip to the Middle East and died onboard ship during his return voyage in June 1841. He was buried at sea, and Turner commemorated the event with his painting *Peace – Burial at Sea*, which was exhibited at the Academy the following year. A death that was more personal to Turner occurred in November 1841 – that of his friend Sir Francis Chantrey. Earlier Chantrey had purchased *Ducal Palace, Dogano with Part of San Georgio, Venice* at the Academy exhibition. Chantrey, who had no children, provided a bequest for the nation to "purchase works of fine art of the highest merit", by British artists or works by foreign artists if executed in Britain. For this he left more than £100,000 (equivalent today to about £7 million).

Napoleonic Wars from 1800 until 1815, and the second after the 1848 Revolution. In the interim, in 1830, he was crowned as King of the French. During his first period of exile, he lived near the Thames at Twickenham, close to Turner's house. Although there is no record of them actually meeting there, it is known that they were acquainted before the 1830s. In the autumn of 1844, Turner watched Louis-Philippe arriving at Portsmouth on a state visit, which he recorded in paint. The next year when Turner was in Normandy, Louis-Philippe invited the artist to dine with him at his château at Eu.

This was to be Turner's last journey on the Continent. During the trip he executed 20 subtle watercolours that together made up the Eu and Tréport Sketchbook.

Below: Tell's Chapel, Lake Lucerne, *watercolour, 1841. Turner appears to have been interested in the legendary Romantic folk hero William Tell.*

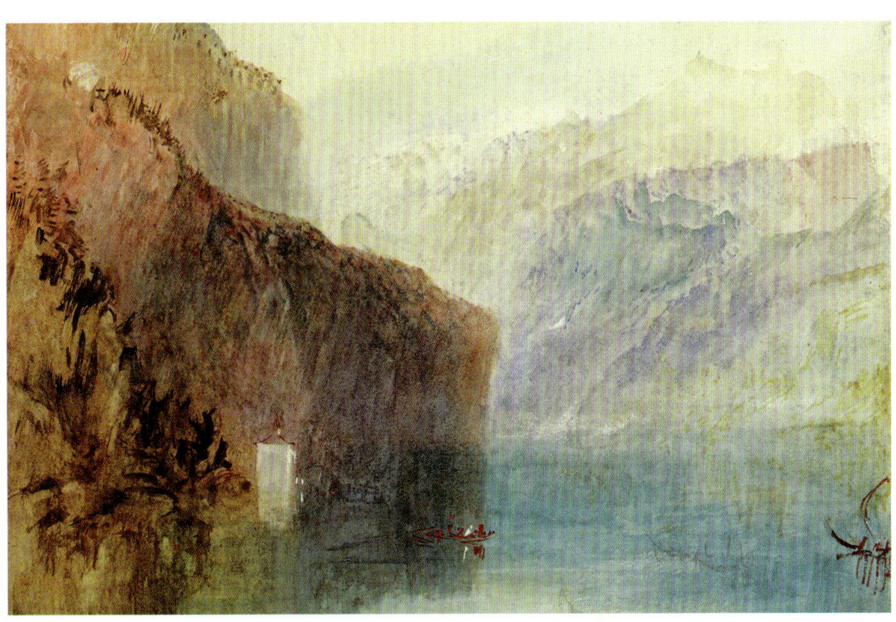

THE FINAL YEARS

During 1846, Turner set up an alternative home with Mrs Booth and was cared for by her in her house in Chelsea, at a time when he was becoming increasingly ill. Despite his poor health he continued to work almost to the end.

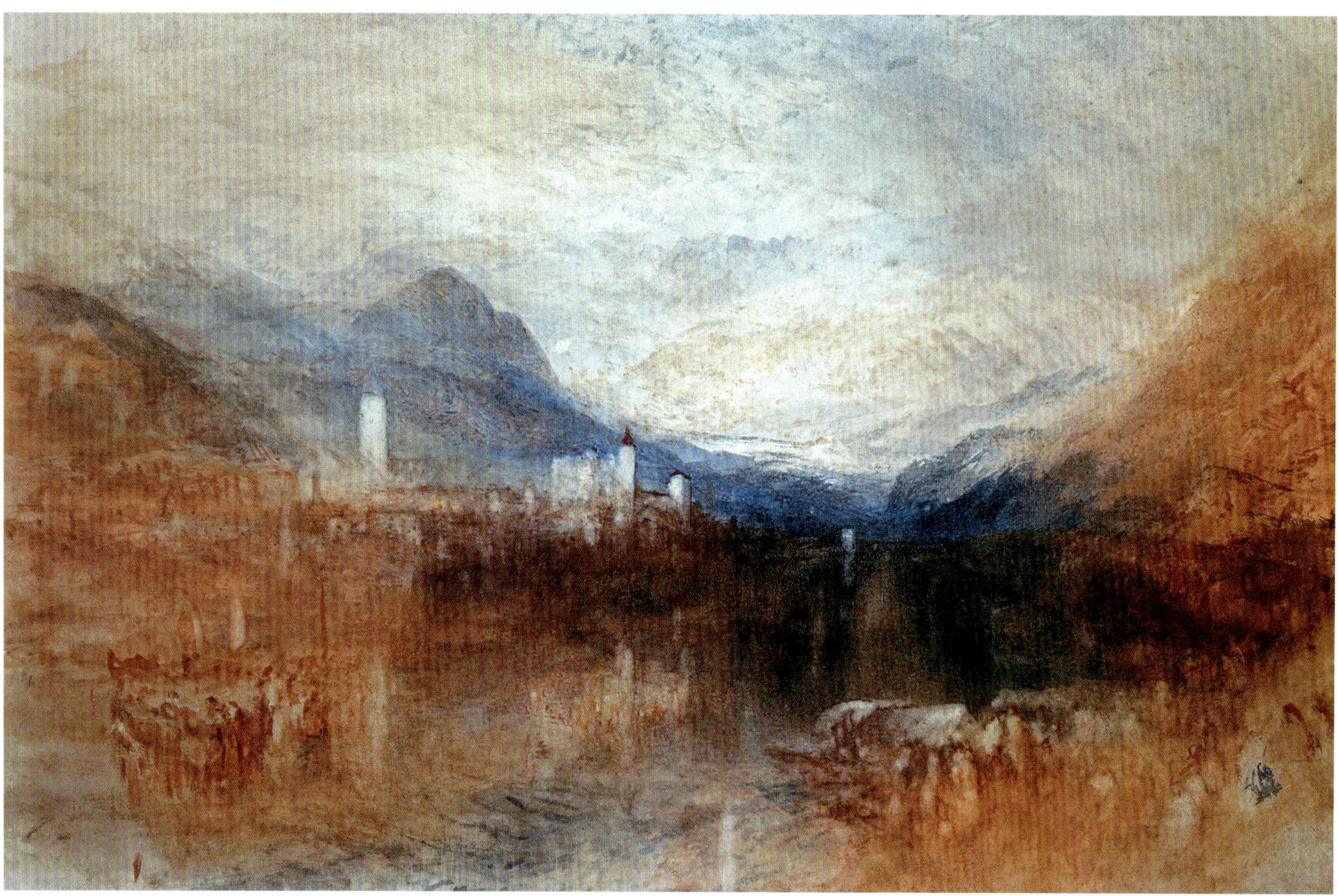

Above: Pallanza, Lake Maggiore (1848–50), *watercolour. A watercolour that encapsulates Turner's oeuvre, distilled into this tranquil topographical scene. A suitable epitaph for a lifetime's work.*

Turner continued to visit Margate on a regular basis, but sometime during the autumn of 1846 he moved into a property overlooking the Thames at Chelsea, leased by Sophia Booth, where they lived together as Mr and Mrs Booth.

A HOUSE IN CHELSEA

At the time Chelsea was a small village on the outskirts of London, with a quiet stretch of river viewed by Turner from the house's roof terrace. Turner set up his studio and in 1848 took on a studio assistant, Francis Sherrell (1826–1916), in exchange for painting lessons.

To the last, Turner was secretive about his personal life among his Academy friends, but it was not difficult to keep this secret since he had by now adopted the habit of staying with the Ruskin and Bicknell families as well. He spent very little time at Queen Anne Street, which was by now becoming dilapidated. The gallery skylight was broken and leaked rain water, resulting in a wet floor and even damage to some of the pictures on display. His housekeeper Hannah Danby was still there and quite used to her master's long absences. However, her face had become infected by a skin condition that made her look decrepit, one visitor remarking "one hardly knew what to feel most, terror or pity".

THE ROYAL ACADEMY

Despite his failing health and age, Turner continued to paint at Chelsea and submit work to the Academy. His last submissions were in 1850, but even in 1851, which was the year of his death, he still managed to attend the Varnishing Days, offering advice to his fellow Academicians. Although Turner never achieved the presidency of the Royal Academy, during 1845 he had occupied the president's chair in place of Shee, who was ill, and was subsequently appointed Deputy President under the acting presidency of his friend George Jones. Turner held this post until the end of 1846,

when he also resigned as Auditor.
Shee died in 1850, the last of the
Academicians elevated at the same
time as Turner, and he was succeeded
by Eastlake.

ILLNESS

Turner had been intermittently ill for
much of his adult life, particularly in the
winter months. In the autumn of 1848
he fell victim to the cholera epidemic
sweeping the country. At the time,
Chelsea was prone to flooding, the
Thames containing a great deal of
sewage. Sophia Booth took Turner
away to Deal on the Kent coast to
recuperate, attended by Dr David Price,
a physician they had known in Margate.
It was, however, a combination of Mrs
Booth's nursing care and the artist's
own robust constitution that enabled
him to make a full recovery.

The couple returned to Margate in
the summer of 1850 where he painted
more large watercolours. In his last
year his diseased teeth were removed
and he was put on a diet of milk and
rum. Dr Price frequently attended
him in Chelsea when required.
Turner ran up a doctor's bill of over
£500, which remained unpaid at
the time of his death. Despite these
setbacks he remained active during
1850, and he went to view the
construction site of Crystal Palace
in London's Hyde Park and visited
at least two fellow artists.

DEATH

The last social function that Turner
attended was a Royal Academy dinner in
May 1851. By the summer he was too
frail to leave his home, the only visitor
being Dr Price, who attended him every
week for the final three months of his
life. Turner died on 19 December,
looking from his bed at a bright winter
sun that greeted him for the last time.

Right: Turner's Burial in the Crypt of
St Paul's Cathedral, *George Jones, oil
on millboard, 1852. From Turner's own
gallery his body was taken to St Paul's
Cathedral, where he was interred on
30th December in the crypt, next to Sir
Joshua Reynolds.*

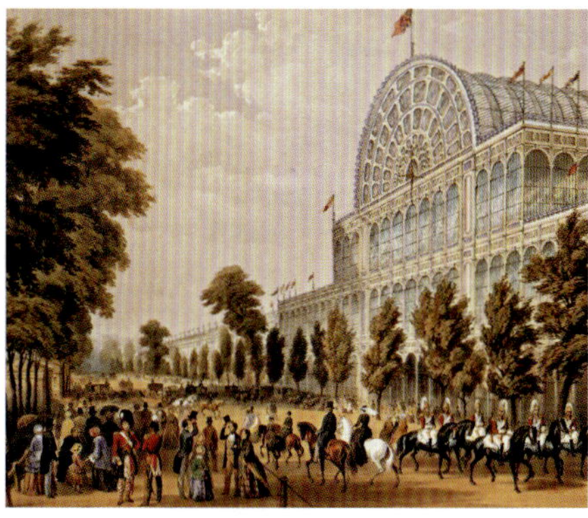

Above: Great Exhibition, 1851: South Side
of Crystal Palace from Near Prince's
Gate, *Brannon and Picken, lithograph,
c.1851. Due to the popularity of the
event, many lithographs were produced.*

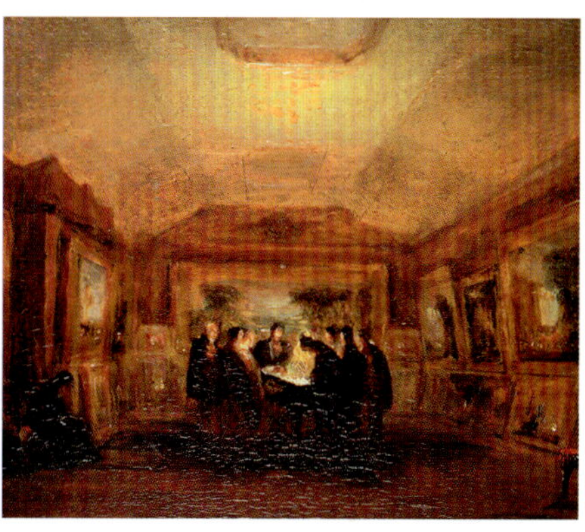

Above: Turner's Body Lying in State,
*George Jones, oil on millboard, 1852. His
body 'lay in state' in his gallery at Queen
Anne Street so that friends and colleagues
could pay their last respects to him.*

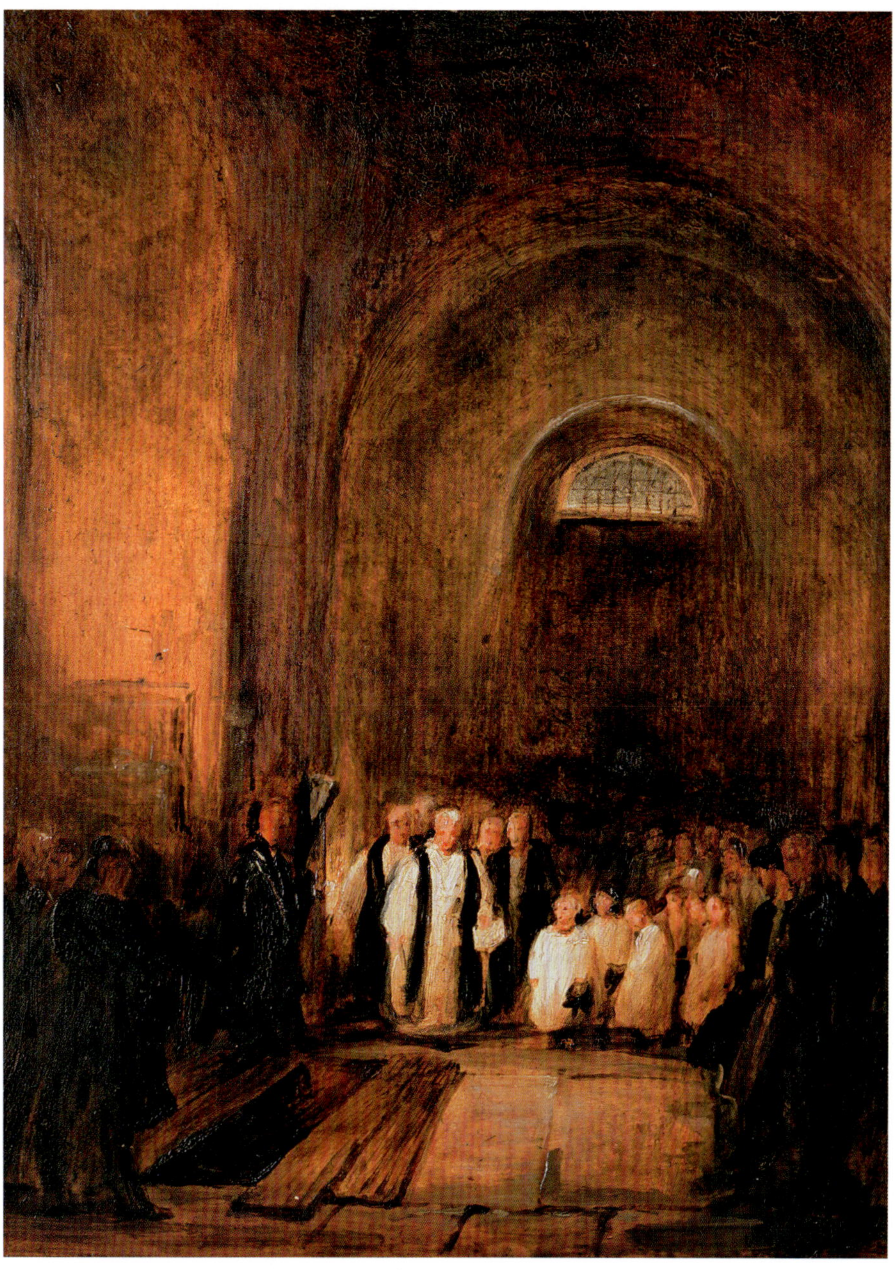

LEGACY AND REPUTATION

Turner's death, his massive collection of paintings and grand charitable ambitions provoked tensions over the execution of his will, with arguments arising between his family and the brotherhood he had established with his fellow artists.

Following Turner's funeral on 30 December 1851, his will was read to the executors at Queen Anne Street, his solicitor Henry Harpur, Hugh Munro, Thomas Griffith and his fellow Academicians Philip Hardwick and George Jones. The other executor was his old friend Henry Scott Trimmer who did not attend.

TURNER'S WILL

After writing his second will in 1831, Turner added a number of codicils. In 1839, he revoked a clause in his will that benefited Sarah Danby and his daughters, indicating that he regarded his brother artists as his family. He made Hannah Danby the sole custodian of his pictures, adding more codicils during the 1840s to enable the building of alms-houses for "the relief of decayed and indigent artists" on his land at Twickenham. Turner also wanted a gallery set up in his own name as an adjunct to the National Gallery to display his pictures. Turner's family disputed the contents of the will on the grounds that he was not of sound mind. The court case was not resolved until 1856, with the family gaining control of his money and property, estimated at £140,000 (about £12 million today).

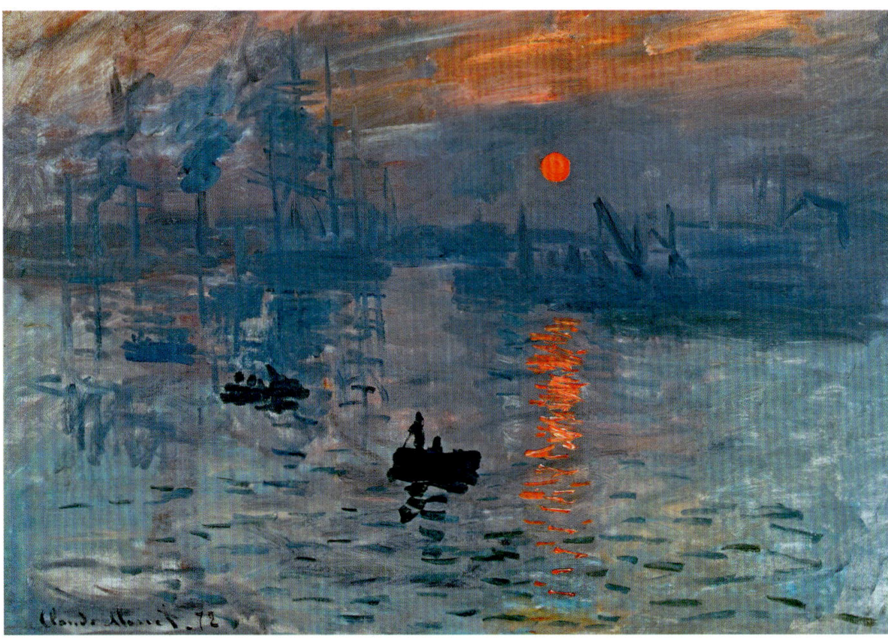

Above: Impression Sunrise, *Claude Monet, oil on canvas, 1872. The painting that led to the use of the term 'Impressionism', a movement that was anticipated in much of Turner's work several decades before.*

His paintings were given to the nation in the form of the 'Turner Bequest'. There were around 300 oil paintings in various states of completion and condition, and nearly 20,000 drawings and watercolours, including his 300 sketchbooks. Most of this work is now in the Clore Gallery at Tate Britain in London. Also, there are nine major works at the National Gallery in London, including the two designated to hang alongside the Claude Lorrain pictures.

Turner's charitable ambitions did not materialize and neither did his desire to create a professorship of landscape painting at the Royal Academy.

HIS LEGACY

Although Ruskin had been named as an executor in Turner's will, he refused to take on that duty, sensing a quarrel. However, he maintained his support of the artist and his work after the issues had been resolved. Ruskin volunteered to sort and catalogue his pictures and in February 1857 a temporary Turner Gallery was created at Marlborough House in London, which showed about

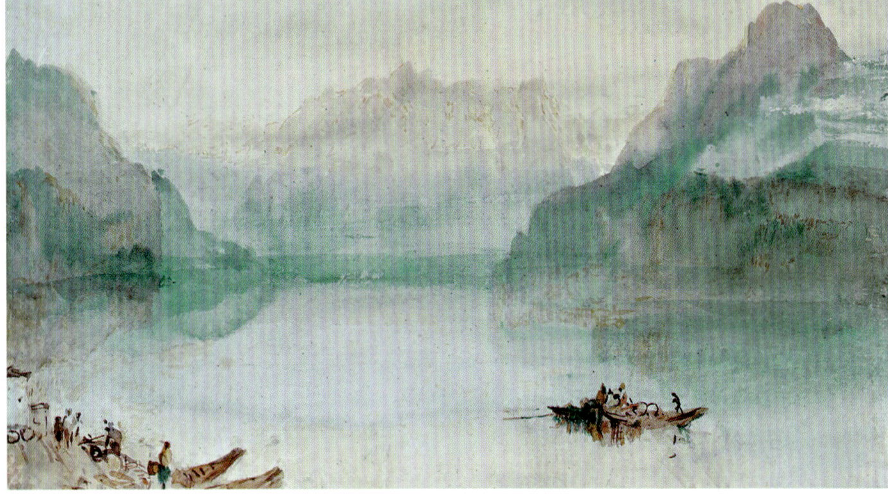

Left: Bay of Uri, Lake Lucerne from Brunnen, *watercolour, 1833. Turner was known to subsequent generations of artists as the 'painter of light', exemplified in this watercolour.*

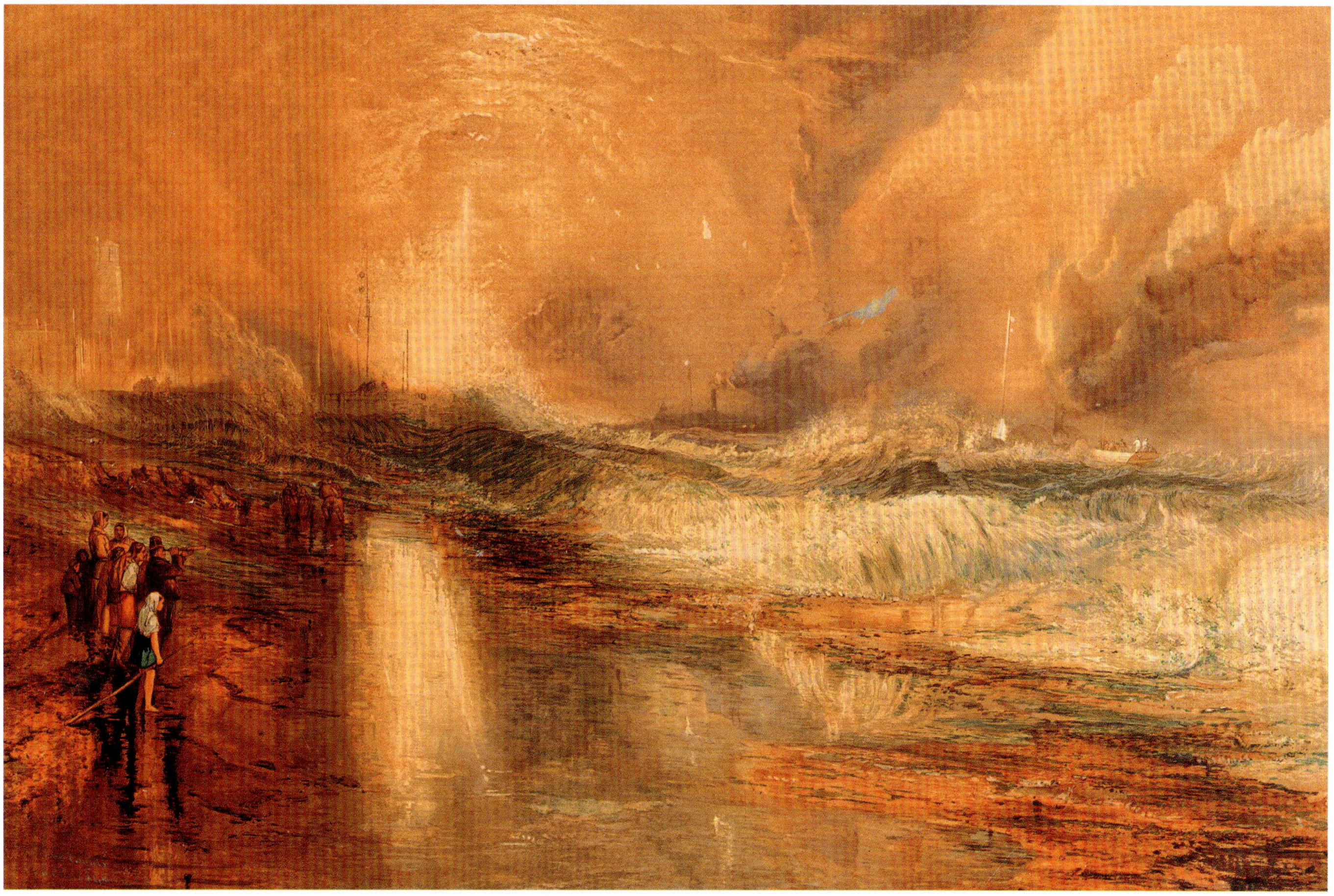

100 watercolours and the same number of oil paintings. The exhibition travelled to Manchester later that year, and Ruskin had selected more work to to show at Marlborough House.

In 1859, the British School Galleries opened at South Kensington Museum, and works were transferred here from Marlborough House. Some work was moved to the National Gallery then installed at the Tate Gallery. Many of Turner's drawings and watercolours were damaged in a flood in 1928, and were moved to the British Museum, where they remain. In 1987, the Tate's Clore Gallery was opened to house his paintings.

INFLUENCE

There is no doubting Turner's influence, both direct and indirect, on subsequent generations of artists, as Claude Lorrain

Right: Battersea Reach from Lindsay House, *JM Whistler, oil on canvas, 1864–71. The fog and mist on the Thames inspired Whistler, and he captured the ethereal effects of light as Turner had done before him.*

had influenced him. Recently there has been an exhibition and discussion about his direct influence on James McNeill Whistler and Claude Monet. However, he influenced others such as Vincent van Gogh indirectly – another northern European artist who responded to the unique light of the Mediterranean. Turner was the first to explore the use of colour for its own sake, showing that it could convey emotion and abstract concepts as well as pictorial representation,

Above: Rockets and Blue Lights, *chromolithograph, 1855. After his death Turner's images continued to be reproduced. This one is on a large scale, reflecting the importance of the original work executed and exhibited in 1840.*

anticipating Wassily Kandinsky's Improvisations by at least 70 years. However, he had many critics during the 20th century, and we have only recently begun again to fully appreciate his genius.

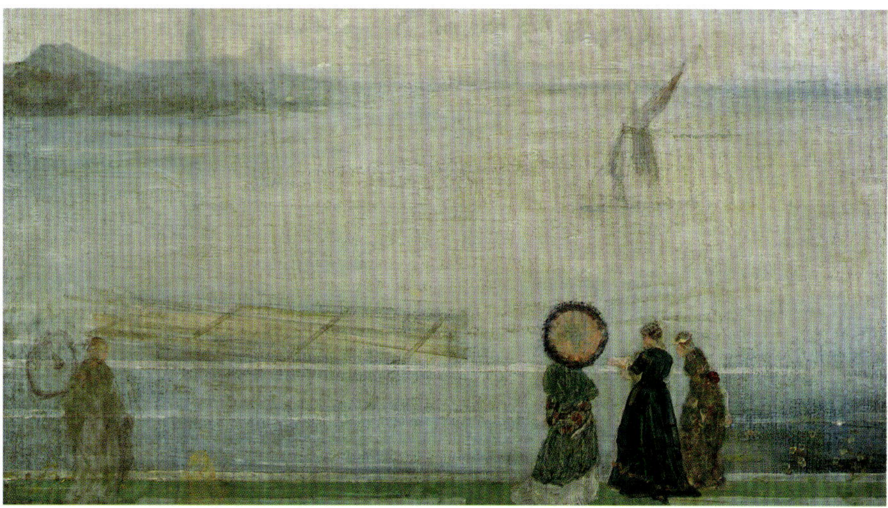

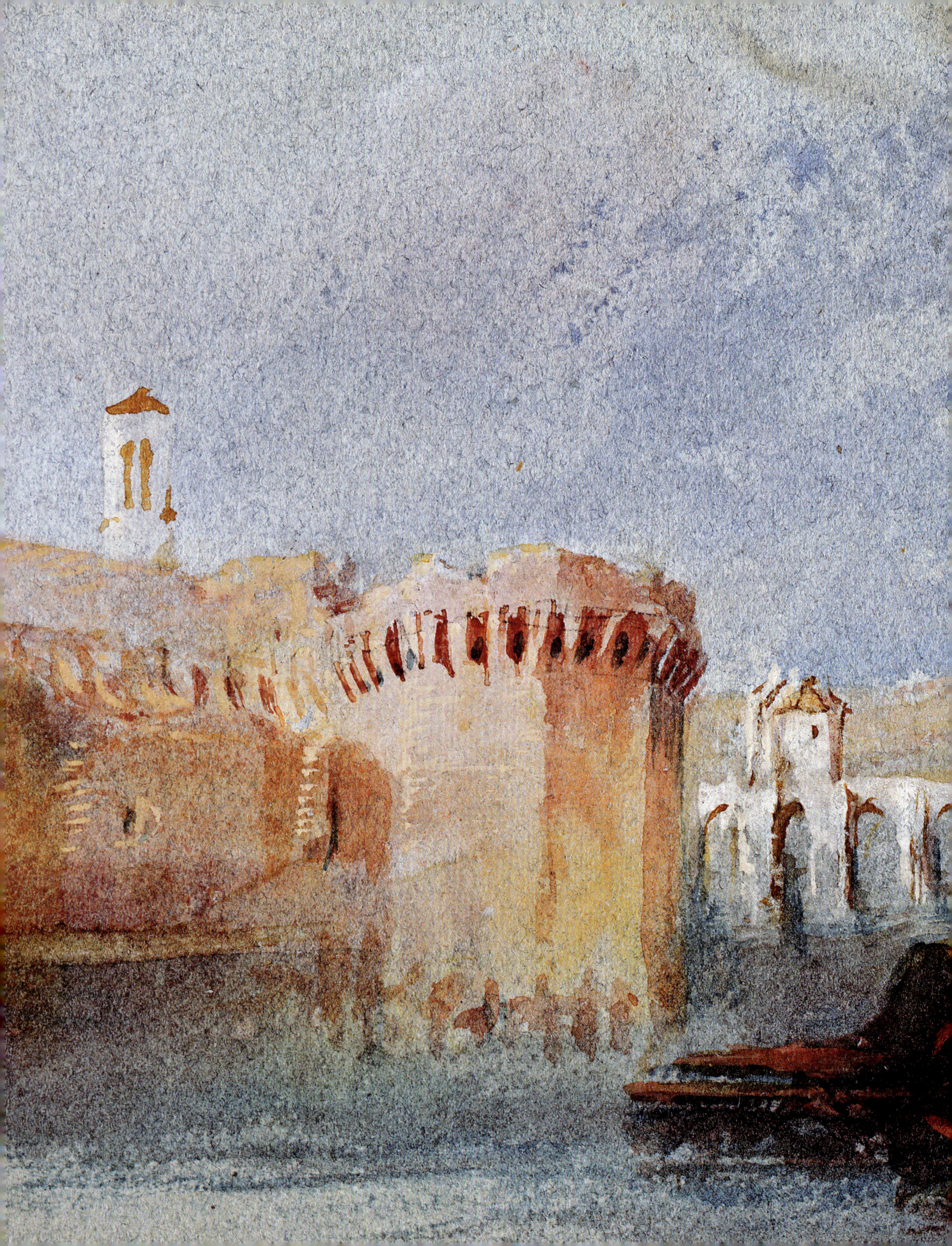

THE GALLERY

Part two of this book examines many of the key works of Turner's oeuvre in chronological order, from his early beginnings as a student at the Royal Academy schools to his final self-reflexive days spent at Chelsea. The Gallery contains many of his best-known works, such as *Rain, Steam and Speed*, as well as many of his lesser-known but equally enthralling paintings. Some are obviously topographically motivated, particularly his early works, while others are more to do with recreating the atmosphere of the landscape that he trusts will find empathy with his viewers. What his pictures all have in common is Turner's loving embrace of the landscape, which had such an extraordinary impact on his life.

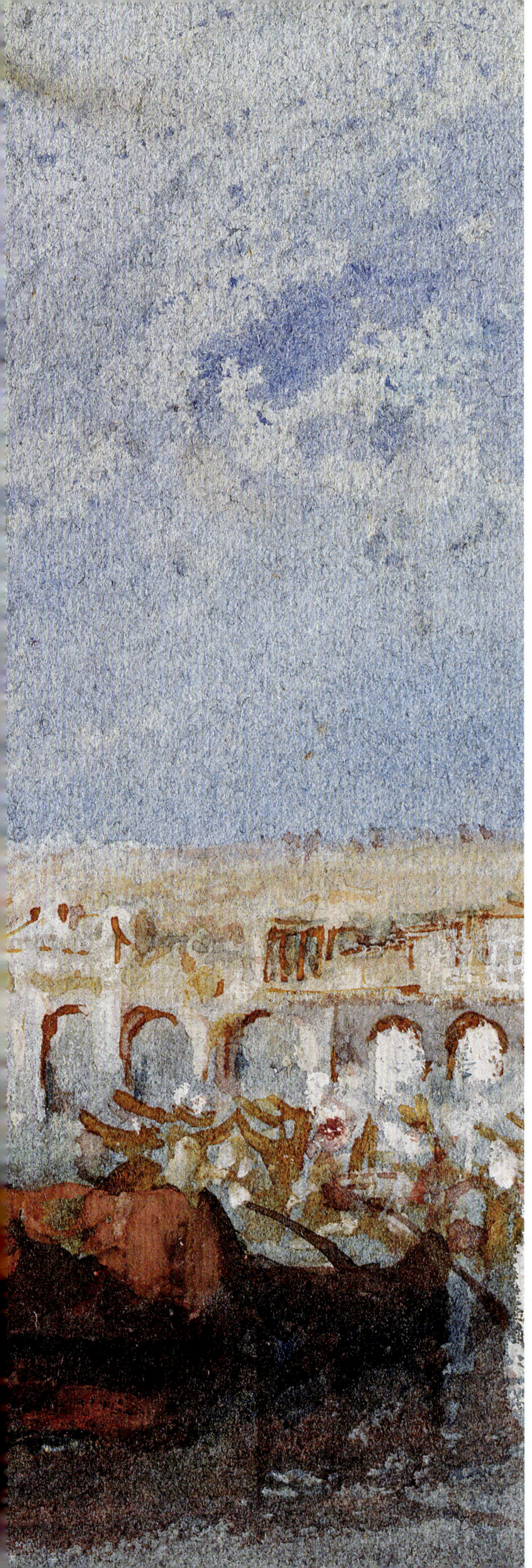

Left: Angers: The Walls of the Doutre with the Tower of the Church of La Trinité, *gouache and watercolour, 1826–8. The magnificent château walls are given prominence in this watercolour because of their importance to the town's defence.*

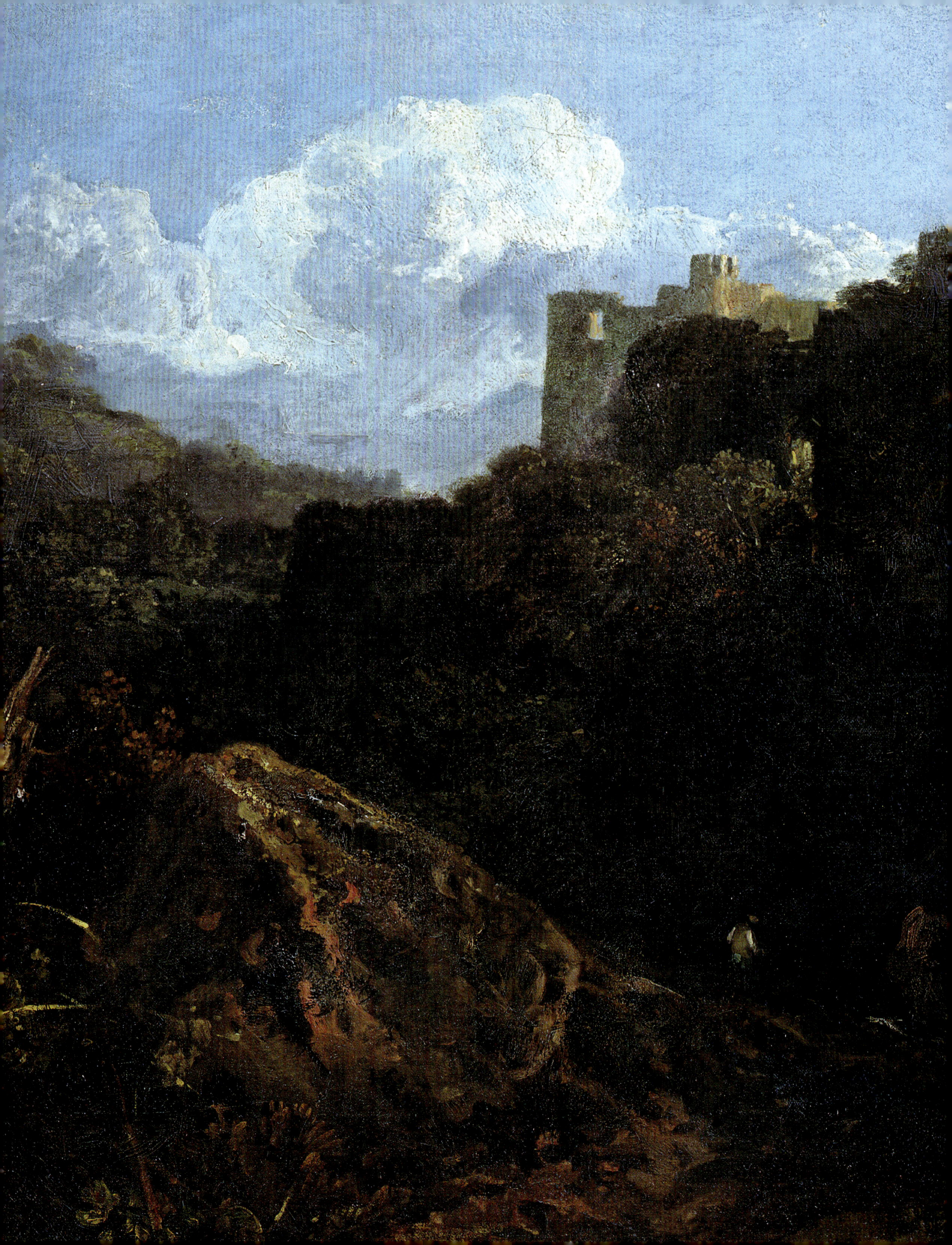

THE EARLY WORKS BEFORE 1800

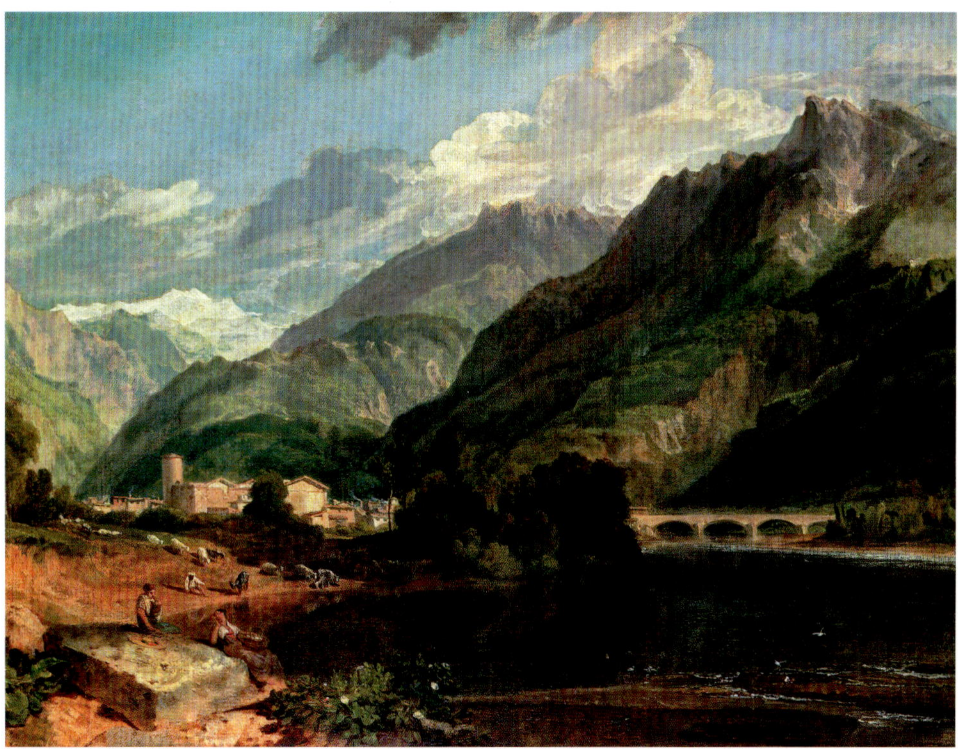

Although his works before 1800 were mainly topographical in nature and used watercolour, Turner had embraced the Picturesque aesthetic in his paintings in accordance with other contemporary artists working in that medium. By the turn of the 18th into the 19th century, Turner had mastered this aesthetic and was already experimenting with alternative notions of Romantic painting using oil. If he were to aspire toward membership of the Royal Academy, he needed to master that medium as well. This section covers his transition from student at the Royal Academy schools to Associate Membership of that august body, a period when he was assimilating the influence of his peers and the Old Masters as a foundation for his own elevation to one of the greatest painters of all time.

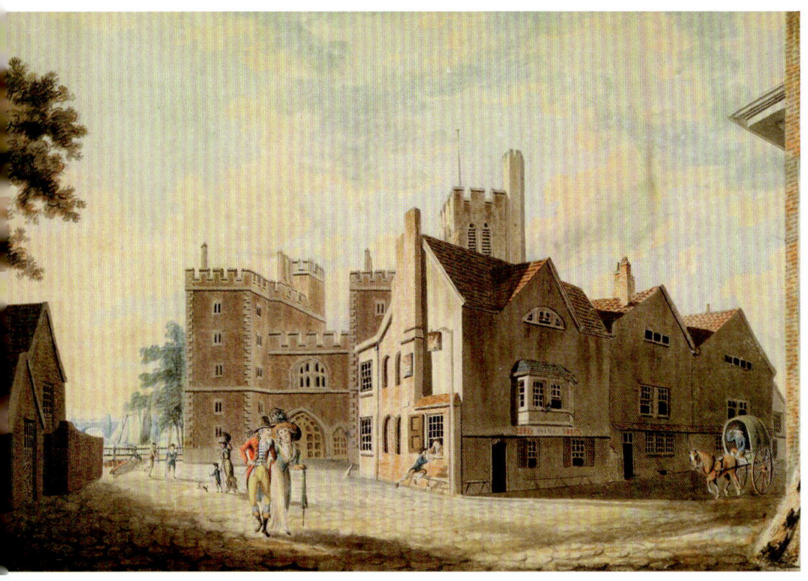

A View of the Archbishop's Palace, Lambeth, 1790, pencil and watercolour, Indianapolis Museum of Art, IN, USA, 27 x 38cm (11 x 15in)

The choice of subject was possibly anecdotal sentiment, since his friends John and Sarah Danby were married at St Mary's Church (shown in the middle distance), alluded to by the couple walking hand in hand in the foreground. The painting was Turner's first watercolour to be exhibited at the Royal Academy in 1790. Although unsold at the exhibition, the Hon Edward Lascelles purchased the picture in 1797.

Interior of St John's Palace, Eltham, 1793, graphite and watercolour, Paul Mellon Collection, Yale Center for British Art, CT, USA, 33 x 27cm (13 x 11in)

This hall, which boasts one of the largest hammerbeam roofs in England, dates back to the 15th century as part of one of the great medieval royal palaces. During the English Civil War, the palace was sacked and left in a completely derelict state, until it was eventually restored in the 1930s. Turner has captured the ruinous state of the hall's return to nature in a Picturesque manner.

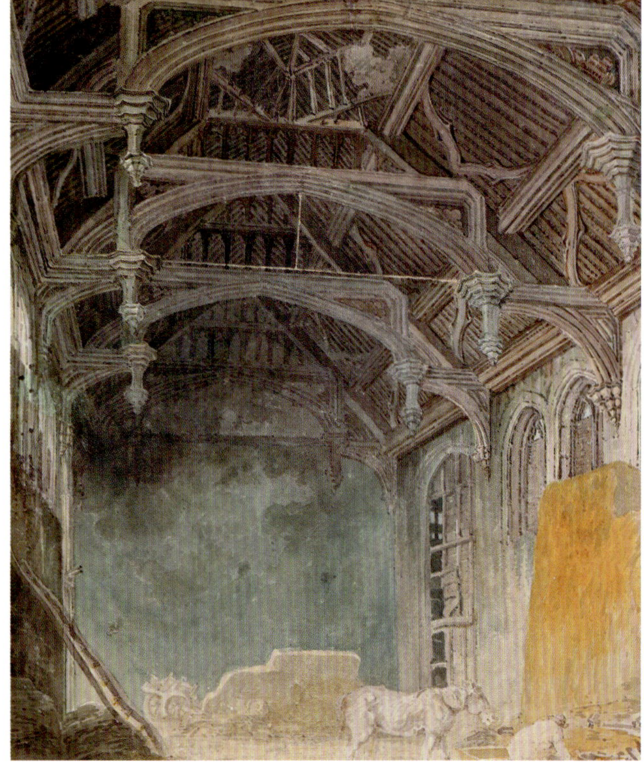

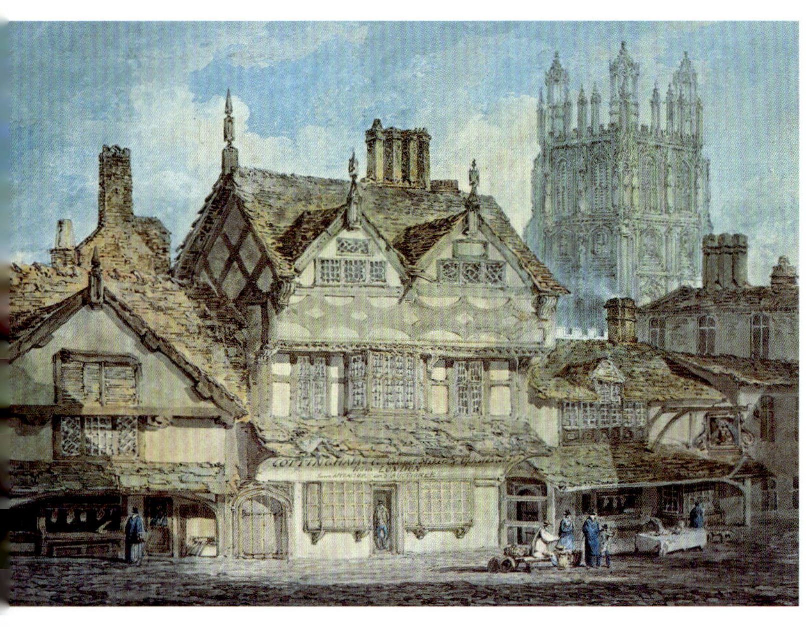

Wrexham, Denbighshire, 1793, watercolour, Victoria and Albert Museum, London, UK, 24 x 32cm (9 x 12½in)

At the time of Turner's birth, Wrexham was little more than a small market town, but by the time of his visit in 1792, it had become one of the pioneering towns of the early Industrial Revolution. For this delightful watercolour though, Turner has chosen to highlight the medieval aspects of the market square, perhaps as a comment on the burgeoning pace of progress.

Clare Hall and the West End of Kings College Chapel, Cambridge, 1793, pencil and watercolour, Paul Mellon Collection, Yale Center for British Art, CT, USA, 20 x 27cm (8 x 11in)

This somewhat unusual view of Clare Hall (later to become Clare College) with Kings College chapel behind shows Turner's ability to approach a motif in new ways. The strange juxtaposition of the early classical proportions of Clare Hall and the late medieval Gothic of the chapel highlights the changes in English architecture in the 16th and 17th centuries.

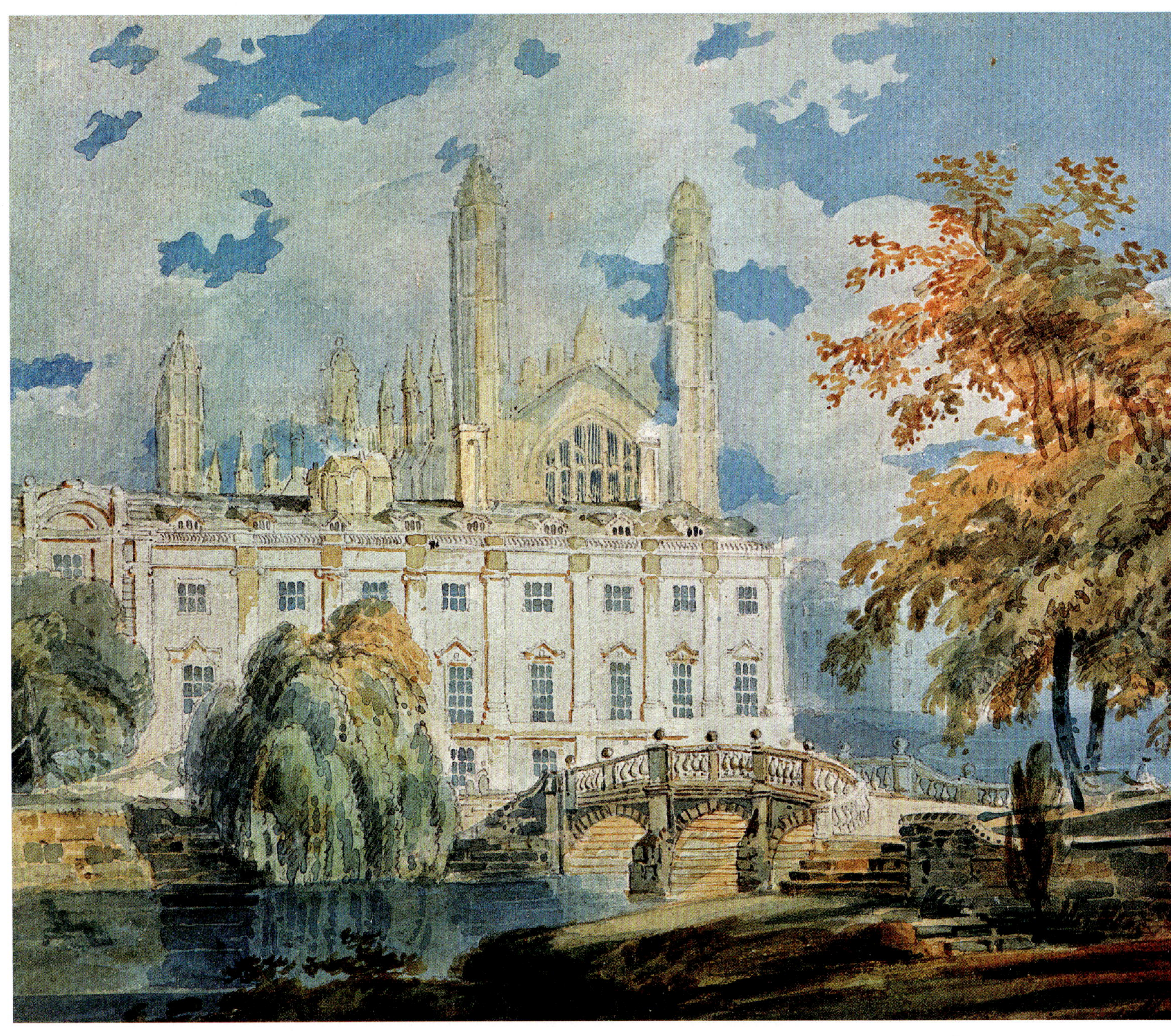

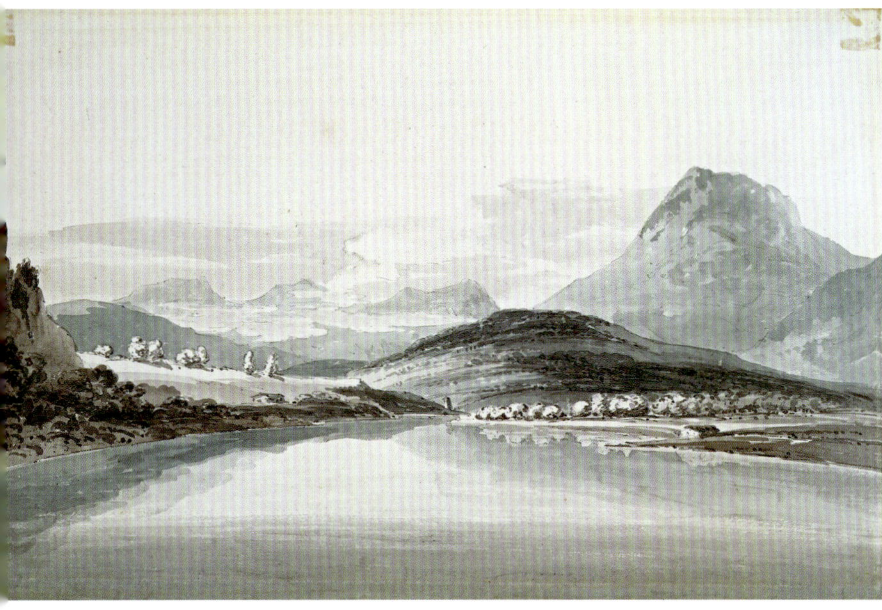

Lake of Klontal, after John Robert Cozens, 1794–7, pencil and watercolour, Leeds Art Gallery, UK, 24 x 37cm (9 x 14½in)

Turner was no exception to the rule that most artists copy their masters while serving their 'apprenticeship'. This painting was a derivative of one produced by the watercolour artist John Robert Cozens (1752–97). Cozens had a profound influence on Turner, Girtin and Constable who thought him a 'genius of landscape'. It is likely that Turner saw this work at the home of Dr Thomas Monro, an enthusiastic collector of Cozens's work. Monro tended Cozens in the last years of his short life, when he became insane.

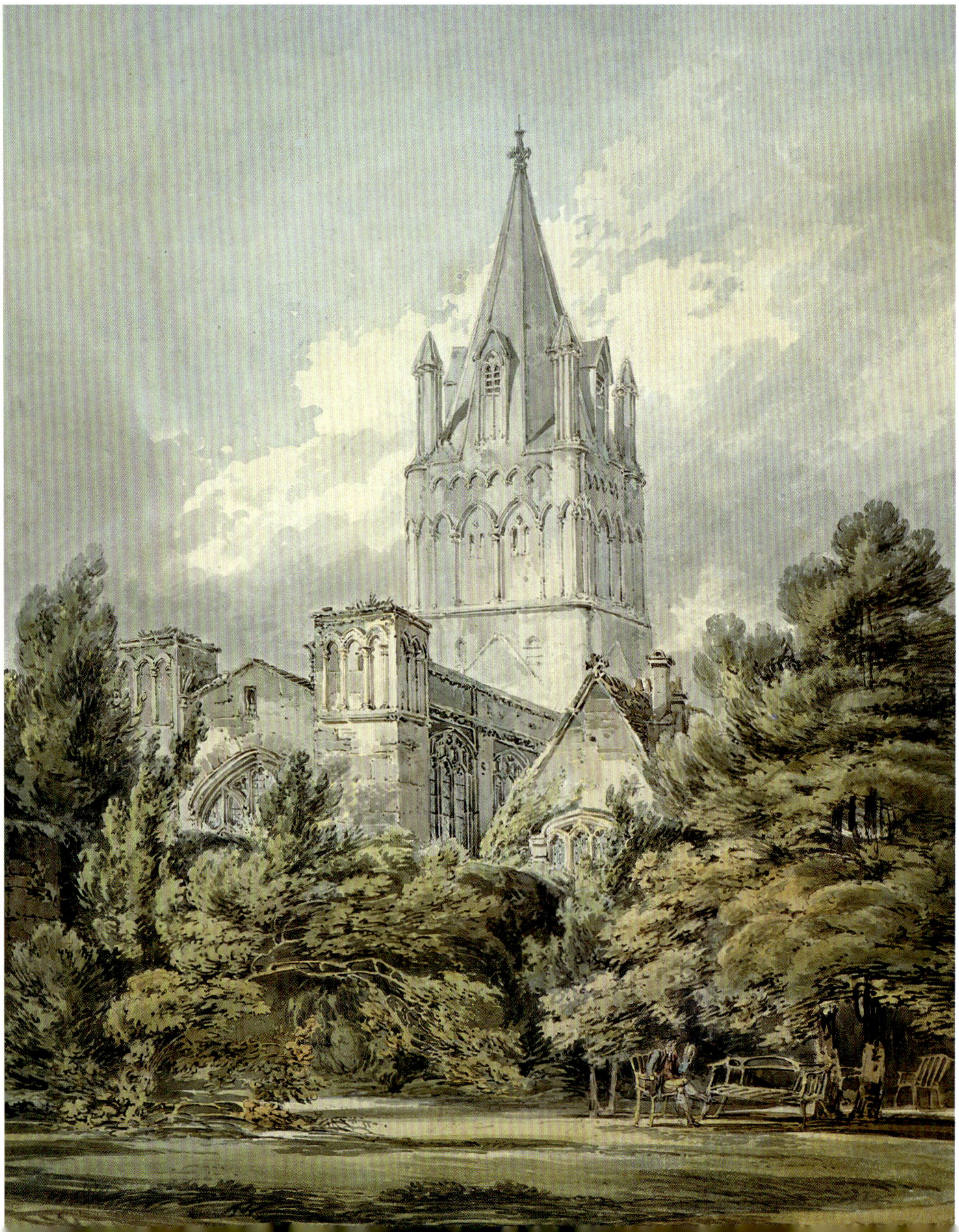

Christ Church, Oxford, 1794, graphite and watercolour, Fitzwilliam Museum, Cambridge, UK, 40 x 32cm (16 x 12½in)

In this watercolour, Turner has elected to depict Christ Church Cathedral, situated in the centre of the College at Oxford. Originally the cathedral was a priory church, elevated to a higher status by Henry VIII during the Reformation, re-founding the College as Christ Church at the same time. The college remains the largest within the University of Oxford.

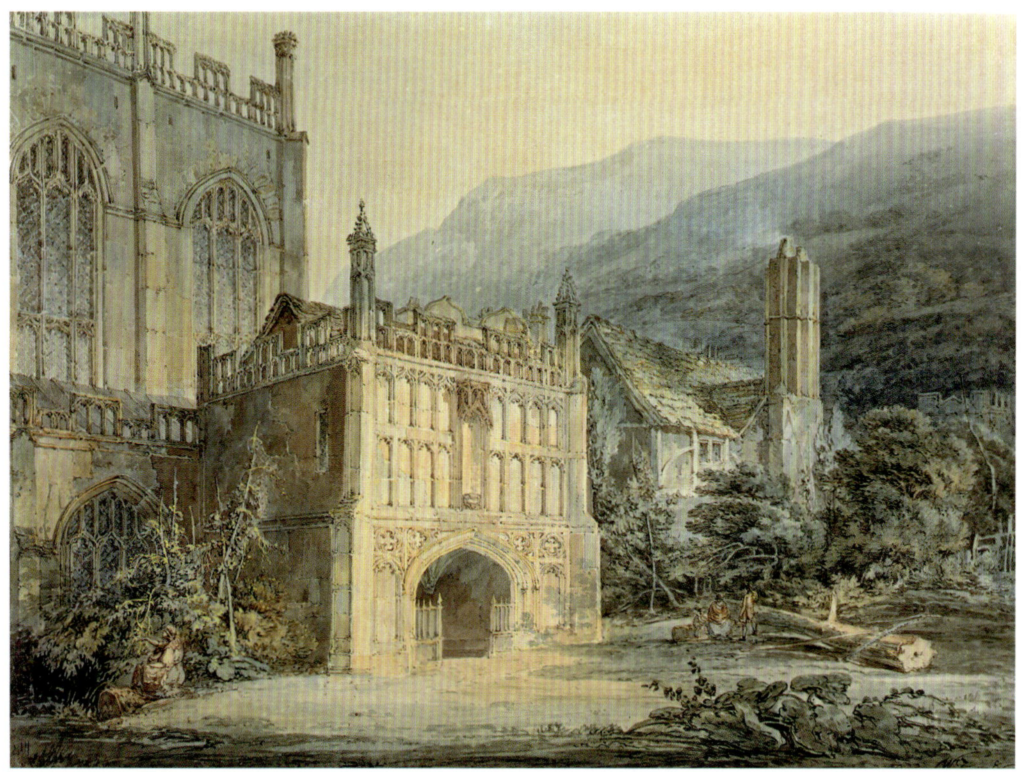

Porch of Great Malvern Abbey, 1794, watercolour, Whitworth Art Gallery, University of Manchester, UK, 23 x 43cm (9 x 17in)

Turner travelled to Great Malvern in the summer of 1793, but there are no actual sketchbooks of the tour. This watercolour, executed and exhibited at the Royal Academy the following year, adopts a Picturesque aesthetic juxtaposing the magnificent Gothic edifice with a humble cottage, set against a mountainous backdrop. The people in the foreground provide a sense of scale to the painting.

Matlock, Derbyshire, 1794, pencil and watercolour, Indianapolis Museum of Art, IN, USA, 11 x 17cm (4 x 7in)

In the summer of 1794, Turner toured the Peak District in search of material for John Walker's *Copper-Plate Magazine*. The artist made about forty drawings of the area in his Matlock Sketchbook but appears to have made only one finished watercolour of the town itself. The watercolour was used by Walker for an engraving the following year.

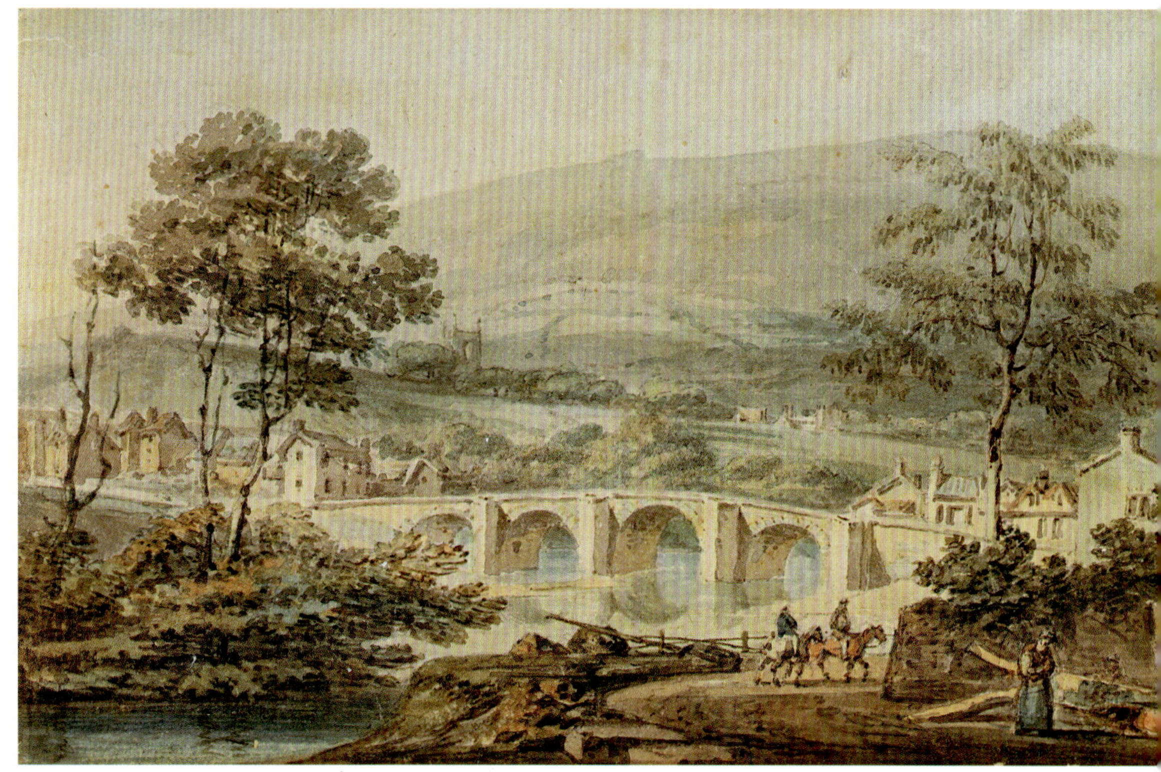

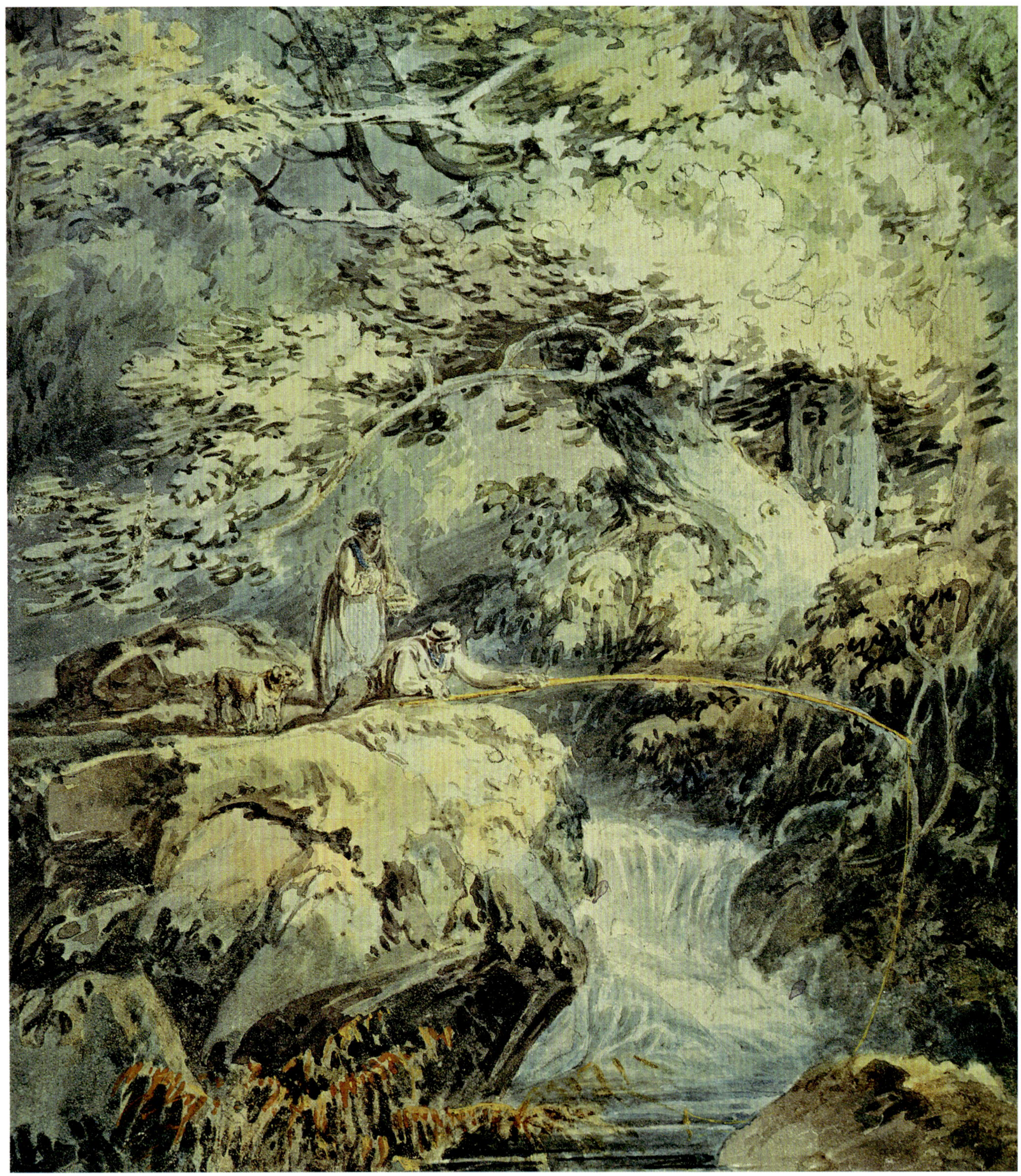

The Angler, 1794,
watercolour and graphite,
Paul Mellon Collection,
Yale Center for British Art,
CT, USA,
23 x 16cm (9 x 6in)

A Picturesque view, exemplified by the gnarled and damaged trees, Turner has depicted one of his favourite pastimes, angling. Little is known about this small work. The picture was never exhibited during his lifetime, suggesting that he executed it purely for pleasure, possibly on site. The title, and absence of a location, would also lend weight to this suggestion.

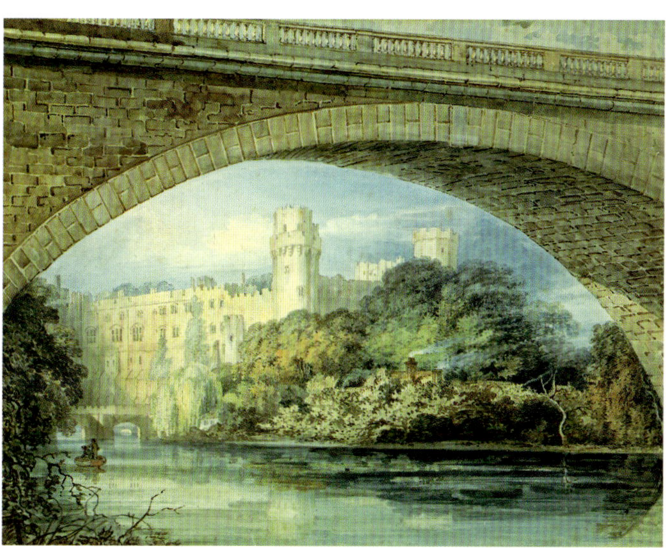

Warwick Castle and Bridge, 1794, pencil and watercolour, Whitworth Art Gallery, University of Manchester, UK, 43 x 53cm (17 x 21in)

The bridge, demonstrating Turner's talent for picture composition, beautifully frames the distant medieval castle. This is emphasized by the clarity of stonework on the bridge, contrasting the castle's ethereal nature, synonymous with much of the artist's later work. Turner was demonstrating his skill at capturing the reflective qualities of water, which was to be a feature of his later paintings.

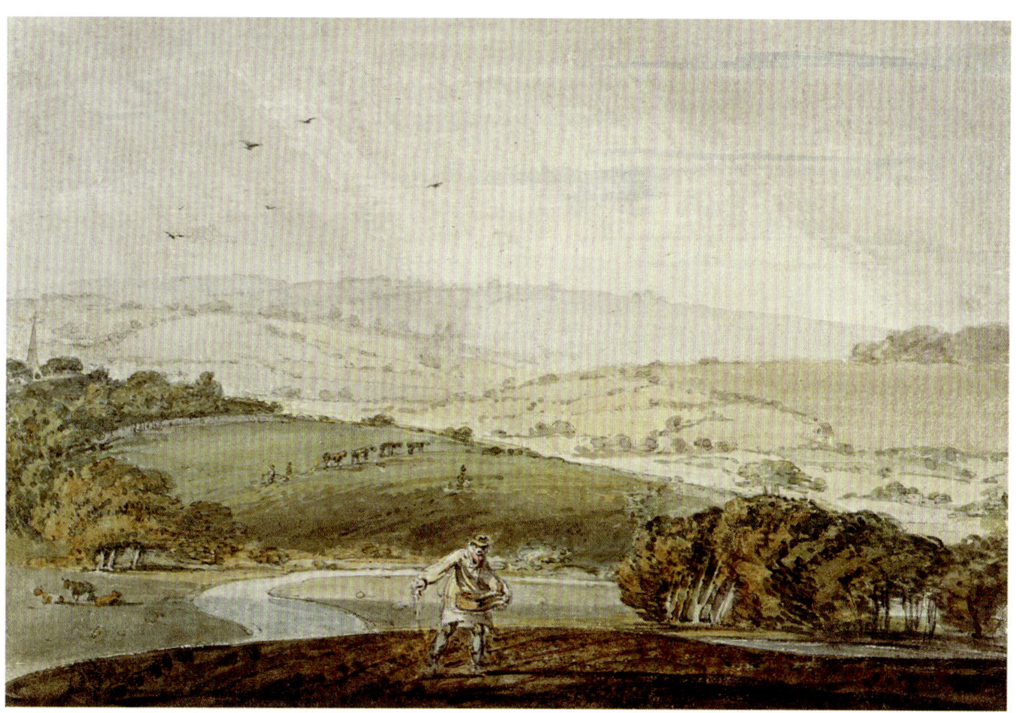

A Farmer Sowing with a River Valley and Rolling Hills Beyond, 1795, watercolour, Private Collection, 13 x 20cm (5 x 8in)

This is a departure for Turner from his topographical views, not being site specific. Instead the artist has centred on the farmer, perhaps highlighting the problems of the Agricultural Revolution. The farmer is still using hand sowing techniques, rejecting available mechanization. The 'rolling hills beyond' may suggest opposition to the Enclosure Acts being discussed in Parliament.

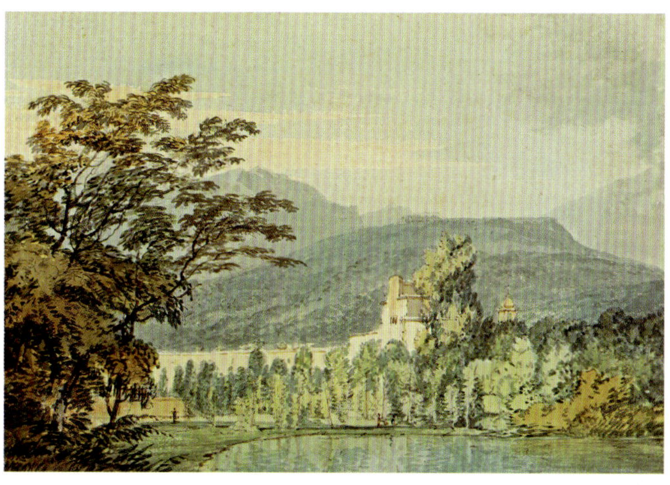

Sir William Hamilton's Villa, 1795, pencil and watercolour, Paul Mellon Collection, Yale Center for British Art, CT, USA, 17 x 24cm (7 x 9in)

Sir William Hamilton (1730–1803) was the British ambassador in Naples. While there, he met Horatio Nelson who was providing protection for the king of Naples, Ferdinand IV. Nelson also met Hamilton's new wife, Lady Emma, thereafter beginning one of the most well documented love affairs in history. Turner did not visit Naples until 1819, and must therefore have used another artist's painting for reference.

A Three Storied Georgian House in a Park, c.1795, wash over graphite, Paul Mellon Collection, Yale Center for British Art, CT, USA, 11 x 28cm (4 x 11in)

During the 1790s, Turner seemed almost obsessed with the execution of drawings and watercolours of houses and buildings. He was equally at home with vernacular buildings as much as the great architectural edifices, such as this unidentified classical building. The park has been landscaped in a 'picturesque' style, a scheme that was introduced by Lancelot 'Capability' Brown, who landscaped many of the fine country houses including Petworth House.

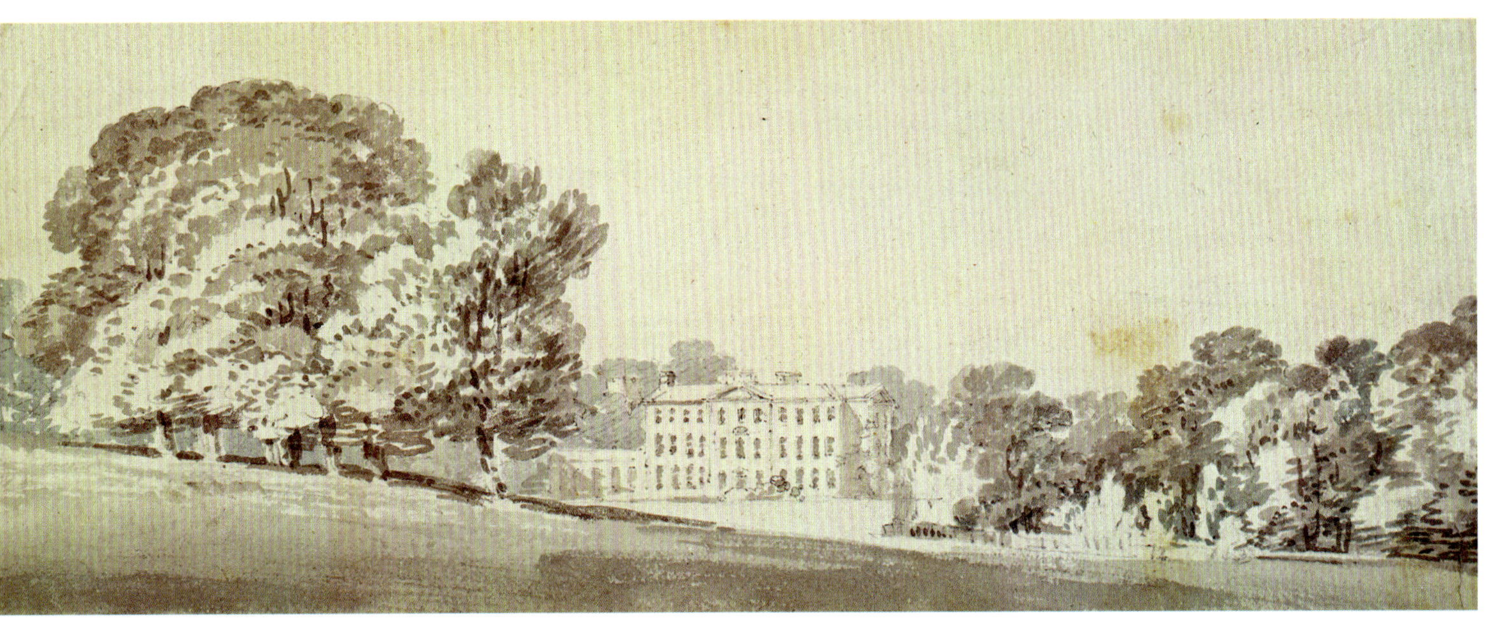

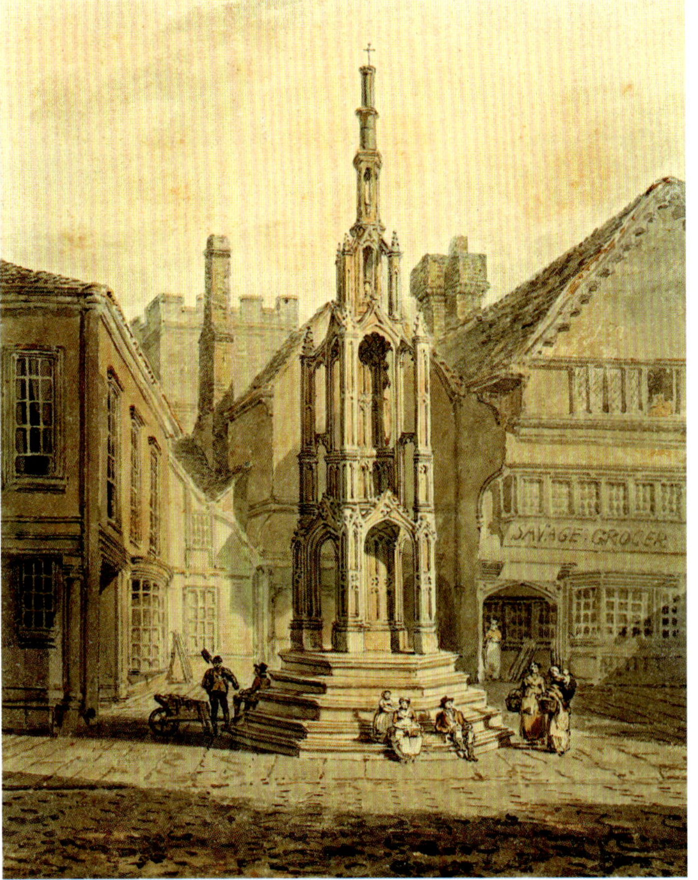

The Buttercross, Winchester, c.1795, watercolour, Whitworth Art Gallery, University of Manchester, UK, dimensions unknown

The Buttercross must have been a fascinating find for Turner during his travels around Wessex because of its history and location among the timber framed houses of Winchester. Most large medieval towns had their own buttercrosses at one time that were normally sheltered venues for the trading of dairy products. Winchester's cross is more significant, celebrating its importance as the ancient capital of England. Among the statues on the cross is King Alfred the Great, the 9th-century king of Wessex.

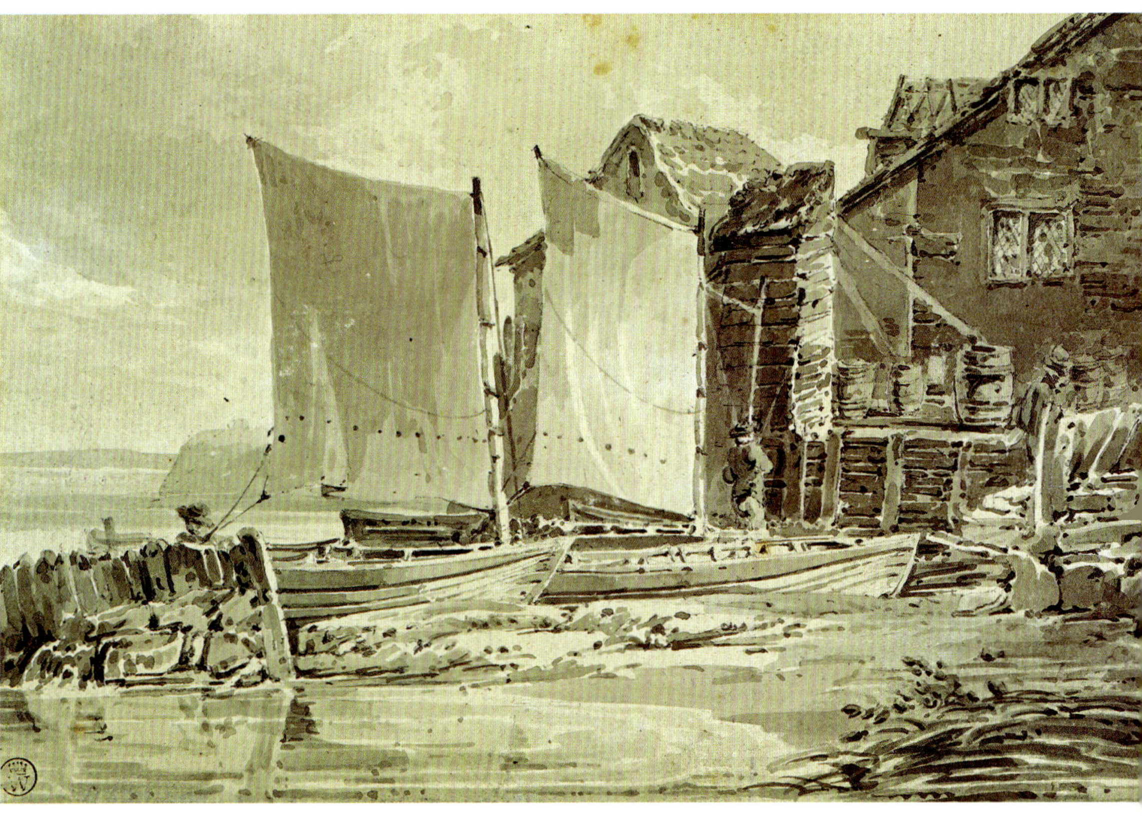

Fisherman's Cottage, Dover, c.1790, pencil and grey wash, Paul Mellon Collection, Yale Center for British Art, CT, USA, 14 x 20cm (5½ x 8in)

A small and concise drawing that is a wonderful example of Turner's mastery of watercolour wash at such an early stage in his career. It is not known exactly when the work was executed suggesting that it was never intended for exhibition purposes, but merely an experiment in laying washes over a drawing. Turner spent his whole life experimenting with watercolour wash.

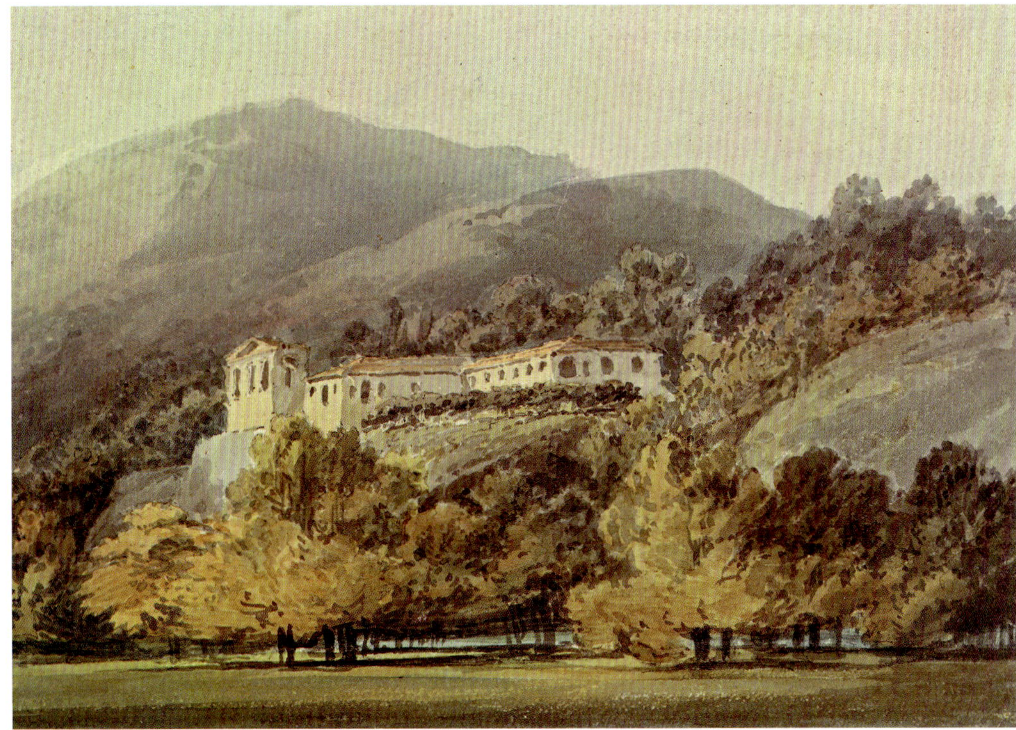

Santa Lucia, a Convent near Caserta, 1795, pencil and watercolour, Paul Mellon Collection, Yale Center for British Art, CT, USA, 15 x 24cm (6 x 9in)

A version of a Continental view by Cozens that Turner must have seen at Dr Monro's house. Turner did not visit Italy until 1819 and relied instead on copying the masters who made the Grand Tour. Caserta is a large town famed for its royal palace, but Cozens has chosen the more modest but beautifully situated convent. It is probably this aspect that appealed to Turner.

Landscape with Trees and Figures, 1796, watercolour, Paul Mellon Collection, Yale Center for British Art, CT, USA, 32 x 43cm (13 x 17in)

This painting is an exercise in draughtsmanship and restrained use of colour that belies Turner's development as a watercolourist. The cool colours are redolent of the artist Francis Towne who was a generation older than Turner. Towne was known in London circles although he failed to become a Royal Academician. By contrast, Turner was still learning his craft and only five years away from Associate Membership at the time of this painting.

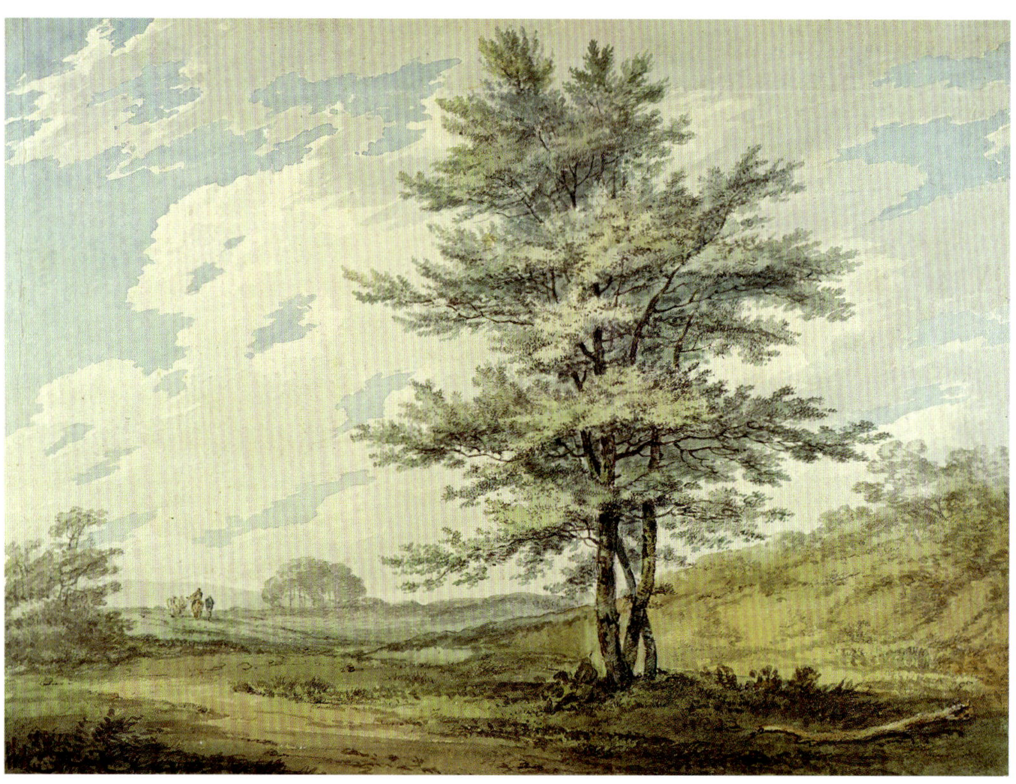

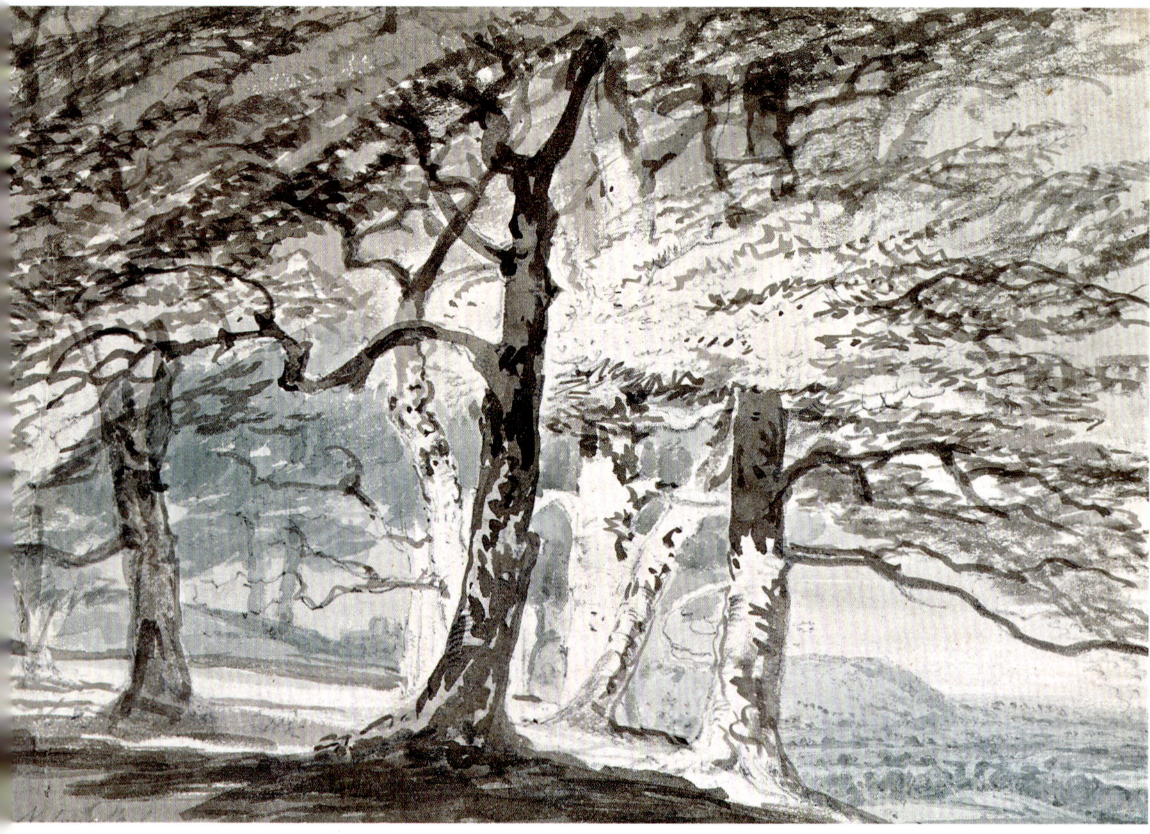

Norbury Park, Surrey, c.1796, pencil and watercolour, Leeds Art Gallery, UK, 18 x 26cm (7 x 10in)

Following the Norman Conquest, Norbury Park was recorded in the Domesday Book of 1085, having been given by William I to the Bishop of Bayeux. The land was used extensively for farming and meadowland and was in the ownership and stewardship of Merton College, Oxford, until the 20th century. Turner has depicted the estate before it became a large conurbation, which occurred after the introduction of the railway network in the mid-19th century.

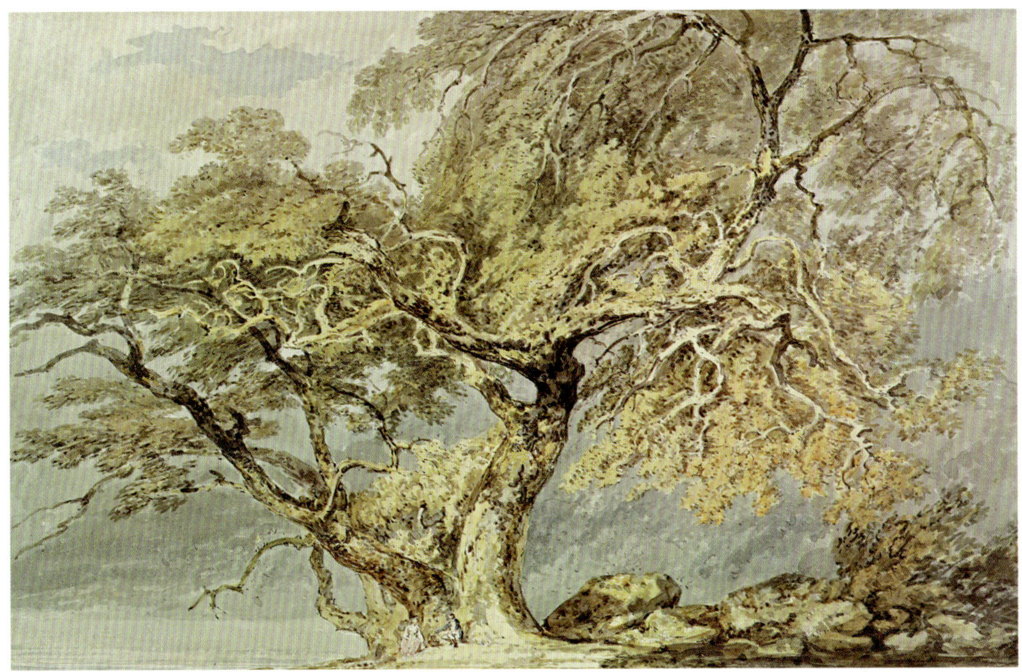

A Great Tree, 1796, pencil and watercolour, Paul Mellon Collection, Yale Center for British Art, CT, USA, 25 x 39cm (10 x 15in)

This watercolour was made on a larger scale than sketchbook size, but does not appear to have been exhibited; it was perhaps an exercise in natural topography. Although the work appears conventional, Turner was by this time using fewer pencil marks, relying more on the watercolour for the detailing. The location is unknown, but it is probably from his Welsh sketchbooks of the time.

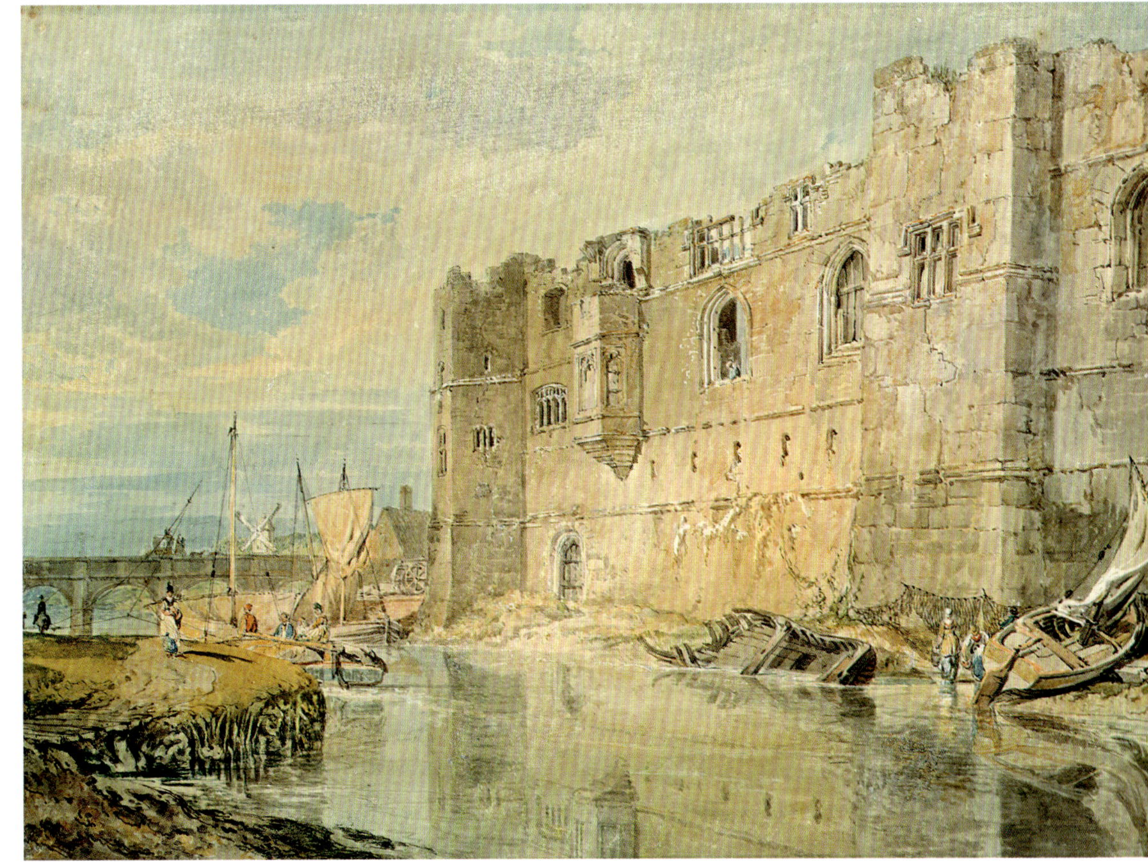

Newark-upon-Trent, 1796, graphite and watercolour, Paul Mellon Collection, Yale Center for British Art, CT, USA, 31 x 43cm (12 x 17in)

The town of Newark has played an influential part in England's history. The Norman castle was built in the 12th century and was significant in the battle between King John (who subsequently died in the castle) and his barons, leading to the signing of Magna Carta. The castle also featured during the Wars of the Roses and the English Civil War.

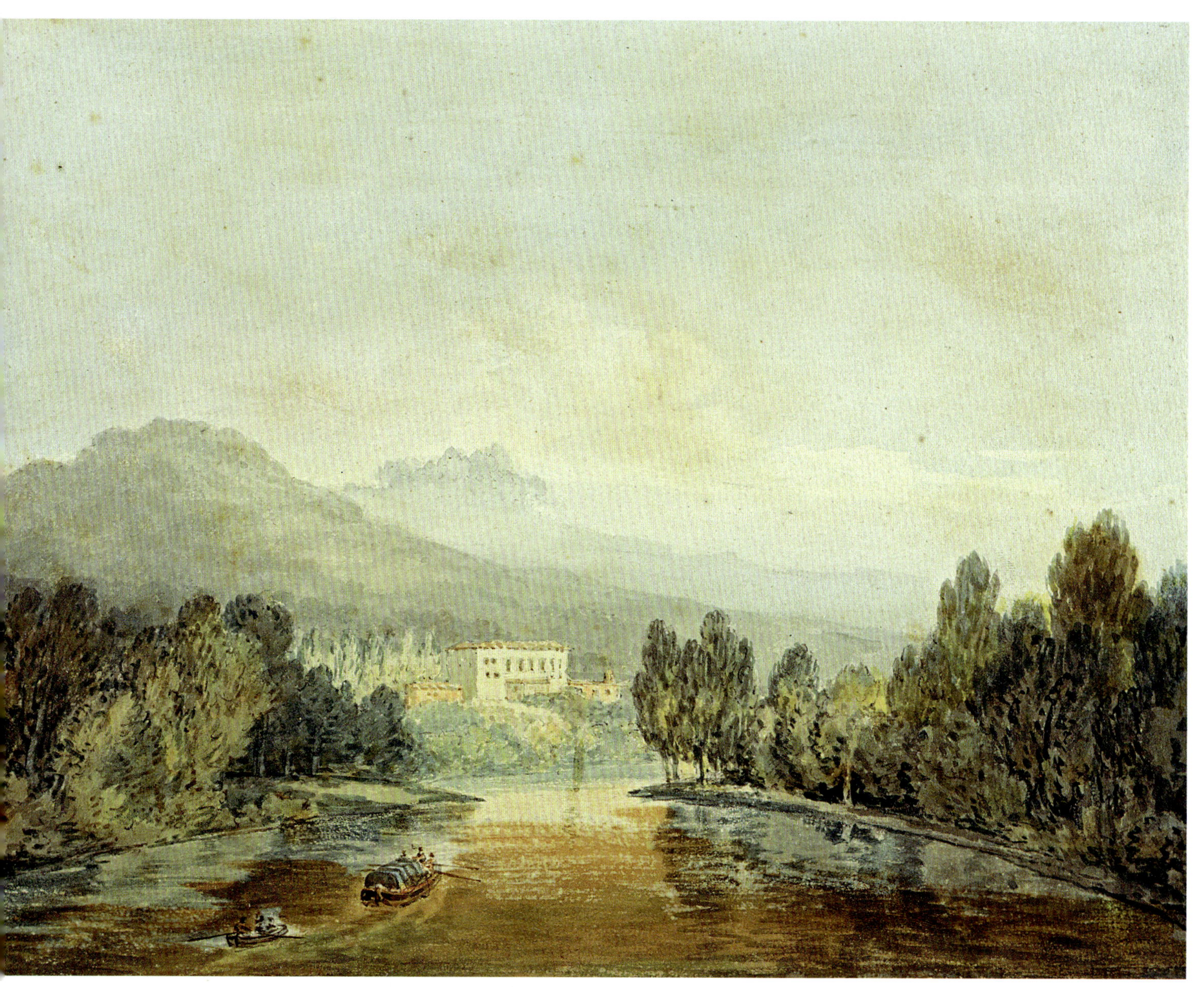

Villa Salviati on the Arno, 1796–7, pencil and watercolour, Paul Mellon Collection, Yale Center for British Art, CT, USA, 18 x 24cm (7 x 9in)

The Villa Salviati is a 15th-century villa built on the site of a medieval castle in the village of Cionfo, just outside Florence on the Arno river. The Tuscan hills in the distance provide a perfect backdrop for this view, which was originally made by an unidentified artist, although it is likely to have been either Francis Towne or John Robert Cozens, both of whom had travelled extensively around Italy.

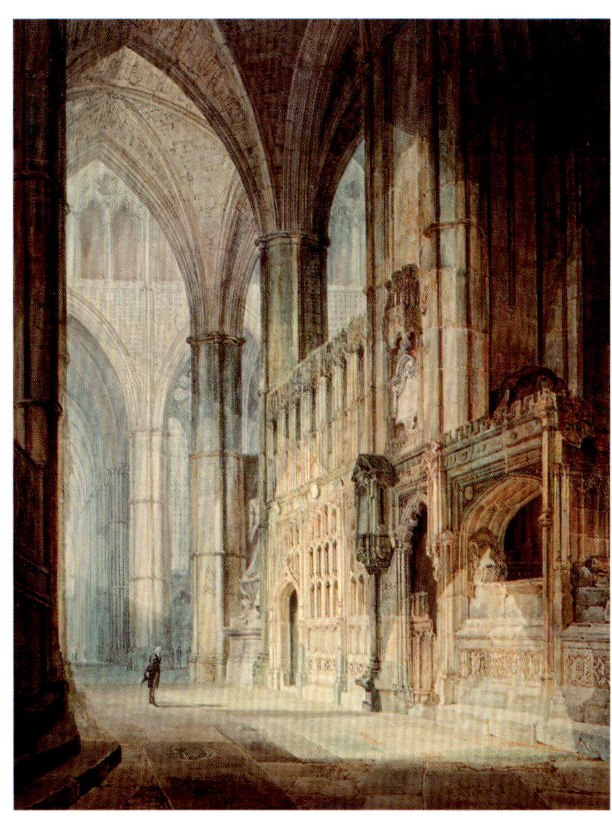

St Erasmus in Bishop Islip's Chapel, 1796, pencil and watercolour, British Museum, London, UK, 55 x 40cm (22 x 16in)

The Tudor chapel is situated in the apse of Westminster Abbey, an important site near the tombs of several kings of England including Edward the Confessor. In the painting, Turner inscribed his own name on a burial tablet in the floor, an early indication of the awareness of his future celebration as a great Englishman. The light coming from the south transept adds to the dramatic effect of the scene.

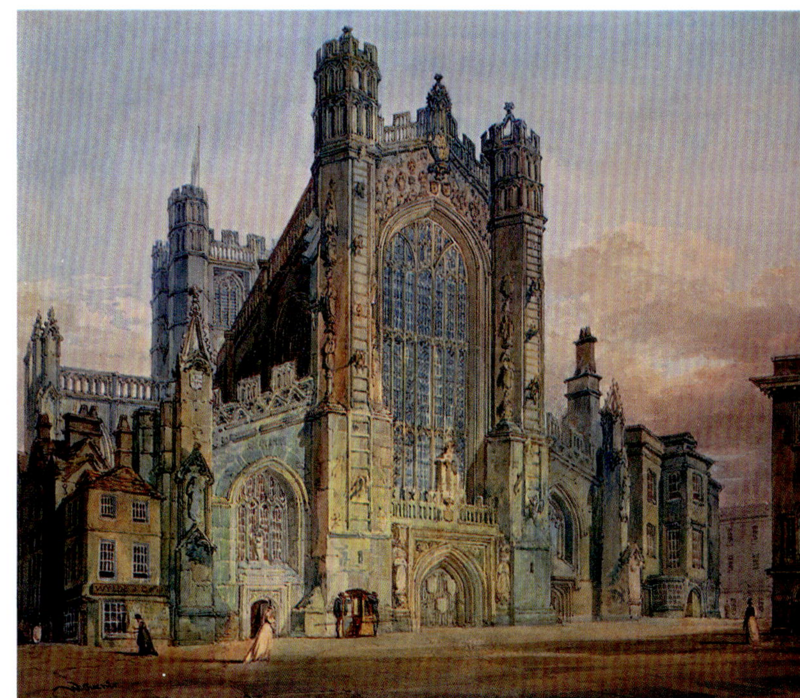

The West Front of Bath Abbey, 1796, watercolour, Victoria Gallery, Bath, UK, 24 x 28cm (9 x 11in)

Bath Abbey is known as the 'Lantern of the West' because of its huge Perpendicular style windows. Turner captures the magnificence of this Gothic abbey dwarfing the Classical façade of the Roman Baths Pump Room on the right. The artist has adopted a low perspective, which highlights the soaring edifice.

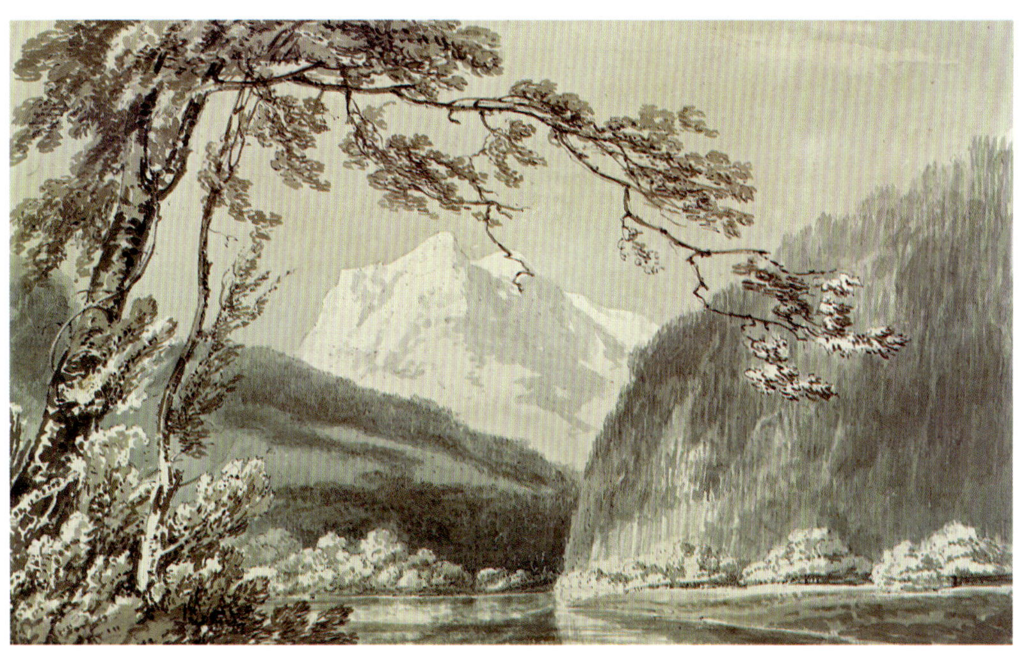

Near Grindewald, c.1796, graphite with blue and grey wash, Paul Mellon Collection, Yale Center for British Art, CT, USA, 24 x 38cm (11 x 15in)

Since Turner's first trip to the Continent was not until 1802, he must have used another artist's work as reference for this exercise. Graphite had been found in the Lake District 200 years before, but was not popular as a medium until the 18th century, superseding the use of black chalk because of quality and supply issues.

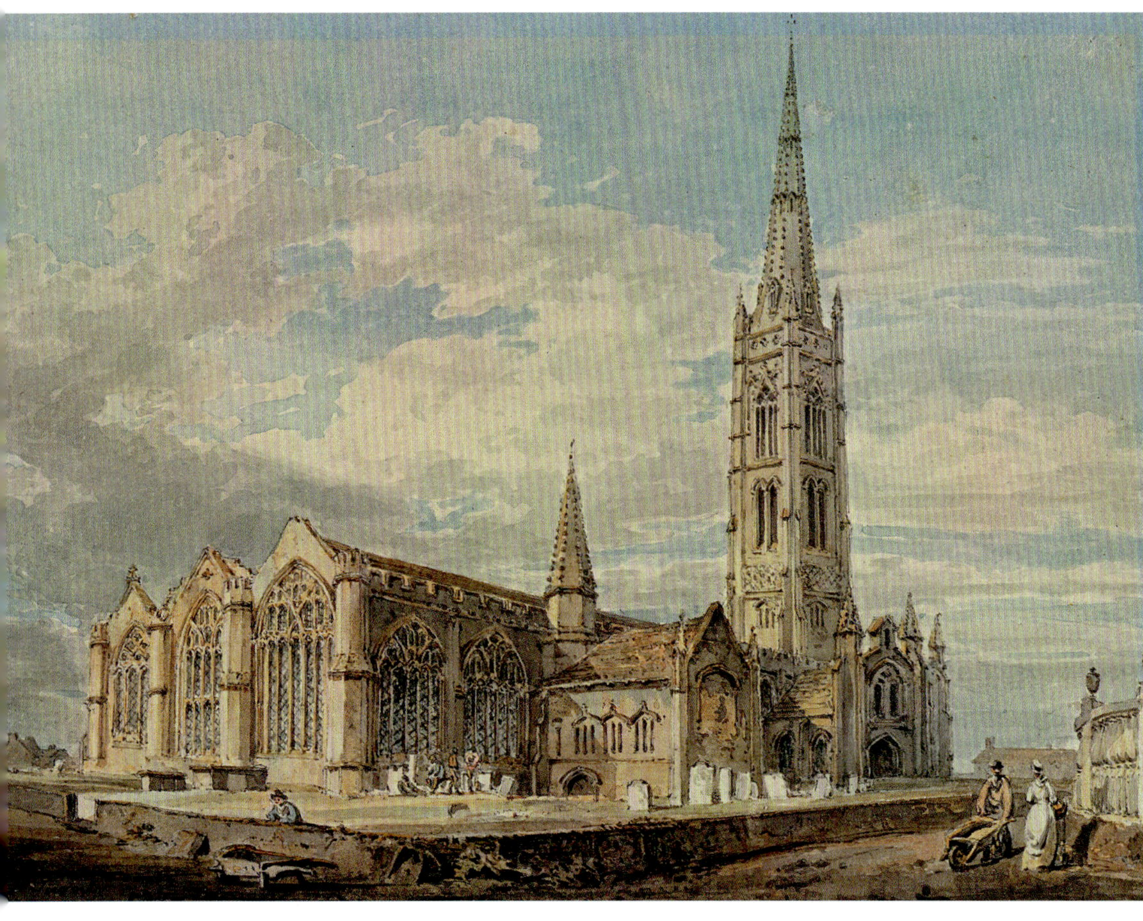

North-east View of Grantham Church, Lincolnshire, 1797, graphite and watercolour, Paul Mellon Collection, Yale Center for British Art, CT, USA, 13 x 18cm (5 x 7in)

At the time this watercolour was executed, Turner appears to have compulsively depicted many cathedrals and churches, possibly triggered by Sir Richard Colt Hoare's commission to paint views of Salisbury. This magnificent cathedral-scale church is dedicated to St Wulfram and was rebuilt in the 12th century. The 13th-century spire was briefly the tallest in England, before being surpassed by that of Salisbury Cathedral.

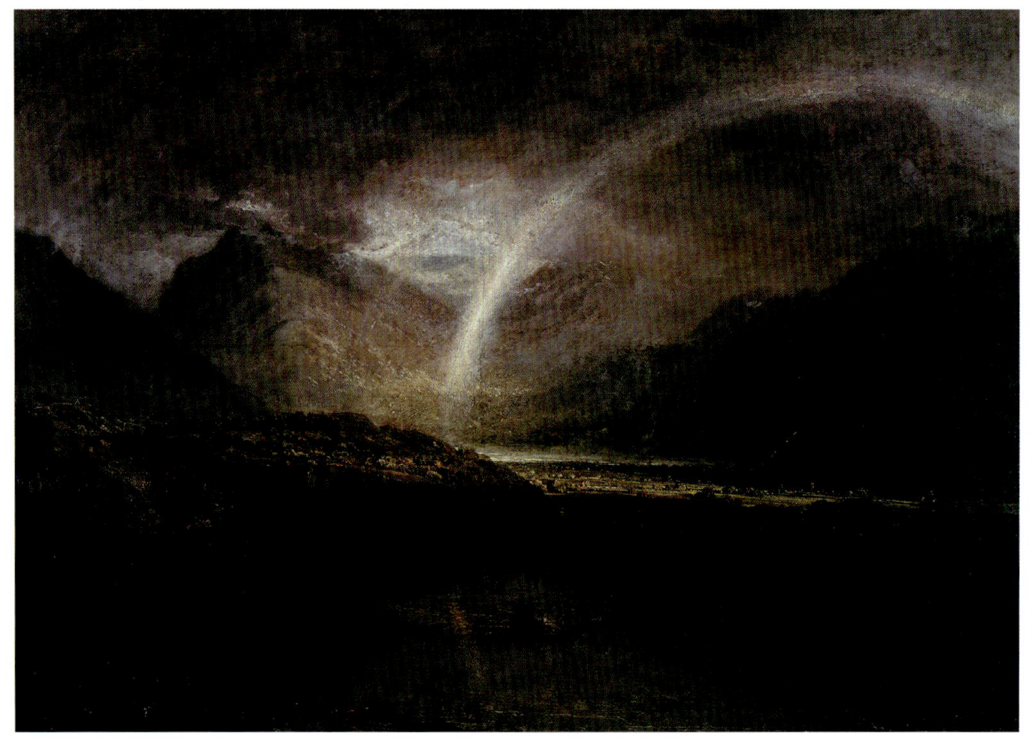

Lake Buttermere with Part of Cromackwater – a Shower, 1798, oil on canvas, Tate Britain, London, UK, 89 x 119cm (35 x 47in)

Turner exhibited this painting at the 1798 Academy exhibition with appended lines from one of James Thomson's poems, *Spring ll*. Turner introduced a rainbow for the first time into his work, and there is the suggestion of a Sublime aesthetic being attempted, although when a fellow artist saw this at the Academy, he remarked that Turner was "a timid man afraid to venture".

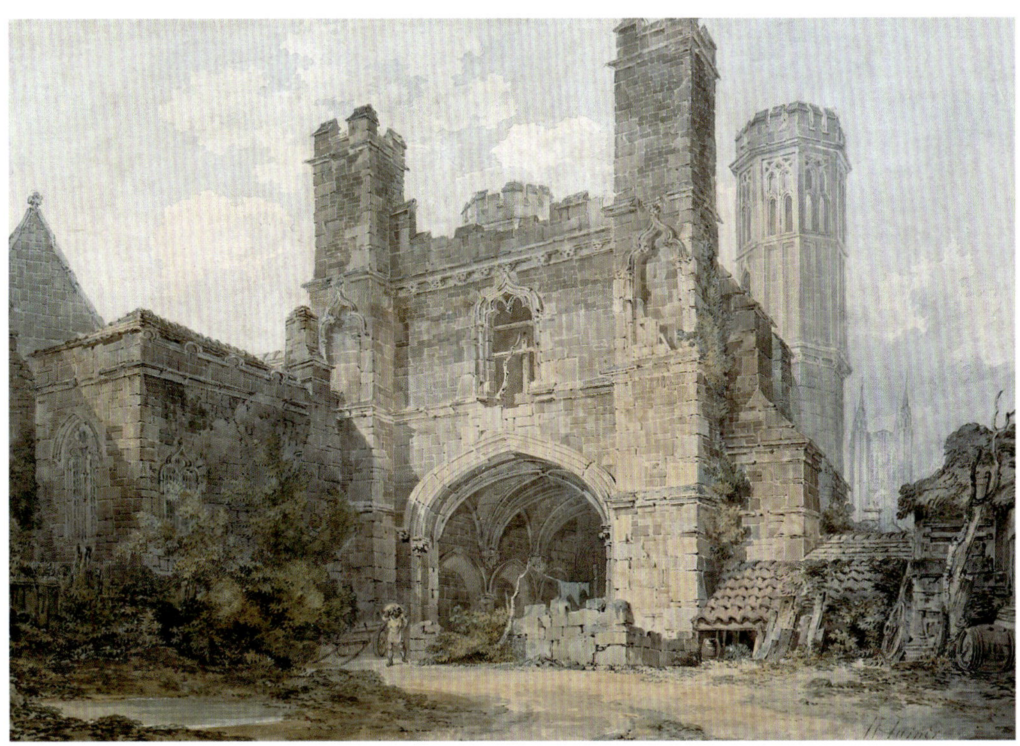

St Augustine's Gate, Canterbury, c.1797, pencil and watercolour, Paul Mellon Collection, Yale Center for British Art, CT, USA, 34 x 49cm (13 x 19in)

This gateway marks the entrance to an abbey founded by St Augustine around the year CE598, when Christianity was first brought to southern England. Henry VIII, who eventually used it as a minor royal palace, dissolved most abbeys and monasteries, including St Augustine's, in the 16th century. In Turner's time, as now, much of the palace remained intact, but the abbey church was destroyed.

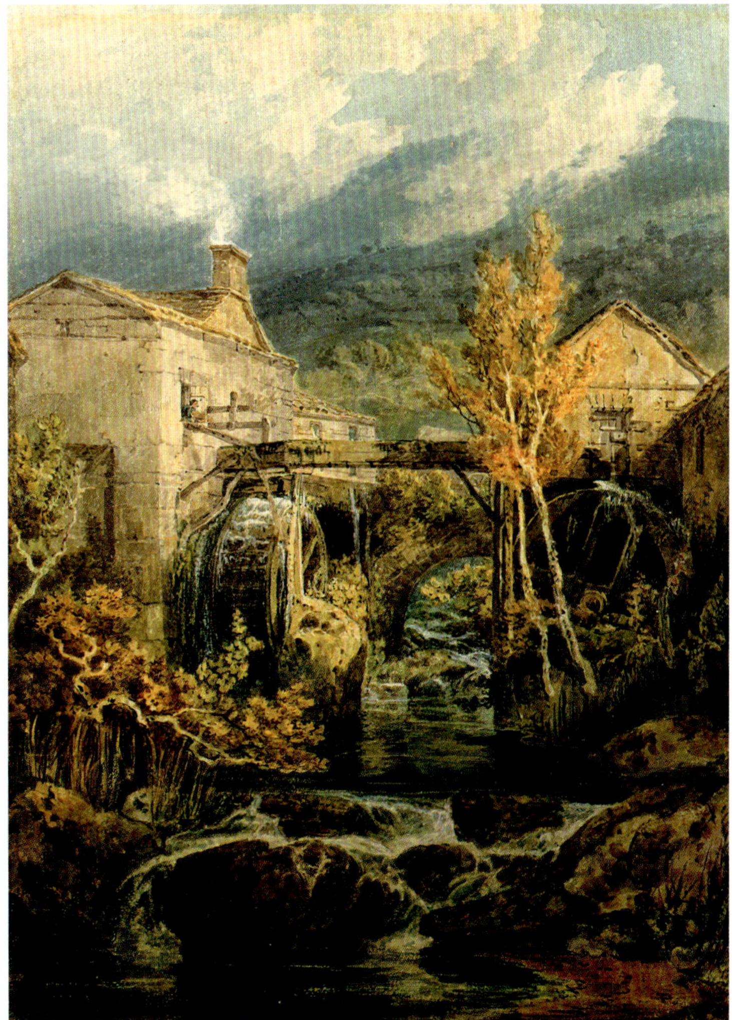

Ambleside Mill, Westmorland, 1798, watercolour, University of Liverpool Art Gallery and Collections, UK, 25 x 37cm (10 x 14½in)

A superbly crafted watercolour that adheres to the Picturesque aesthetic, this picture was exhibited at the 1798 Royal Academy exhibition. The medieval mill is close to a 20m (70ft) high waterfall, Stock Ghyll Force, which powered several mills in this area of the Lake District. As well as providing inspiration for Turner, the area also inspired the Romantic poet William Wordsworth, who lived close by.

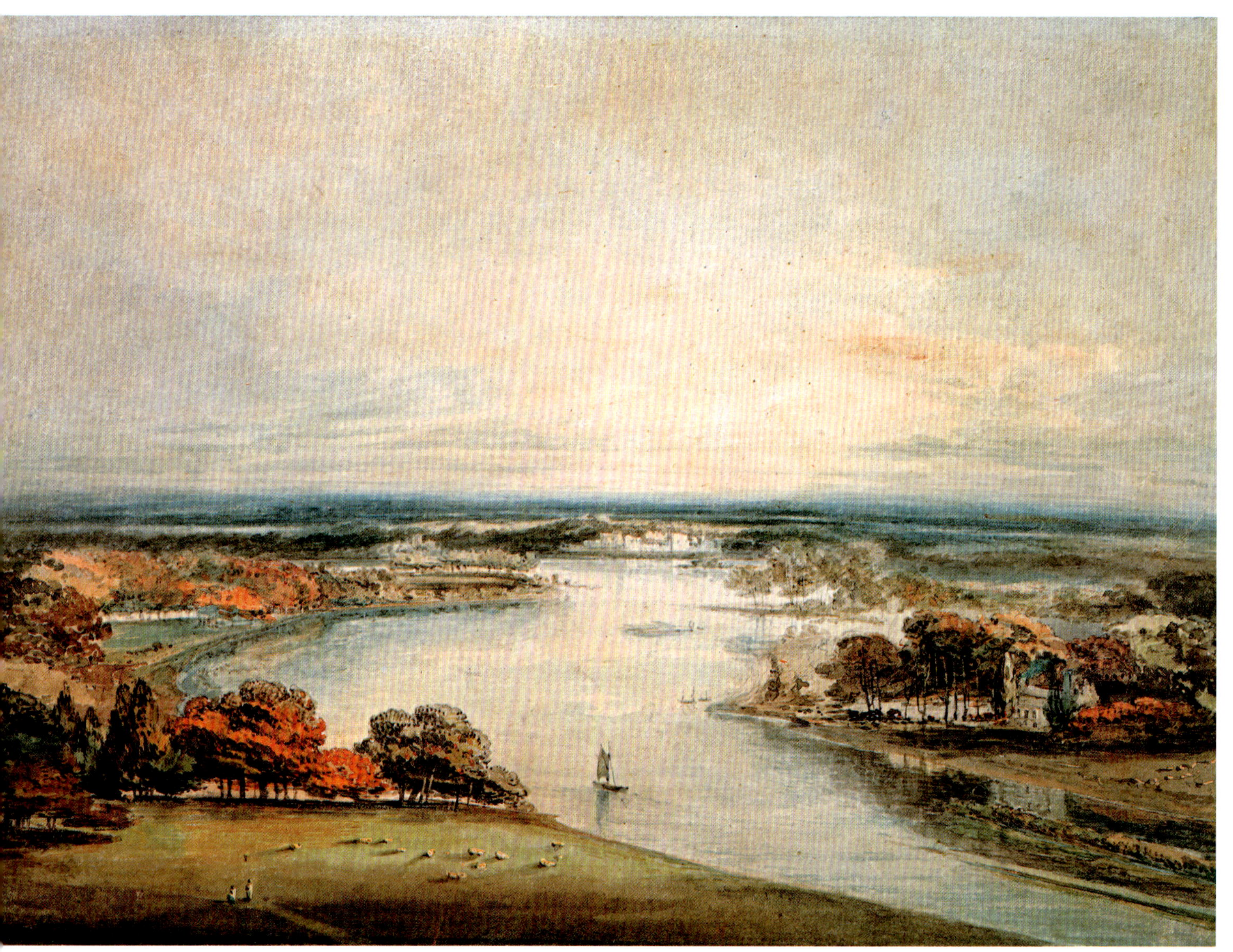

The Thames from Richmond,
1796–8, watercolour,
Private Collection,
dimensions unknown

The River Thames played a
significant part in Turner's
oeuvre. From his boyhood
days in London and
Brentford, until his last days

at Chelsea, the Thames
was never very far away
and continued to be
an inspiration for him.
It seems likely that this
restful watercolour was
executed as a contemplative
piece, during a convalescent
period following his illness
in 1796.

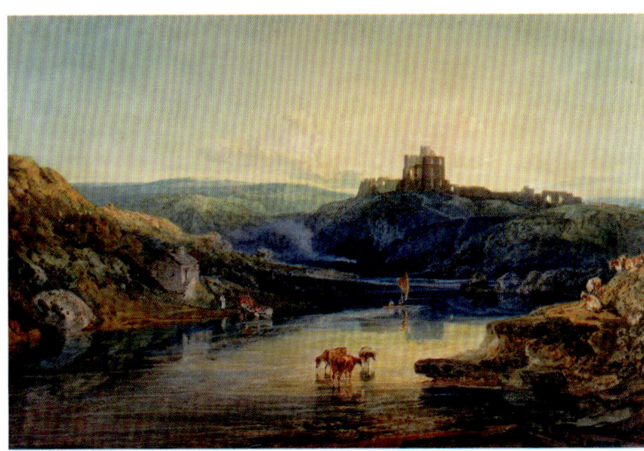

Norham Castle: Summer's Morn, 1798, pencil, watercolour and bodycolour, Cecil Higgins Art Gallery, Bedford, UK, 51 x 74cm (20 x 29in)

Norham Castle became one of Turner's favourite motifs, this watercolour being the first example. The castle, on the River Tweed, a natural border between England and Scotland, had strategic importance during the medieval wars between the two countries. By the end of the 16th century the castle had fallen into a ruinous state, providing a Picturesque setting for Turner's watercolour.

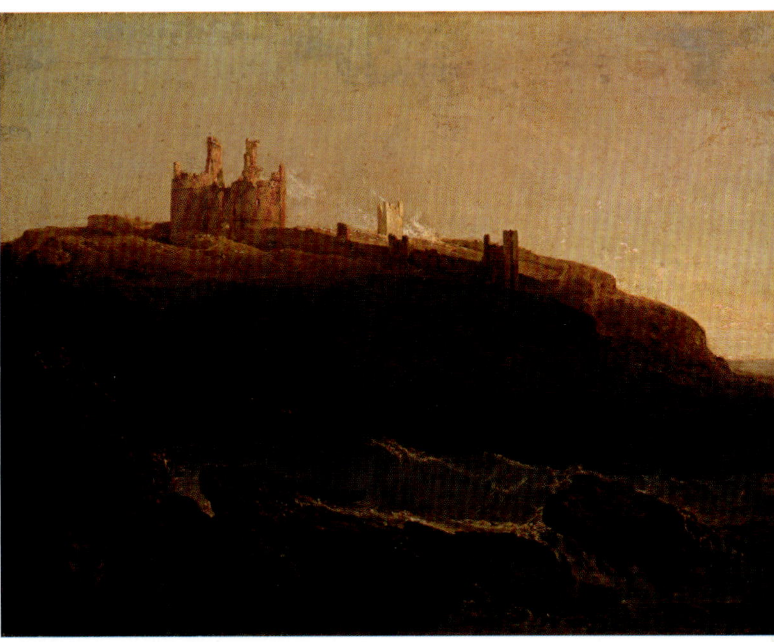

Dunstanborough Castle, Sunrise after a Squally Night, 1798, oil on canvas, National Gallery of Victoria, Melbourne, Australia, 92 x 123cm (36 x 48in)

In the summer of 1797, Turner visited the north of England on a sketching tour that included Dunstanborough. The style of this resultant painting is not dissimilar to that of Richard Wilson, as one critic noted when it was favourably received at the Royal Academy exhibition of 1798. This view of the castle appeared as an engraving in Turner's *Liber Studiorum*, published in 1808.

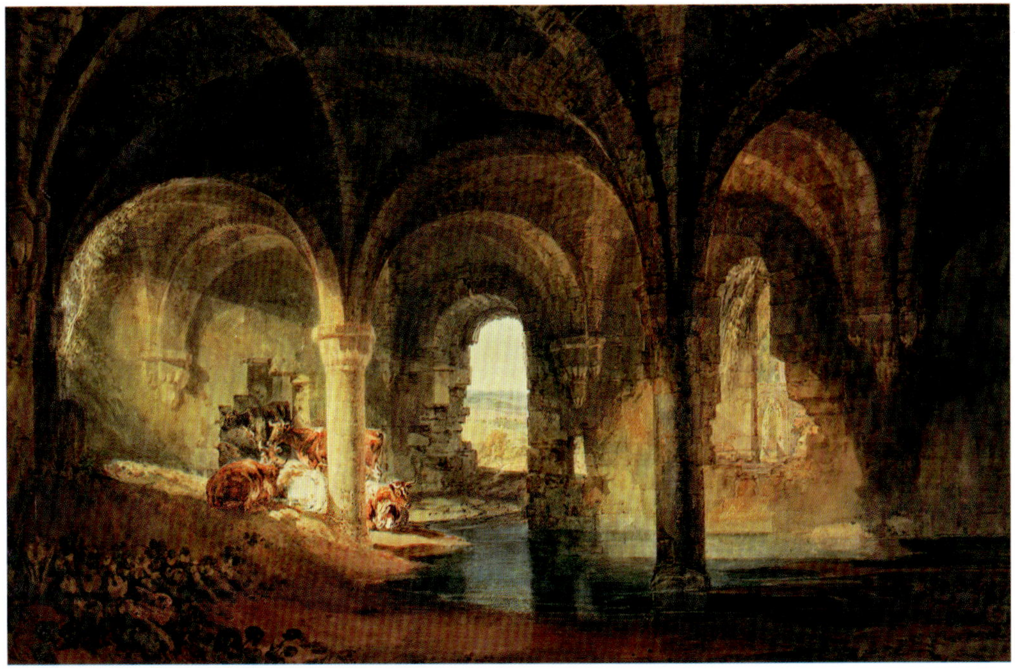

Refectory of Kirkstall Abbey, 1798, watercolour, Sir John Soane Museum, London, UK, 45 x 65cm (18 x 25½in)

At the Royal Academy exhibition of 1798, Turner showed several watercolours depicting Christian sites that included this view of a ruined abbey. With growing confidence, the artist began using larger sheets of paper for his watercolours, producing an exemplary work in architectural detail and light effects. Mrs Soane, wife of Turner's fellow Academician, John Soane, bought the picture in 1804.

Bridge over the Usk, Monmouthshire, c.1799, watercolour, Victoria and Albert Museum, London, UK, 41 x 76cm (16 x 30in)

This tranquil watercolour belies the importance of the small town of Usk, barely visible in the picture, which is dominated by the medieval stone bridge that spans the River Usk. Once a Roman settlement, the town and castle were a strategic stronghold in disputes between the Welsh and English. Turner has depicted a scene when the river is low, making it fordable.

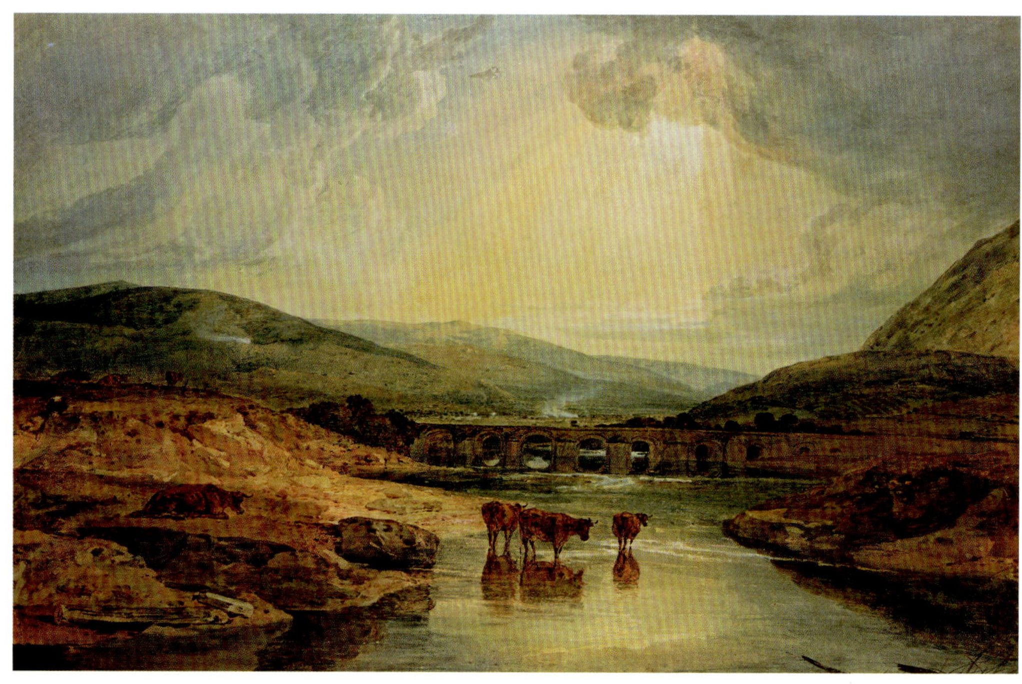

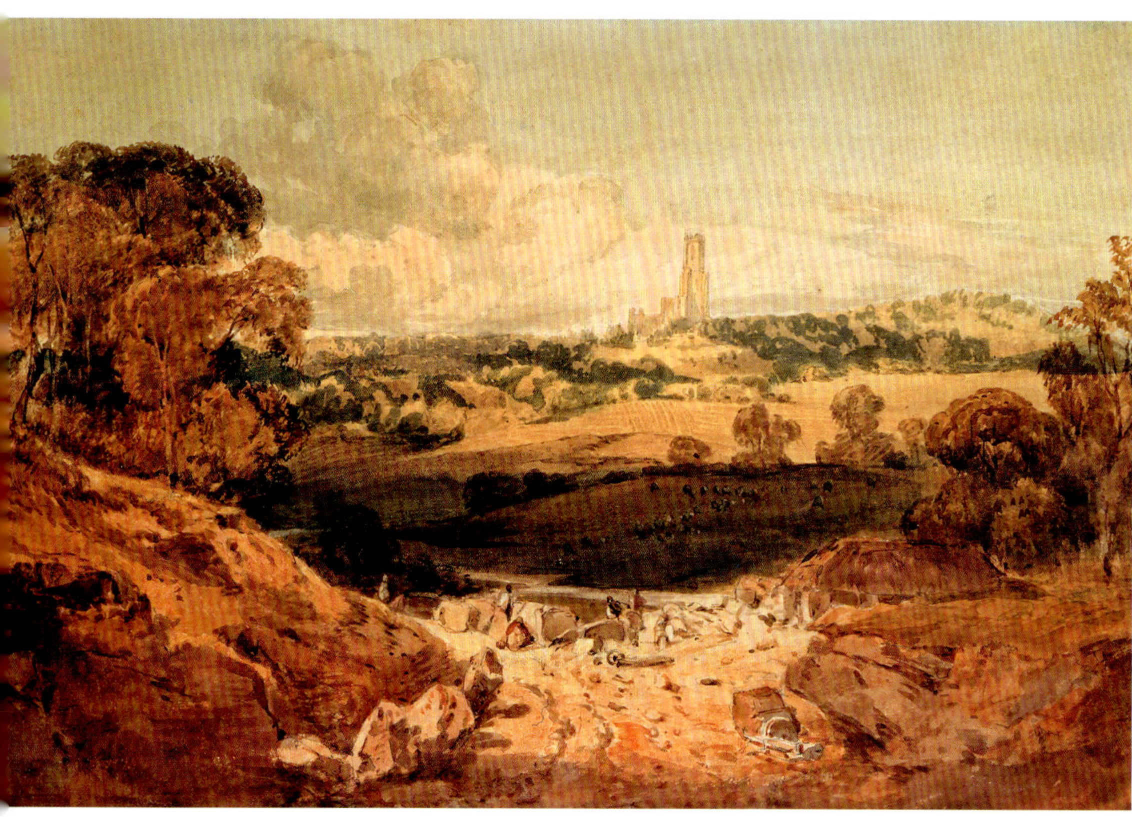

View of Fonthill from a Stone Quarry, 1799, watercolour and ink, Leeds Art Gallery, UK, 30 x 45cm (12 x 18in)

In the summer of 1799, Turner was invited to see the construction of Fonthill Abbey, intending to make a series of drawings and a painting for its owner, the wealthy William Beckford. The massive neo-Gothic country house was completed in 1813, and Beckford lived alone there until 1822, but following the collapse of the tower in 1825, the building was demolished.

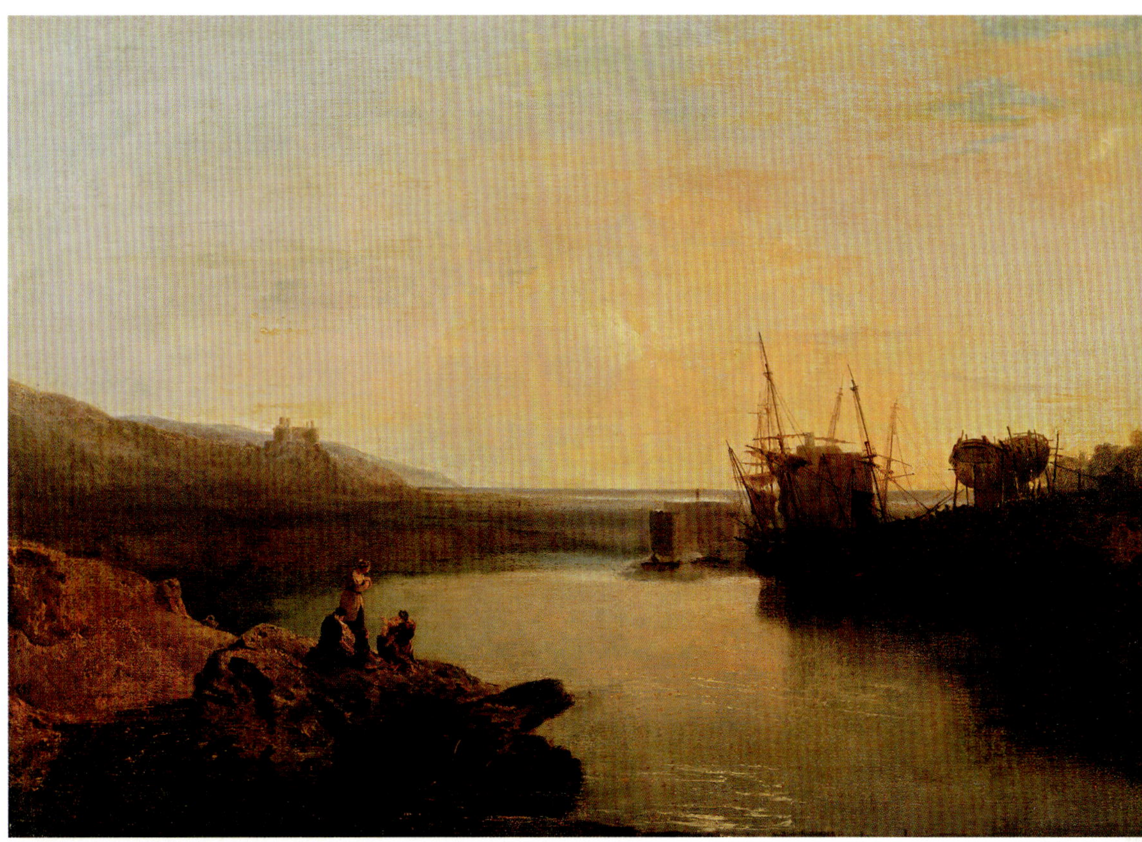

Harlech Castle from Twgwyn Ferry: Summer's Evening, Twilight, 1799, oil on canvas, Paul Mellon Collection, Yale Center for British Art, CT, USA, 87 x 119cm (34 x 47in)

When this picture was exhibited at the Academy in 1799, one critic immediately noticed its similarity to the paintings of Claude Lorrain and Richard Wilson, two of Turner's artistic heroes. The painting was shown with appended lines from Milton's epic poem *Paradise Lost*. As Turner later explained in a lecture, "we cannot make good painters without some aid from poesy".

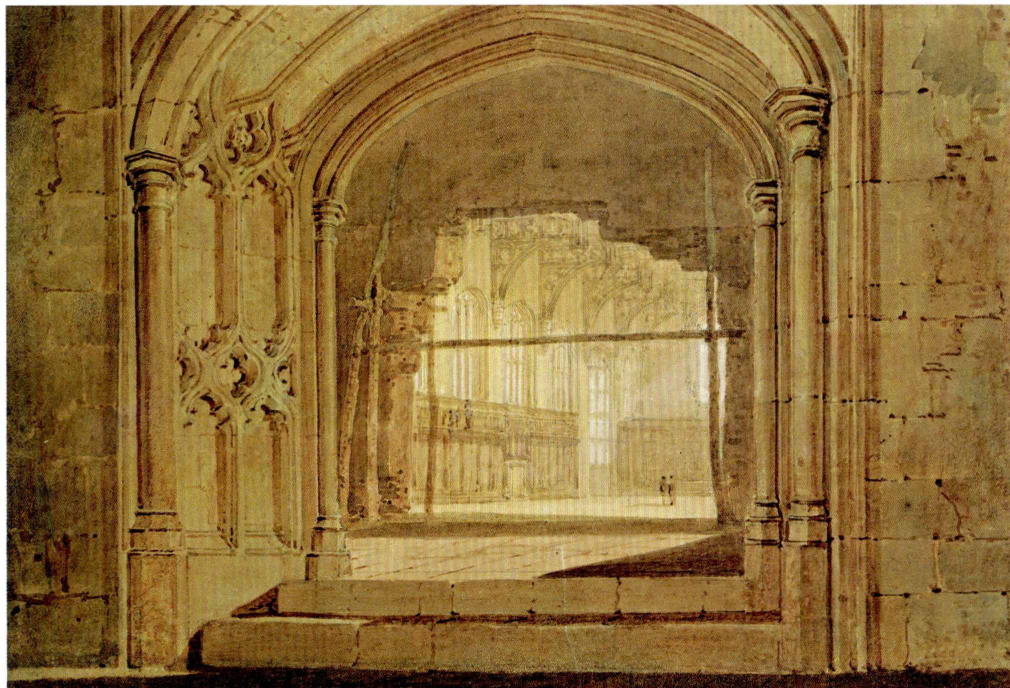

Christ Church Hall, Oxford, 1800, watercolour, Leeds Art Gallery, UK, 22 x 32cm (9 x 12½in)

The Tudor doorway depicted here by Turner leads into the huge dining hall at Christ Church College, Oxford. Cardinal Wolsey had the hall built in 1529 when he founded the original Cardinal College, but following his fall from royal favour, all of Wolsey's property was confiscated by Henry VIII, who re-founded his college as Christ Church in 1546.

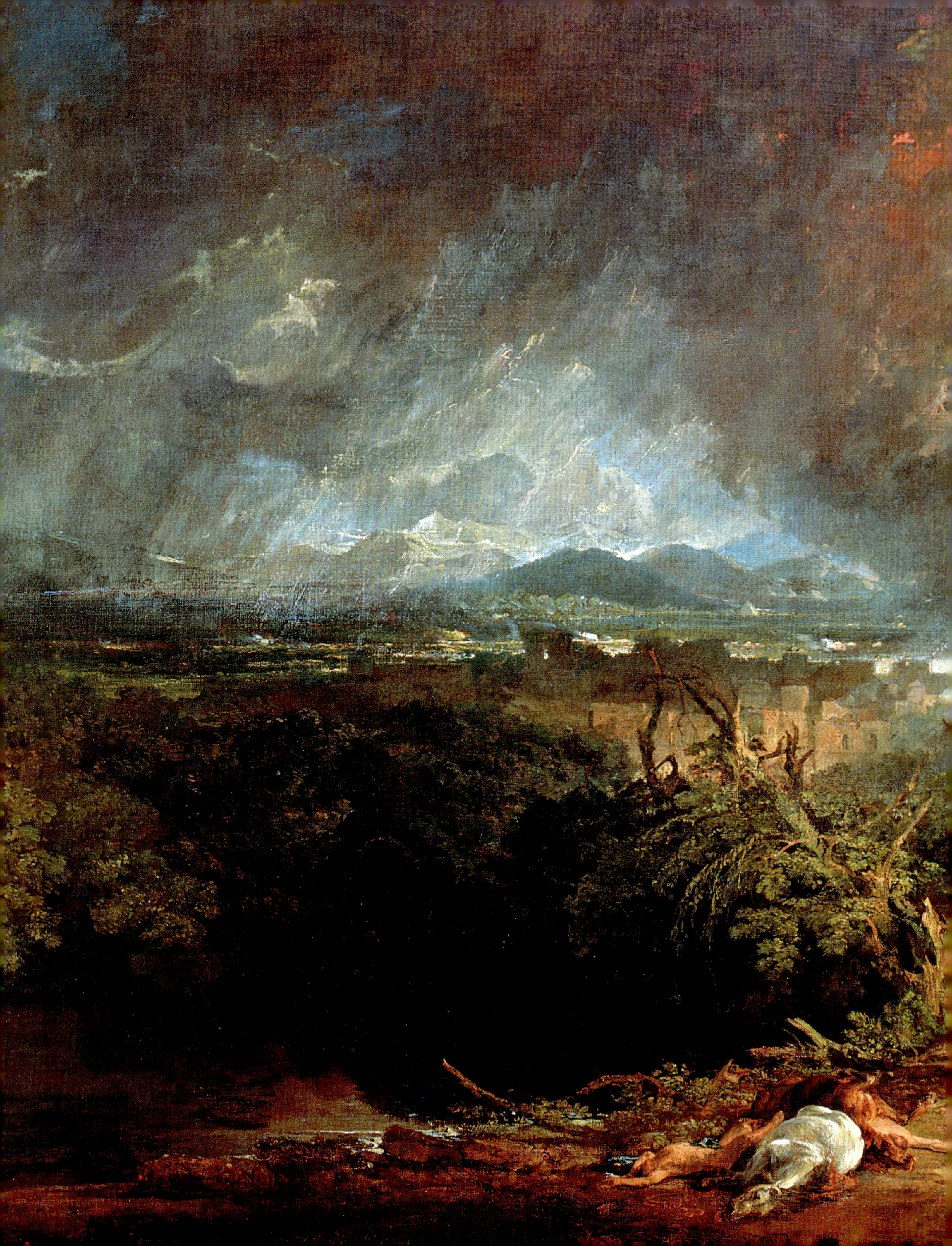

AN ACADEMICIAN
1800–1810

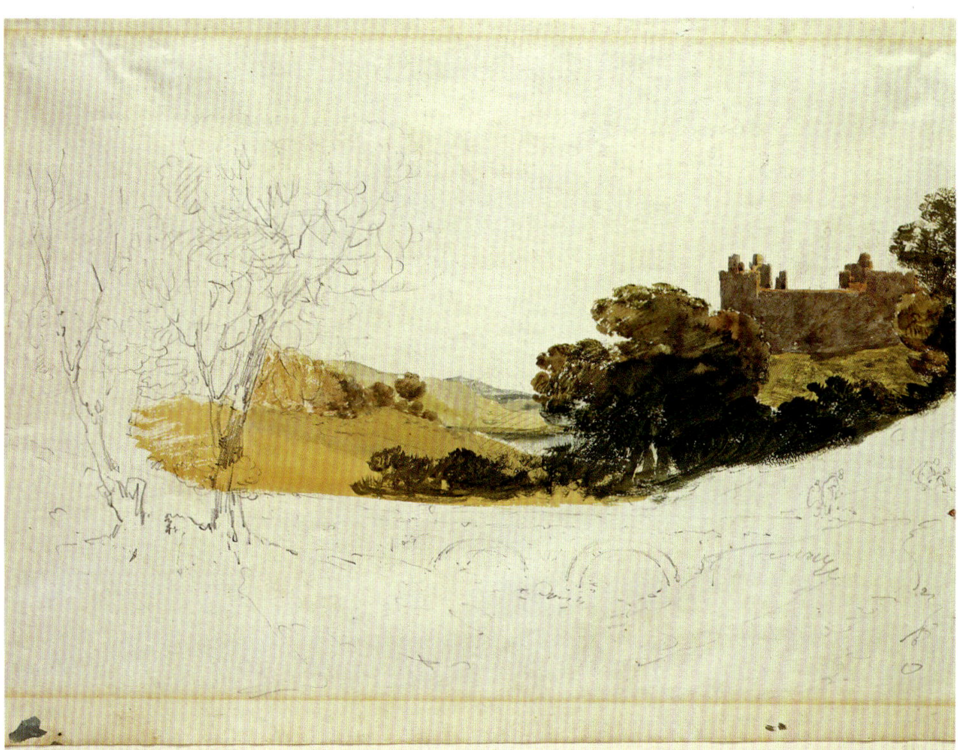

In accordance with his new status as an Associate Academician, Turner began to produce large-format oil paintings including several seascapes that are now considered among his masterpieces. His elevation to full Academy status just two years later reflects the awe in which his contemporaries held him as an artist of the English School of Painting. It was at this time that Turner made the first of his journeys abroad. In addition, he saw the potential of reproducing his paintings as prints for financial gain, as well as a way of promoting his work.

Above: Linlithgow Palace, Scotland, *pencil and watercolour, 1801.*
A partially completed work in progress with the emphasis on the castle that demonstrates Turner's working method. The palace was largely destroyed by the Duke of Cumberland during the Jacobite rebellion of the mid-18th century. Although it is in a ruinous state, Turner shows its majestic skyline.
Left: The Fifth Plague of Egypt, *oil on canvas, 1800. This painting was Turner's most imaginative work to date when it was exhibited at the Academy in 1800.*

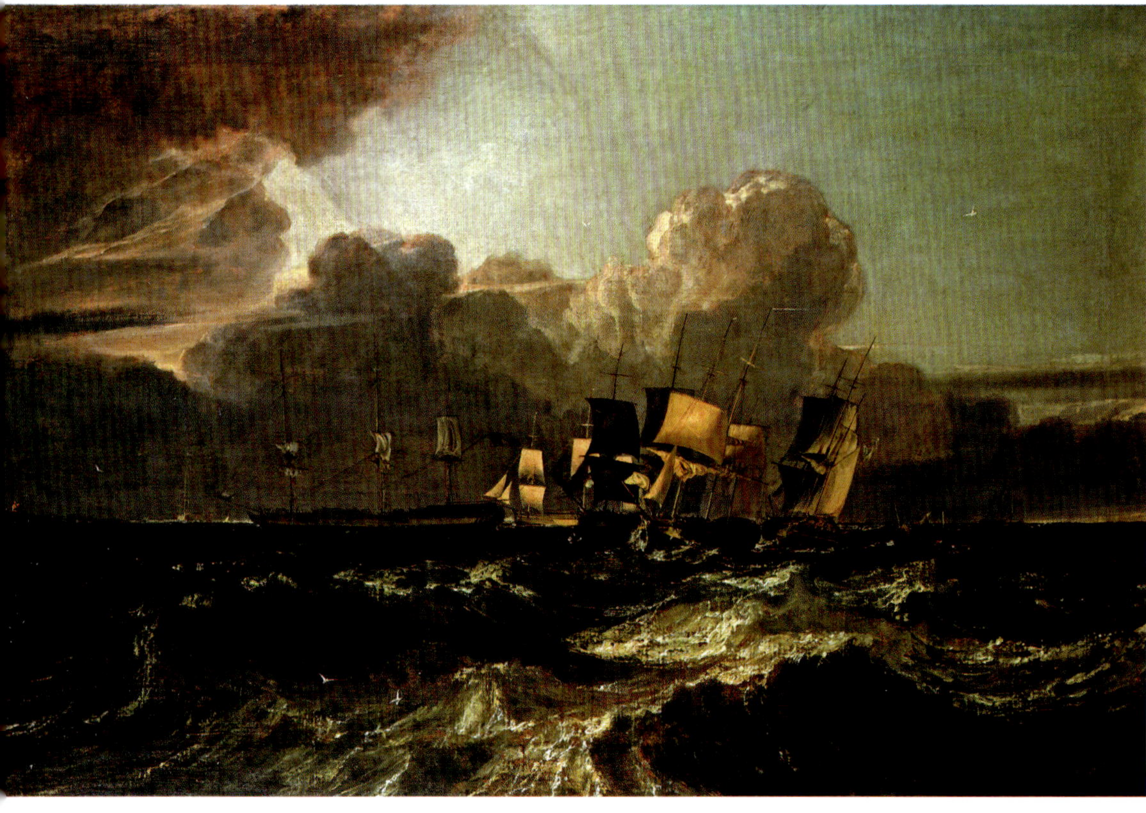

Ships Bearing up for Anchorage (The Egremont Sea-piece), 1802, oil on canvas, Petworth House, Sussex, UK, 119 x 180cm (47 x 71in)

The Earl of Egremont bought this painting from the Academy exhibition in 1802, the first of his many purchases of Turner's work. The painting was worked up from several sketches made in the Calais Pier Sketchbook, in which Turner recorded much of the immense detail and consideration given to this masterpiece of seascape painting. The picture remains at its original home, Petworth House.

Calais Pier, with French Poissards Preparing for Sea: An English Packet Arriving, 1803, oil on canvas, National Gallery, London, UK, 172 x 240cm (68 x 94in)

This picture is a visual account of Turner's first sea voyage across the English Channel, during his first visit to France in 1802. When exhibited at the Academy in the following year, it was generally well received, one critic remarking that the artist had "an eye to see and mind to feel the beauties of nature and art".

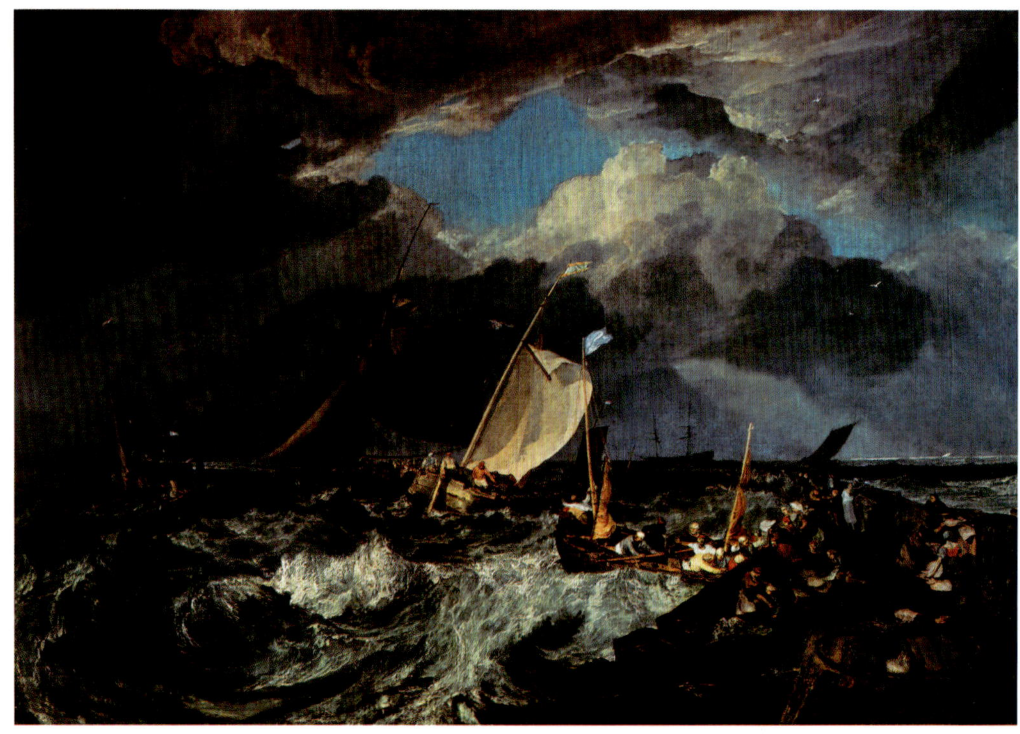

Durham Castle, 1801,
watercolour, Leeds
Art Gallery, UK,
40 x 25cm (16 x 10in)

The fact that Turner has
omitted the cathedral from
his view suggests that he was
more interested in the
ethereal effects of light on a
misty morning than any real
topographical considerations.
The detail of the houses
in the foreground has also
been diminished with
the focus of attention
on the skyline and the tonal
values of the limited palette.

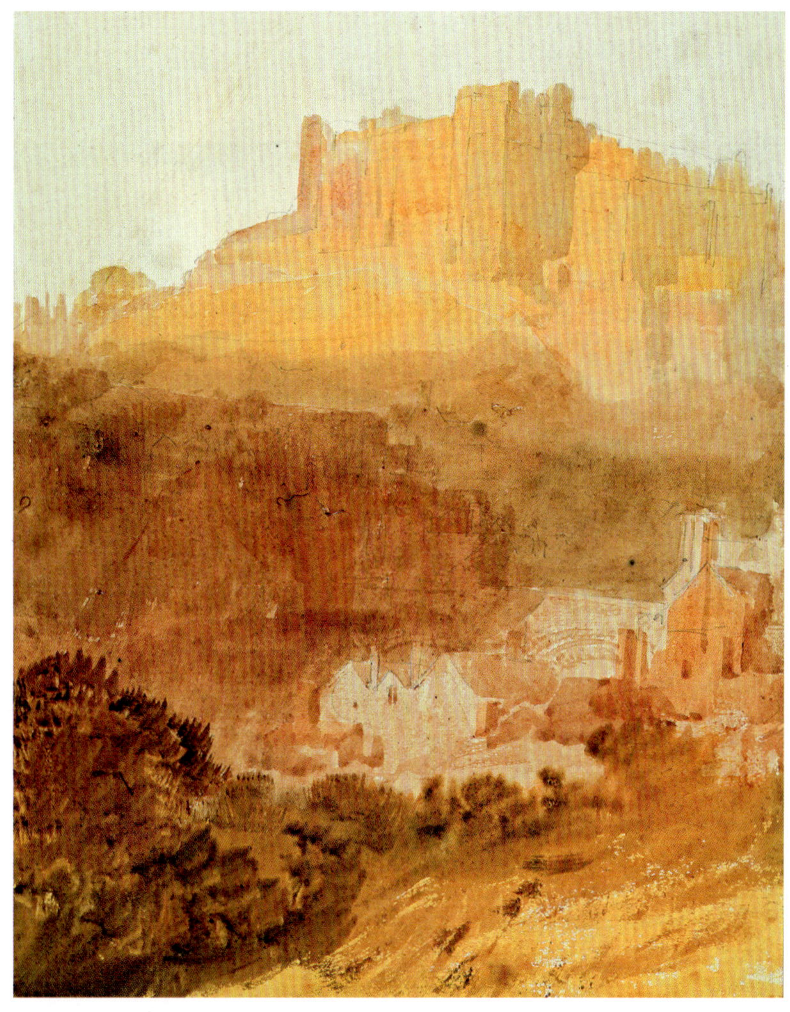

*Fishermen upon a Lee-shore in
Squally Weather*, 1802,
oil on canvas, Southampton
City Art Gallery, UK,
92 x 122cm (36 x 48in)

Having now become a full
member of the Academy,
Turner carefully selected his
first submissions as an
Academician for that year's
exhibition. This picture was
one of four submitted, two
history paintings and two
seascapes, all of which refer
in some way or other to
mortal danger. Reflecting his
new status, Turner signed
his pictures JMW in place
of William.

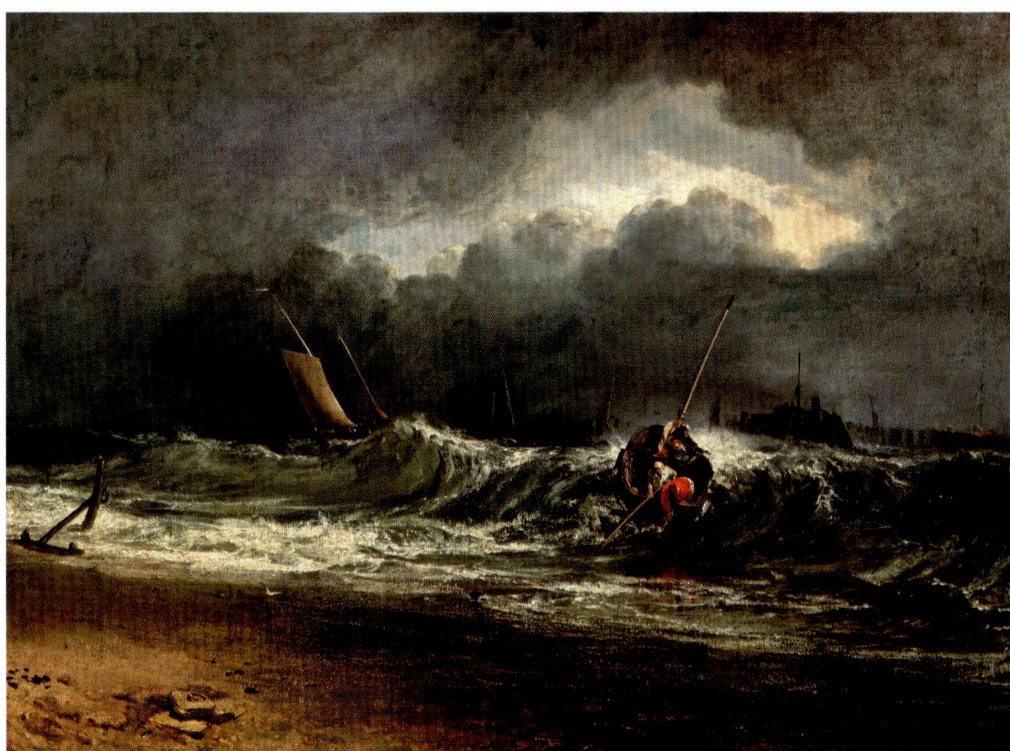

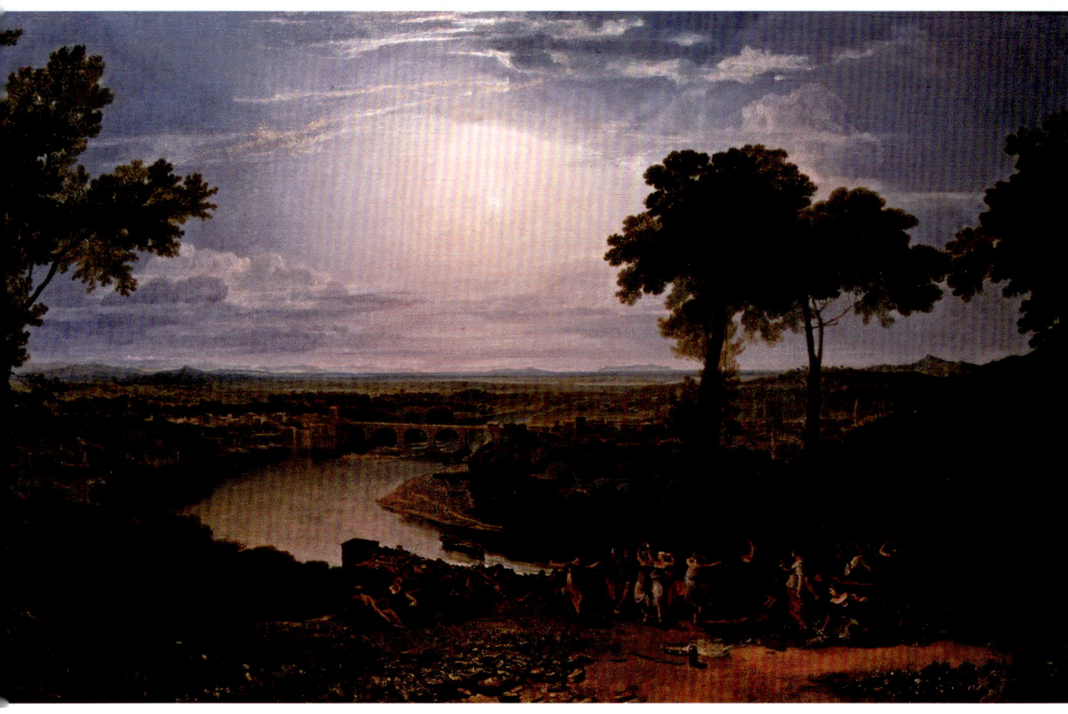

The Festival upon the Opening of the Vintage at Macon, 1803, oil on canvas, Sheffield Galleries and Museums, UK, 146 x 238cm (57 x 94in)

As a result of Turner's visit to the Louvre in Paris in 1802, the artist produced this picture, his most Claude-inspired work to date. One critic remarked in fact that the artist had "surpassed that master in the richness and forms of some parts of his picture". Turner's arch critic Sir George Beaumont was however unconvinced by this apparent redolence.

Fishmarket on the Beach, 1802–4, oil on canvas, Private Collection, 45 x 59cm (18 x 23in)

Although modest in size and not exhibited in Turner's lifetime, *Fishmarket on the Beach* is a good example of the artist's early genre paintings. The picture's early provenance is also sketchy but it was probably owned by Sir John Boyd, the son of a wealthy wine merchant who was one of Turner's early patrons and sponsored his first trip to the Continent.

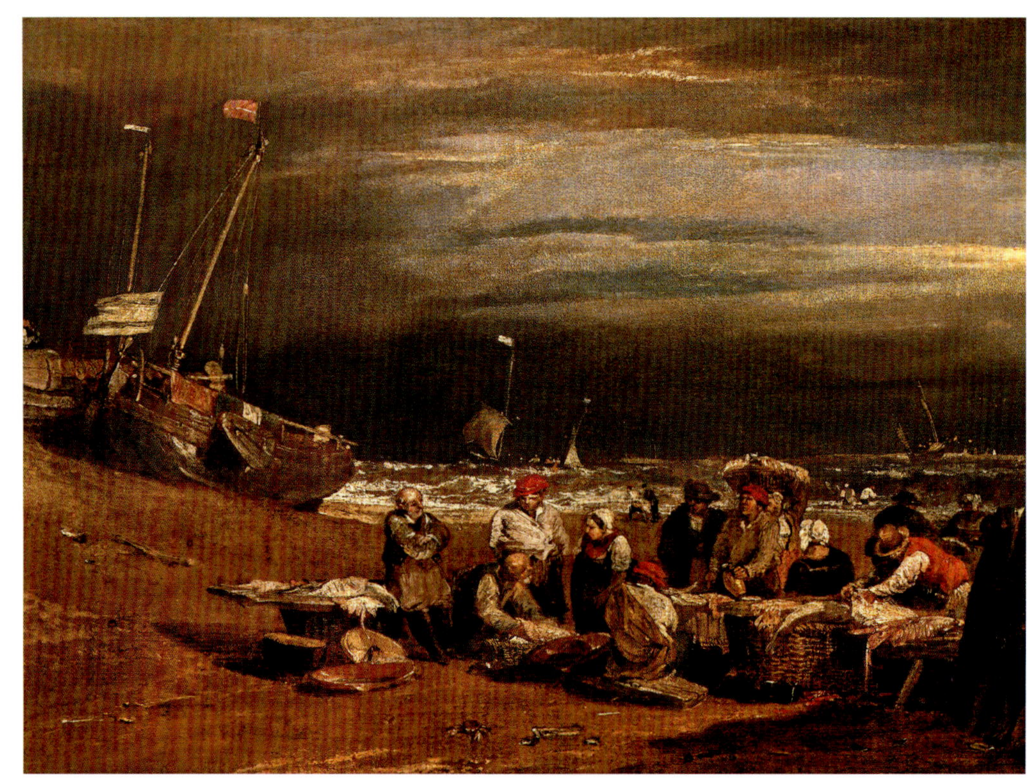

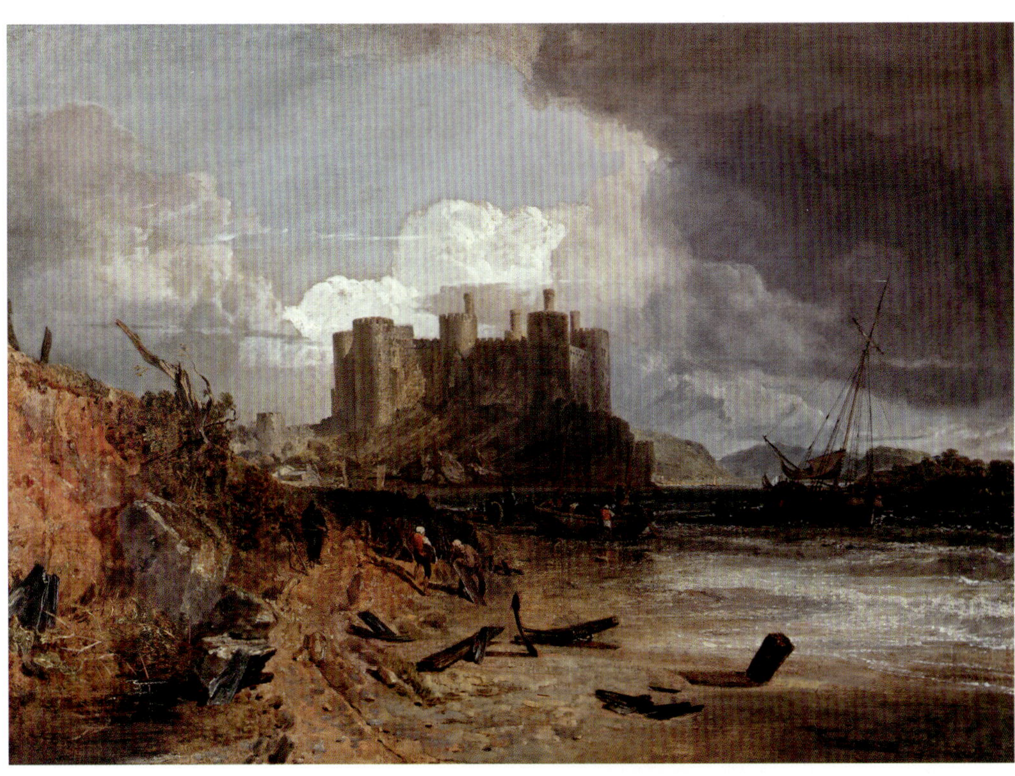

Conway Castle, 1803, oil on canvas, Private Collection, 104 x 140cm (41 x 55in)

Unusually, this large picture was not submitted for exhibition at the Royal Academy. In fact it was purchased by William Leader, who already owned two of Turner's watercolours of this subject and may well have commissioned the artist to execute this oil. The picture was, however, exhibited after Turner's death, firstly at the British Institute in 1855 and then at the Royal Academy in 1877.

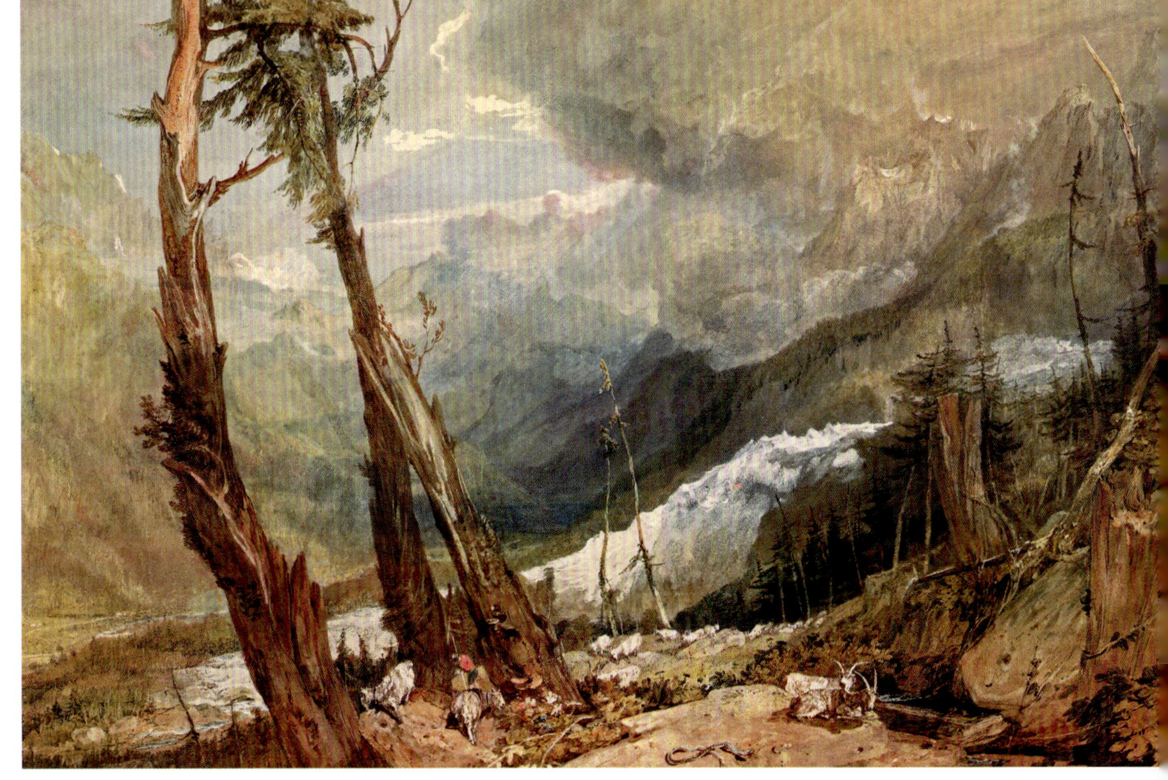

Glacier and Source of the Arveron Going up to the Mer de Glace, 1803, watercolour and graphite with scraping out, Paul Mellon Collection, Yale Center for British Art, CT, USA, 71 x 104cm (28 x 41in)

Turner used a technique in his watercolours called 'scraping out', in which, having applied washes to the paper, he then 'scraped out' the colour in certain areas to reveal the white paper underneath. This was useful in highlighting white areas such as snow-covered mountains. The effect was starker and more dramatic than the previous method of applying white bodycolour highlights.

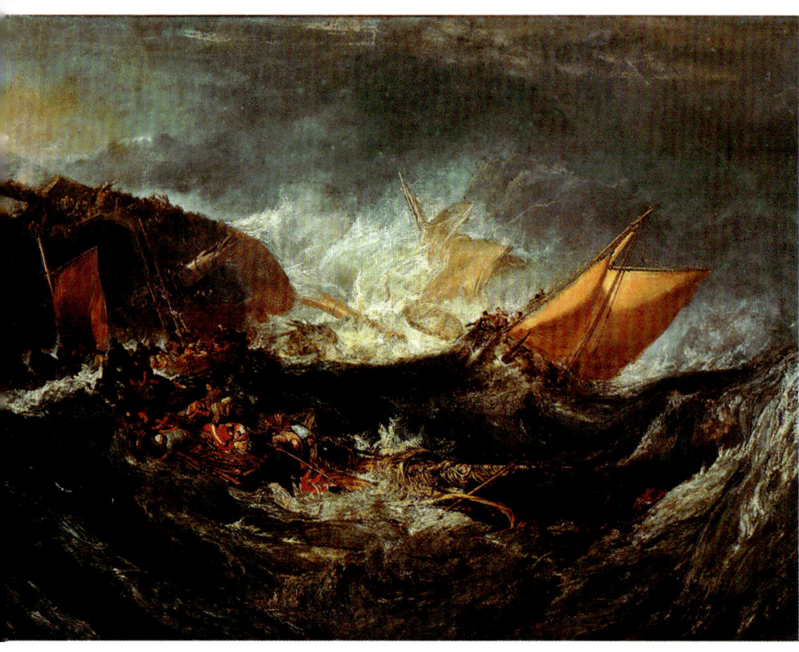

Shipwreck of the Minotaure *on Haack Sands, c.*1805–10, oil on canvas, Gulbenkian Foundation, Lisbon, Portugal, 173 x 241cm (68 x 95in)

This painting is more commonly known as *Wreck of a Transport Ship* but has been variously titled when it was exhibited several times after Turner's death. The work was probably derived from details of his *Wreck Sketchbook* (number 1) that the artist made during 1805–6. The painting has had only two owners in its lifetime. The first was Lord Yarborough who commissioned the painting, paying Turner £300 for the work; the second was Calouste Gulbenkian, the wealthy businessman who purchased it from the Yarborough Estate in 1920.

Old Margate Pier, 1804, oil on panel, Agnew and Sons, London, UK, 25 x 41cm (10 x 16in)

There is no record of the pictures displayed in Turner's gallery for its inaugural exhibition, but there is a consensus that this was one of them. Samuel Dobree apparently admired this small painting and Turner gave it to him as a gift with the larger works that he had purchased.

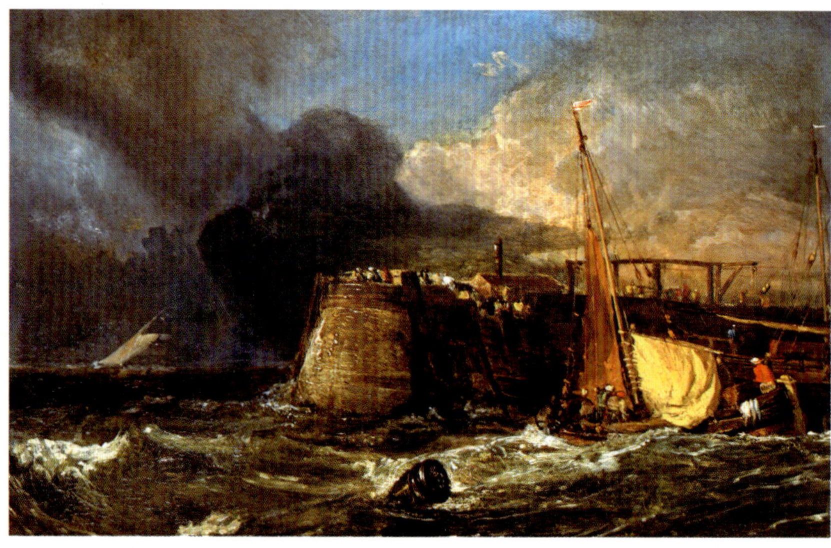

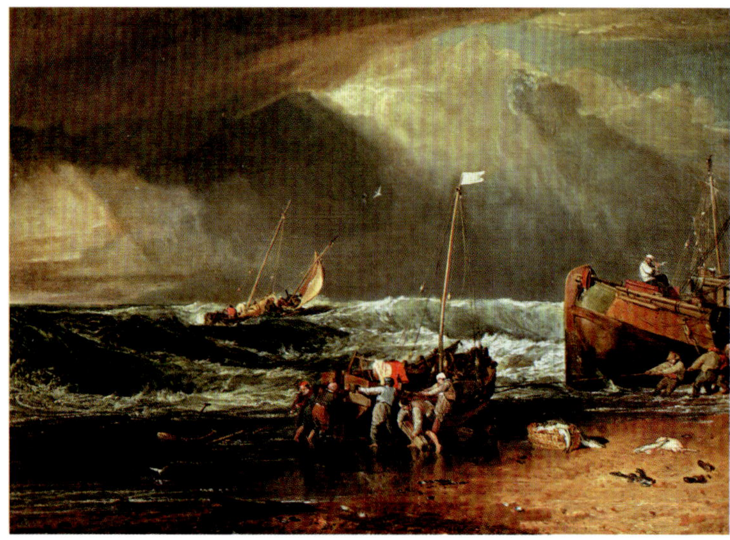

A Coast Scene with Fishermen Hauling a Boat Ashore (The Iveagh Sea-piece), 1804, oil on canvas, Kenwood House, London, UK, 91 x 122cm (36 x 48in)

This picture has often been confused with an earlier work, *Fishermen upon a Lee-shore in Squally Weather*, both pictures having been purchased by the banker Samuel Dobree and their subsequent histories conflated. The brewing magnate, Sir Edward Guinness, later Lord Iveagh, purchased the painting in 1888, placing it in his London home, Kenwood House, where it still remains as part of the Iveagh Bequest.

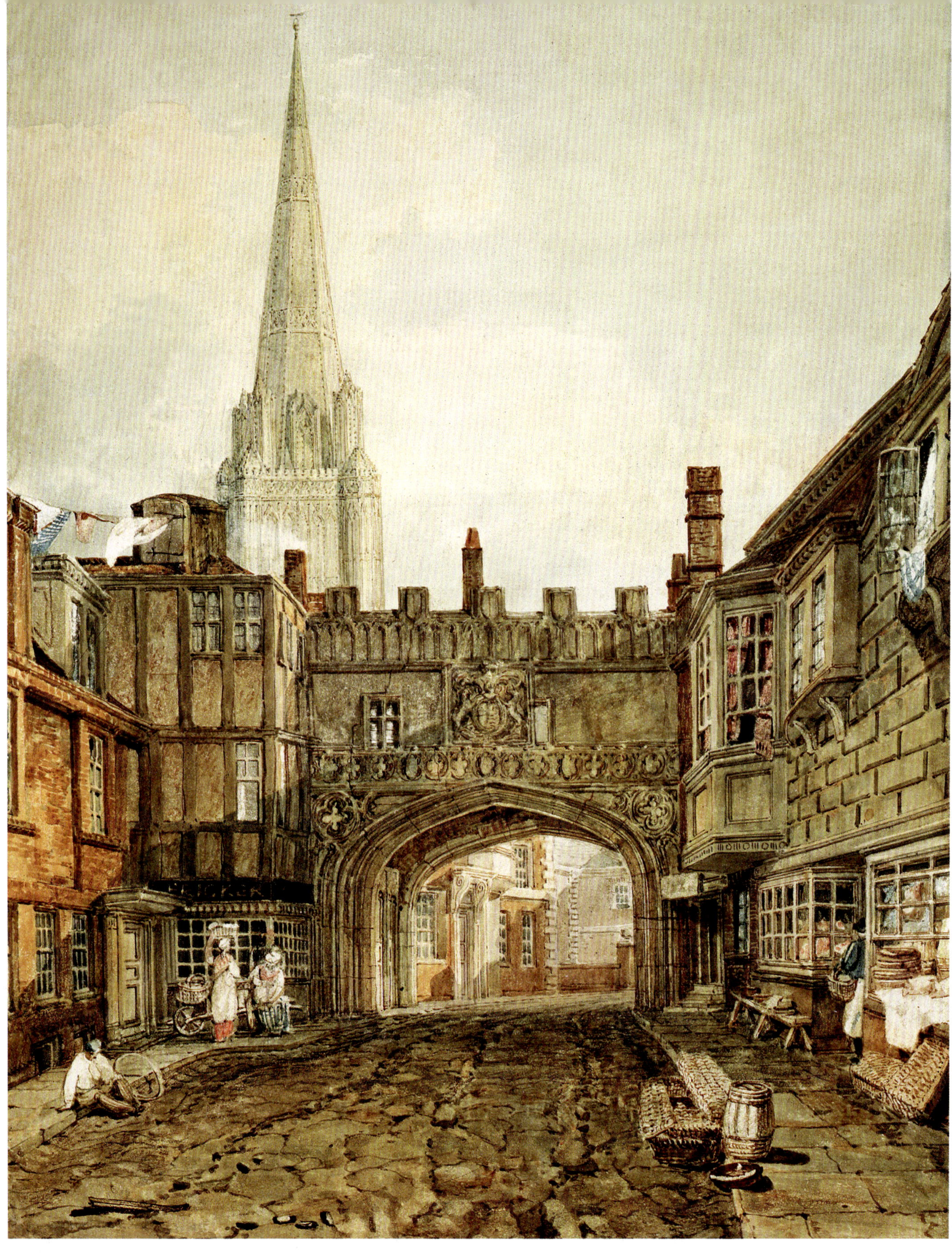

Gateway to the Close, Salisbury, 1802–5, graphite and watercolour, Fitzwilliam Museum, Cambridge, UK, 32 x 46cm (12½ x 18in)

This watercolour was among the last to be painted as part of the commission by the wealthy banker Richard Colt Hoare for Views of Salisbury. The main gateway to the close dates back to the 14th century and originally contained a small jail for minor felons. It was also the home of the porter, who was responsible for locking the main gate at night.

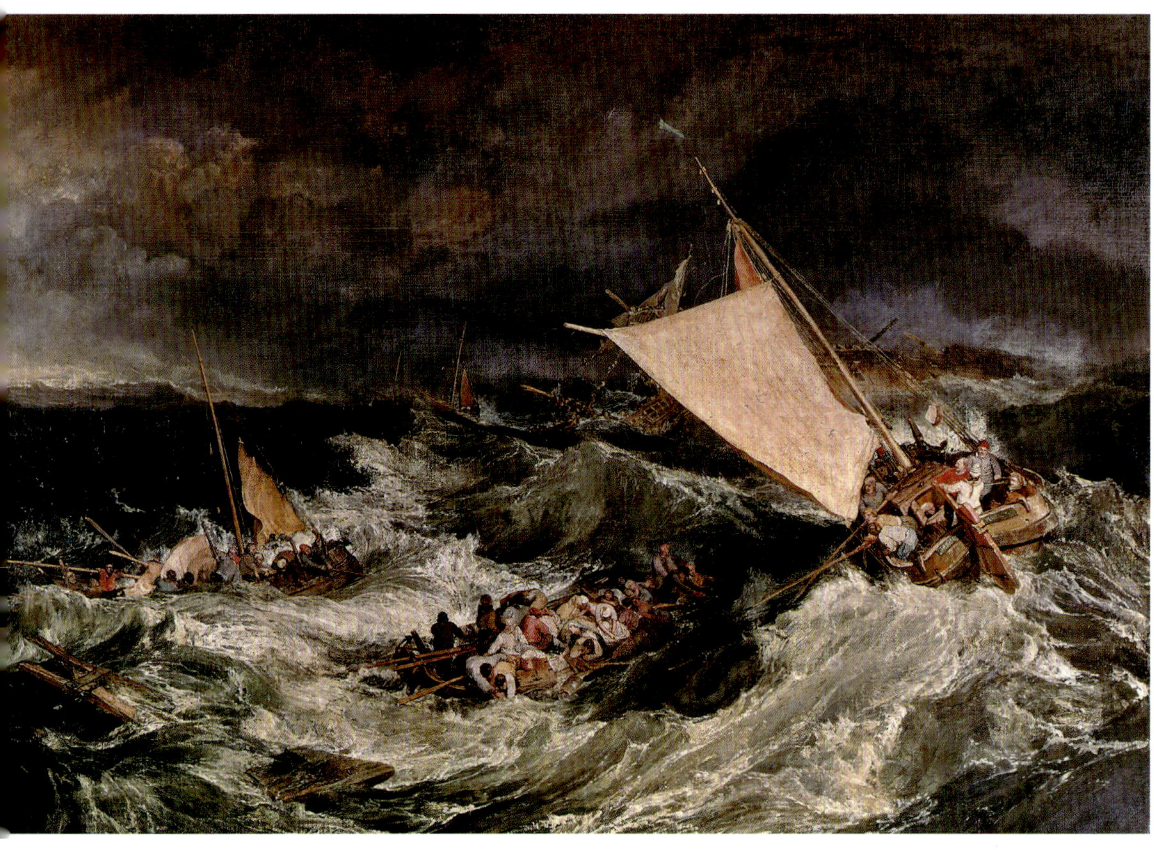

The Shipwreck, 1805,
oil on canvas, Tate Britain,
London, UK,
171 x 242cm (67 x 95in)

Against a background of the
Napoleonic Wars, when
France was threatening to
invade England, Turner
embarked on a series of
marine paintings that
embraced the notion of
disaster. Sensing the public
readiness for such an image,
the artist worked with the
engraver Charles Turner to
produce a large-scale
mezzotint of *The Shipwreck*
that was published in 1807.

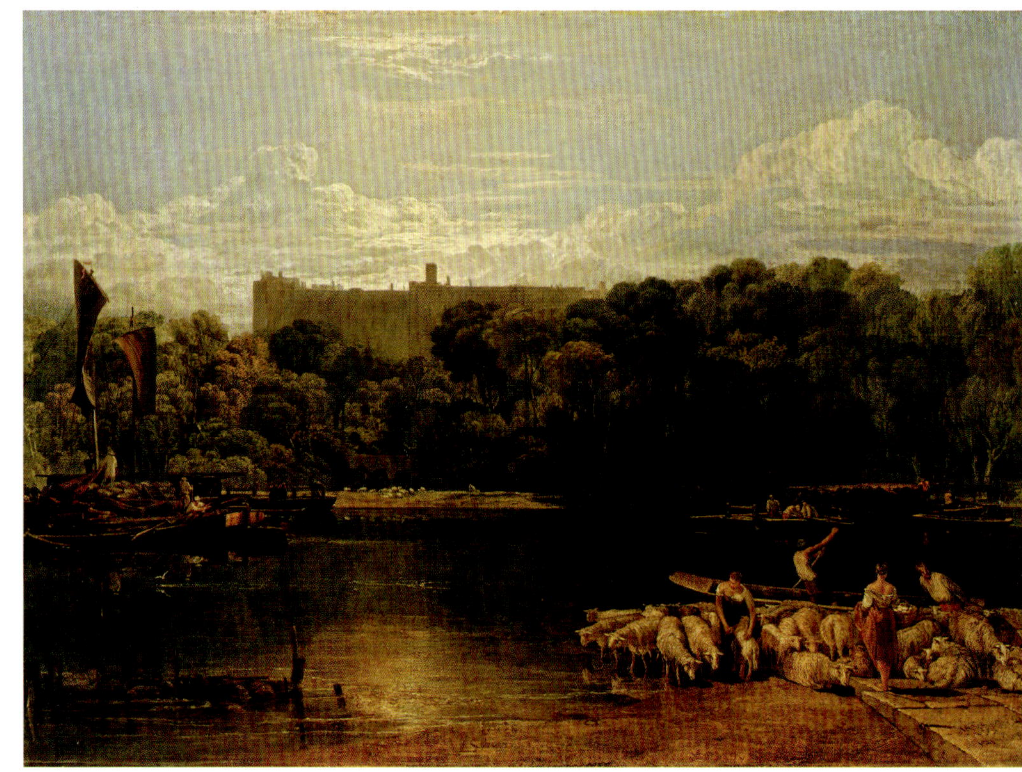

*Windsor Castle from the
Thames*, *c*.1805,
oil on canvas, Petworth
House, Sussex, UK,
86 x 122cm (34 x 48in)

This painting was signed
JMW Turner, Isleworth,
indicating that he was living
at Sion Ferry House at the
time of its execution.
Interestingly in this picture,
Turner has forsaken the
typical view of Windsor
Castle, obliterating the
Round Tower with trees,
suggesting that he was more
interested in depicting
a Classical Arcadian
landscape than producing a
topographical representation.

Artist's Studio, 1809, pen, ink and watercolour, British Museum, London, UK, 19 x 30cm (7½ x 12in)

It is unclear as to who the artist is in this almost mocking caricature of an artist's studio, although it may well be self-deprecating. Turner has, however, captured the chaotic atmosphere in a studio which he achieves using a bravura style that suggests speed and economy of effort not dissimilar to his own working methods.

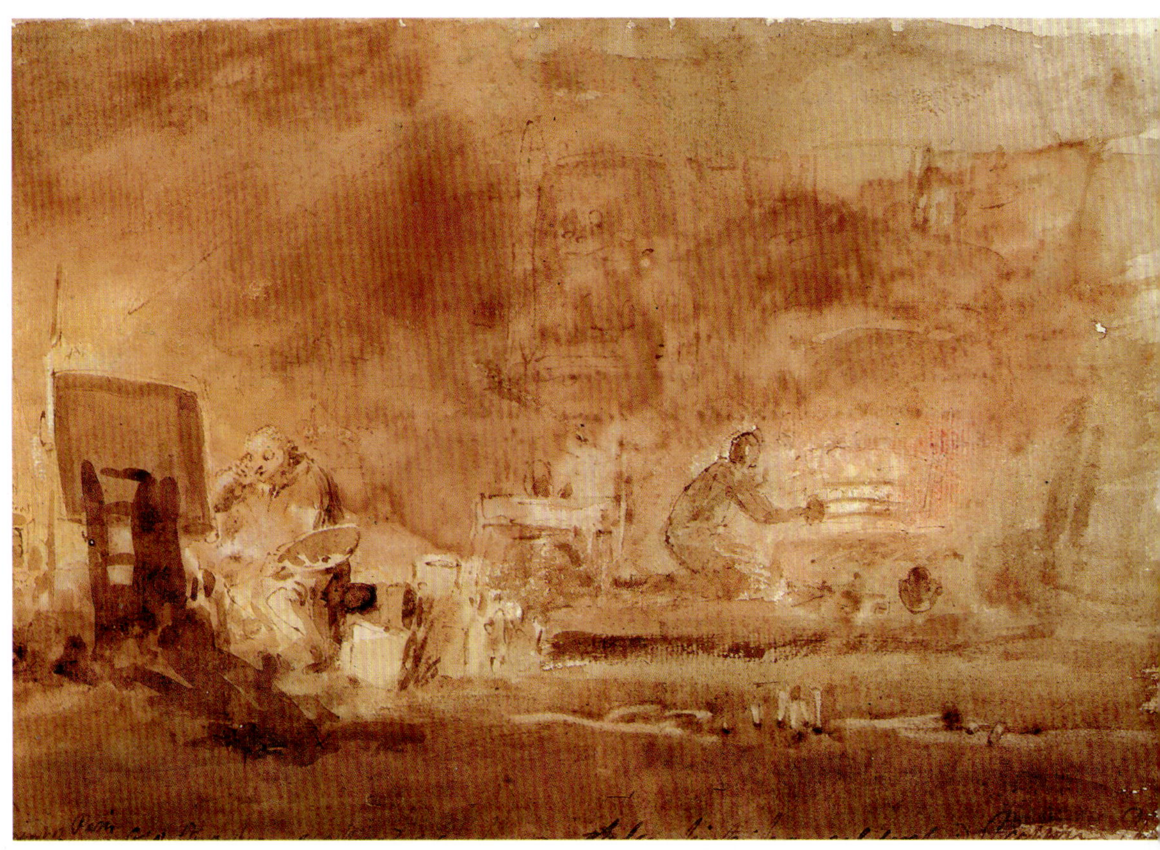

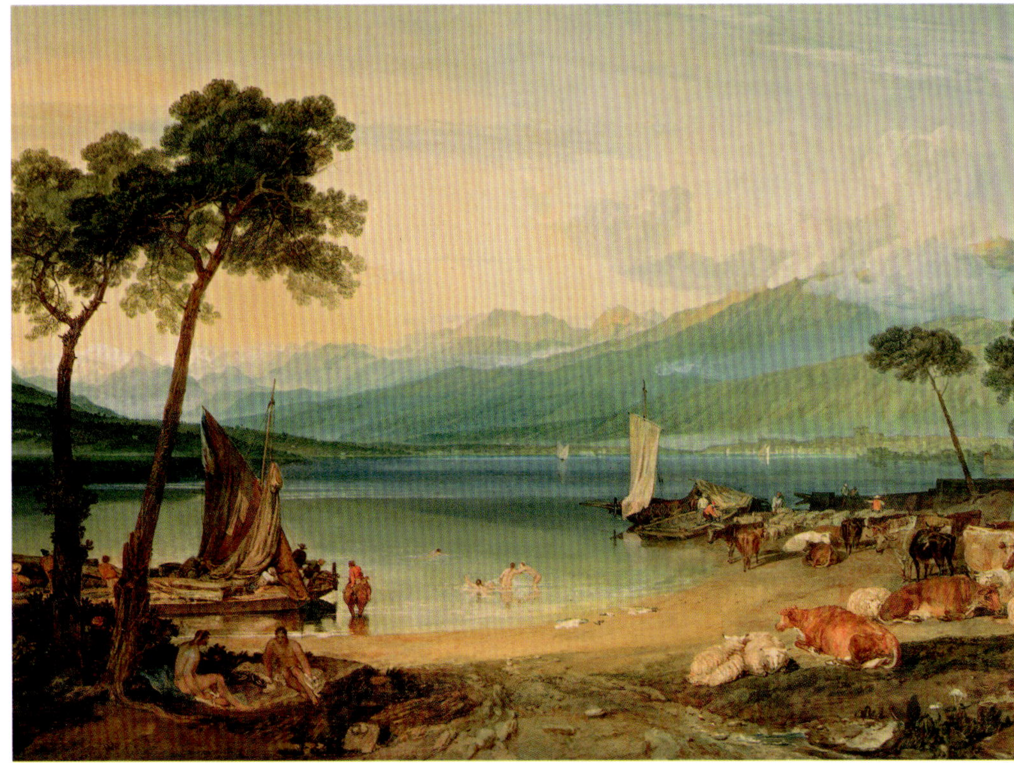

Lake Geneva and Mont Blanc, 1802–5, watercolour and ink, Paul Mellon Collection, Yale Center for British Art, CT, USA, 73 x 114cm (29 x 45in)

Turner painted this idealized pastoral landscape in the Classical tradition from the sketchbook that he made on his first trip to the Continent in 1802. It demonstrates his ability to combine physical features, that are not necessarily indigenous, in order to create effect, typical of artists in the Romantic period. The picture indicates the influence of the British painter Richard Wilson, whom Turner much admired.

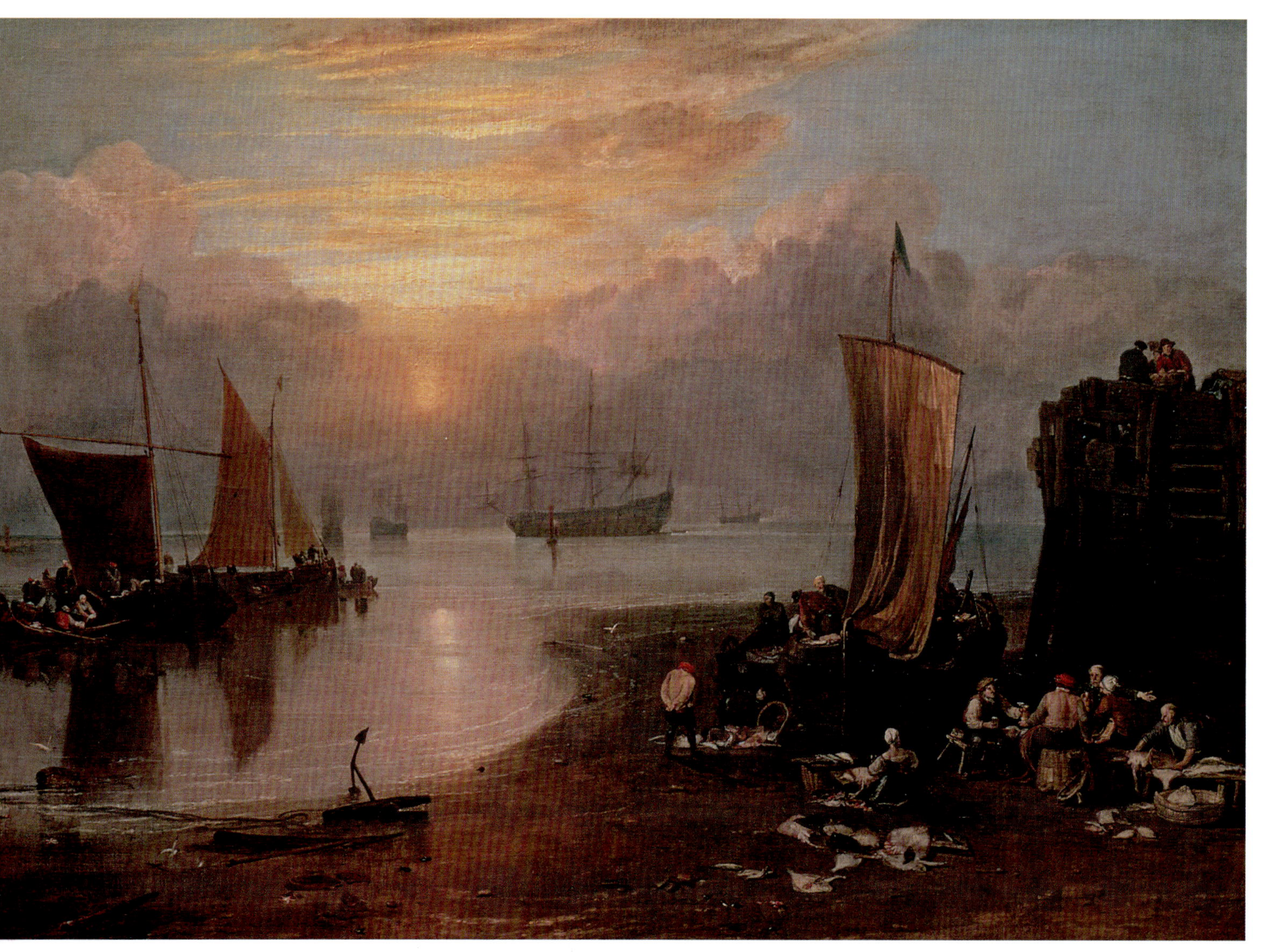

Sun Rising through Vapour: Fishermen Cleaning and Selling Fish, 1807, oil on canvas, National Gallery, London, UK, 135 x 179cm (53 x 70in)

Turner purchased this picture when it came up for auction in 1827, having originally been sold to Sir John Leicester in 1818. The artist was aware of the significance of the painting, and in his second will of 1831 he replaced *The Decline of the Carthaginian Empire* with this picture, to be given to the National Gallery as part of his legacy.

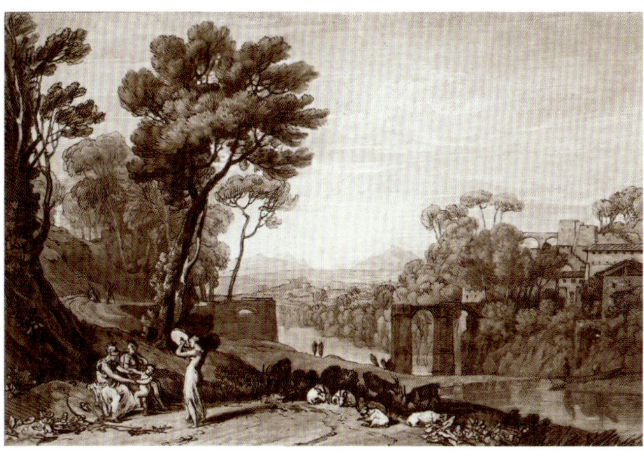

The Woman and the Tambourine, 1808, etching and mezzotint, Fitzwilliam Museum, Cambridge, UK, 19 x 26cm (7½ x 10in)

Turner's *Liber Studiorum* was published in June 1807 as the first in a series of five etched plates to demonstrate different aspects of landscapes. This plate, the second of the five, represented the 'Elevated' or 'Epic Pastoral' (EP), and the artist referred to the work as his "EP Bridge" and also his "Claude EP". Later, Ruskin was less favourable in his comments and referred to it as imbecilic.

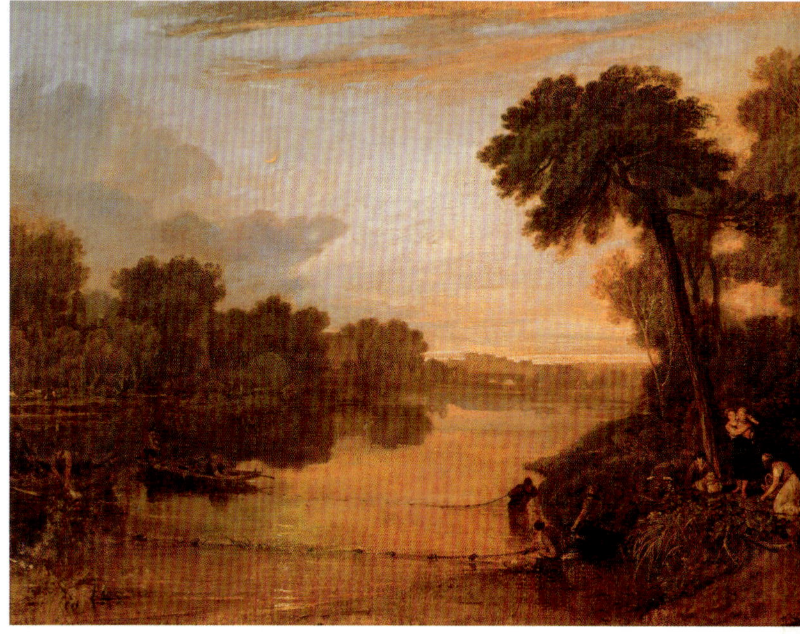

The Thames near Windsor, Evening: Men Dragging Nets on Shore, 1807, oil on canvas, Petworth House, Sussex, UK, 89 x 119cm (35 x 47in)

This is an example of Turner mixing landscape and genre painting, a significant shift in subject matter for early 19th-century artists. It is, however, a Romantic and idealized work redolent of Classical painting that accorded with Academy tradition. Windsor Castle can just be seen in the far distance behind Windsor Bridge, which was replaced in 1822.

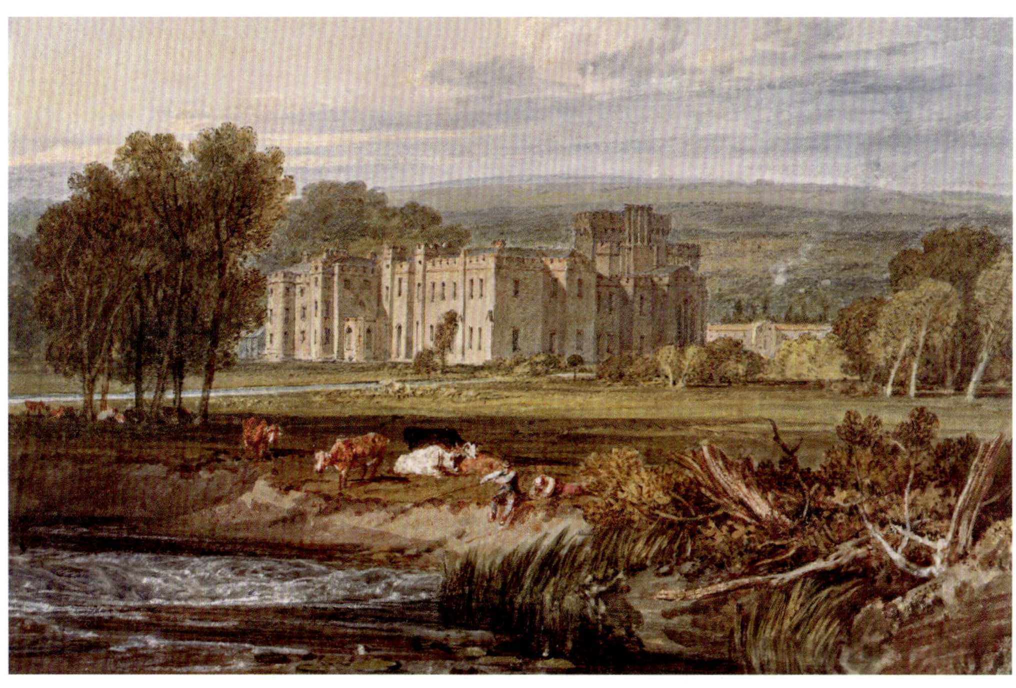

View of Hampton Court, Herefordshire, from the South-east, 1806, graphite and watercolour, Paul Mellon Collection, Yale Center for British Art, CT, USA, 20 x 31cm (8 x 12in)

Not to be confused with the palace of the same name on the outskirts of London, this castellated country house dates from the early 15th century, and was built by Sir Rowland Lenthall, who had fought alongside Henry V at the Battle of Agincourt. The house was altered in the 19th century after John Arkwright purchased it.

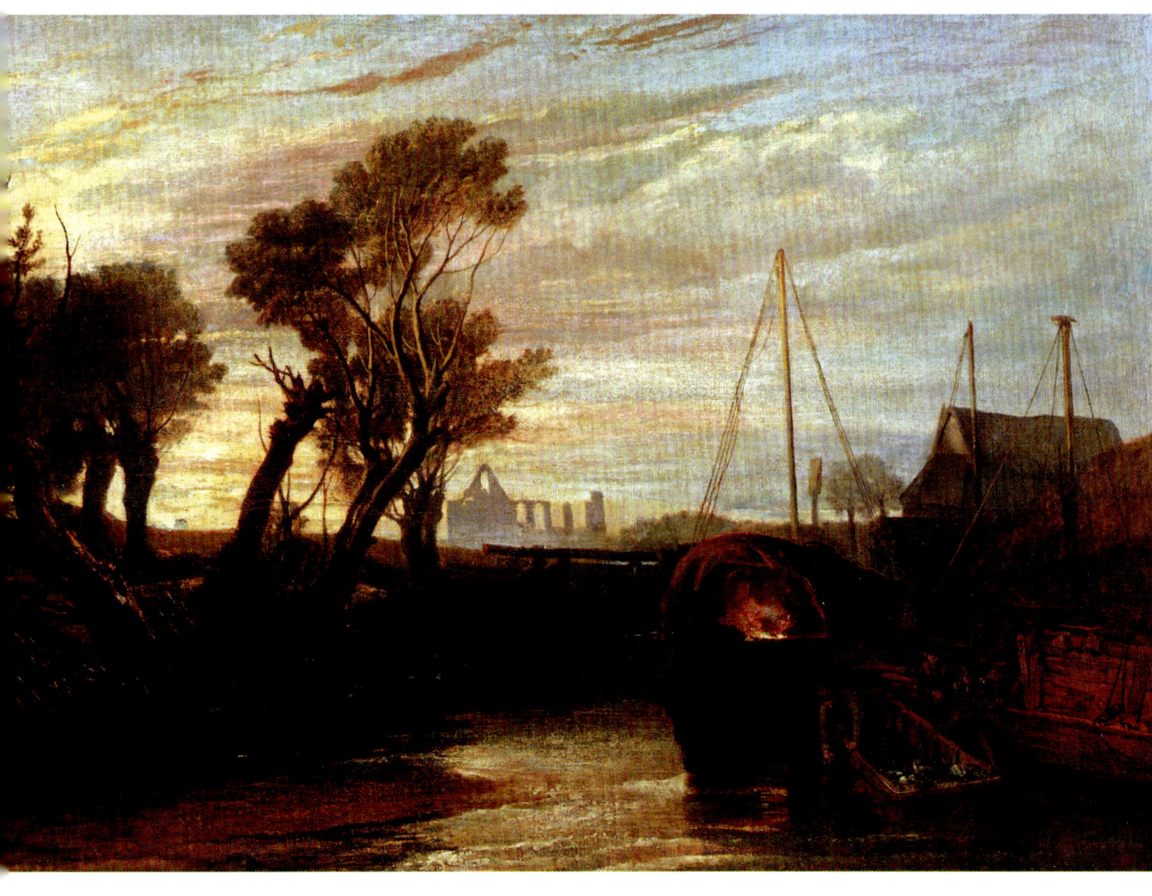

Newark Abbey, 1807,
oil on canvas, Paul Mellon
Collection, Yale Center for
British Art, CT, USA,
92 x 123cm (36 x 48in)

It is unclear whether this
picture was exhibited at
Turner's own gallery in 1807,
which would have been its
only public showing during
the artist's lifetime while he
still owned it. Having been
originally purchased by Sir
John Leicester, who then
showed it to the public in his
own gallery, it was then sold
at auction after his death to
the court painter Sir Thomas
Lawrence. The picture
changed hands several more
times after that.

*The Bridge in Middle
Distance*, 1808, etching and
mezzotint, Fitzwilliam
Museum, Cambridge, UK,
21 x 29cm (8 x 11in)

The bridge referred to
in this plate from Turner's
Liber Studiorum is Walton
Bridge across the Thames,
a favourite motif of the
artist, who had recently
acquired land along the
river on which to build
a house for himself.
The bridge appeared
several times in a number
of his important later
works. Here it provides
a backdrop to a
Claudian landscape that
Turner has designated
'Elevated Pastoral'.

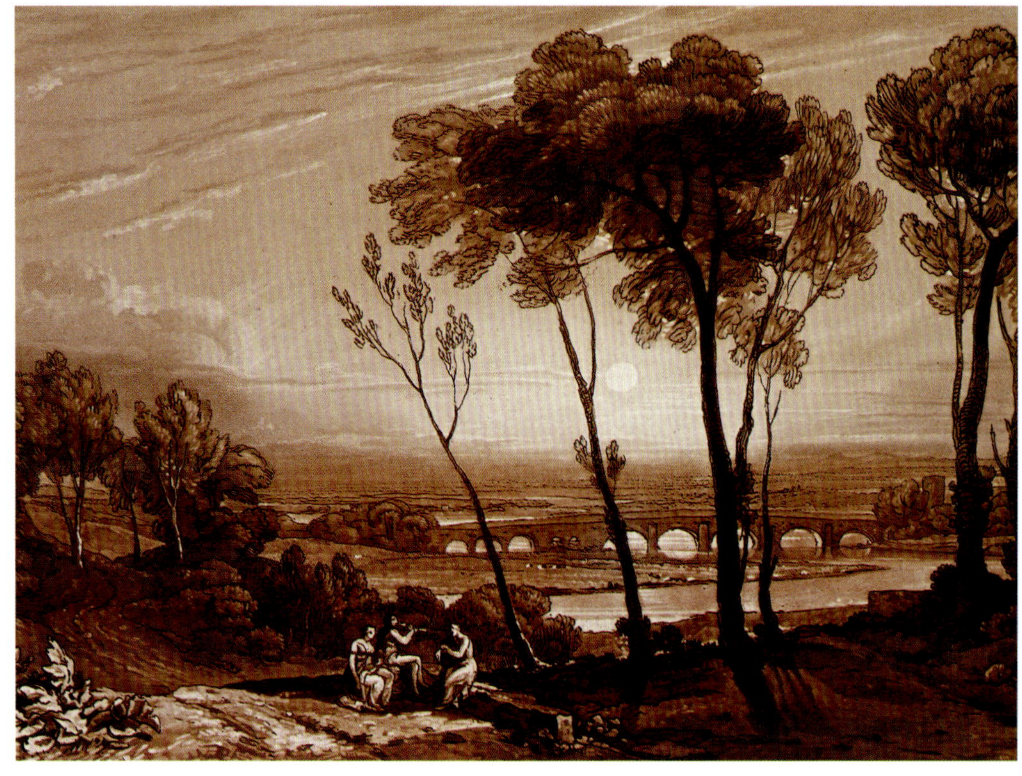

The Thames at Eton, 1808, oil on canvas, Petworth House, Sussex, UK, 60 x 90cm (24 x 35in)

Lord Egremont purchased this picture, and three others, from Turner's gallery exhibition of 1808. The artist had spent the previous summer along the Thames valley, making a number of sketches of this area in his Eton and Windsor Sketchbook. This painting demonstrates the influence of Jan van Goyen, the 17th-century Dutch painter who specialized in river scenes.

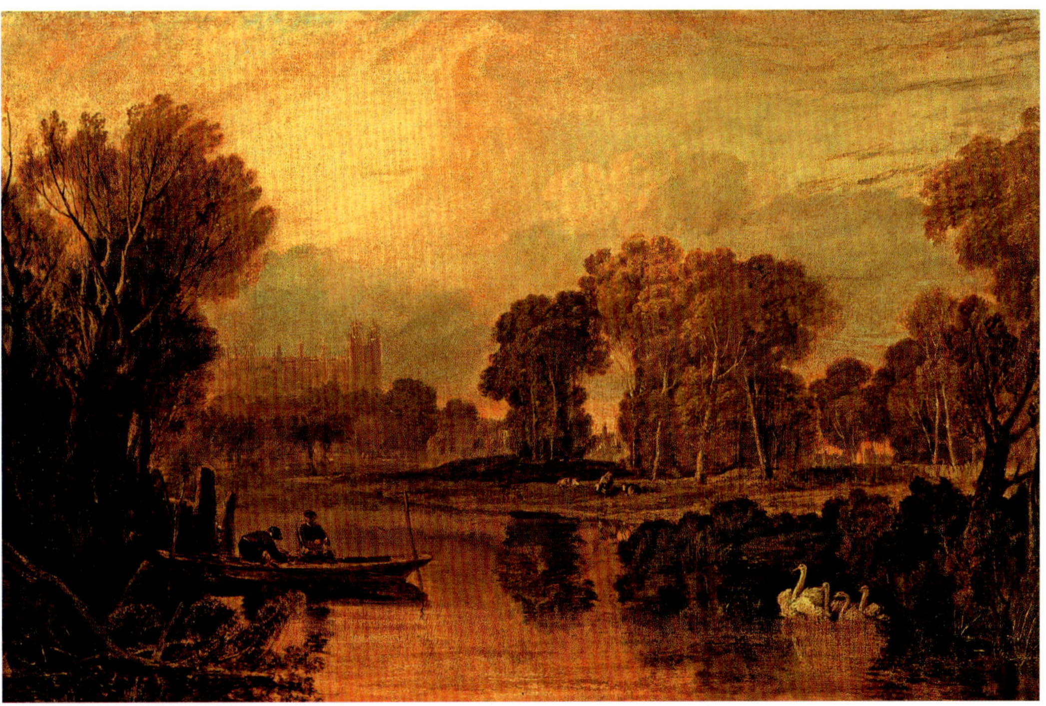

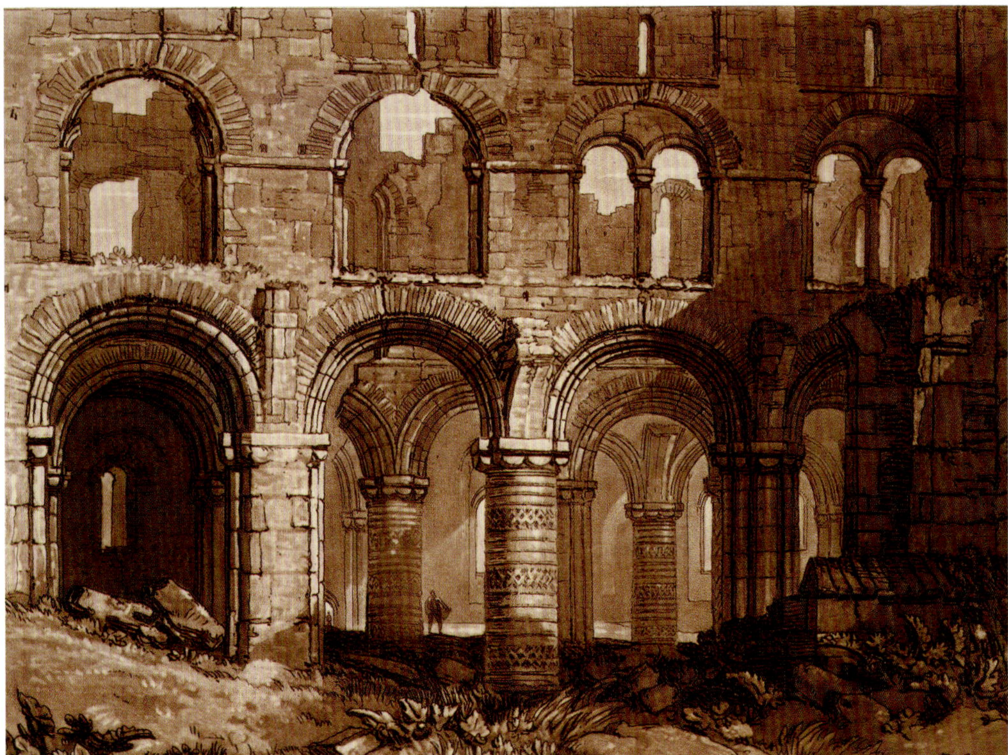

Holy Island Cathedral, from the *Liber Studiorum*, 1808, etching, Fitzwilliam Museum, Cambridge, UK, 21 x 29cm (8 x 11in)

The *Liber Studiorum* was an ambitious publishing project initiated by Turner, based loosely on Claude Lorrain's *Liber Veritatis* or 'Book of Truths', in order to illustrate and compartmentalize landscape composition. The first series of five etchings were produced in 1807, each representing one aspect of pastoral, architectural, historical, marine or mountainous landscape. Charles Turner reproduced this image for the second issue.

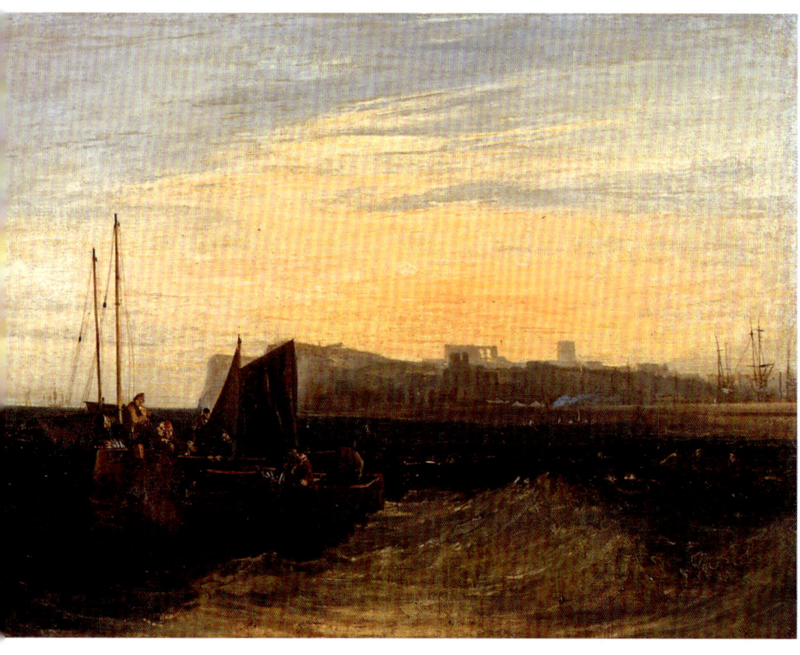

Margate, 1808, oil on canvas, Petworth House, Sussex, UK, 90 x 121cm (35 x 48in)

Another of Lord Egremont's purchases from Turner's gallery in 1808, this picture apparently was either untitled or retitled later, the only written verification for its location being John Landseer's contemporary *Review of Publications in Art*, which is slightly ambiguous, and additional circumstantial evidence concerning the boat. Turner's contrasted forms of detailed foreground and misty townscape provide a dynamic narrative to the scene.

Fishing upon Blythe Sand, Tide Setting In, 1809, oil on canvas, Tate Britain, London, UK, 89 x 119cm (35 x 47in)

Although this painting had several exhibition outings during Turner's lifetime, including at the Academy, it remained unsold at his death and became part of the Bequest in 1856. In fact Turner's old adversary, Sir George Beaumont wanted to buy the painting, but he had the 'proud pleasure' to refuse to sell it to him because of his acerbic remarks concerning some of his previously exhibited pictures.

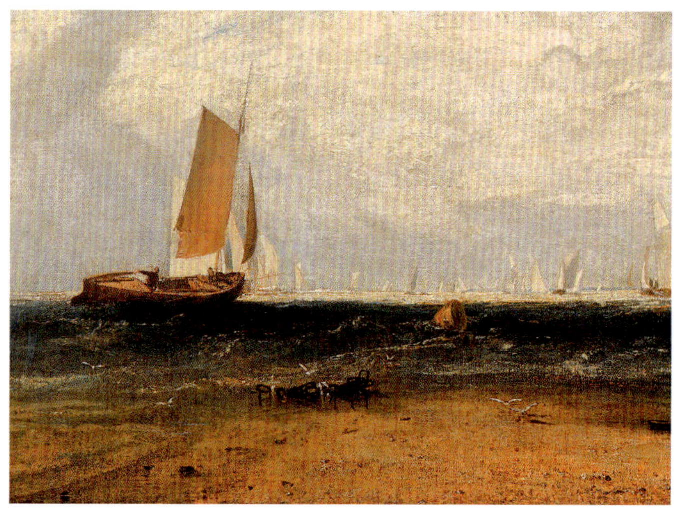

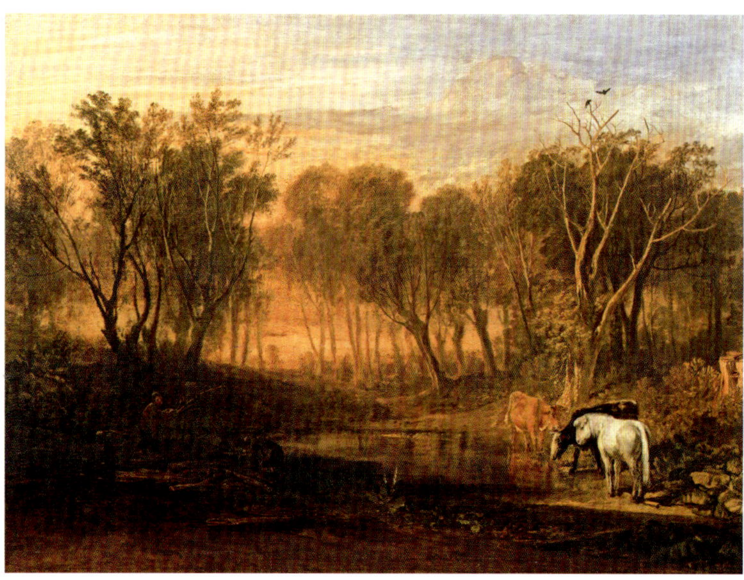

The Forest of Bere, 1808, oil on canvas, Petworth House, Sussex, UK, 89 x 119cm (35 x 47in)

This woodland area once formed part of Lord Egremont's estate before being sold off. The figures in the foreground (barely seen) may have been working for Egremont, tanning on his estate. Turner may well have had this in mind when he executed the painting, since Egremont purchased it as part of his haul of 1808.

Bolton Abbey, Yorkshire, 1809, watercolour, University of Liverpool, UK, 28 x 39cm (11 x 15in)

One can immediately discern the influences of previous generations of classical landscape artists in this work by Turner. It adopts the Picturesque aesthetic, depicting one of the many ruined priory churches that were destroyed in the 16th century, amid an idealized Arcadian landscape. Turner probably visited this area in Yorkshire while he stayed at Farnley Hall with his friend Walter Ramsden Fawkes for the first time in the summer of 1808.

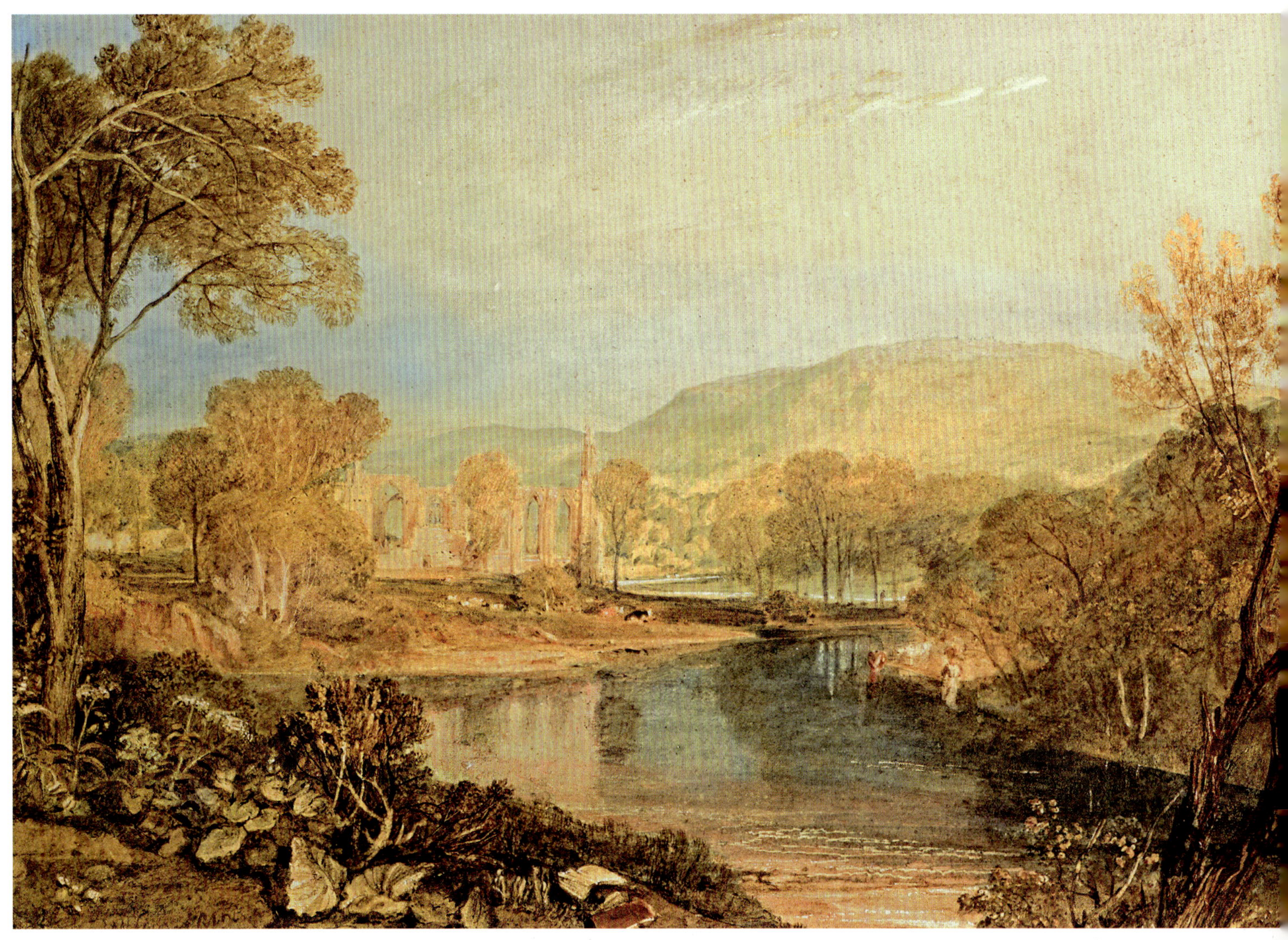

The Sun Rising through Vapour, c.1809, oil on canvas, University of Birmingham, UK, 69 x 102cm (27 x 40in)

Walter Fawkes purchased this painting directly from Turner. The preliminary drawing for the painting is in the Spithead Sketchbook from 1807, but the date of execution is unclear and it is not known if the picture was exhibited in the artist's lifetime, although it is likely that it was shown in his own gallery in 1809. It may well have been a commission from Fawkes who already owned the *Victory* painting.

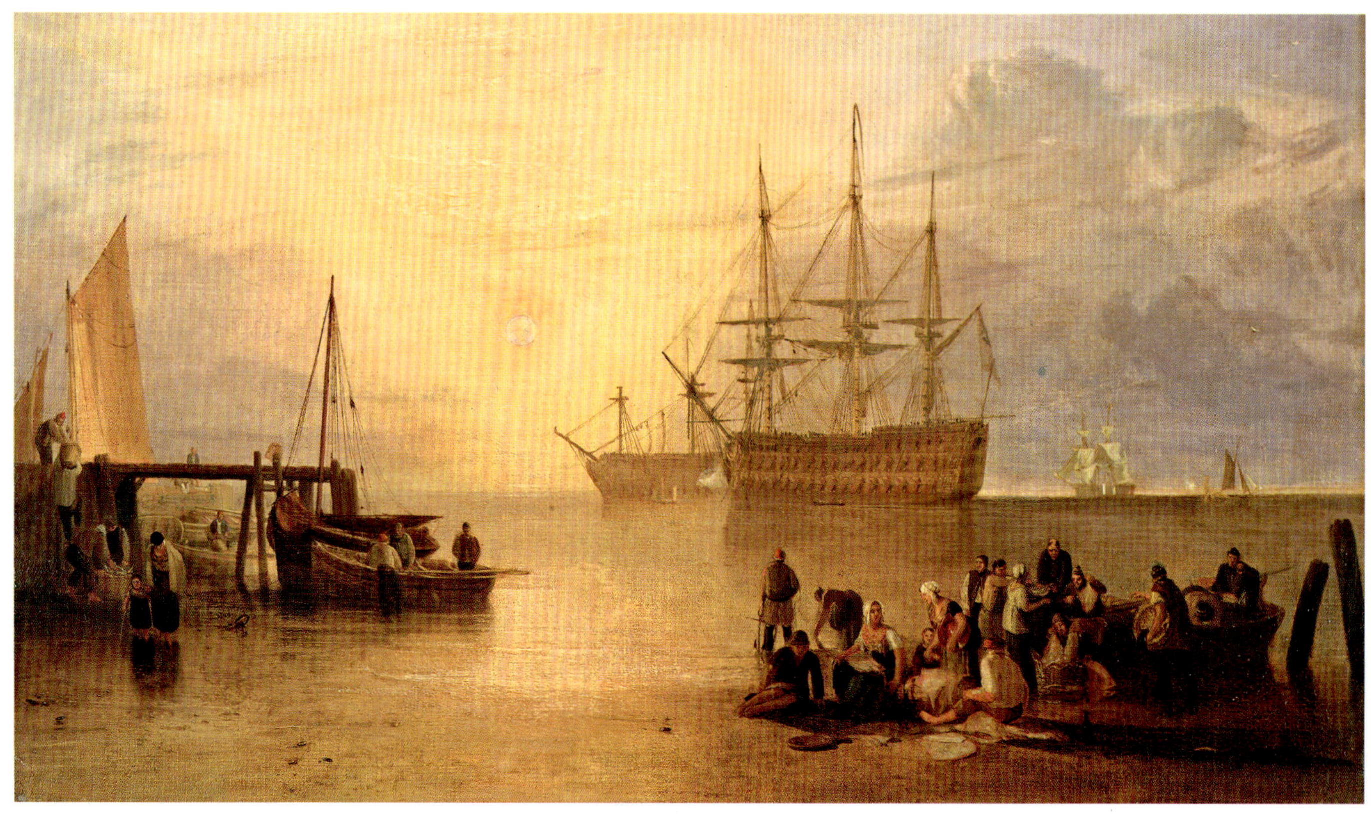

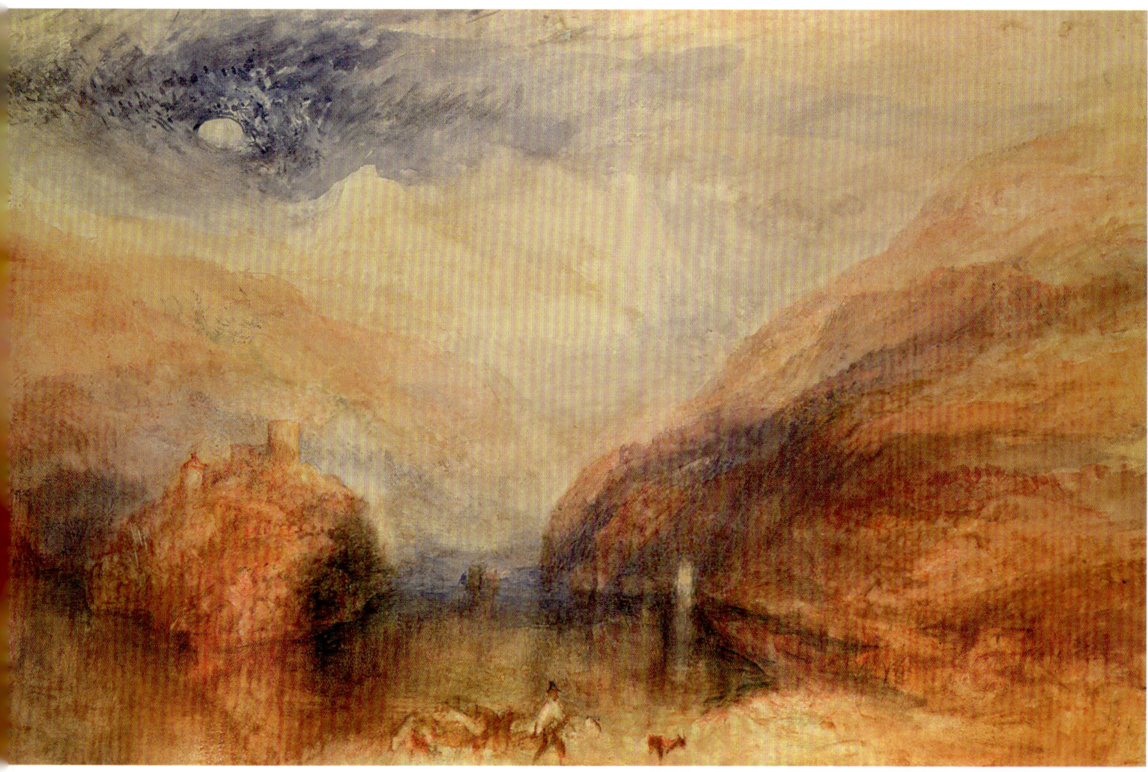

The Lake of Brienz, 1809, watercolour, British Museum, London, UK, 39 x 56cm (15 x 22in)

By this time, Turner had moved away from the Sublime aesthetic used in the earlier Alpine pictures, to one that was more Arcadian in concept, using the mountains as a backdrop to an idyllic social scene. This may well have reflected the relative calm in the area, following the withdrawal of French troops in 1803 and the establishment of the Swiss Confederation, under the Act of Mediation signed by Napoleon.

Grand Junction Canal at Southall Mill, 1810, oil on canvas, Private Collection, 92 x 122cm (36 x 48in)

A painting that is so redolent of Dutch 17th-century landscape paintings has nevertheless one of Turner's hallmarks, the coloured evening sky. The mill itself no longer exists and it is said that the artist sketched it one evening on a return journey from his friend Henry Scott Trimmer's house close by. The image was published in 1811 in the sixth edition of *Liber Studiorum* as *Windmill and Lock*.

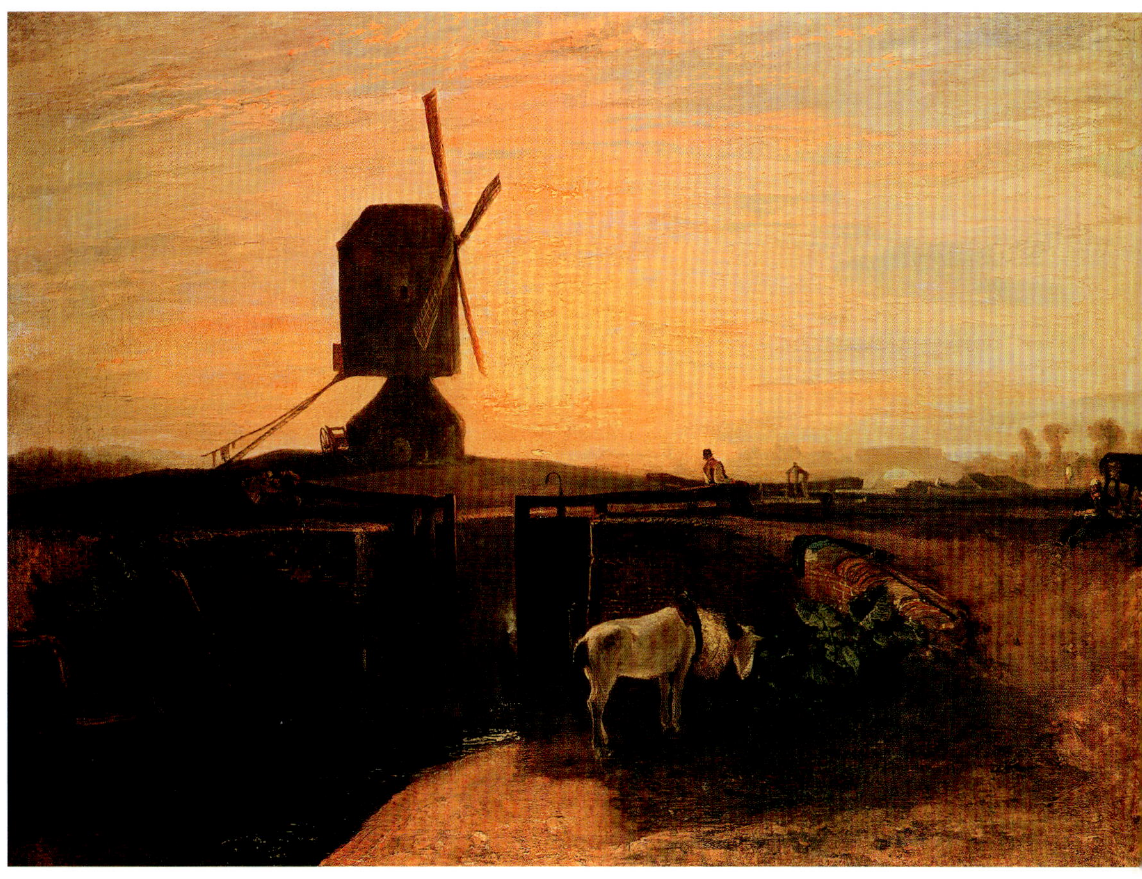

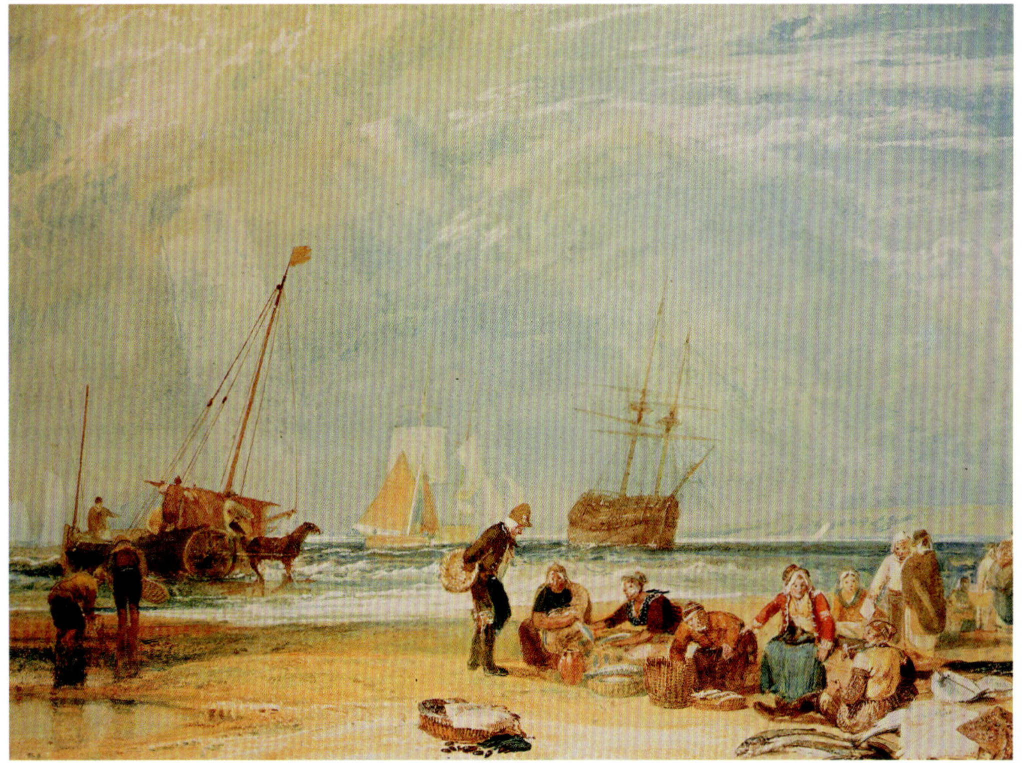

Fishmarket on the Sands, Hastings, 1810, watercolour, Private Collection, 28 x 39cm (11 x 15in)

Without any visible landmarks, it is difficult to identify the location of this painting. He had, however, been visiting Sussex in the summer of 1810 and made copious drawings and sketches in his Hastings Sketchbook. He also painted an oil of similar nature, which also refers to the town of Hastings, although again there are no visible landmarks to identify the town. The viewer is therefore forced to engage with this wonderful genre painting for its own sake.

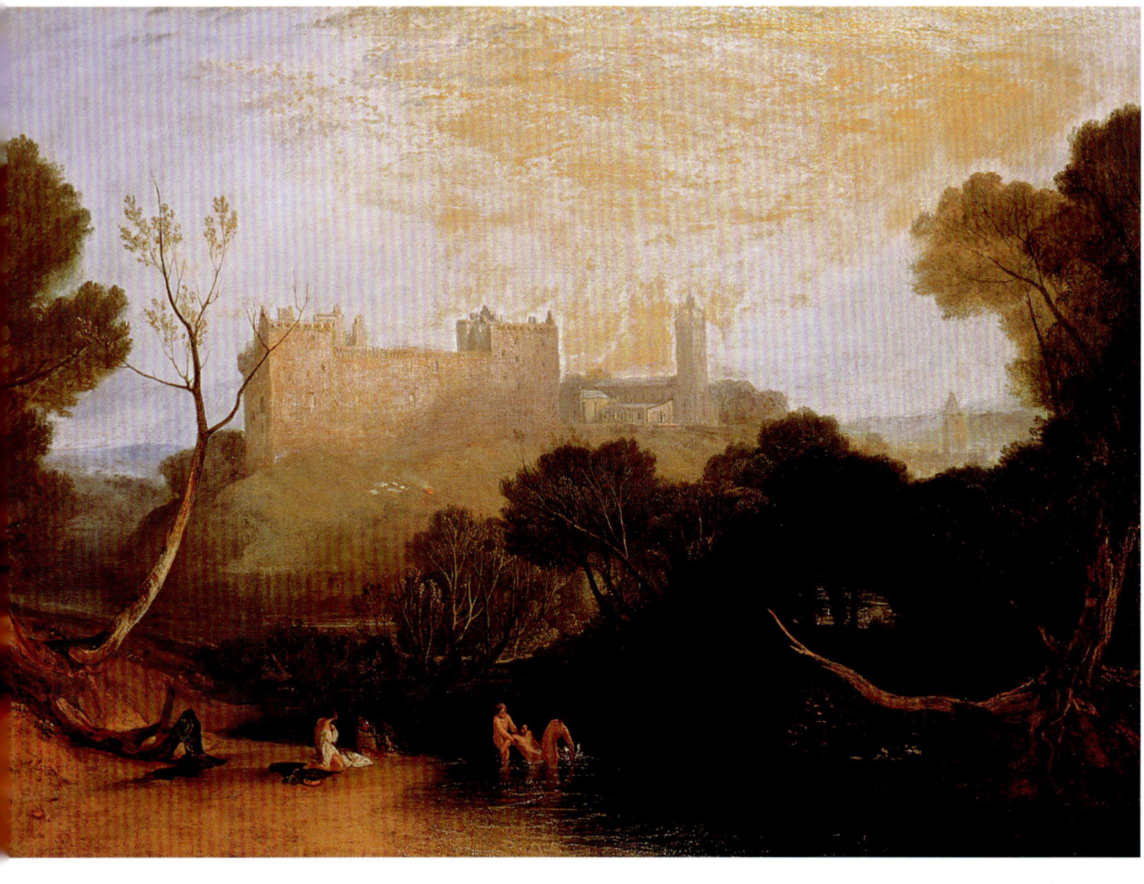

Linlithgow Palace, 1810,
oil on canvas, Walker Art
Gallery, National Museums,
Liverpool, UK,
91 x 122cm (36 x 48in)

At the time of this painting,
the palace lay in ruins, having
been destroyed by the Duke
of Cumberland's troops
during the Jacobite Rebellion
of the mid-18th century.
Previously the Scottish royal
family had used the palace,
situated conveniently
between Edinburgh and
Stirling Castles. Linlithgow
Palace was the birthplace
of Mary Queen of Scots
in 1542.

*Scarborough Town and Castle:
Morning, Boys Catching Crabs*,
*c.*1810, watercolour, Art
Gallery of South Australia,
Adelaide, Australia,
69 x 102cm (27 x 40in)

Exhibited at the Academy in
1811, this watercolour was
purchased by Turner's friend
and long-time patron Walter
Fawkes. From a painting
dated 1819 of Fawkes'
drawing room by John
Buckler, *Scarborough* can be
readily identified as taking
pride of place among several
smaller works, providing
evidence of the esteem
in which the patron
held Turner.

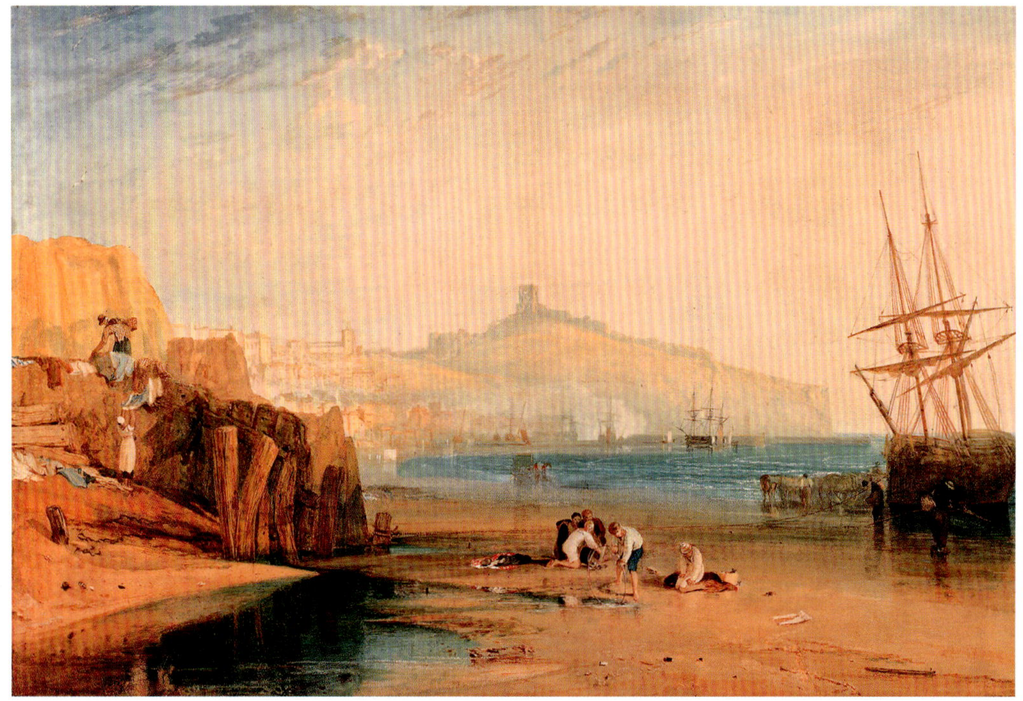

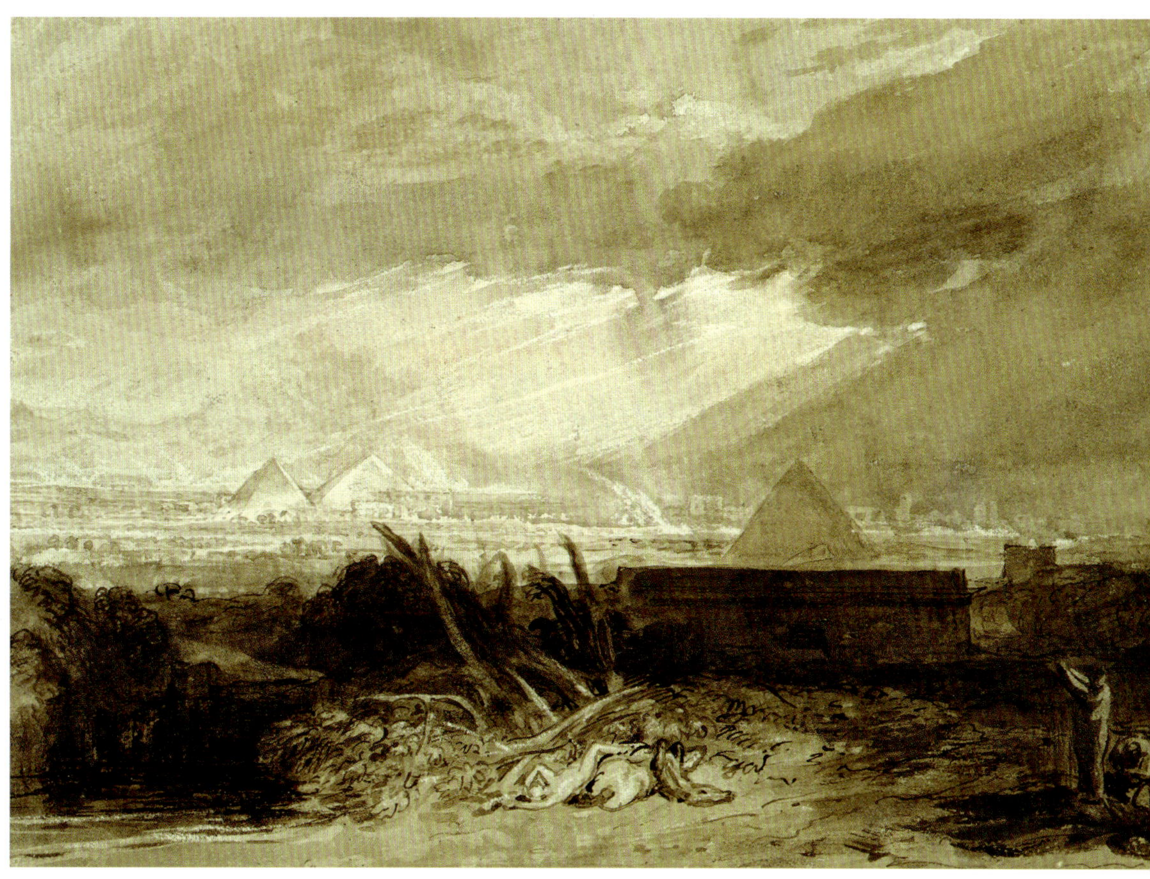

The Fifth Plague of Egypt, 1806–10, pen and ink and wash, British Museum, London, UK, 19 x 26cm (7½ x 10in)

In this reworking of the previous large-scale oil executed in 1800, Turner appears to have reused the motif as an exercise in monochromatic paint handling. Charles Turner translated this version into an engraving for the third edition of *Liber Studiorum*, to represent aspects of historical landscape composition. The picture is factually inaccurate though, since Turner is depicting the seventh rather than the fifth plague.

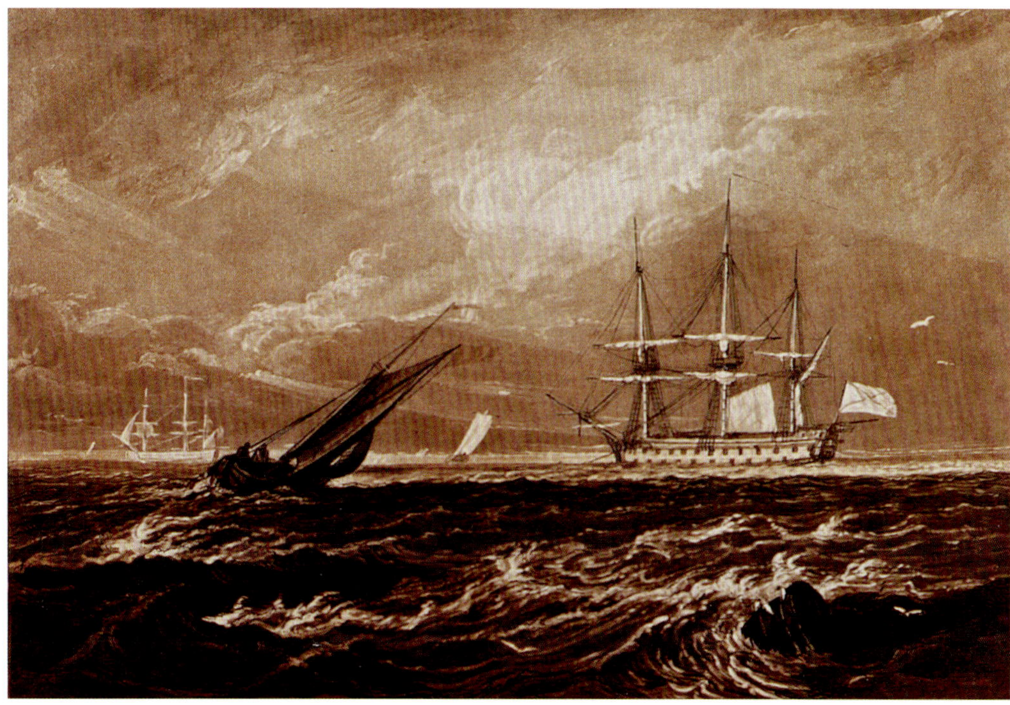

The Leader Sea-piece, c.1809, engraving and mezzotint, Paul Mellon Collection, Yale Center for British Art, CT, USA, 18 x 26cm (7 x 10in)

The original painting (now lost) was executed between 1807 and 1809 for William Leader, from which an etching was made by Turner and engraved by Charles Turner, for the *Liber Studiorum*. The only record of the painting's existence was the record on the etching: "Original sketch of a picture for W. Leader". The engraving shown here was a later impression.

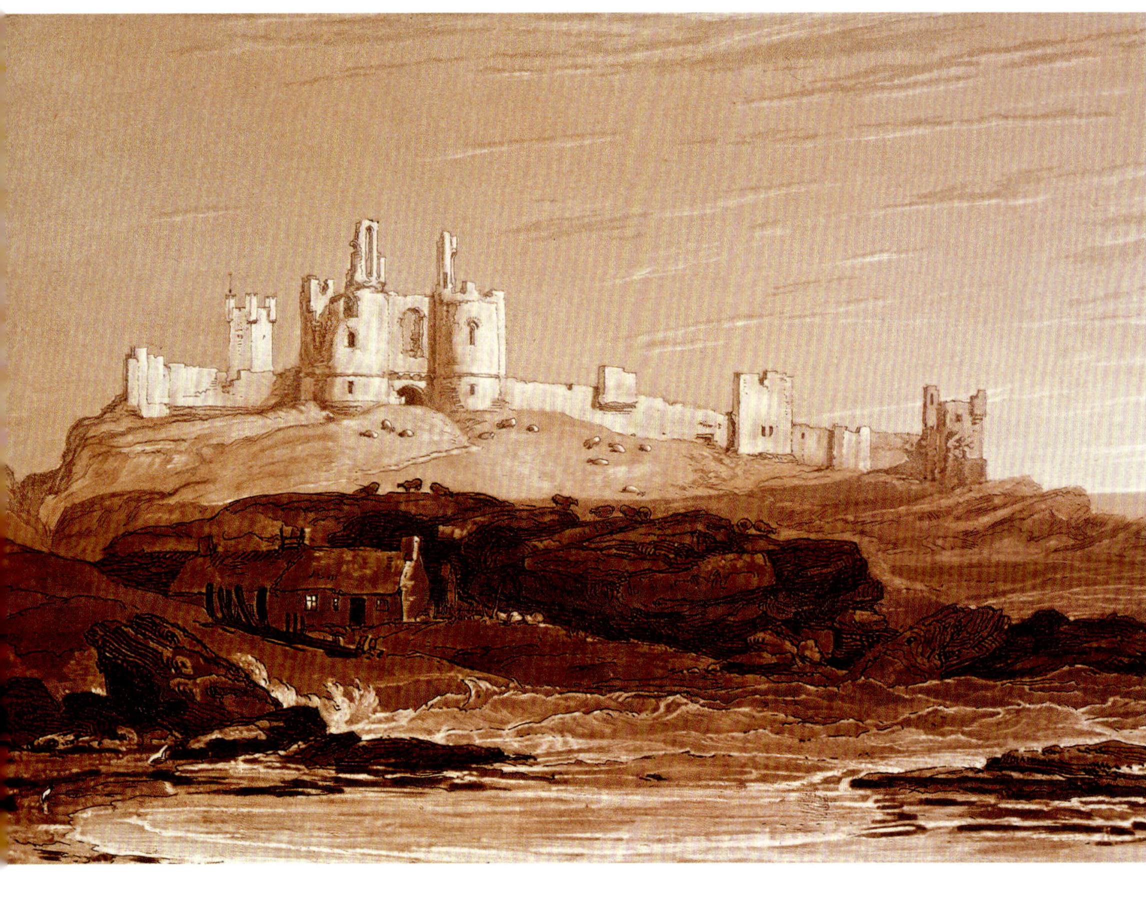

Dunstanborough Castle, 1808, etching, Fitzwilliam Museum, Cambridge, UK, 21 x 29cm (8 x 11in)

Part three of *Liber Studiorum* was published in June 1808 and included the plate shown here which was used to demonstrate architecture within the landscape painting tradition. However, Turner also draws our attention to the sharp contrasts of the picture. The pale sky and the regular ordered forms of the sunlit castle contrast sharply with the dark and unpredictable sea, which is emphasized by its irregular forms.

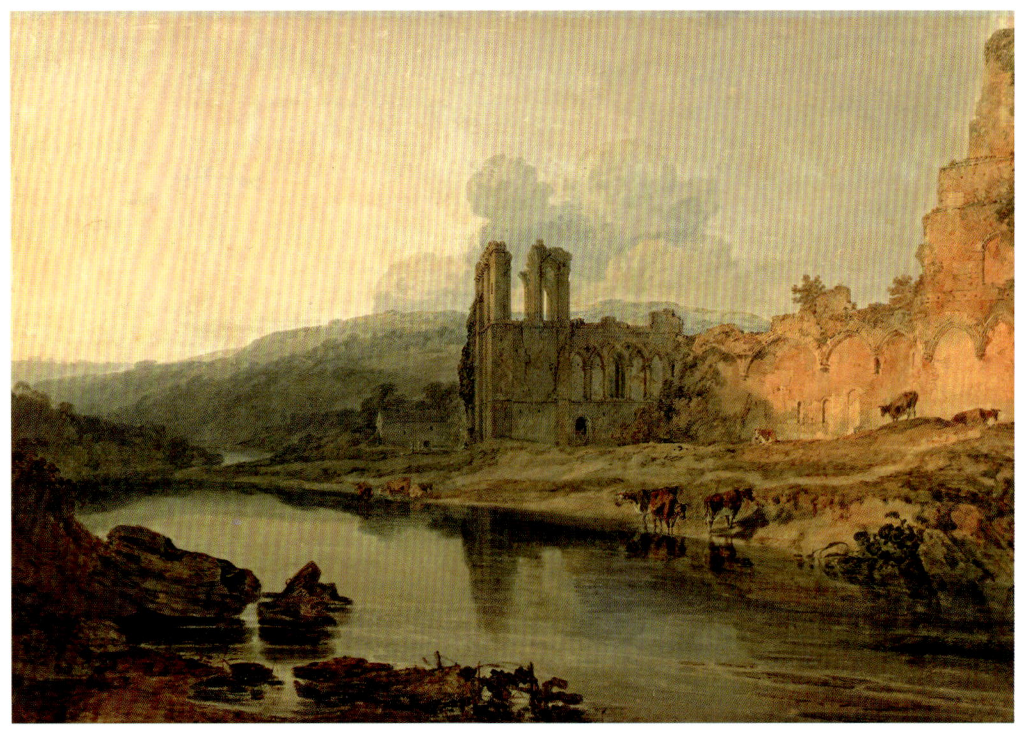

St Agatha's Abbey, Easby, 1800, watercolour, Whitworth Art Gallery, University of Manchester, UK, 63 x 89cm (25 x 35in)

Often referred to simply as Easby Abbey, this one like most others in England was dissolved by Henry VIII in the 16th century and left to ruin. Fortunately the 7th-century Celtic 'Easby Cross' was salvaged and can now be seen in the Victoria and Albert Museum in London. Turner's depiction shows the ruin alongside the River Swale, a superb example of the Picturesque aesthetic.

A Beech Wood with Gypsies Seated Round a Campfire, 1799–1801, oil on paper laid on panel, Fitzwilliam Museum, Cambridge, UK, 19 x 28cm (7½ x 11in)

The location of this wood and the date of the work are unclear. This suggests that these were unimportant considerations for Turner, who may well have sketched these woods as an experiment in painting in oil on paper. The subsequent laying down of the work on a wooden support indicates that he was pleased with the result and wished to preserve the work.

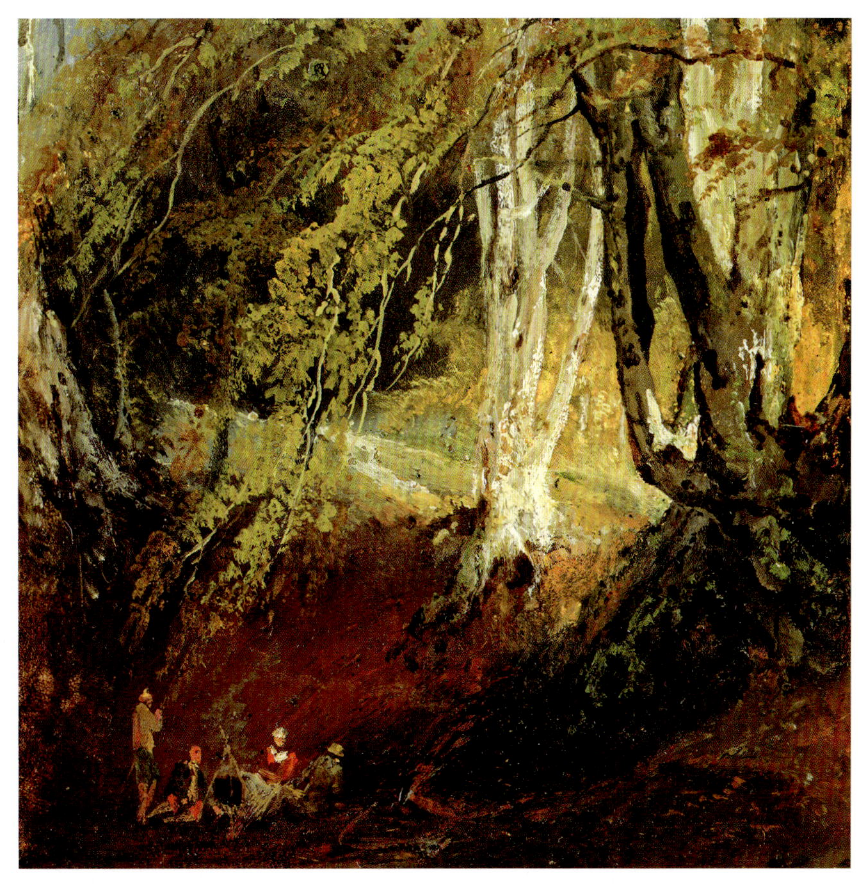

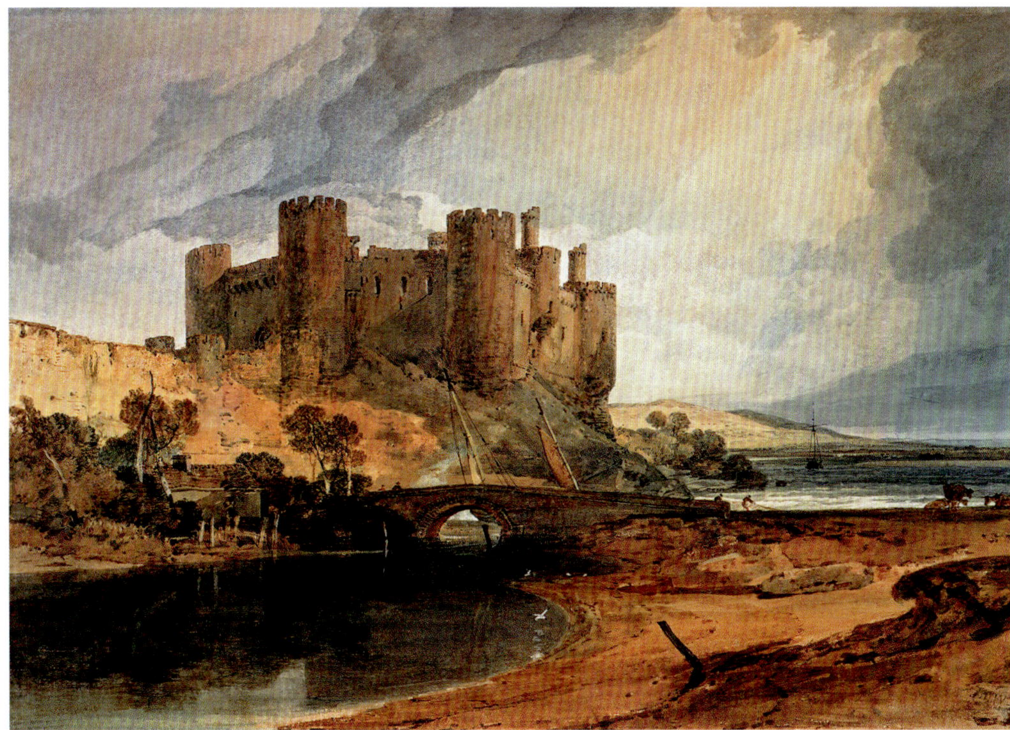

Conway Castle, 1802–3, pencil and watercolour, Whitworth Art Gallery, University of Manchester, UK, 43 x 63cm (17 x 25in)

On his tour of North Wales and Hereford in 1798, Turner filled his Hereford Court Sketchbook with nearly 200 drawings, including several of Conway Castle. From these drawings, the artist produced several watercolours including this one, another example of his exploitation of the Picturesque aesthetic, containing the right ingredients: a ruinous castle, an old bridge, a cottage and a river.

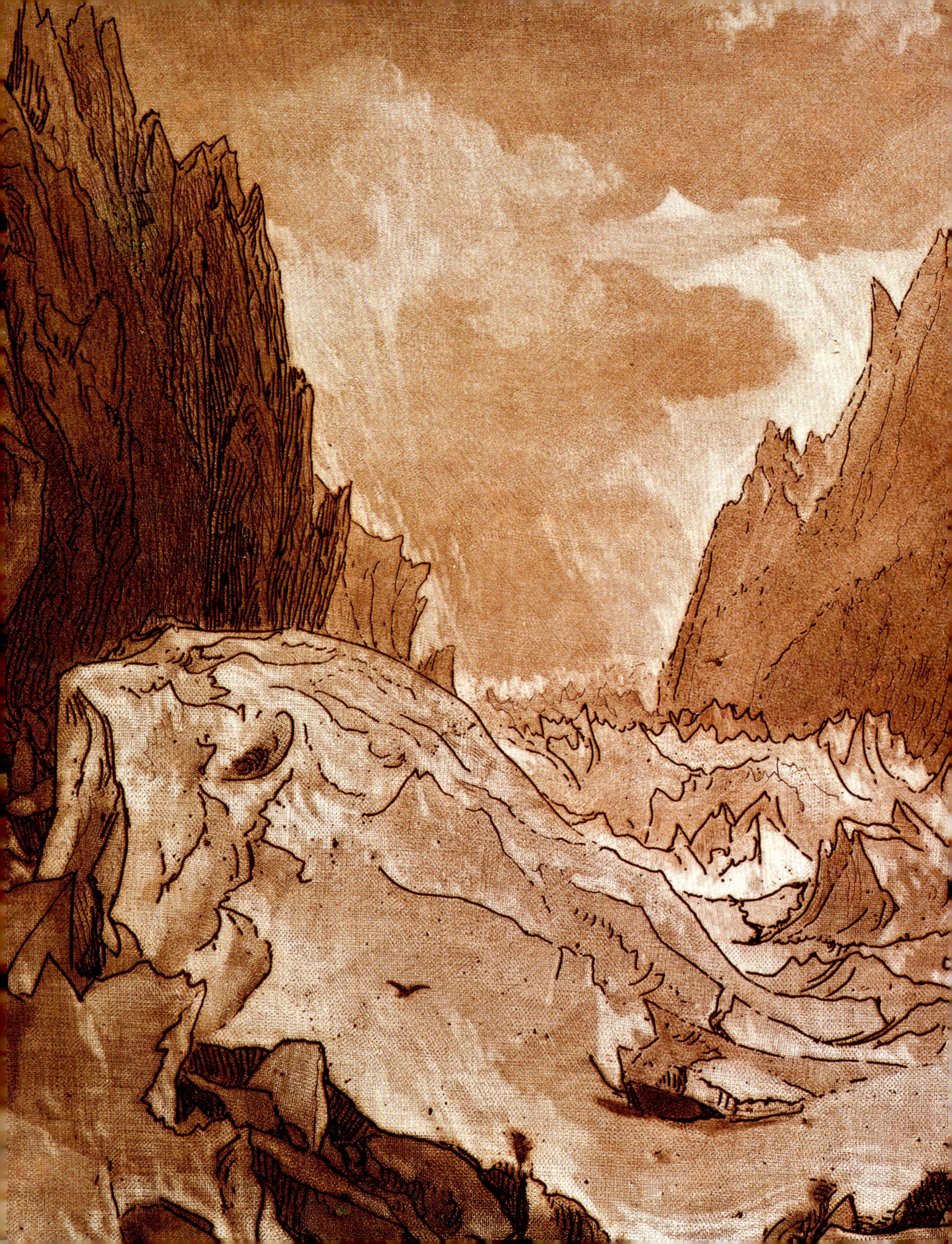

THE HEROIC PERIOD 1811–1820

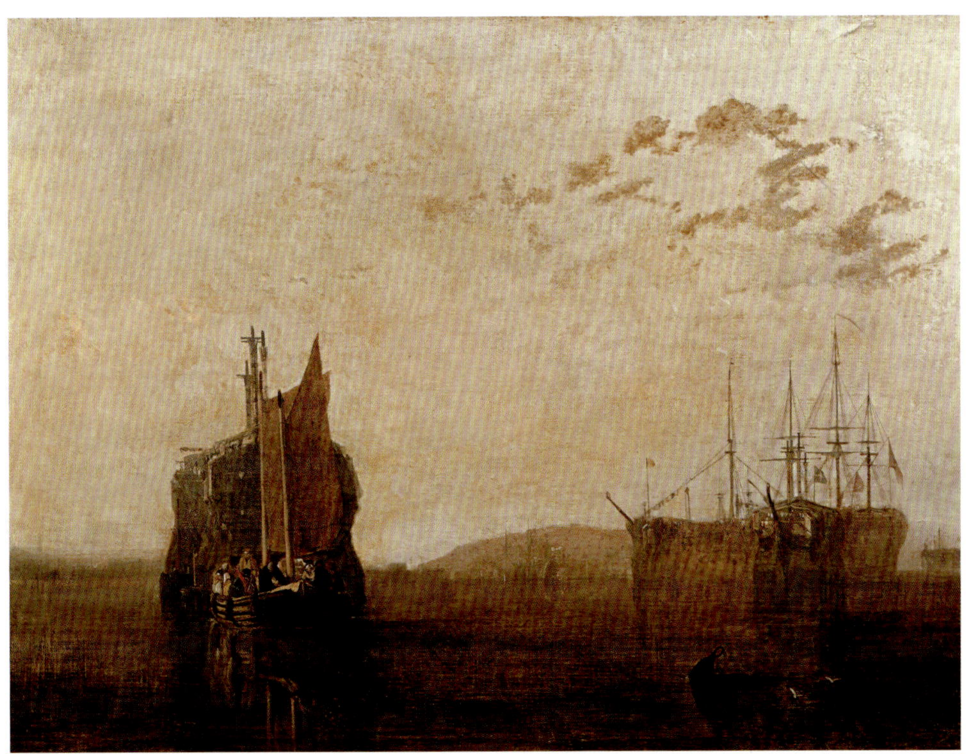

Now an established Academician, Turner began to paint some epic mythological scenes, such as his *Dido Building Carthage*, inspired in part by Britain's victories over Napoleon. He became interested in the inequalities of his society and also painted genre subjects that idealized ordinary folk. Many of these pictures were reproduced as engravings for mass consumption, adding to their power as political statements. With the end of the Napoleonic wars, Turner was now free to explore Europe and fully discover the potential for the Sublime aesthetic in the Alpine region.

Above: Hulks on the Tamar, *c.1812, oil on canvas. Turner visited this area on the border of Devon and Cornwall in the summer of 1811 for the recent commission of* Picturesque Views in England in Wales.
Left: Mer de Glace, Chamonix, *1812, etching and mezzotint. A number of the* Liber Studiorum *images were both etched and engraved by Turner himself including the one shown here, which appeared in the tenth edition to represent the depiction of 'mountains' in landscape painting.*

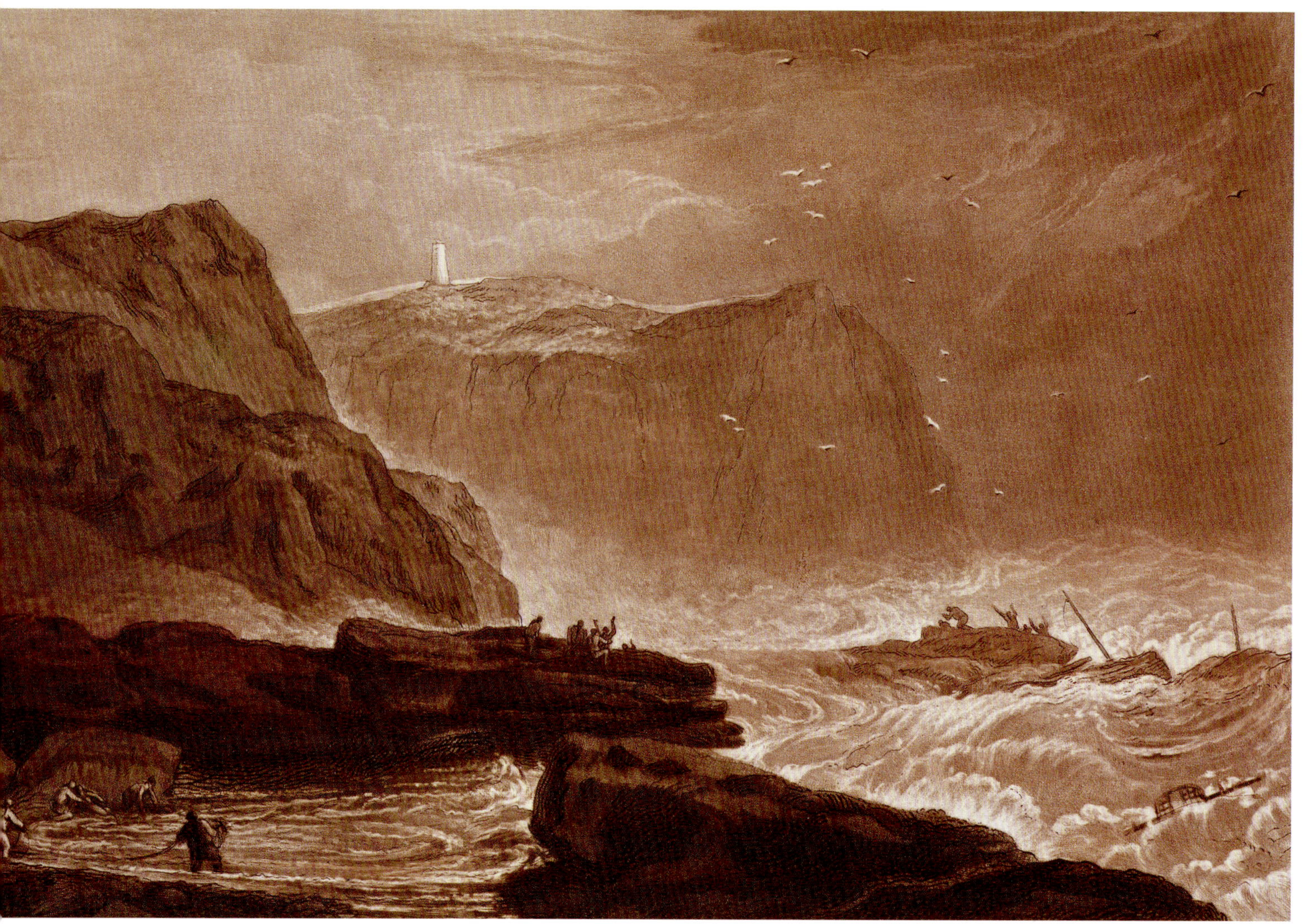

Coast of Yorkshire, 1811, etching from *Liber Studiorum*, Fitzwilliam Museum, Cambridge, UK, 21 x 30cm (8 x 12in)

This etching and mezzotint was made for the *Liber Studiorum* after a monochromatic watercolour Turner had made in 1806–7.

The subsequent engraving for the *Liber* was signed "Turner RAPP", reflecting his position as Professor of Perspective at the Academy, and was published for the fifth edition. The location is Whitby, famous in Turner's time as a major port for whaling vessels.

Woodland Scene, c.1811,
watercolour,
Private Collection,
23 x 28cm (9 x 11in)

The whereabouts of this
woodland is unclear, but is
likely to be at either of the
two homes of Lord
Egremont: Petworth in
Sussex or Cockermouth in
Cumbria, where Turner
spent the previous summer.
Turner's preoccupation
was not topographical
accuracy, however, he
needed a break from the
'business' and seems to
have enjoyed painting a
number of these small
watercolours for his own
personal pleasure.

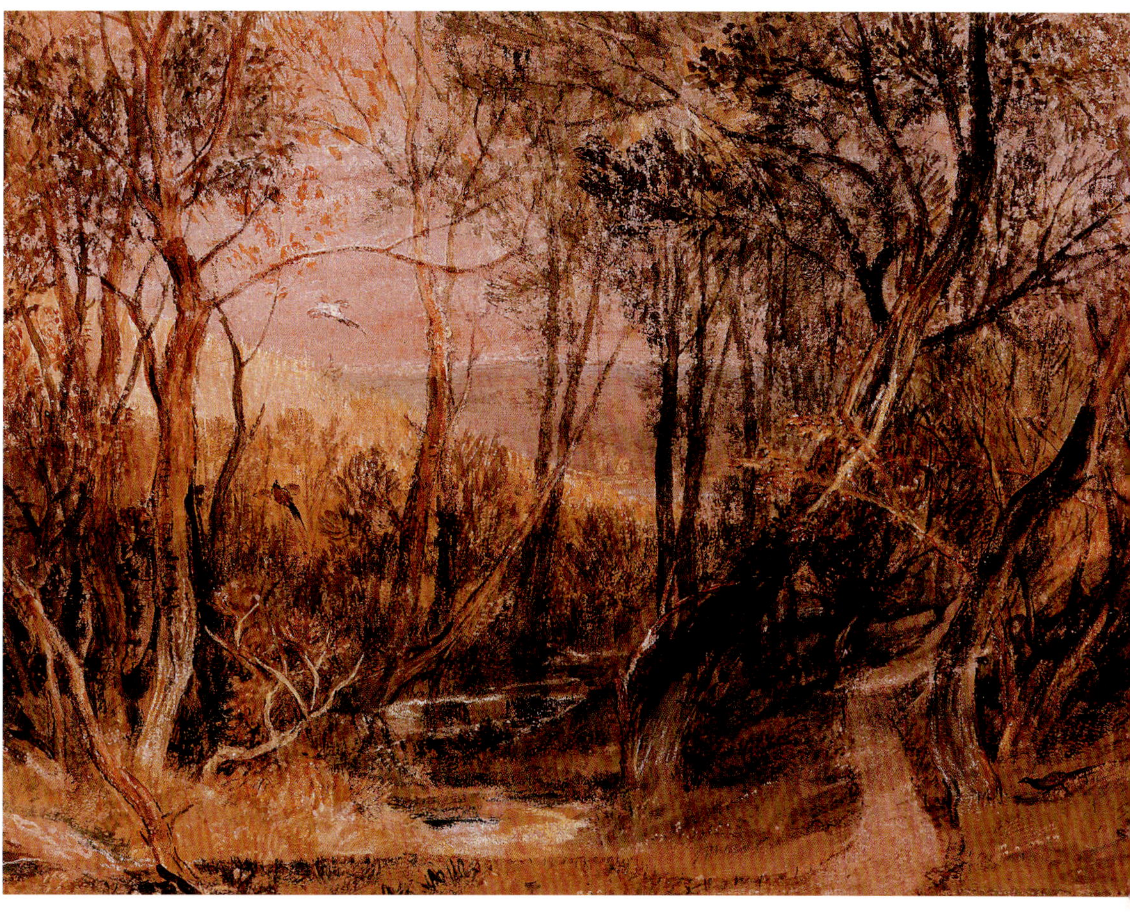

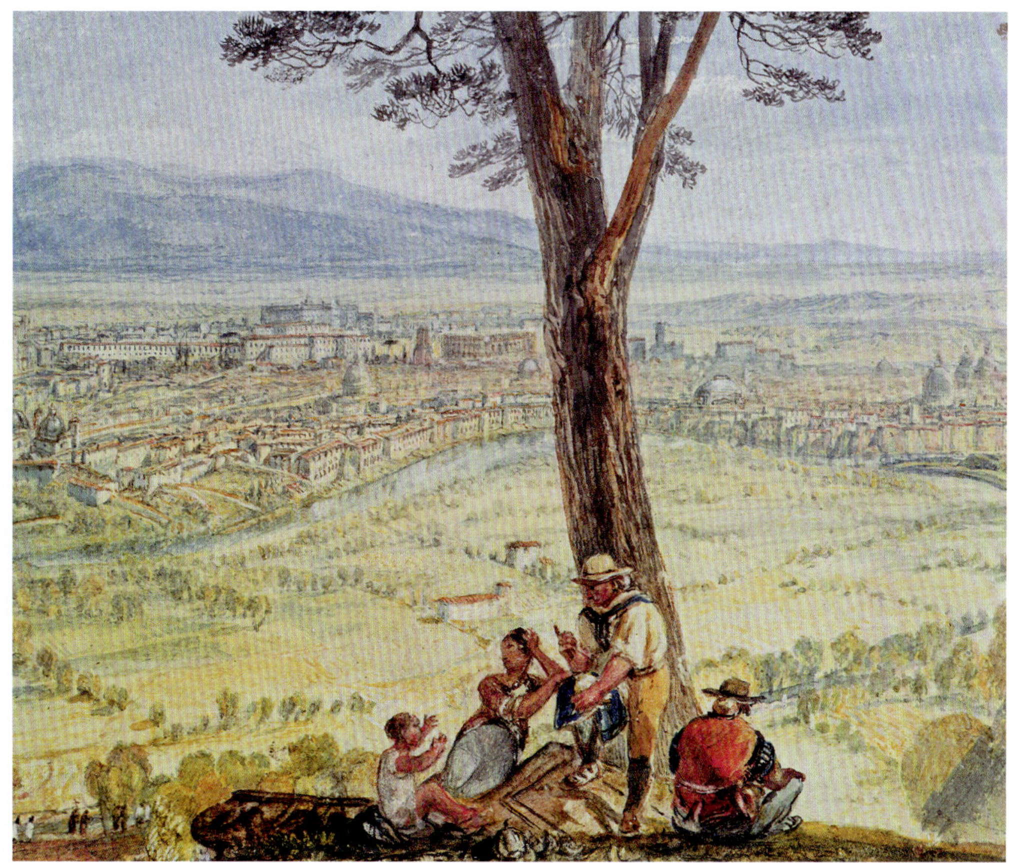

Rome from Monte Mario,
1818, pencil and
watercolour, Paul Mellon
Collection, Yale Center
for British Art, CT, USA,
14 x 22cm (5½ x 9in)

Taken from a drawing by
James Hakewill, Turner
executed a series of Italian
scenes for *A Picturesque Tour
of Italy* for Longman. The
Monte Mario is the highest
of the hills surrounding the
city and takes its name from
a 16th-century cardinal who
owned a villa there.
The Monte Mario is not one
of the original seven hills on
which Rome was built.

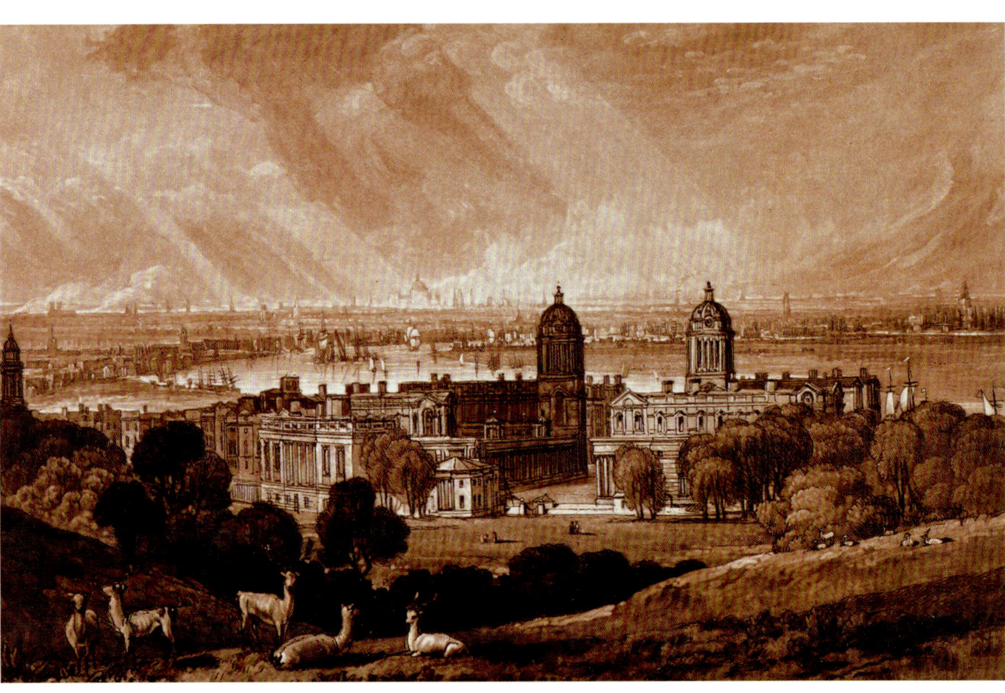

London from Greenwich, 1811, engraving, Paul Mellon Collection, Yale Center for British Art, CT, USA, 21 x 29cm (8 x 11in)

Taken from the painting of 1809, this view of Greenwich was engraved for the fifth edition of *Liber Studiorum*, to represent the architectural aspects of landscape composition. The view includes the Royal Naval Hospital in the middle ground, with St Paul's Cathedral and the City churches in the background, all designed by Sir Christopher Wren.

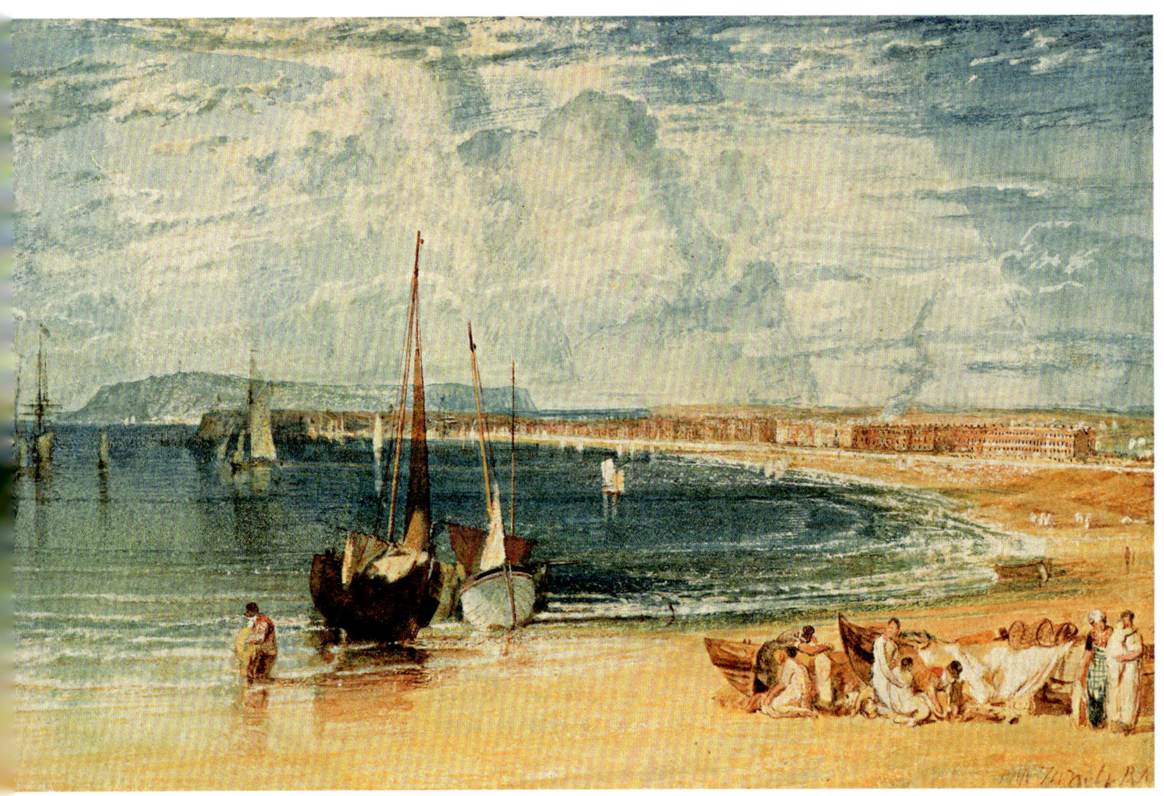

Weymouth, 1811, watercolour, Paul Mellon Collection, Yale Center for British Art, CT, USA, 17 x 22cm (7 x 9in)

This watercolour was reproduced as one of the images for *Picturesque Views on the Southern Coast of England*, commissioned and engraved by the Cooke brothers and issued in 1814. Turner embarked on the series in 1811, travelling to Dorset, Devon and Cornwall in search of suitable views, which he continued to develop until 1826 when he argued with the brothers over mismanagement of the publication.

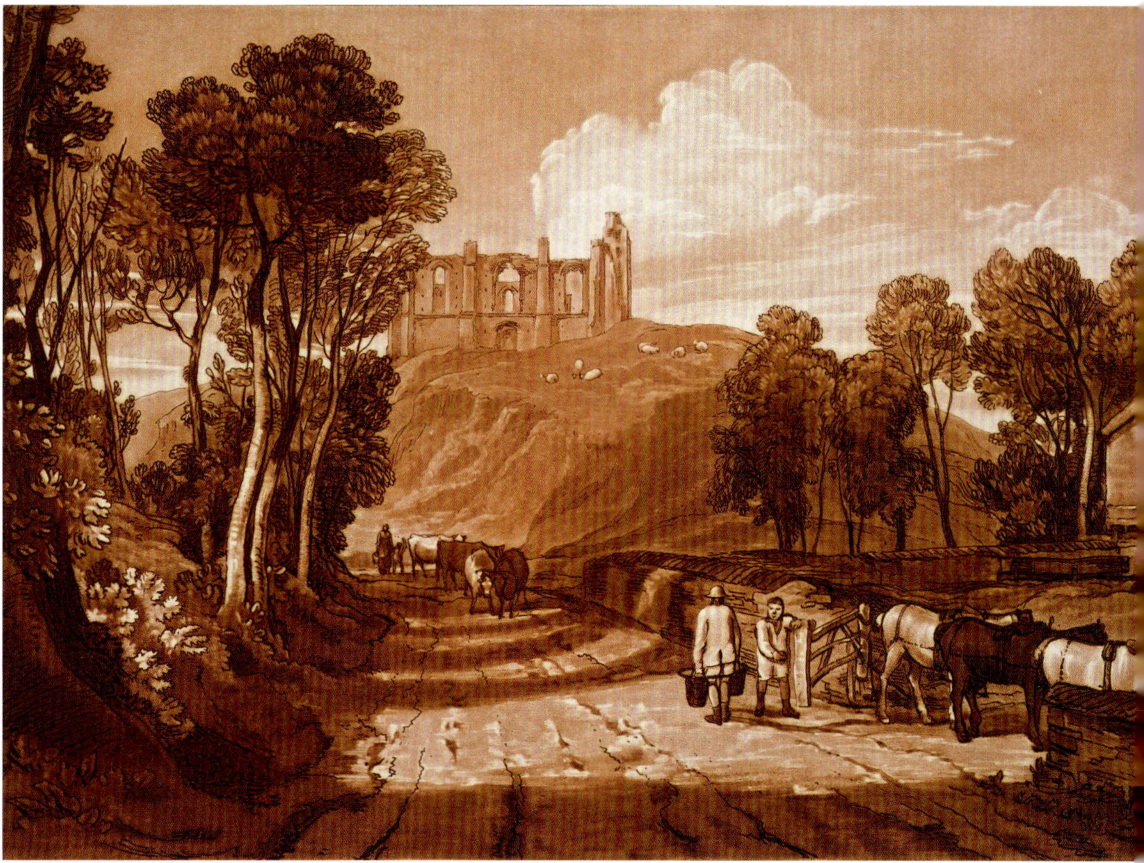

St Catherine's Hill, Guildford, Surrey, 1811, etching, Fitzwilliam Museum, Cambridge, UK, 21 x 29cm (8 x 11in)

The ruined chapel provides a Picturesque setting for this etching used in the *Liber Studiorum* to denote 'Elevated Pastoral'. The original chapel's legend is that two sisters, Catherine and Martha, built it with their own hands, along with another on St Martha's Hill. The one shown here dates from the 13th century and was built by the rector of St Nicolas' Church in Guildford.

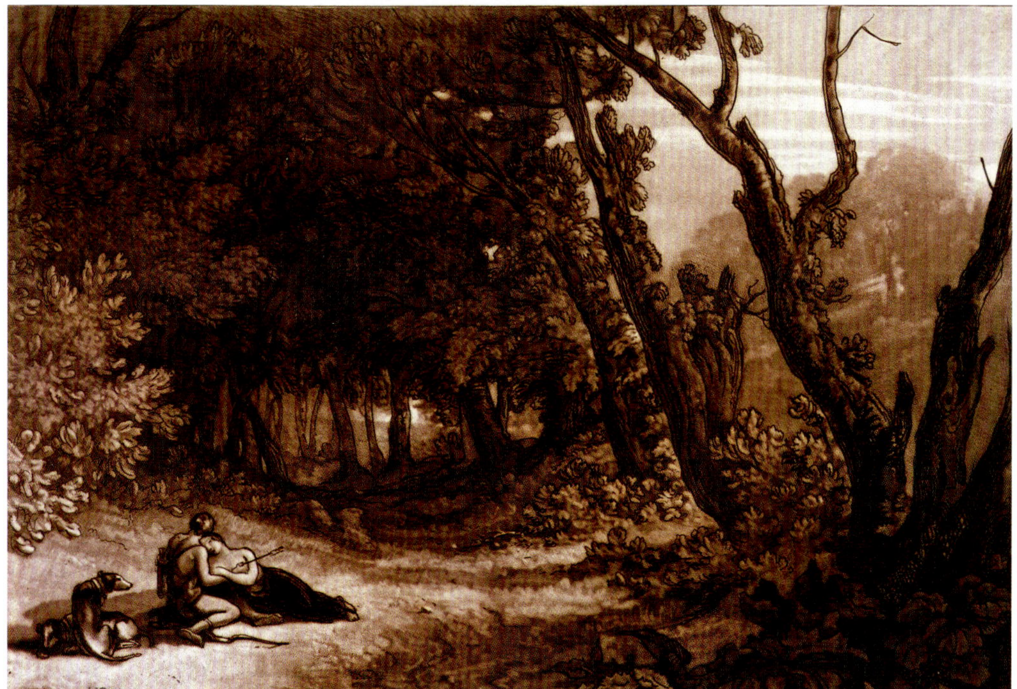

Procris and Cephalus, 1812, etching and mezzotint, Fitzwilliam Museum, Cambridge, UK, 22 x 29cm (9 x 11in)

Designed for the *Liber Studiorum*, this etching represents history painting, which according to Sir Joshua Reynolds was the most significant use of landscape in painting. The scene is the death of Procris who is married to the hunter Cephalus, also depicted. After Procris emerges from the bush to surprise her husband he accidentally kills her mistakenly thinking that she is a wild animal.

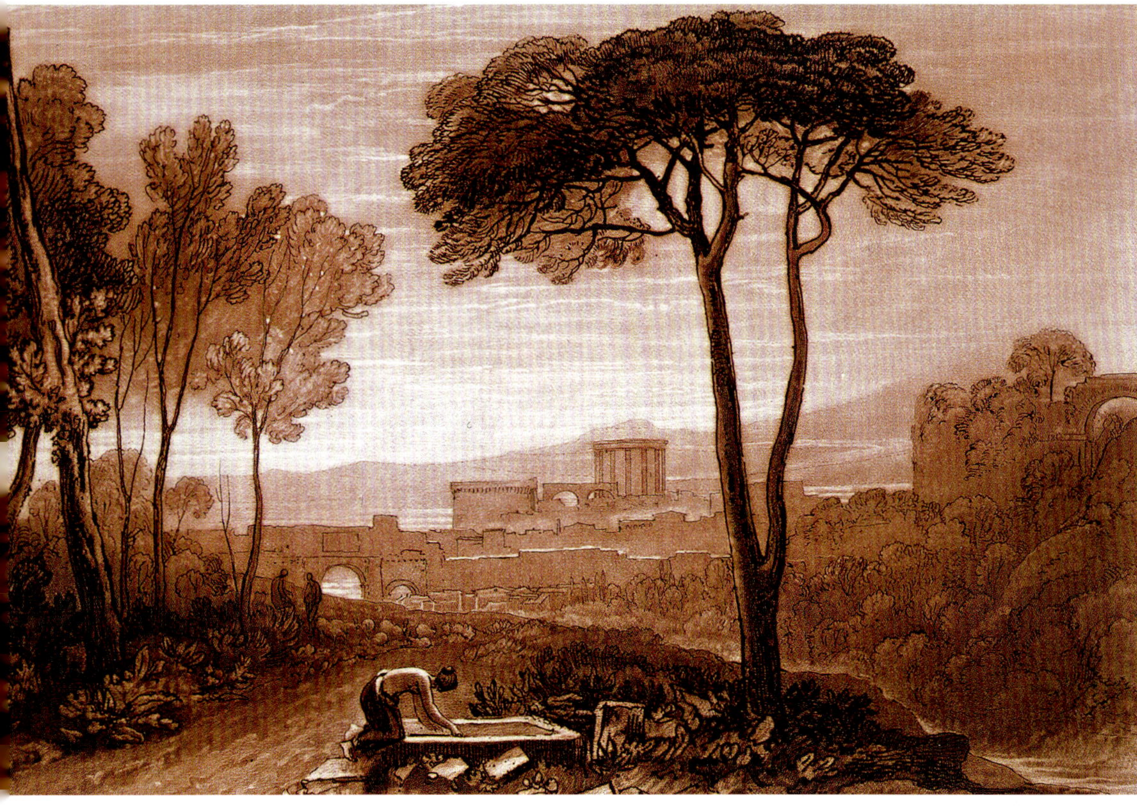

Scene on the Campagna, 1812, etching, Fitzwilliam Museum, Cambridge, UK, 21 x 29cm (8 x 11in)

Published in February of 1812 as part of the *Liber Studiorum* series, this image represents the 'Elevated Pastoral' of landscape painting. The original watercolour for this was created in 1808 and possibly originally called 'Hindoo [sic] Ablutions'. When it was engraved, Turner referred to it as 'Say's tall tree' after the engraver William Say. The scene is heavily borrowed from Claude Lorrain's Pastoral landscapes.

Snow Storm: Hannibal and His Army Crossing the Alps, 1812, oil on canvas, Tate Britain, London, UK, 146 x 238cm (57 x 94in)

Turner was aware of the importance of showing this painting – arguably his most important to date – to good effect at the Academy, haranguing his colleagues to hang it at the right height, under threat of withdrawal for failing to comply. The painting explored Turner's new compositional ruse, the central vortex, which is a key motif in many of his subsequent works.

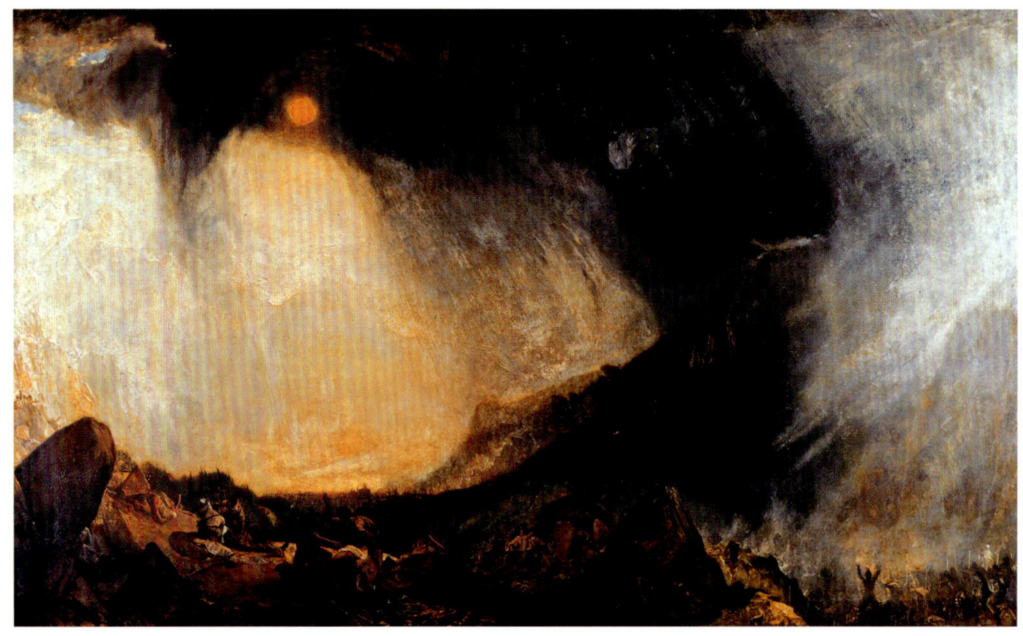

Poole, Dorset, with Corfe Castle in the Distance, 1812, watercolour and bodycolour, Private Collection, 14 x 22cm (5½ x 9in)

As part of the *Picturesque Views on the Southern Coast of England* series, Turner produced this watercolour of Poole Bay with Corfe Castle in the distance. The castle, parts of which dated from the 11th century, was besieged and destroyed by Parliamentary forces during the English Civil War, leaving it in a ruinous condition. Turner saw this view as according with a Picturesque aesthetic.

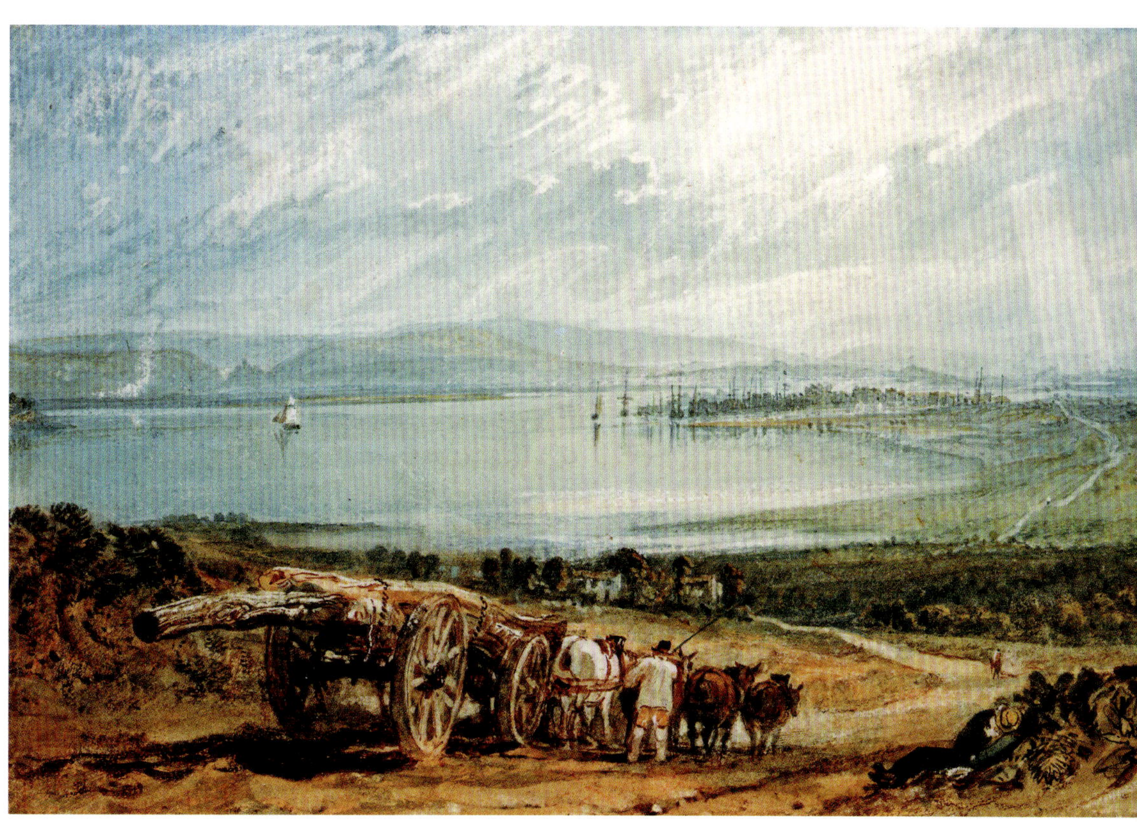

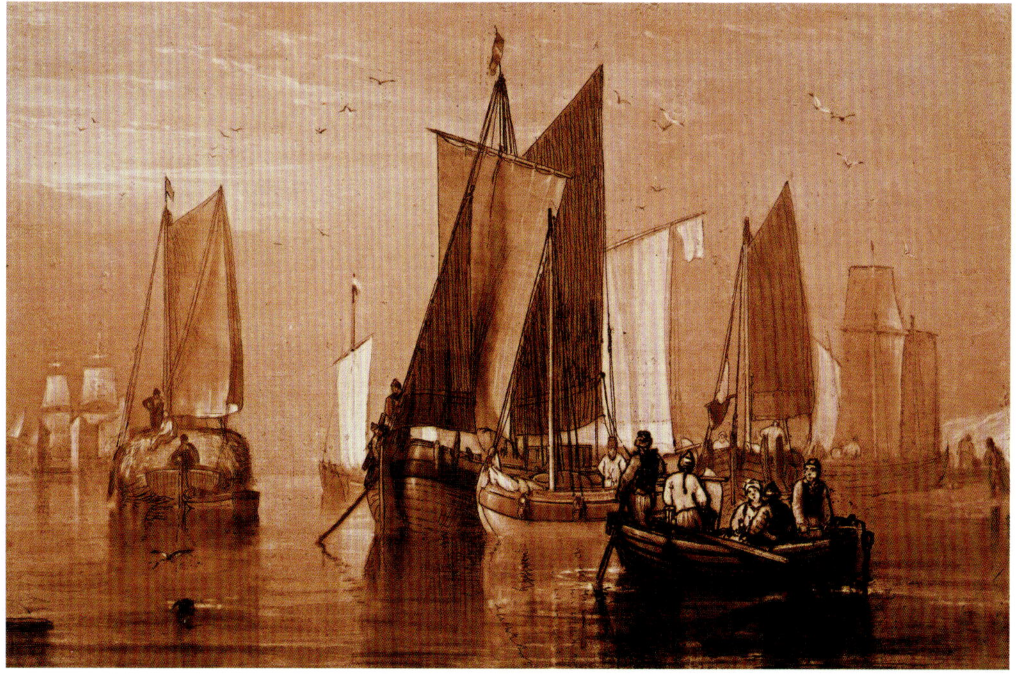

Calm, 1812, etching from *Liber Studiorum,* Fitzwilliam Museum, Cambridge, UK, 21 x 30cm (8 x 12in)

Turner himself laboured on the production of the aquatint and mezzotint from the soft ground etching that he had originally produced for the *Liber Studiorum*. He worked through 14 stages to achieve the effect of calm, which he used to represent probably his most resolved evocation of a marine composition for the *Liber*. His style is redolent of the 17th-century Dutch marine painters he so admired.

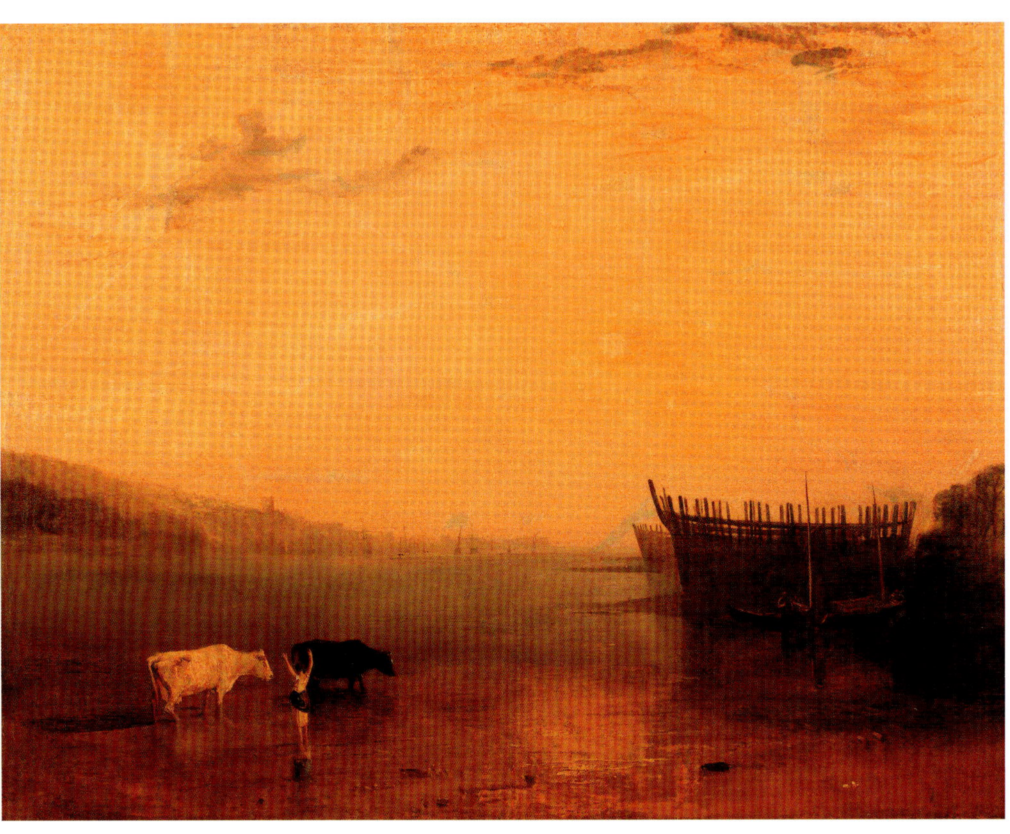

Teignmouth Harbour, Devon, 1812, oil on canvas, Petworth House, Sussex, UK, 90 x 121cm (35 x 48in)

From his Corfe to Dartmouth Sketchbook, Turner worked up two paintings of Teignmouth: a watercolour that was reproduced in the *Picturesque Views on the Southern Coast of England* series, and this oil painting, exhibited at Turner's own gallery and purchased from there by Lord Egremont in 1812. This painting was well received, with one critic remarking on its "extraordinary merit".

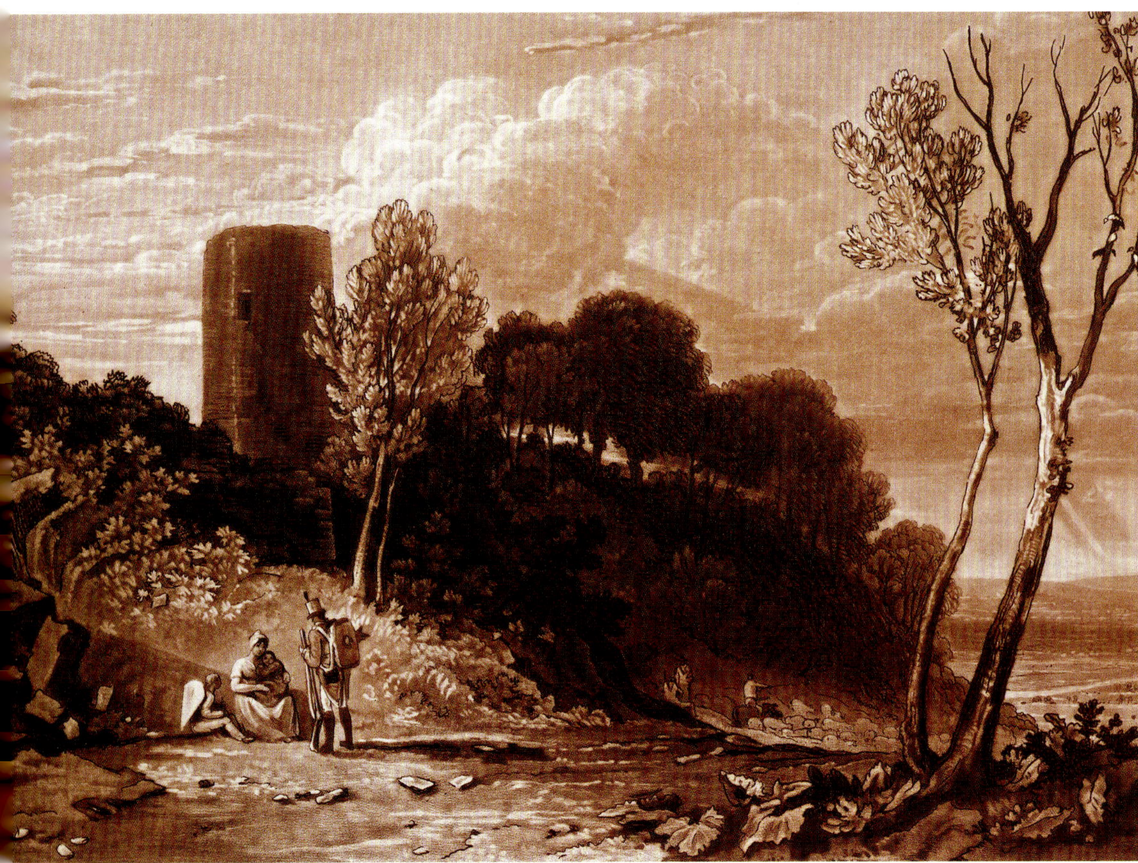

Winchelsea, 1812, etching and mezzotint, Fitzwilliam Museum, Cambridge, UK, 18 x 26cm (7 x 10in)

Engraved by JC Easling, this image appeared in the ninth edition of the *Liber Studiorum* published in April 1812 to represent the Pastoral aspects of landscape painting. The soldier in the picture appears to be relating his adventures in the Napoleonic wars and may well be en route to rejoining his regiment at the port where they were constructing a defensive canal to repel any planned invasion.

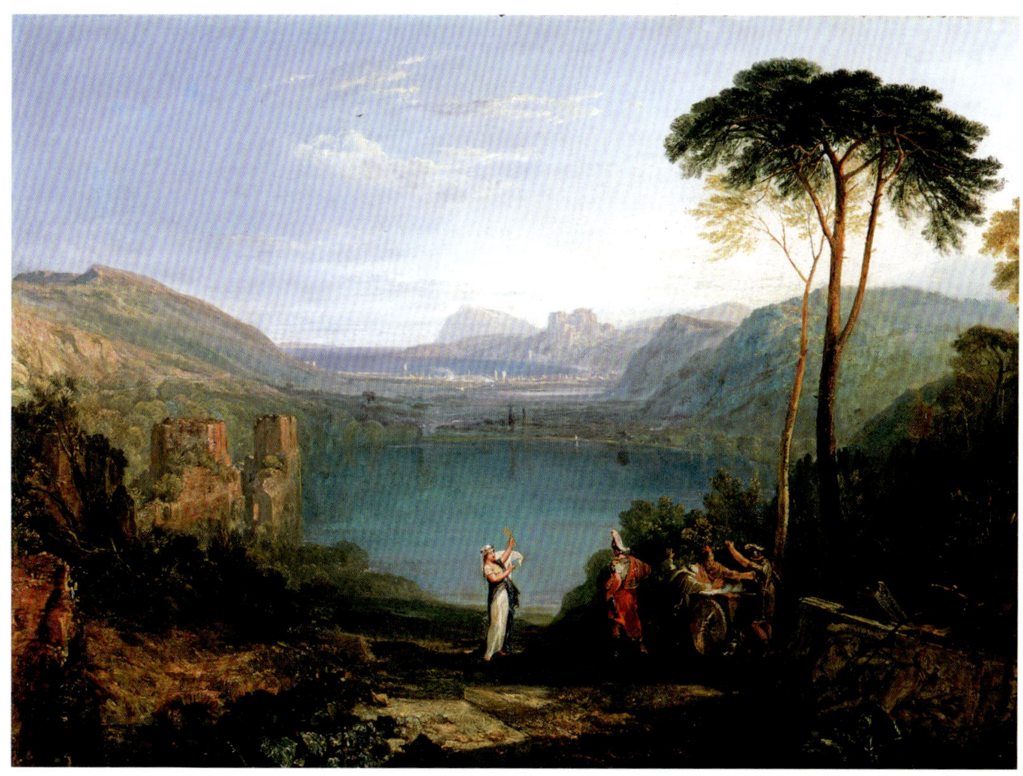

Lake Avernus: Aeneas and the Cumaean Sibyl, 1814–15, oil on canvas, Paul Mellon Collection, Yale Center for British Art, CT, USA, 72 x 97cm (28 x 38in)

Painted on commission for Sir Richard Colt Hoare, who paid one hundred and fifty guineas for it, the work was not exhibited in public until the mid-20th century. Turner had painted an earlier version of this in 1798 that was based on a sketch given to him by Hoare, and it is unclear whether the first version had been rejected by him, but it remained in the artist's possession forming part of the 1856 bequest.

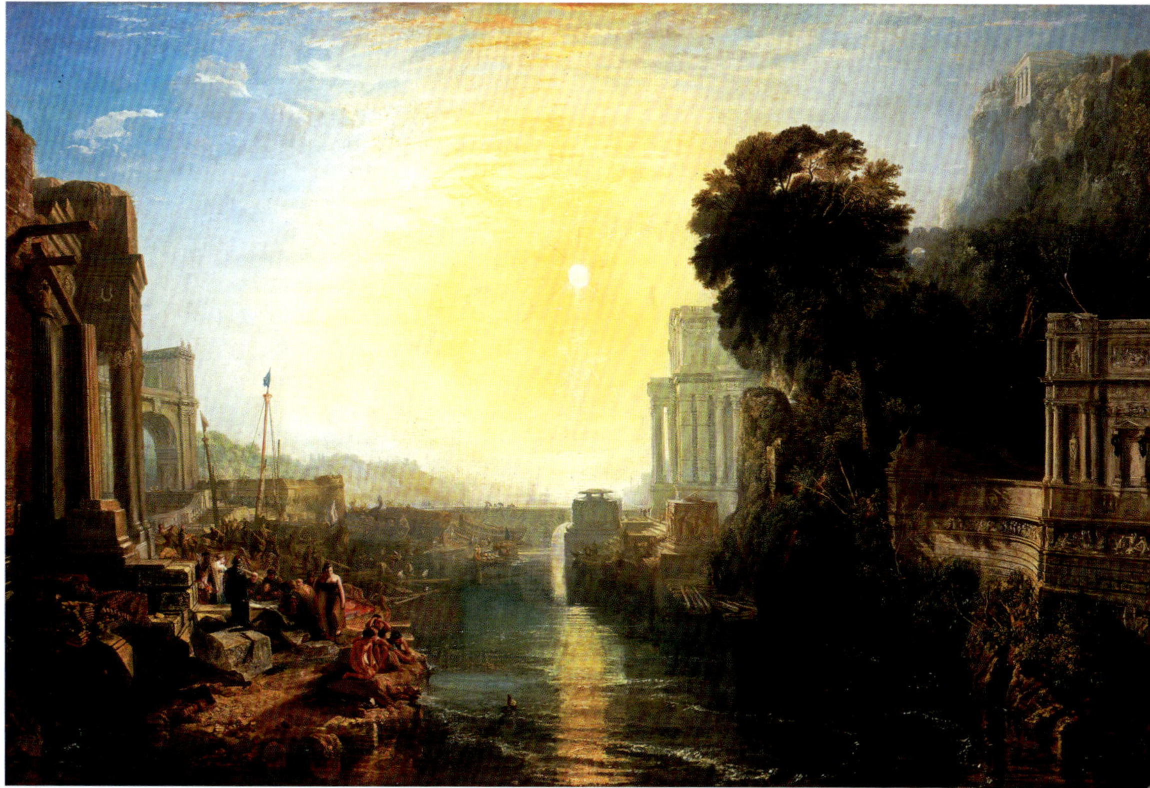

Dido Building Carthage: The Rise of the Carthaginian Empire, 1815, oil on canvas, National Gallery, London, UK, 156 x 230cm (61 x 91in)

Turner must have considered the poignancy of this subject at a time when England, having been at war with France for over twenty years, was almost bankrupt and trying to rebuild her status as the world's major economic power. The central theme of the picture is optimism, symbolized by the sunrise, and tells the story of an ancient civilization working together for the common good.

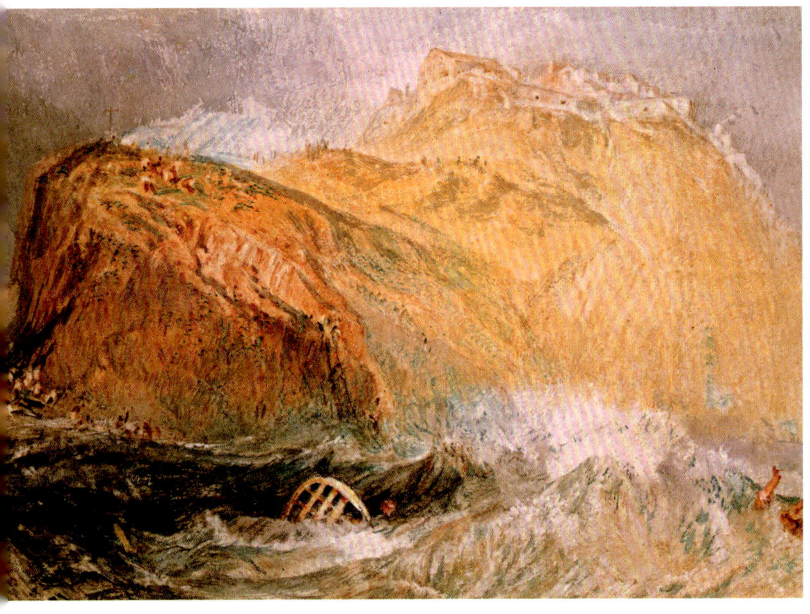

Tintagel Castle, 1815,
watercolour,
Private Collection,
16 x 24cm (6 x 9in)

The ruinous castle on the headland provided a perfect backdrop for this Romantic seascape by Turner, embracing aspects of the Sublime aesthetic. Tintagel is virtually an island, attached to mainland Cornwall by a narrow strip of land, facing the full might of the Atlantic Ocean. Consequently there are often mountainous seas that prove perilous for ships, an aspect that Turner captures well.

Head of a Heron, c.1816,
pen and ink with
watercolour,
Leeds Art Gallery, UK,
25 x 29cm (10 x 11in)

Turner developed a keen interest in natural history after visiting Farnley Hall, the home of Walter Fawkes, who had a passion for ornithology. Fawkes commissioned the artist to produce a series of 20 watercolour drawings for *The Farnley Book of Birds*. Turner's subsequent interest is manifest in several of his landscape paintings at this time and later.

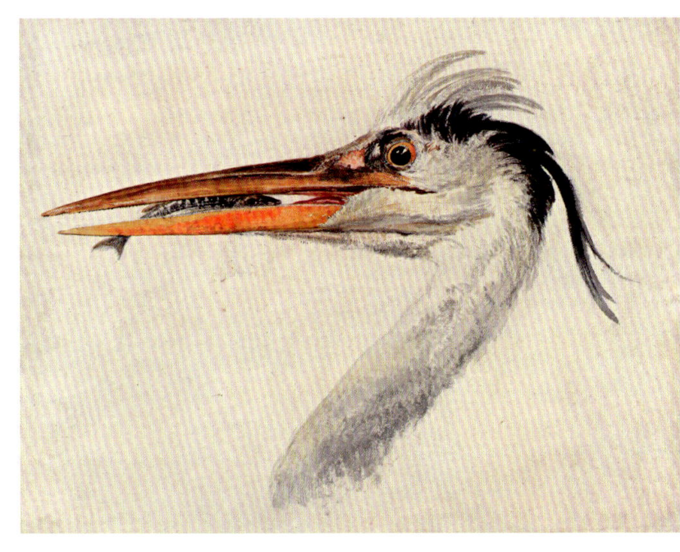

Robin, c.1816,
pencil and watercolour
on paper,
Leeds Art Gallery, UK,
14 x 18cm (5½ x 7in)

This watercolour formed part of the *The Farnley Book of Birds* compiled for Richard, the youngest son of Walter Fawkes, who was to die in a hunting accident. His older brother Hawksworth (referred to by Turner affectionately as "Hawkey") was one of very few people to ever set foot in the artist's studio to witness his working practices, while he was staying at Farnley Hall.

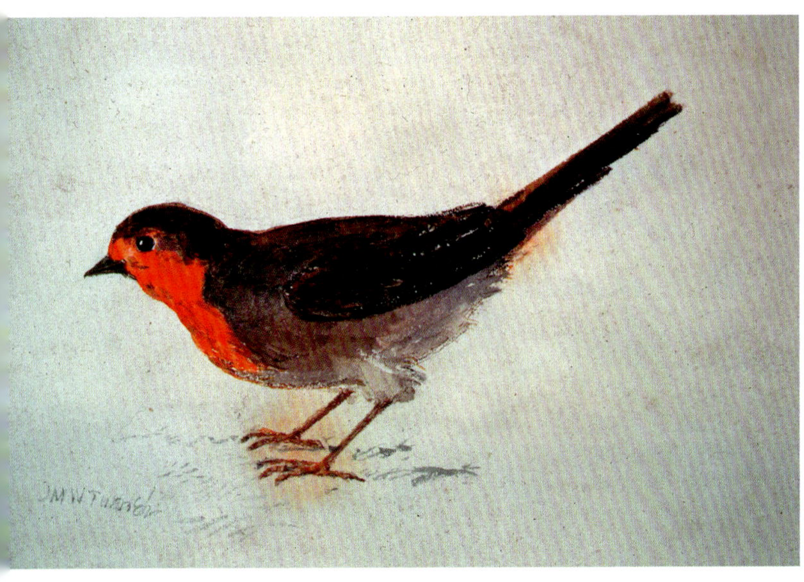

Bow and Arrow Castle, Isle of Portland, c.1815, oil on panel, University of Liverpool Art Gallery and Collections, UK, 15 x 23cm (6 x 9in)

The ruined castle in the background was established in the 11th century by King William II (Rufus) and gets its name from the style of windows used for his archers. It is also sometimes referred to as Rufus Castle.

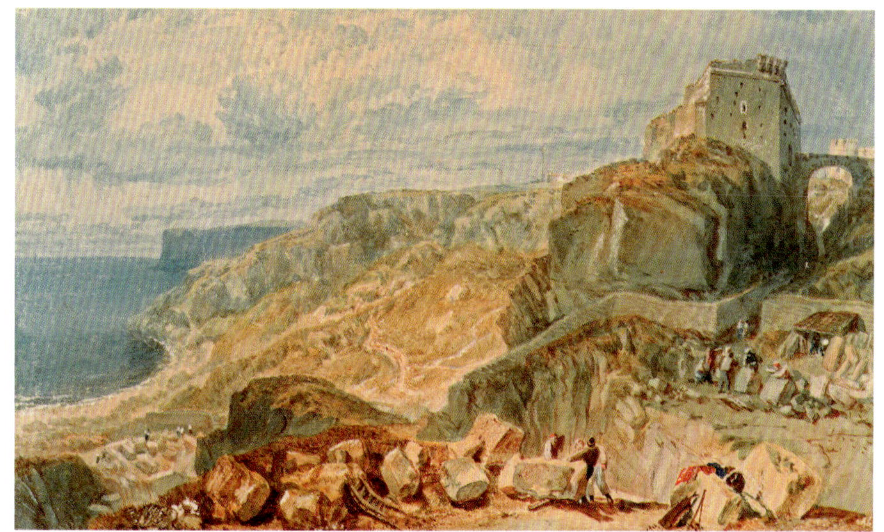

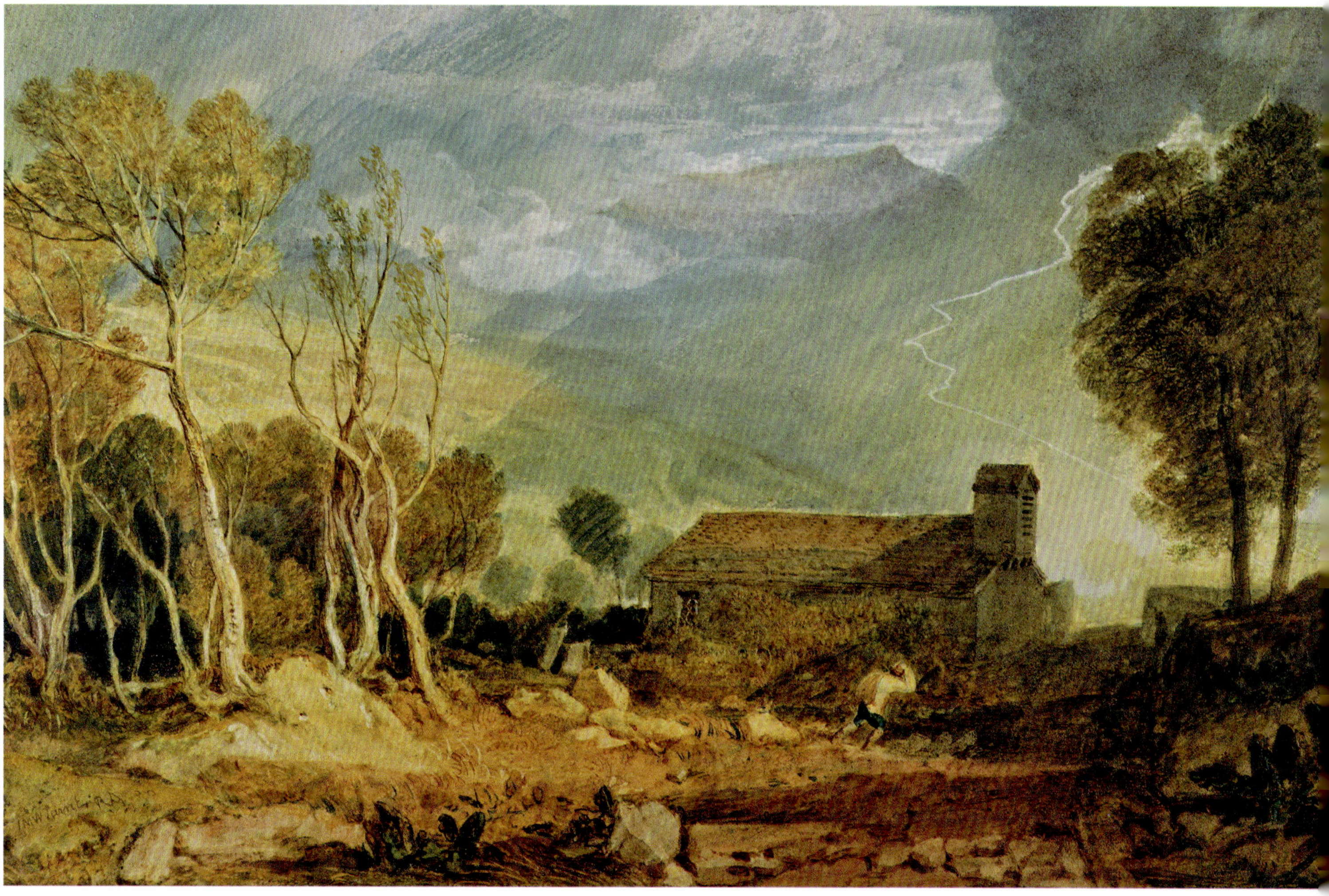

Patterdale Old Church, 1810–15, watercolour and graphite, Paul Mellon Collection, Yale Center for British Art, CT, USA, 28 x 40cm (11 x 16in)

Every year between 1810 and 1815, Turner visited Yorkshire to stay with Walter Fawkes, often leaving Farnley Hall for the day in search of views to sketch. This picture is the result of one outing, a view toward Ingleborough, one of the highest peaks in England, providing a backdrop to an old church in the village of Patterdale.

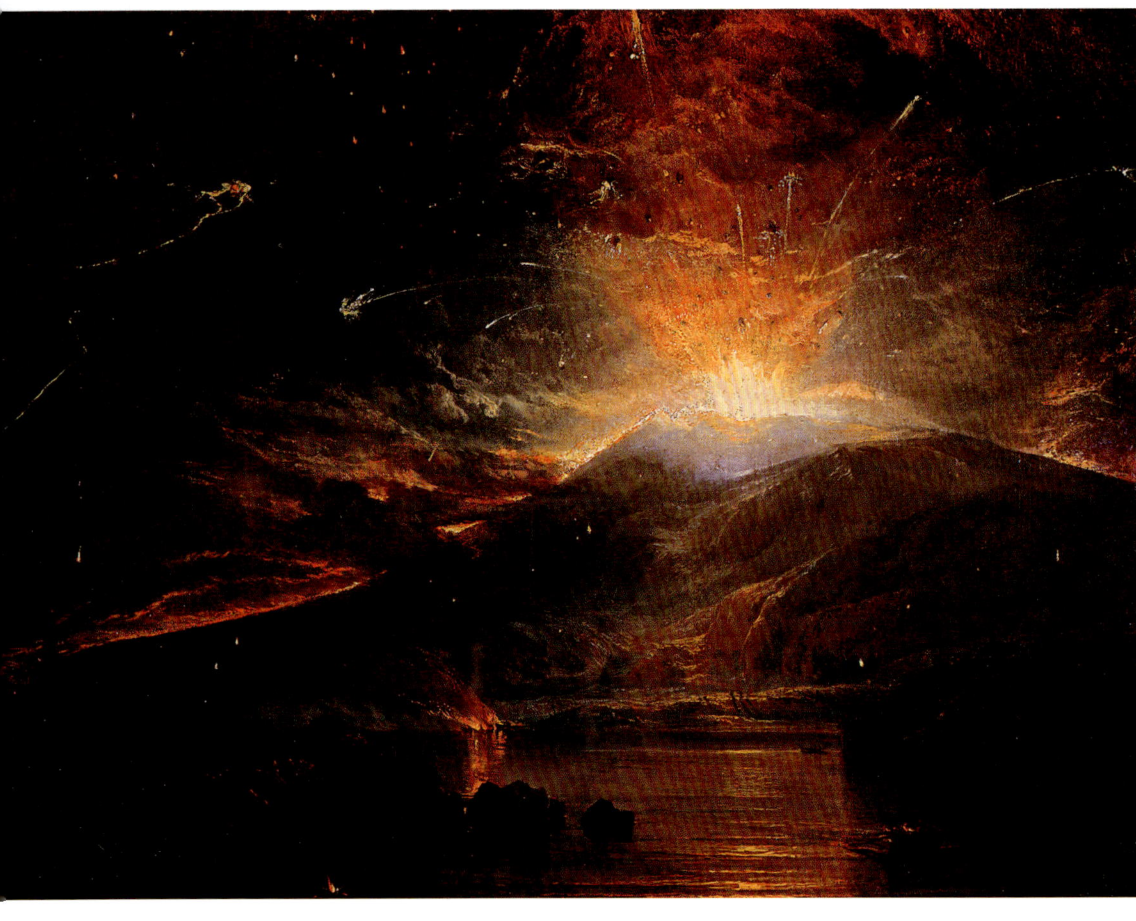

The Eruption of the Soufrière Mountains, in the Island of St Vincent, at Midnight on the 30th April 1812, 1815, oil on canvas, Liverpool Art Gallery, UK, 80 x 105cm (31 x 41in)

Working only from a sketch made on the spot by a gentleman, Hugh Keane, and the various press reports of the eruption, Turner borrowed the Sublime aesthetic of Joseph Wright of Derby to create a sense of the volcano's power. When the picture was shown at the Academy in 1815, it was well received, and Charles Turner published a mezzotint of the image later that year.

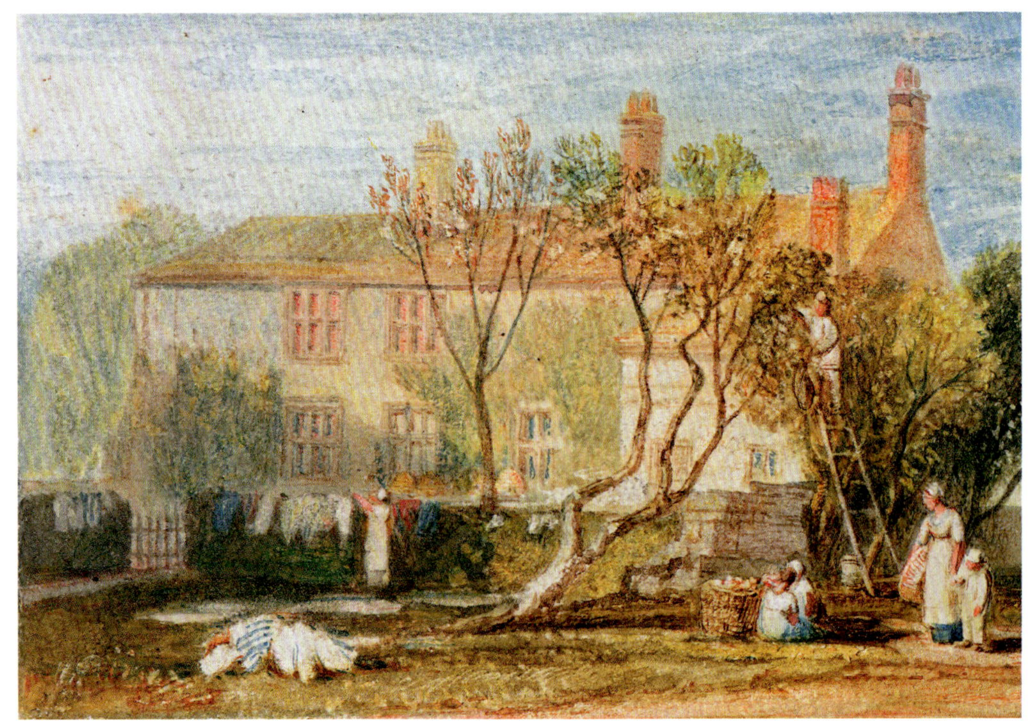

Steeton Manor House, c.1815–18, watercolour, Paul Mellon Collection, Yale Center for British Art, CT, USA, 11 x 16cm (4 x 6in)

An unusual genre picture by Turner executed while he was staying at nearby Farnley Hall with Walter Fawkes. Some parts of the manor house date from the 15th century, but it was extensively remodelled just before Turner painted this picture, suggesting he may have been commissioned. The scene anticipates the High Victorian period's embrace of sentimental rural scenes.

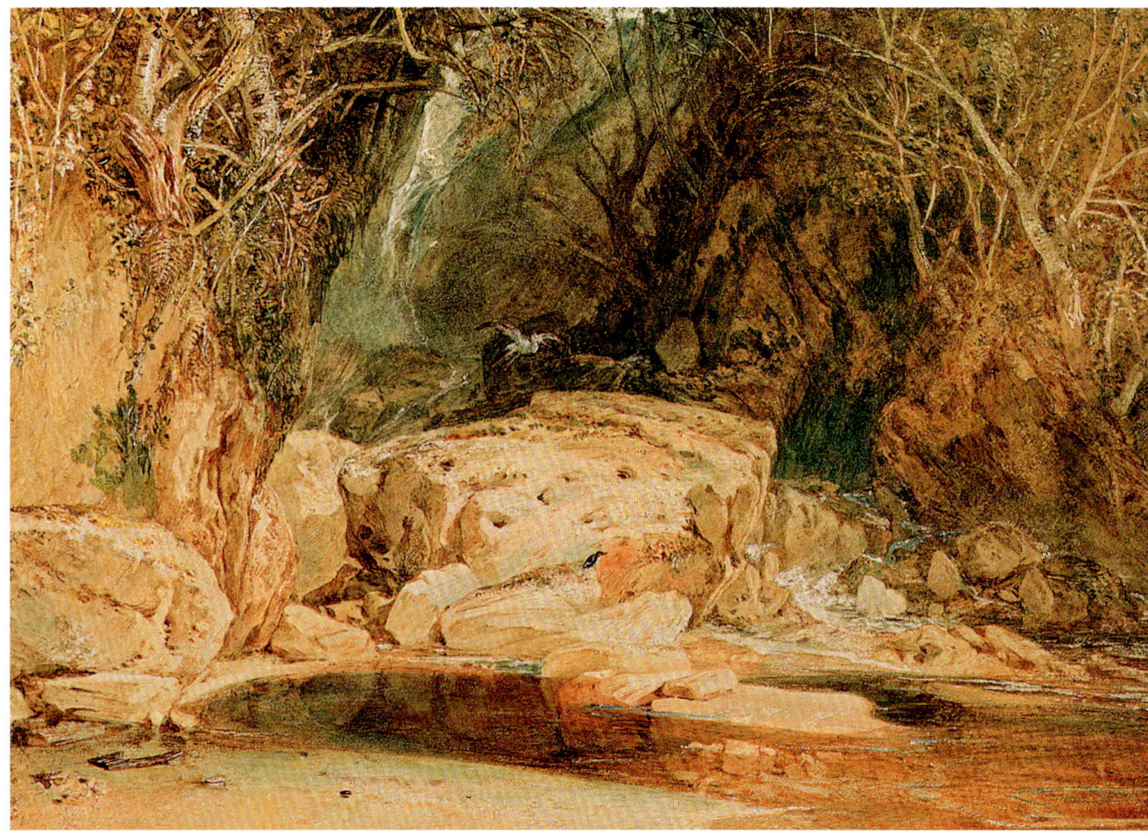

Lonely Dell, Wharfedale,
*c.*1815, watercolour,
Leeds Art Gallery, UK,
28 x 40cm (11 x 16in)

A reflective piece of watercolour painting, this work was executed while Turner was staying with his friend Walter Fawkes in Yorkshire. The artist filled six sketchbooks with material from Yorkshire during his visits to Farnley Hall in the years 1815 to 1818. A 'Dell' is an old English word meaning 'small valley', Wharfedale being one of the Yorkshire Dales or valleys.

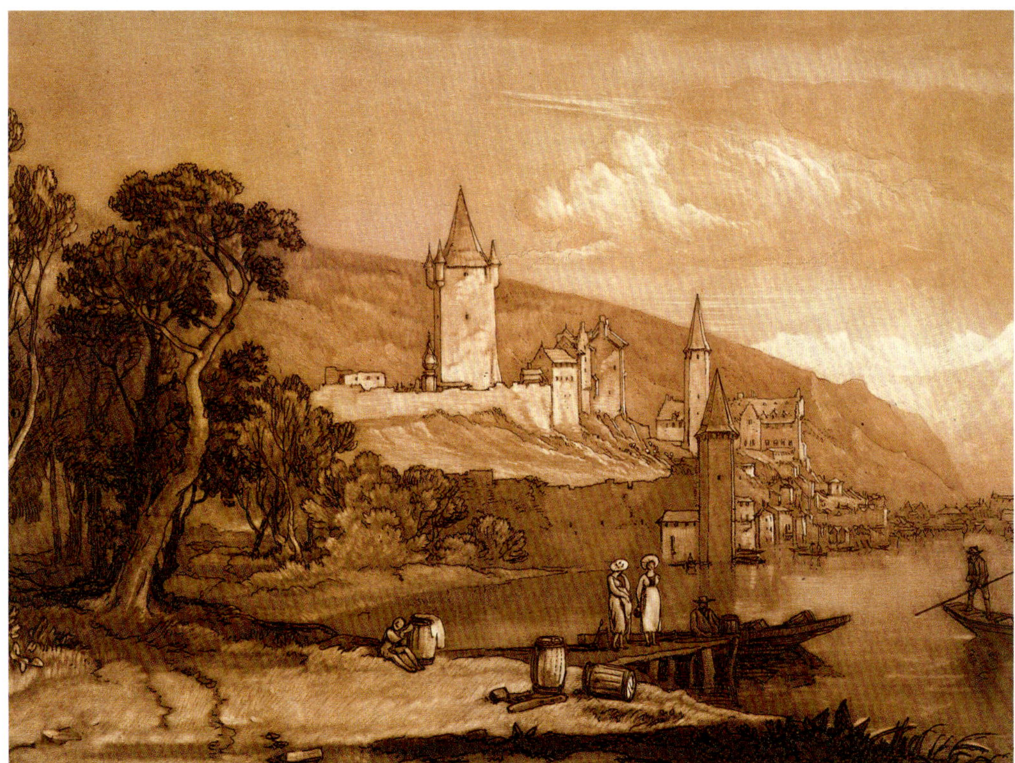

The Town of Thun, 1816,
etching and mezzotint,
Fitzwilliam Museum,
Cambridge, UK,
18 x 26cm (7 x 10in)

Thun, with its 12th-century castle as a focal point, is a town situated on the edge of a lake of the same name where it joins the River Aere. It was built by Duke Bertold V of Zähringen, who established the town as a strategic part of the Holy Roman Empire. Thomas Hodgetts engraved the image for the 12th *Liber Studiorum* series to represent architecture. Hodgetts' mezzotint is a departure from previous examples in its textural quality.

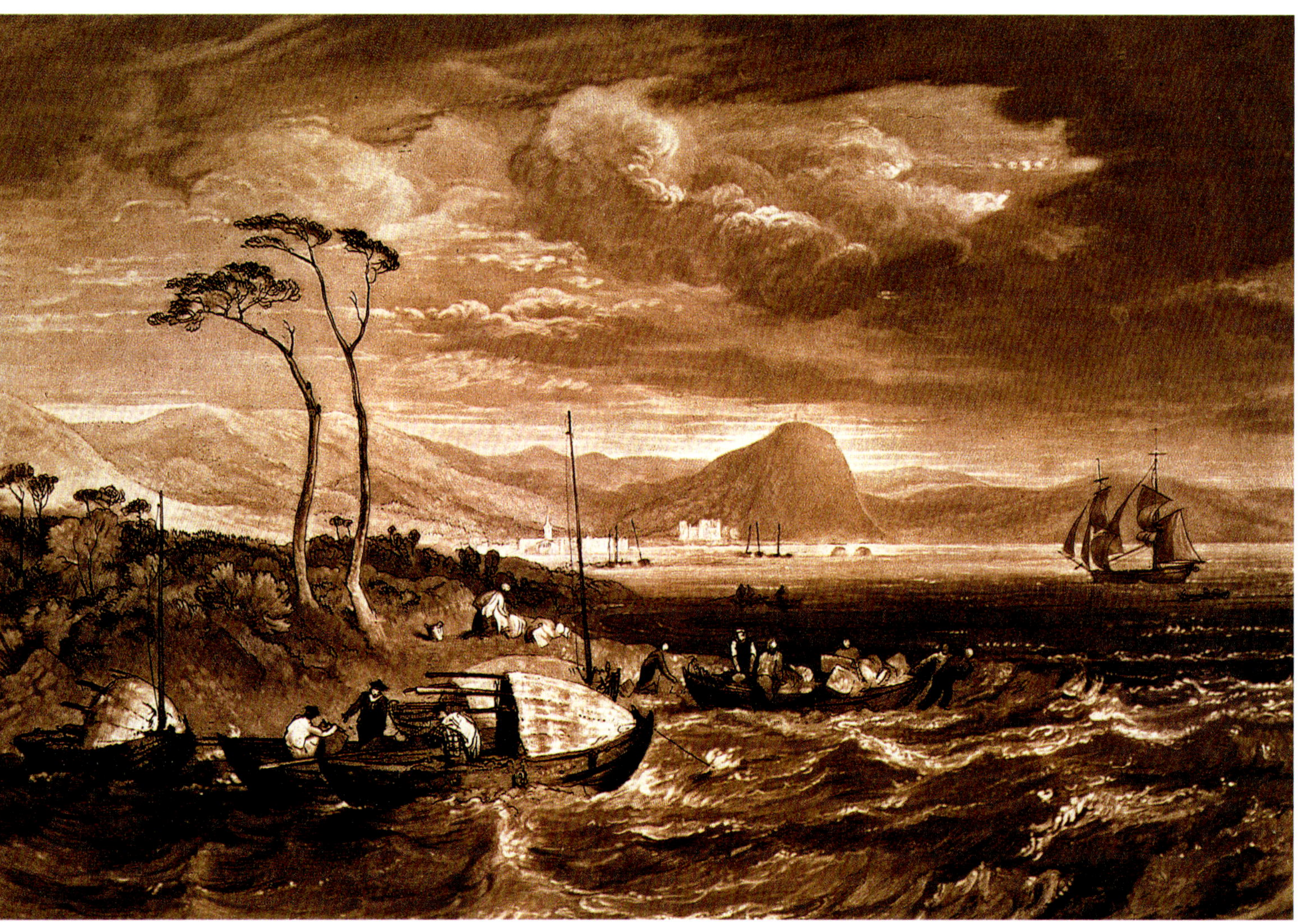

Inverary Castle, 1816,
etching and mezzotint,
Fitzwilliam Museum,
Cambridge, UK,
21 x 29cm (8 x 11in)

From the penultimate series
of *Liber Studiorum*, engraved
by Charles Turner, which
represents 'marine' subjects
in landscape painting, this
image depicts the shoreline
around the West Coast of
Scotland. In the distance are
the town and castle, which
had only been built about
50 years before as the
ancestral home for the
Dukes of Argyll. The town
grew up around the castle
and was therefore very
modern in Turner's day.

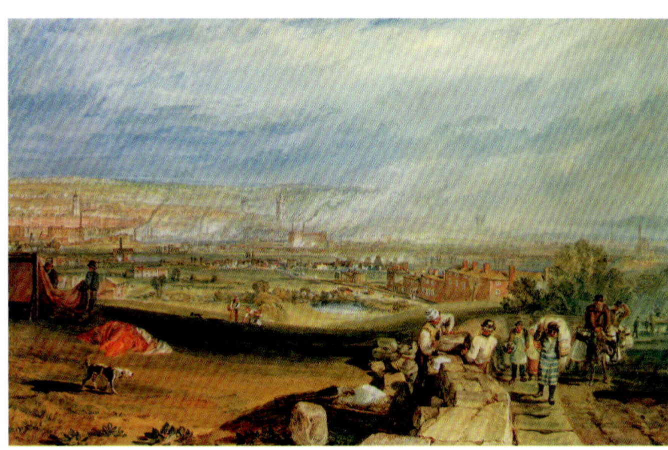

Leeds, 1816, watercolour,
Paul Mellon Collection,
Yale Center for British Art,
CT, USA,
29 x 43cm (11 x 17in)

Turner may have executed
this watercolour to
celebrate the completion of
the 204km- (127-mile-) long
Leeds to Liverpool canal in
1816. The artistic emphasis
is on industry, Leeds seeing
a meteoric rise in the
building of mills and
factories at this time, and
a population rise from
30,000 at the end of the
18th century to 150,000
by 1840.

Dumblain Abbey, 1816,
etching, Fitzwilliam
Museum, Cambridge, UK,
21 x 29cm (8 x 11in)

To emphasize the
architectural aspects of his
treatise, Turner created this
image of a ruined medieval
abbey for his *Liber Studiorum*.

To contrast the majesty of
the building, he included a
group of women washing at
the river's edge, which also
provides a sense of scale for
the composition. Thomas
Lupton, who later
commissioned Turner in *The
Harbours of England* series,
engraved this image.

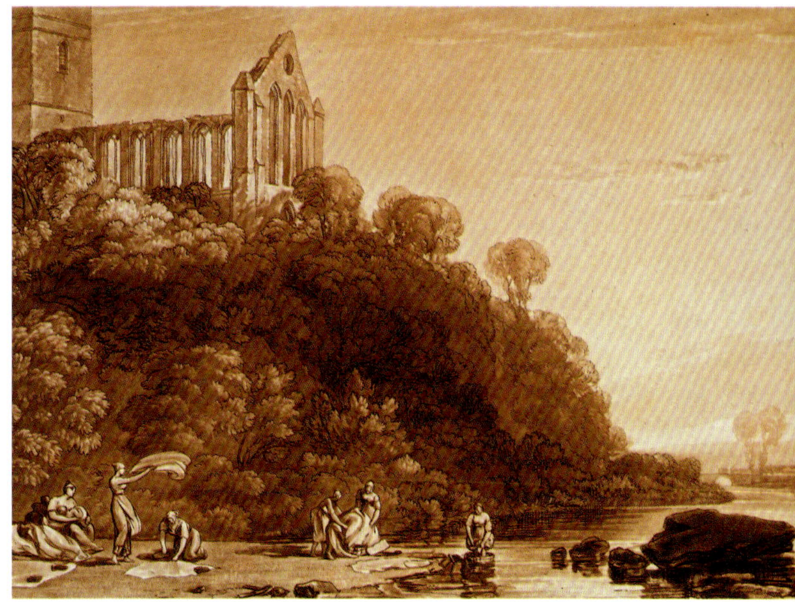

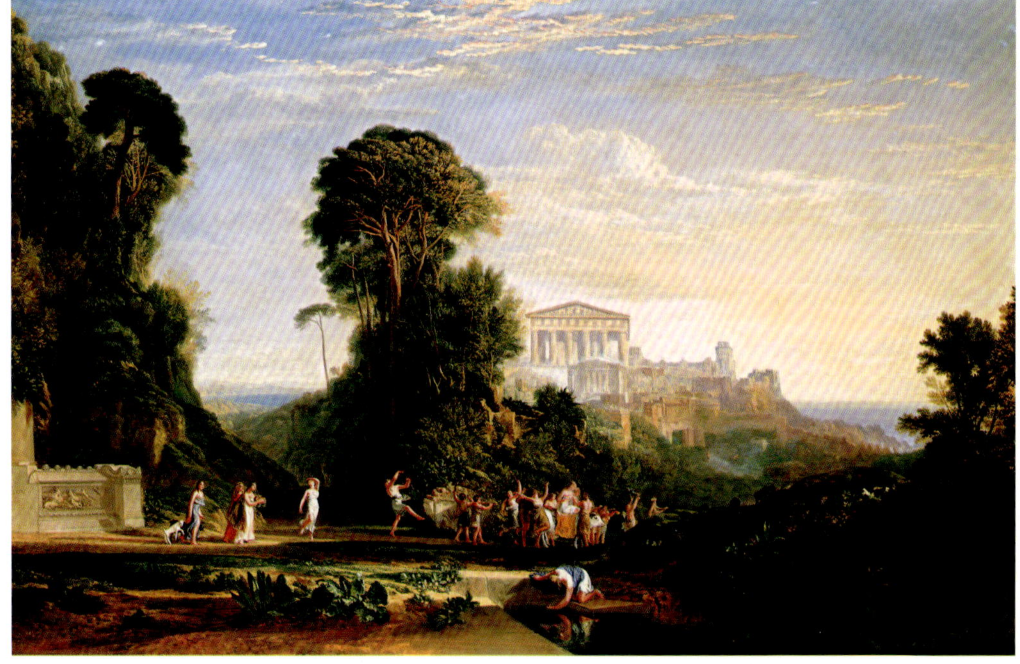

*The Temple of Jupiter:
Panellenius Restored*, 1816,
oil on canvas,
Private Collection,
46 x 70cm (18 x 28in)

At the Academy exhibition
of 1816, Turner showed two
paintings, this and a
companion piece, based on
the ruined temple at Aegina.
This one shows the restored
temple, making an interesting
contrast of ancient and
modern aspects of Greek
culture. The reference for
the work was a drawing
provided by Henry Gally
Knight, a friend of the
Romantic poet Lord Byron.

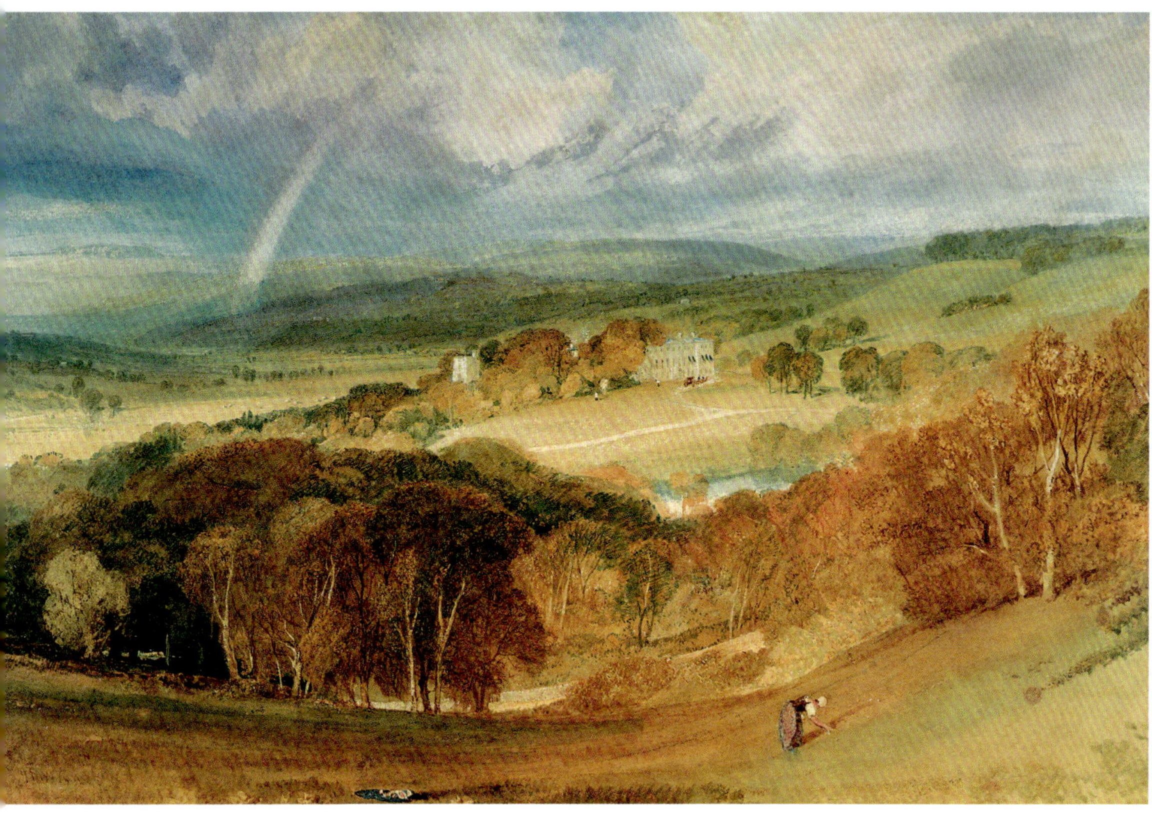

The Vale of Ashburnham,
1816, watercolour,
University of Liverpool
Art Gallery, UK,
36 x 55cm (14 x 22in)

Ashburnham Place, as seen
in this watercolour, was
once the home of the Earls
of Ashburnham. It was
demolished in the 1950s
after the family were unable
to maintain its upkeep.
The watercolour was
commissioned by 'Mad Jack'
Fuller, the local Member of
Parliament, as part of a
series of paintings of Sussex
that were to be made into a
set of prints.

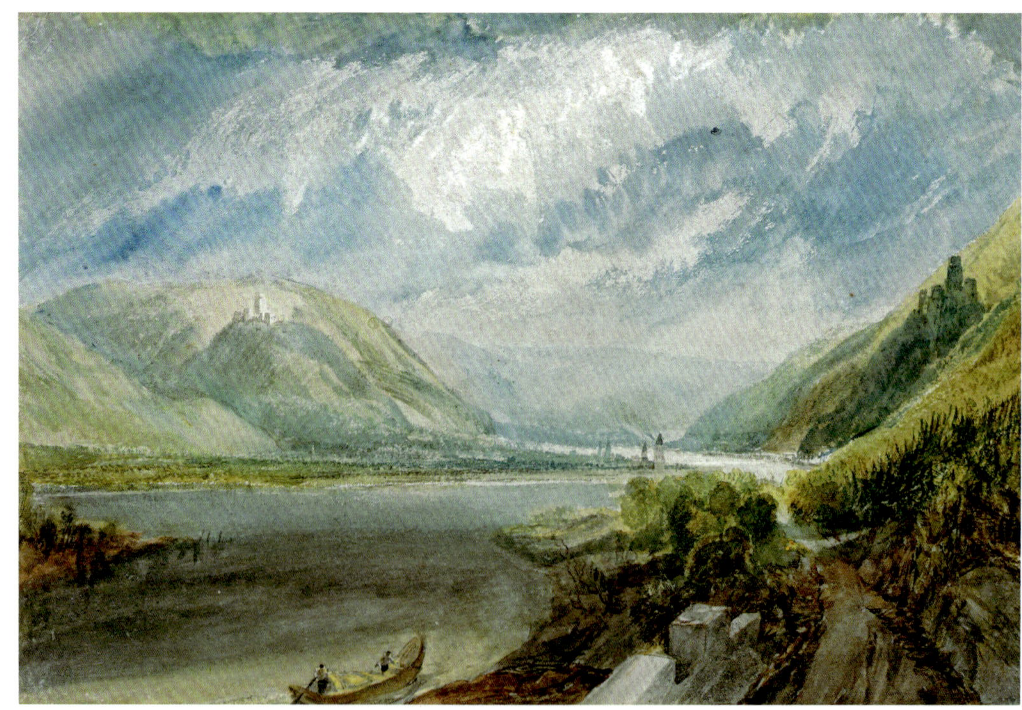

*Junction of the Lahn and the
Rhine*, 1817,
watercolour and
bodycolour,
Private Collection,
20 x 31cm (8 x 12in)

During the Napoleonic
Wars this part of Prussia
had been annexed to
France, but as a result of the
Congress of Vienna in 1814,
was subsequently occupied
by the Russians. At the time
of this painting, the Prussians
had regained much of their
territory after helping to
defeat Napoleon at
Waterloo. Turner's picture
reflects that sense of
peace and stability.

Remagen and Linz, 1817,
watercolour and
bodycolour, Indianapolis
Museum of Art, IN, USA,
18 x 32cm (7 x 13in)

Remagen and Linz are
adjacent towns along the
River Rhine. This beautifully
executed watercolour
demonstrates the appeal
of the location for tourists.
By placing a group of
tourists at bottom right of
the picture plane, Turner
cleverly invites the viewer
into the pictorial space to
share the spectacular view.

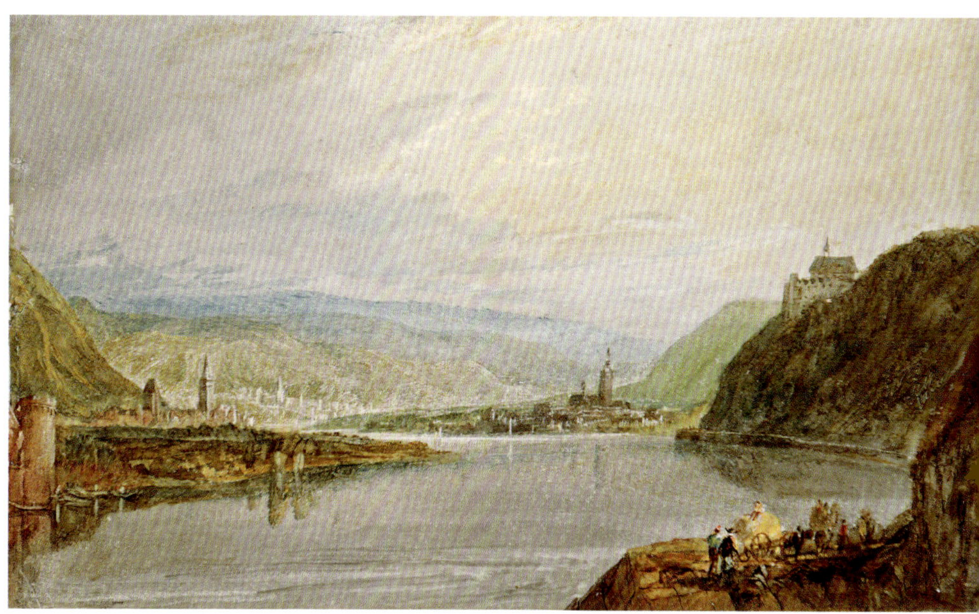

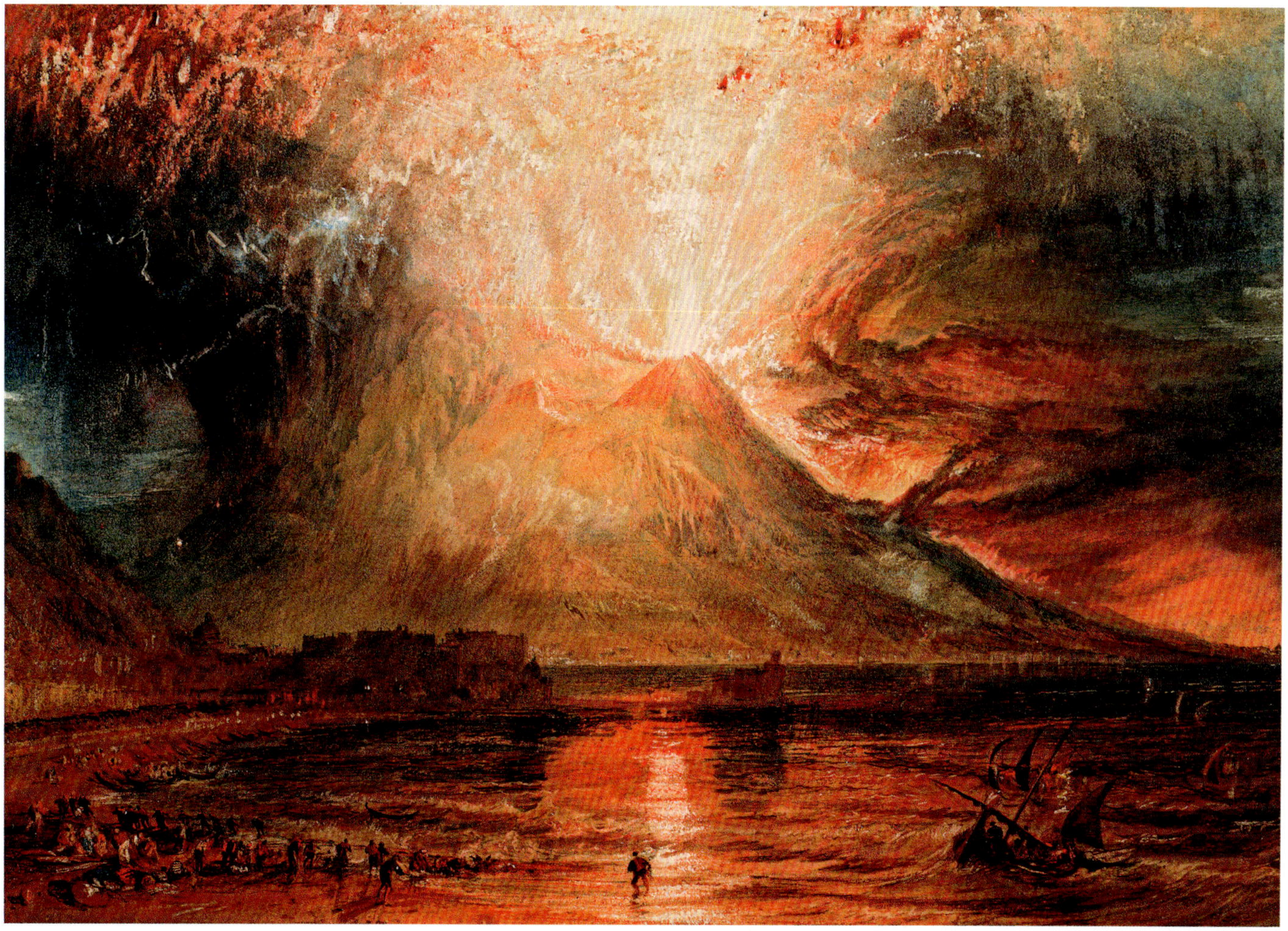

Mount Vesuvius in Eruption,
1817, watercolour, Paul
Mellon Collection, Yale
Center for British Art, CT,
USA, 29 x 40cm (11 x 16in)

Mount Vesuvius was, and
still is, one of the most
volatile volcanoes in the
world. In Turner's day it
was often in the news
because it was continually
erupting, with a severe
eruption occurring in 1794.
Although Turner had not, at
the time of this watercolour,
visited Italy, there were
many pictorial references
available including Joseph
Wright of Derby's picture
of 1774–6.

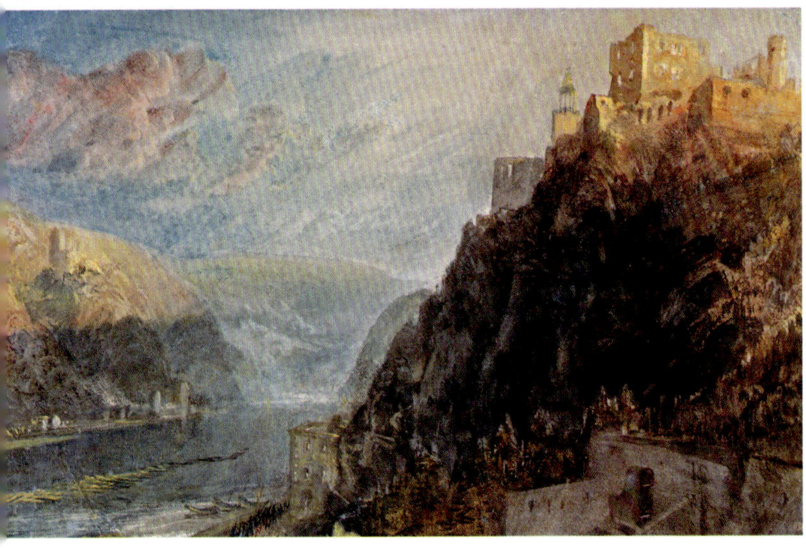

Rheinfels Looking to Katz,
1817, watercolour and
bodycolour, Paul Mellon
Collection, Yale Center
for British Art, CT, USA,
20 x 37cm (8 x 15in)

Aside from this picturesque
location with its recently
ruined castle, destroyed by
the French in 1794, Turner

may well also have enjoyed
the salmon fishing in this
area. The River Rhine
narrows considerably at
this point to about one-
third of its normal width
as it winds its way around
the famous Lorelei Rock,
which is a dangerous and
difficult stretch to navigate
by boat.

Burg Sooneck with Bacharach
in the Distance, 1817,
watercolour and
bodycolour on grey paper,
British Museum, London, UK,
22 x 36cm (9 x 14in)

Turner obviously liked this
watercolour since he
recreated the scene in a
larger format in 1820 as one
in a series of Rhineland views
for a patron, Sir John
Swinburne. Sir John's son,
Edward, became a friend of
Turner's and received
drawing lessons from him.
Walter Fawkes acquired the
smaller version, shown here.

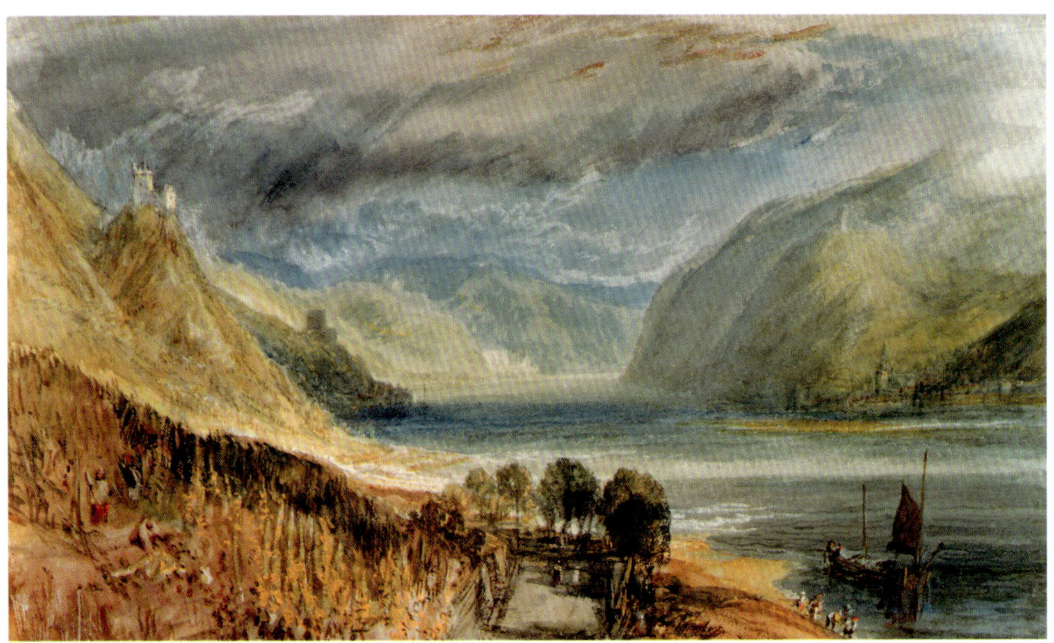

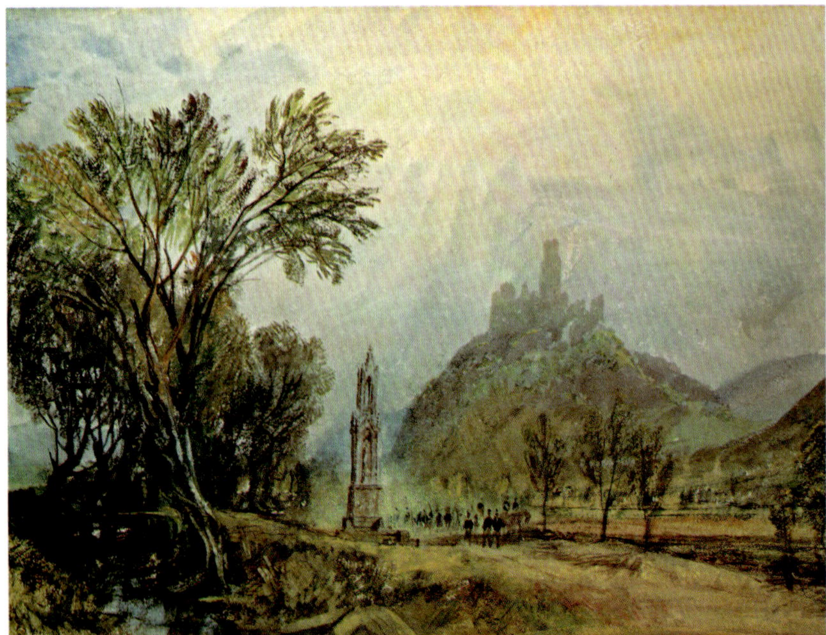

The Hochkreuz and
Godesberg, 1817,
watercolour and bodycolour,
Private Collection,
20 x 30cm (8 x 12in)

Looking at this tranquil
watercolour, it is hard to
imagine that this area now
forms part of the German
city of Bonn. Turner's painting
focuses on the two landmarks
that are still present today, the
Celtic cross at Hochkreuz
and the ruins of the castle
at Godesberg.

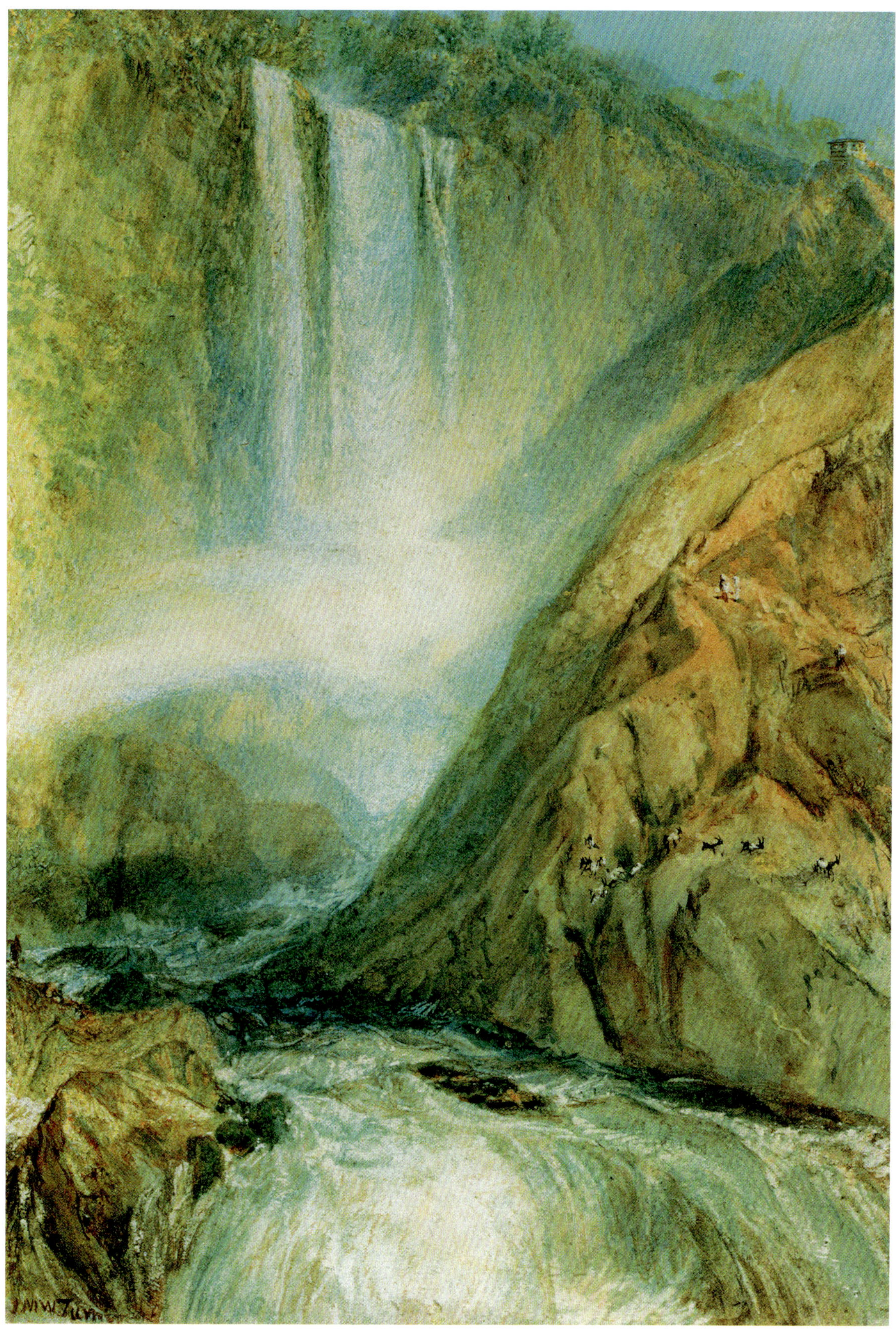

The Falls of Terni, 1817,
watercolour,
Blackburn Museum, UK,
14 x 22cm (5½ x 9in)

Since Turner did not visit Italy until two years after this watercolour was executed, he is likely to have copied and adapted the motif from the work of John Cozens. Turner's image was published as an engraving in 1819, after he had assured himself of its accuracy during his visit that year.

The Lorelei Rock, 1817, watercolour, Leeds Art Gallery, UK, 20 x 31cm (8 x 12in)

The narrowest part of the River Rhine in Germany is here at St Goarshausen. It is one of the most hazardous stretches of the river, with ships often running aground. Legend has it that the water nymphs known as Lorelei or Rhinemaidens lured the mariners off course, leading to the headland being called the Lorelei Rock.

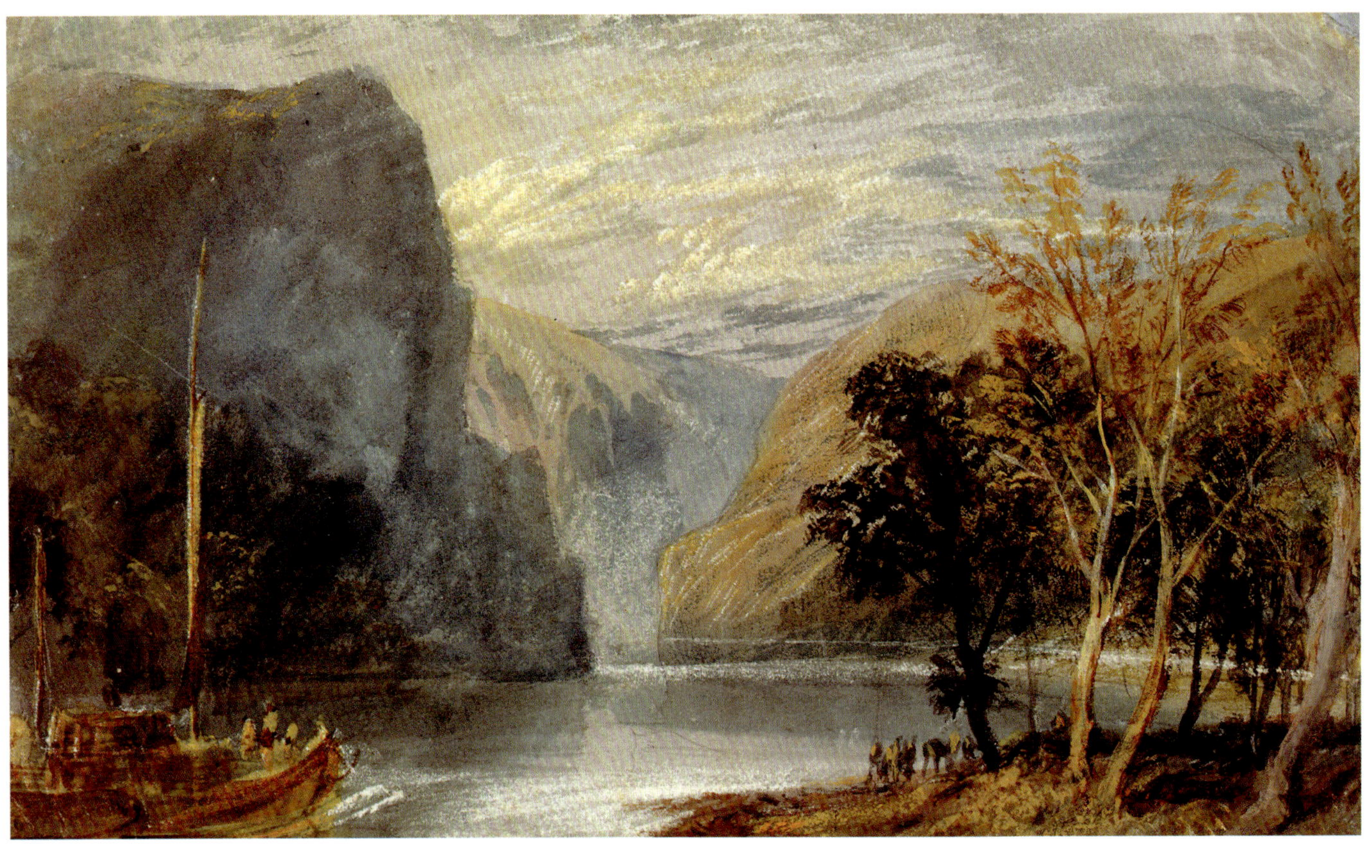

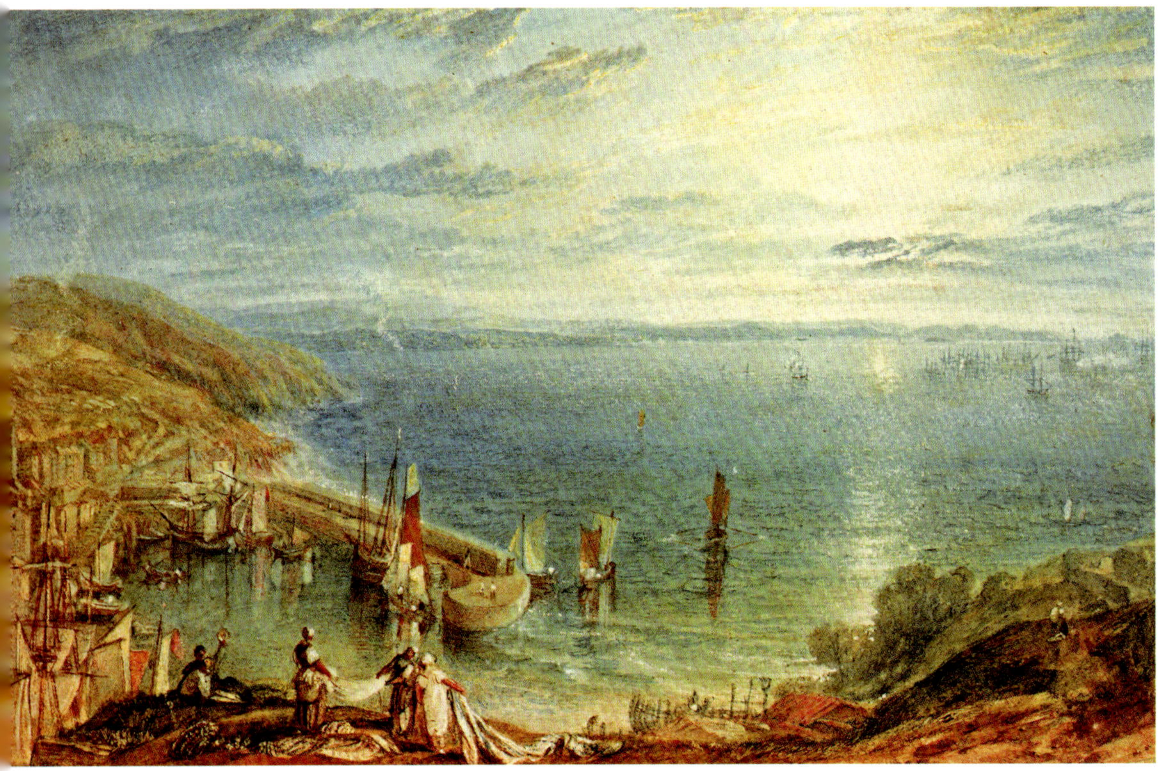

Torbay from Brixham, 1817, watercolour, Fitzwilliam Museum, Cambridge, UK, 16 x 24cm (6 x 9in)

Of note in this watercolour is the fishing trawler shown inside the harbour wall. At the time this picture was painted, Brixham, with its 4,000 inhabitants, had become a major fishing port adapted to commercial fishing using trawlers. In the foreground are a group of women opening the used nets for drying in the sun.

Florence from the Ponte alla Carraia, 1816–17, watercolour, Whitworth Art Gallery, Manchester, UK, dimensions unknown

Turner produced this detailed topographical watercolour of Florence two years before he even went to the city.

The image was made into an engraving, published in 1818. The commission came from the publisher John Murray, who paid

Turner for a series of watercolours based on drawings by James Hakewill, an architect and a skilled draughtsman.

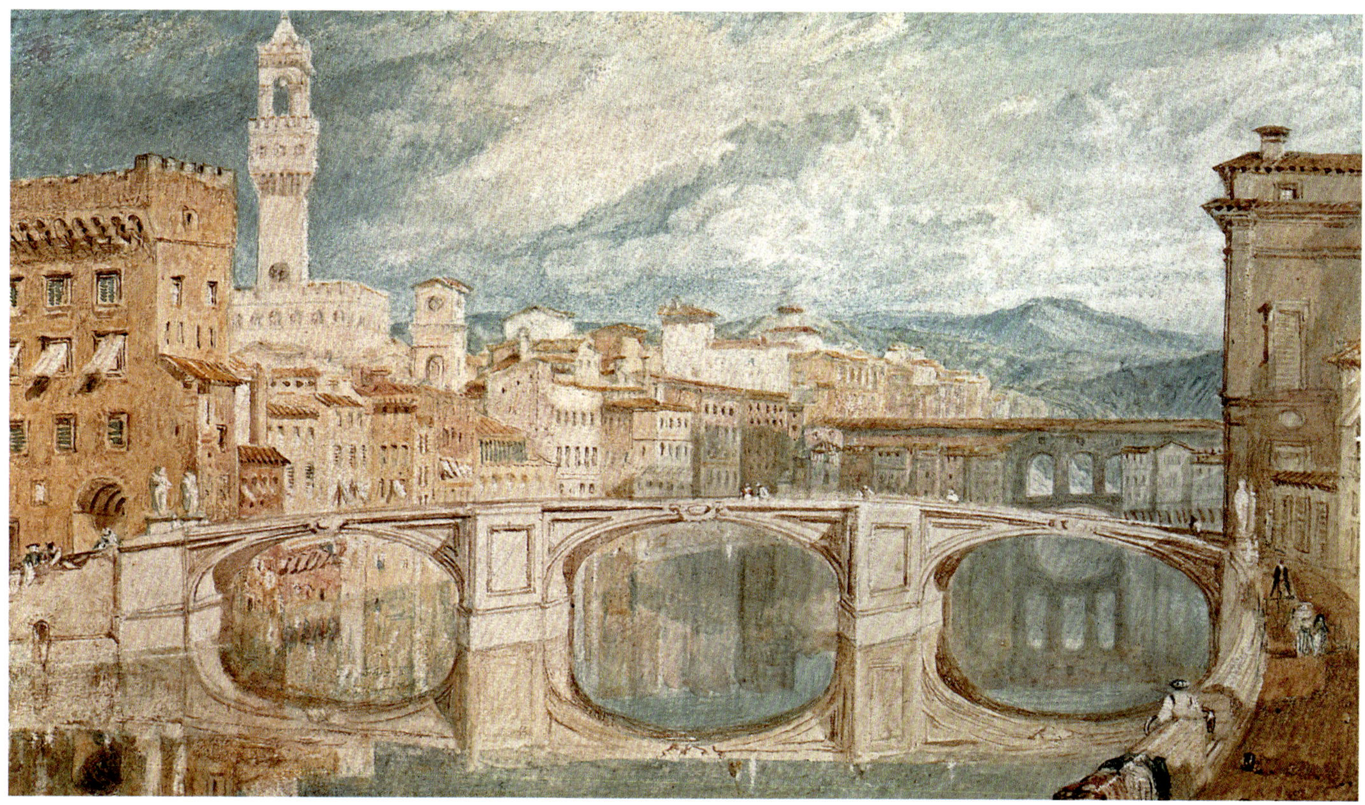

Winchelsea, Sussex and the Military Canal, 1817, watercolour, Private Collection, 13 x 20cm (5 x 8in)

Even in medieval times, this stretch of coastline had been continuously threatened by French invasion. Napoleon, with his huge forces, posed an even greater threat and it was decided in 1804 to build a 30-km- (20-mile-) long canal for defensive purposes. Seawater would be used to fill the canal to provide an impassable moat-like barrier, behind which a rampart would be made from the excavated earth.

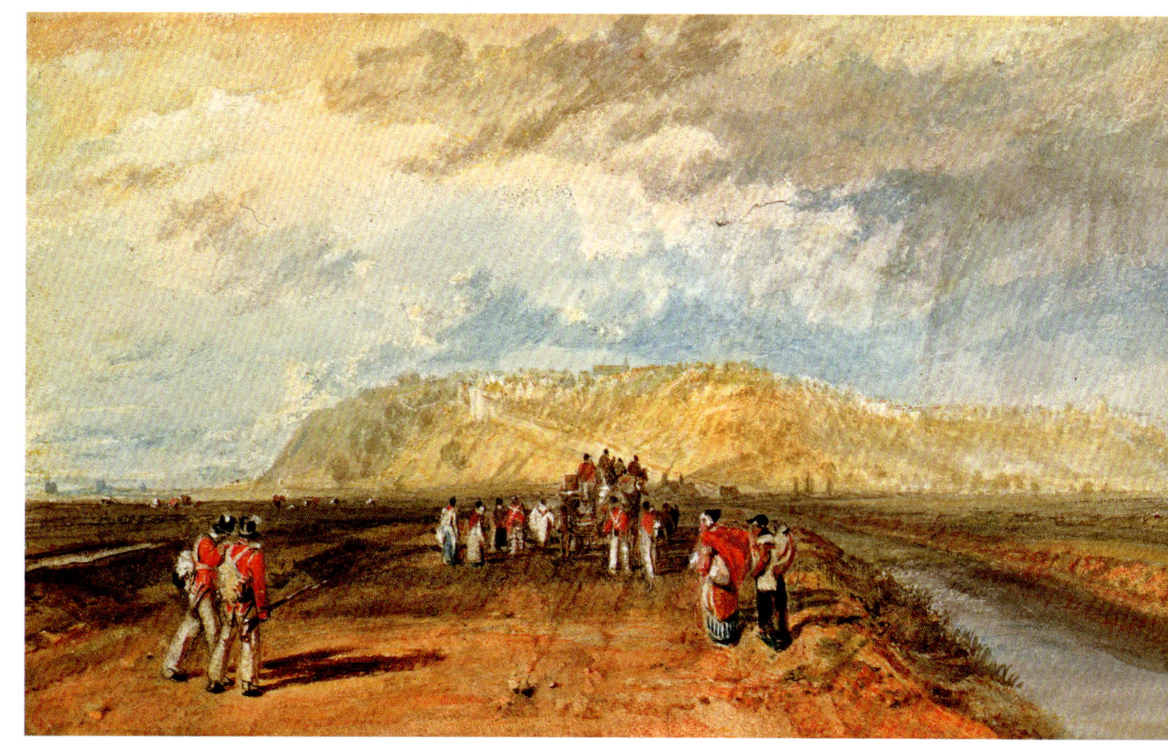

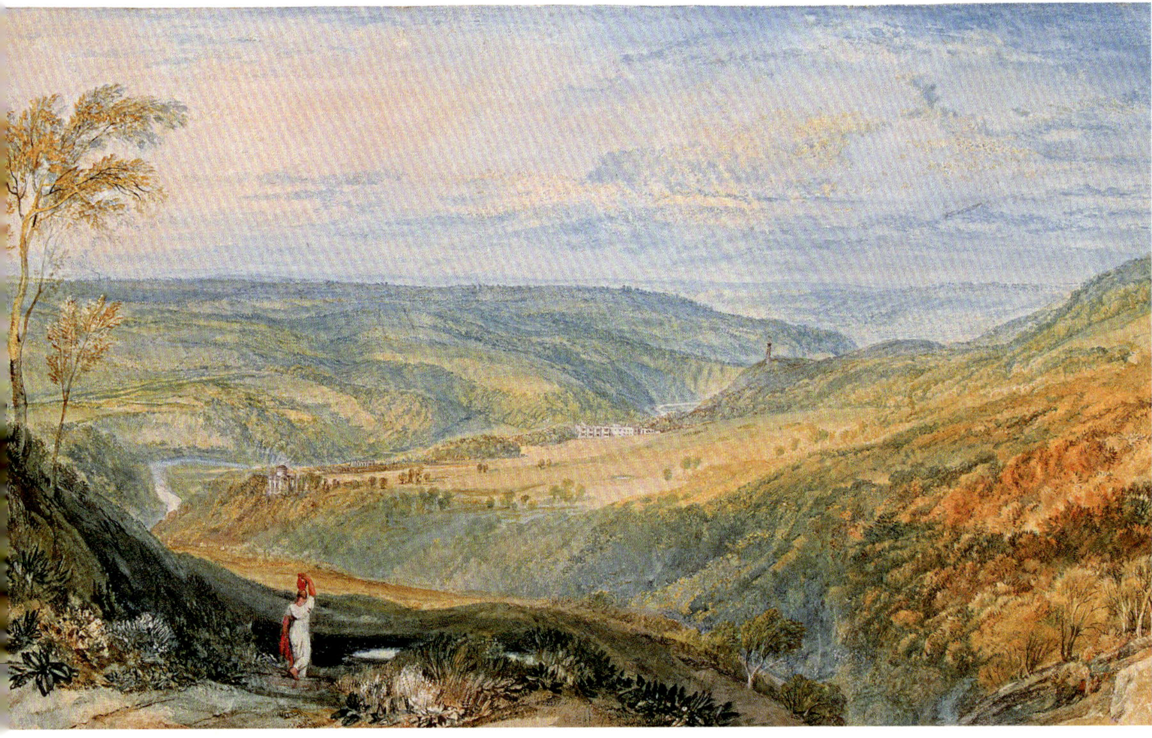

Gibside, County Durham from the South, 1817, watercolour, Bowes Museum, Durham, UK, 26 x 43cm (10 x 17in)

The estate in the distance of Turner's watercolour is Gibside, owned by the Bowes family since the 17th century. In the 18th century, the present manor house was built when Mary Bowes married the ninth Earl of Strathmore, John Lyon. In Turner's time the Bowes-Lyon family managed the estates, but in the 20th century they were forced to sell because of death duties.

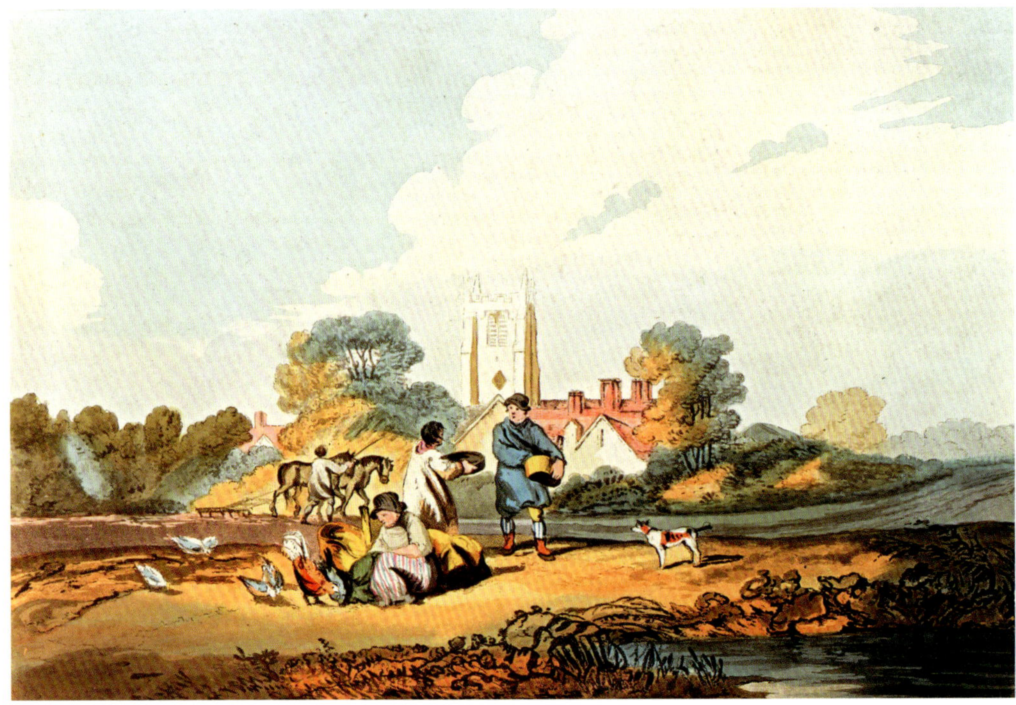

Autumn Sowing Grain, 1818, hand coloured etching and aquatint, Victoria and Albert Museum, London, UK, dimensions unknown

The advantage of aquatint over conventional etching is that tonal variations can be made to the picture. To achieve this, a resin is applied to the surface of the copper plate that will resist the acid etch, to create larger areas of tone. Thus in aquatint, the emphasis is on tonal effect rather than the specific detail achieved in etching.

Borthwick Castle, 1818, watercolour, Indianapolis Museum of Art, IN, USA, 16 x 24cm (6 x 9in)

One of the largest medieval castles in Scotland, it was built for Sir William Borthwick in the 15th century. Mary Queen of Scots visited the castle in 1563, seeking the protection of the sixth Earl of Borthwick while fleeing the Scottish court after her contentious marriage to the Earl of Bothwell. The castle was attacked in 1650 by Oliver Cromwell and subsequently abandoned.

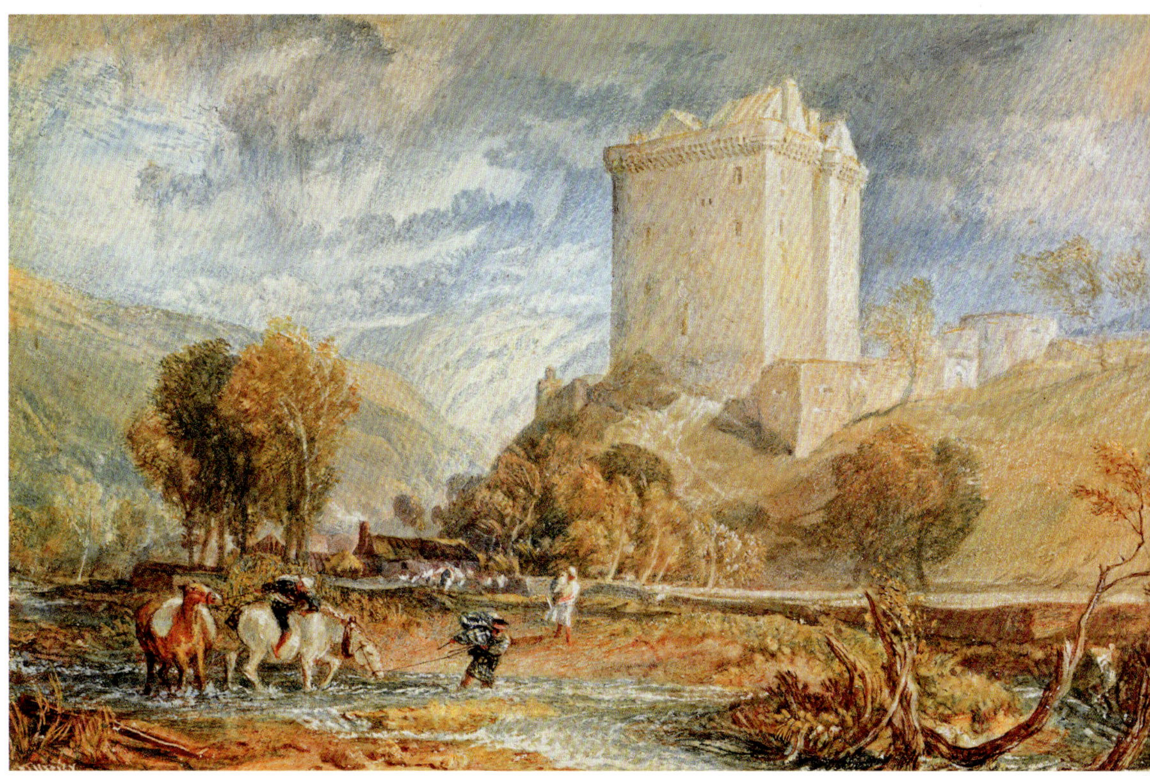

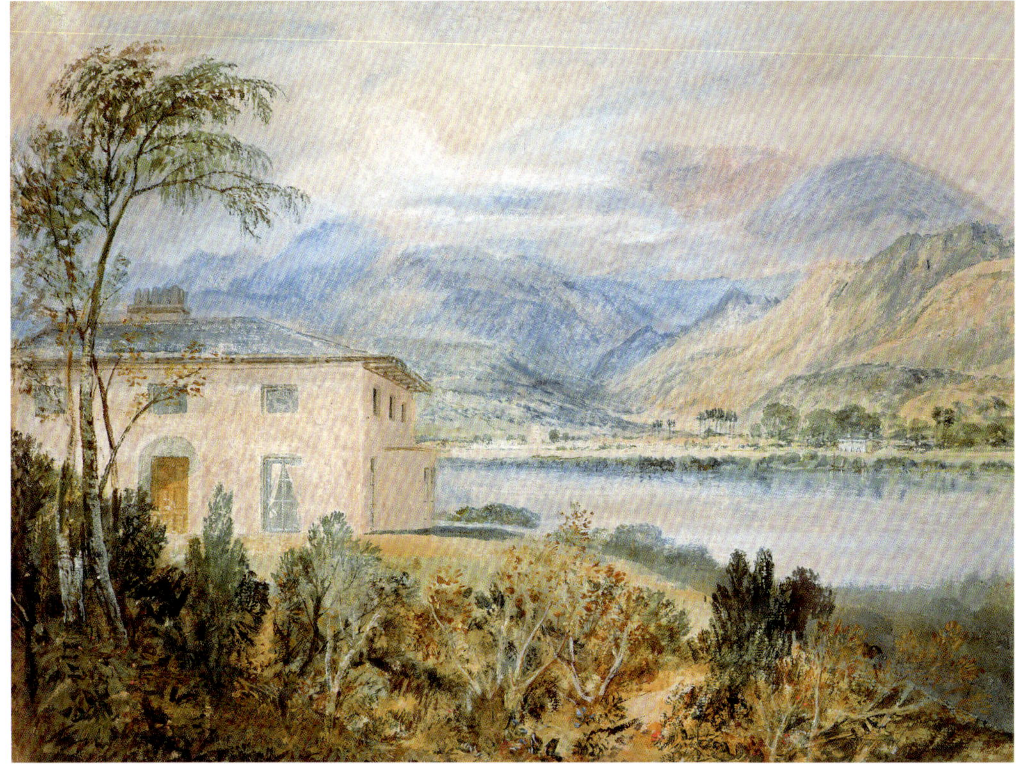

Tent Lodge by Coniston Water, 1818, watercolour and bodycolour, Fitzwilliam Museum, Cambridge, UK, 50 x 66cm (20 x 26in)

Coniston Water is the third largest of the lakes in the area of north-west England known as the Lake District. Famed for its stunning scenery, which includes mountains and lakes, in Turner's time it was the inspiration for a number of artists and poets such as William Wordsworth and Samuel Taylor Coleridge. Turner made several trips to the area between 1797 and 1831.

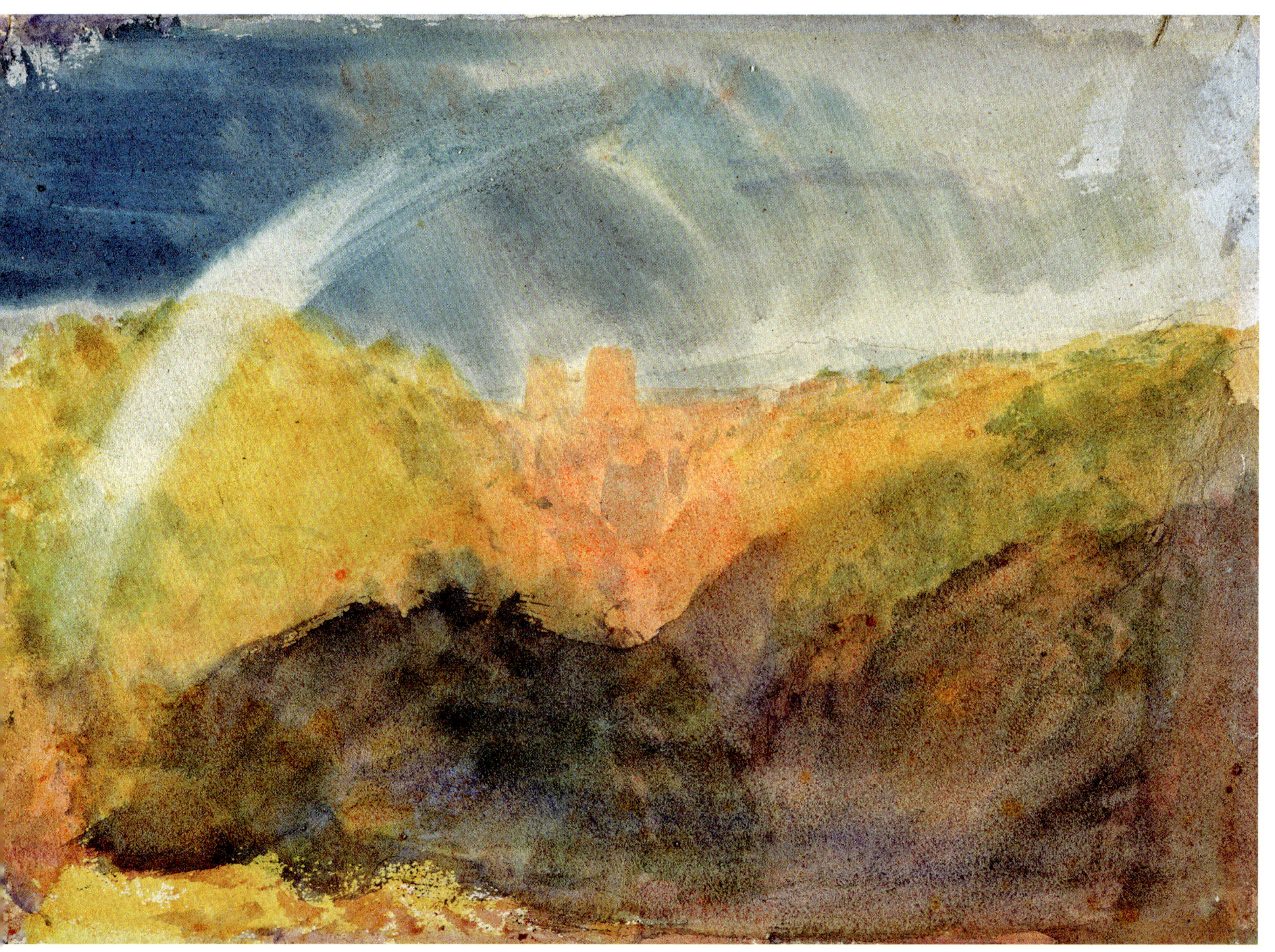

Crichton Castle (Mountainous Landscape with a Rainbow), 1818, graphite and watercolour, Paul Mellon Collection, Yale Center for British Art, CT, USA, 17 x 24cm (7 x 9in)

During 1818, Turner completed two watercolours of the ruined Crichton Castle, which is situated only a couple of miles from Borthwick Castle. The work shown here is a preliminary sketch made before working up a second watercolour that was subsequently used to illustrate Walter Scott's *Provincial Antiquities of Scotland*. Nevertheless, Turner does succeed in capturing the ethereal nature of the light.

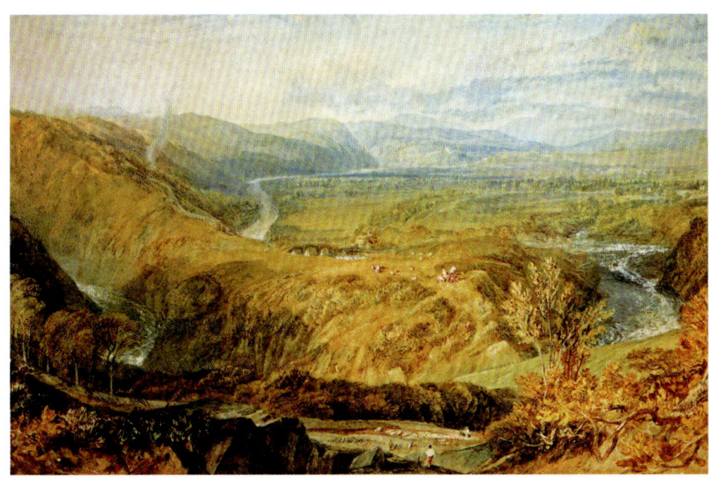

The Crook of Lune, Looking towards Hornby Castle, 1816–18, watercolour and bodycolour, Courtauld Institute, London, UK, 29 x 43cm (11 x 17in)

Turner's view looks along the valley of the River Lune toward the 13th-century Hornby Castle. The meandering Lune, as shown in the watercolour, takes the form of a shepherd's crook, an example of the kind of topography that Turner found particularly attractive. The image was used by the Reverend Doctor Thomas Whitaker for his *History of Richmondshire*, which was published in 1821.

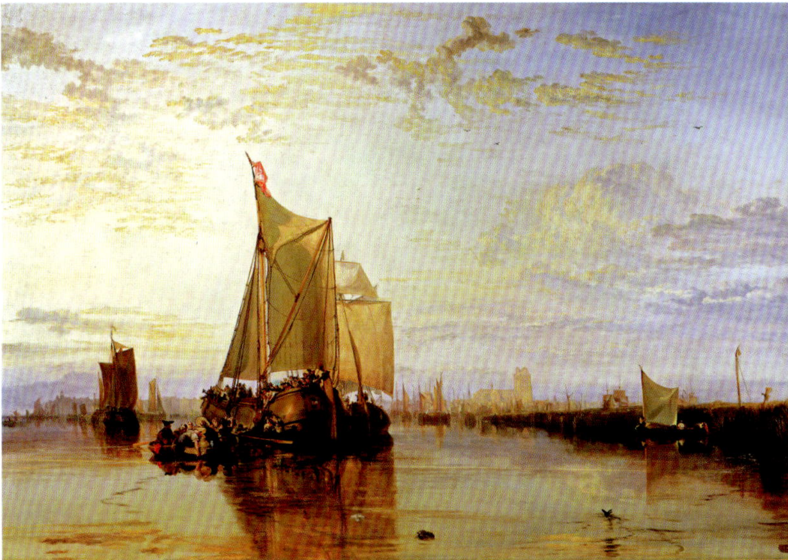

Dort or *Dortrecht: The Dort Packet-boat from Rotterdam Becalmed*, 1818, oil on canvas, Paul Mellon Collection, Yale Center for British Art, CT, USA, 158 x 234cm (62 x 92in)

Turner made several sketches of this scene when he stayed at Rotterdam before returning from his Rhine tour. Walter Fawkes purchased this painting for 500 guineas at the Royal Academy exhibition of 1818, and placed it at Farnley Hall where it remained until 1966. Fawkes was apparently persuaded to buy the picture by his son and heir Hawksworth.

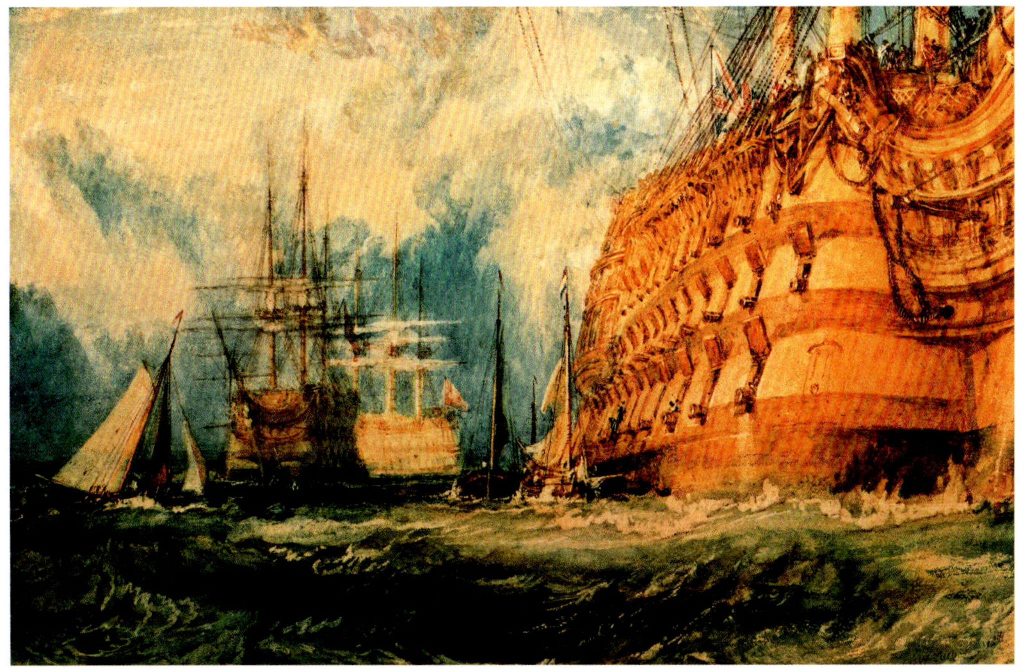

A First Rate Taking in Stores, 1818, pencil and watercolour, Cecil Higgins Art Gallery, Bedford, UK, 29 x 40cm (11 x 16in)

An accurate record of Turner's painting method exists for this watercolour, its execution witnessed by Hawksworth Fawkes, while the artist was staying at Farnley Hall. He recalled that Turner began by soaking the paper in watercolour before scratching at it in a frenzy, until "gradually and as if by magic, the lovely ship, with all its exquisite minutia [sic] came into being".

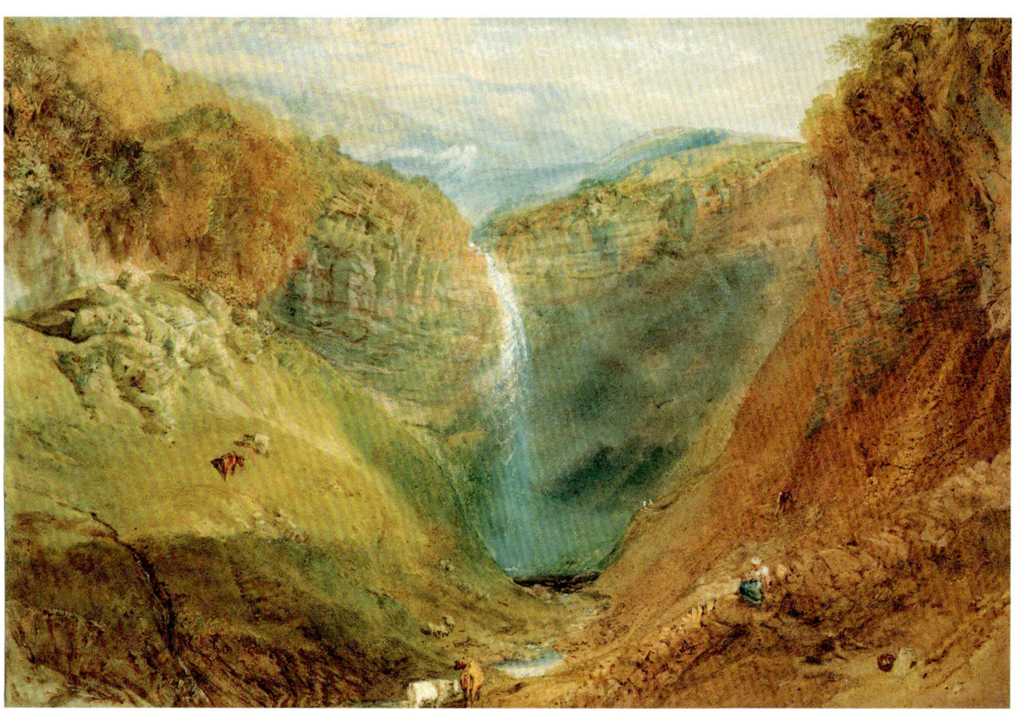

Hardraw Fall, 1816–18, graphite and watercolour, Fitzwilliam Museum, Cambridge, UK, 29 x 42cm (11 x 16½in)

One of England's highest continuous waterfalls, Hardraw Falls is sited in the Yorkshire Dales, which Turner visited in the summer of 1816, one of several locations that he explored from his base at Farnley Hall for the *History of Richmondshire* commission. The waterfall is apparently best seen after heavy rainfall, which Turner had certainly experienced during that summer!

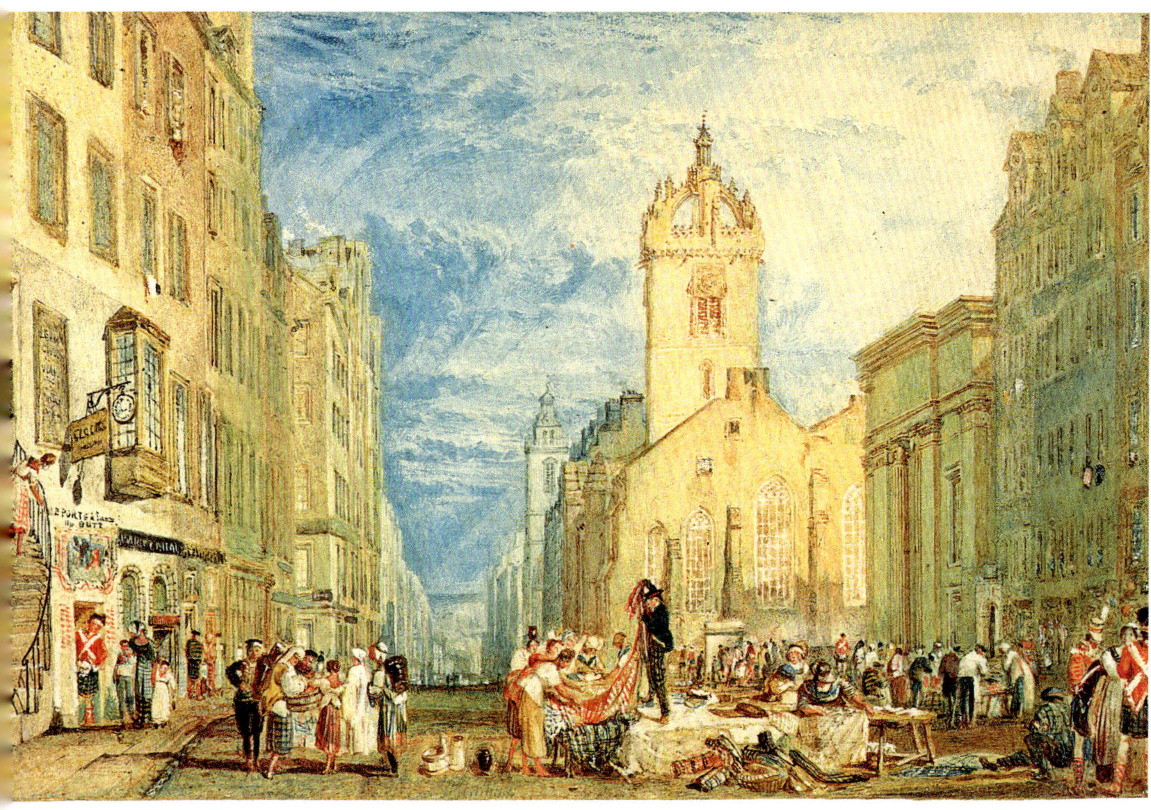

High Street, Edinburgh, c.1818, watercolour, pen, ink and graphite, Paul Mellon Collection, Yale Center for British Art, CT, USA, 17 x 25cm (7 x 10in)

In October 1818, Turner travelled north to Scotland to collect material for the *Provincial Antiquities of Scotland* commission. He made more than 400 sketches on this tour, resulting in a series of drawings completed by 1821. Turner has depicted the busy High Street with plenty of human activity in the Scottish capital city. St Giles' Cathedral dominates the Edinburgh skyline.

Lancaster Sands, 1818,
watercolour, Birmingham
Art Gallery, UK,
28 x 37cm (11 x 15in)

The figures shown in this
watercolour are crossing the
sands at Morecambe Bay at
low tide to avoid a long
detour. Their path is marked
out with a series of 'brobs'
made from laurel leaves
pushed into the wet sand.
Guides, who knew the sands
well and could avoid
the areas of quicksand,
placed them there.

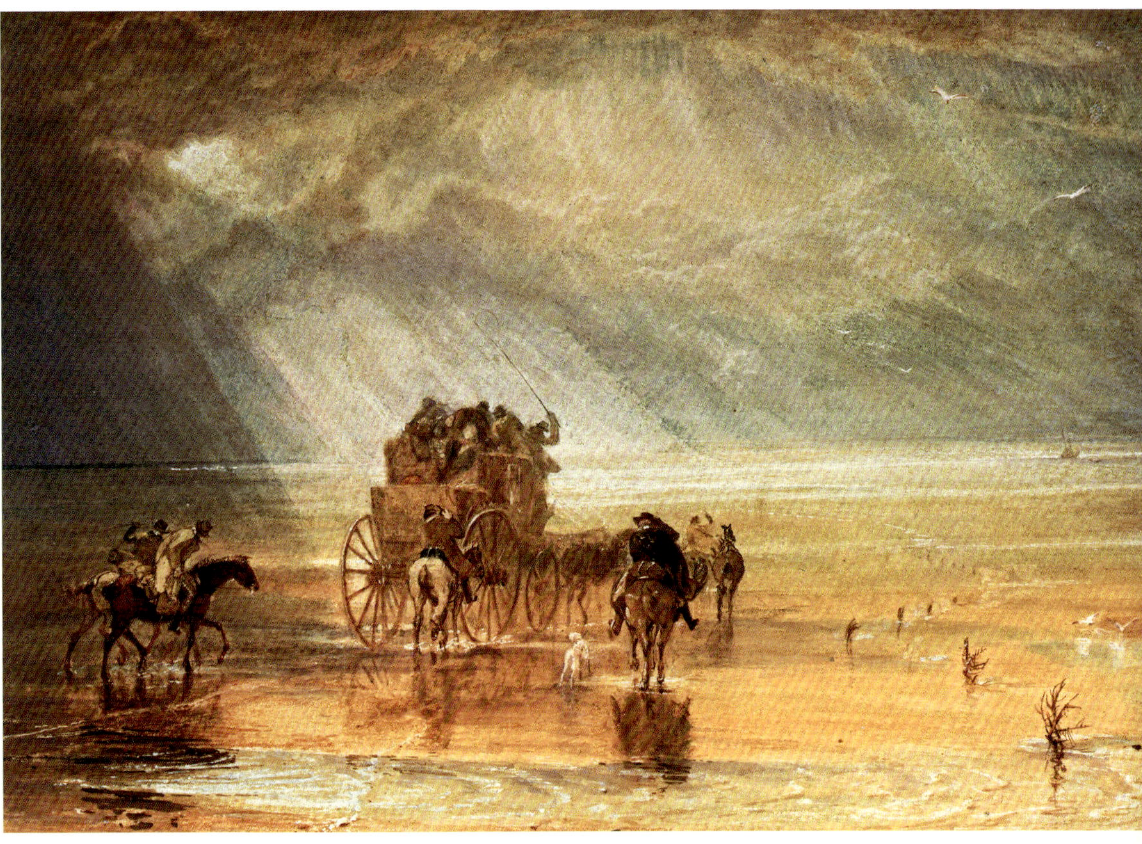

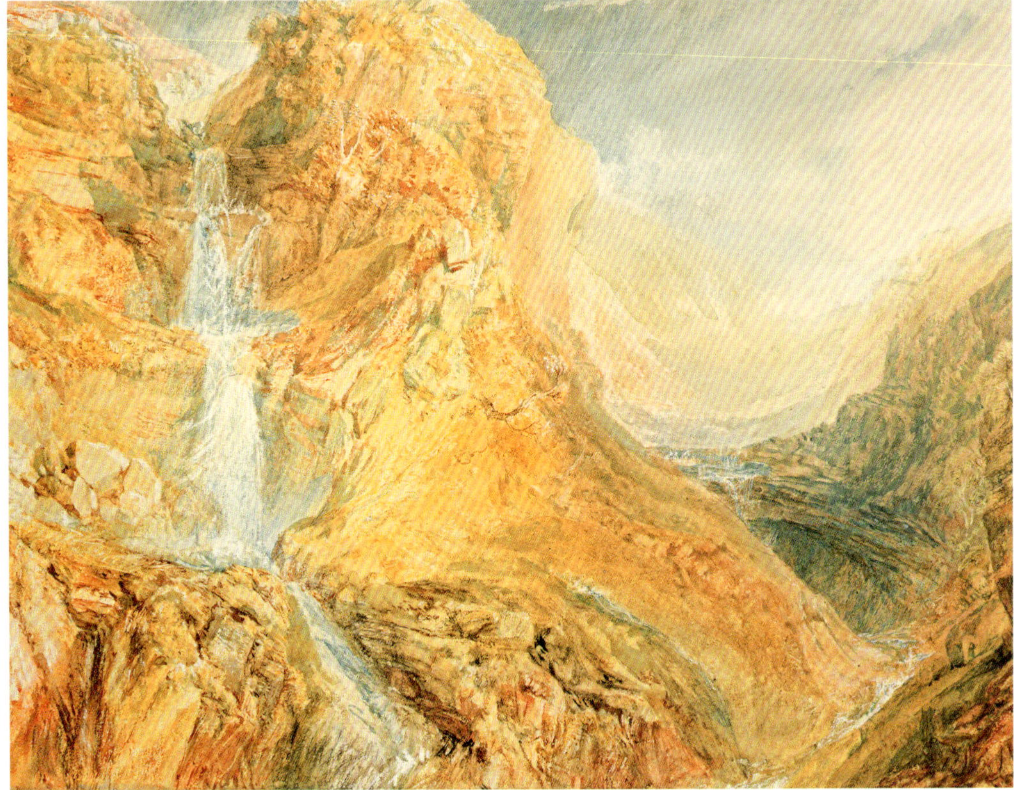

Mossdale Fall, Yorkshire,
1816–18, watercolour and
scratching out, Fitzwilliam
Museum, Cambridge, UK,
29 x 42cm (11 x 16½in)

In his book *Modern Painters*,
John Ruskin referred to
Turner's Yorkshire series of
watercolours as having
"great solemnity and
simplicity of subject…the
drawing manly but careful,
the minutiae sometimes
exquisitely delicate". Ruskin
may well have been
describing this watercolour,
which he owned. Turner
has used 'scratching out' to
great effect in this work
to highlight the waterfall
and imbue it with a sense
of movement.

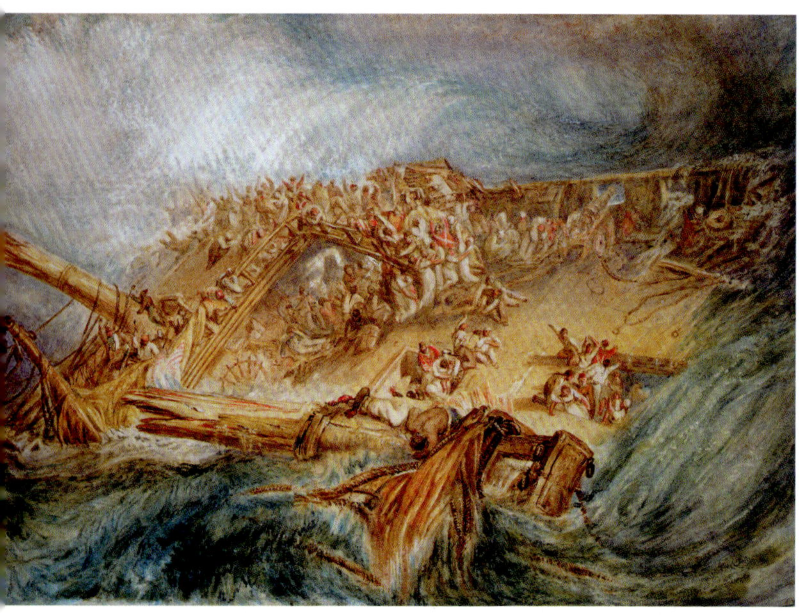

The Loss of an East Indiaman, 1818, watercolour, Cecil Higgins Art Gallery, Bedford, UK, 28 x 40cm (11 x 16in)

This disaster picture refers to a ship belonging to the East India Company, an organization set up for the purposes of trading between England and the Indian subcontinent. The Company was set up in the early 17th century, and by the 19th had achieved a monopoly on trade, and control of Indian territory. The 1813 Charter Act transferred that power to the British Crown.

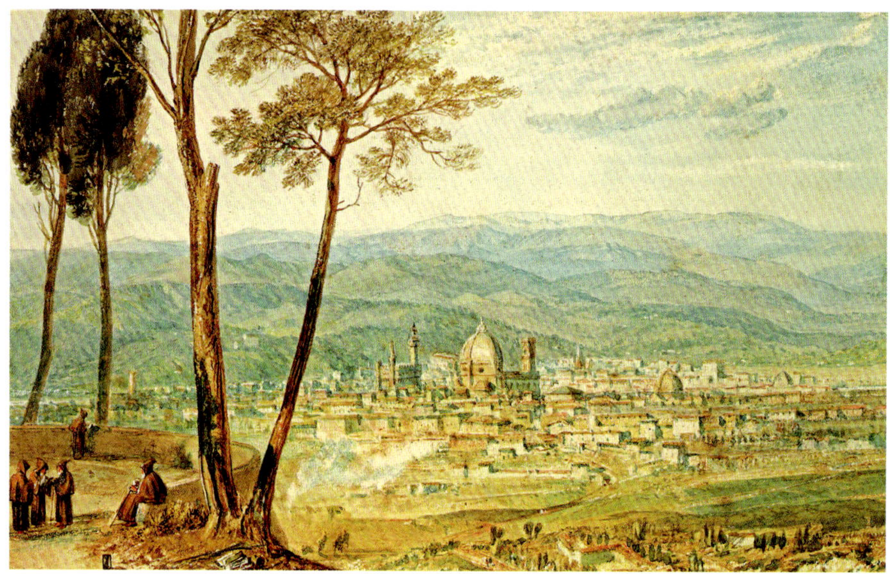

Florence from the Road to Fiesole, 1818, watercolour, Private Collection, 14 x 21cm (5½ x 8in)

It is difficult to believe that Turner executed this detailed watercolour drawing a year before he had even been to Italy for the first time. Nevertheless he conveys the topographical detail accurately with the recognizable 15th-century Duomo taking centre stage in the distant city.

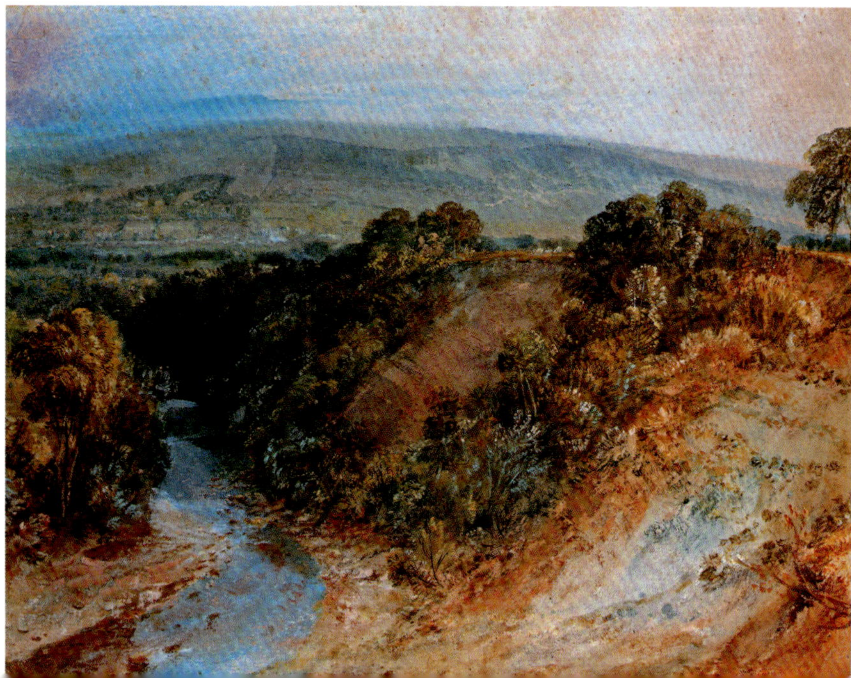

The Valley of the Washburn, 1818, watercolour, Leeds Art Gallery, UK, 173 x 216cm (68 x 85in)

The Otley Chevin shown here in the background was the ridge that Turner saw during a thunderstorm at Farnley Hall. The storm influenced the painting of *Snow Storm: Hannibal and his Army Crossing the Alps*. The village of Otley is shown at the foot of the Chevin. Close by is Farnley Hall.

*Valley of the Wharfe with
Otley in the Distance,
watercolour, c.1818,
Private Collection,
30 x 45cm (12 x 18cm)*

Painted during one of
Turner's visits to this area
when he was staying with
Walter Fawkes, this
watercolour is now in a
private collection but
may well have once been
owned by Fawkes and
his family as one of the
so-called 'Wharfedales'.
After Fawkes' death in 1825,
many of the family assets
were sold to clear
his debts.

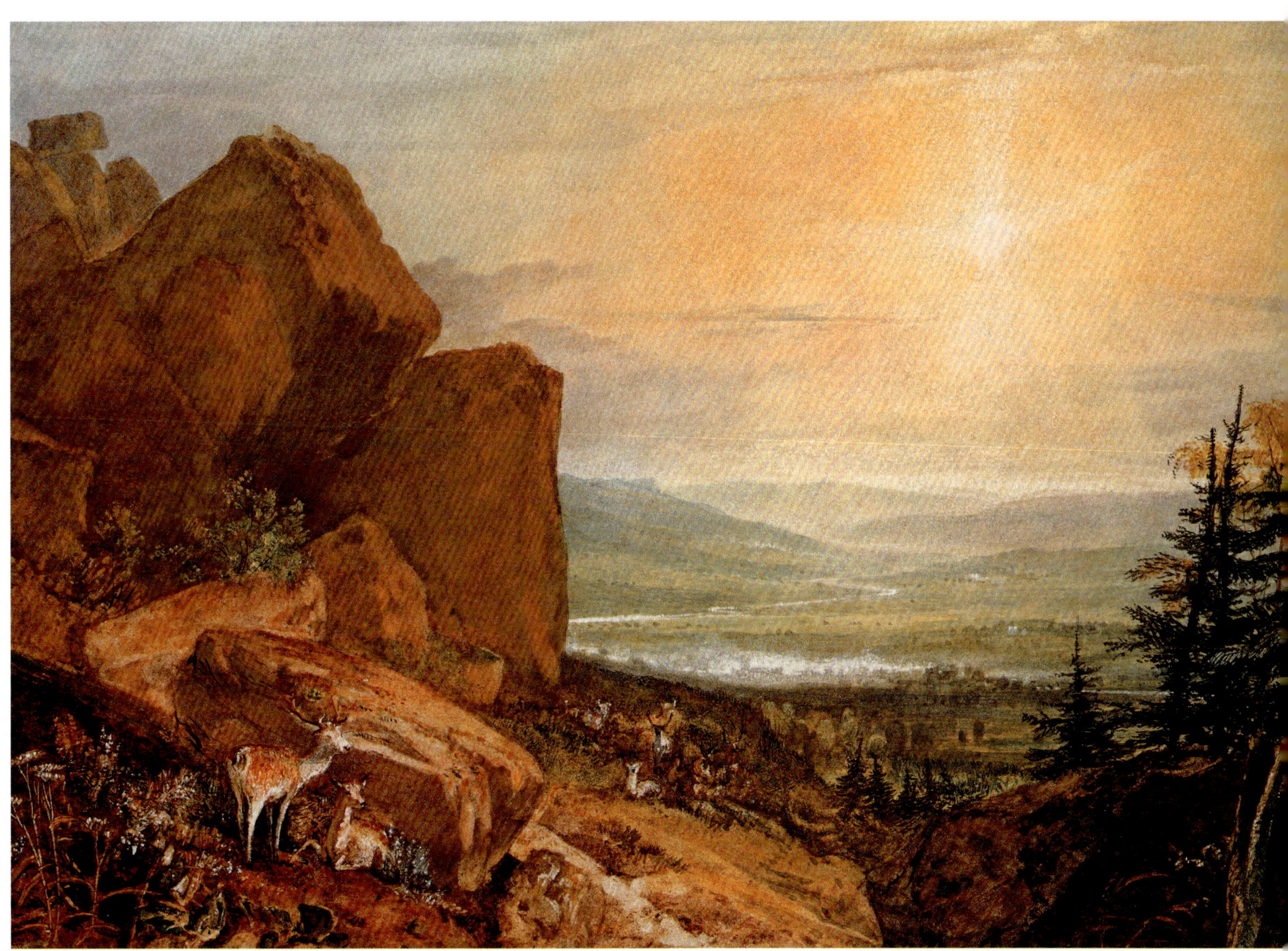

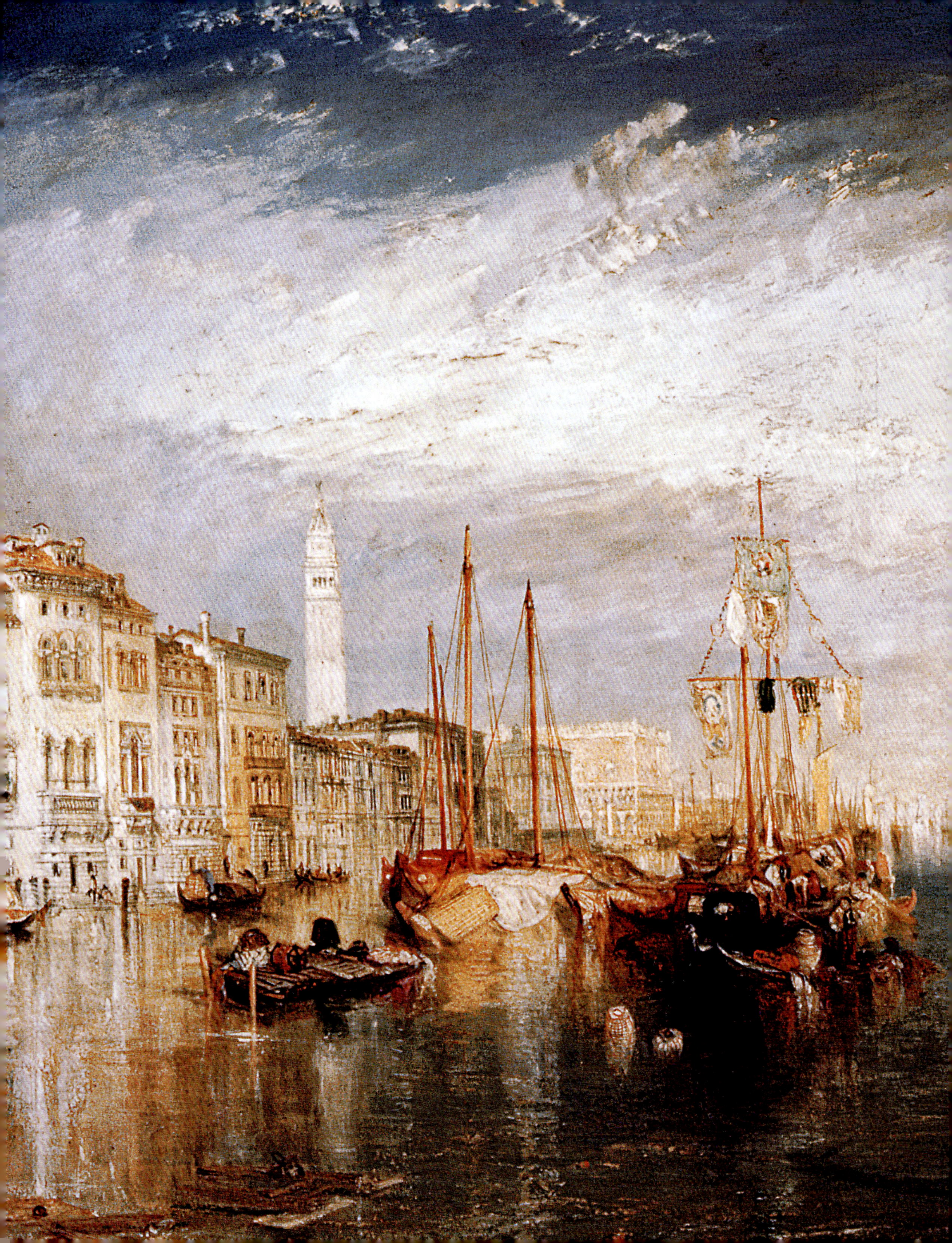

VENETIAN LIGHT 1821–1830

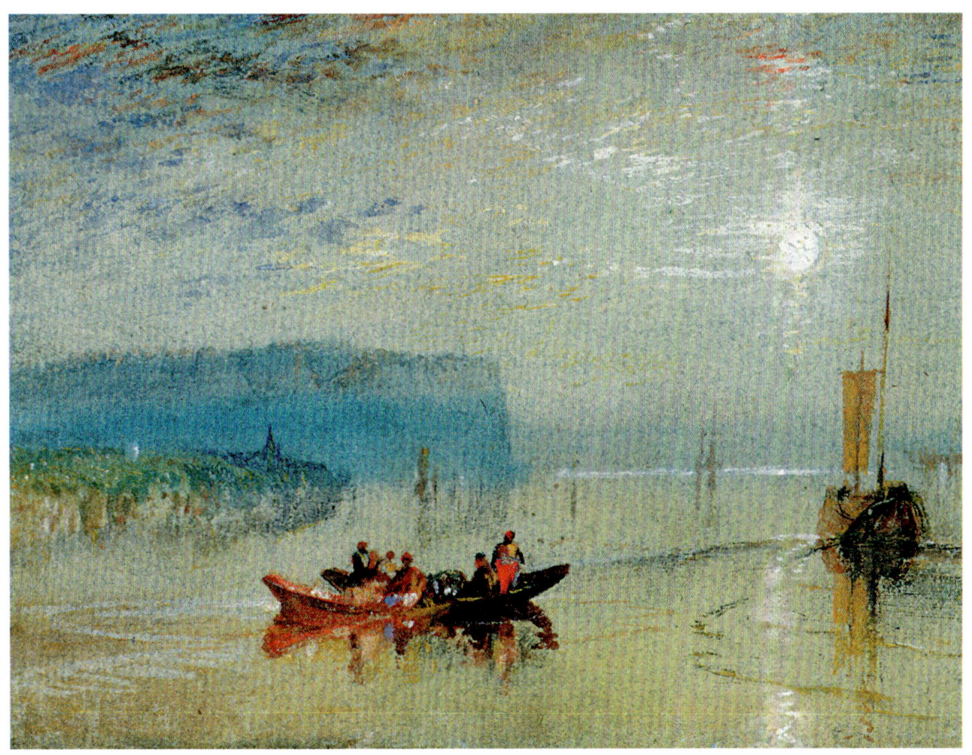

The decade following Turner's first visit to Italy in 1819 was arguably the most exciting for both the artist and his audience. The ever changing English light excited Turner most in the landscape, but in Italy, particularly Venice, he found a yet more exciting phenomenon, the effect that its light had on the reception of colour. Its intensity offered Turner new challenges to the way that he, and his audience, would see colour. The Venetian light would not only affect the way he painted Italian scenes but would also lead to the next decade's experiments in colour in all his work. As in some of his English landscapes, Turner was prepared to sacrifice topographical accuracy in order to capture the essence of a place, exemplified by his Venetian paintings.

Above: Scene on the Loire, near the Côteaux de Mauves,
watercolour, bodycolour, pen and ink, c.1826–30. This painting shares
some of the other ethereal qualities synonymous with Venice.
Left: Venice, from the Porch of Madonna della Salute, *oil on canvas,*
1835. Despite visiting Venice in 1819, Turner did not begin painting
the motif in oils until the 1830s.

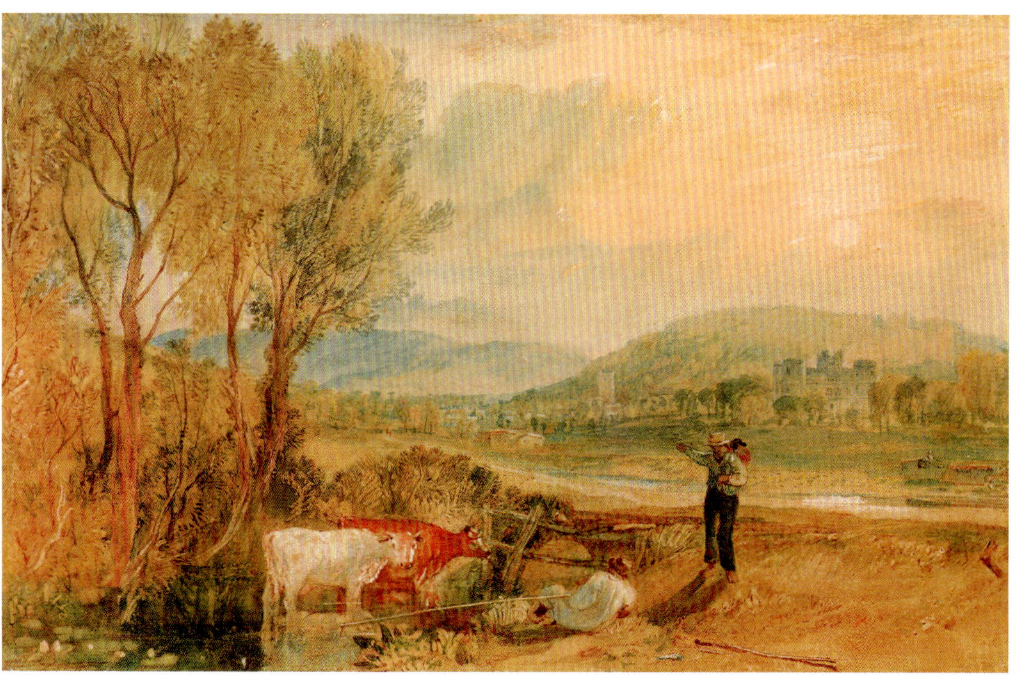

Lulworth Castle, Dorset, 1820, watercolour, Paul Mellon Collection, Yale Center for British Art, CT, USA, 16 x 24cm (6 x 9in)

At the time of this painting, Lulworth Castle was owned by the Weld family, who purchased it in the 17th century from the Duke of Norfolk and still own it today. Turner brings a sense of the Pastoral to the view by including some cattle, possibly en route to market. This image was engraved as part of the *Picturesque Views* series.

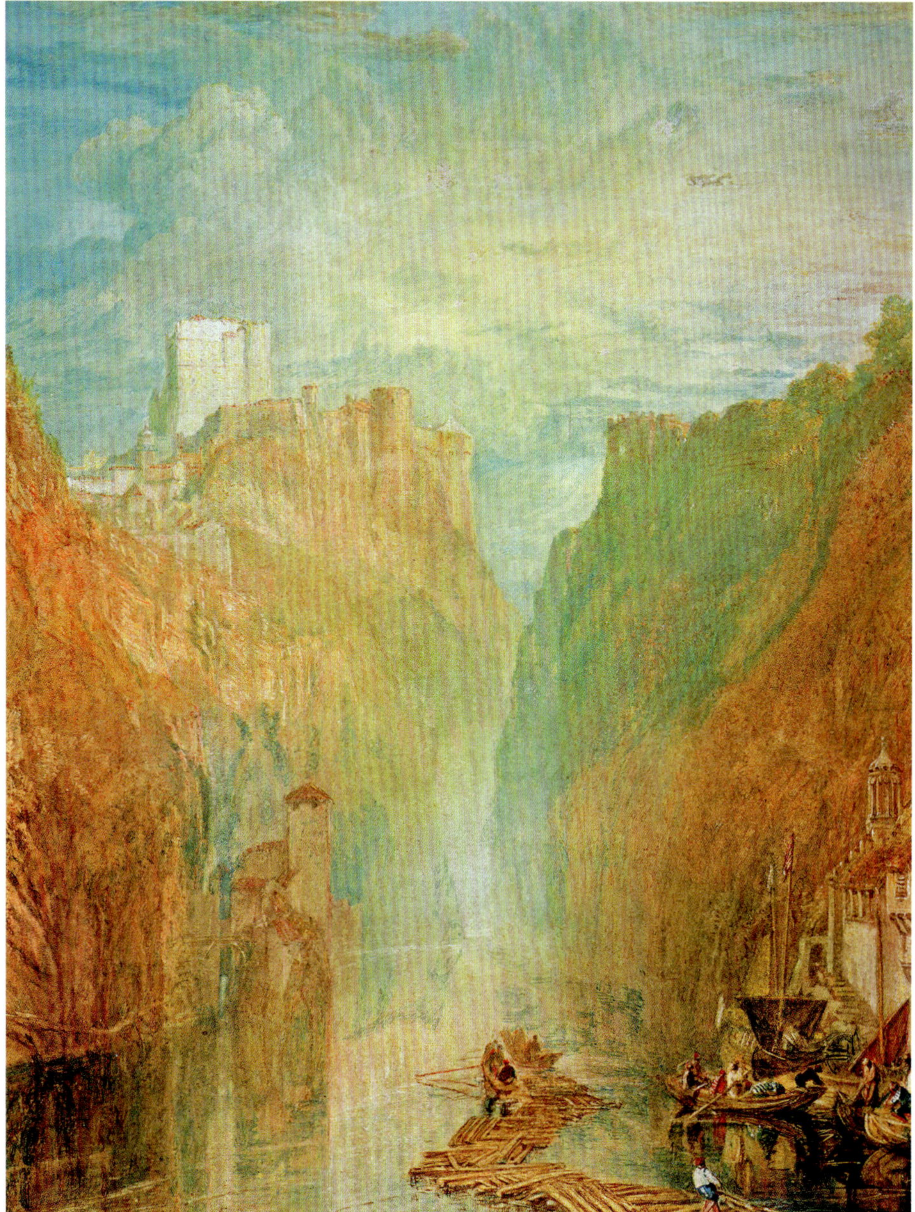

On the Upper Rhine, 1820, watercolour, Bolton Museum, UK, 35 x 45cm (14 x 18in)

That Turner should not be geographically specific in his title suggests that he wanted his viewer to be more in awe of the Sublime aspects of the view than its topography. The artist has provided a boat and crew to give the gorge a sense of scale, its majesty emphasized by the strong sunlight at the centre of the picture and the castles sitting atop.

Shipping Scene with Fishermen, 1815–20, brown ink and wash, Paul Mellon Collection, Yale Center for British Art, CT, USA, 22 x 29cm (9 x 11in)

This watercolour is an exemplary exercise in monochromatic wash. With no apparent pencil outline, Turner applied a number of washes of variant dilutions of ink to create this painting. He achieved the white areas using various techniques. The large white sail in the centre was probably masked out, but he also rubbed out areas using stale bread and scratched out using his thumbnail.

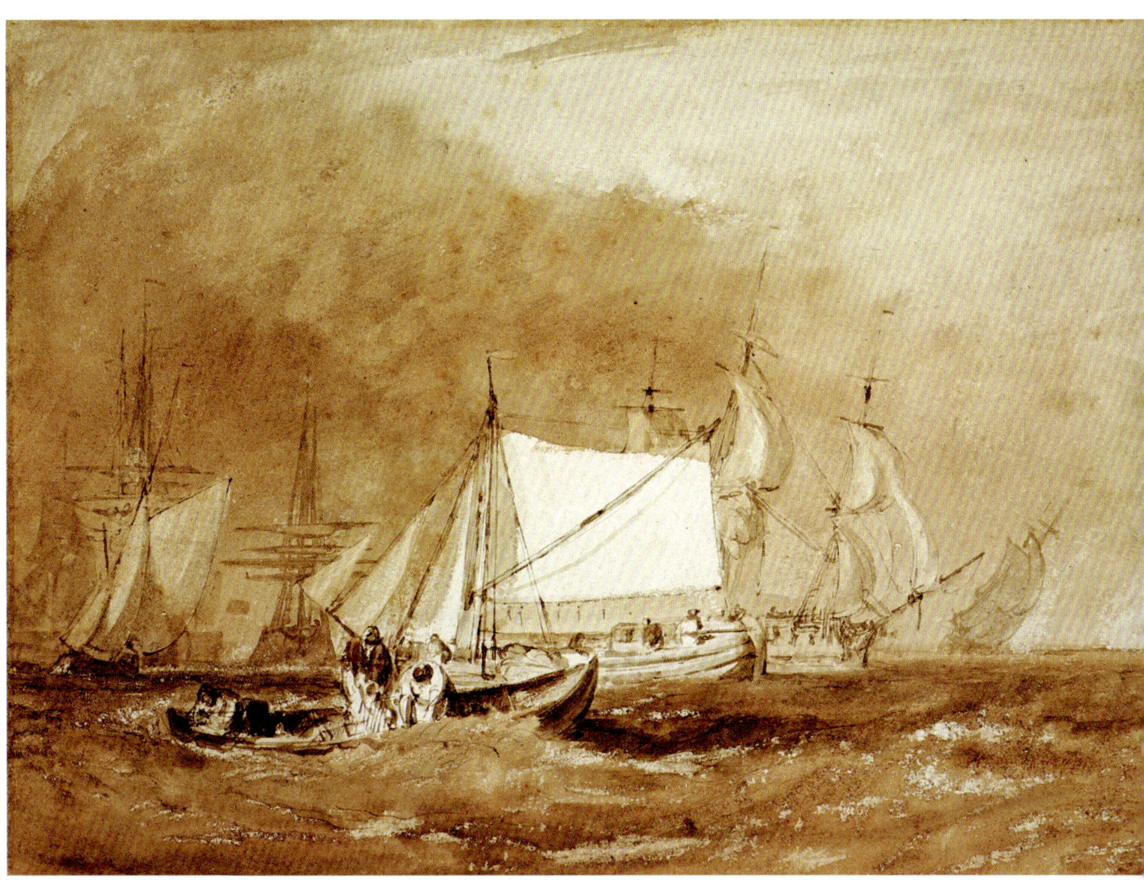

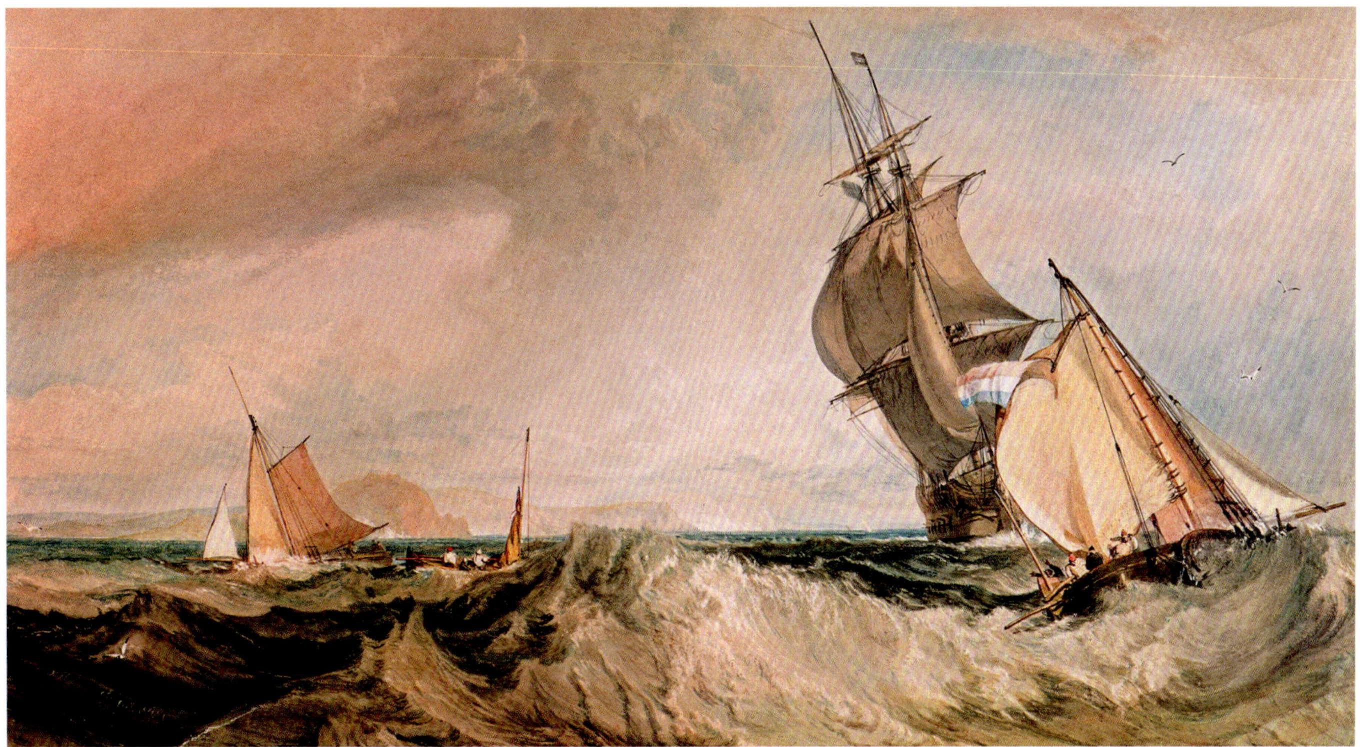

Off St Alban's Head, 1818–22, watercolour, Harrogate Museum, UK, 40 x 67cm (16 x 26in)

Although never issued as an engraving, the painting may have been executed originally for that purpose. Turner may have sailed along the coast of England in the summer of 1821, and included this Dorset location. He depicted a small Dutch fishing vessel running too close to a man-o'-war ship of the fleet.

Venice, the Rialto, 1820–1, watercolour, Indianapolis Museum of Art, IN, USA, 29 x 41cm (11 x 16in)

This is a modestly sized watercolour for such a highly detailed subject. Turner executed the work on his return from Venice in 1820.

The work was completed possibly after discussion with Walter Fawkes, who bought a number of Italian watercolours from the artist. Turner's contemporaries had also painted this view, but none were imbued with the same sense of place as this watercolour.

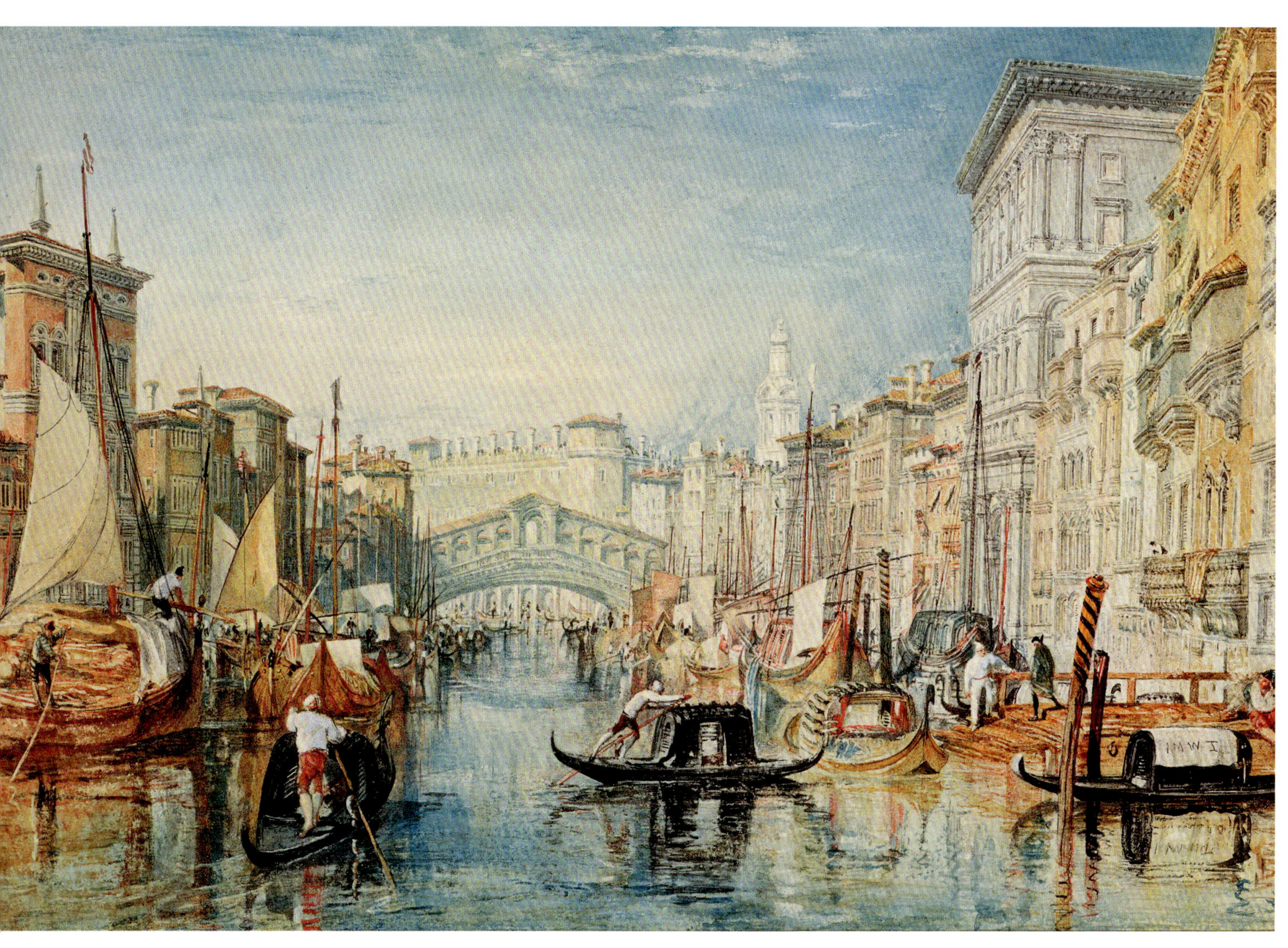

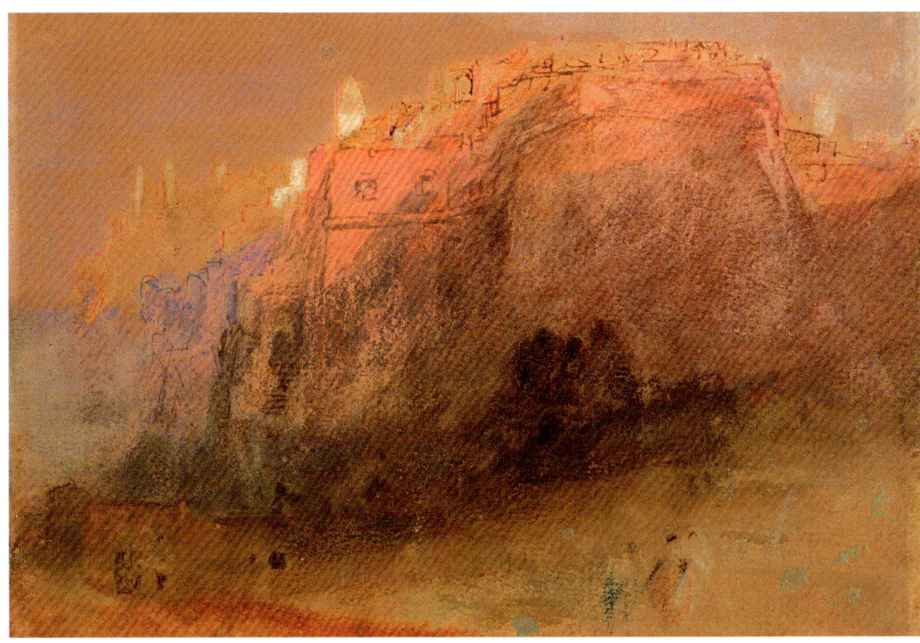

Luxembourg, 1825,
watercolour and bodycolour,
Paul Mellon Collection,
Yale Center for British Art,
CT, USA,
14 x 20cm (5½ x 8in)

In 1825, Turner made a visit to
the Low Countries including
Luxembourg City, known as
the 'Gibraltar of the North'
due to its strong fortifications.
During the Napoleonic Wars
the French had laid siege
to the castle, shown in this
watercolour. Under the 1815
Treaty of Paris, Luxembourg
came under the control of the
Prussian military.

*Fishing Boats at Sea, Boarding
a Steamer off the Isle of
Wight*, 1827,
Indian ink and watercolour,
Private Collection,
dimensions unknown

A rapidly made sketch using
ink for the detail over a plain
sepia wash, then highlighted
with white for the sail and
cloud outline. Turner
achieved the complete
artistic enterprise with
economy of line, an example
of his mastery of the
medium, as yet unsurpassed.

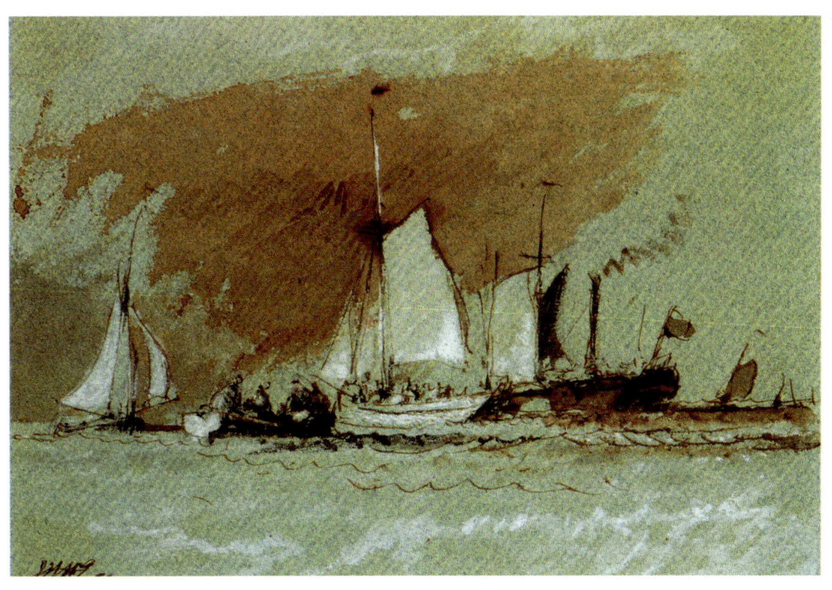

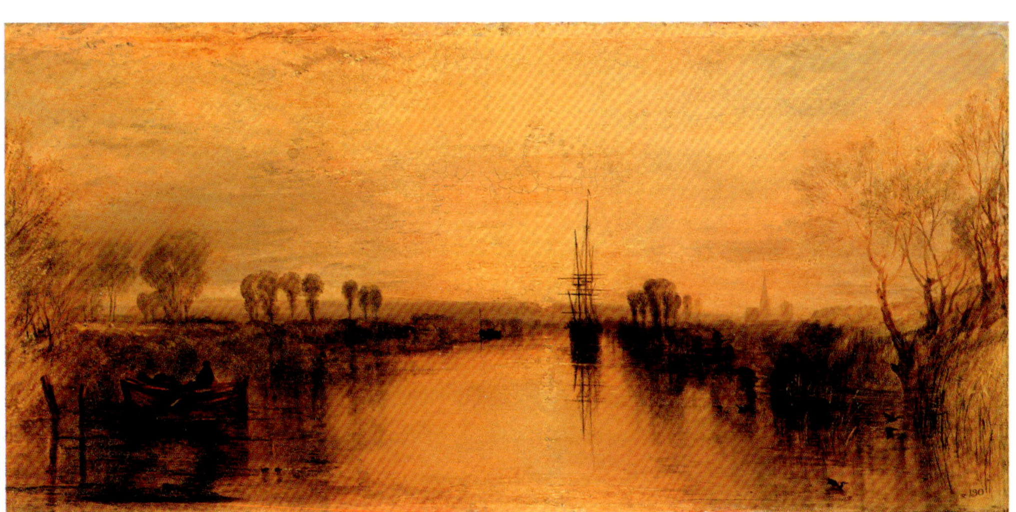

Chichester Canal, 1829, oil
on canvas, Petworth House,
Sussex, UK,
64 x 132cm (25 x 52in)

One of four paintings
commissioned by Lord
Egremont for his dining
room at Petworth. There is
an oil sketch dated 1828
of *Chichester Canal*, now
hanging in the Tate Britain,
suggesting that Turner was
working on the commission
for at least a year.

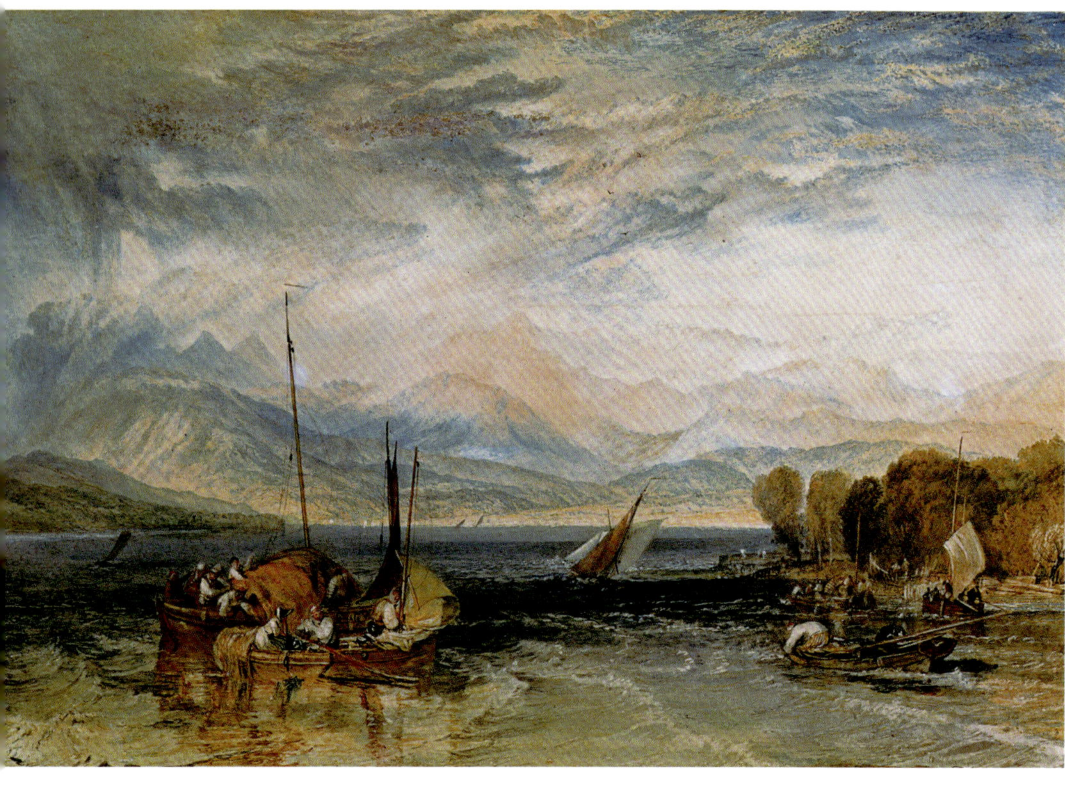

Windermere, 1821,
watercolour, Abbot Hall
Gallery, Kendal, UK,
29 x 41cm (11 x 16in)

Windermere is fed by
several rivers and is the
largest natural lake in
England, being 16.9km
(10.5 miles) long. The lake
is, however, only 400m
(a quarter of a mile) wide
in places, making it long
and narrow. Turner's view
is in the pre-railway era
and therefore not subject
to the hordes of tourists
that descended on the
place after 1847.

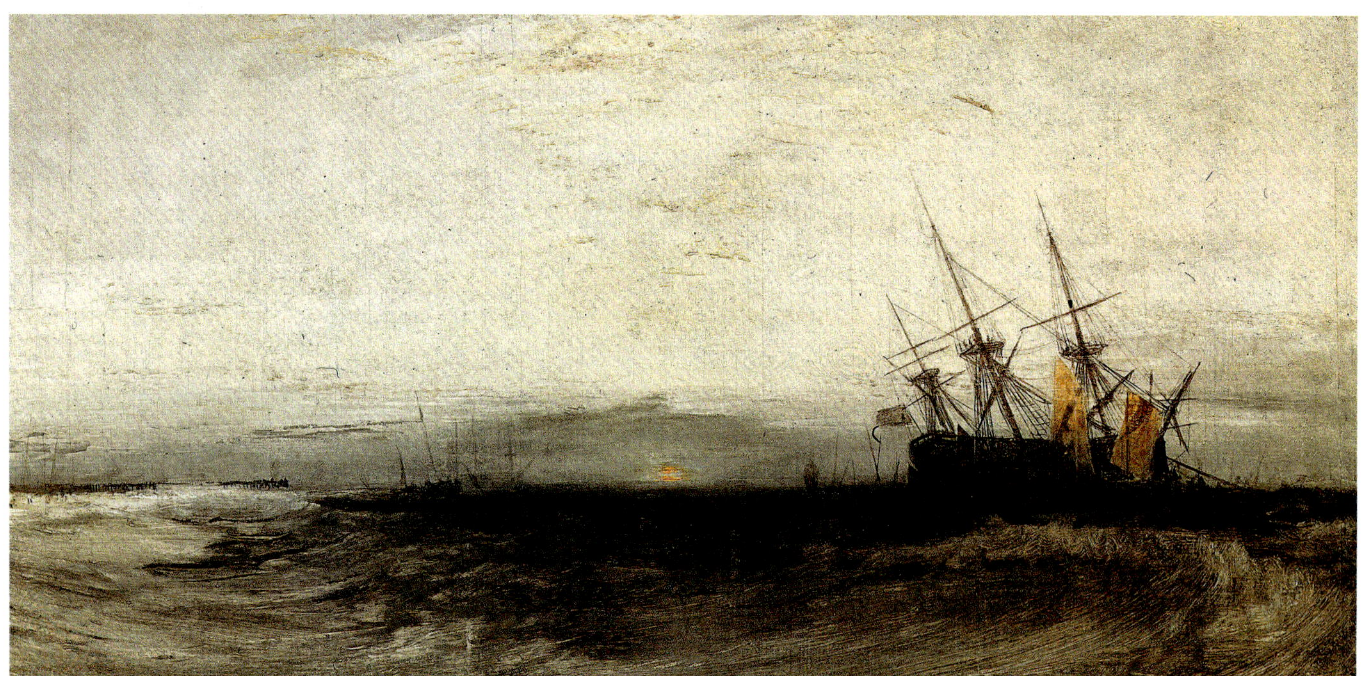

A Ship Aground, 1828,
oil on canvas, Tate Britain,
London, UK,
70 x 136cm (28 x 53½in)

The 2:1 format used in this
painting is similar to the
pictures executed for Lord
Egremont at Petworth. It is
unclear why the picture was
painted but it may have
been an alternative image
for Egremont to consider. In
any event it was not
exhibited in Turner's lifetime
and formed part of the
bequest after his death.

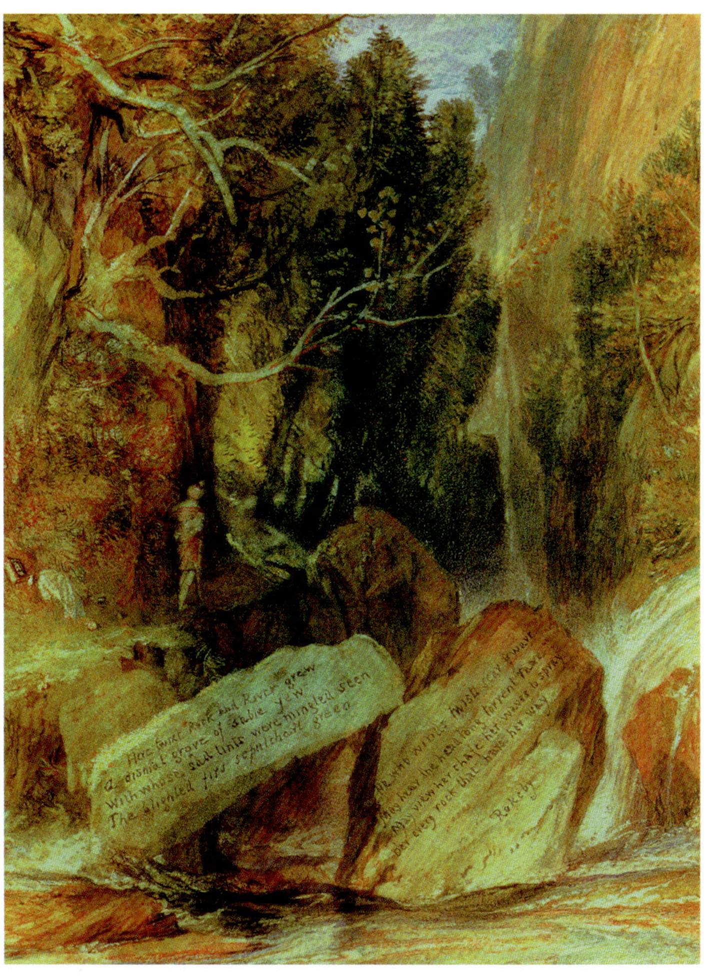

Rokeby, 1822, watercolour,
Cecil Higgins Art Gallery,
Bedford, UK,
14 x 20cm (5½ x 8in)

Rokeby Park was the home
of BS Morritt, a close friend
of Sir Walter Scott, who
used the house and grounds
as the setting for his epic
poem *Rokeby*. Turner's
watercolour probably
depicts a scene from the
poem, as suggested by
the text on the rocks in the
foreground. Morritt was an
art lover and purchased the
Velázquez painting *The Toilet
of Venus*, also known as the
'Rokeby' Venus.

Newcastle, *c.*1823,
watercolour, British
Museum, London, UK,
15 x 22cm (6 x 9in)

During 1817, Turner made a
number of sketches of this
city while staying with
Thomas Bowes-Lyon, the
Earl of Strathmore. The
artist has depicted a vibrant
city that was becoming
prosperous through
shipbuilding and also
the exporting of coal.
On the right of the picture
is the Norman castle and
in front of that is All Saints'
Church with its lofty
spire, which was
completed in 1796.

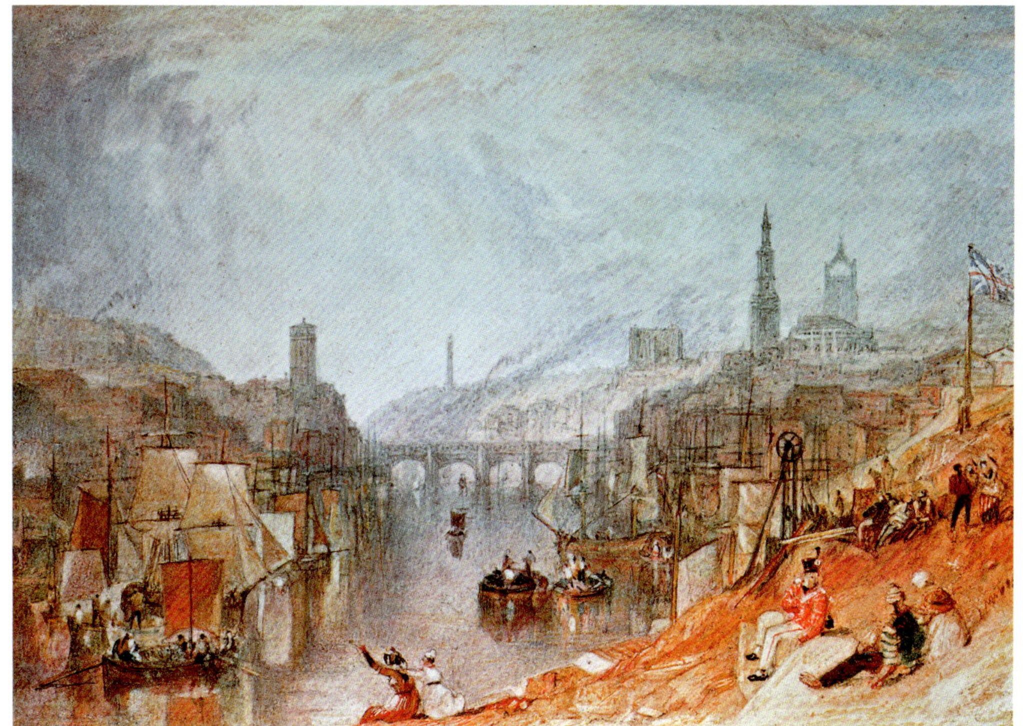

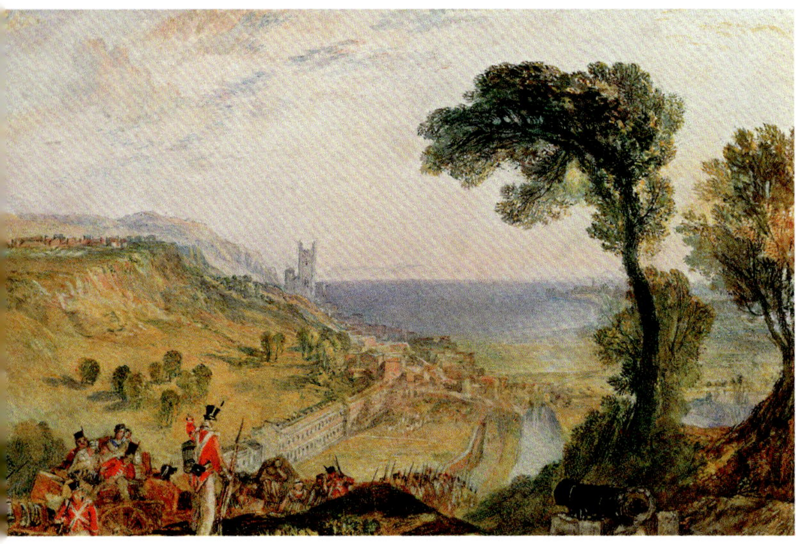

Hythe, Kent, 1824, watercolour, Guildhall Art Gallery, London, UK, 14 x 23cm (5½ x 9in)

In the distant left of the picture is the port of Dover with its famous white cliffs. The soldier in the foreground points in this direction, but perhaps he is thinking beyond to France and retelling tales of the Napoleonic wars. At the bottom of the hill is the recently completed military barracks to facilitate the building and garrison of the military canal.

Norham Castle on the River Tweed, 1824, watercolour, British Museum, London, UK, 16 x 22cm (6 x 9in)

This watercolour, probably the brightest and most detailed, was one of several undertaken by Turner, the motif being a particular favourite. The partially ruined castle located on the border of England and Scotland witnessed many of the battles between the two countries. Turner has added a kilted Scotsman on the bank of the River Tweed, which forms the border.

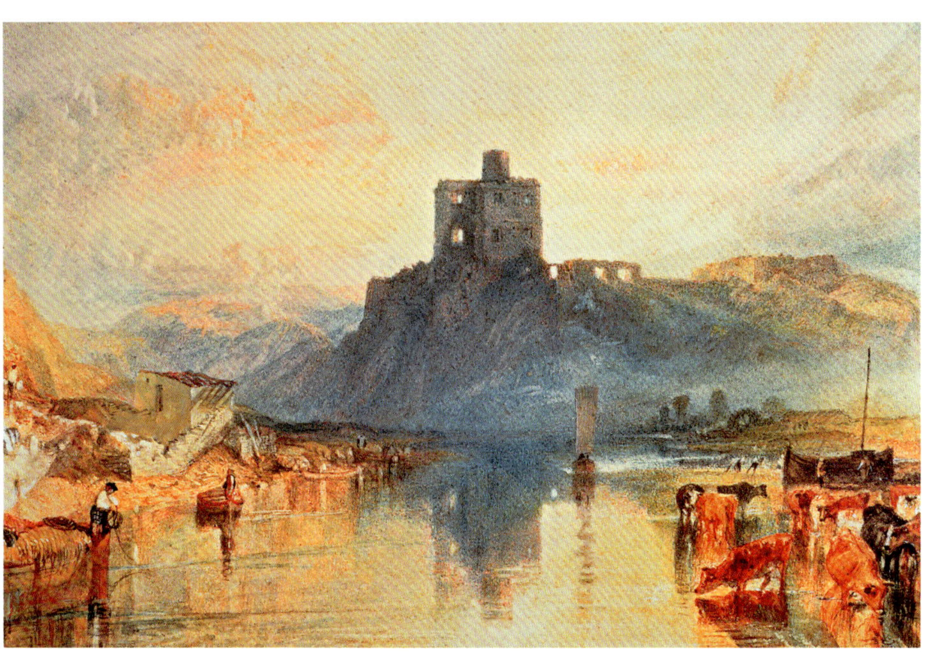

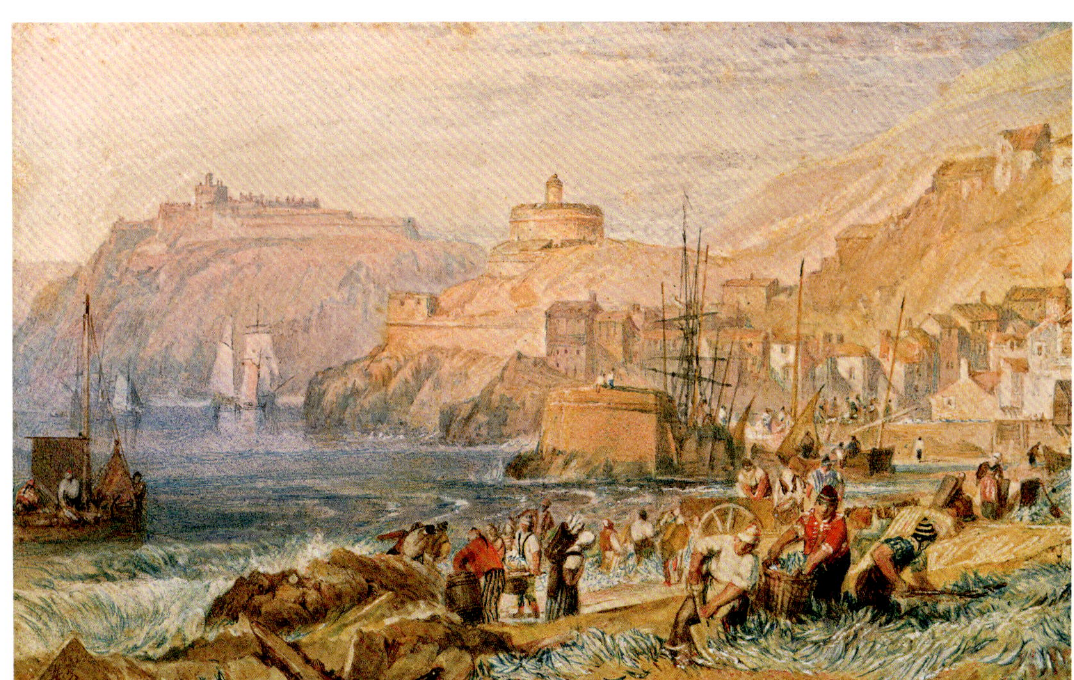

St Mawes, Cornwall, 1823, watercolour, Paul Mellon Collection, Yale Center for British Art, CT, USA, 14 x 22cm (5½ x 9in)

Henry VIII built St Mawes Castle, seen at the centre, and Pendennis Castle in the distance, in the 1540s as strategic defensive positions to repel an attack by the Spanish, who were seeking to reinstate Catholicism in England.

The Bay of Baiae, Apollo and the Sybil, 1823, oil on canvas, Tate Britain, London, UK, 145 x 238cm (57 x 94in)

John Ruskin described this picture in his *Modern Painters* as illustrating the "vanity of human life". Having visited Baiae, on the southern coast of Italy, in 1819, Turner was moved to record the landscape with a tale from mythology that foretells man's downfall as a consequence of his corruption. Despite being exhibited at the Academy, the picture was unsold at Turner's death.

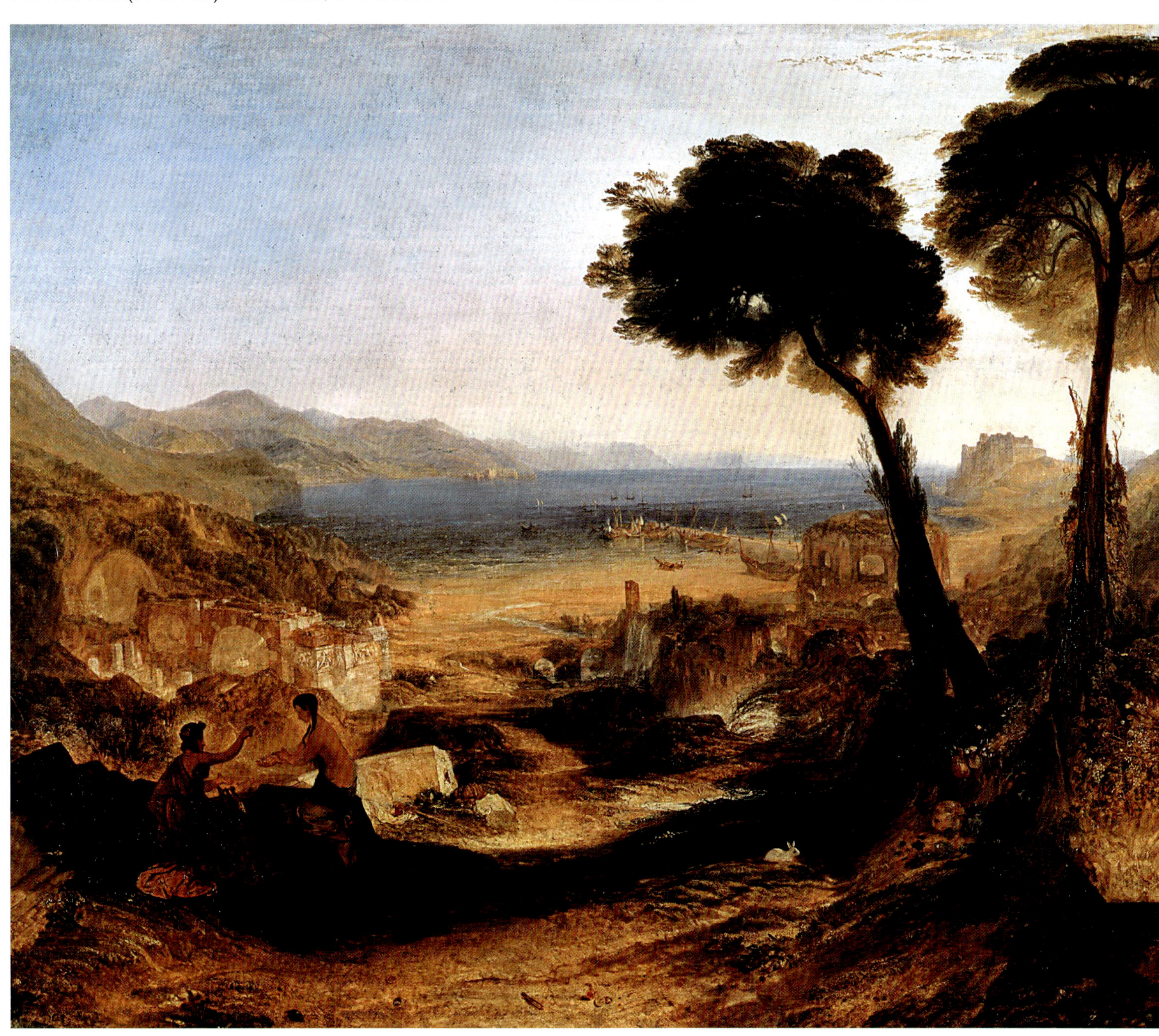

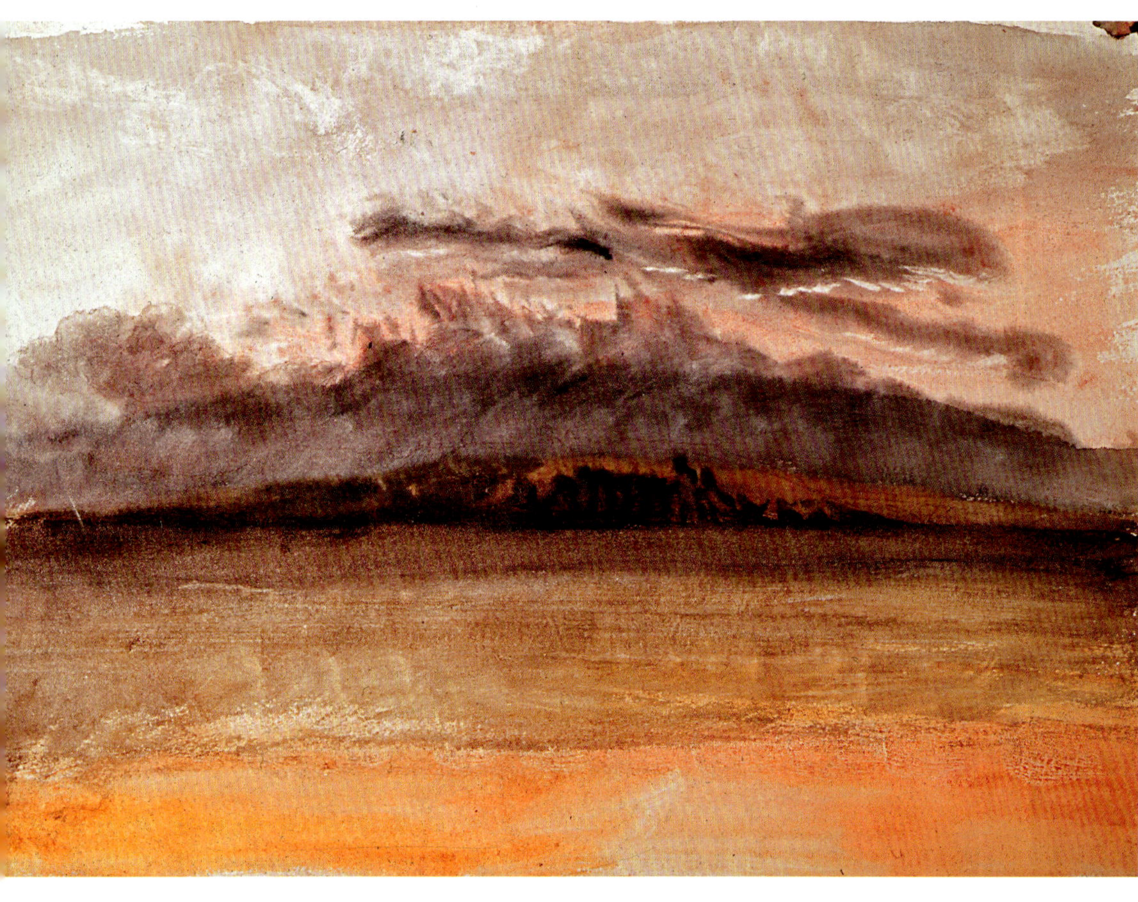

Storm Clouds: Sunset with a Pink Sky, watercolour and pencil, *c.*1824, Tate Britain, London, UK, 24 x 35cm (9 x 14in)

An example of Turner exploring the use of colour for its own sake and an exercise in applying watercolour washes. His experiment here demonstrates both hard and soft edge techniques; he carefully controlled wet washes by moving the pigment around with a wet brush. Often he moved the colour around until he "expressed the idea in his mind".

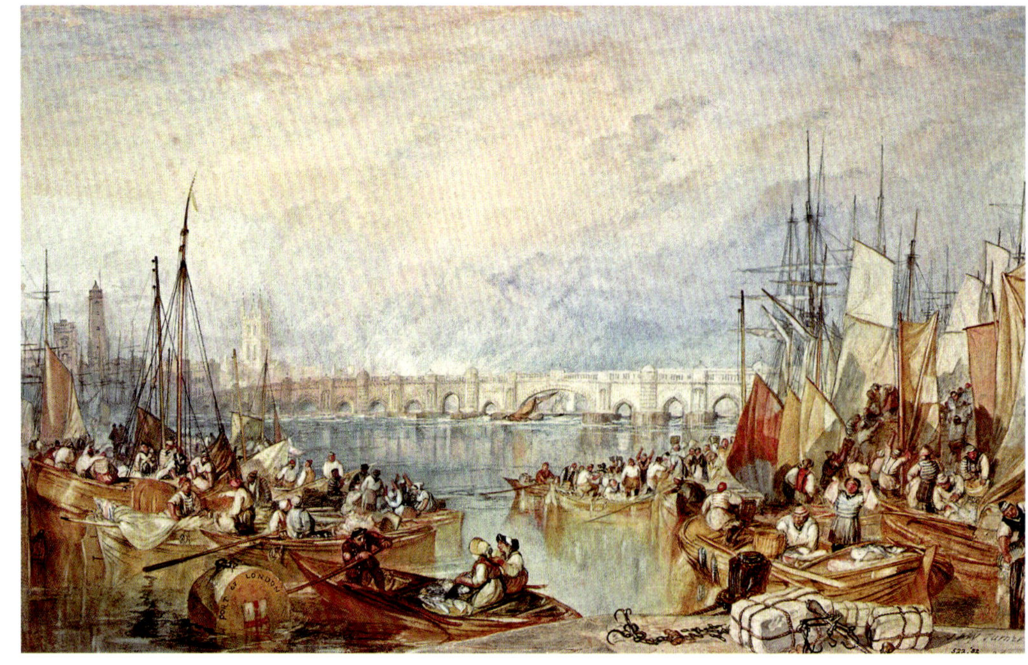

The Port of London, 1824, watercolour, Victoria and Albert Museum, London, UK, 29 x 45cm (11 x 18in)

This watercolour is a rare view of the old London Bridge before it was demolished in 1831. The bridge, which dated from the 13th century, had a number of houses and shops on it, which were removed in the 1760s for safety reasons. At the same time, a wider central arch was created from two smaller ones to allow for the river flow and prevent the river from freezing in winter.

Dartmouth Cove with Sailor's Wedding, 1825, watercolour, Private Collection, 27 x 39cm (11 x 15in)

Turner has captured a snapshot of this happy occasion showing several of the sailors having probably drunk too much, the one in the foreground now asleep from intoxication. Others are waving their arms and possibly singing, happy to be home from the war and its aftermath. The bawdiness of the scene is a sharp contrast to the ethereal effects of the soft landscape in the distance.

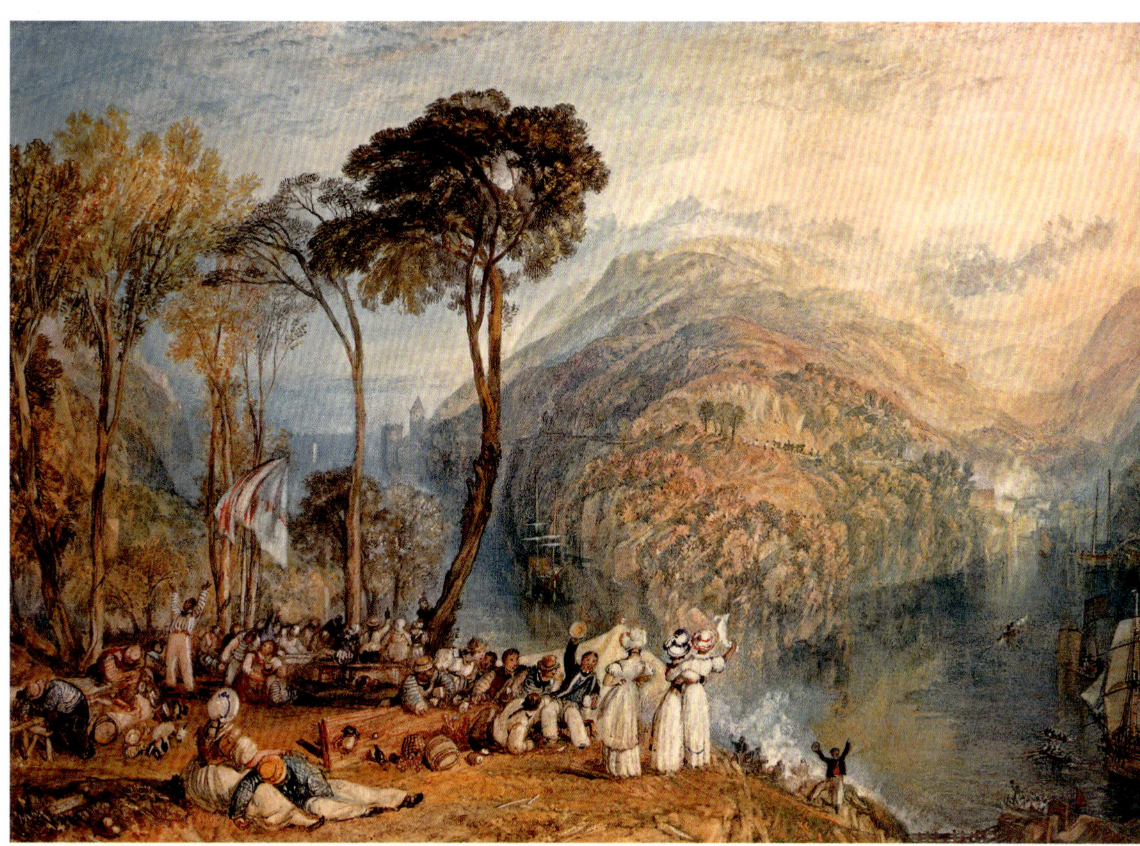

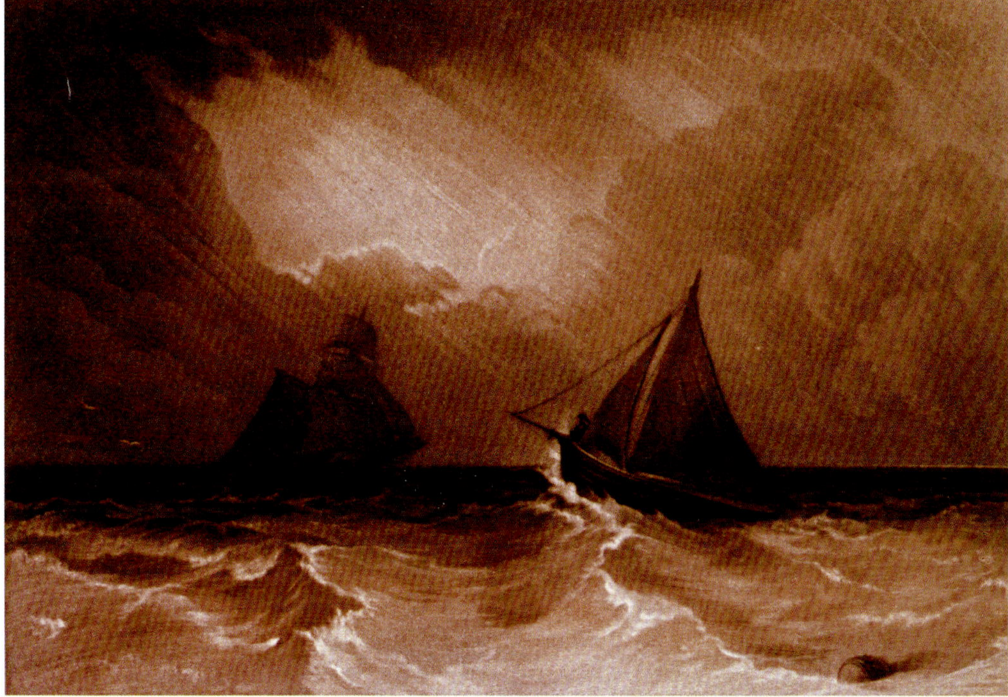

Ship and Cutter, c.1825, mezzotint, Fitzwilliam Museum, Cambridge, UK, 20 x 25cm (8 x 10in)

Turner created this mezzotint for his *Little Liber Studiorum* series of 12 engravings, Turner's attempt at producing and marketing his own prints. The series was relatively unknown in his lifetime, however, compared with *The Picturesque Views in England and Wales* and *The Harbours of England* series that appeared around the same time.

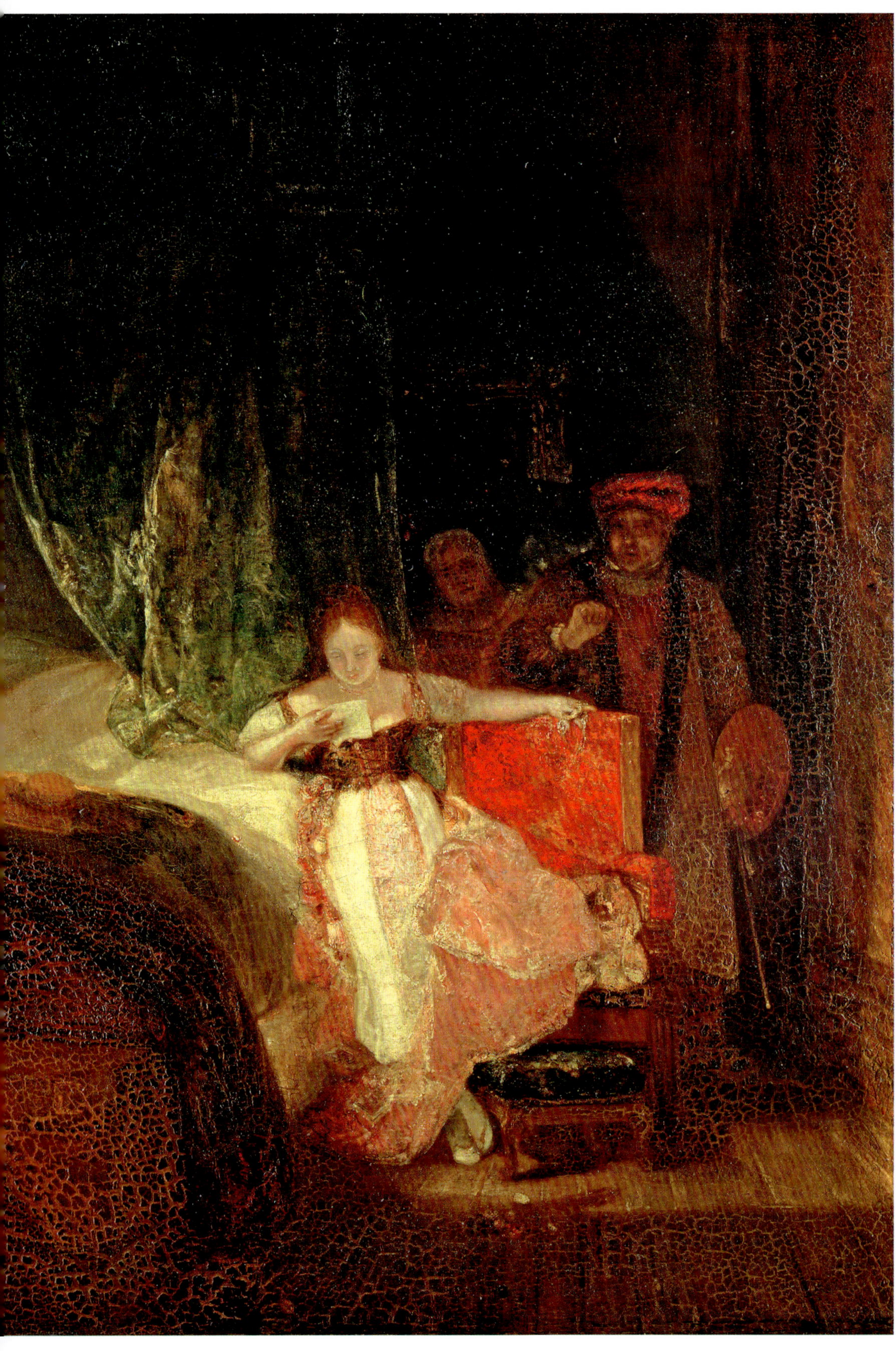

Rembrandt's Daughter,
1827, oil on canvas,
Harvard University,
MA, USA,
90 x 122cm (35 x 48in)

Hawksworth Fawkes bought
this painting two years after
his father's death to hang at
Farnley Hall, the last of
Turner's works to be
purchased for that purpose.
Turner took inspiration for
the painting from
Rembrandt's *Joseph Accused
by Potiphar's Wife*, owned at
the time by his fellow artist
Sir Thomas Lawrence.
Turner's picture was not well
received at the Academy
exhibition of 1827.

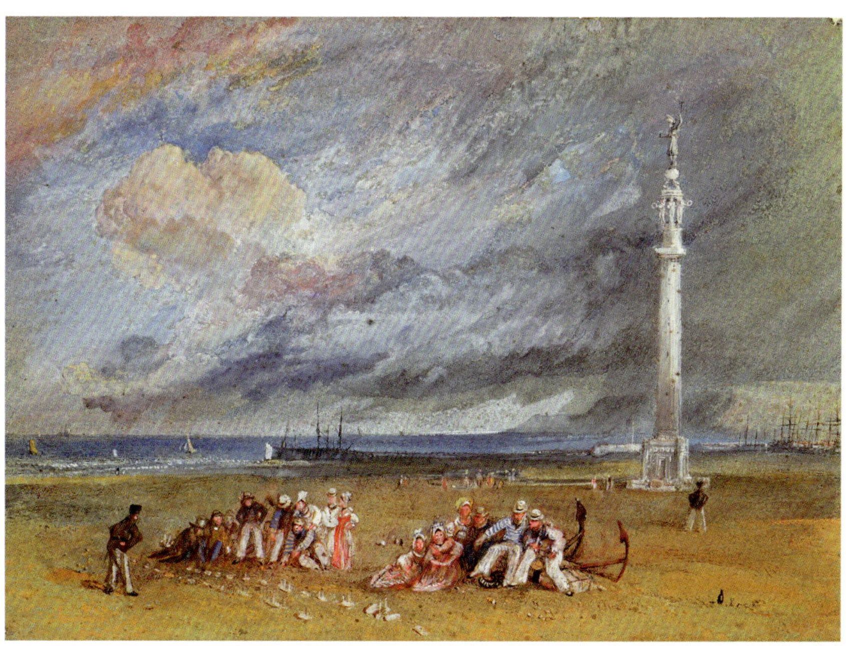

Yarmouth Sands, c.1827,
watercolour and
bodycolour, Fitzwilliam
Museum, Cambridge, UK,
19 x 25cm (7½ x 10in)

A group of mariners are
engaged in a re-enactment
of a battle scene, possibly
Trafalgar, on the beach in
front of a group of ladies.
Turner alludes to this battle
by including the monument
to Lord Nelson, which was
unveiled in 1817 to
commemorate his famous
victory. The passing clouds
overhead reinforce the end
of hostilities with France.

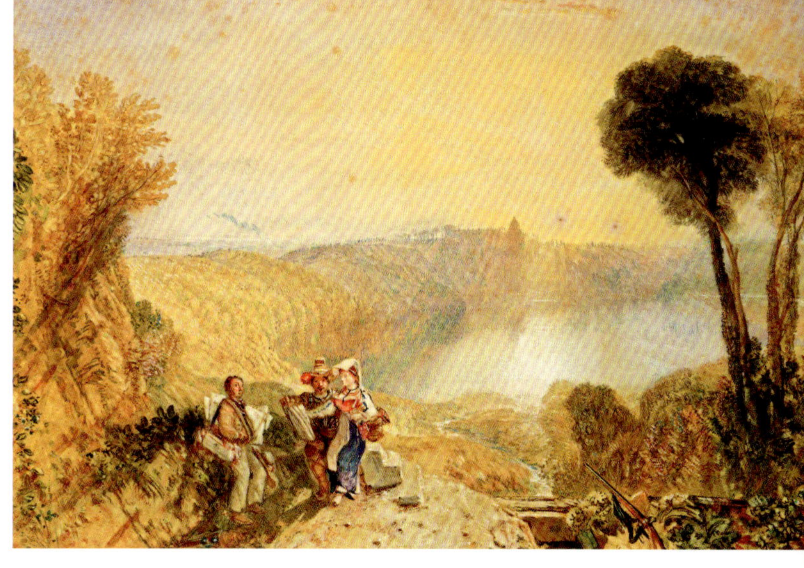

Lake Albano, c.1828,
watercolour,
Private Collection,
29 x 41cm (11 x 16in)

Turner continually used the
reference material from his
tours, even many years later,
as demonstrated by this
work, completed nine years
after his first visit to Italy.
The lake is situated just
south of Rome in the
Alban Hills of Lazio, and
overlooks the Castel
Gandolfo where the Pope
has had a summer residence
since the 17th century.

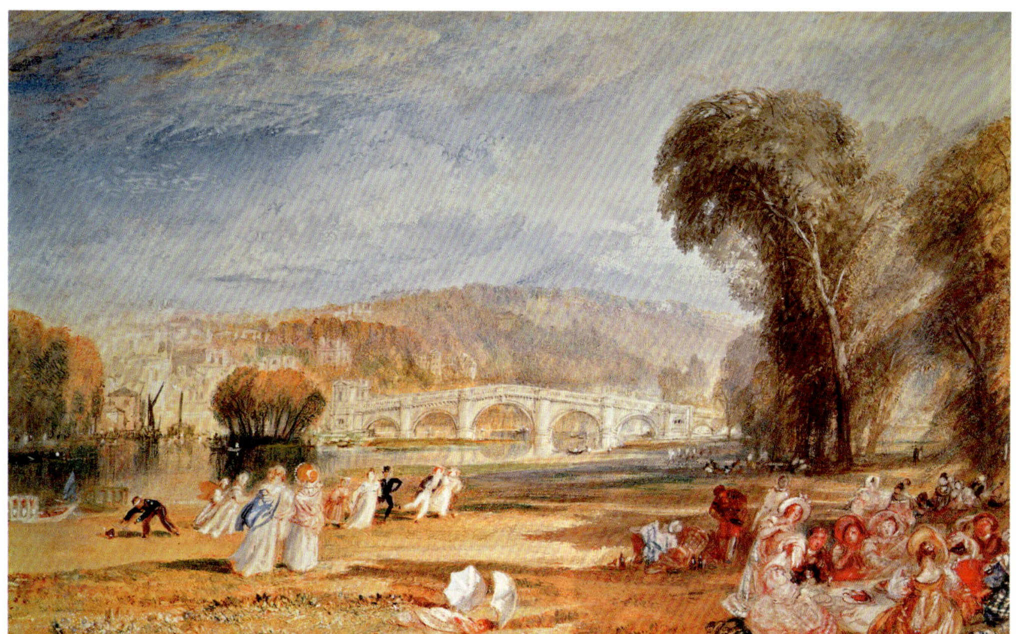

Richmond Hill and Bridge,
1828, watercolour and
bodycolour, British
Museum, London, UK,
29 x 44cm (11 x 17in)

The hill and 18th-century
bridge provide the perfect
backdrop to this picnic scene.
The group of people on the
left contrast with the serenity
of the River Thames and
the picnickers. The scene is
redolent of the 18th-century
French Rococo artist,
Antoine Watteau.

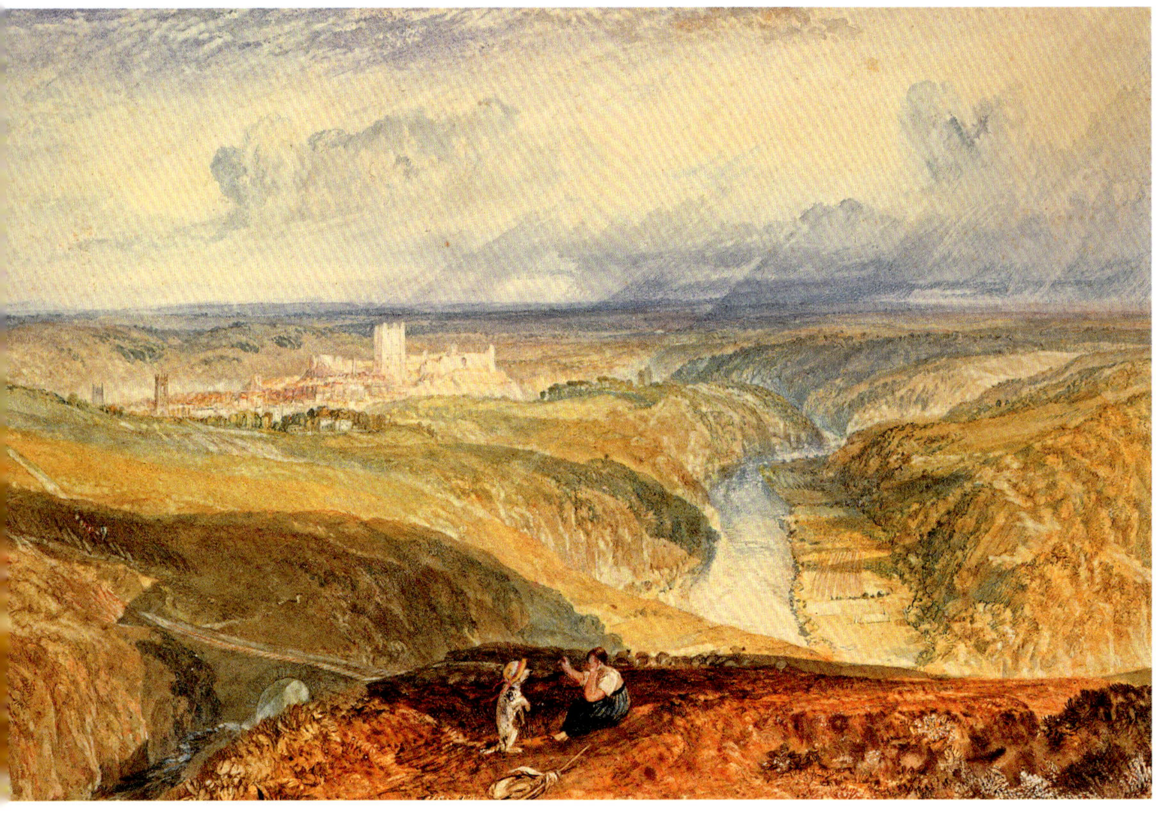

Richmond, Yorkshire, 1826–8, graphite and watercolour, Fitzwilliam Museum, Cambridge, UK, 28 x 40cm (11 x 16in)

Turner completed two watercolour views of this area, both of which appeared in *Picturesque Views in England and Wales* in 1828. In both images, Turner has depicted a country girl, this one being a shepherdess. The artist has wittily depicted her sheep dog wearing the girl's bonnet and teasing its owner. The Norman castle at Richmond in the middle distance dominates the skyline.

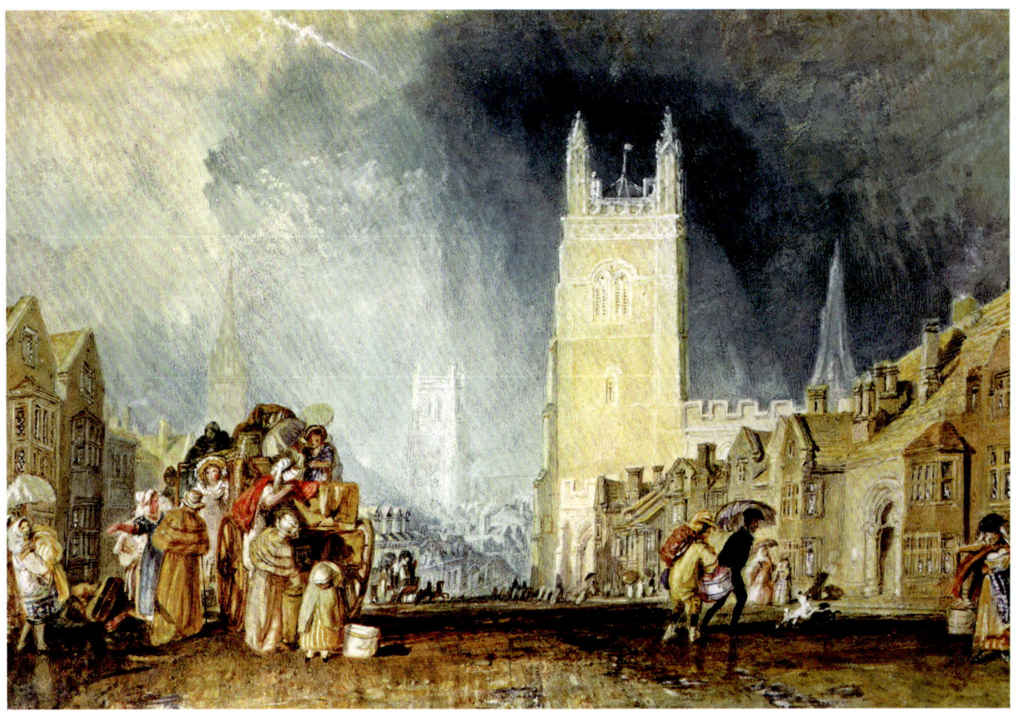

Stamford, Lincolnshire, 1828, watercolour, Usher Gallery, Lincoln, UK, 29 x 42cm (11 x 17in)

In Turner's day, Stamford was a busy coaching stop en route to York, that he must have stayed at on his way to the north of England. He has captured the scene of a busy street with two coaches, the people enduring a heavy downpour. The rain is about to subside as suggested by the strong sunlight that is making the Gothic tower of St Martin's Church glow.

East Cowes Castle, the Seat of J Nash Esq: the Regatta Beating to Windward, 1828, oil on canvas, Indianapolis Museum of Art, IN, USA, 91 x 121cm (36 x 48in)

One of a pair of paintings executed for a commission by the architect John Nash while Turner was staying with him on the Isle of Wight off the south coast of England. At the Royal Academy Exhibition in 1828, for which Turner was on the committee, this painting was criticized by the *Morning Herald* as having a sea "more like marble-dust than living waters". By contrast the other picture was well received.

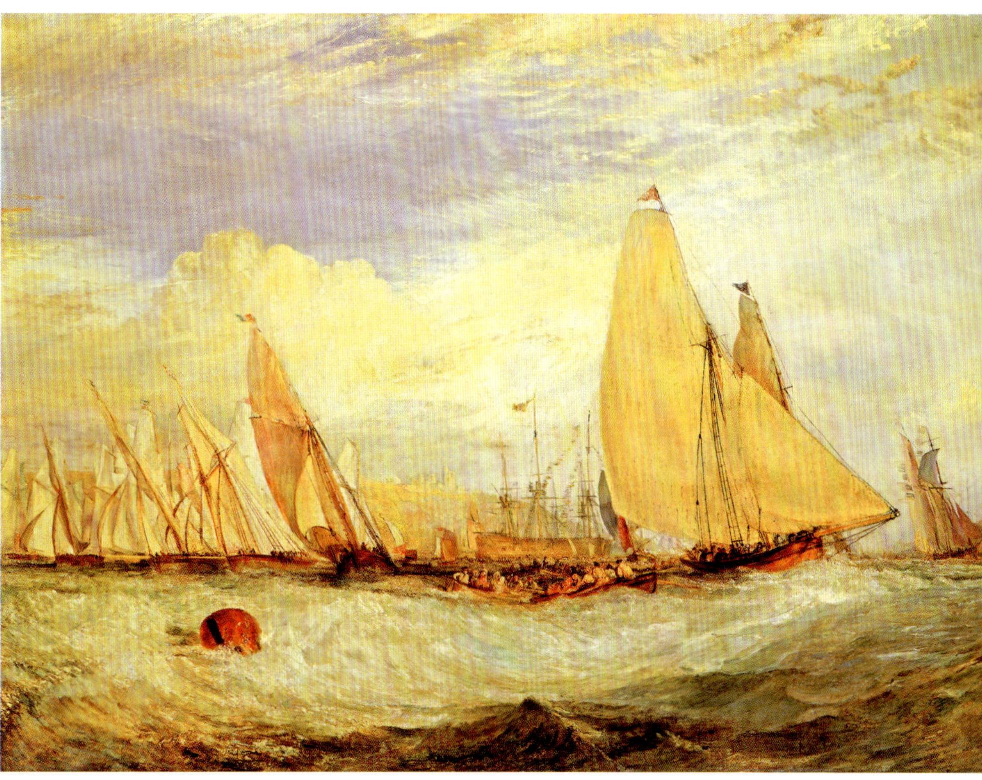

Bedford, 1829, watercolour, Private Collection, 35 x 49cm (14 x 19in)

Since this is his only known painting of this town, Turner must have executed it solely for the purpose of its reproduction in *Picturesque Views in England and Wales*. He has, however, included a group of people fishing, his own favourite pastime. The River Ouse is crossed by a new bridge erected in 1813, shown in this watercolour, together with the medieval church of St Paul's.

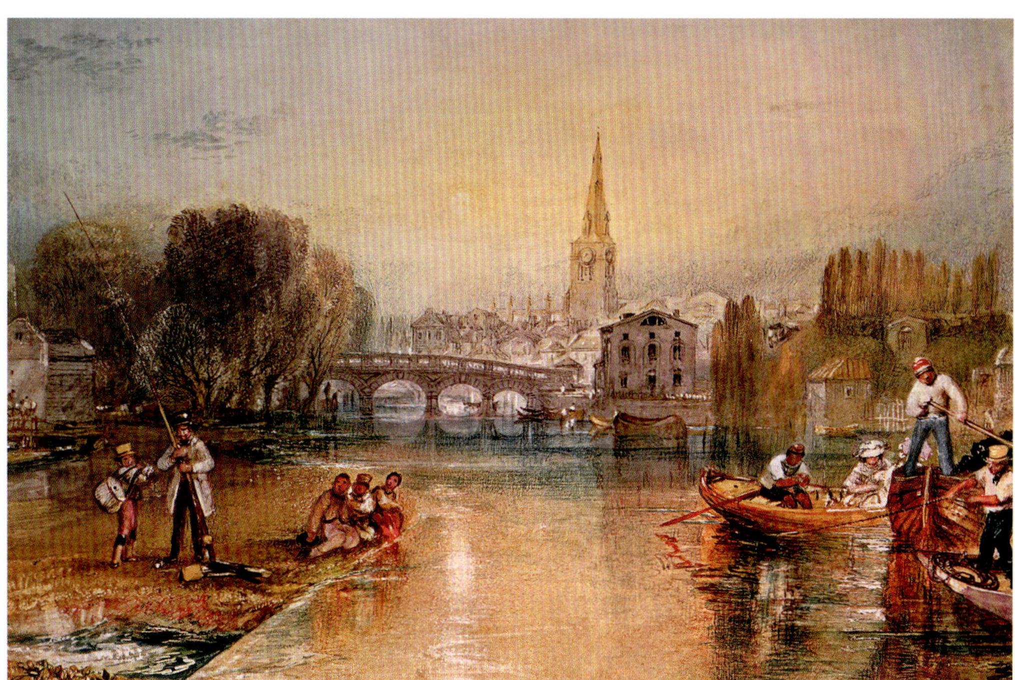

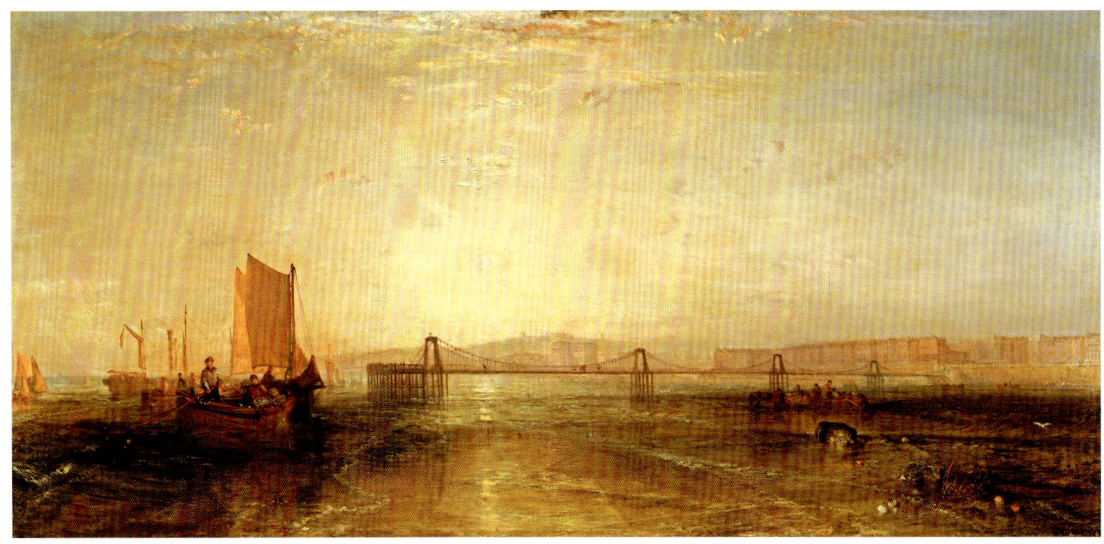

Brighton from the Sea, 1829, oil on canvas, Petworth House, Sussex, UK, 64 x 132cm (25 x 52in)

Commissioned by Lord Egremont, this painting still hangs at Petworth House, although it is now owned by Tate Britain. The view shows the Royal Suspension Chain Pier, erected a few years earlier. Egremont was one of the venture capitalists involved in the scheme, hence the commission.

The Dockyard, Devonport, c.1829, watercolour and bodycolour, Harvard University, MA, USA, 30 x 44cm (12 x 17in)

John Ruskin owned this watercolour and remarked on the "breaking up of the warm rain-clouds of the summer, thunder passing away to the west", possibly a metaphor for the end of war and a return to peace. The scene is located at the Royal Navy dockyards, where ships were being dismantled and the sailors were being paid off following the end of the Napoleonic Wars.

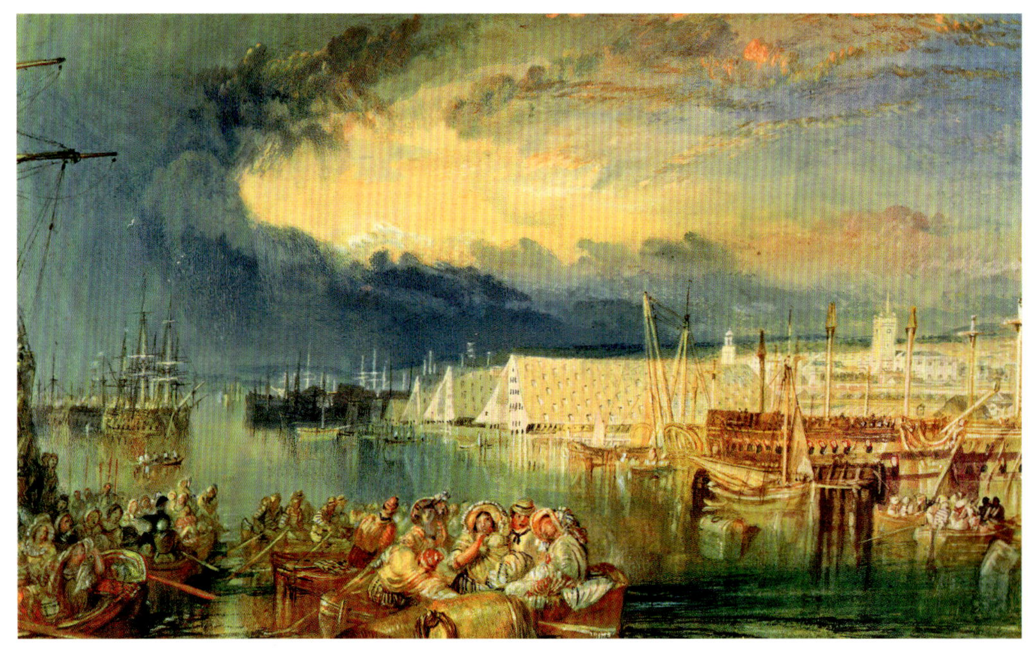

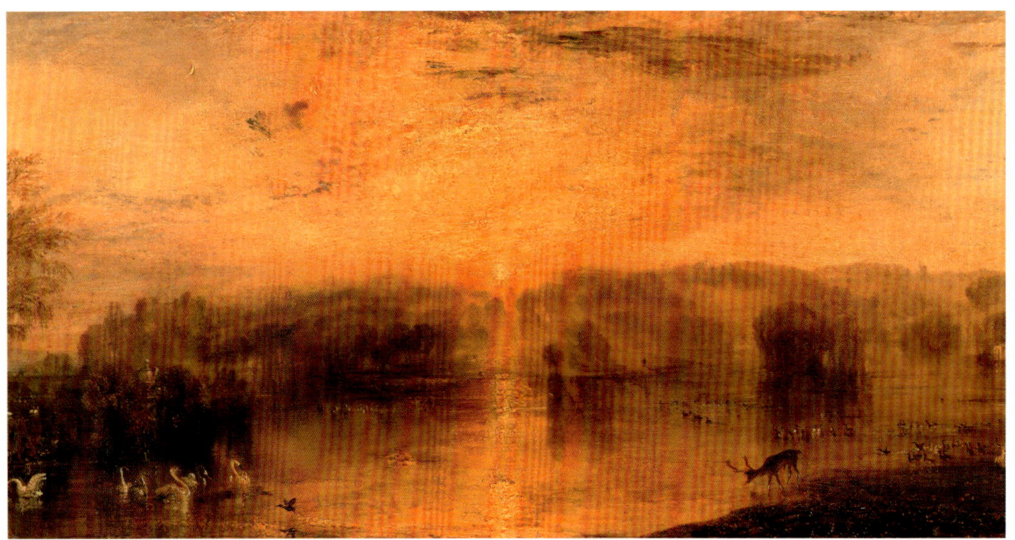

The Lake, Petworth: Sunset, a Stag Drinking, 1829, oil on canvas, Petworth House, Sussex, UK, 64 x 132cm (25 x 52in)

In August 1827, Turner was commissioned by Lord Egremont for a series of pictures for his dining room, including this one. An indistinct oil sketch exists of this view, in which he seems to have been working on the composition and colour scheme for the finished work.

Messieurs les Voyageurs on their Return from Italy (Par la Diligence) in a Snowdrift upon Mount Tarare, 1829, watercolour and bodycolour, British Museum, London, UK, 55 x 75cm (22 x 29½in)

A strange bilingual title is given to this masterful watercolour that recalls an event that Turner experienced while he was returning from his European tour in January 1829. The autobiographical aspect of the event is the inclusion of the artist himself with his back to the viewer, his notable form with top hat silhouetted against the blazing fire. The painting was exhibited at the Royal Academy in 1829.

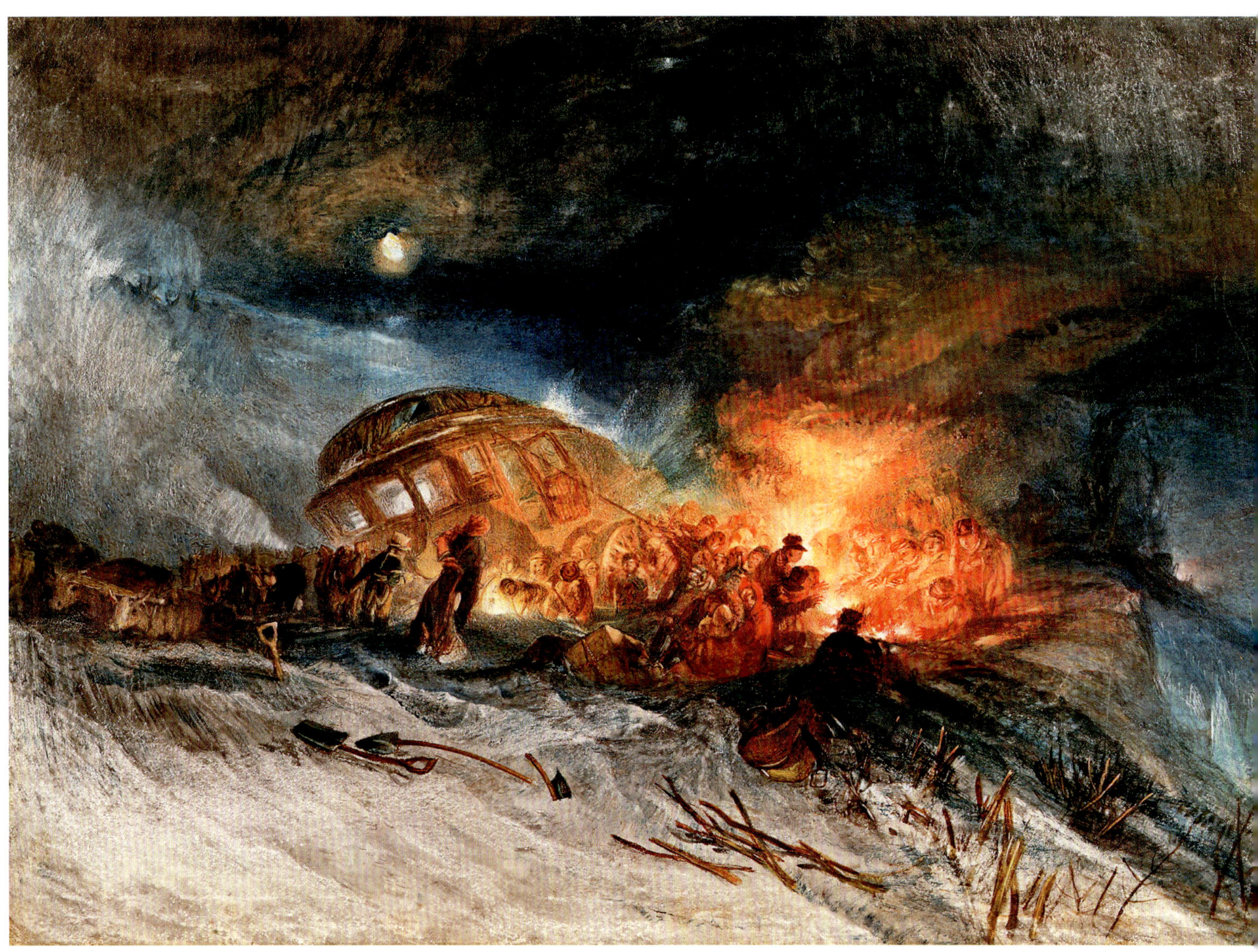

Ulysses Deriding Polyphemus – Homer's Odyssey, 1829, oil on canvas, National Gallery, London, UK, 133 x 203cm (52 x 80in)

Turner began considering the theme of The Odyssey as early as 1807 but had not made any preliminary sketches until 1828 when he visited Italy. It may be that the heightened colour that Turner has used is as a result of the 15th-century frescoes that he had seen in Florence. However, his heavy use of colour was derided in London as "unnatural tawdriness".

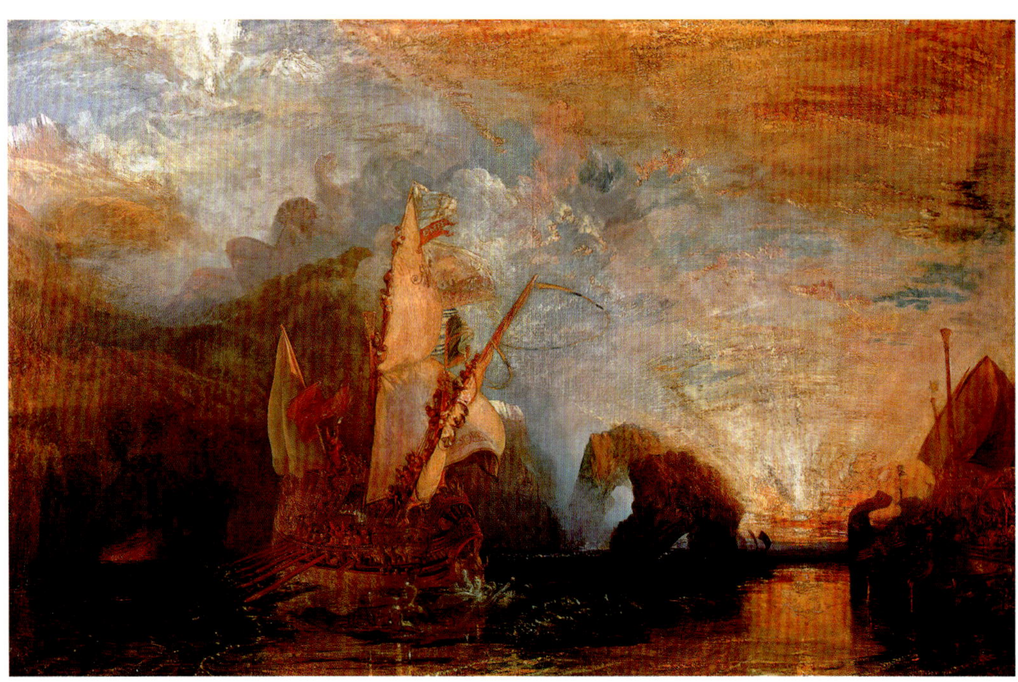

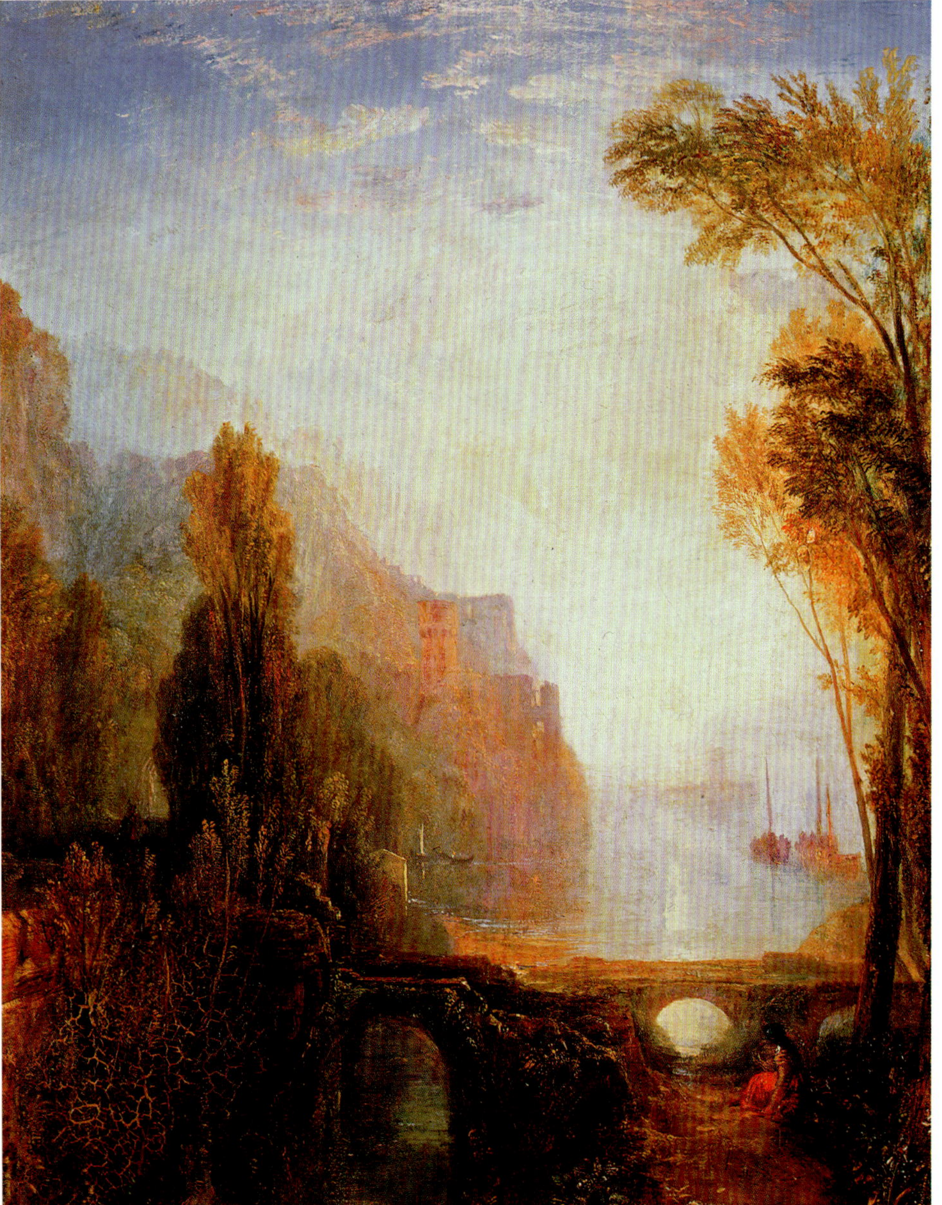

The Banks of the Loire, 1829, oil on canvas, Worcester Art Museum, MA, USA, 53 x 71cm (21 x 28in)

Following his tour of the Loire in 1826, Turner executed many sketches and watercolours of the surrounding area. He also created some oil paintings in succeeding years including this one that was exhibited at the Royal Academy in 1829. The painting was commissioned by General Sir James Willoughby Gordon and his wife, and is a typically Claudian landscape depicting a rural idyll rather than a recognized topography.

Holy Island, Northumberland,
1829, watercolour,
Victoria and Albert
Museum, London, UK,
29 x 43cm (11 x 17in)

Christianity came to England during the 7th century when St Aidan founded a monastery at Lindisfarne, which is often referred to as 'Holy Island'. The cathedral shown on the left of the watercolour was destroyed during the Reformation in the 16th century. In the distance is Lindisfarne Castle, destroyed during the English Civil War of the 17th century. At low tide one can walk between the two sites.

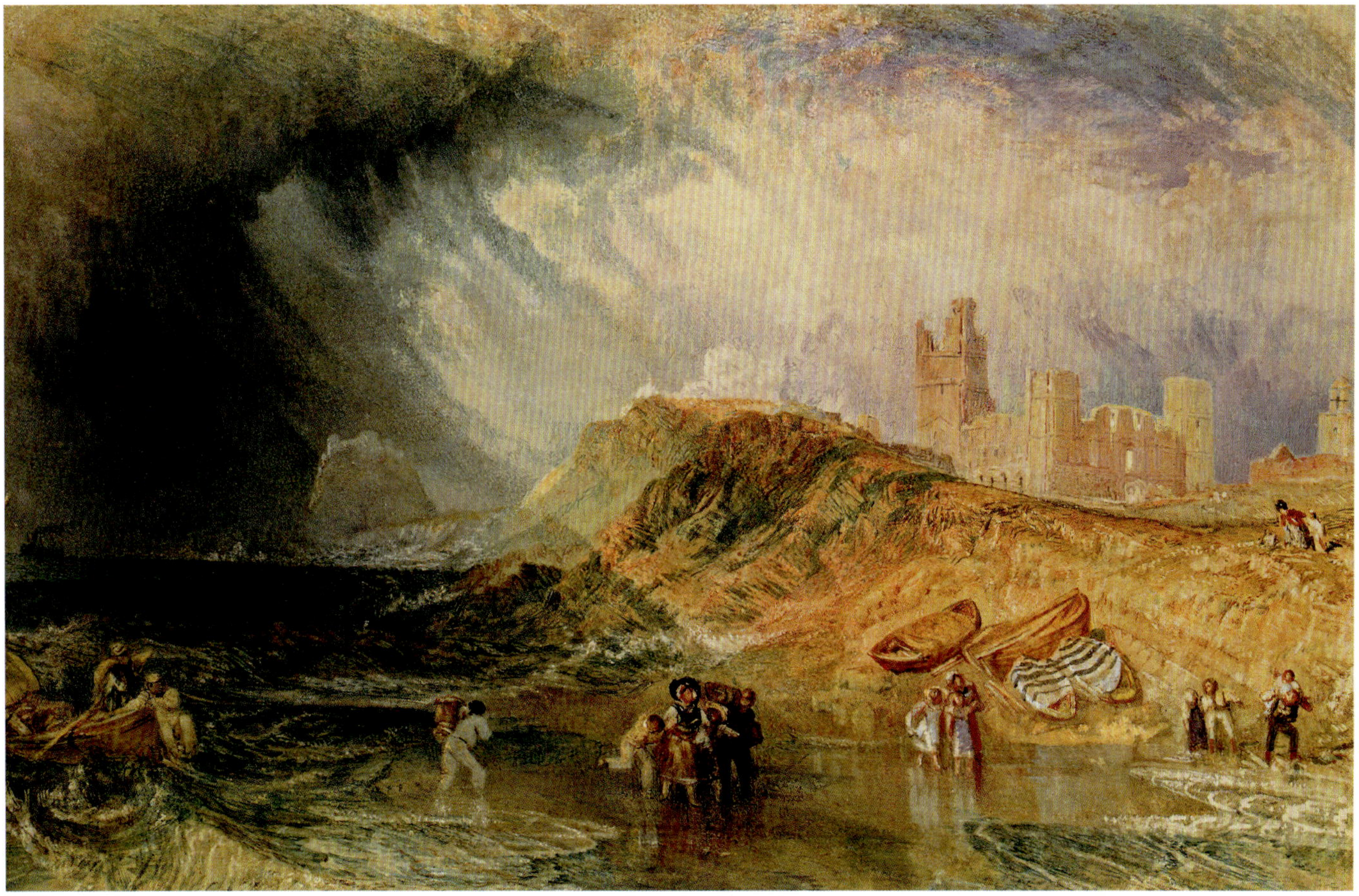

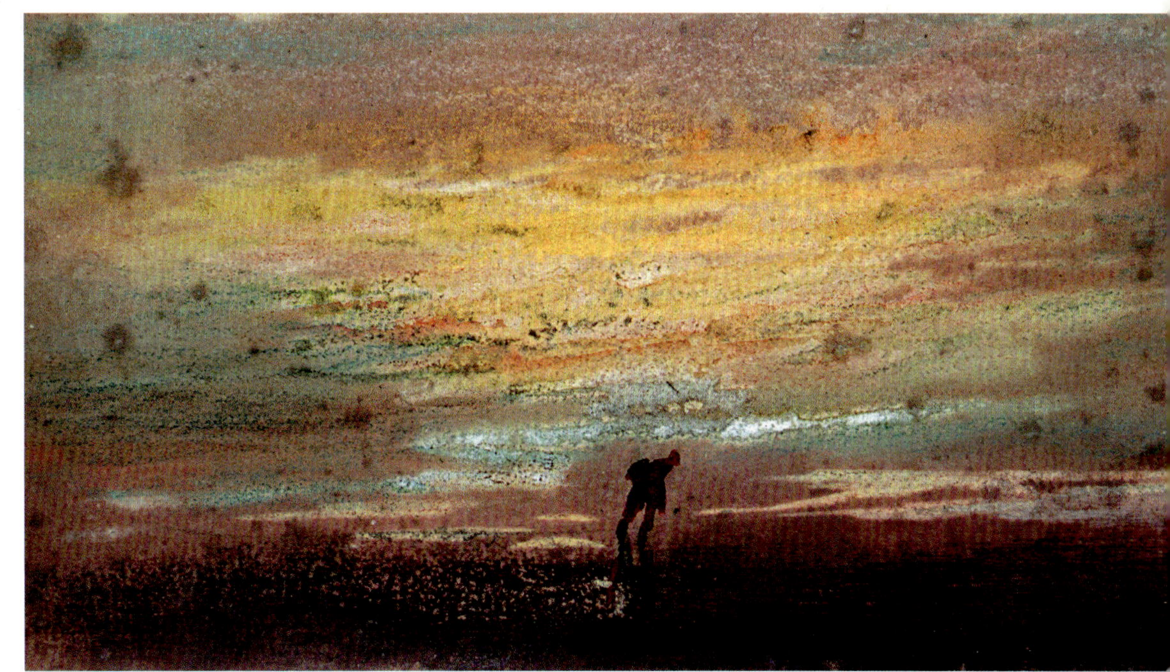

*Study of Sunlight, c.*1830,
watercolour, Victoria and
Albert Museum, London, UK,
9 x 19cm (3½ x 7½in)

This tiny work has to be appreciated not only as a study of the effect of light, but also as an intimate reflection of the artist's mood at the time. In 1829, the artist's father died and left Turner during the 1830s with a sense of his own inevitable mortality. During the same decade he witnessed the demise of some of his friends and colleagues, including John Constable and Sir John Soane.

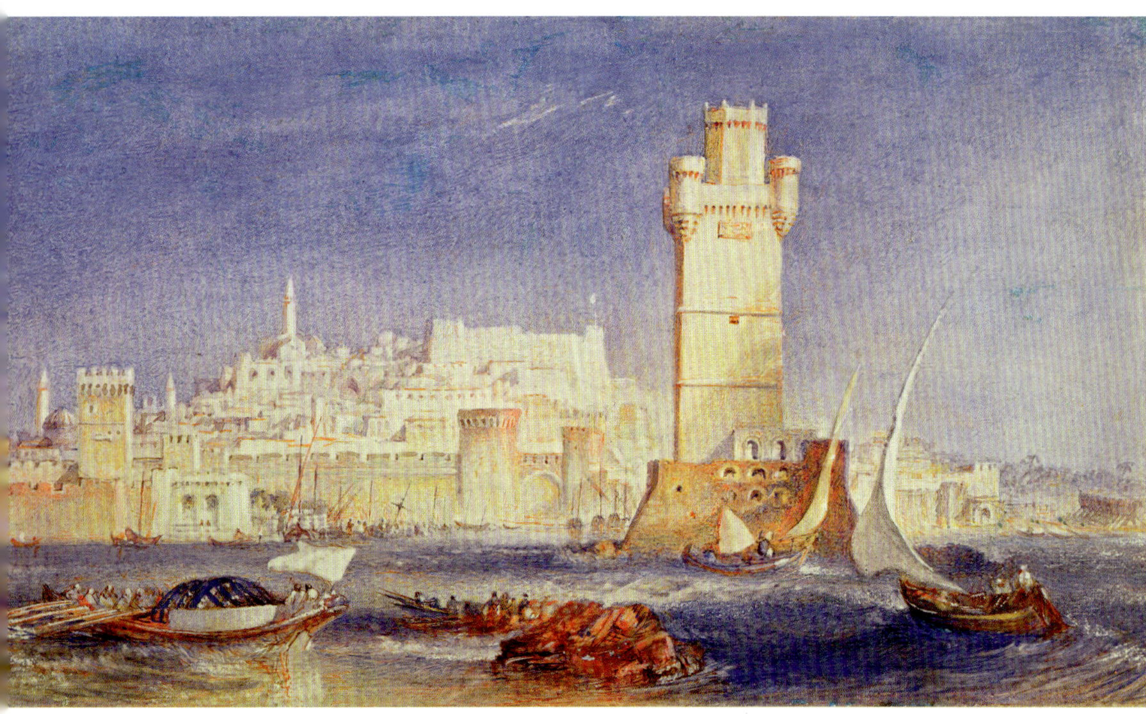

Rhodes, 1830, watercolour,
Paul Mellon Collection,
Yale Center for British Art,
CT, USA,
13 x 23cm (5 x 9in)

Turner never visited Greece
or its islands but managed to
conjure up this perfect image
of Rhodes harbour from a
drawing supplied to him by
William Page. The work was
published in a collection of
landscapes to illustrate *The
Life and Works of Lord Byron.*
The Greeks considered
Byron, the Romantic poet
who had died in Greece in
1824, a national hero.

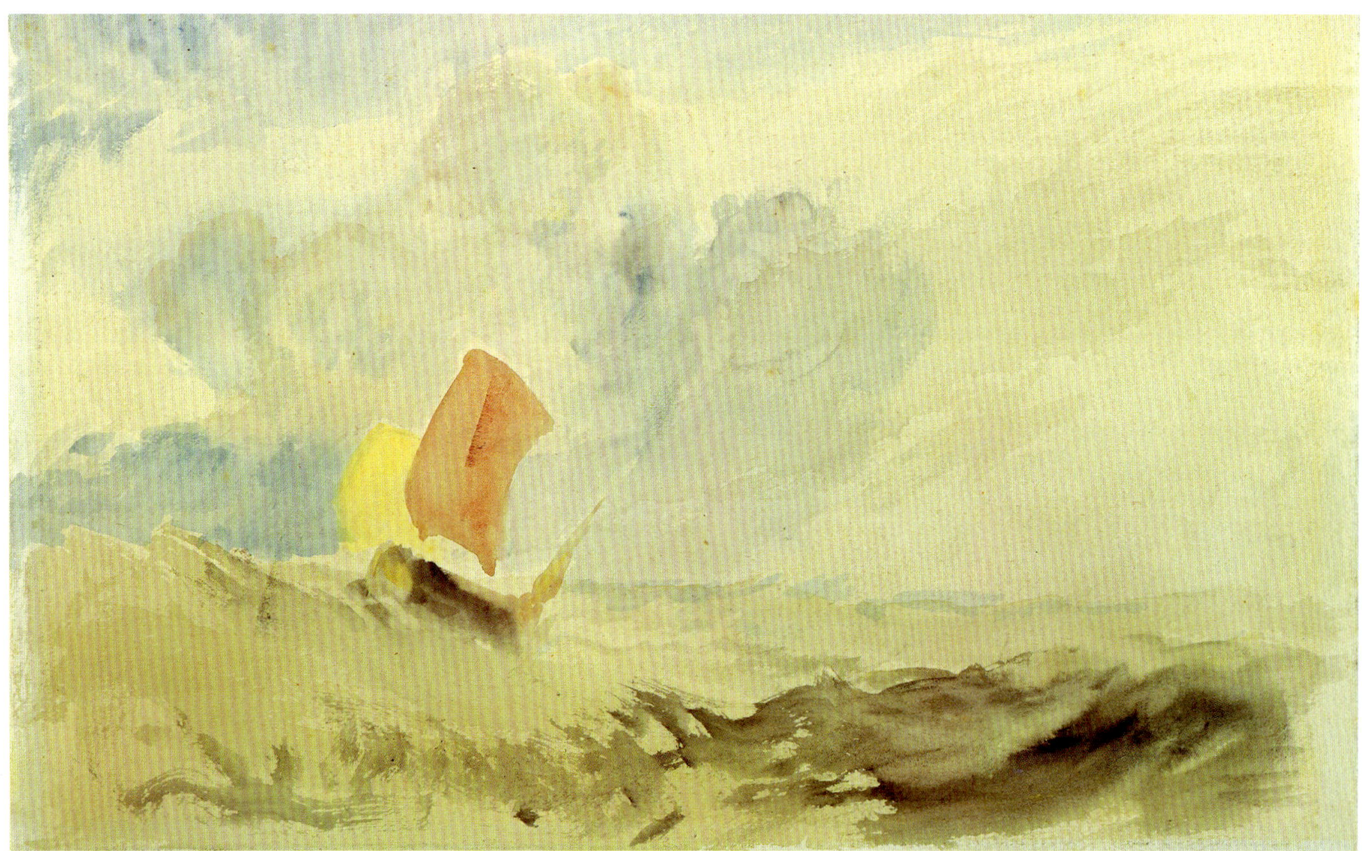

*A Sea-piece – A Rough Sea
with a Fishing Boat*, 1830,
watercolour, Paul Mellon
Collection, Yale Center for
British Art, CT, USA,
20 x 29cm (8 x 11in)

Most people today accept
the idea of paring away
superfluous detail in a picture
to leave abstracted forms
that can easily be interpreted.
For Turner's contemporaries,
this would have been more
difficult, as they were not
used to such brevity in
painting. Similar paintings
stayed in his studio until
after his death.

Calais Sands at Low Water: Poissards Collecting Bait, 1830, oil on canvas, Bury Art Gallery, Lancashire, UK, 69 x 106cm (27 x 42in)

Clearly derived from Turner's experiments with watercolour washes, this oil painting is somewhat mournful, a reflection on the loss of the artist's father, but possibly a homage to the English painter Richard Parkes Bonington, who had died tragically at the age of only 26 in 1828. Bonington had spent some of his youth in Calais and was well known for his landscapes of northern France.

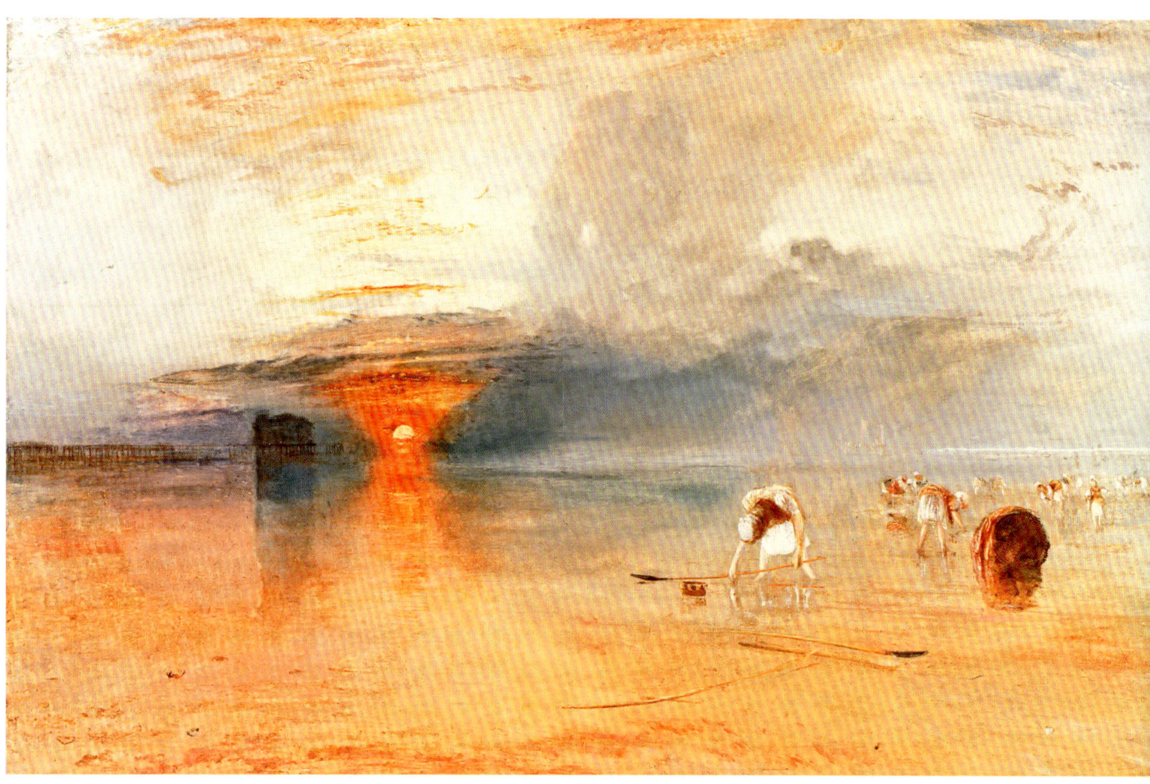

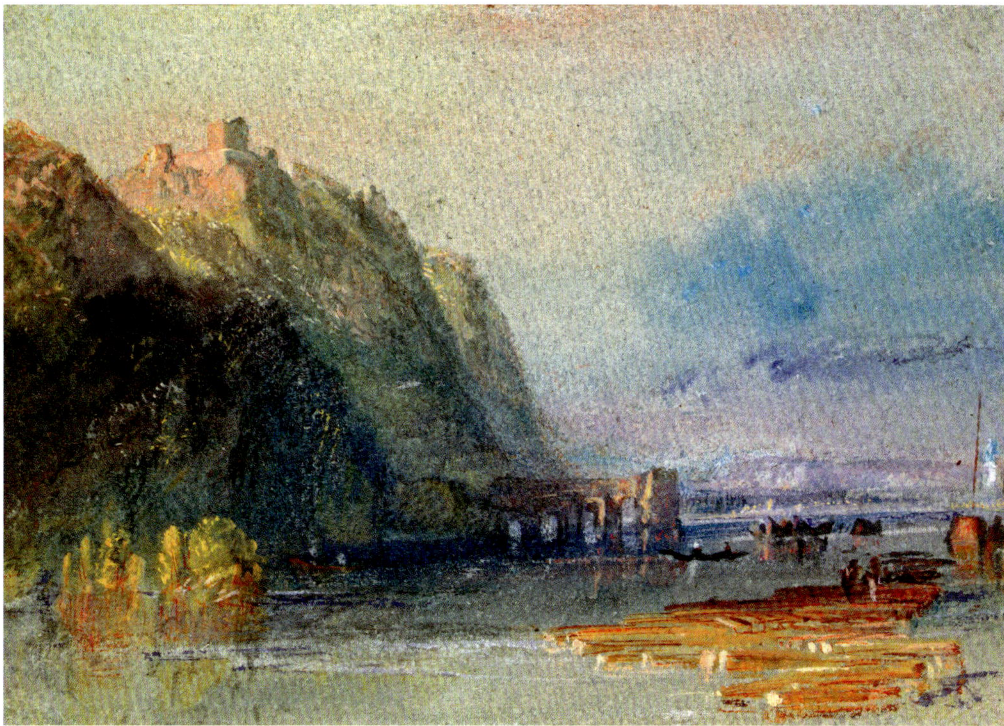

Château Hamelin, 1830, watercolour and pen with scratching out, Ashmolean Museum, Oxford, UK, 14 x 19cm (5½ x 7½in)

Little now remains of the fortress at the top of the hill in Turner's picture, which was of such strategic importance during the Hundred Years War between England and France. Sketches for this work and others around Champtoceaux were executed in a boat on one of the widest stretches of the Loire. The work was reproduced as an engraving in 1833.

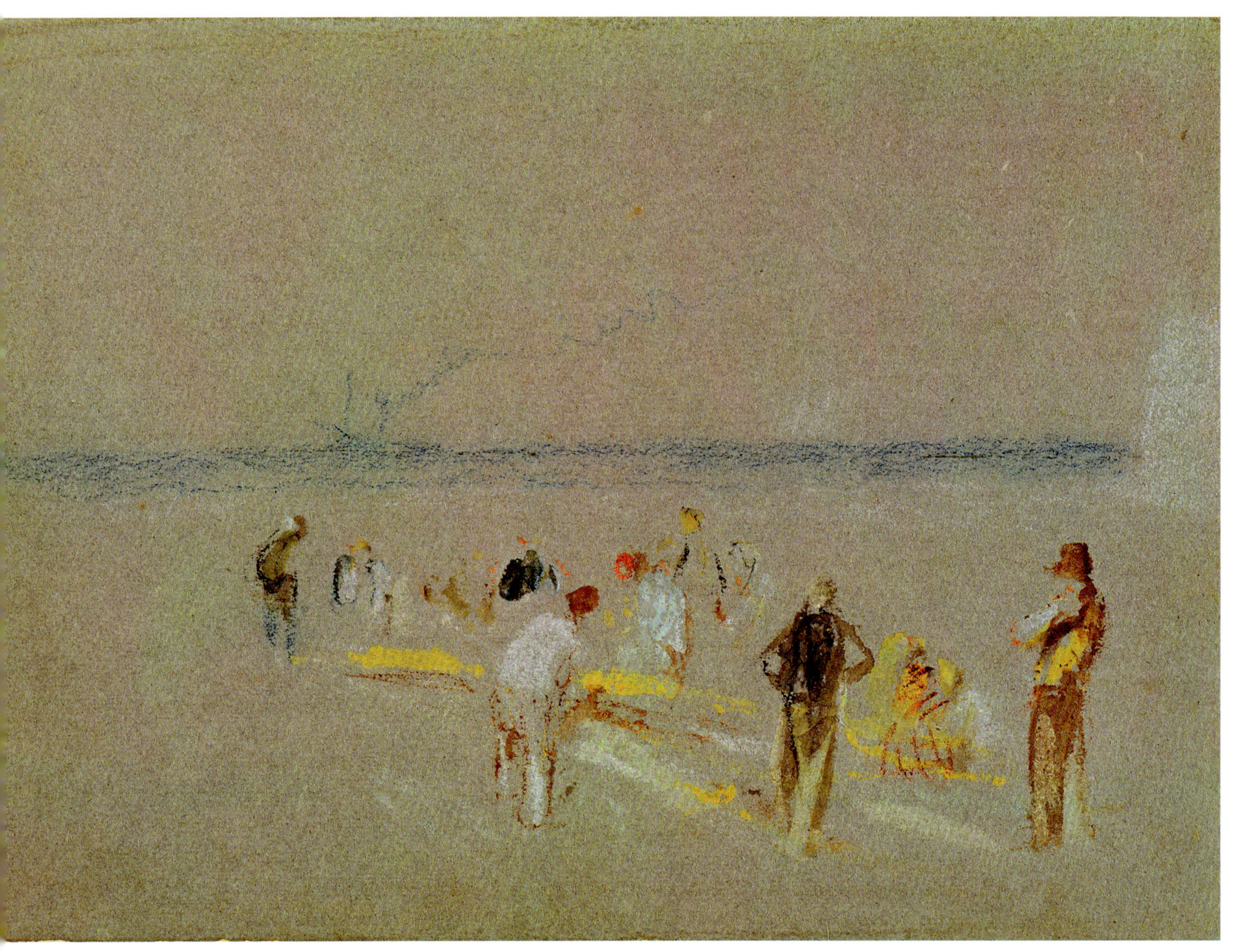

Cricket on the Goodwin Sands, 1828–30, watercolour, bodycolour and chalk, Paul Mellon Collection, Yale Center for British Art, CT, USA, 14 x 19cm (5½ x 7½in)

This small-scale watercolour drawing perfectly depicts this quintessentially English game on the beach, with the minimum of pictorial detail. The gentleman in the top hat may well be Turner himself, as ever enjoying playing games with young people. The scene belies the dangers of this stretch of coast in Kent where many ships have been wrecked and lives lost.

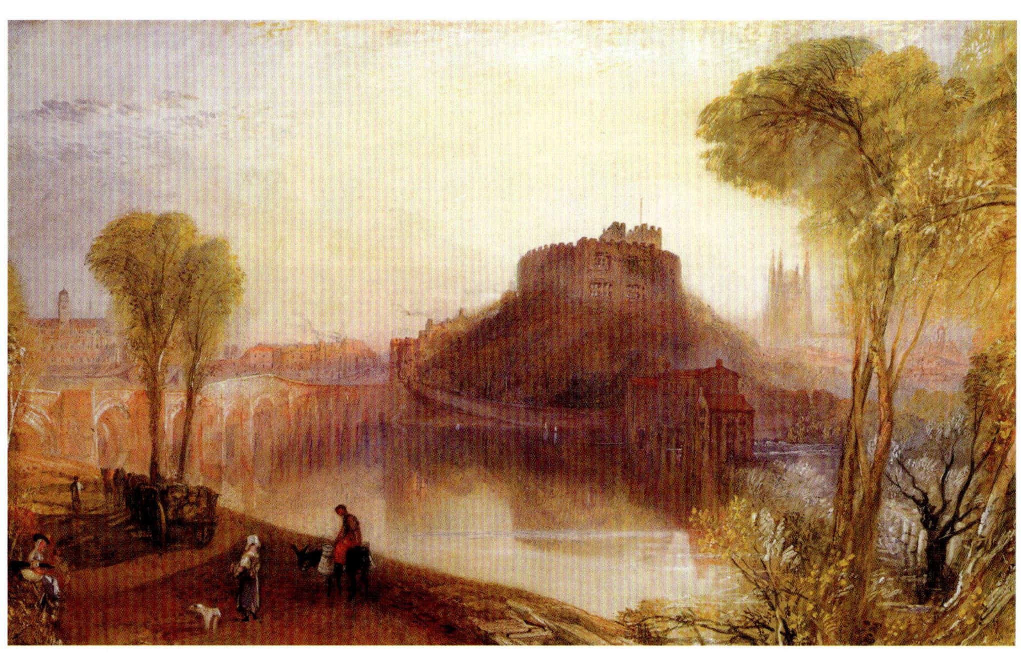

Tamworth Castle, 1830,
pencil and watercolour,
Private Collection,
29 x 45cm (11 x 18in)

Engraved later as part of the
Picturesque Views series, this
is the only painting by Turner
of Tamworth Castle as the
central motif, suggesting that
it was only created for the
purpose of reproduction.
The watercolour perfectly
depicts a well-preserved
example of a Norman motte
and bailey castle from the
11th century, that was at one
time a manorial home.

Côteaux de Mauves, 1830,
watercolour, Ashmolean
Museum, Oxford, UK,
14 x 19cm (5½ x 7½in)

The unusual boat depicted
in this watercolour is in fact
a Loire barge, known as a
gabarre, which was based on
a Viking design of the 9th

century. It was equipped
with a flat-bottomed keel,
which was ideal for the
shallow parts of the rivers,
and also it had a very
large rudder to make
steering easier. By contrast,
Turner travelled along
the Loire in a steam-
powered ship.

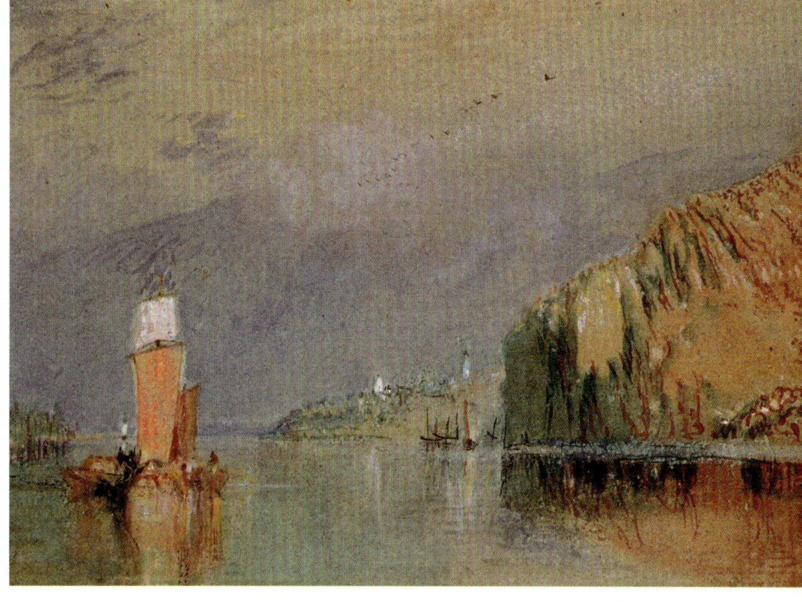

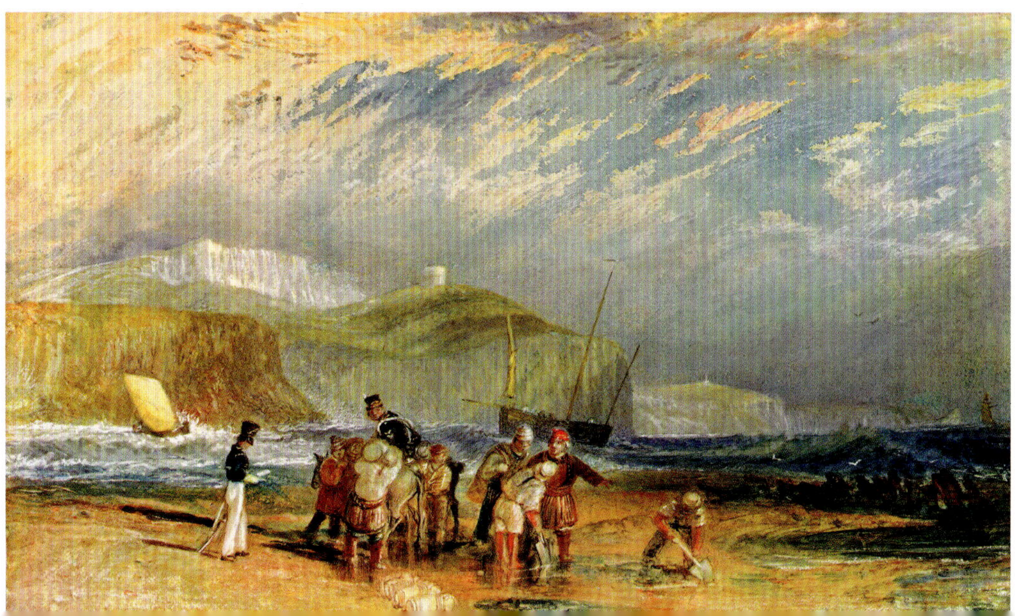

*Folkestone Harbour and
Coast to Dover*, c.1830,
watercolour and
bodycolour, Paul Mellon
Collection, Yale Center
for British Art, CT, USA,
29 x 45cm (11 x 18in)

Turner depicts customs men
apprehending smugglers.
Shortly after this picture was
painted, the Coastguard
service came into being to
help to eliminate smuggling.

Fishermen on a Weir, c.1830, watercolour, bodycolour, pencil and chalk, Paul Mellon Collection, Yale Center for British Art, CT, USA, 14 x 19cm (5½ x 7½in)

Between 1830 and 1835 Turner created a sketchbook called Fishing at the Weir, containing about forty drawings. He also made this coloured sketch. Turner visited so many rivers in England and France at this time that it is impossible to know the weir's exact location. Clearly his agenda was not topographical but rather to capture the mood of his favourite pastime, fishing.

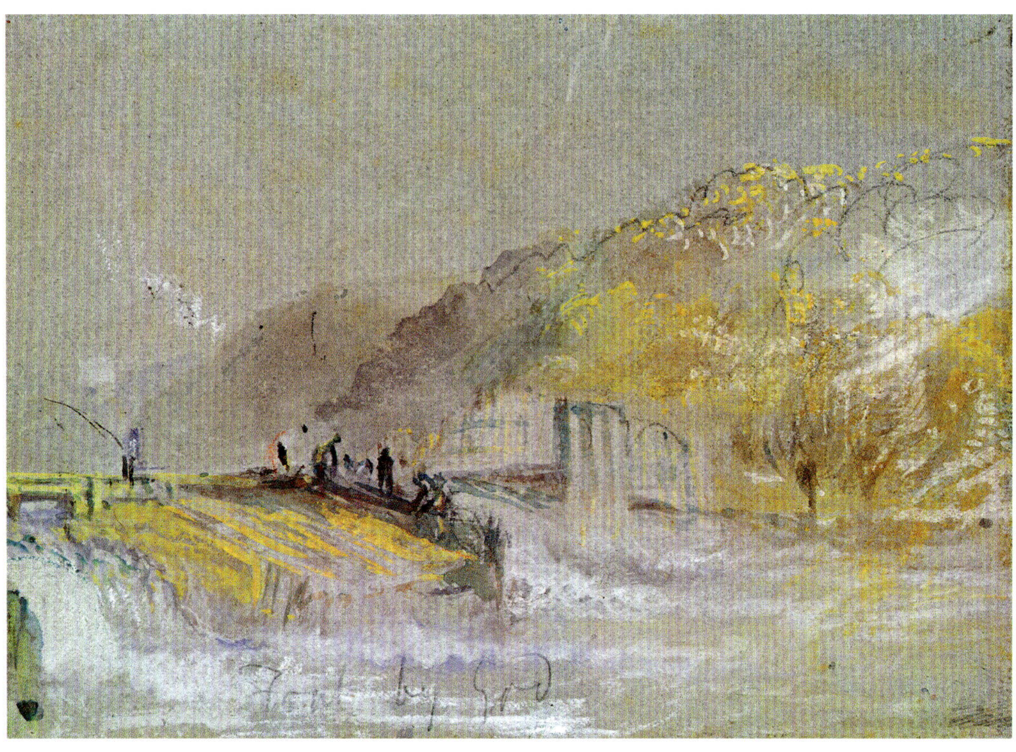

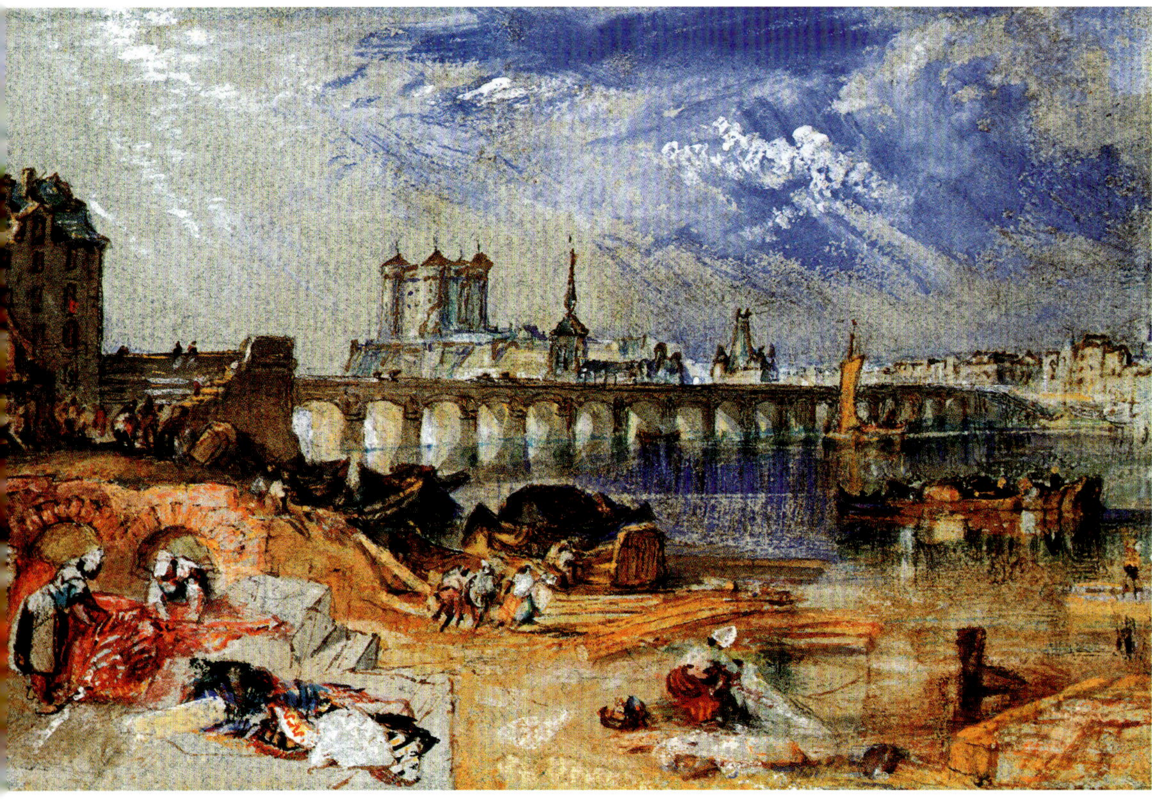

Saumur, c.1830, watercolour, Private Collection, 13 x 19cm (5 x 7½in)

The huge bridge spanning the Loire is the focal point for Turner's watercolour. Behind is the Château de Saumur, a fortress originally built by the English King Henry II, who was also the ruler of this region in the 12th century. The French used the château during the Napoleonic Wars, firstly as an army barracks and then later as a prison.

Ship Aground, Brighton,
c.1830, watercolour and
bodycolour, Paul Mellon
Collection, Yale Center
for British Art, CT, USA,
14 x 19cm (5½ x 7½in)

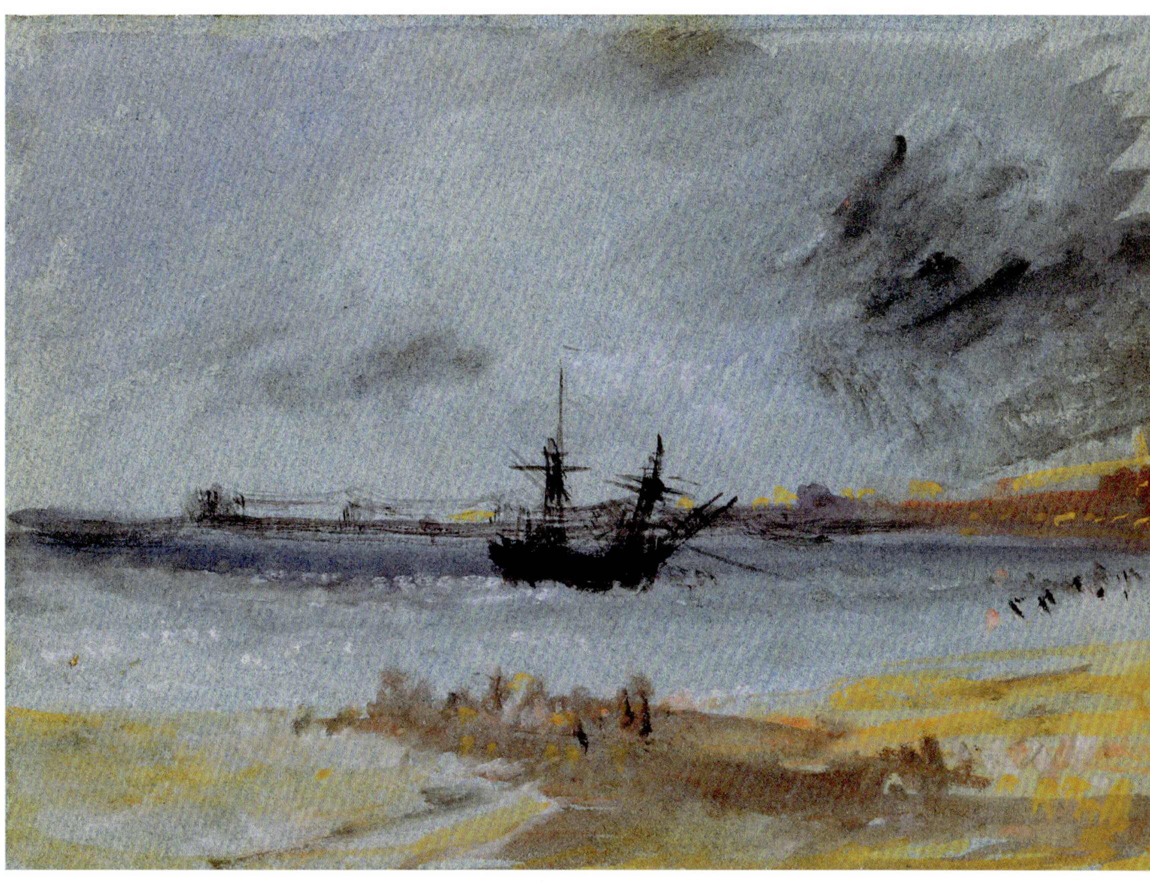

Brighton had become a
popular resort at this time,
following the first visit to this
former fishing village by the
Prince Regent in 1783.
Originally he rented a
farmhouse where he
conducted his long affair with
Mrs Fitzherbert, but by 1815
he had instructed the
architect John Nash to
redesign a new palace, since
known as the Royal Pavilion.

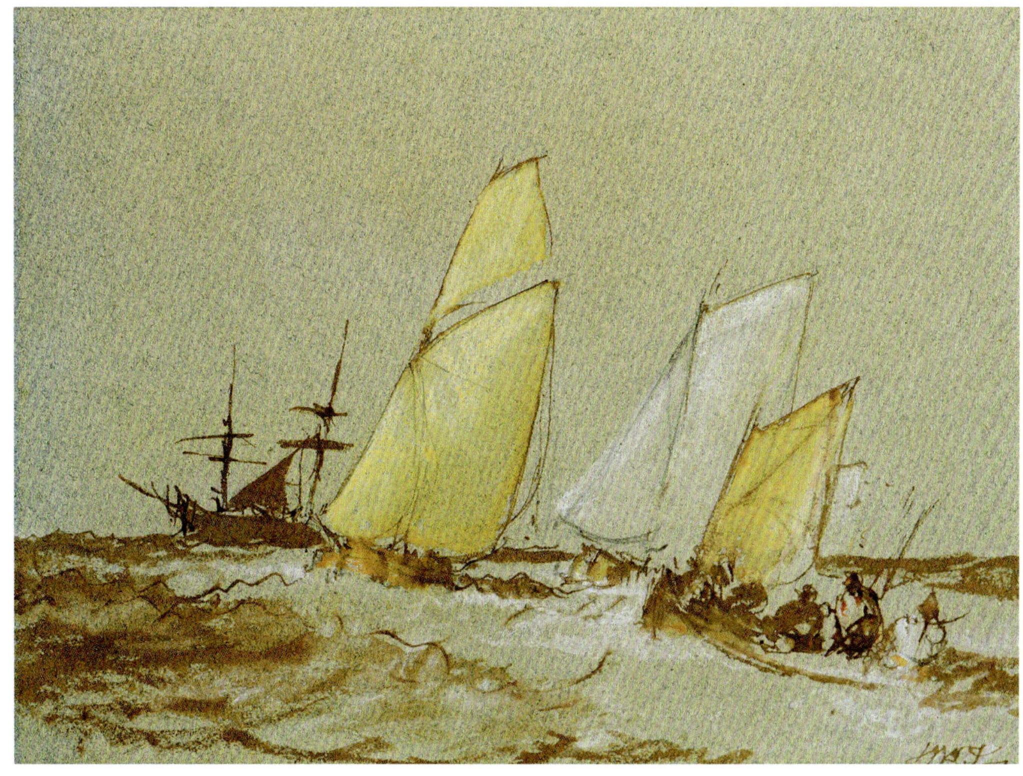

Shipping, 1828–30,
bodycolour and ink on
blue paper, Paul Mellon
Collection, Yale Center
for British Art, CT, USA,
14 x 19cm (5½ x 7½in)

Either side of visiting
Petworth in the summer
of 1828 to work on his
commission for Lord
Egremont, Turner must have
visited several places on the
Sussex coast. These were
recorded in his Brighton,
Newhaven and Cowdray
Sketchbook. Among the one
hundred or so drawings was
this small coloured exercise
on coloured paper, showing
both brevity of mark and
minimum use of colour.

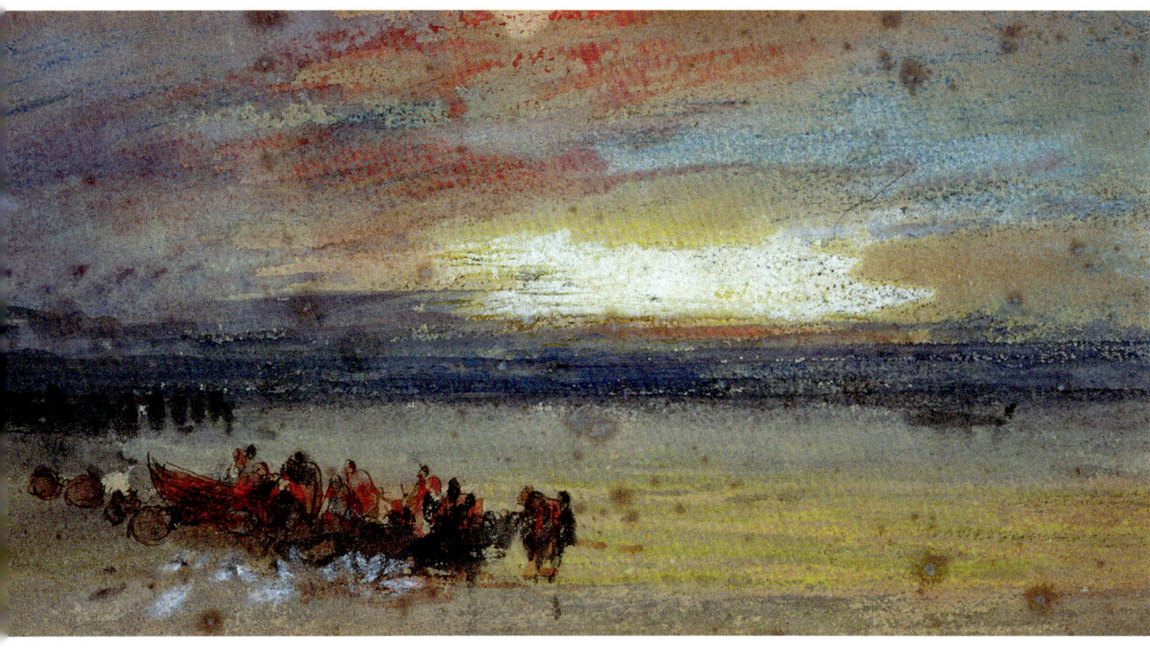

*Shore Scene, Sunset, c.*1830, watercolour, Victoria and Albert Museum, London, UK, 10 x 19cm (4 x 7½in)

Although not strictly speaking a miniature, this tiny watercolour has at least one of its traits, the quality of detail. This scene of confrontation between a soldier and a group of nine smugglers around their boats and some contraband behind the breakwater, provides a foil for the glorious sunset, which was probably Turner's real agenda for this painting.

Shoreham, 1830, watercolour, Blackburn Museum, Lancashire, UK, 51 x 93cm (20 x 37in)

The detail for this watercolour was taken from the Brighton and Arundel Sketchbook that Turner made in 1824, possibly with the Ports of England series in mind. This is a genre picture focusing on the shipbuilding industry that Shoreham was renowned for at the time.

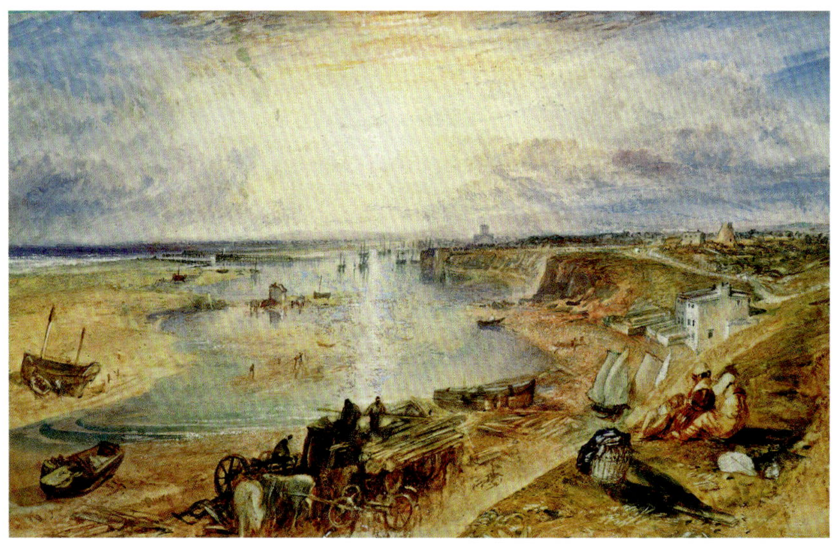

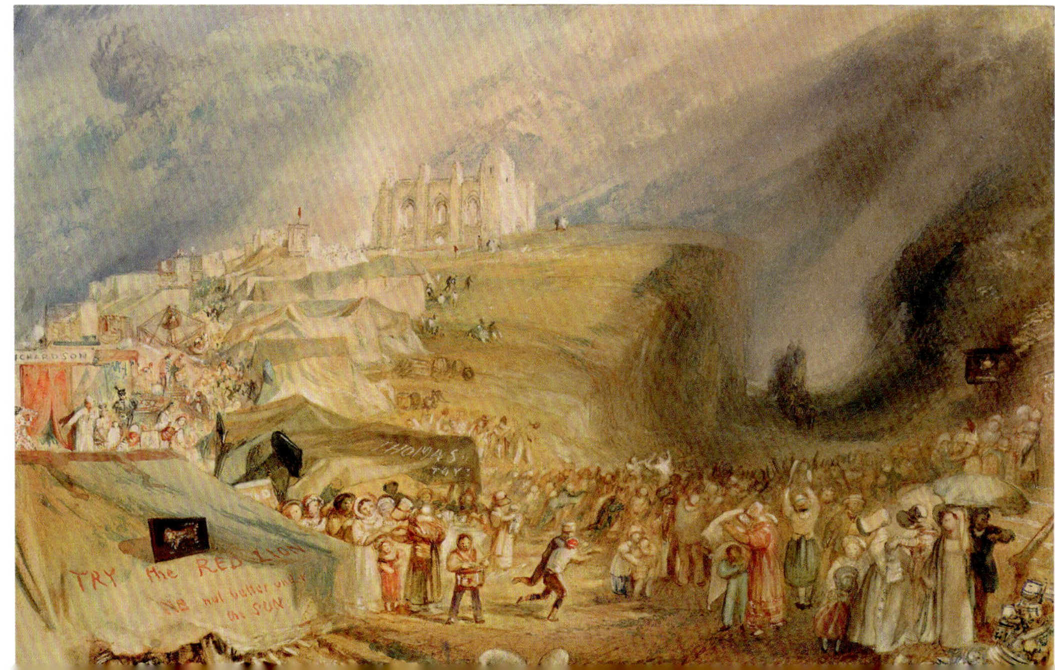

St Catherine's Hill, Guildford, Surrey, 1830, graphite and watercolour, Paul Mellon Collection, Yale Center for British Art, CT, USA, 30 x 45cm (12 x 18in)

The scene depicts a fair held every year at St Catherine's Hill since the 14th century. The ruined chapel provided a Picturesque element, and Turner added a touch of the Sublime on the right of the picture as a coach travels through dark rain clouds.

Sunset, 1830, watercolour, Private Collection, dimensions unknown

A study in watercolour that anticipates Impressionism in style, it is nevertheless a work of reflection. Having recently lost his father and acted as pall-bearer at a friend's funeral, Turner was in a reflective mood at this time and began to consider his own mortality. The painting was possibly executed at Margate, where he began to stay for long periods in the company of Sophia Booth.

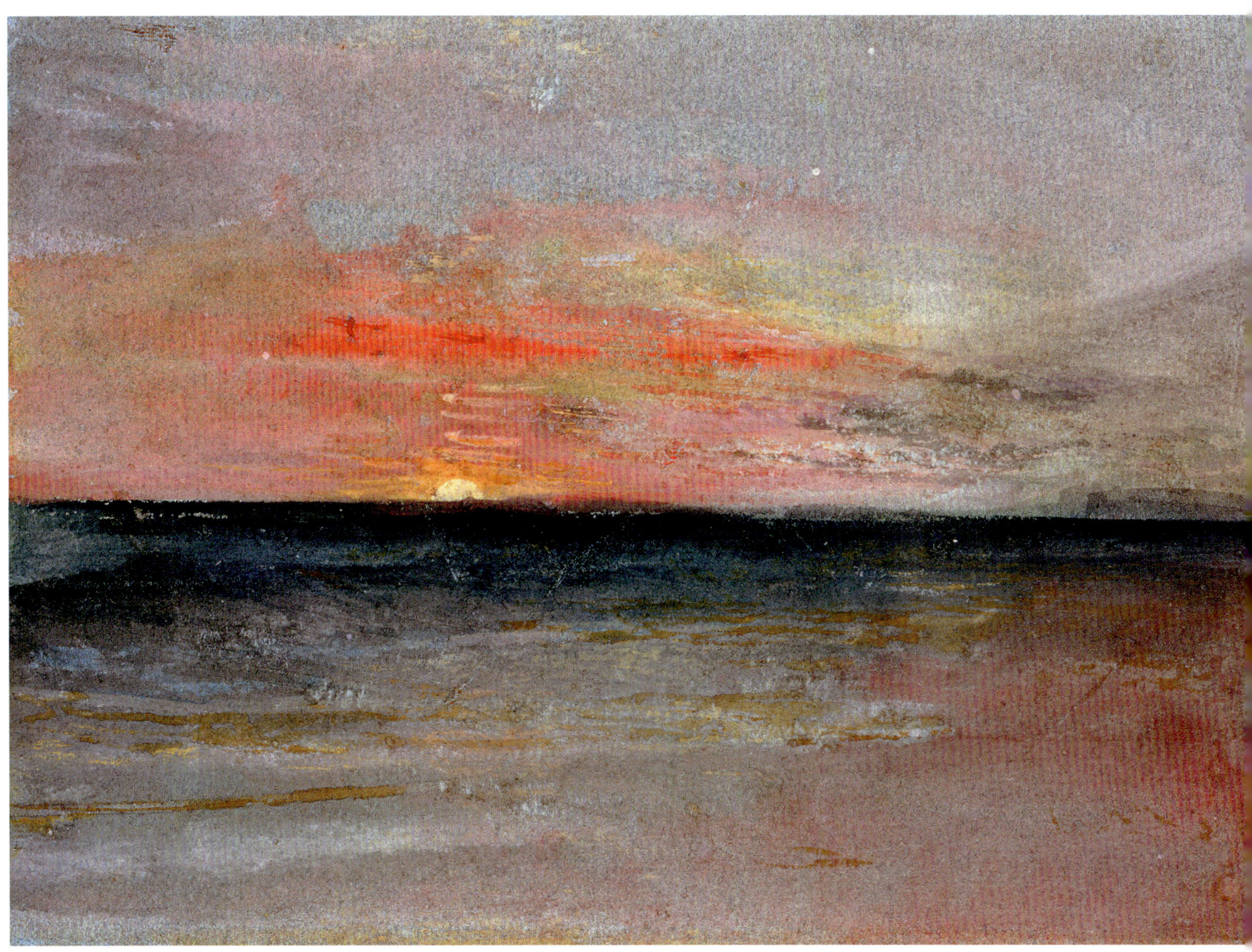

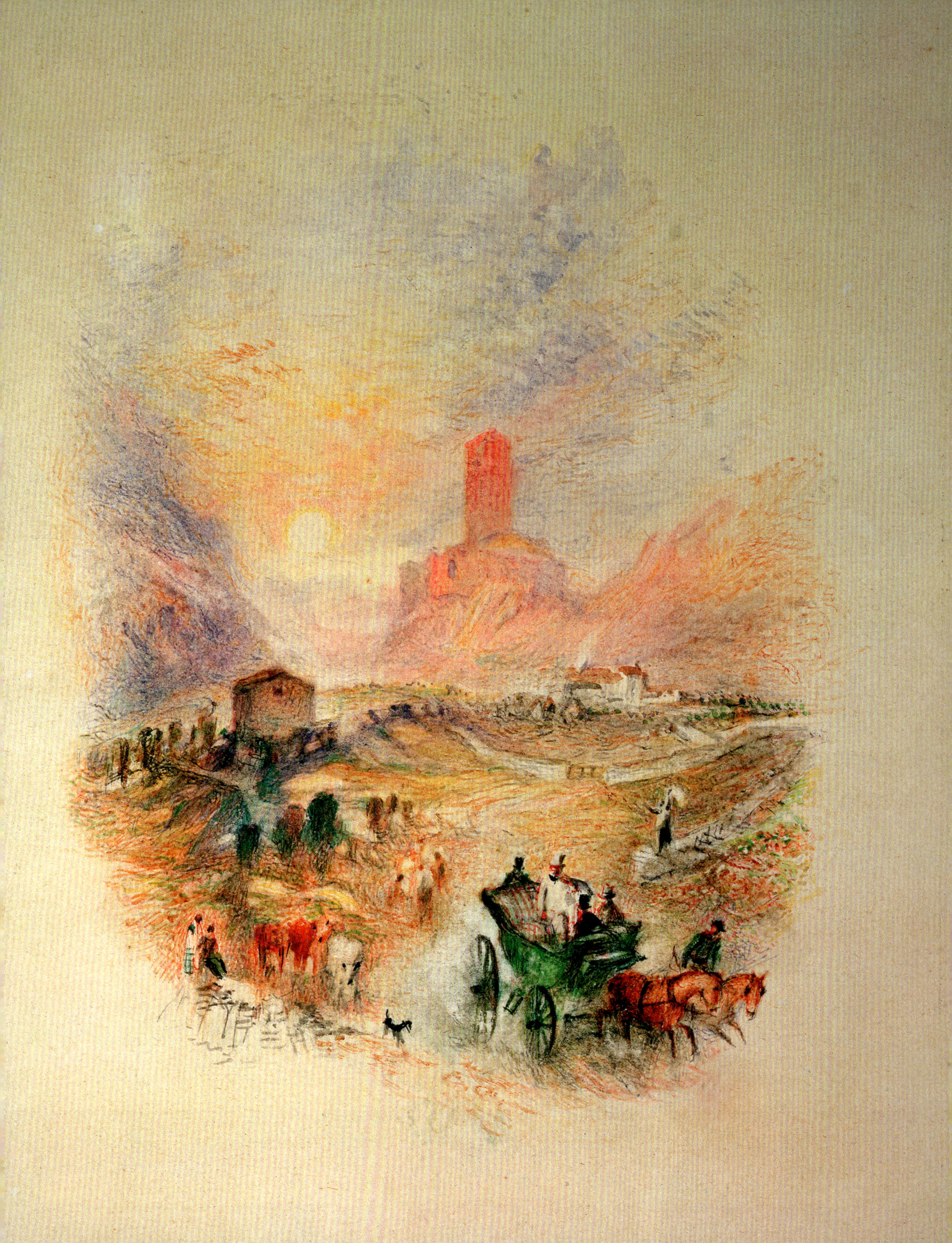

EXPERIMENTS IN COLOUR AND FORM 1831–1840

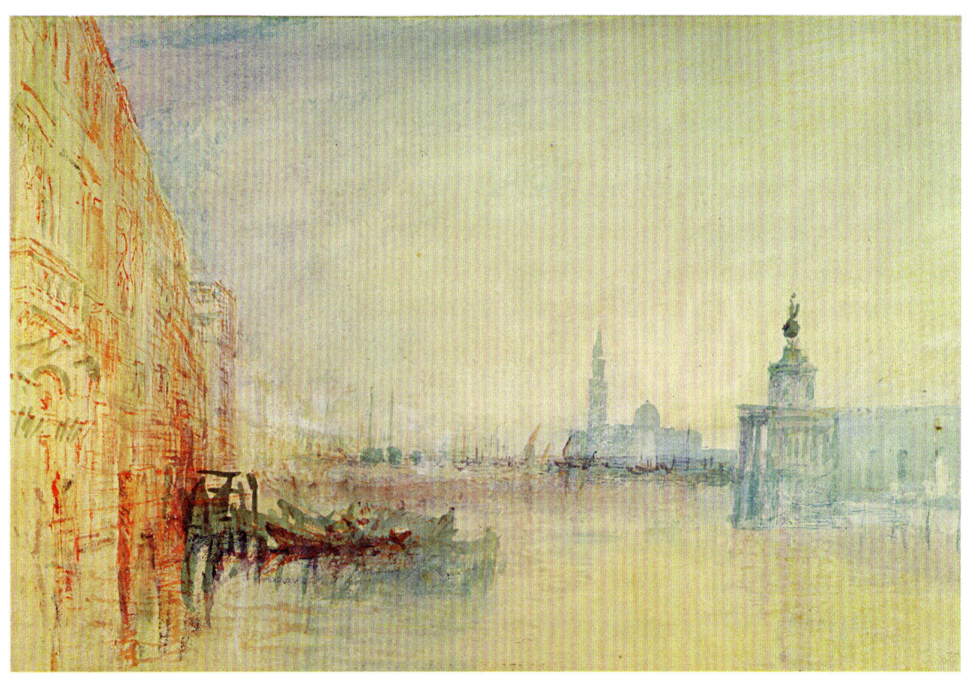

Turner's exposure to the Italian light in the previous decade, and again in this one, encouraged him to experiment with his palette, creating paintings that appeared strange and even controversial to English sensibilities, using unnatural colour. He also began to remove the superfluous detail of a motif to create many of his most ethereal landscapes that lacked topographical detail but were highly charged with atmosphere and emotion. This was Turner's own response to the Sublime aesthetic popularized by other artists, which he brought to a new level of human engagement.

Above: Venice, the Mouth of the Grand Canal, *watercolour on paper, c.1840. The ethereal quality of Turner's watercolours was achieved to greatest effect in Venice, particularly at sunset and sunrise.*
Left: Walter Scott Visiting Smailholm Tower, *watercolour, 1832. Turner presented this intricate small vignette to Scott as a memento of their visit to the Tower in 1831. Turner has depicted himself, Scott and Cadell riding in the carriage. The vignette was sent to Scott.*

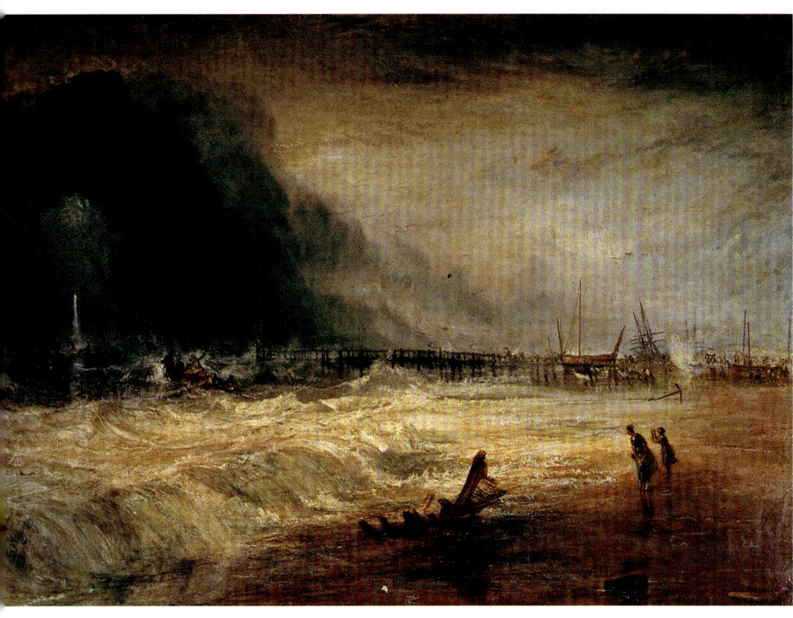

Lifeboat and Manby Apparatus, 1831, oil on canvas, Victoria and Albert Museum, London, UK, 91 x 122cm (36 x 48in)

Whenever the occasion arose, Turner loved to demonstrate the modernity and technology of his age.

The Manby Apparatus had first been used in 1808. It consisted of a mortar used to fire a shot with a line attached from a rescue point to a distressed ship. The system was adapted for use by the lifeboat service, which had been launched in 1824.

Paris: Hôtel de Ville, 1833, watercolour with sepia ink, Indianapolis Museum of Art, IN, USA, 23 x 20cm (9 x 8in)

Sir Walter Scott's *Life of Napoleon* was published in 1827, and was so successful that it was decided to create a new illustrated edition to which Turner would contribute a number of watercolour drawings, including this one. It was published in 1834. Turner chose the Hôtel de Ville as one image, the scene of revolutionary events leading up to the ascendancy of Napoleon's regime.

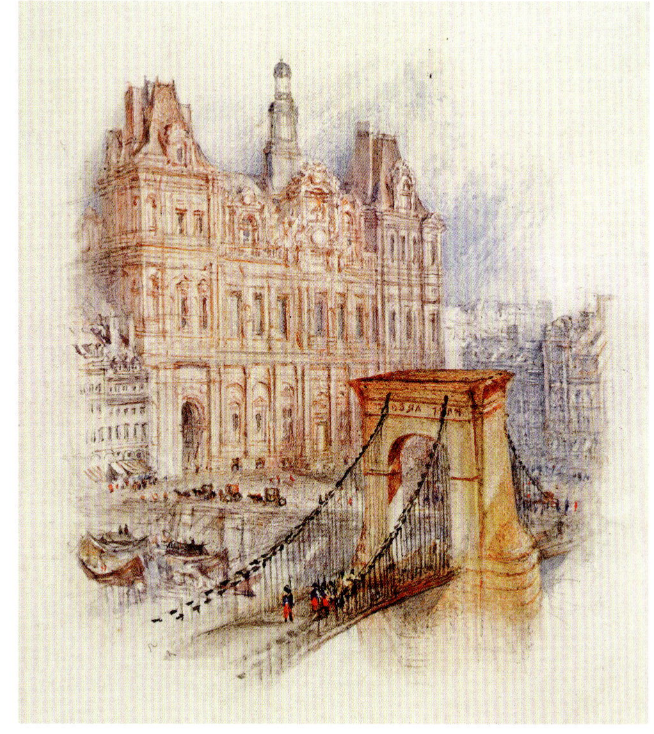

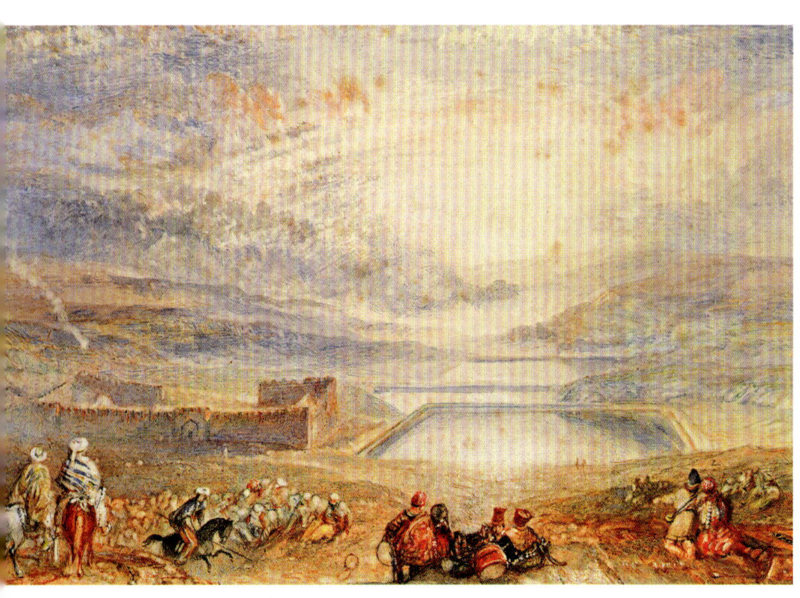

Solomon's Pools, 1834–5, watercolour, Fitzwilliam Museum, Cambridge, UK, 14 x 21cm (5½ x 8in)

These pools were most likely built during the Roman occupation of the Holy Land, and given the name because of a biblical reference. They are located near the town of Bethlehem, their construction probably overseen by Herod. Since that time they have been a site of pilgrimage and tourism, as suggested in Turner's watercolour, which was published in *Landscape Illustrations of the Bible*.

Neapolitan Fisher Girls Surprised, Bathing by Moonlight, 1840, oil on canvas, Private Collection, 65 x 80cm (26 x 31in)

Critics of the time were derogatory in their remarks concerning the six oil paintings submitted by Turner to the Academy exhibition of 1840. This painting was purchased at the exhibition by Robert Vernon, who sold it two years later, possibly as a result of the critical remarks made about the light being too bright for a moonlit scene. *Blackwood's Magazine* was also very critical, unable "to find any fisher-girls at all".

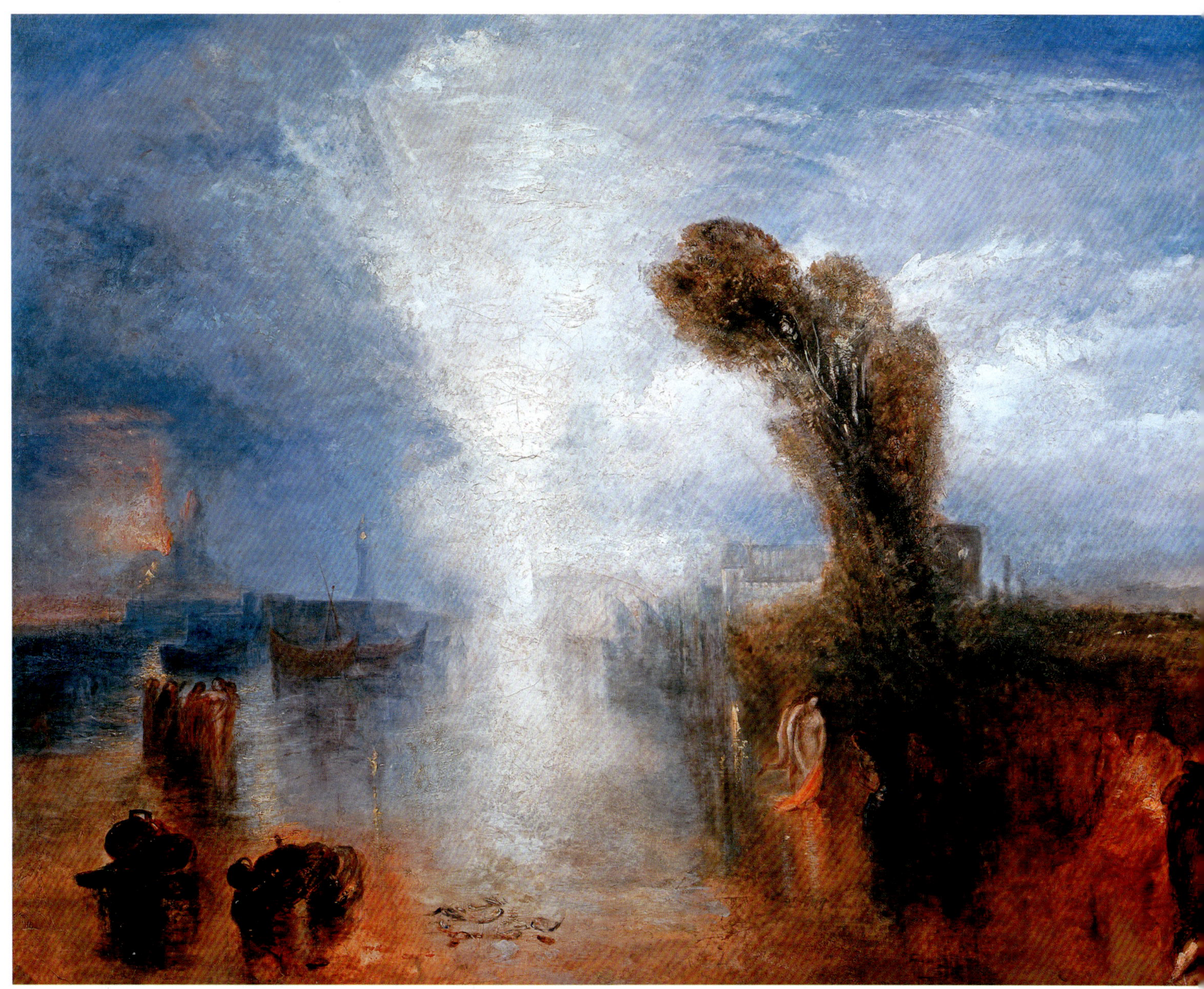

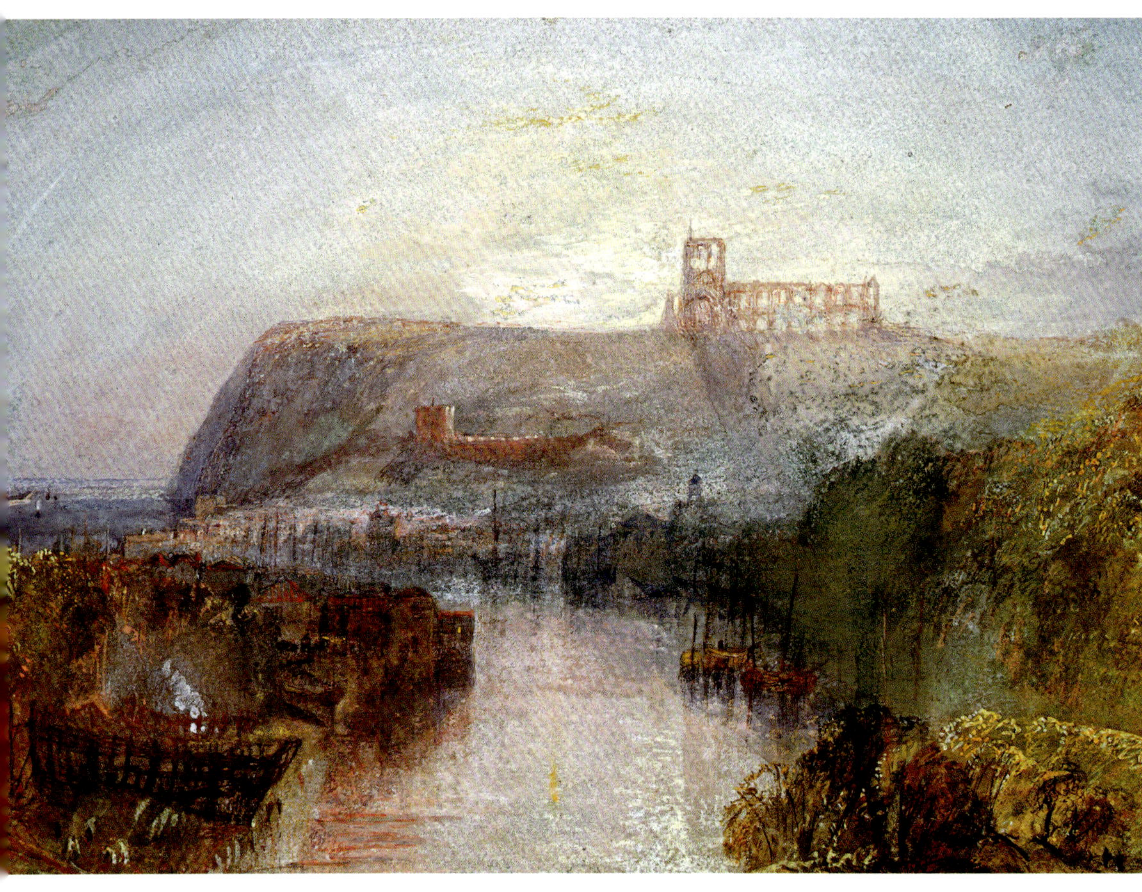

Whitby, 1830, watercolour,
Private Collection,
17 x 25cm (7 x 10in)

Turner considered Whitby an
important motif from 1801
when he first visited the site,
using images for his *Liber
Studiorum* and *The Harbours
of England* series. The key
factors in this are the
presence of a ruined
abbey on the headland
and shipping in the bay and
harbour. The town was
important at this time
as a centre for the
whaling industry.

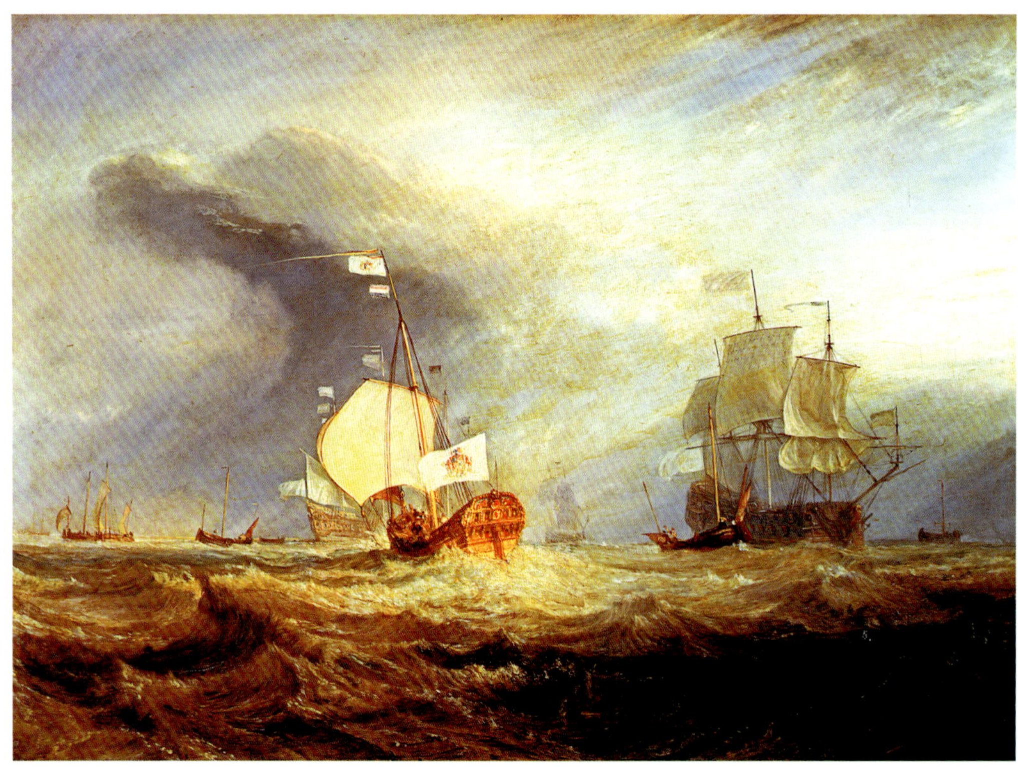

*Admiral von Tromp's Barge at
the Entrance of the Texel in
1645*, 1831, oil on canvas,
Sir John Soane's
Museum, London, UK,
90 x 121cm (35 x 48in)

Given the relatively recent
successes against France
during the Napoleonic Wars,
it seems odd that Turner
would select a scene that
depicts the ascendancy of
the Dutch navy during the
war with Britain in the 17th
century. To underpin the
narrative the artist has also
chosen a typically Dutch
style of painting, perhaps a
rebuff to the critics of his
Rembrandt pastiches.

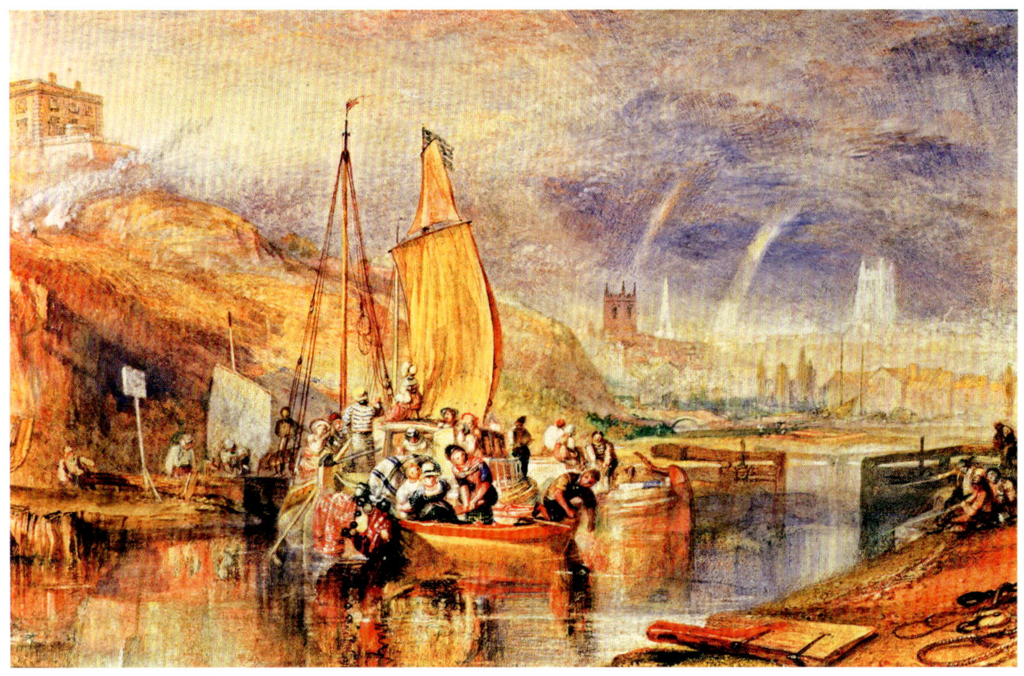

Nottingham, 1831, watercolour, Nottingham Castle Museum and Art Gallery, UK, 31 x 46cm (12 x 18in)

Turner has reinterpreted an earlier watercolour of this scene executed in 1795. The painting has a political dimension, the artist including a scene of burning arable stubble on the left of the picture. This alludes to the mob rioting and burning at Nottingham Castle in protest at the rejection of the parliamentary Reform Bill in 1831. The Bill was enacted the following year.

Upnor Castle, 1831, watercolour, Whitworth Art Gallery, University of Manchester, UK, 29 x 44cm (11 x 17in)

Another example of Turner's fascination with the war against the Dutch in the 17th century is this watercolour depicting the blockade across the channel of the River Medway. The castle, being a military fort, was instrumental in providing firepower in the event of a naval strike by the Dutch, but had shut down its artillery battery in 1827.

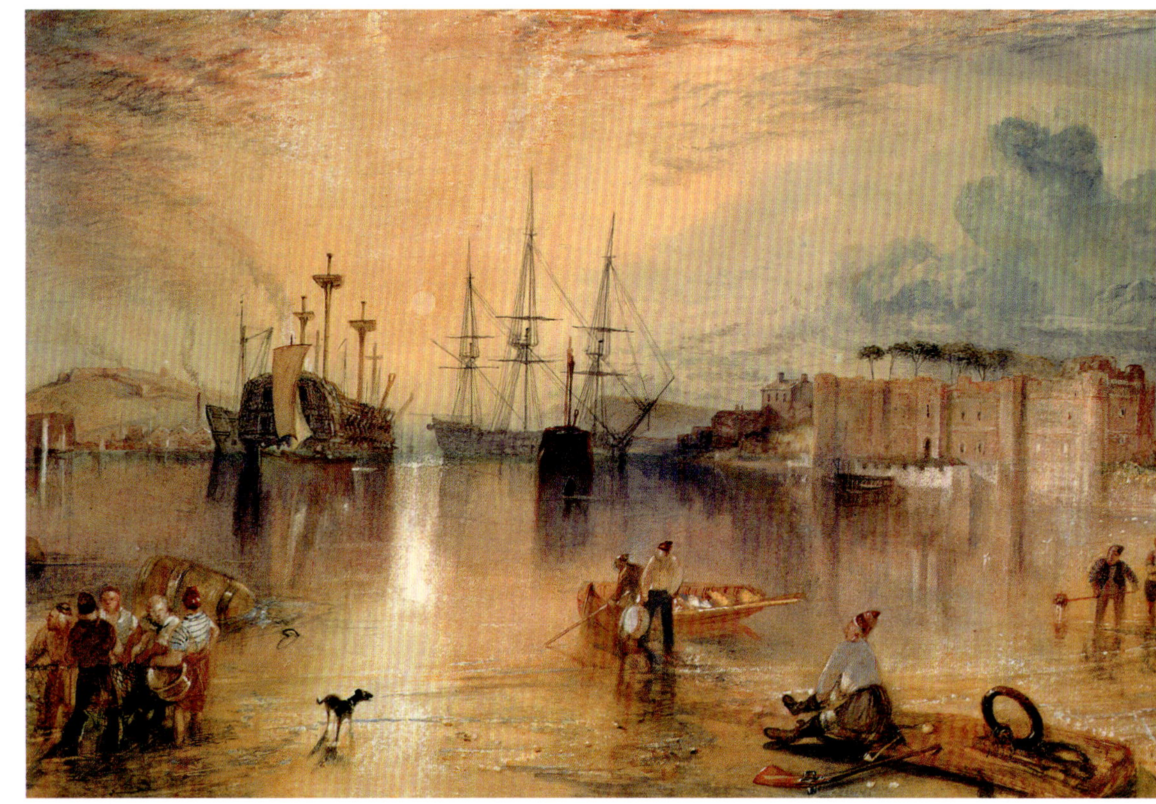

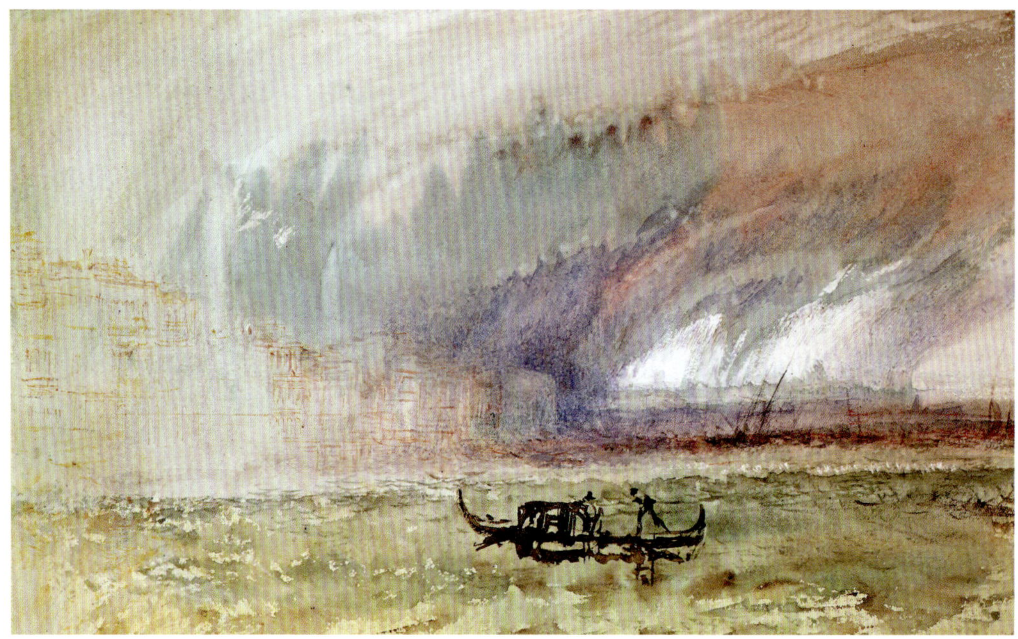

Venice, a Storm, 1840, watercolour, British Museum, London, UK, 22 x 32cm (9 x 13in)

This is an exercise in restrained technique in colour and motif. It is possible to engage with the drama against the Venetian skyline in the distance and the sense of isolation that the gondolier feels as he negotiates the difficult waters of the open lagoon. In the middle distance, Turner has suggested a tall ship with her sails down almost in the eye of the storm.

Ely Cathedral, 1831, watercolour, Private Collection, 30 x 41cm (12 x 16in)

This picture seems to be a topographical scene, but it is charged with political innuendo, set in the context of the new Reform Act. The boy in the foreground represents the working classes, who were disenfranchised in the political system. He is throwing stones toward the church, which had adopted a conservative view of the status quo. Turner was in favour of reform.

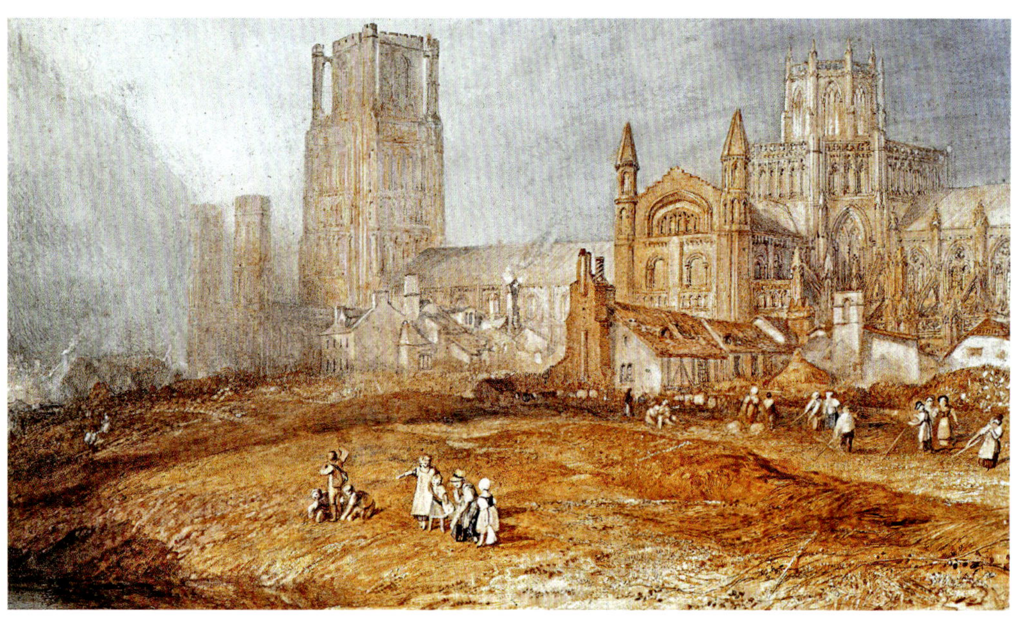

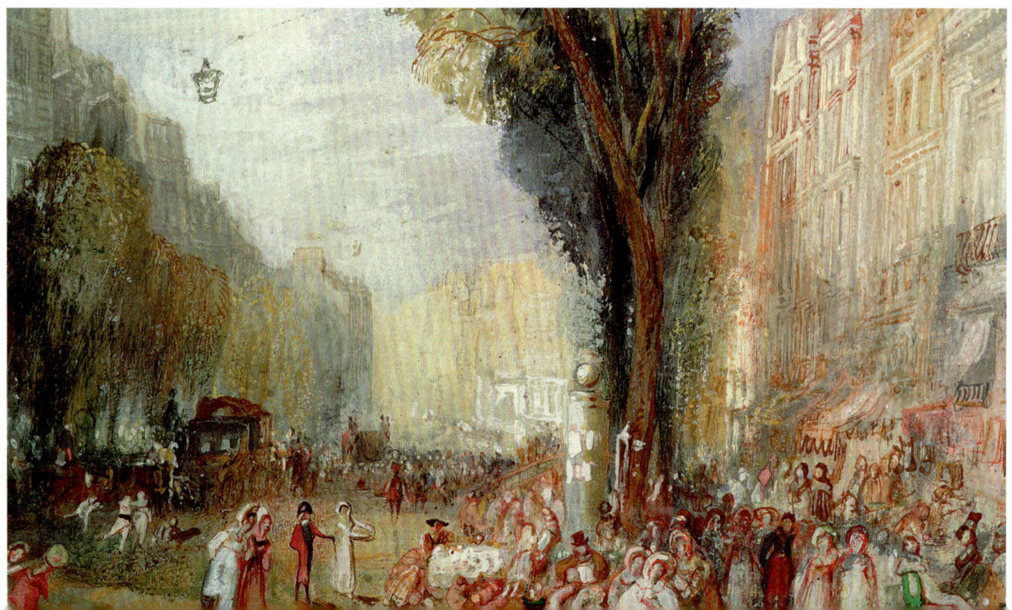

Boulevard des Italiennes, 1832, bodycolour, Private Collection, 13 x 18cm (5 x 7in)

Despite a cholera epidemic, Turner visited Paris in 1832 and was captivated by the colour and gaiety of the city after the revolution in 1830, which saw the restoration of a monarchy. This watercolour anticipates the excitement, if not the style, experienced by the Impressionist painters of modern urban life, a generation later.

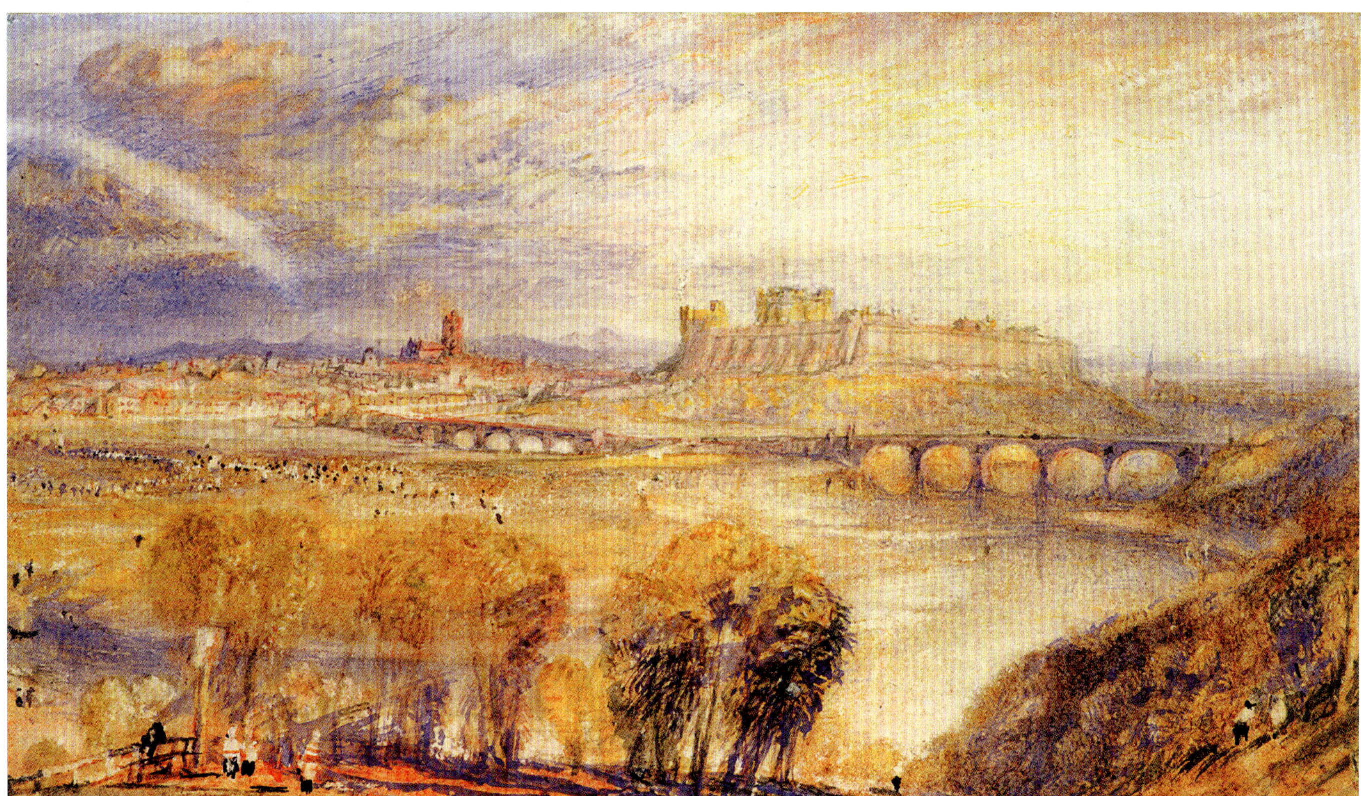

Carlisle, 1832, watercolour, Paul Mellon Collection, Yale Center for British Art, CT, USA, 8 x 14cm (3 x 5½in)

The castle depicted by Turner in the background has played a significant role in British history for 900 years. William II built it in the 11th century because of its strategic position on the border of England and Scotland. It served as a prison for Mary Queen of Scots and was also instrumental in the last Jacobite rebellion of 1745.

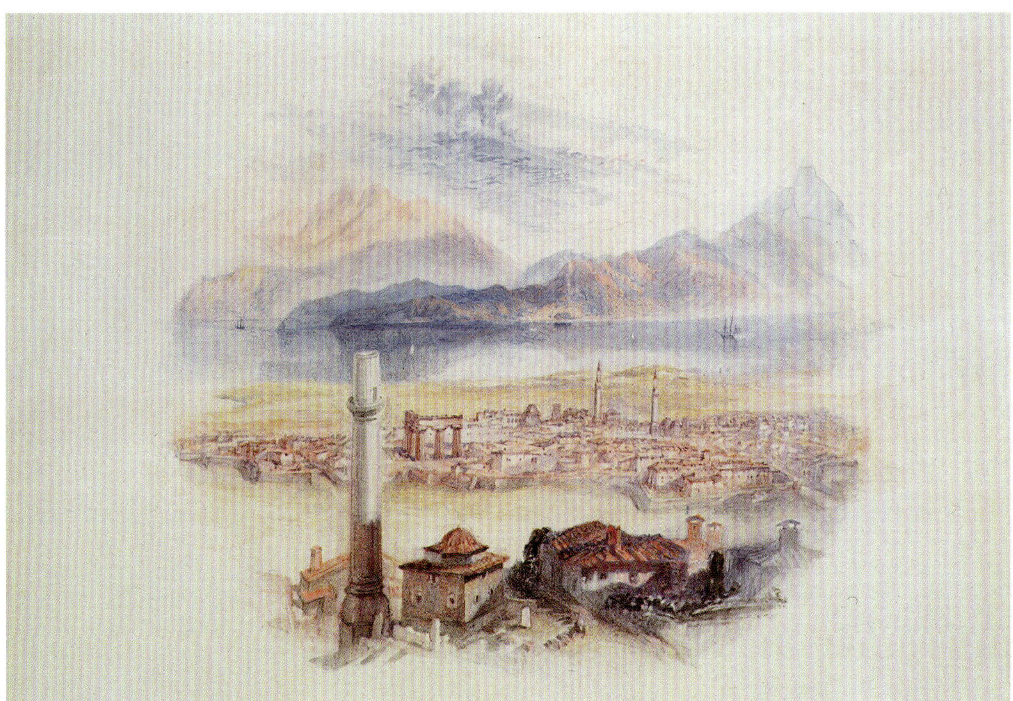

Corinth from the Acropolis, 1831–2, graphite and watercolour, Fitzwilliam Museum, Cambridge, UK, dimensions unknown

The inclusion of a minaret in the foreground of this vignette by Turner is a stark contrast to the Greek classical buildings in the background, which are symbolic of the Ottoman rule since 1458. The work is inspired by Lord Byron's poem, and the Greek War of Independence from the Ottoman Empire, finally achieved in 1832 after a long conflict.

Dudley, Worcester, 1832,
watercolour and
bodycolour, Lady Lever Art
Gallery, Liverpool, UK,
29 x 43cm (11 x 17in)

Here the artist has captured
the very essence of the
Industrial Revolution, with
laden barges and smoking
factory chimneys. The scene
is at twilight, a recurring
motif in Turner's paintings of
the 1830s, depicting the
presence of both a setting
sun and a moon, symbolizing
the passing of an old age, as
suggested by the horse on
the right, and the dawning of
a darker modern age.

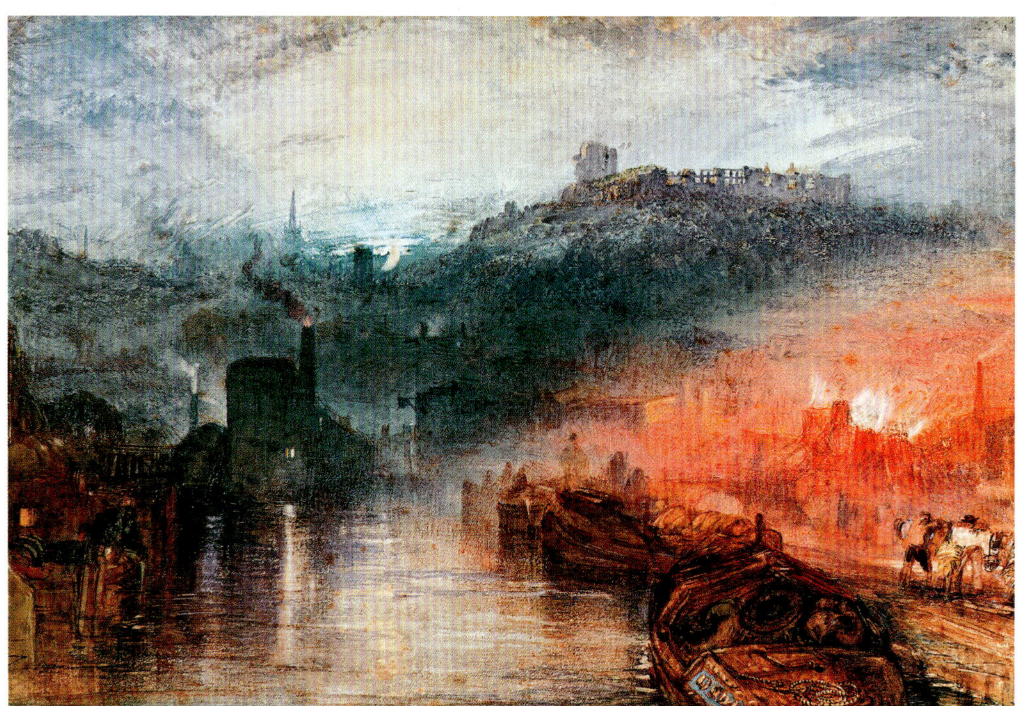

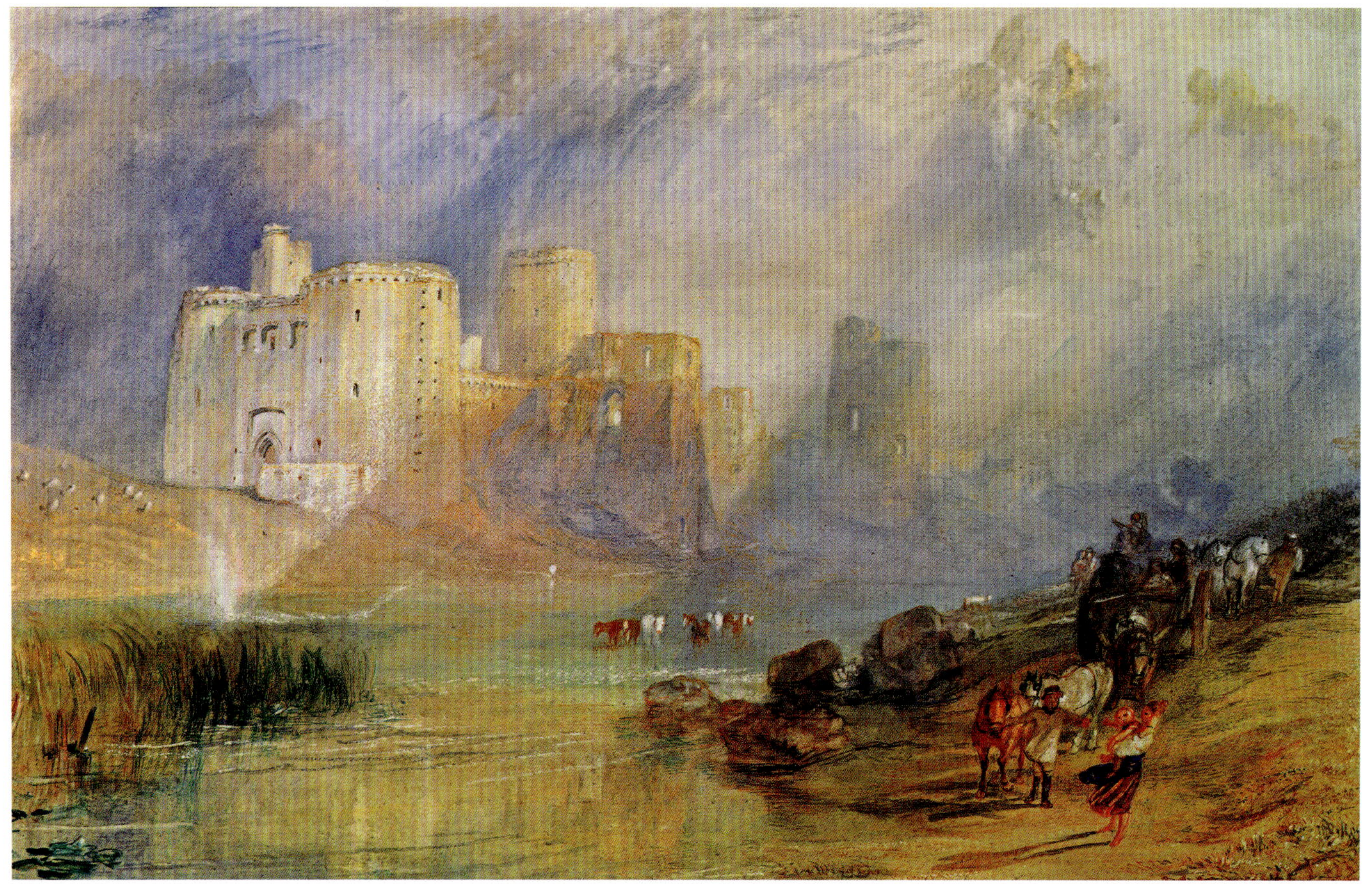

Kidwelly Castle, 1832,
watercolour, Harris
Museum, Preston, UK,
29 x 45cm (11 x 18in)

Turner beautifully captures
the changing light in his
depiction of the castle
during a passing storm.
The juxtaposition of the
complementary colours of
yellow and mauve creates
a mysterious contrast to the
more easily defined sunlit
castle front, adding to the
transient effect. The figures
emphasize the effect, some
still in part shadow, and
others bathed in the
emerging strong sunlight.

Staffa, Fingal's Cave, 1832, oil on canvas, Paul Mellon Collection, Yale Center for British Art, CT, USA, 91 x 121cm (36 x 48in)

Unsold at the Academy exhibition of 1832 despite its good reviews, this picture was purchased by Colonel James Lenox of New York in 1845, designating it the first of Turner's paintings to enter an American collection. Turner decided to go and see the recently discovered Fingal's Cave in Scotland after visiting Sir Walter Scott to discuss suitable illustrations for his *Poetical Works*.

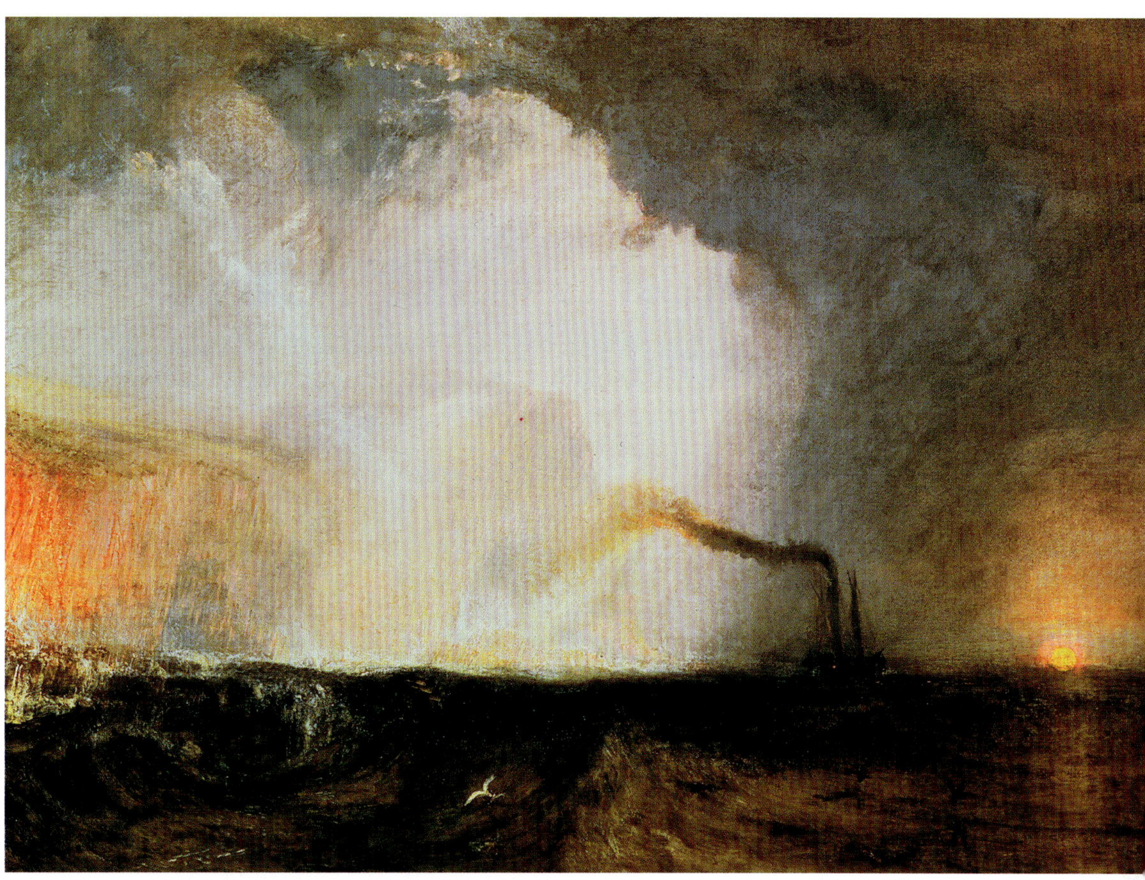

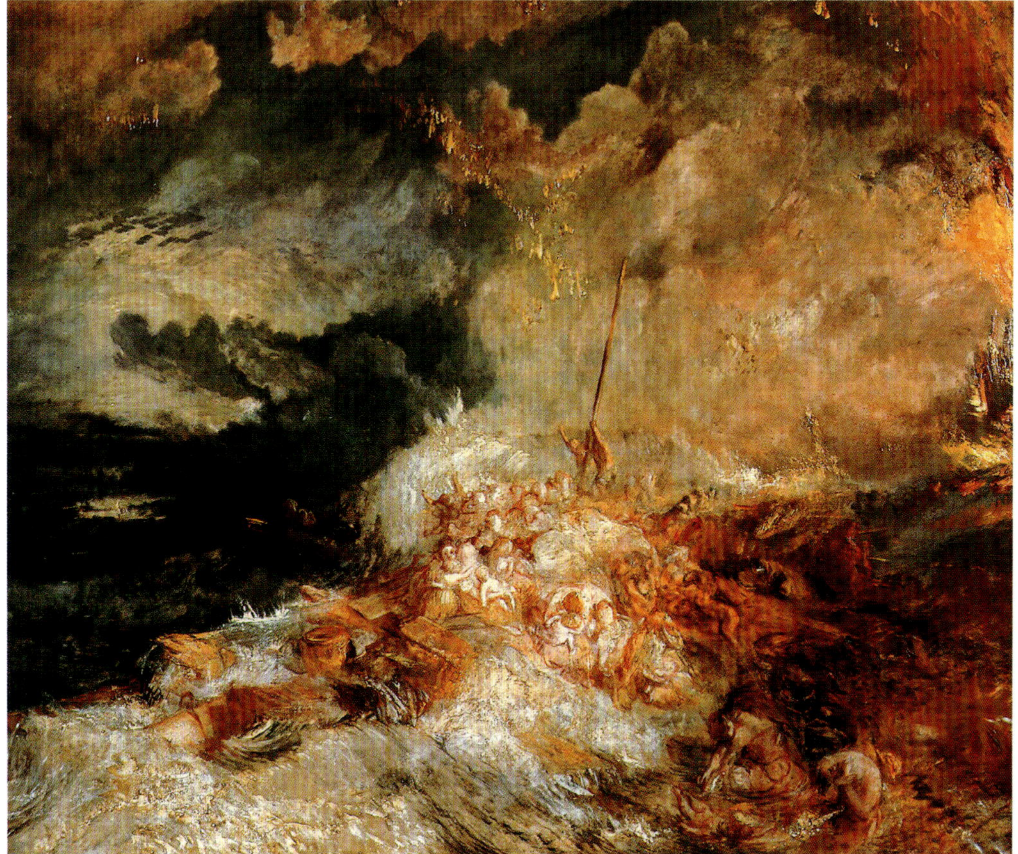

*Fire at Sea, c.*1835, watercolour, Private Collection, dimensions unknown

During 1834, Turner created his Fire at Sea Sketchbook to use as reference material for future seascapes. It is not known what motif he used for these sketches but it seems likely that it was a combination of his travel across the English Channel in July and the burning of the Houses of Parliament in October. The watercolour shown here was made into an engraving after Turner's death.

Design for an Illustration for Scott's "Lady of the Lake", Loch Achray, 1832, pencil, pen, ink and watercolour, Paul Mellon Collection, Yale Center for British Art, CT, USA, 21 x 29cm (8 x 11in)

A delightful vignette used to illustrate Sir Walter Scott's epic poem *The Lady of the Lake*, written in 1810 and based on Arthurian legend, but with the action taking place in the Scottish Highlands as shown here. The poem was very successful and spawned a number of other creative works such as Franz Schubert's *Liederzyklus vom Fräulein vom See*, and Rossini's opera, *La Donna del Lago*.

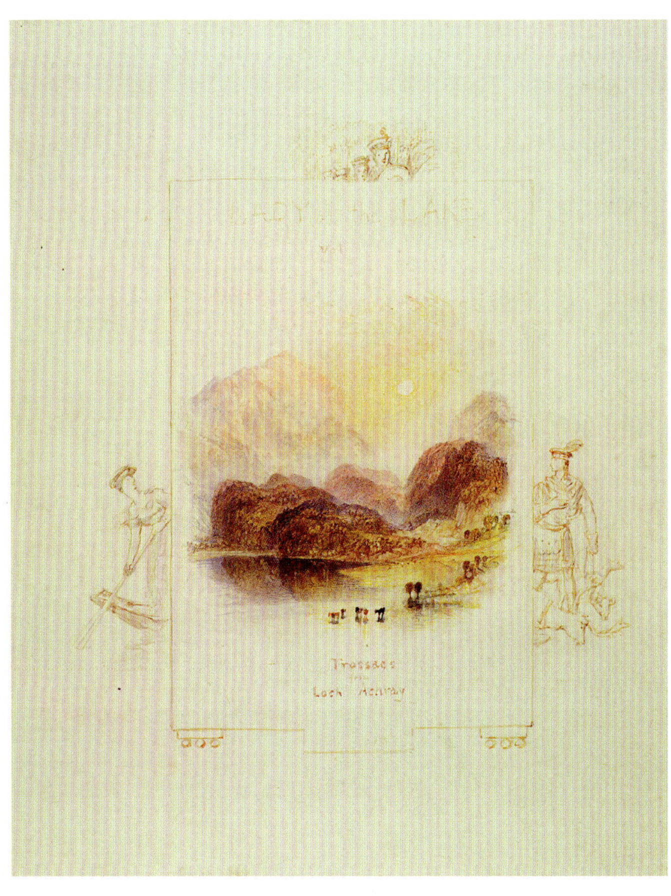

Helvoetsluys: Ships Going out to Sea, 1832, oil on canvas, Tokyo Fuji Art Museum, Japan, 91 x 122cm (36 x 48in)

Although shown at the Royal Academy exhibition of 1832, this painting was not sold until purchased by the whaling entrepreneur, Elhanan Bicknell, in 1844. The scene is at the naval station of Helvoetsluys, in the Netherlands. The port became famous as the departure point for William of Orange when he claimed the English throne in 1688, following the Glorious Revolution. At the time of this painting, a new canal had been built between Helvoetsluys and Rotterdam.

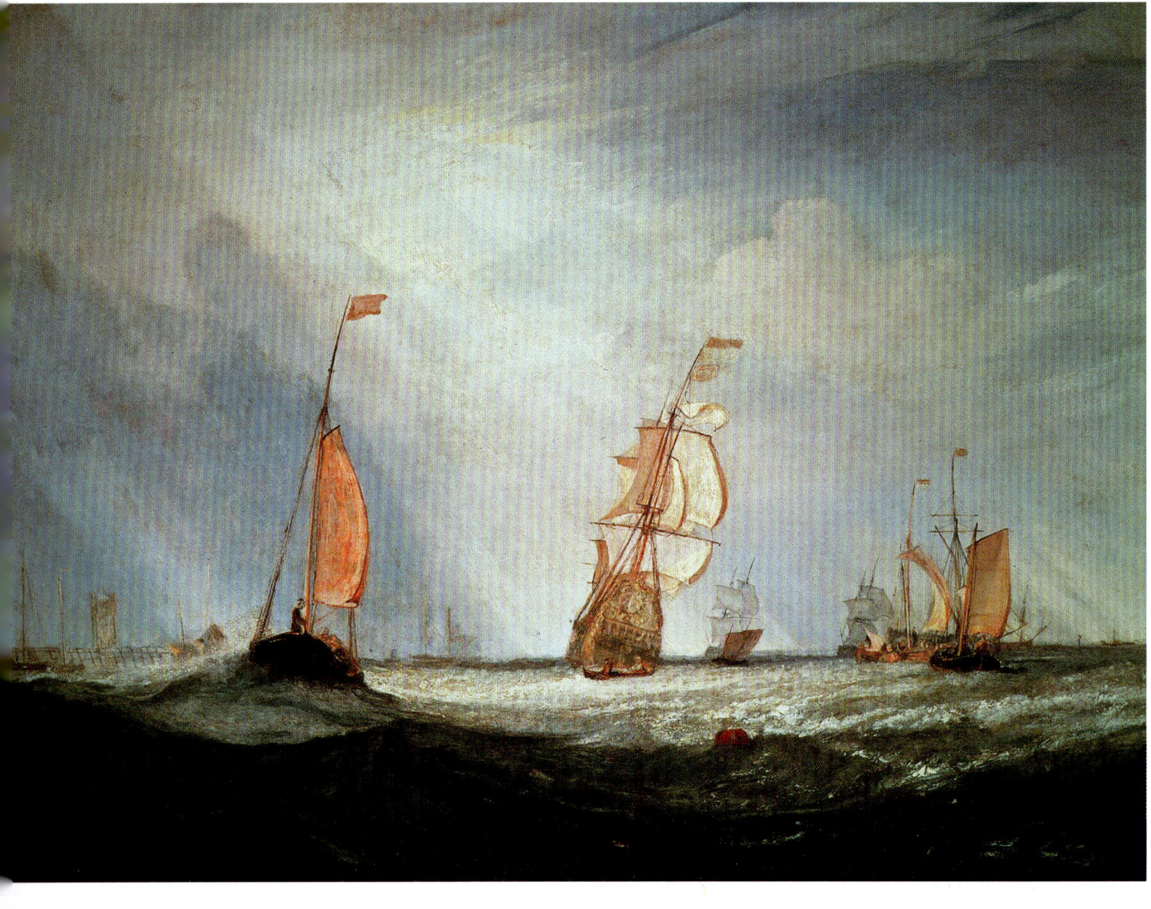

Fort Augustus, Loch Ness,
1833, watercolour,
Private Collection,
13 x 10cm (5 x 4in)

This vignette was used to
illustrate Scott's *Poetical
Works*, depicting the modern
Caledonian Canal and the
infamous Loch Ness behind.
The canal was constructed
between 1803 and 1822 and
linked several lochs to create
a 100km- (62-mile-) long
waterway for commercial
traffic. The Fort was
named after the Duke of
Cumberland, who was
responsible for the merciless
suppression of the Jacobites
in the 18th century.

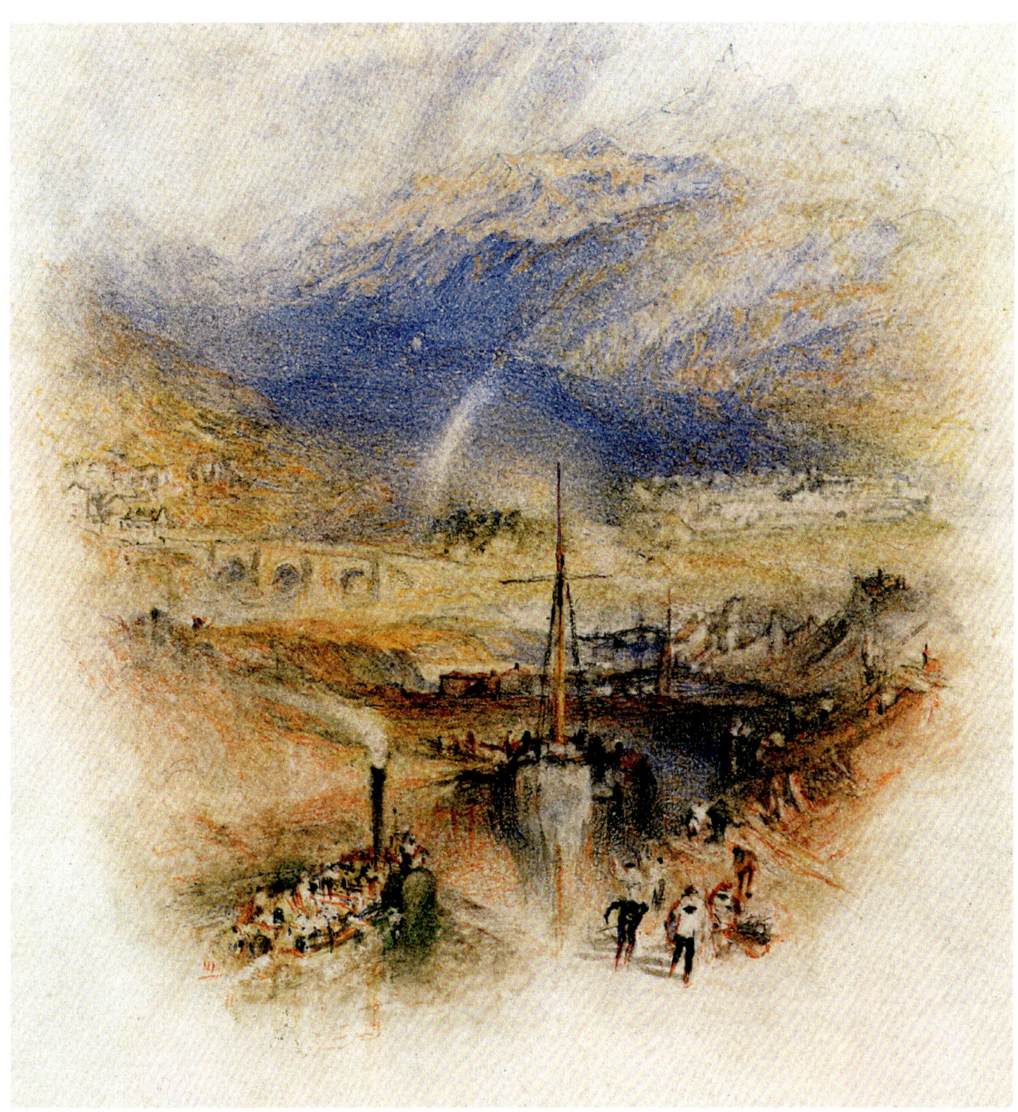

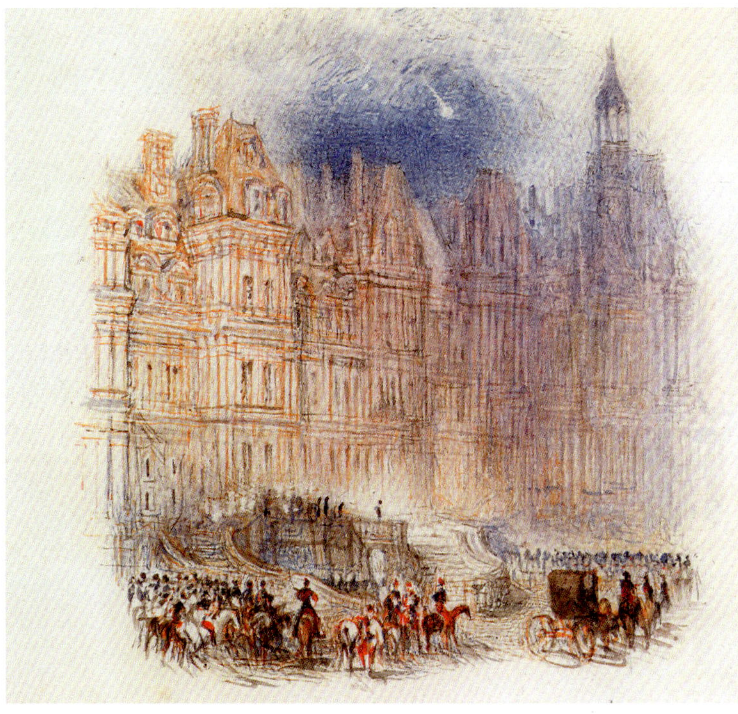

*Fontainebleau: The Departure
of Napoleon*, 1833,
watercolour, Indianapolis
Museum of Art, IN, USA,
13 x 18cm (5 x 7in)

A key moment in the
Napoleonic Wars was the
Treaty of Fontainebleau,
signed in 1814, in which the
emperor lost sovereignty
over France and instead was
granted similar status on the
Mediterranean island of Elba.
Turner captured the scene in
this tiny vignette used to
illustrate Scott's *Poetical
Works*, the writer referring
to him as a "strangely
mingled character".

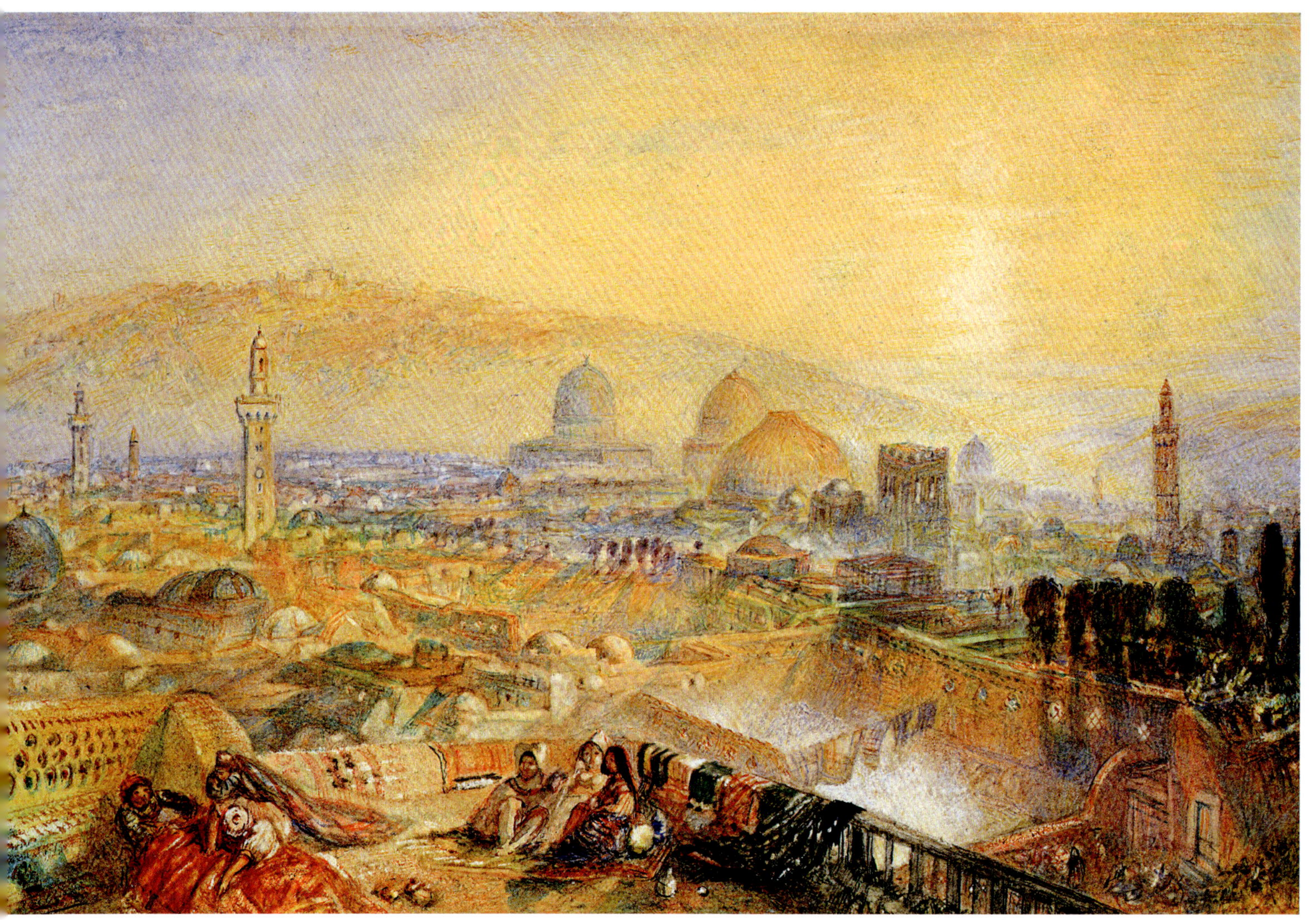

Jerusalem from the Latin Convent, 1832–3,
watercolour,
Private Collection,
14 x 20cm (5½ x 8in)

While in Paris during 1832, Turner met the French painter Eugène Delacroix who, along with several other British and European artists, had a passion for Orientalist painting. Turner never visited the Middle East and was not persuaded to participate in the depiction of Oriental subjects. He did, however, complete a small number of topographical views such as this, probably from studying other Orientalist paintings.

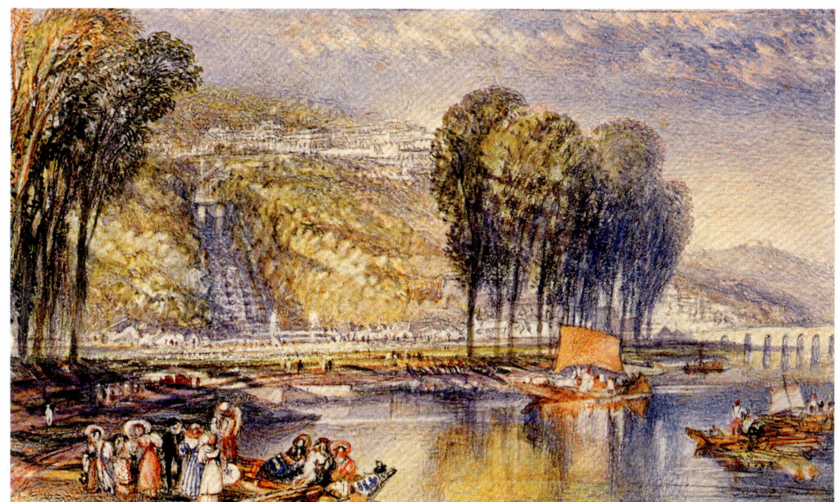

St Cloud, 1832–3,
watercolour, Fitzwilliam
Museum, Cambridge, UK,
9 x 15cm (3½ x 6in)

Another image for Scott's
Life of Napoleon, this
depicts the château where
Napoleon was proclaimed
Emperor of France in 1804.
Earlier it had been the site of
the *coup d'état* by Napoleon
against the French *Directoire*.
The original building dates
from the 17th century.

Ullswater, 1833,
watercolour,
Private Collection,
33 x 43cm (13 x 17in)

Arguably the prettiest if
not the largest of the
English lakes, Ullswater
was a constant source of
inspiration to the Romantic
poet William Wordsworth,
who wrote perhaps his
most famous poem,
Daffodils, after a visit. Turner
has depicted a hot
day, emphasized by the
scantily clad milkmaids in
the foreground and the
need for the cattle to
stay in the water.

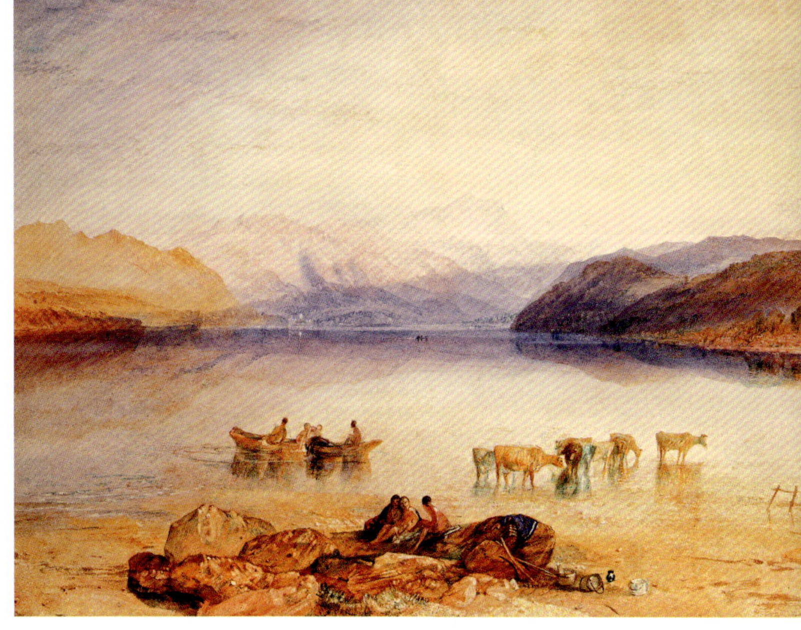

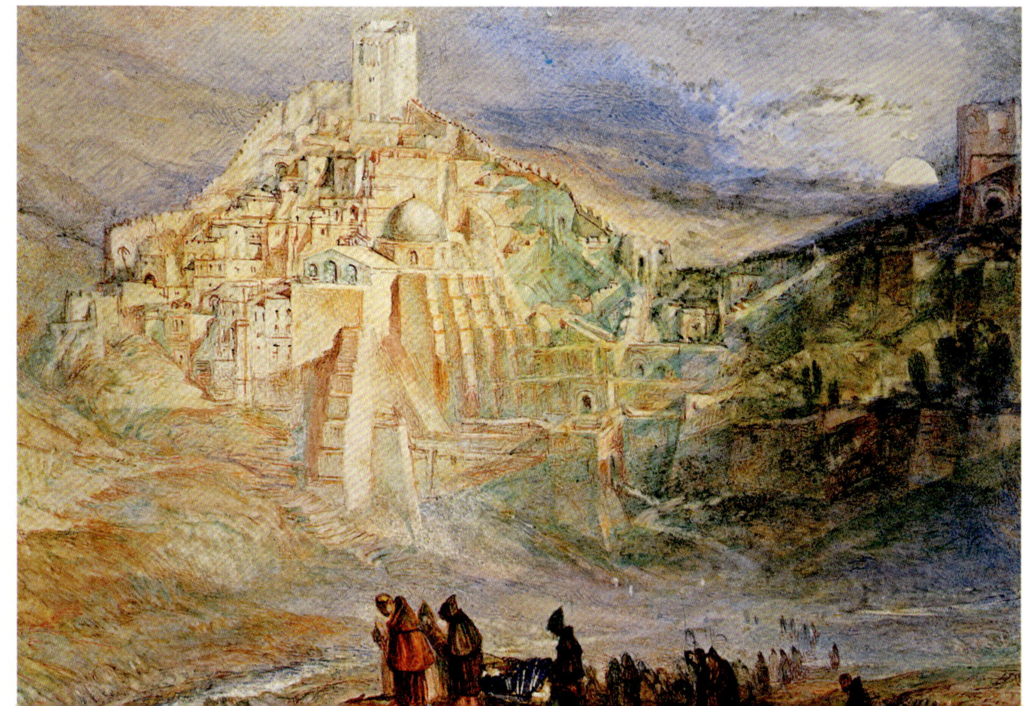

*Wilderness of Engedi and
Convent at Santa Saba*,
1832–4, watercolour,
Private Collection,
15 x 20cm (6 x 8in)

Founded in the 5th century,
this monastery is one of the
oldest in existence and
despite its name is a male
only order. This watercolour,
along with others by Turner
and his contemporaries, was
made into a print that
contributed to *Landscape
Illustrations of the Bible*,
published in 1836.

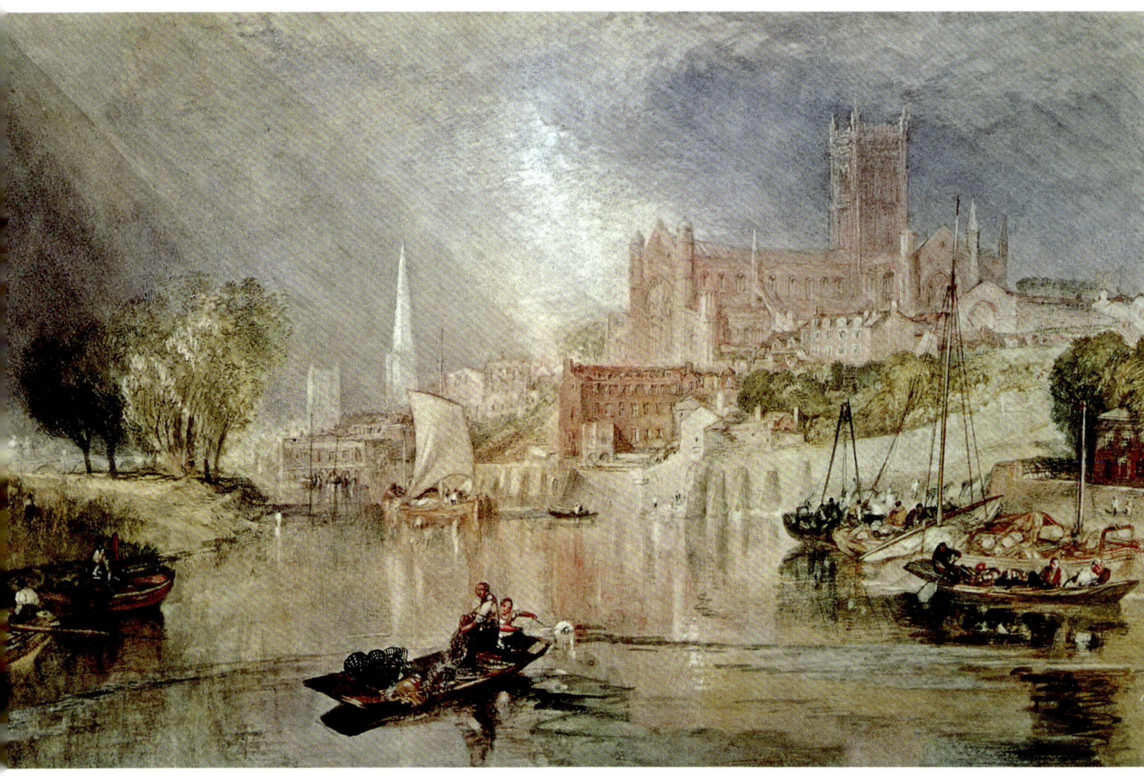

Worcester, 1834, watercolour and bodycolour, British Library, London, UK, 29 x 44cm (11 x 17in)

From a series of sketches he made on a tour of this region in 1830, Turner has worked up a magnificent watercolour with the cathedral illuminated by the sun after a storm. Turner's picture is not, however, just concerned with historical anecdote despite Worcester's heritage. The town was now part of the Industrial Revolution, with its famous porcelain factory established in 1750 and the opening of the Worcester and Birmingham Canal in 1815.

Abbeville, 1834, watercolour, Private Collection, 11 x 14cm (4 x 5½in)

This vignette was created as one of the illustrations for *The Prose Works of Sir Walter Scott* published between 1834 and 1836. It depicts the main church of St Vulphran, erected in the 15th century, a monument to Gothic architecture. The towers of the church dominate the townscape, which Turner uses to great effect, dwarfing the peasant women sitting in the market square dressed in traditional Normandy style hats.

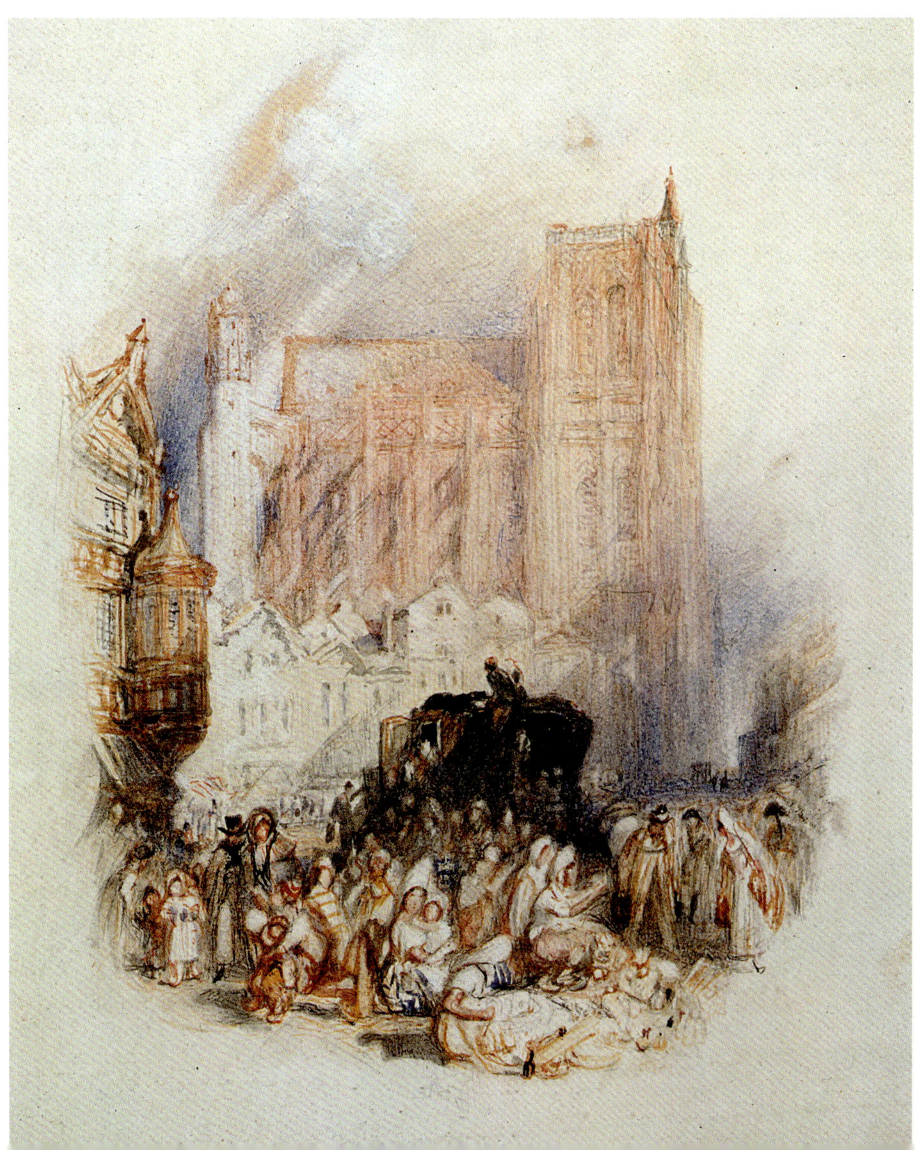

Flint Castle, North Wales,
1834, watercolour, National
Galleries of Wales, Cardiff,
UK, 28 x 40cm (11 x 16in)

For the first edition of his
Liber Studiorum, Turner
produced an etching of Flint
Castle. He repeated the
motif as a watercolour in
the 1820s, but this scene of
shrimp fishermen in the
morning has to be one of
the finest examples of the
mature style he developed
in the 1830s, incorporating
an astute use of colour.

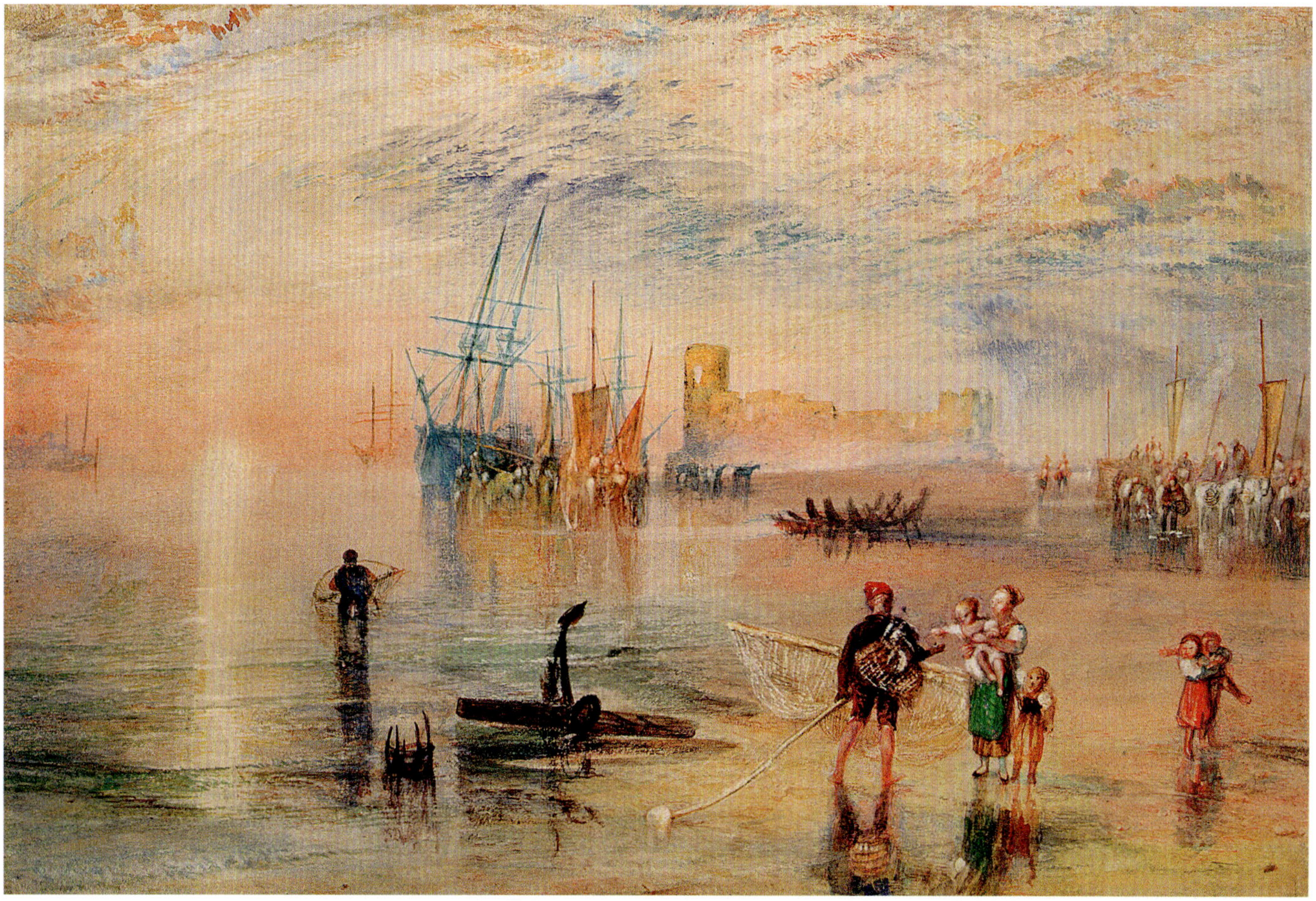

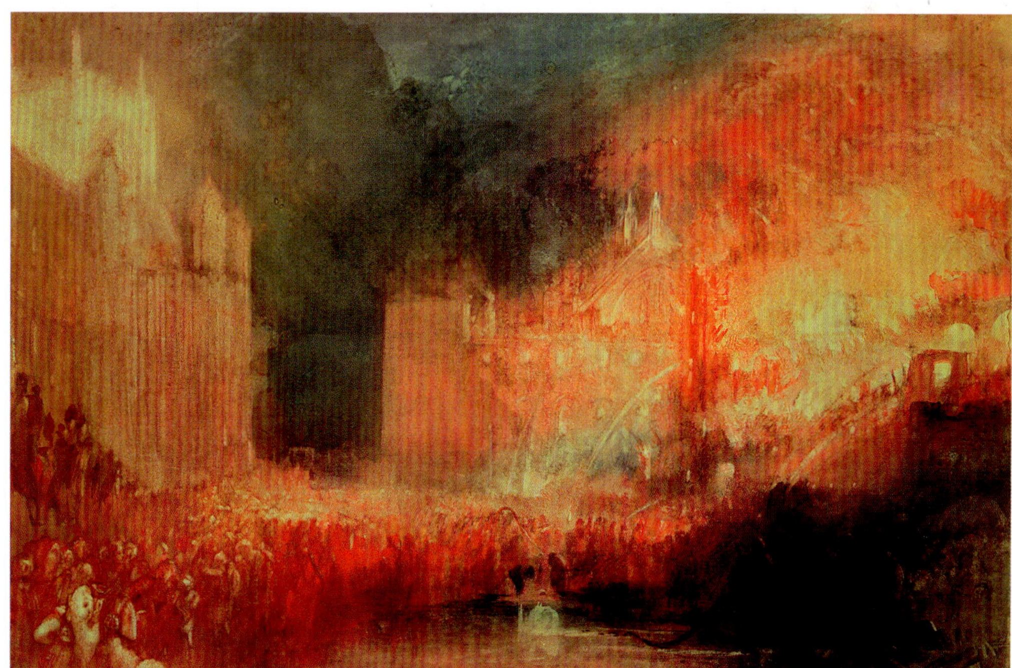

*The Burning of the Houses of
Parliament,* 1834,
watercolour,
British Museum, London, UK,
30 x 44cm (12 x 17in)

Turner spent most of the
night at the scene of
the destruction of the Palace
of Westminster, sketching the
details of the event and filling
two sketchbooks with
drawings, some coloured. He
was one of the thousands of
people who turned out to
see the spectacle, which
Turner has recorded here,
with figures silhouetted
against the intense heat and
brightness of the fire.

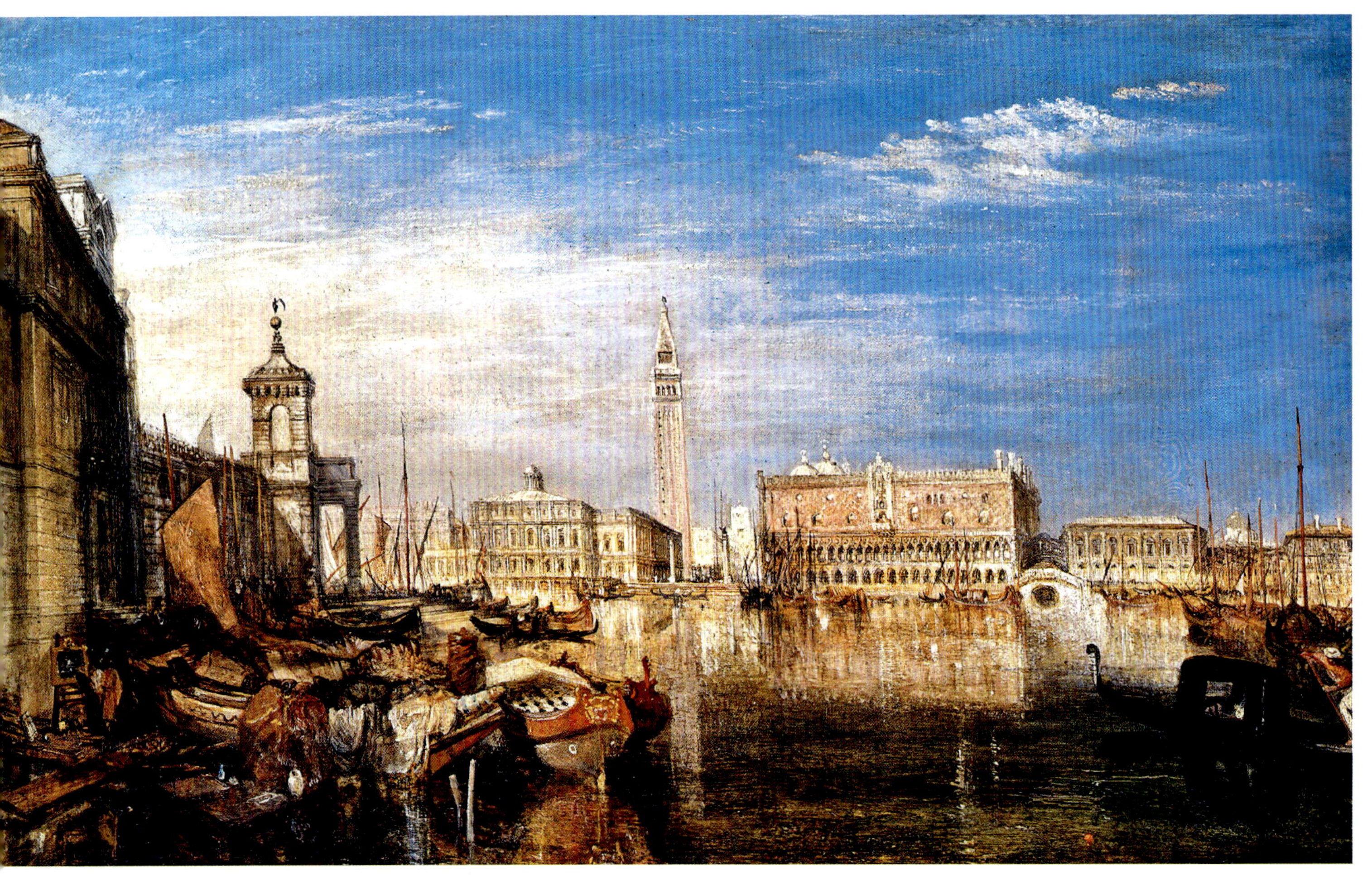

Bridge of Sighs, Ducal Palace, and Custom House: Canaletti Painting, 1833, oil on mahogany, Tate Britain, London, UK, 51 x 83cm (20 x 33in)

As homage to the great 18th-century Italian artist, Turner has included him at his easel on the left side of his own painting.

Aligning himself with a master of the motif in this way demonstrates Turner's belief in his own genius. This was the first of his oil paintings of Venice despite the fact that his first trip there was in 1819; he spent the intervening 12 years perfecting a watercolour technique that adequately represented the extraordinary Venetian light.

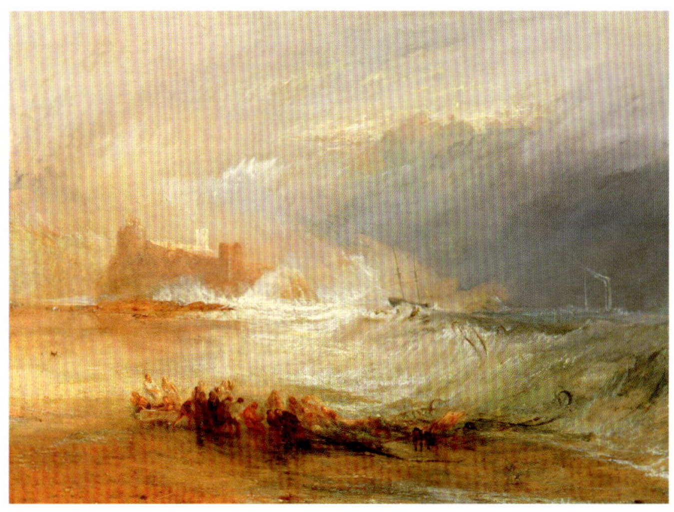

Wreckers – Coast of Northumberland, with a Steamboat Assisting a Ship off Shore, 1834, oil on canvas, Paul Mellon Collection, Yale Center for British Art, CT, USA, 90 x 121cm (35 x 48in)

The exact event that inspired this painting is not known, but it may have been one that Turner witnessed. The castle in the background is probably Dunstanborough, in an area that Turner had been visiting and recording since 1798. Wrecking – the taking of goods from a shipwreck site – was often a lucrative activity for economically deprived coastal areas in Britain.

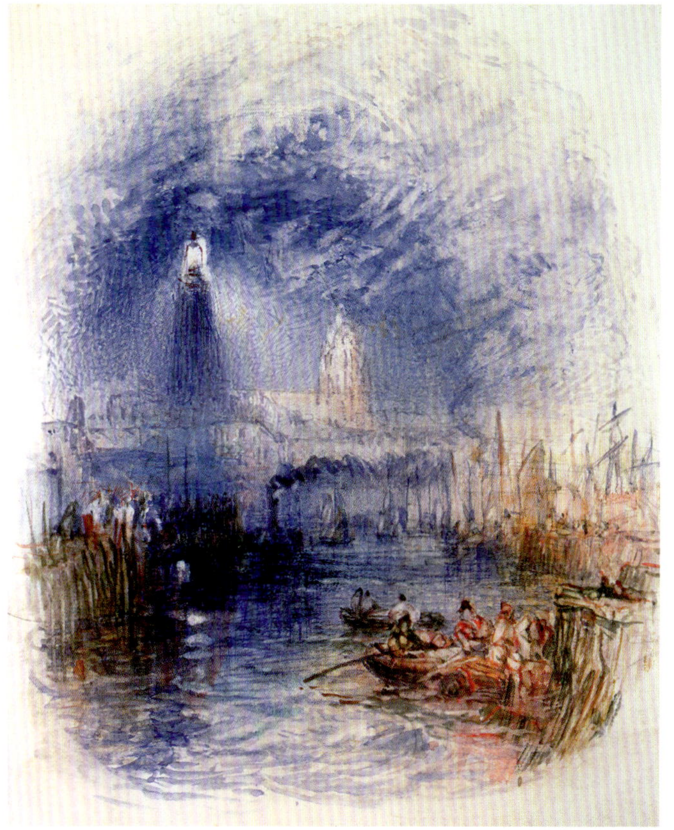

Calais, 1834–6, intaglio print, Private Collection, 15 x 29cm (6 x 11in)

One of two French vignettes made for *The Prose Works of Sir Walter Scott* (the other being Abbeville), this print shows perfectly the benefits of tonal engraving when depicting a night scene such as this. The watch tower lights eerily pick out the figures in the rowing boats, and highlight the smoke belching from the tugboat. This was replaced a decade later by a new lighthouse. In the distance is the Gothic church of Notre Dame.

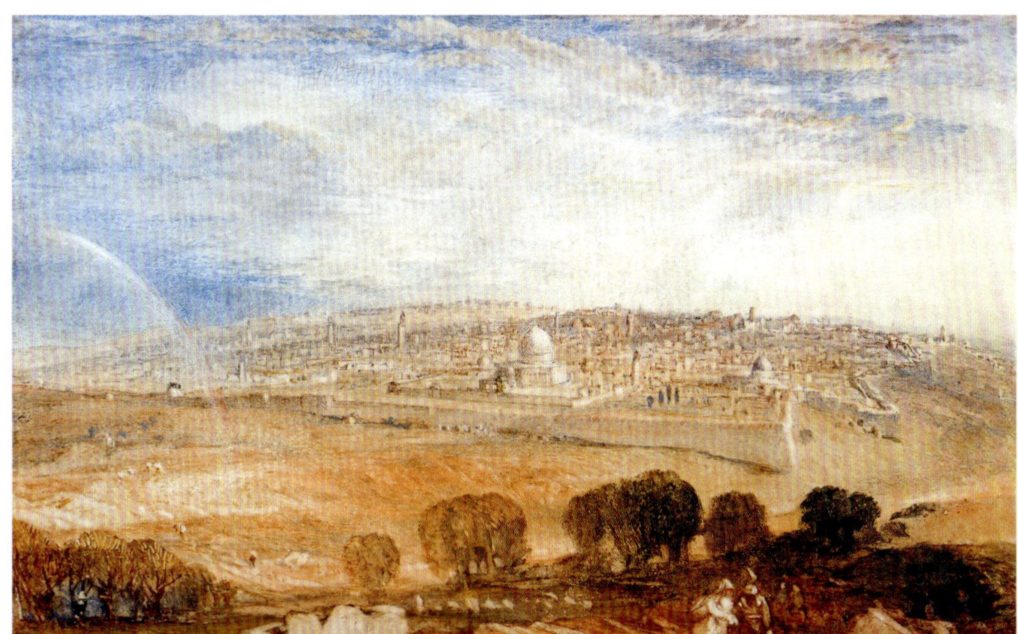

Jerusalem from the Mount of Olives, c.1835, watercolour, Israel Museum, Jerusalem, Israel, 137 x 250cm (54 x 98in)

Intended for use in *Landscape Illustrations of the Bible*, this painting must have been created using references, since Turner had not visitd the Holy Land. The view is from the Mount of Olives, a site of religious significance.

Oxford from North Hinksey,
1835–40, watercolour,
Manchester Art Gallery, UK,
35 x 52cm (14 x 20in)

Turner had been visiting
Oxford since the 1780s, yet
he still managed to find
something new to say in his
work of the 1830s with a
series of sparkling and even
daring watercolours of the
city and its environs. This
view of the city of "dreaming
spires" is from the village of
North Hinksey, to the west.
In the centre of the
background, the dome of
the Radcliffe Camera can
just be seen.

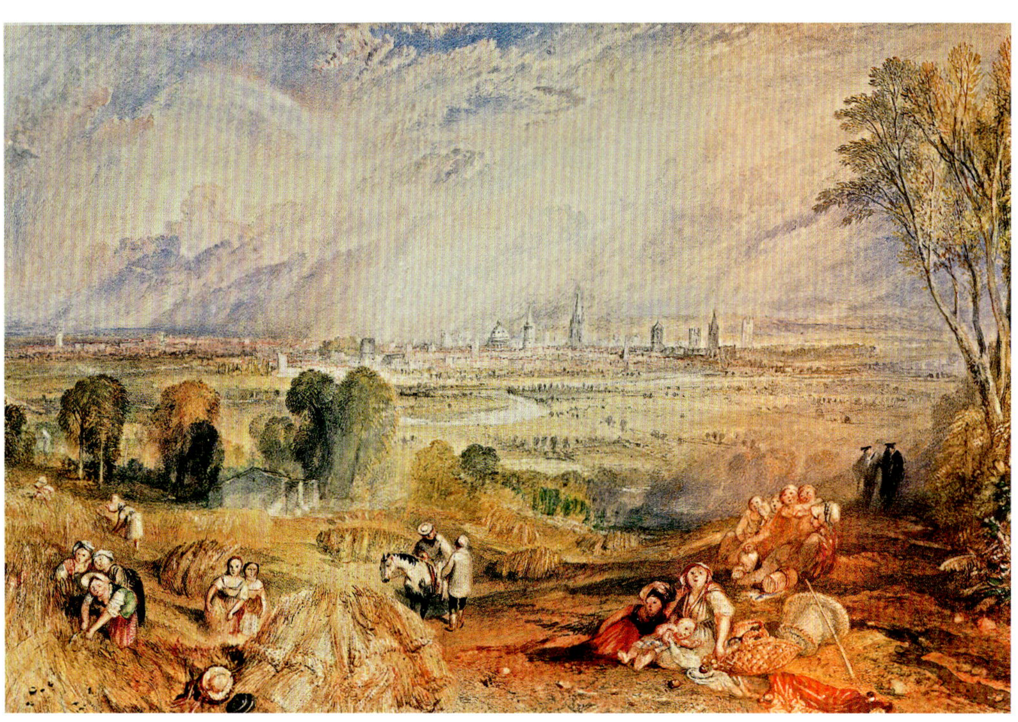

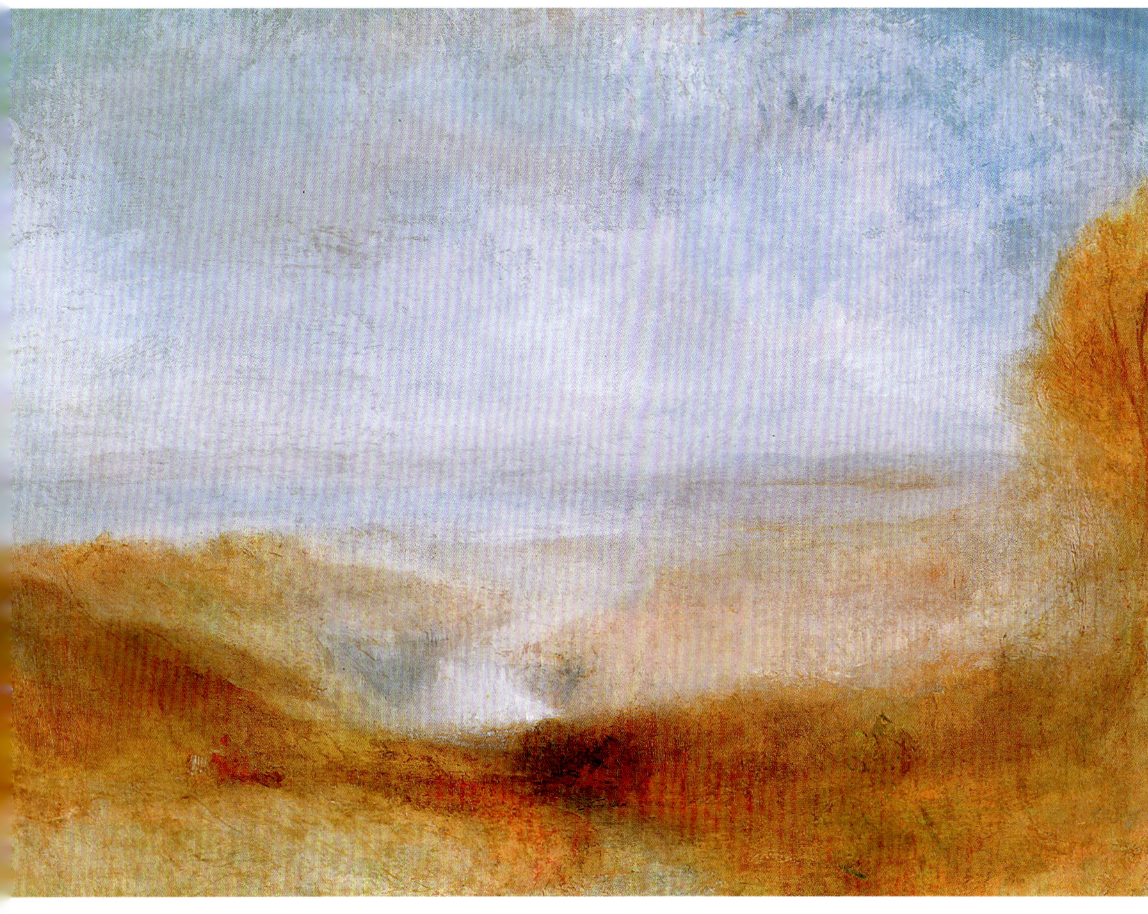

*Landscape with a River and a
Bay in the Distance*, 1835–40,
oil on canvas,
Musée du Louvre, Paris,
93 x 123cm (37 x 48in)

Unusually this oil painting
was not executed for
exhibition purposes or to
satisfy a commission,
suggesting that Turner
intended leaving the work to
the nation as part of his
bequest. In the event it was
acquired by M. Camille
Groult sometime in the late
19th century and displayed
in an exhibition in Paris as an
example of the English
School of Painting. It was
subsequently admired
by Camille Pissarro and
his son Lucien.

A Sailing Boat off Deal, c.1835, oil on millboard, National Museum and Gallery of Wales, Cardiff, UK, 23 x 30cm (9 x 12in)

Turner is supposed to have given this picture, along with another of similar subject and date, to his landlady in Margate, Mrs Sophia Booth. The artist was making frequent visits to this part of the Kent coast at this time. The painting is much looser in style than previous versions and the use of millboard as a ground suggests that this was a preparatory or experimental sketch.

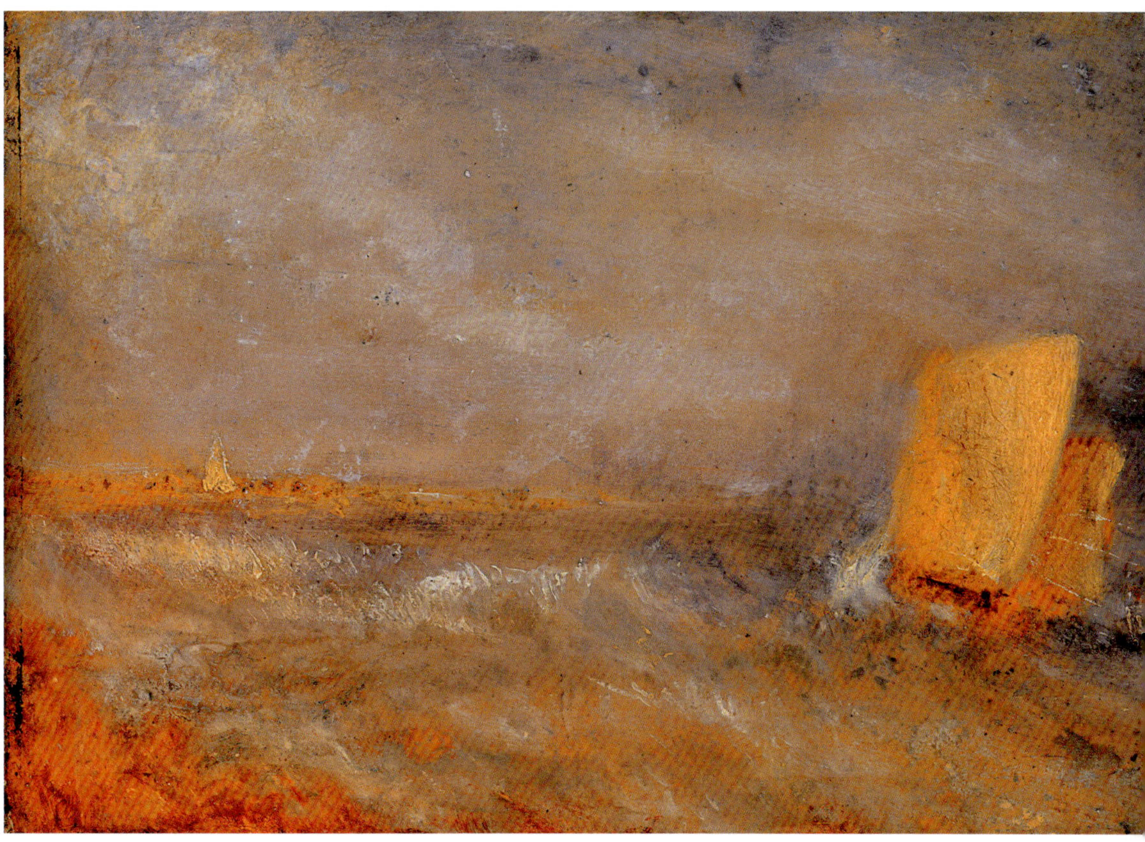

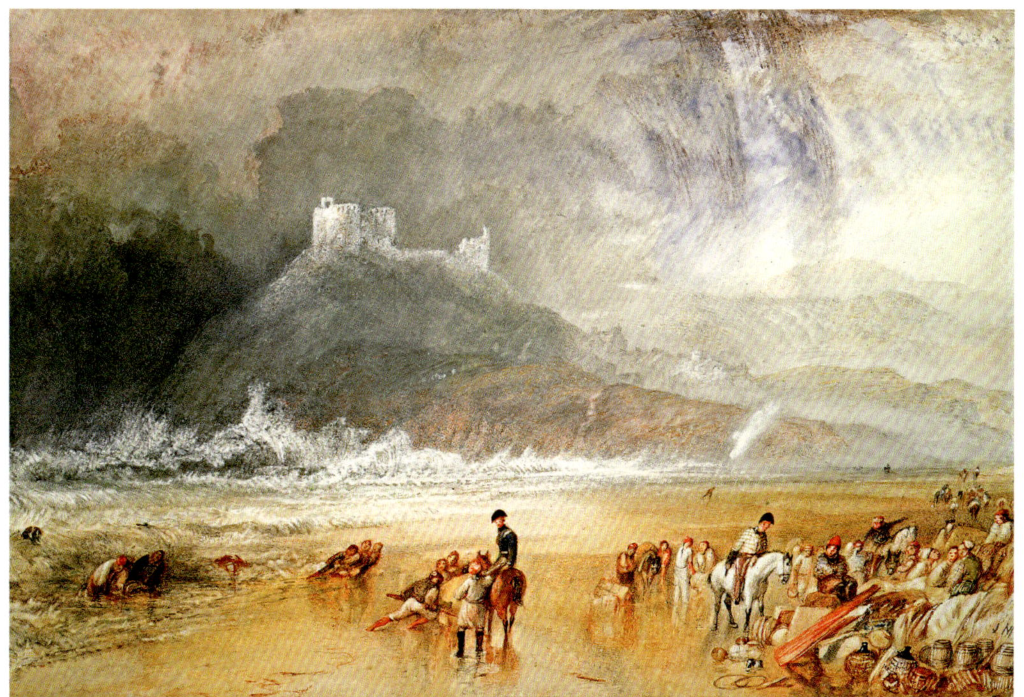

Criccieth Castle, 1835, watercolour, British Museum, London, UK, 29 x 43cm (11 x 17in)

This castle was strategically important during the war between England and Wales in the 13th century, being the stronghold of the last native Prince, Llywelyn ap Gruffydd. Turner has depicted the castle on a higher mound than in actuality to provide a backdrop for his portrayal of a shipwreck scene, in which an officer on horseback is haranguing the victims.

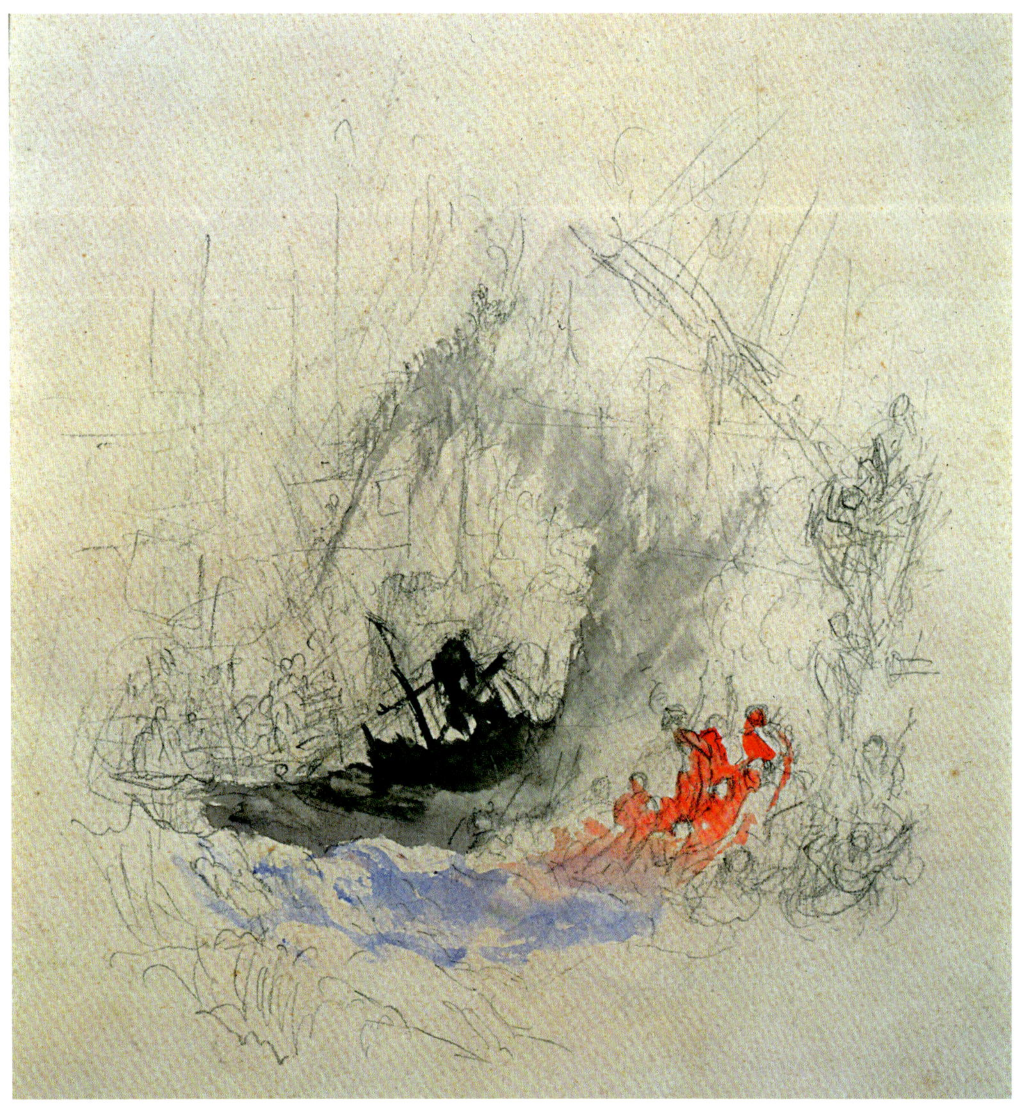

Fire at Sea, a Design for a Vignette, 1835, pencil and watercolour, Private Collection, 21 x 18cm (8 x 7in)

A swirling vortex, as found in much of Turner's later work, makes its appearance in this 'Design for a Vignette'. It was executed at a time when the artist created a series for *The Keepsake*, a popular periodical. The fully worked-up version of this depicts a ship on fire with a group of women in the water pleading for help.

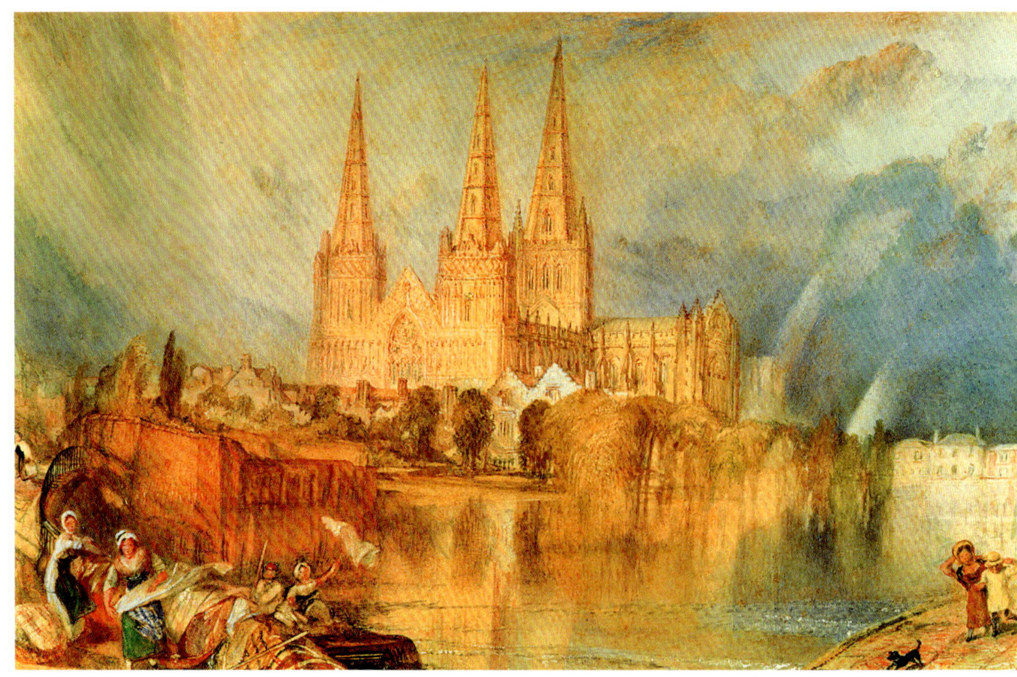

Lichfield, 1835, watercolour, Private Collection, 29 x 44cm (11 x 17in)

Unfortunately this view of Lichfield was never engraved as part of the *Picturesque Views* series. Turner has chosen to bathe this post-storm view in a golden light, the central focus being the magnificent cathedral. It is one of the earliest Gothic cathedrals in England, begun in 1195, and replacing the heavier built Norman church. It is most notable for being the only cathedral in England with three spires.

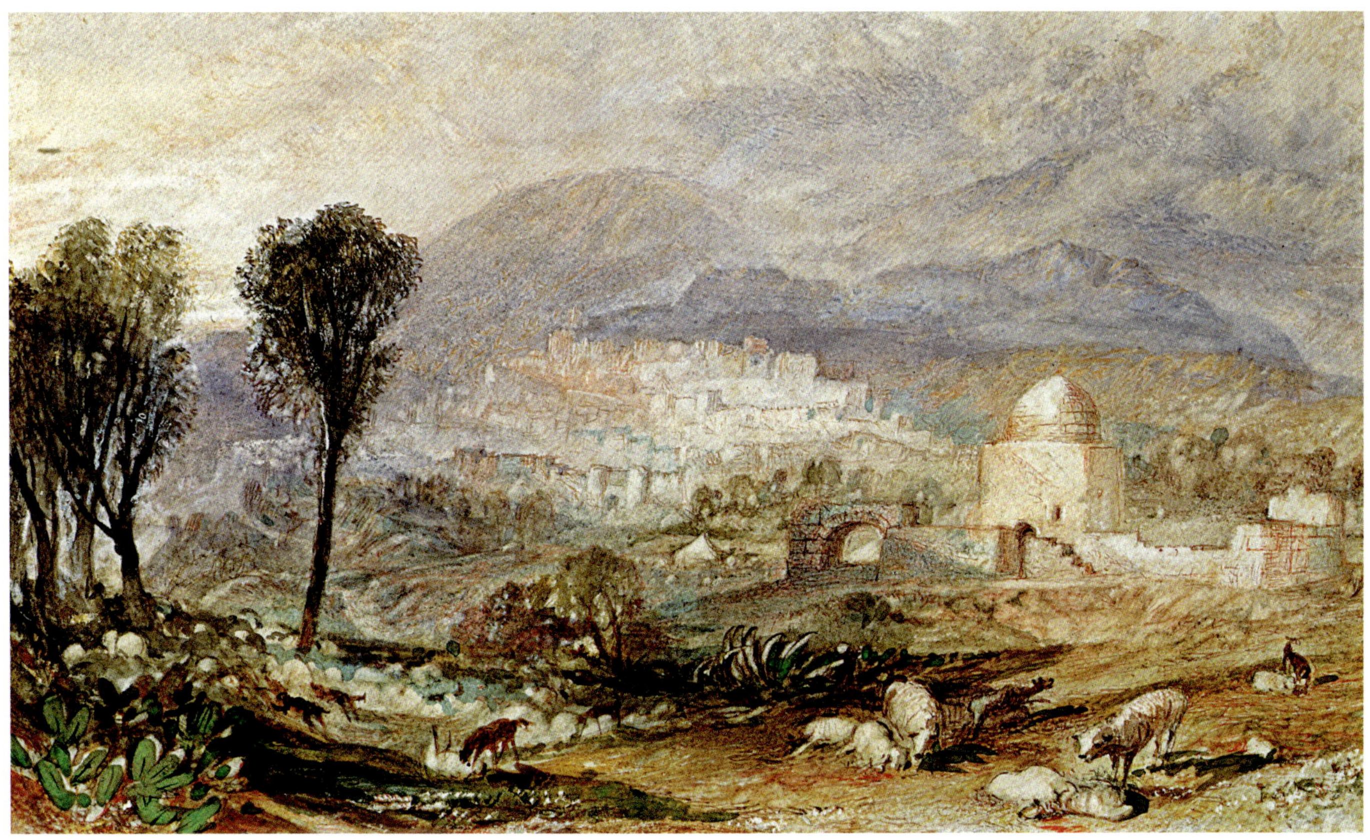

Rachel's Tomb at Ramah, 1835, watercolour, Blackburn Museum, Lancashire, UK, 14 x 19cm (5½ x 7½in)

Turner executed a number of paintings from his imagination, of suitable subjects for *Landscape Illustrations of the Bible*, a venture by the publisher John Murray. Turner must have seen engravings of the site to create this accurate watercolour. The site has been one of pilgrimage for more than 3,000 years, particularly for infertile women praying that Rachel will intercede with God on their behalf.

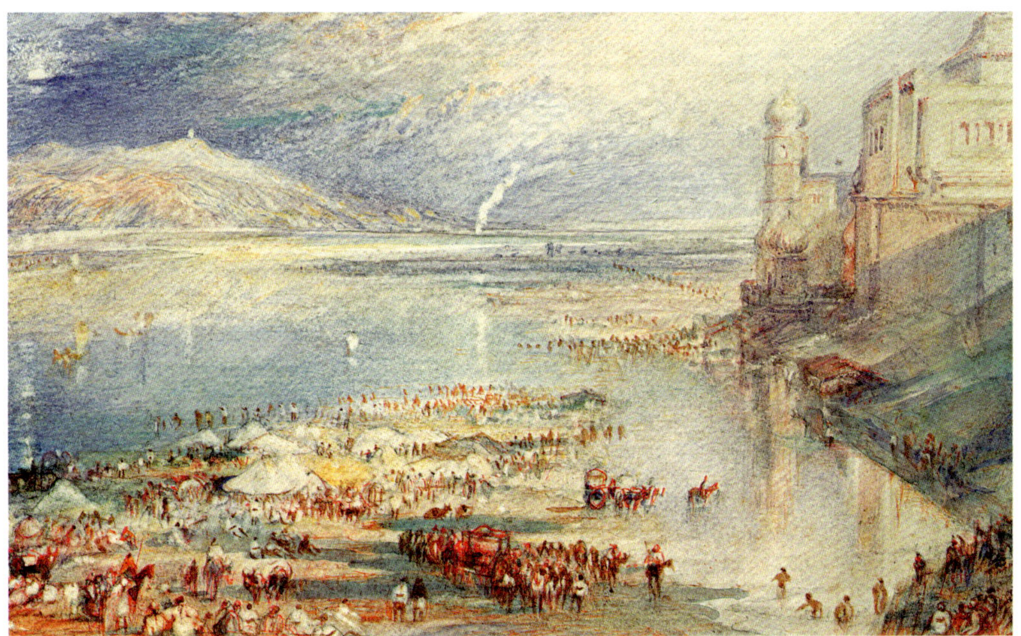

Part of the Ghaut at Hurdwar, 1835, watercolour and bodycolour, Leeds Art Gallery, UK, 14 x 21cm (5½ x 8in)

From Turner's own imagination, this wonderfully crafted picture depicts the steps down to the sacred River Ganges at Hurdwar in India. Hurdwar is one of the most sacred Hindu sites, one of four, supposedly, where the elixir of immortality, Amrita, was accidentally spilled into the river. This made the city a site of pilgrimage.

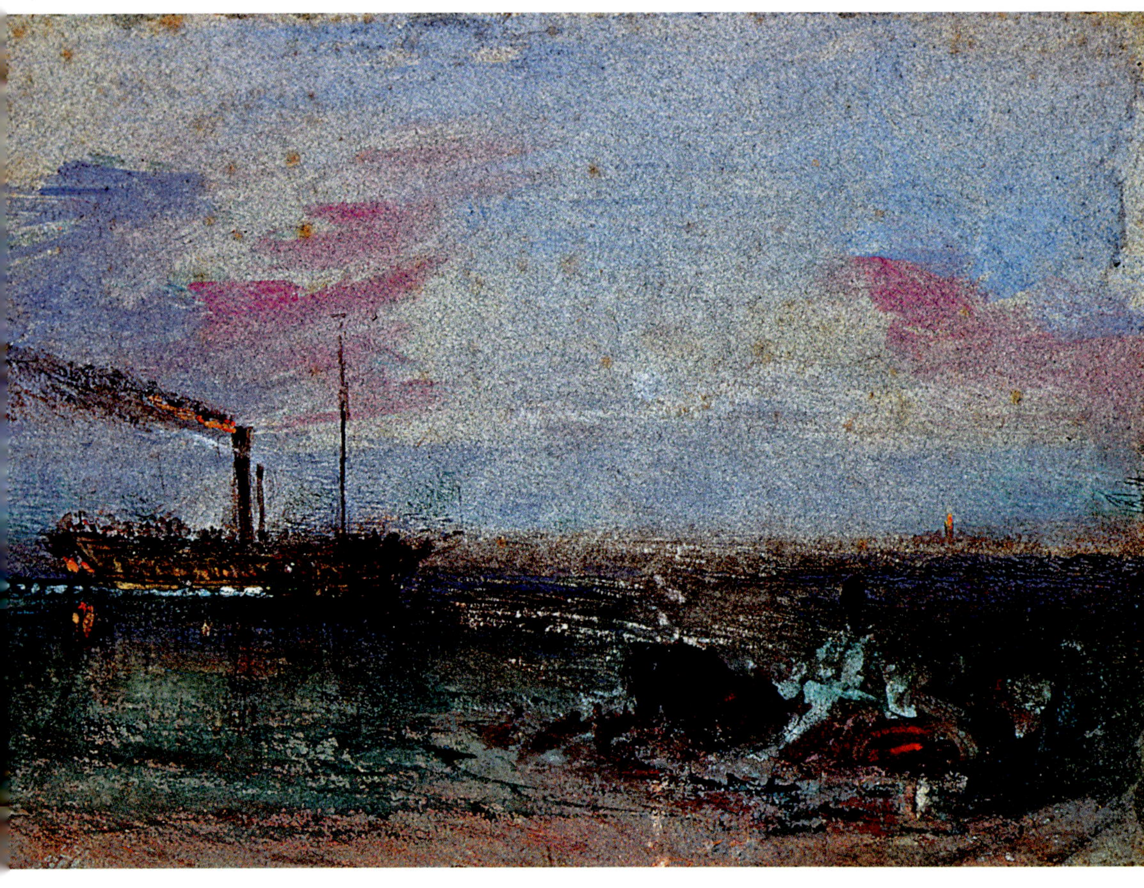

Seascape with a Boat, c.1835,
watercolour,
chalk and bodycolour,
Sheffield Art Gallery, UK,
14 x 19cm (5½ x 7½in)

The indistinct figures in the foreground force the viewer to engage with the packet boat at sea, its chimney belching smoke as it makes rapid headway along the coast. These ships were used to carry mail, cargo and sometimes passengers around the coast of Britain. This one is also equipped with a sail that can be unfurled at sea when additional speed is needed.

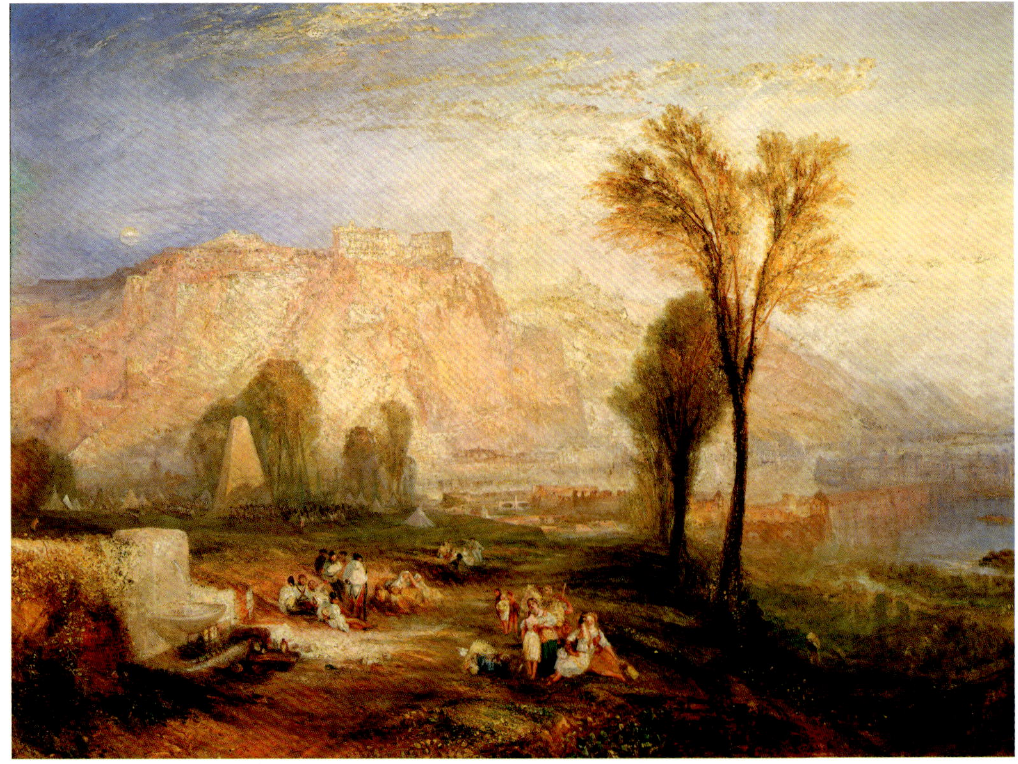

The Bright Stone of Honour (Ehrenbreitstein) and Tomb of Marceau, from Byron's 'Childe Harold', 1835, oil on canvas, Private Collection, 93 x 123cm (37 x 48in)

Turner revisited the site of this tomb near Koblenz in 1834, ostensibly to look for other views for a different project. This painting was a commission from the engraver John Pye, who held on to the picture for several years in order to perfect the subsequent engraving for an illustration of Byron's epic, and sometimes autobiographical, narrative poem, *Childe Harold's Pilgrimage*.

Music Party, East Cowes Castle, c.1835, oil on canvas, Tate Britain, London, UK, 90 x 121cm (35 x 48in)

The location for this unfinished painting is likely to have been the Octagon Room at East Cowes Castle on the Isle of Wight. Turner stayed there in 1827 as the guest of the architect John Nash and his wife, who was an accomplished musician. Turner made many sketches of family life at the castle, and it is possible that he painted this as a tribute to Nash, who died in 1835.

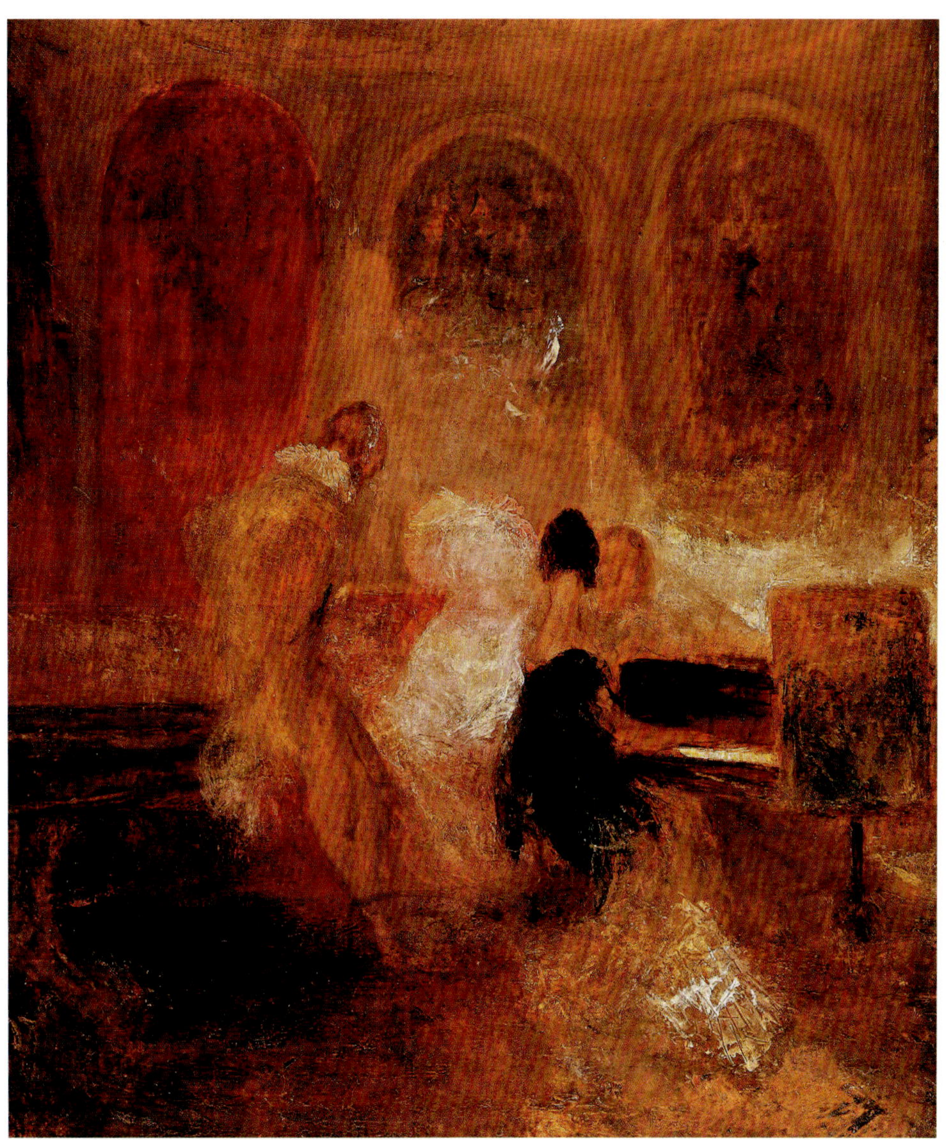

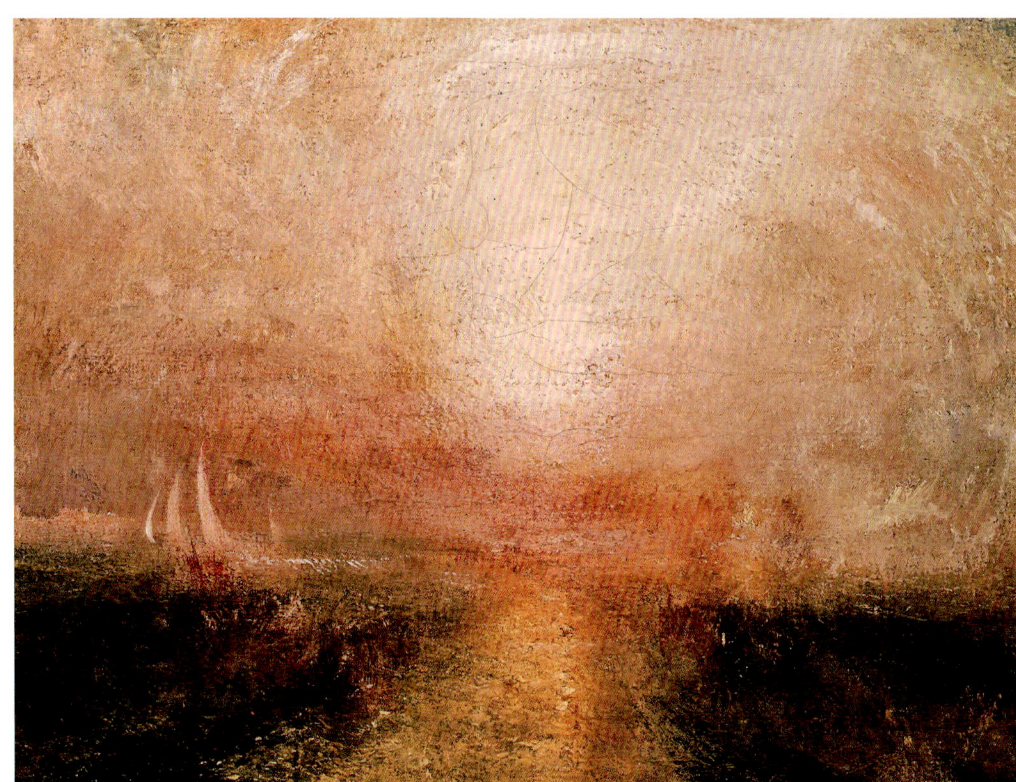

Yacht Approaching the Coast, 1840, oil on canvas, Tate Britain, London, UK, 102 x 142cm (40 x 56in)

The title and the coastline give no real clue as to the location of this scene, although a closer examination of the painting reveals that a series of gondola-like shapes have been over-painted, suggesting that the city in the distance is possibly Venice. The picture was never shown in Turner's lifetime and became a part of his bequest in 1856.

Brenva Glacier, Val d'Aosta,
1836, watercolour,
Private Collection,
19 x 30cm (7½ x 12in)

Brenva Glacier is on the east face of Mont Blanc, thus on the Italian side of the Alps. The mountain, the highest in Europe, had been climbed for the first time at the end of the 18th century, and the site thereafter received many visitors on both the French and the Italian sides. The 'ownership' of the summit has been debated and argued over ever since.

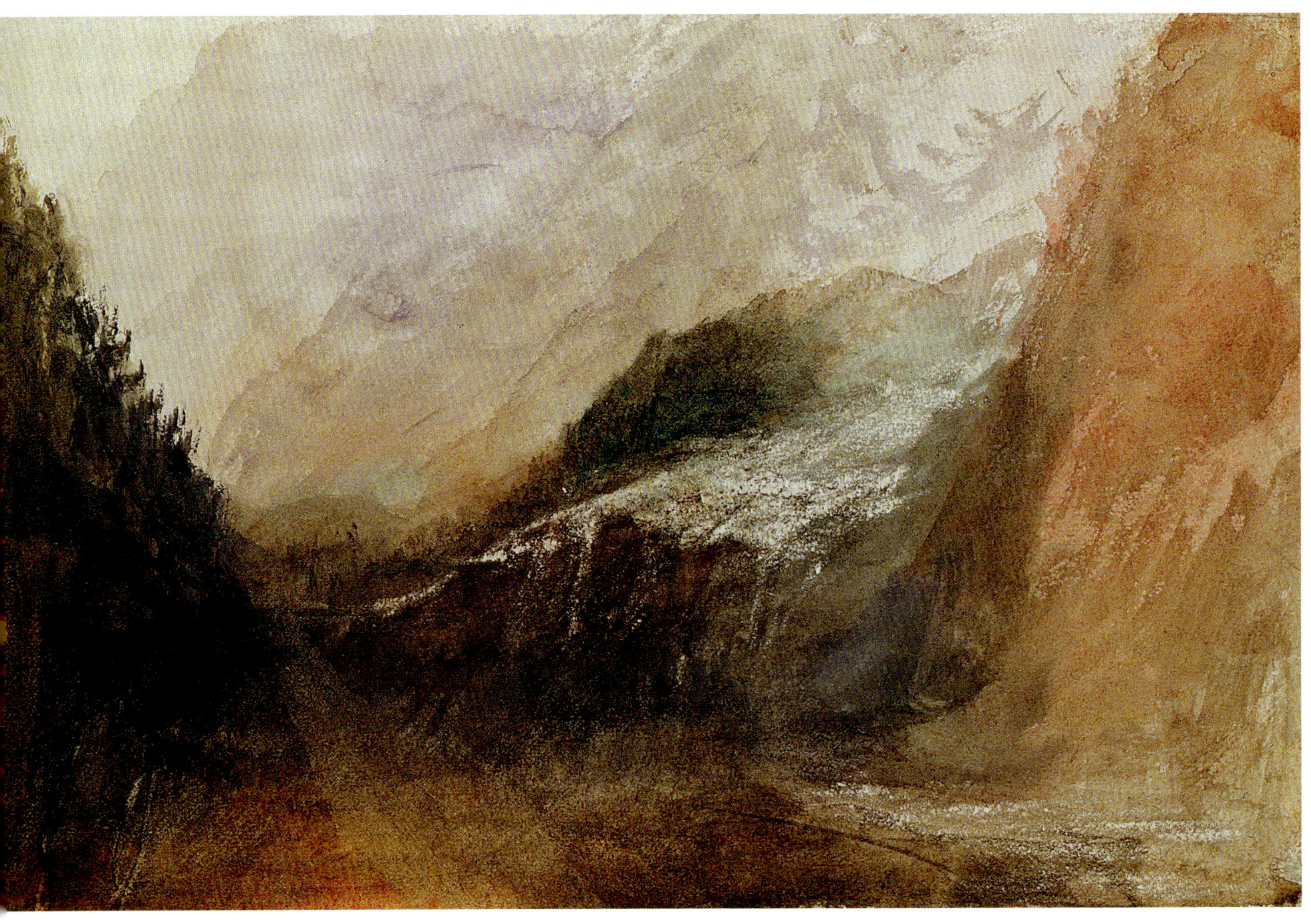

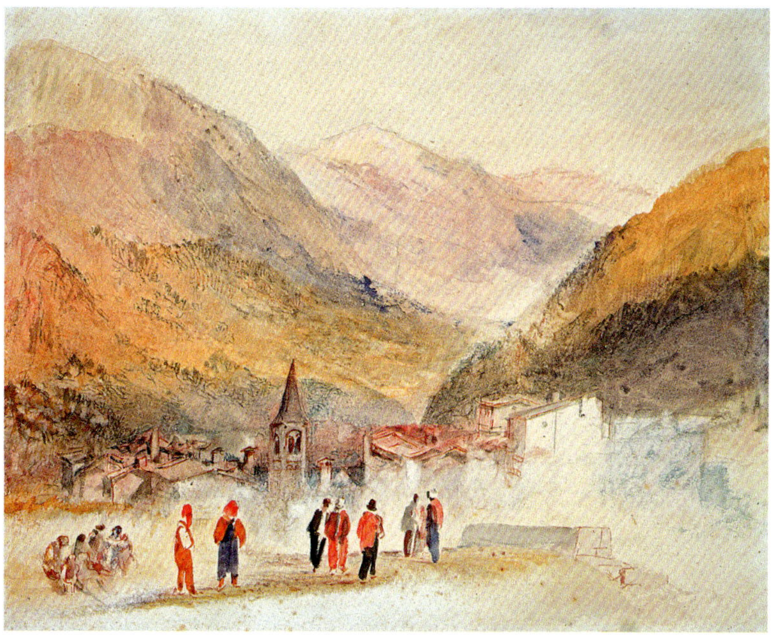

Pré-Saint-Didier, 1836, watercolour, Fitzwilliam Museum, Cambridge, UK, 23 x 28cm (9 x 11in)

This delightful watercolour depicts the height of summer with no snow on the top of the mountains in the town of Pré-Saint-Didier, which, despite its French sounding name, is in the Val d'Aosta in Italy. Turner has shown the popularity of the venue with tourists visiting the town, which is set high up in the mountain range at over 1,000m (3,280ft).

St Michael's Mount, 1836, watercolour, University of Liverpool, UK, 31 x 44cm (12 x 17in)

The castle is on an island, accessible only at low tide. Its Picturesque quality provided a perfect backdrop to the main theme of Turner's watercolour: wreckers trying to salvage timbers from a shipwreck. The artist has created a vortex shape that frames another vulnerable-looking ship.

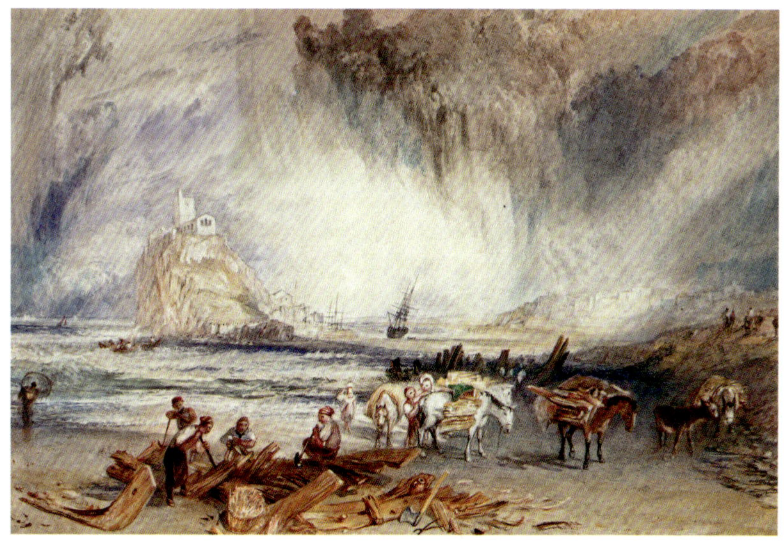

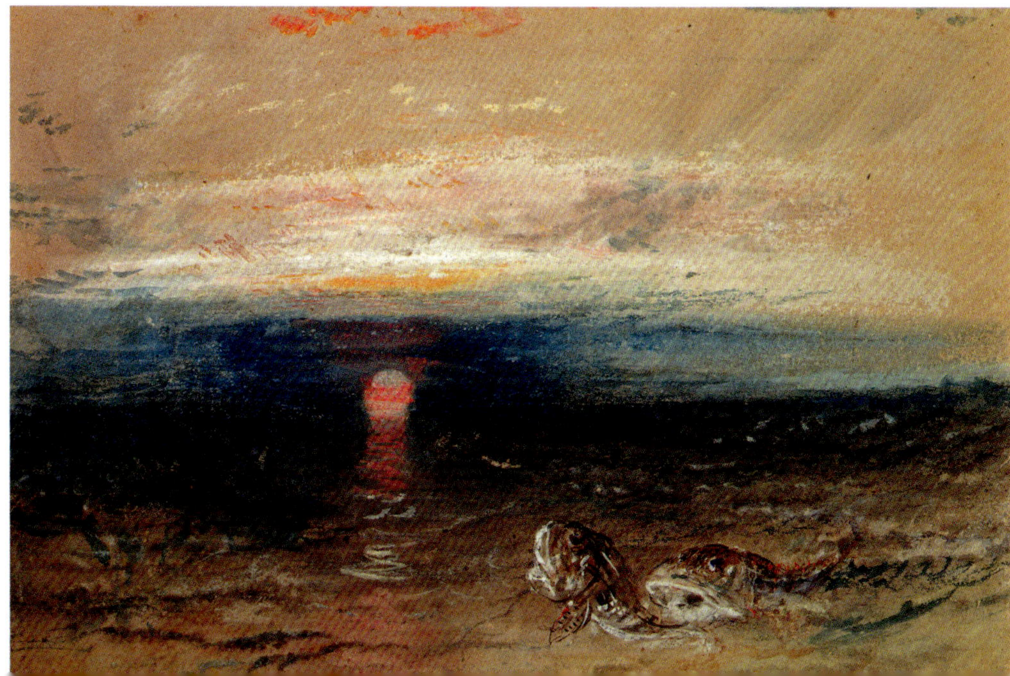

Sunset at Sea, with Gurnets, c.1836, watercolour, bodycolour and chalk, Whitworth Art Gallery, University of Manchester, UK, 22 x 28cm (9 x 11in)

As the title suggests, Turner draws our attention to the focal points of the picture, the cool sunset and the rather strange-looking gurnets or gurnards. Their pectoral fins resemble a bird's wings, hence their alternative name of sea robins.

*View along an Alpine Valley,
possibly Val d'Aosta,
c.*1836, watercolour,
Private Collection,
23 x 32cm (9 x 12in)

The juxtaposition of the
bright yellow and gold in
the foreground, and the blue
distance, helps to create a
sense of space in the picture.
The blue recedes in the
background and the yellow
brings the foreground into
prominence. For Turner,
this use of colour was
instinctive, but in the early
20th century artists such
as Wassily Kandinsky
formulated these ideas.

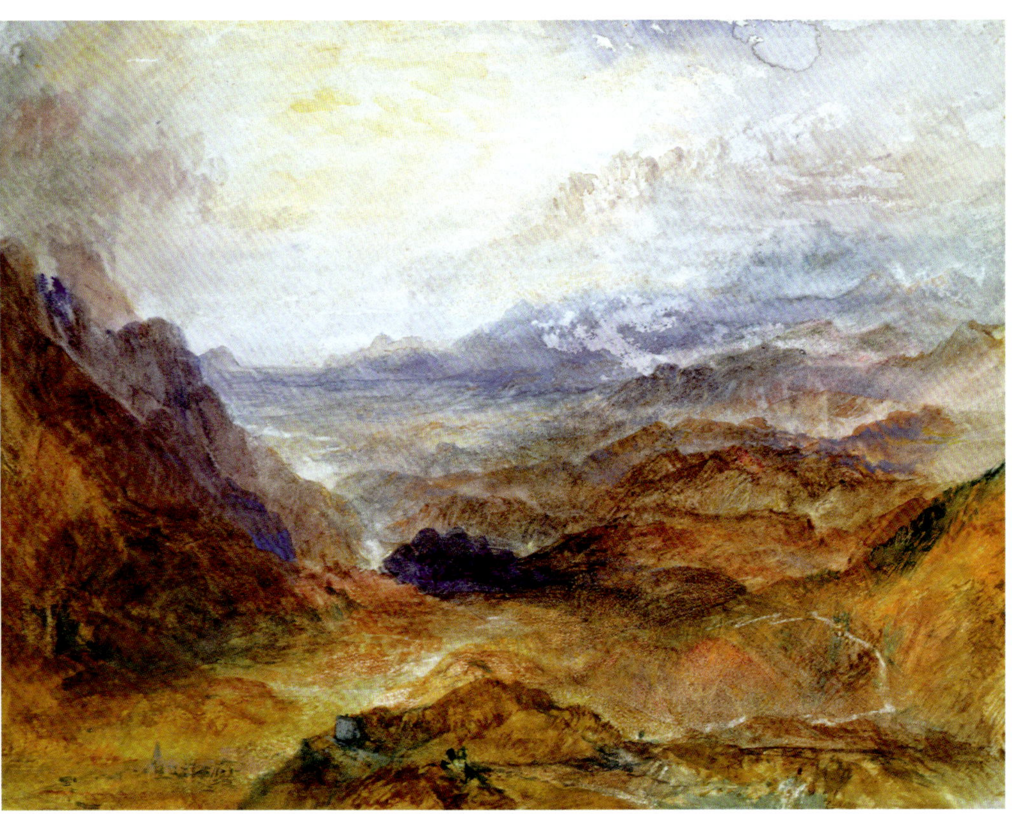

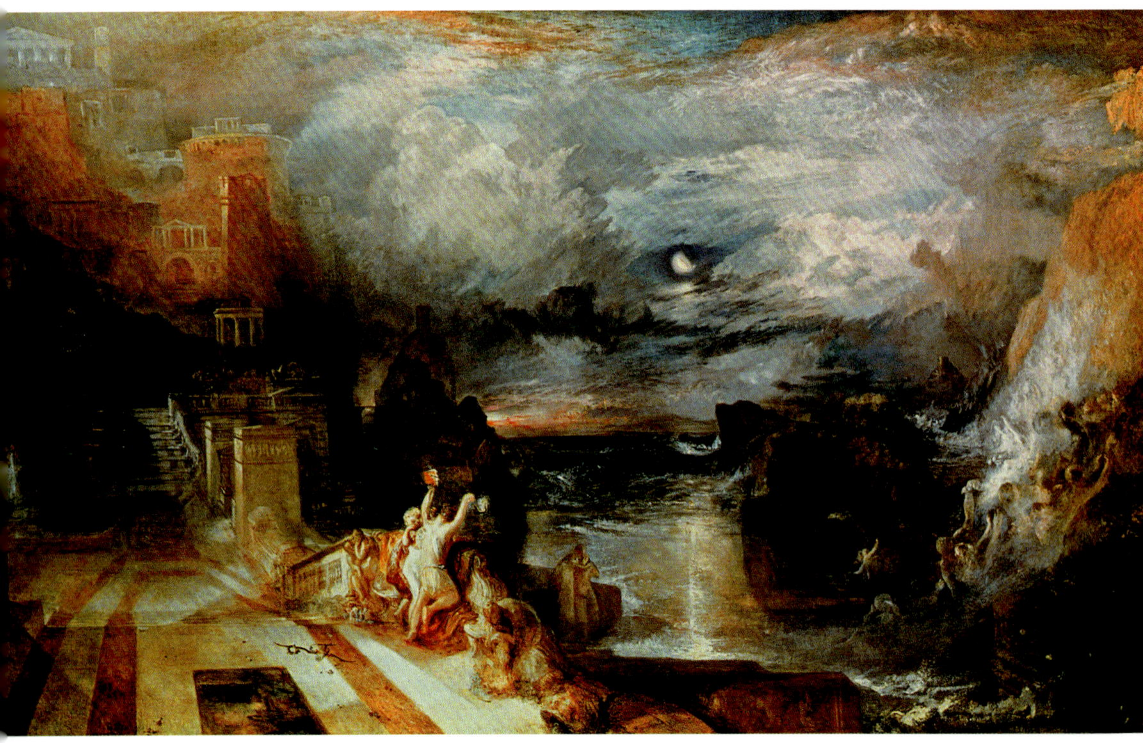

*The Parting of Hero and
Leander*, 1837, oil on canvas,
National Gallery,
London, UK,
146 x 236cm (57 x 93in)

Turner has created a
dramatic *mise-en-scène* with
juxtaposed areas of light and
dark, and the Sublime
aspects of natural
phenomena. The work is
situated in a fictional Greek
landscape to underpin the
source of the story of Hero
and Leander by the ancient
writer Musaeus. Turner
appended words from his
own poem to the picture
when it was exhibited at
the Academy.

Town and Lake of Thun,
*c.*1838, watercolour,
Cecil Higgins Art Gallery,
Bedford, UK,
23 x 29cm (9 x 11 in)

Passenger ships were in use
on the lake after 1835
despite their omission from
Turner's watercolour. Instead
he has concentrated on the
town of Thun, in the central
north-east region of
Switzerland, with the Alpine
range in the distance. Apart
from its origins as part of the
Holy Roman Empire, as a
historical town it is
unremarkable, but is typical
of an Alpine resort.

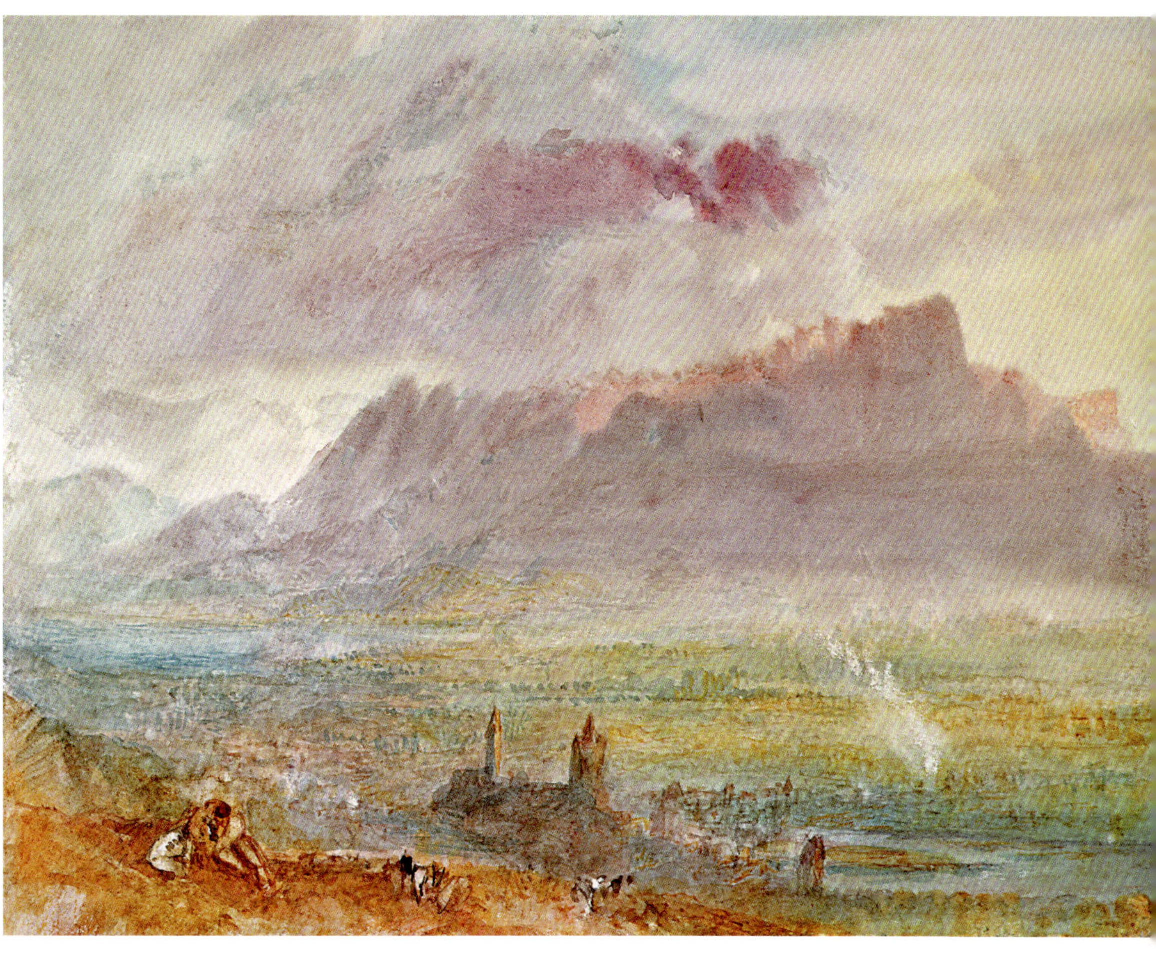

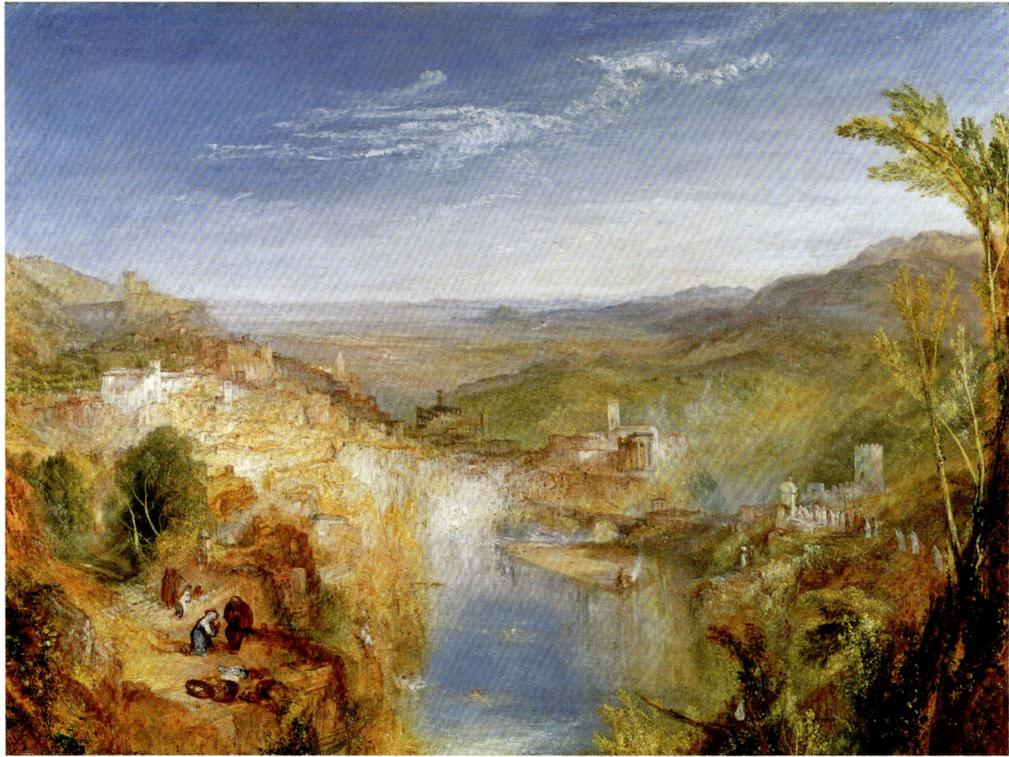

Modern Italy – The Pifferari,
1838, oil on canvas,
Kelvingrove Art Gallery
and Museum,
Glasgow, Scotland, UK,
93 x 123cm (37 x 48in)

Turner exhibited this picture
and *Ancient Italy – Ovid
Banished from Rome* at the
Academy exhibition of 1838.
Both ended up in the
collection of Munro of
Novar, but this one was a
protracted transaction, after
the artist had already agreed
to sell the painting to
Reverend Daniell for a
reduced price. Daniell died
before he could pay for the
painting, and Munro
purchased it in 1842.

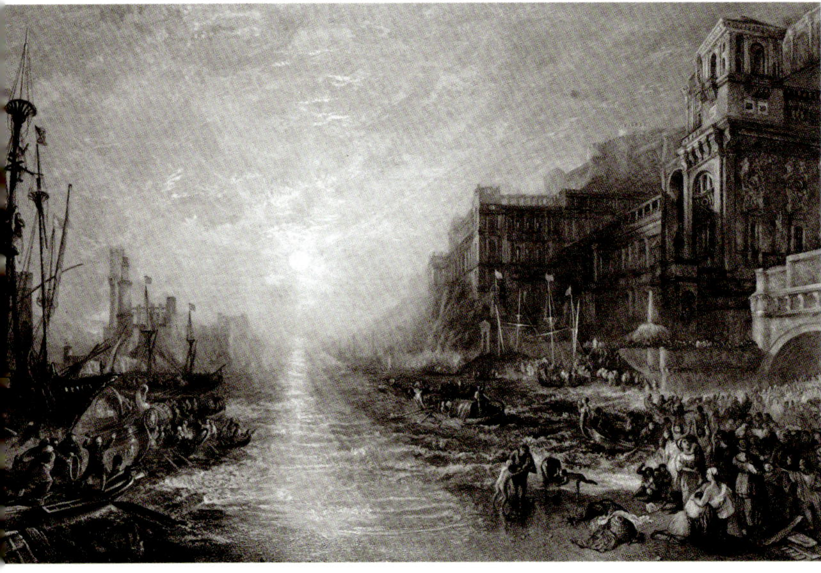

The Embarkation of Regulus, Ancient Carthage, 1838, etching, Paul Mellon Collection, Yale Center for British Art, CT, USA, 52 x 64cm (20 x 25in)

This fine line engraving by D Wilson was published in 1838 and does justice to Turner's *Regulus*. The image tells of the mission that the Roman consul Regulus undertook to negotiate the release of the Carthaginian prisoners held in Rome. He returned to Carthage having failed in the mission and was punished by having his eyelids removed and being tortured to death.

The Fighting Temeraire, Tugged to her Last Berth to be Broken up, 1838, oil on canvas, National Gallery, London, UK, 91 x 122cm (36 x 48in)

Arguably the most famous of Turner's paintings, this was unsold at the Royal Academy exhibition and remained in the artist's possession until he died. Despite her French name, the *Temeraire* was a British man-o'-war that saw distinguished service at Trafalgar. The melancholic image was noted by one contemporary as "…a scene, which affects us almost as deeply as the decay of a noble human being".

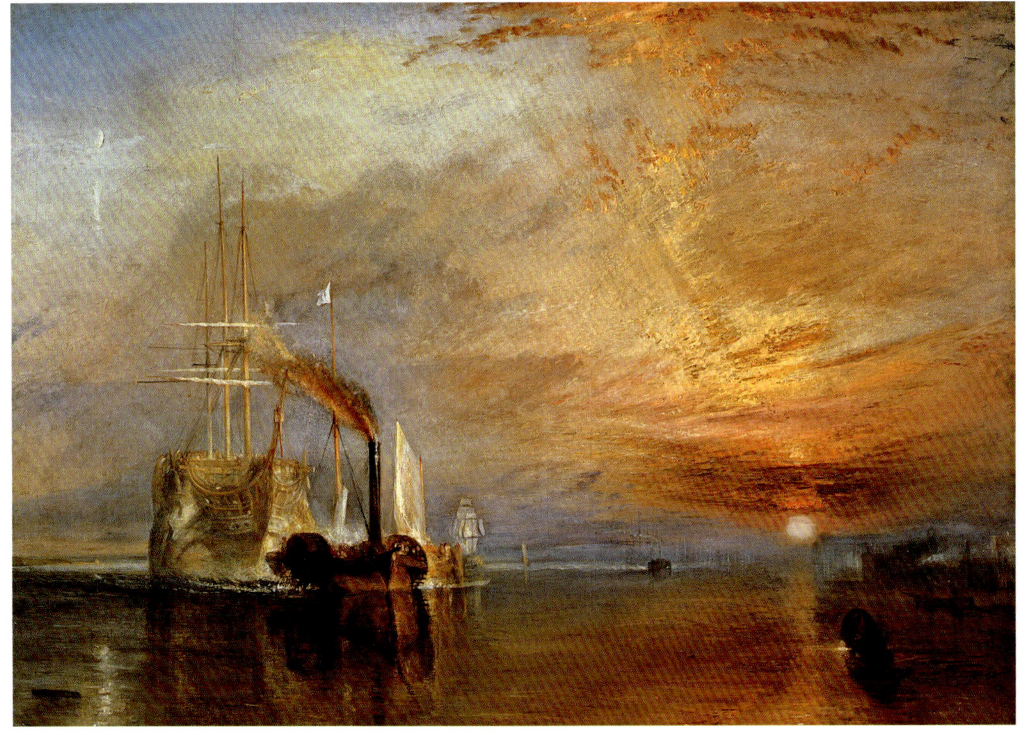

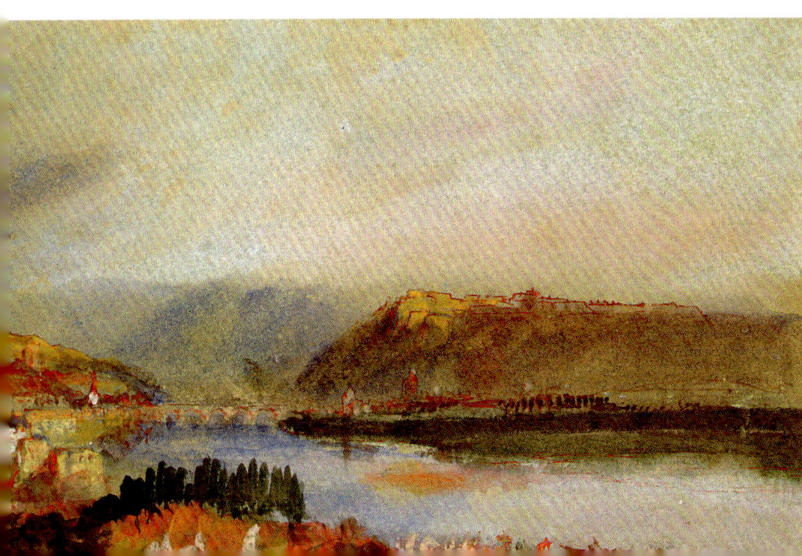

Givet from the North, 1839, watercolour and bodycolour, Private Collection, 13 x 19cm (5 x 7½in)

The town of Givet is in the Ardennes region of France, very close to the Belgian border on the River Meuse. Turner visited this area in 1824, filling his Givet and Fort Charlemont Sketchbook. Fort Charlemont was built by Charles V, the Holy Roman Emperor during the first half of the 16th century. The Empire was dissolved during the Napoleonic Wars.

Grey Sea, Boat Running Ashore, c.1840, watercolour on paper, Leeds Art Gallery, UK, 25 x 37cm (10 x 15in)

This tiny painting is a wonderful example of Turner's restrained use of a limited palette that still manages to depict the movement and power of the sea, the grey tones adding to its coldness. There is a correlation between the brevity of mark used to define the boat and the actuality of seeing a boat from a distance, Turner reminding us that all too often our eyes deceive us, effectively filling in the blanks of what we actually see.

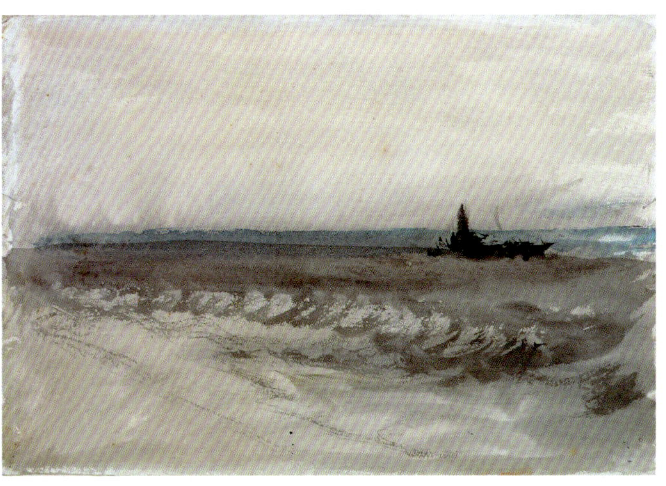

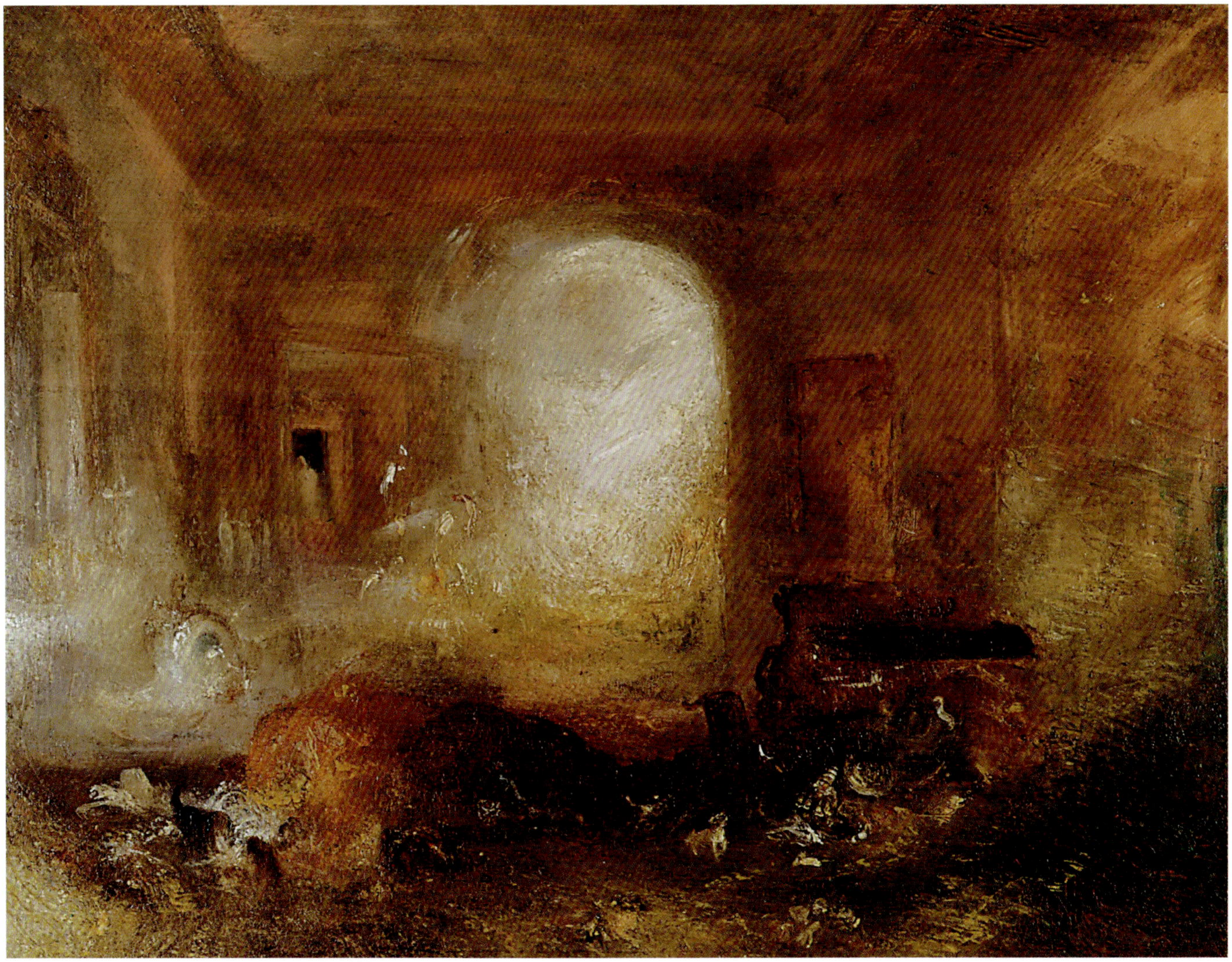

Interior of a Great House: The Drawing Room, East Cowes Castle, c.1830, oil on canvas, Tate Britain, London, UK, 91 x 122cm (36 x 48in)

This canvas is apparently unfinished and the subject of it is uncertain. It has been suggested that it is a collage of different aspects of the house. An alternative explanation is that the painting represents a house that was ransacked during the English Civil War.

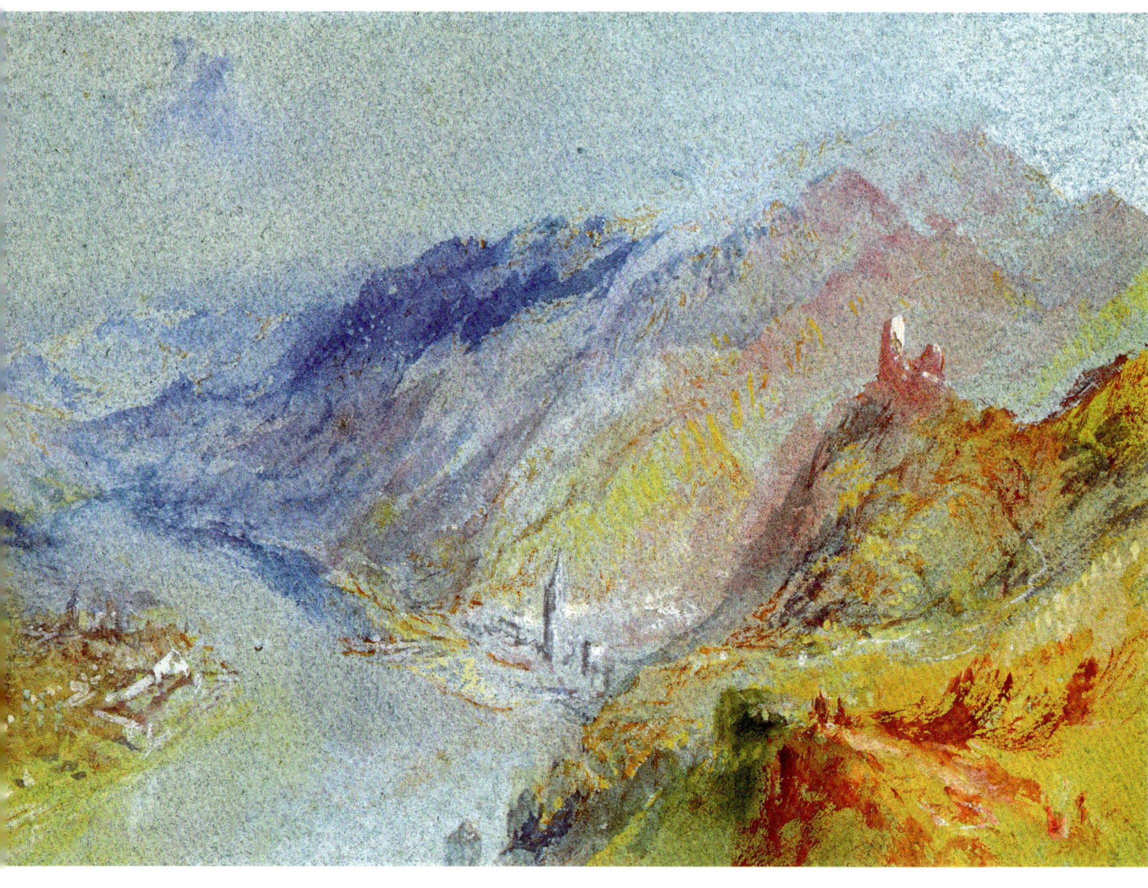

The Castle of Trausnitz overlooking Landshut, 1840, watercolour and bodycolour, Private Collection, 13 x 18cm (5 x 7in)

Perched high on a ridge and overlooking the town of Landshut, Trausnitz Castle dates from the 13th century and was the ancestral home for the dukedom of Bavaria, in southern Germany. The town, on the River Isar, is not far from Munich, and Turner travelled around this whole area on his return journey from Venice in the autumn of 1840.

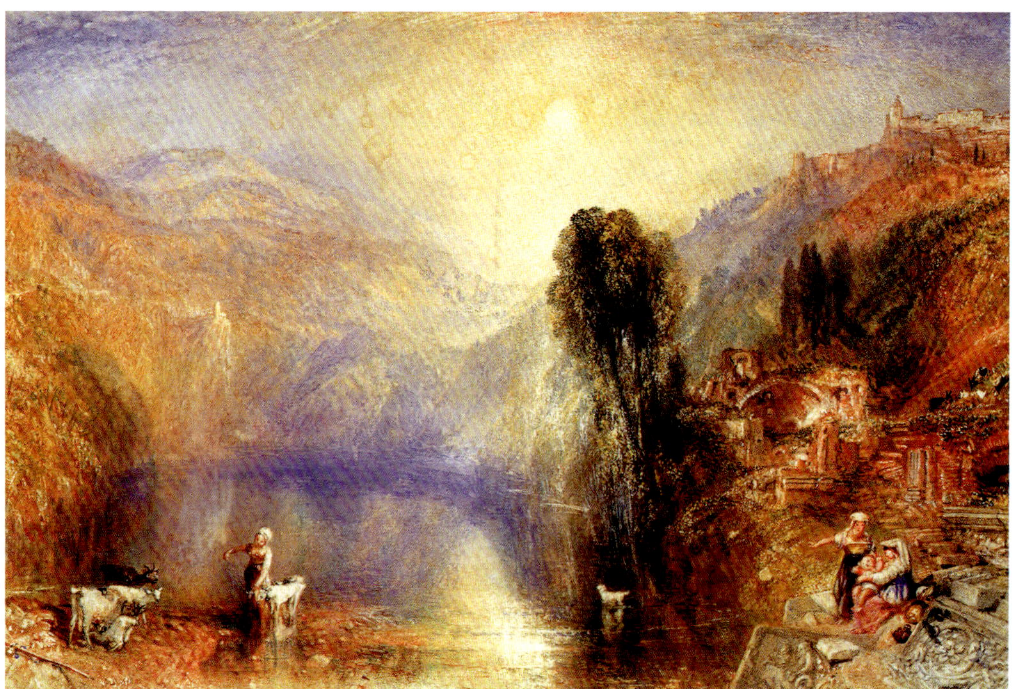

Lake Nemi, 1840, watercolour, British Museum, London, UK, 35 x 52cm (14 x 20in)

Lake Nemi had been a continual motif for Turner from the time he studied *Dr Monro's Album of Italian Views* in 1794, when he interpreted Cozens' watercolours. His Gandolfo to Naples Sketchbook included several references to Lake Nemi. The 1828 watercolour, which is similar in composition to the one shown here, lacks the subtlety of colour typical of his mature style.

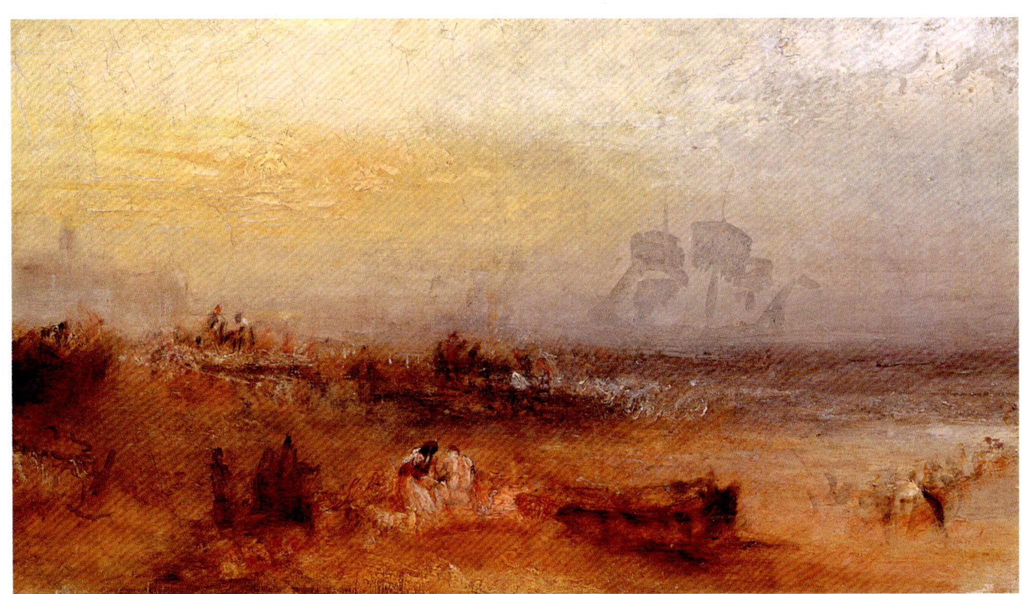

Morning after the Wreck, 1835–40, oil on canvas, National Museum and Gallery of Wales, Cardiff, UK, 38 x 61cm (15 x 24in)

This is a difficult picture to date and attach provenance to before 1880. The painting depicts a group of people who are either victims, or more likely wreckers, picking their way through property washed up ashore on the morning tide. Turner has also included a ghostly presence of the ship that has foundered.

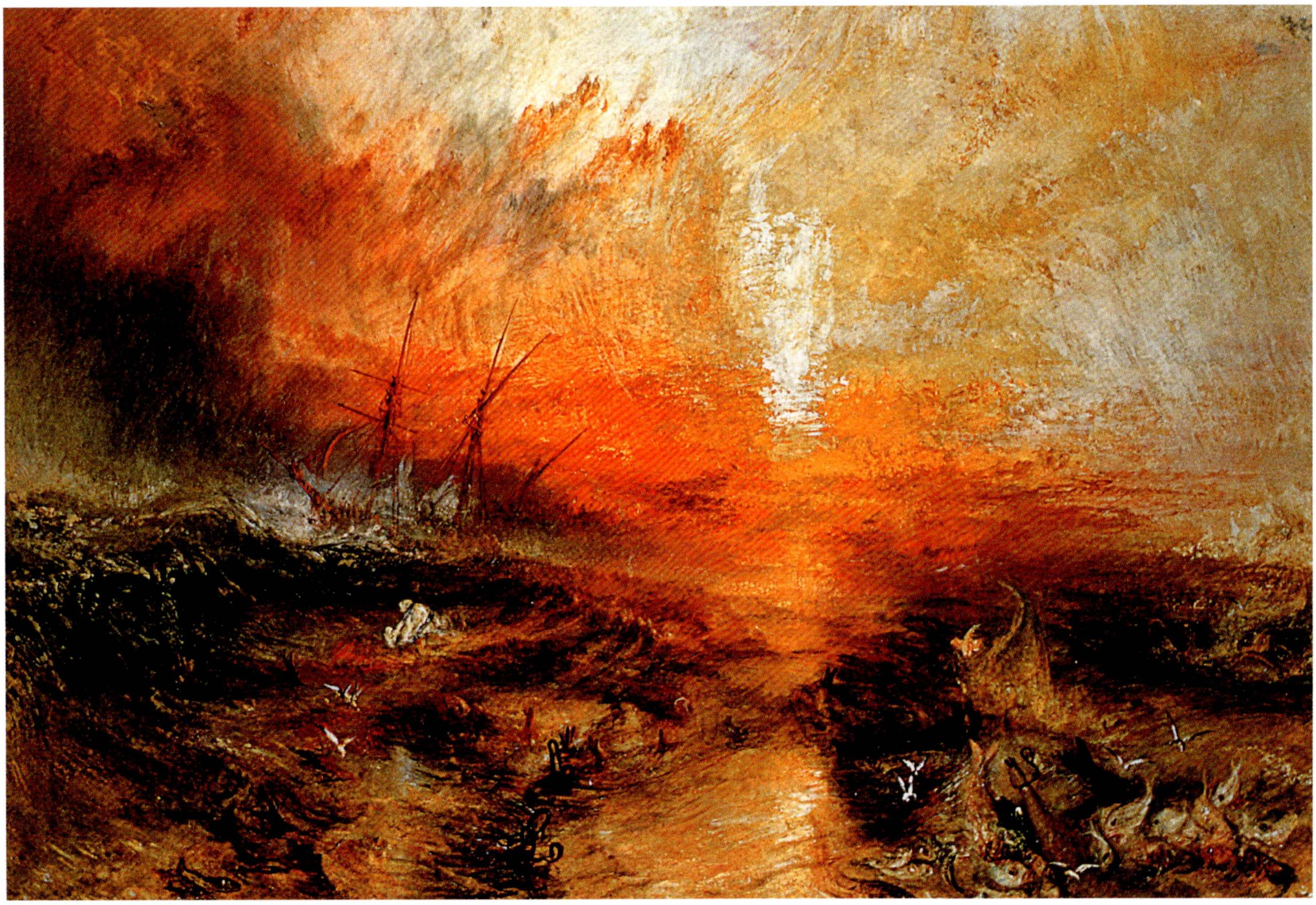

Slavers Throwing Overboard the Dead and Dying – Typhoon Coming on, 1840, oil on canvas, Burstein Collection, 91 x 123cm (36 x 48in)

Despite its slating in the press and mockery because of its long title, this painting, which came to be commonly known as *The Slave Ship*, was recognized by Ruskin as the ultimate masterpiece of Turner's mature style. Ruskin's father, acting upon his son's advice, purchased the painting through Turner's dealer, Thomas Griffiths. Mr Ruskin subsequently gave it to his son, who wrote about the painting, in his role as Turner's apologist, in his *Modern Painters.*

Storm at Sunset, Venice, 1840, watercolour and bodycolour, Fitzwilliam Museum, Cambridge, UK, 22 x 32cm (9 x 13in)

Away from the canals and gondolas, one of the main ships used in Venice during Turner's time was the *bragozzo*, a flat-bottomed sailing boat that was used mainly for fishing. The billowing sail depicted by Turner in this watercolour, deftly painted with a single masterly brushstroke, adds to the drama of the storm, which is already suggested by the multicoloured clouds depicted above the lagoon.

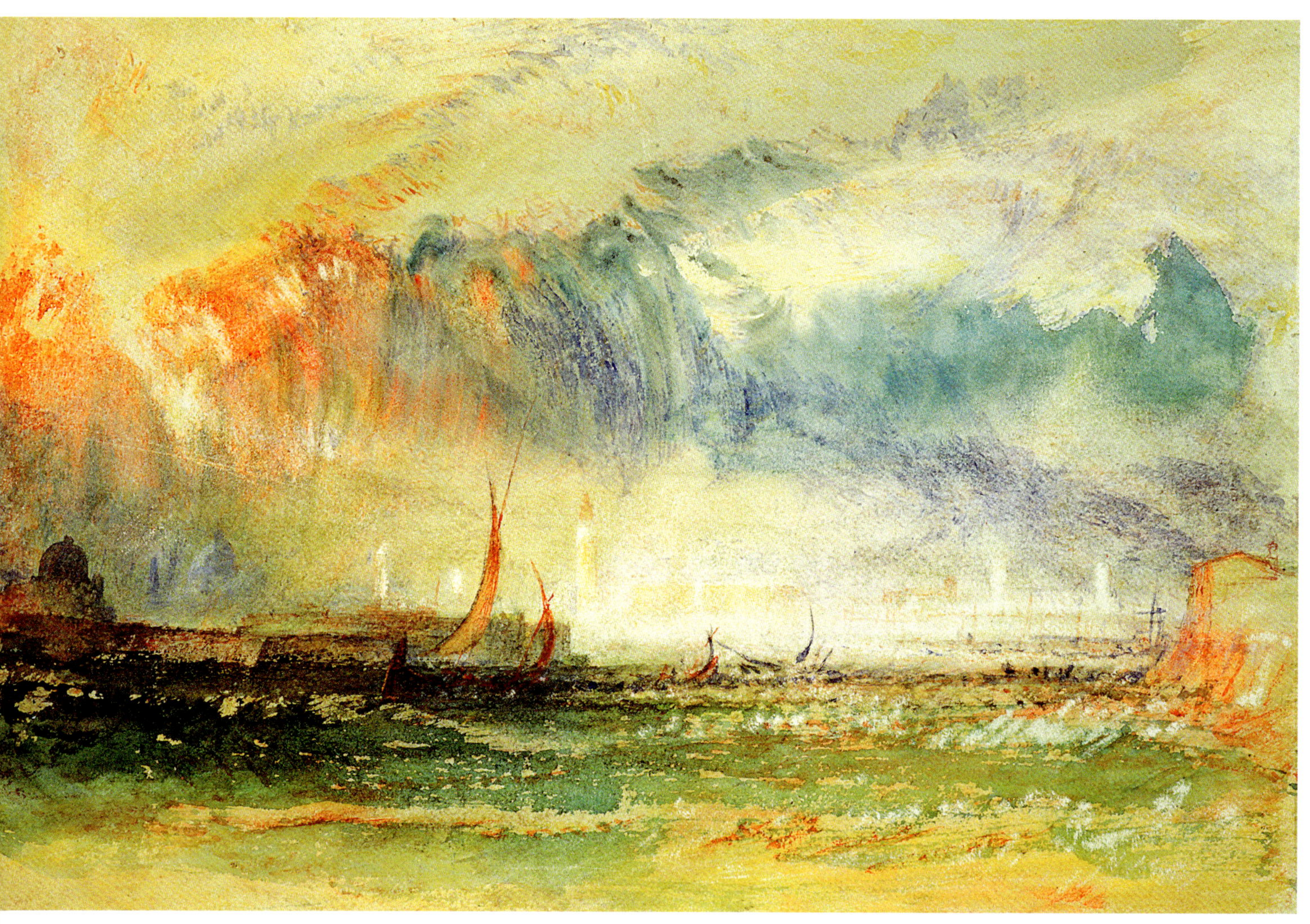

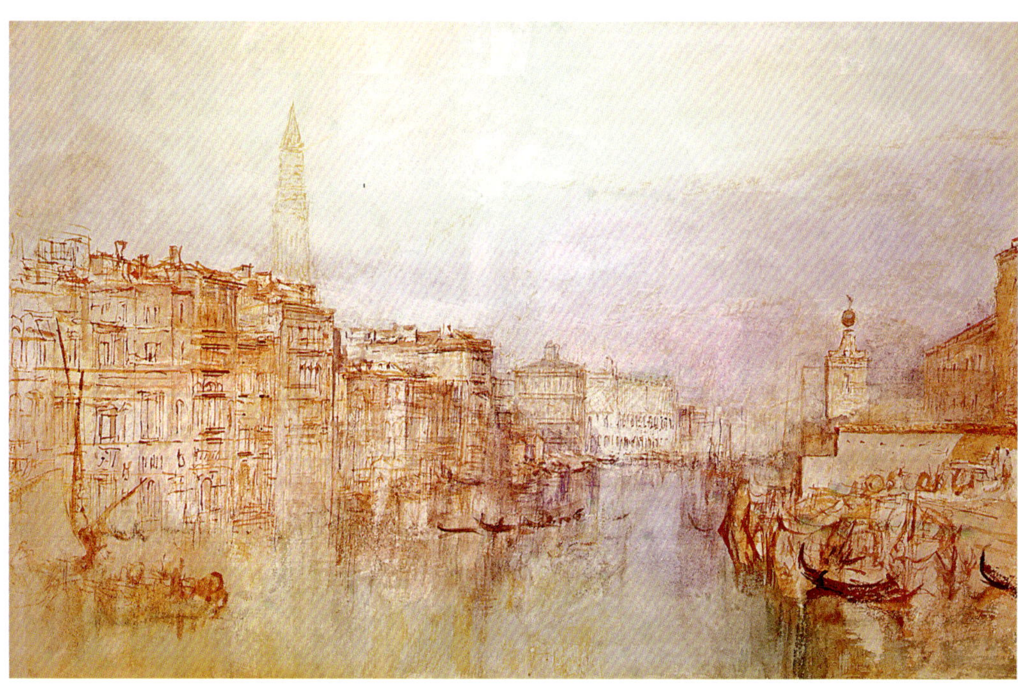

The Grand Canal Looking towards the Dogana, 1840, watercolour, British Museum, London, UK, 22 x 32cm (9 x 13in)

This is one of Turner's most delicate Venetian pictures, balancing topographical detail with atmosphere. The soft pastel washes emphasize the ethereal early morning light. Behind the solidity and dynamism of the gondolas on the right of the picture is the Dogana di Mare, the customs house erected in the 17th century. Above the palazzos on the left is the Campanile di San Marco.

Venice, 1840, oil on canvas, Victoria and Albert Museum, London, UK, 61 x 91cm (24 x 36in)

This oil painting was created for John Sheepshanks, one of Turner's later patrons, and exhibited at the Royal Academy in 1840. Sheepshanks gave more than 500 pictures to the Victoria and Albert Museum in 1857 to create a core of English art that included several works by Turner and John Constable.

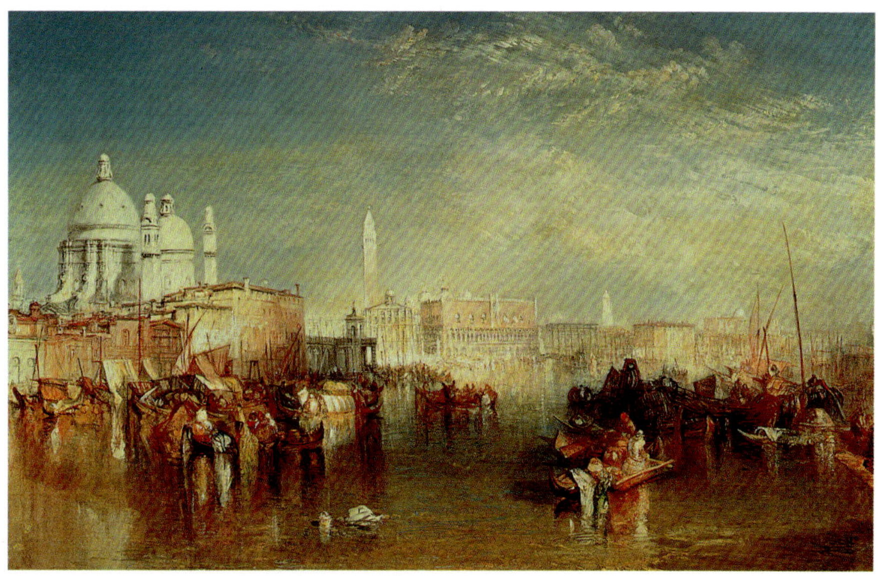

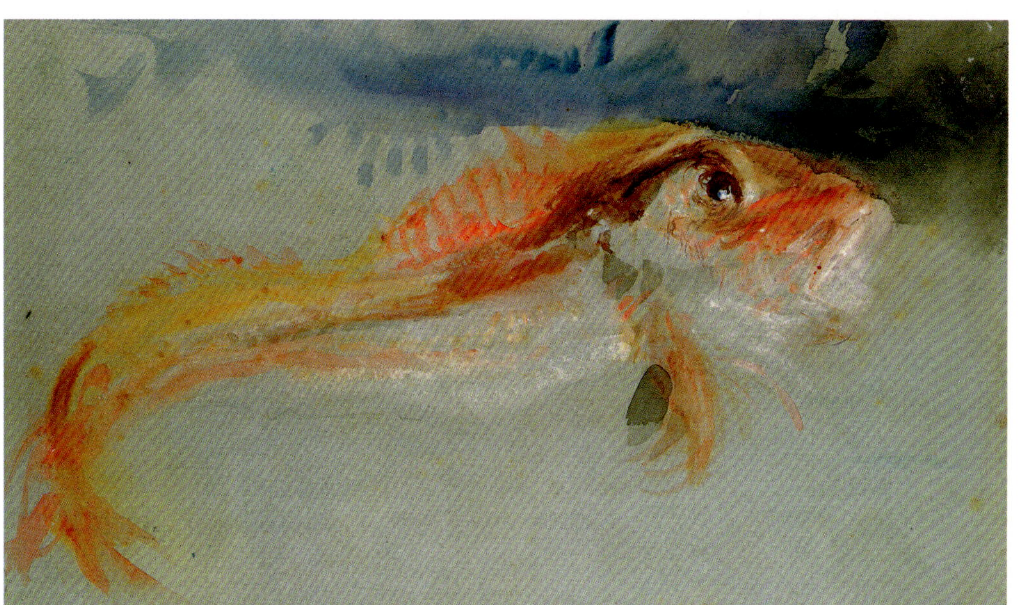

*Study of a Gurnard, c.*1840, watercolour, Victoria and Albert Museum, London, UK, 18 x 28cm (7 x 11in)

Turner's interest in natural history appears to have been limited to birds and fish. There are more than 100 varieties of gurnard – mainly found in the Atlantic Ocean feeding on small crustaceans. They were considered an inexpensive source of food.

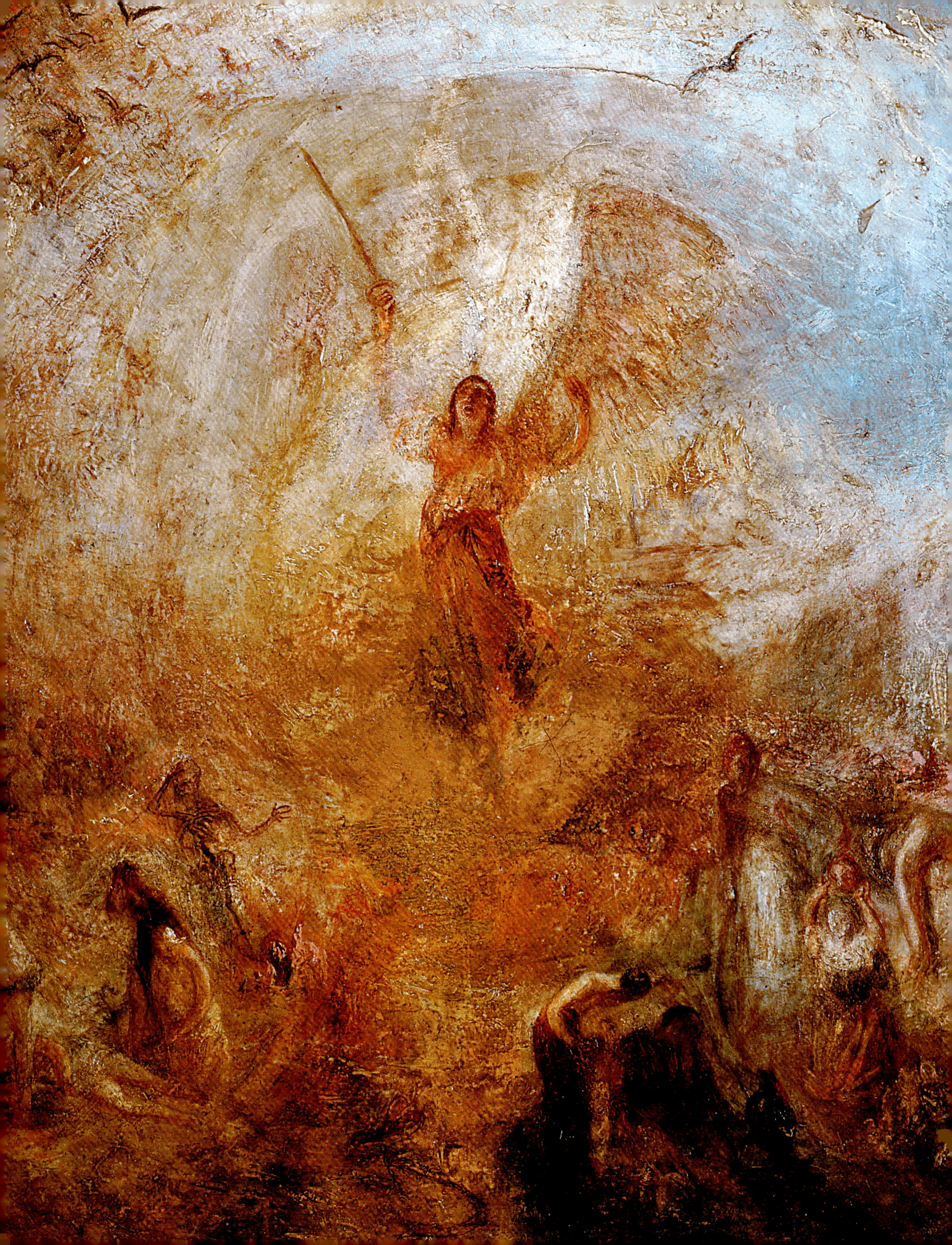

THE FINAL DECADE 1841–1851

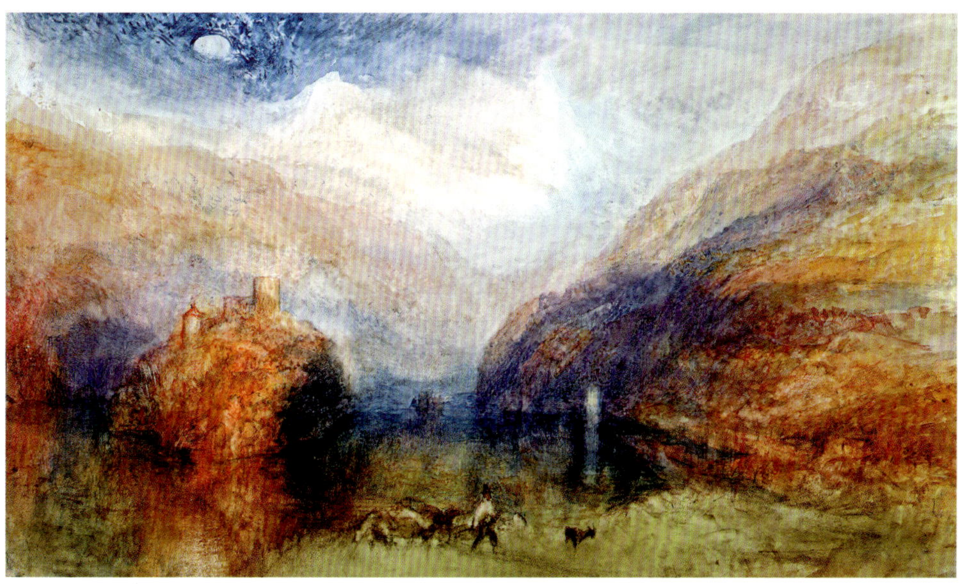

The last years of Turner's life did not see a letting up of his creative talents. Spurred on perhaps by Ruskin's polemic and his own self-belief, Turner refused to submit to his ageing body and continued ill health, embarking instead on four gruelling tours of Switzerland. In this period he painted many works that are now considered among his greatest, including *Rain, Steam and Speed* – a suitable swansong to arguably the greatest English landscape painter.

Above: The Lauerzersee with the Mythens, *watercolour and ink, 1848. It would be difficult to comprehend from Turner's watercolour that this area had been the scene of utter devastation, following a landslide in 1806.*
Left: The Angel Standing in the Sun, *oil on canvas, 1846. Turner appended lines from the Book of Revelation and a poem by Samuel Rogers to this painting for the Academy exhibition. Despite its golden colour, the work is essentially one of pessimism, the archangel Michael, the Christian angel of death, overlooking the figures below, which include Adam and Eve weeping over the body of Abel.*

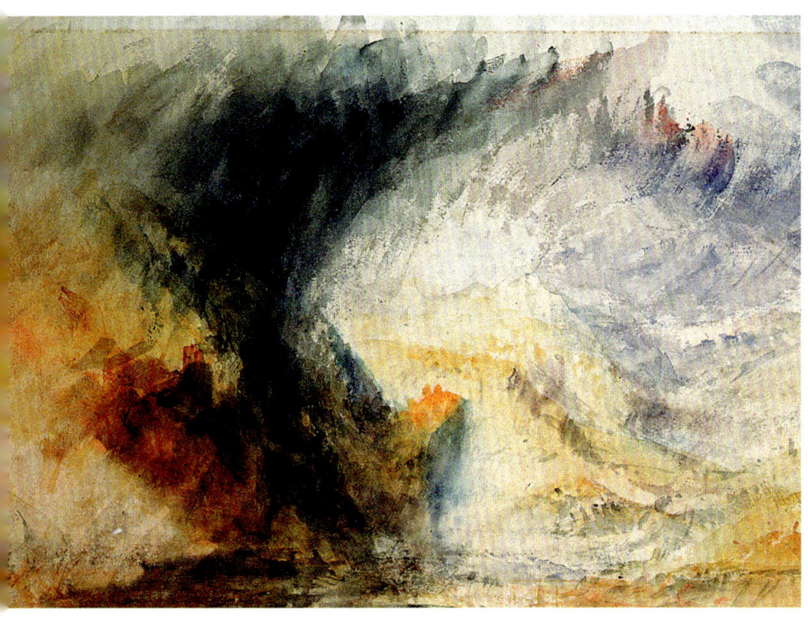

Mount St Gotthard, c.1840, Leeds Art Gallery, UK, 21 x 29cm (8 x 11in)

Named after a 10th-century saint, this mountain pass was one of the most difficult to negotiate, as, up until the 19th century, there was only an old medieval wooden bridge in place. Turner had already gathered most of the reference material for this watercolour during his tour of 1819, his later versions coming from his subsequent tours of the 1840s.

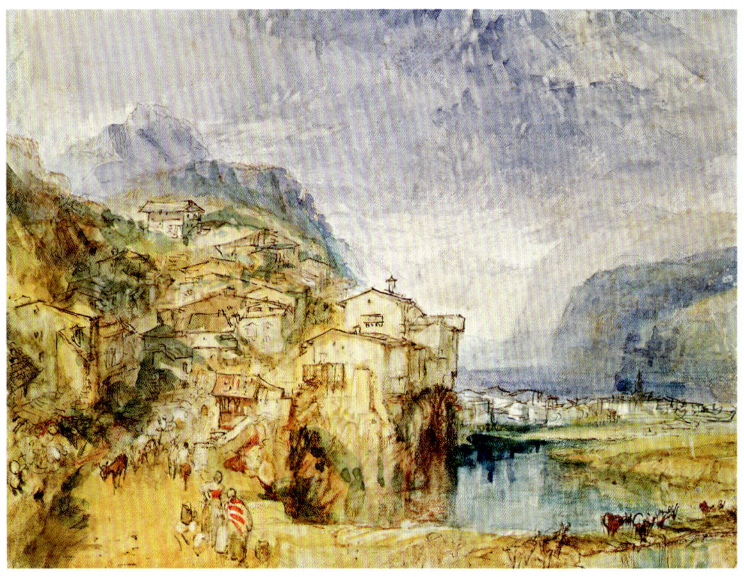

Brunnen, Lake Lucerne in the Distance, 1843, graphite and watercolour, Fitzwilliam Museum, Cambridge, UK, 23 x 29cm (9 x 11in)

The River Muota enters Lake Lucerne at Brunnen, an area associated with the legend of William Tell. He was a 14th-century folk hero whose rebellious acts brought about the Swiss Confederation that lasted until Napoleon's invasion in the late 18th century.

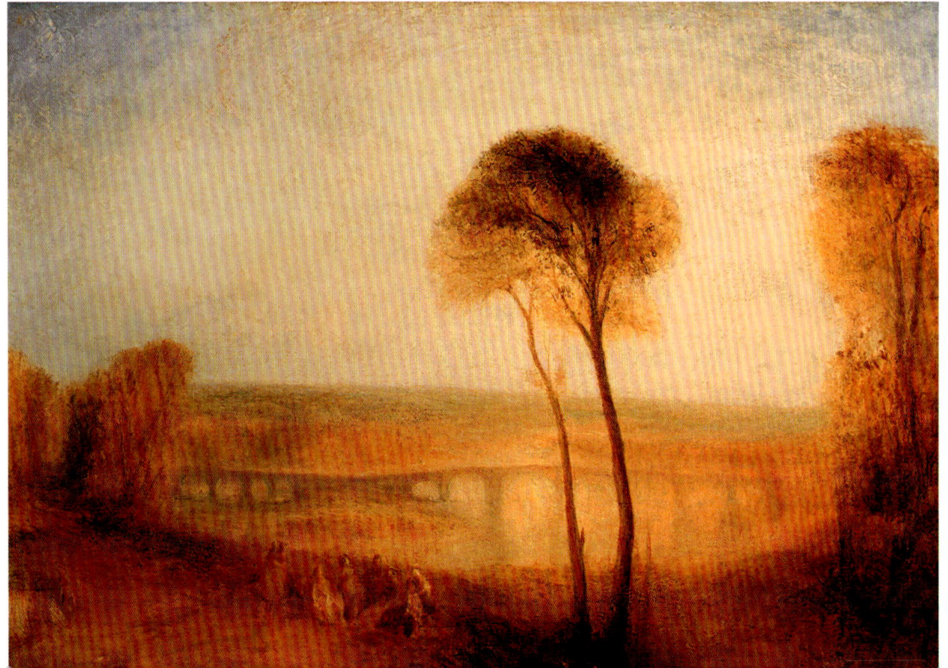

Landscape with Walton Bridges, 1845, oil on canvas, Private Collection, 88 x 118cm (35 x 46in)

Not exhibited until the 20th century, Turner left no clue as to the location of the scene and it was assumed to be a Claudian style landscape of Italy. Scholarship in the 20th century, however, revealed that it was of the reach and bridges across the River Thames at Walton.

View of Venice: The Ducal Palace, Dogana and Part of the San Giorgio, 1841, oil on canvas, Allen Memorial Art Museum, Oberlin College, OH, USA, 64 x 93cm (25 x 37in)

This painting was purchased by Turner's friend and fellow Academician Sir Francis Chantrey, while it was being painted on one of the Royal Academy's Varnishing Days. The picture was one of three of Venice exhibited at the Academy that year. Unfortunately Chantrey died a few months after buying the picture.

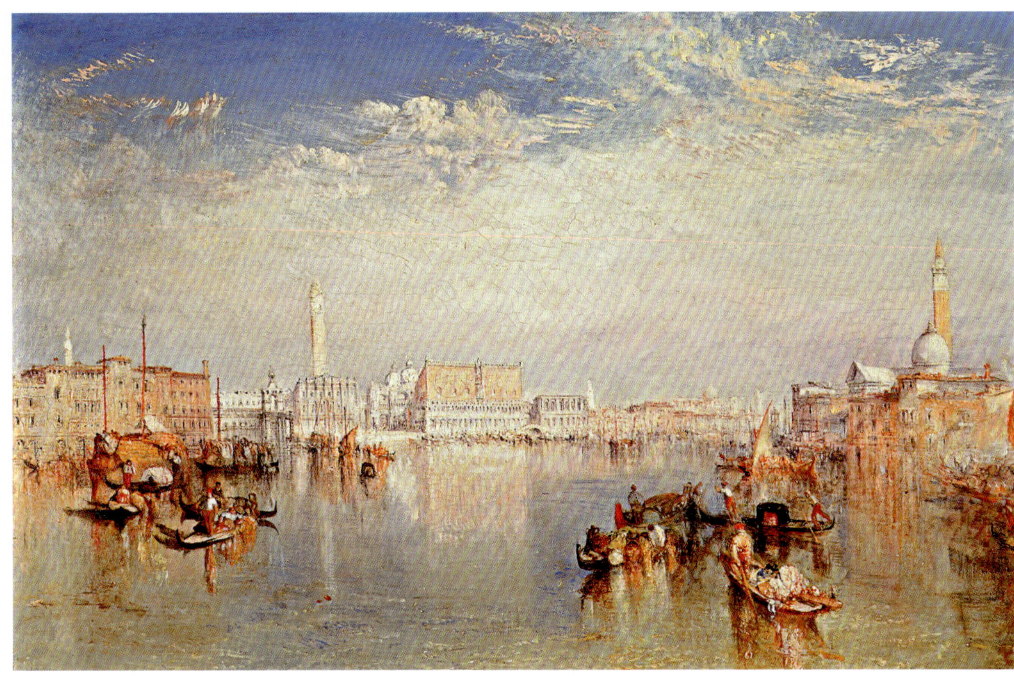

Oberhofen, Lake Thun, c.1848, watercolour, Indianapolis Museum of Art, IN, USA, 38 x 55cm (15 x 22in)

Located on the northern shore of Lake Thun, Oberhofen is one of the most picturesque towns in the Swiss Alps. The castle, which dates back to the medieval period, dominates this scene, and is captured perfectly by Turner, who has also retained the feeling of the rural idyll of the community.

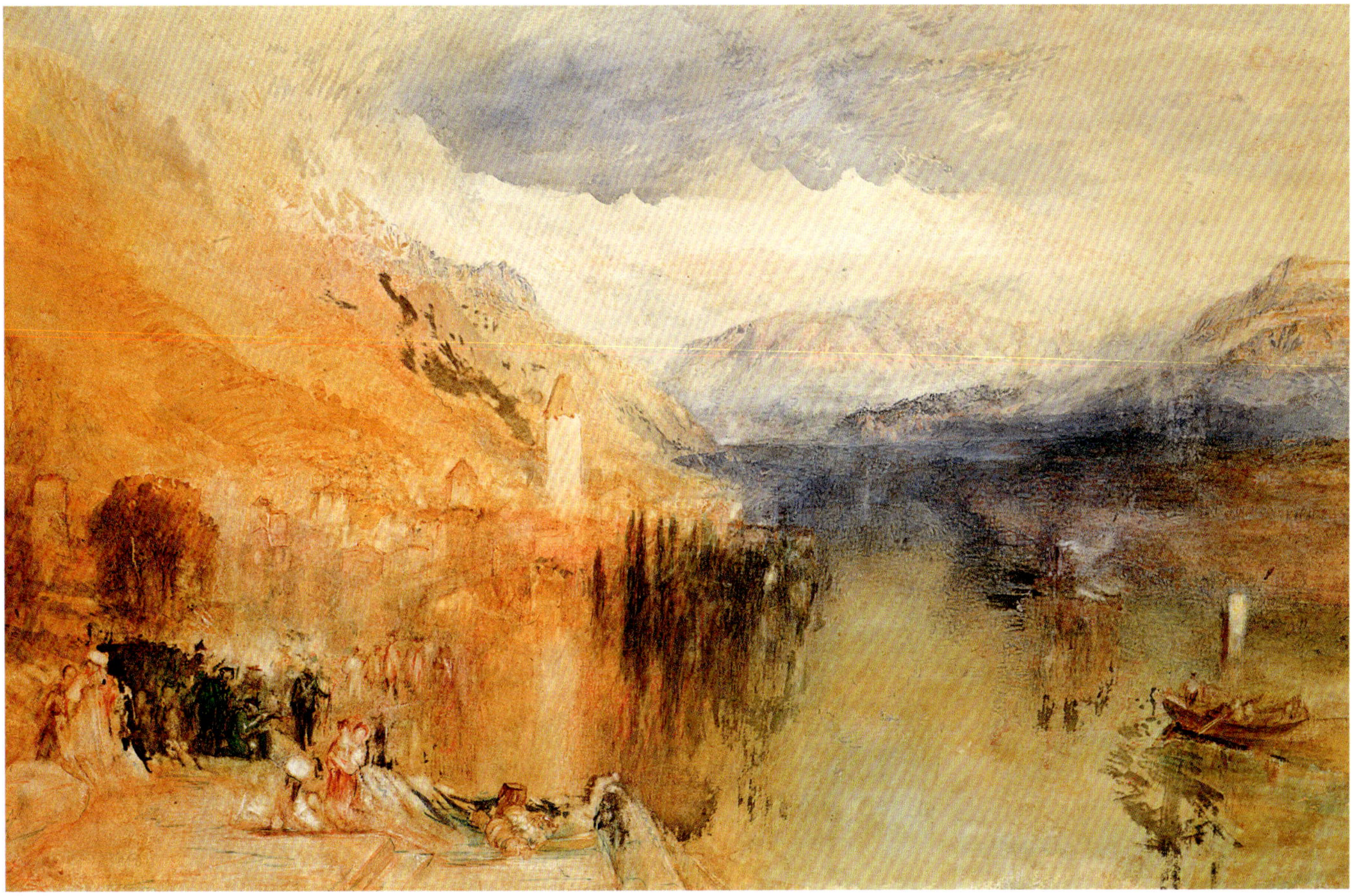

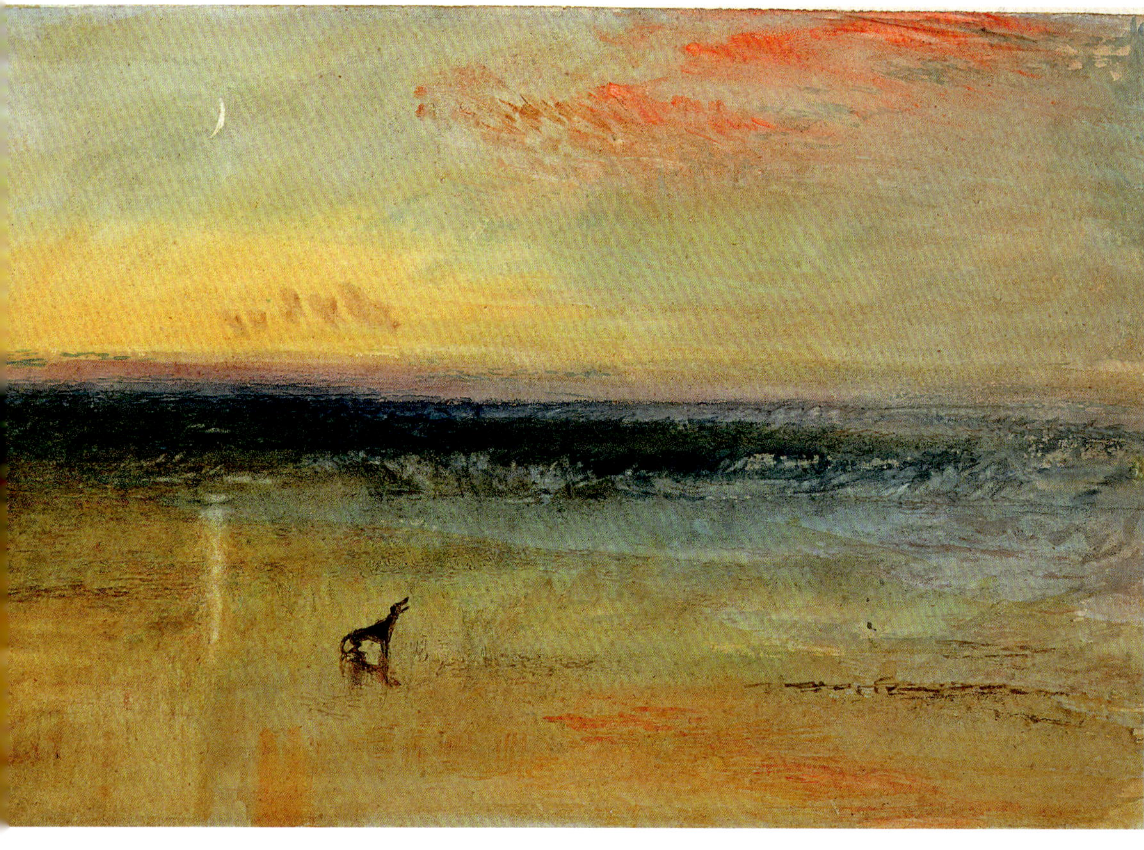

Dawn after the Wreck,
*c.*1841, watercolour,
bodycolour and red chalk,
Courtauld Institute
of Art, London, UK,
25 x 37cm (10 x 15in)

John Ruskin referred to this watercolour as "one of the saddest and most tender" of Turner's paintings. The location is most likely Margate. Turner has depicted a hound baying on a desolate seashore, perhaps lamenting the loss of life following a shipwreck. Daybreak has been heightened with the addition of red chalk in the yellow sky, reflected in the wet sand of the beach.

Falls of the Rhine at
Schaffhausen, 1841,
watercolour and ink,
Indianapolis Museum
of Art, IN, USA,
23 x 29cm (9 x 11in)

The falls at Schaffhausen are among the largest in Europe and Turner made the trip here several times, beginning in 1802. He created several versions of the motif from this time, increasingly Sublime in nature. (There are several versions around 1841 that are exceptional in their Sublime qualities.) In this version the lone figure is dwarfed and, like Turner, can only marvel at the majesty of the falls.

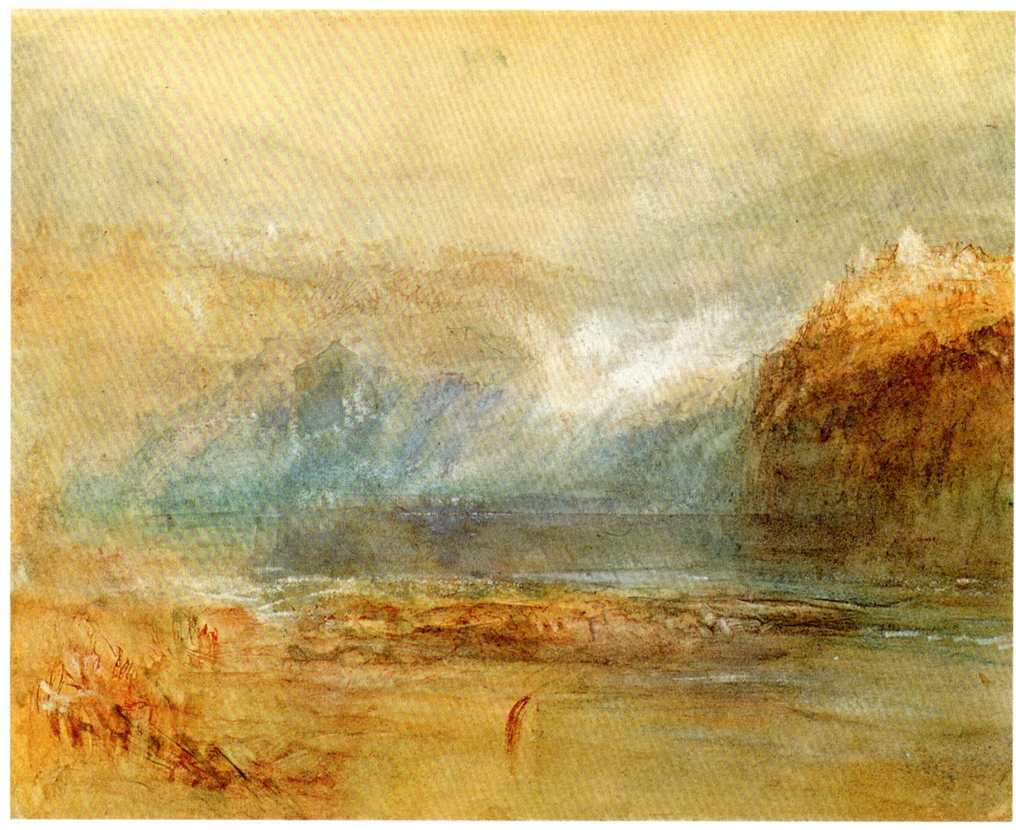

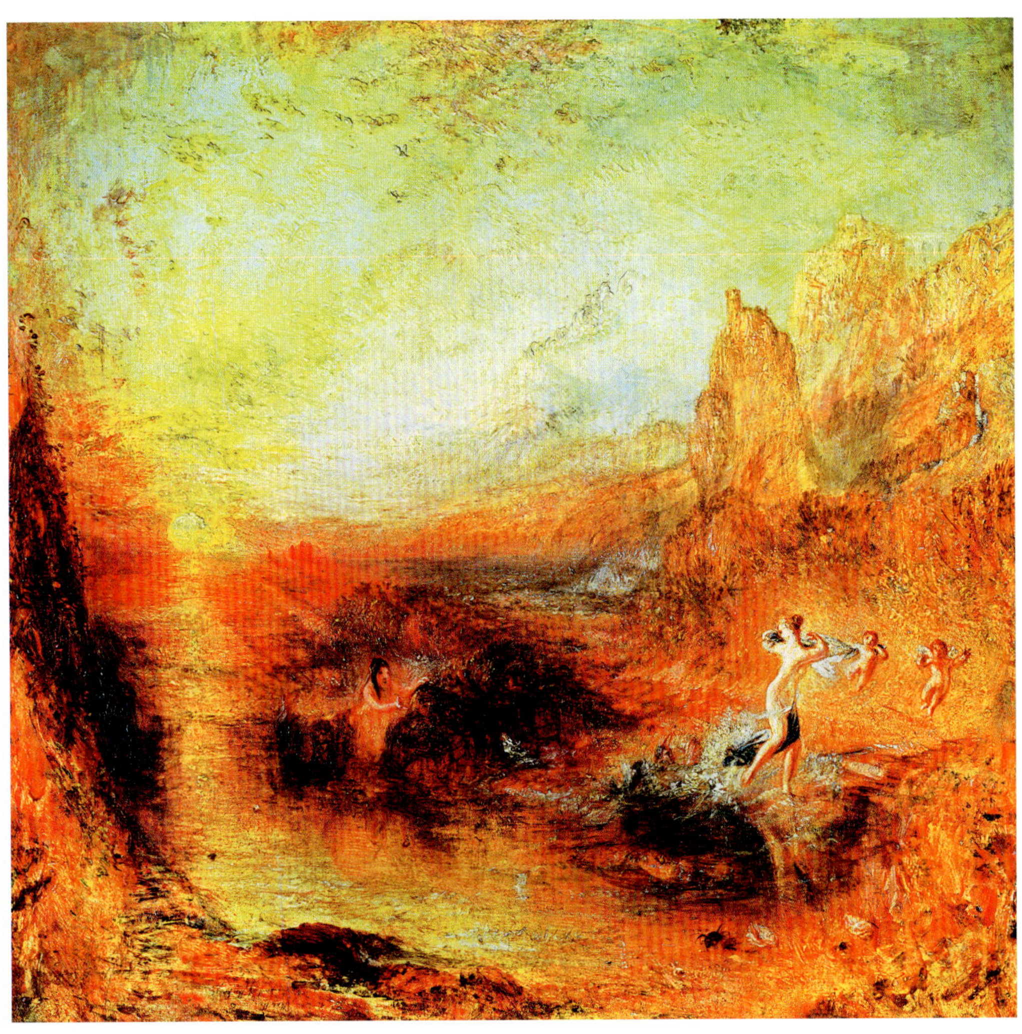

Glaucus and Scylla (from Ovid's *Metamorphoses*), 1841, oil on panel, Kimbell Art Museum, Fort Worth, TX, USA, 79 x 78cm (31 x 31in)

This canvas is almost square, which is unusual for a landscape piece. This is probably due to Turner's decision to place a circular gilt slip over the canvas and exhibit it at the Academy as a round picture, one of two shown, the other being *Dawn of Christianity*, of similar dimensions and shape. There the similarities end, *Glaucus and Scylla* being warm in tone and the other much cooler.

Lucerne from the Walls, 1841–2, watercolour, Lady Lever Art Gallery, Liverpool, UK, 30 x 45cm (12 x 18in)

One of the most famous sights in the city of Lucerne is the *Wasserturm* or water tower next to the *Kapellbrücke* (Chapel Bridge), which crosses the River Reuss. Turner has, however, preferred to set these in the far distance, concentrating instead on the medieval Old Town walls and their watchtowers overlooking the newer part. Also in the distance is the twin-towered church that is dedicated to Lucerne's patron saint, St Leodegar.

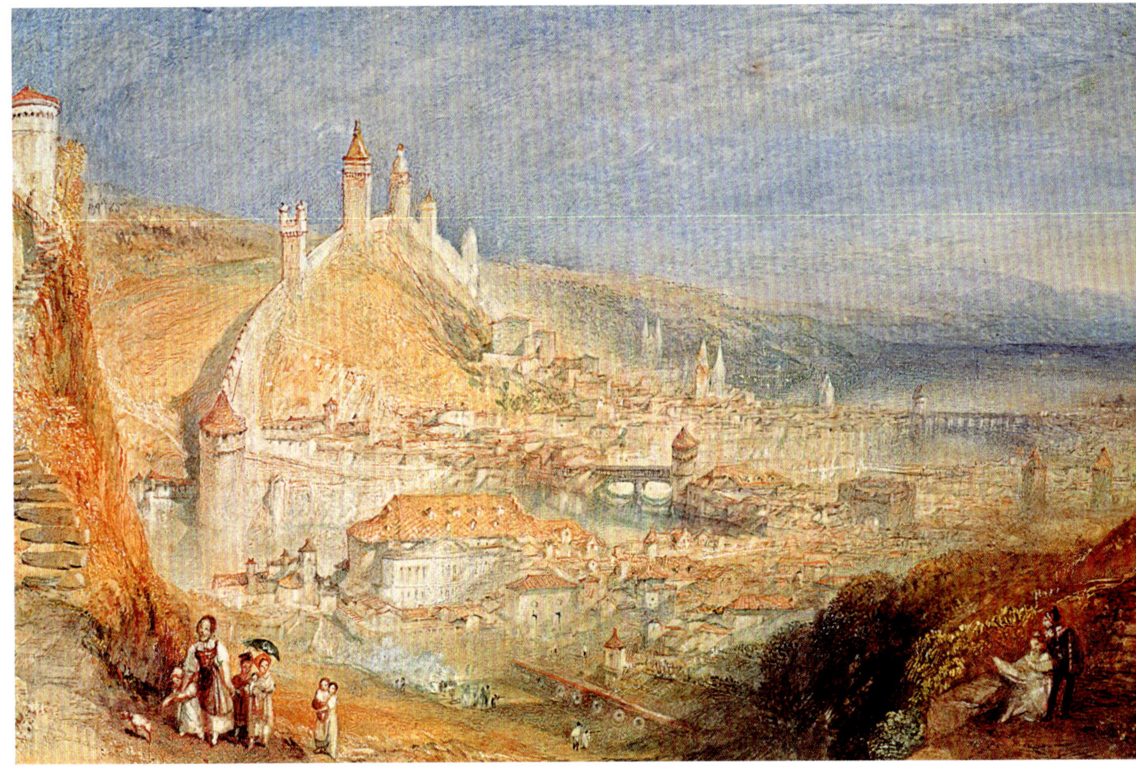

Lake Constance, 1842,
watercolour,
York Art Gallery, UK,
30 x 45cm (12 x 18in)

Lake Constance is one of the largest lakes in the Alpine region, nestling at 395m (1,295ft) above sea level on the borders of Germany, Switzerland and Austria. Significantly, the River Rhine runs through it. Because of its location, there have been border disputes between the three countries. Turner's picture shows the town of Constance on the western edge of the lake.

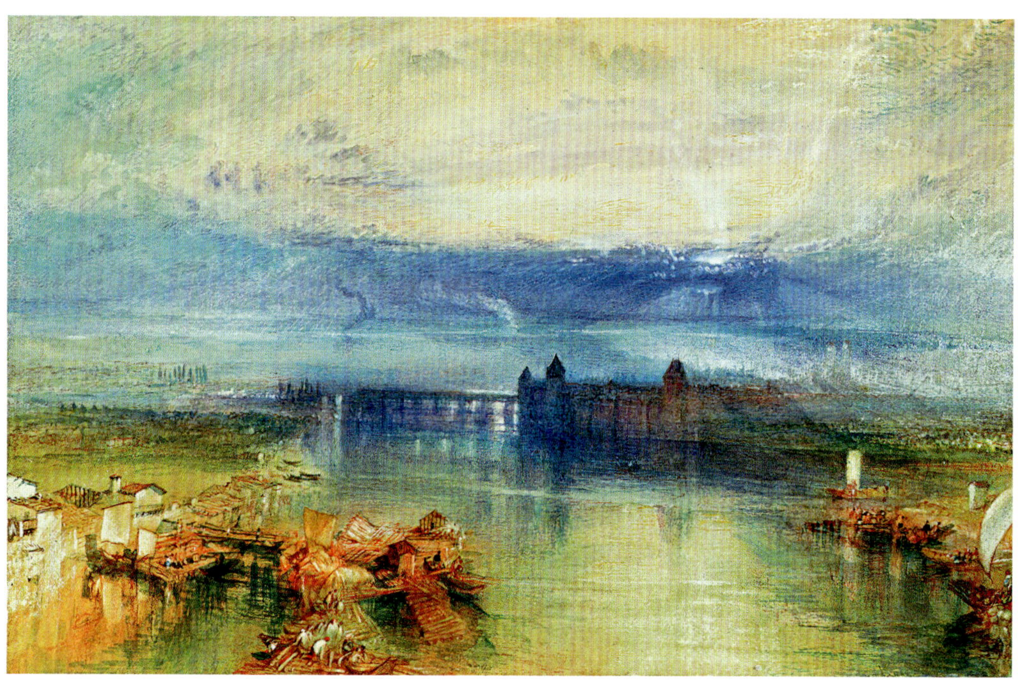

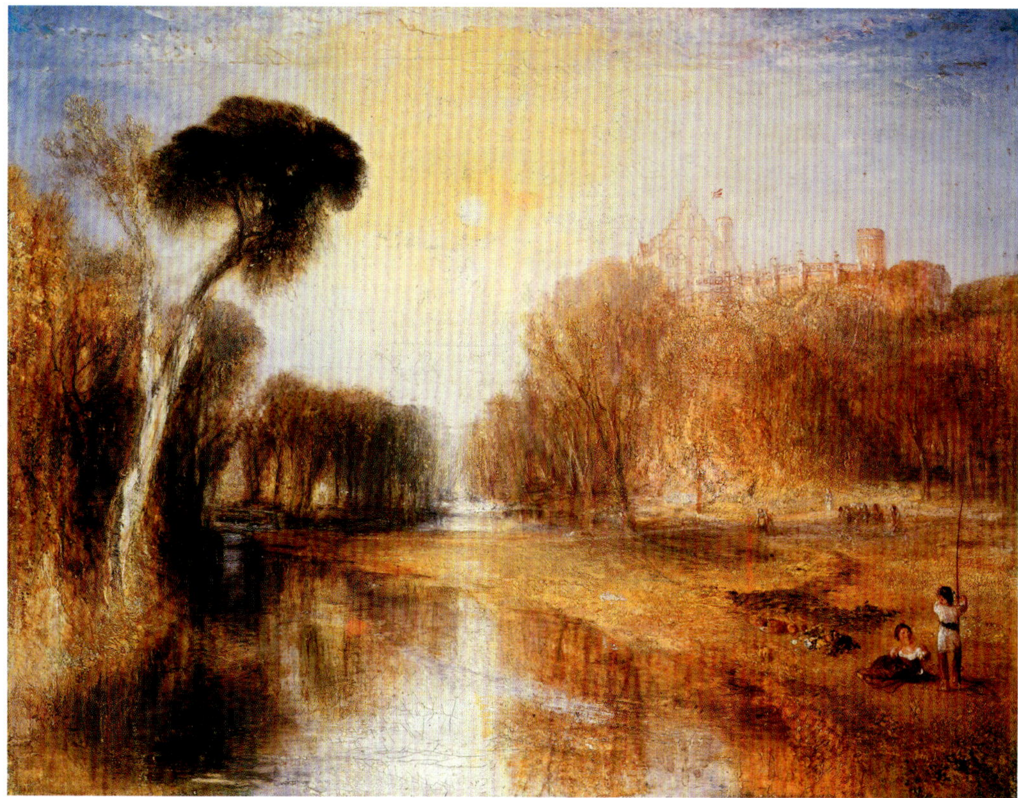

Schloss Rosenau, Seat of HRH Prince Albert of Coburg, 1841, oil on canvas, Walker Art Gallery, Liverpool, UK, 97 x 125cm (38 x 49in)

Perhaps seeking to curry royal favour, Turner, returning to England from Venice, stopped off at this town in the autumn of 1840. The Rosenau Castle, seen in Turner's picture on the right above the tree line, was the birthplace of Prince Albert, who earlier that year had married Britain's Queen Victoria. Despite the artist's best efforts, the royal family did not buy the painting.

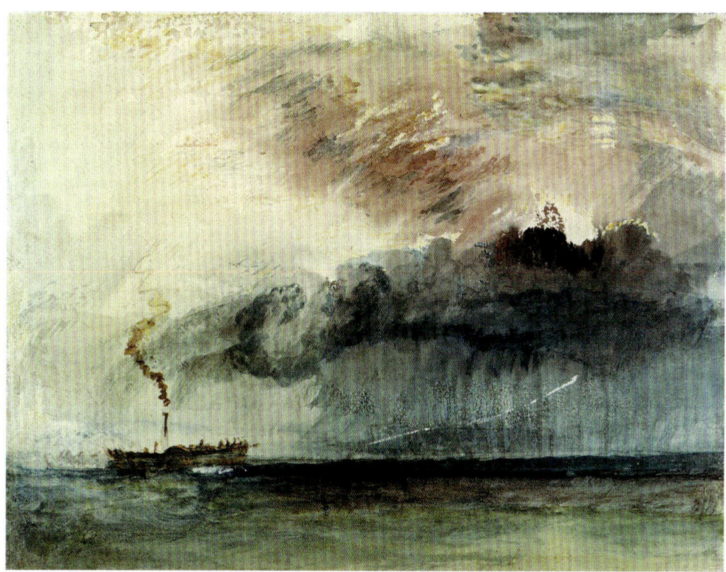

Steamboat in a Storm, 1841, pencil and watercolour, Paul Mellon Collection, Yale Center for British Art, CT, USA, 23 x 30cm (9 x 12in)

The location for this watercolour is not known, but it may be Venice. The dominance of blue gives a cool feel to the picture, the boat making 'full steam ahead' to escape the storm clouds and head into brighter skies. Turner has used a 'scratching out' technique to emphasize the waves.

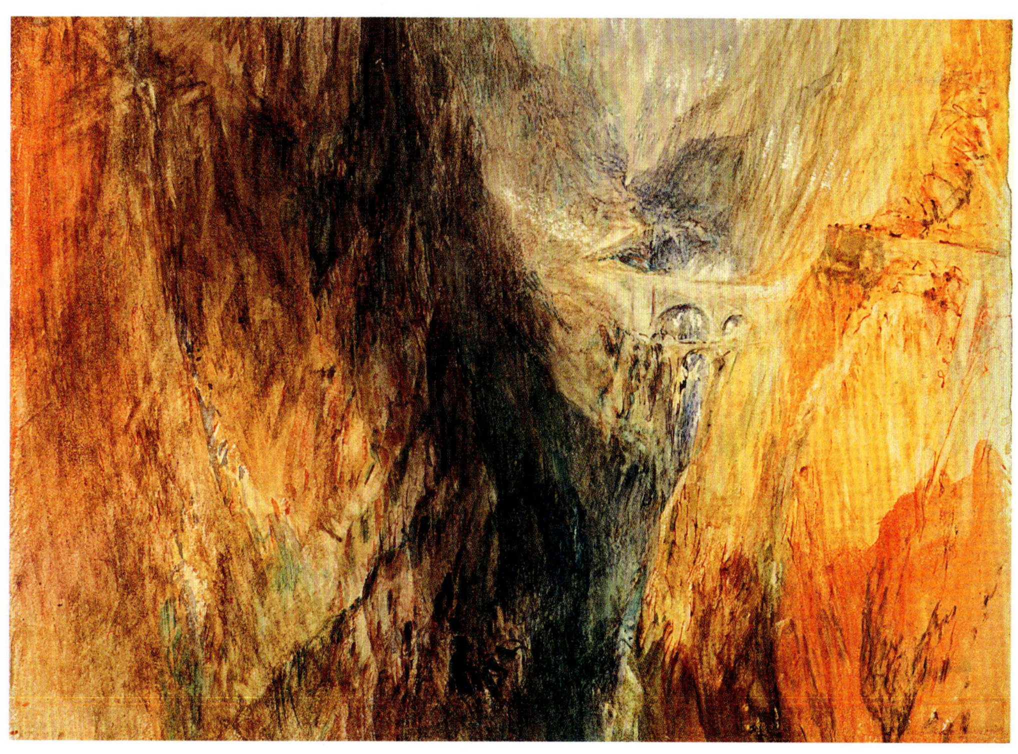

*The Devil's Bridge, St Gotthard, c.*1841, watercolour and ink, Fitzwilliam Museum, Cambridge, UK, 24 x 31cm (9 x 12in)

Because it was the main access route to the St Gotthard Pass, over the dangerous River Reuss, a wooden bridge had been in situ since the 13th century. This was replaced by a stone bridge in the 16th century which was destroyed during the Napoleonic Wars. It was finally replaced by a new stone bridge, which opened in 1830 and is depicted in Turner's watercolour.

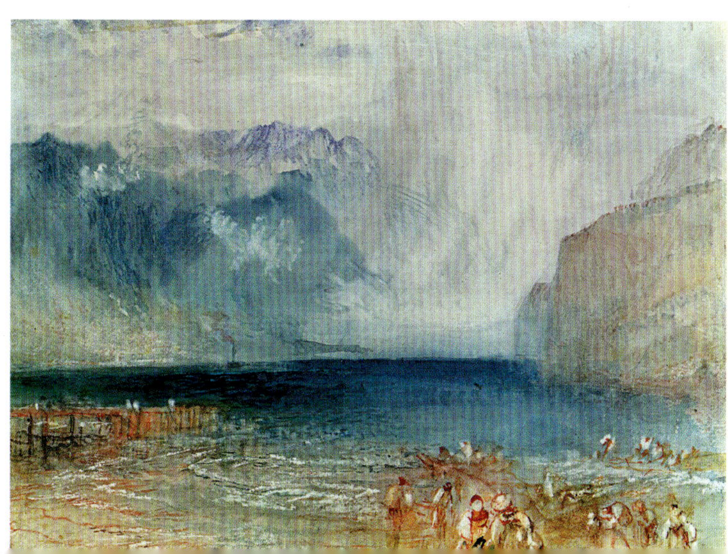

The First Steamer on the Lake of Lucerne, 1841, watercolour, University College, London, UK, 23 x 29cm (9 x 11in)

Described as possibly the most beautiful of the lakes in Switzerland, Lucerne has certainly the most variety, with mountains on all sides and forests to the shoreline in many places. The lake is irregular in shape, providing a surprise for the tourist around each bend. Having seen the potential for tourism, the authorities began providing steam ship cruises around the lake in the 19th century.

The Lake of Lucerne, Moonlight, the Rigi in the Distance, 1841, watercolour and bodycolour, Whitworth Art Gallery, University of Manchester, UK, 23 x 31cm (9 x 12in)

For Turner, the main quality of Lake Lucerne was the sense of tranquillity that the surroundings afforded him, as recorded in this watercolour. In 1841, he was 67 years old and not enjoying the best of health. The fresh, clean air and stress-free environment proved a tonic for the artist, and he returned here for the next three summers.

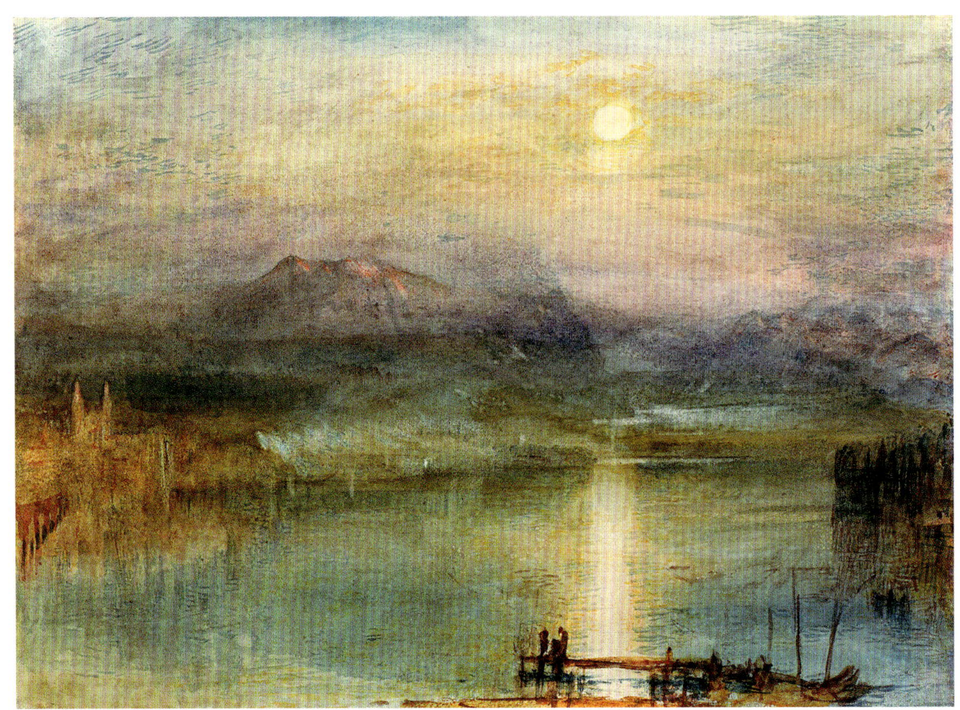

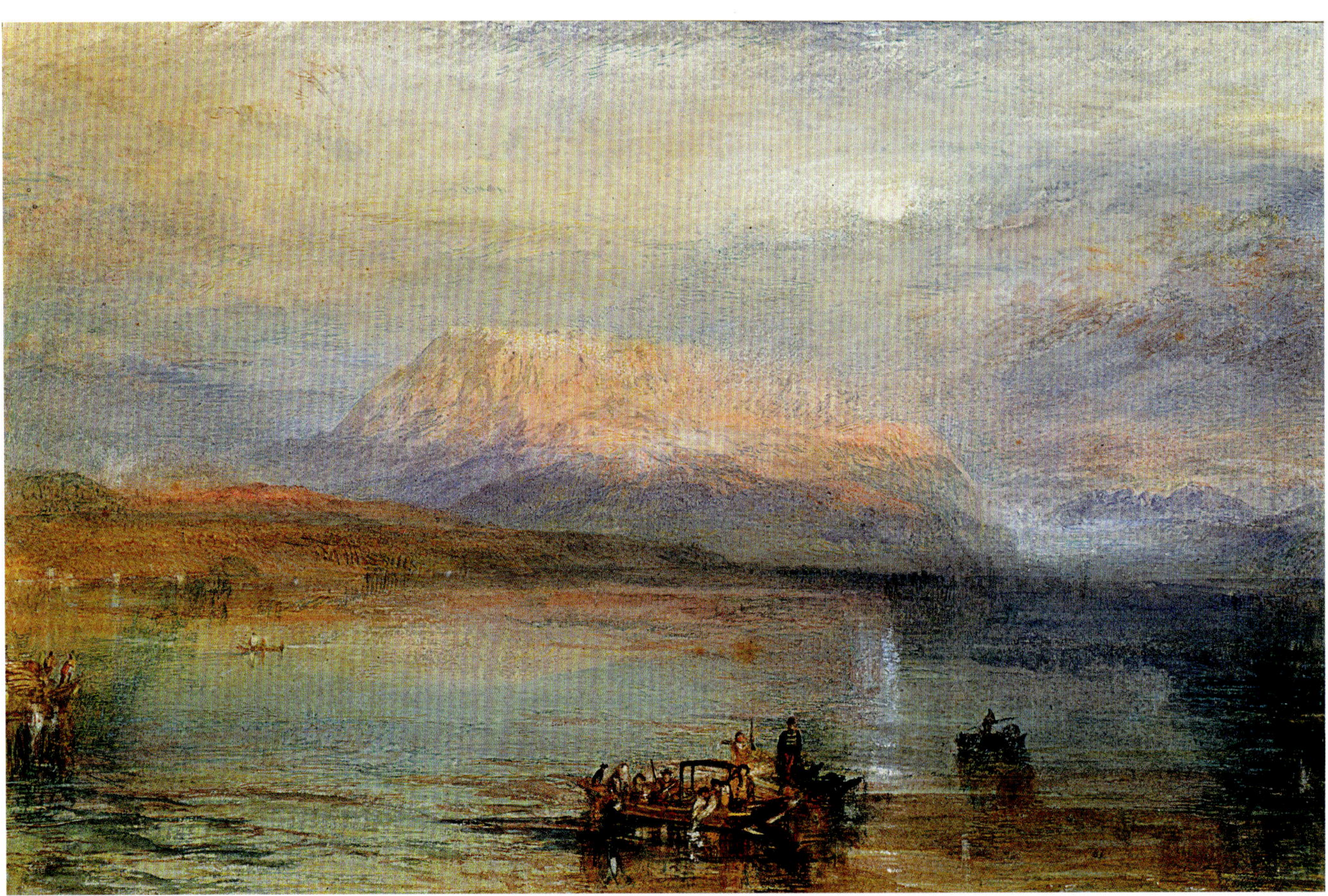

The Red Rigi, 1842, watercolour, National Gallery of Victoria, Melbourne, Australia, 31 x 46cm (12 x 18in)

Known as the 'Queen of the mountains', Rigi is part of the Alps, next to Lake Lucerne in central Switzerland. Turner stayed at the Schwan Inn, from where he sketched and executed watercolour studies of the mountain, a motif he was to repeat many times up until his death less than 10 years later. Hugh Munro of Novar purchased this picture, like so many others of its kind.

Convent du Bonhomme, Chamonix, 1836–42, watercolour, Fitzwilliam Museum, Cambridge, UK, 24 x 30cm (9 x 12in)

In the early 19th century, tourism had become an important part of Chamonix life, its growth gradually replacing agriculture as the economic mainstay of the area in the 20th century. Chamonix is located at the foot of Mont Blanc, the highest mountain in Europe, a mecca for tourists in both the summer and winter. Turner's picture is a pre-tourism rural idyll.

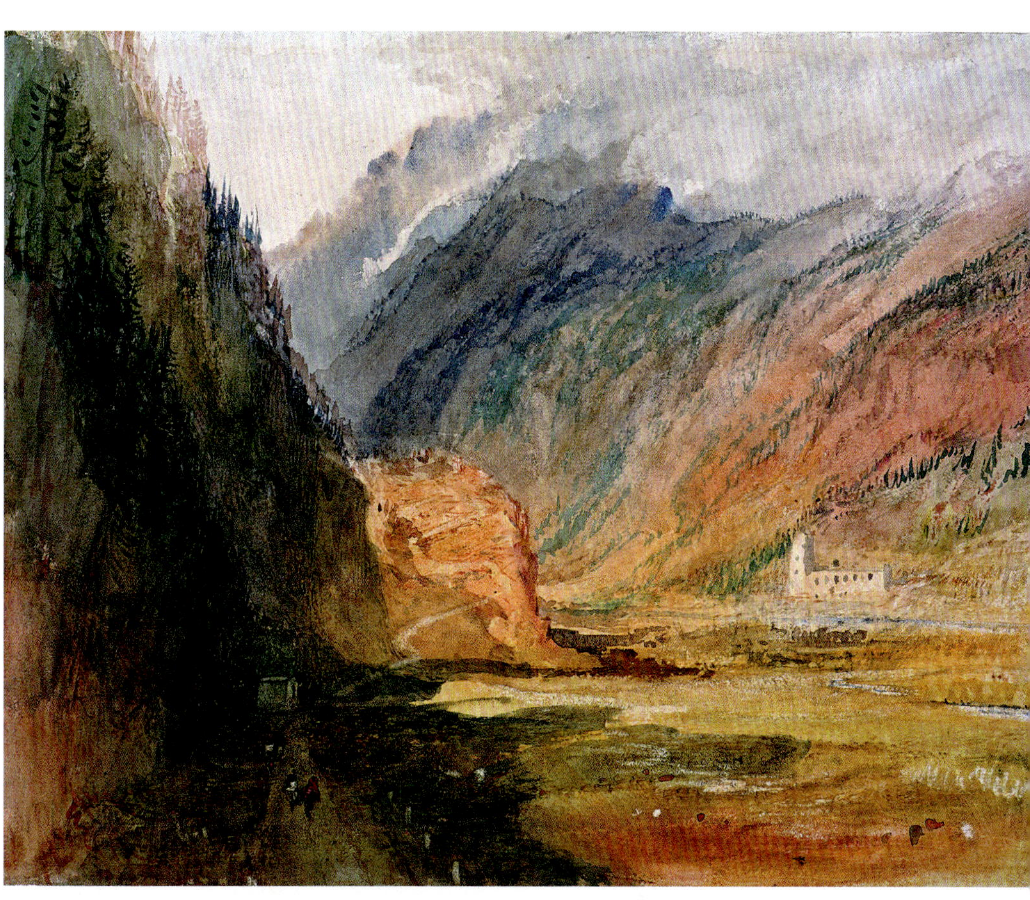

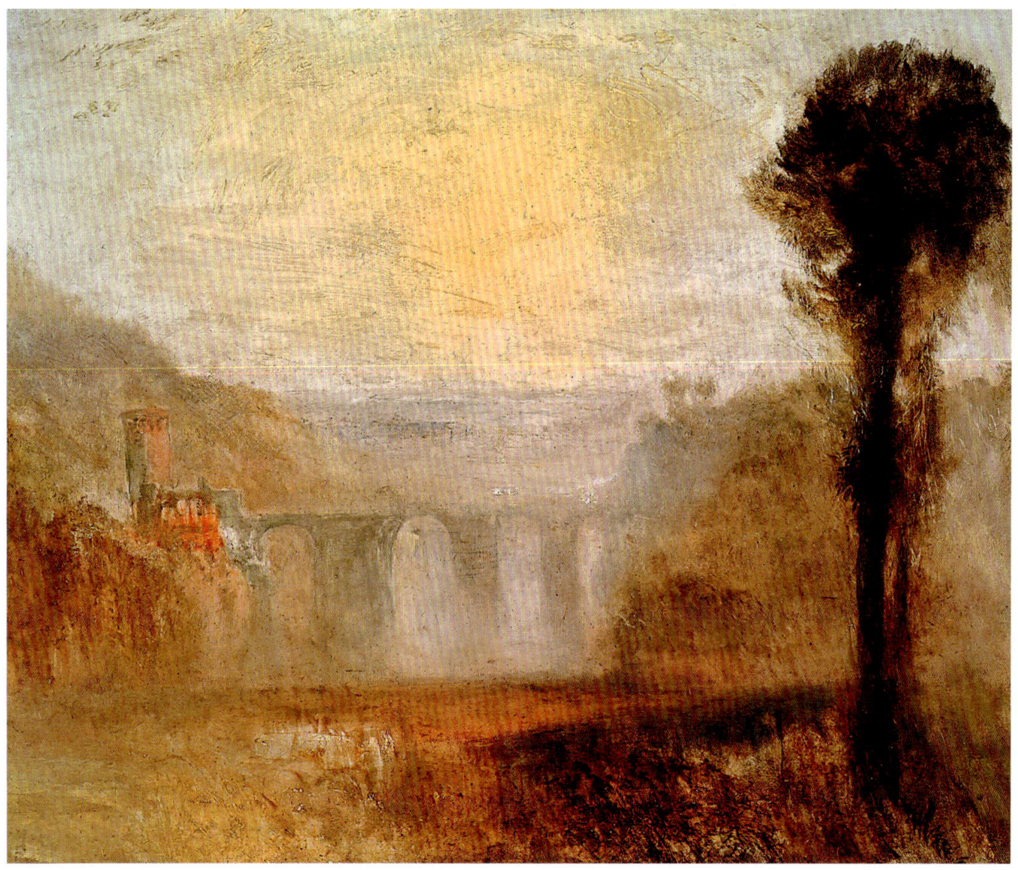

*The Ponte delle Torri, Spoleto, Italy, c.*1840, oil on canvas, Tate Britain, London, UK, 91 x 122cm (36 x 48in)

This painting was not exhibited in public until 1936 and was part of Turner's bequest. The motif for the work was taken from his Rome Sketchbook of 1819 and is a reworking of one of the *Liber Studiorum* plates. The painting reflects Turner's aspiration, the search for a tranquil Claudian-style landscape.

Zurich, 1842,
watercolour, British
Museum, London, UK,
30 x 46cm (12 x 18in)

This watercolour appears to
be the summation of a life's
study into topography, urban
life, reflective light and the
Romantic. Here we see the
birth of a modern city (albeit
a slightly romanticized view),
its inhabitants – who have
shaken off their past under
the *Zuriputsch* of 1839 –
going about their daily lives.
The medieval walls have been
torn down in preparation for
the formation of the Swiss
Federal State.

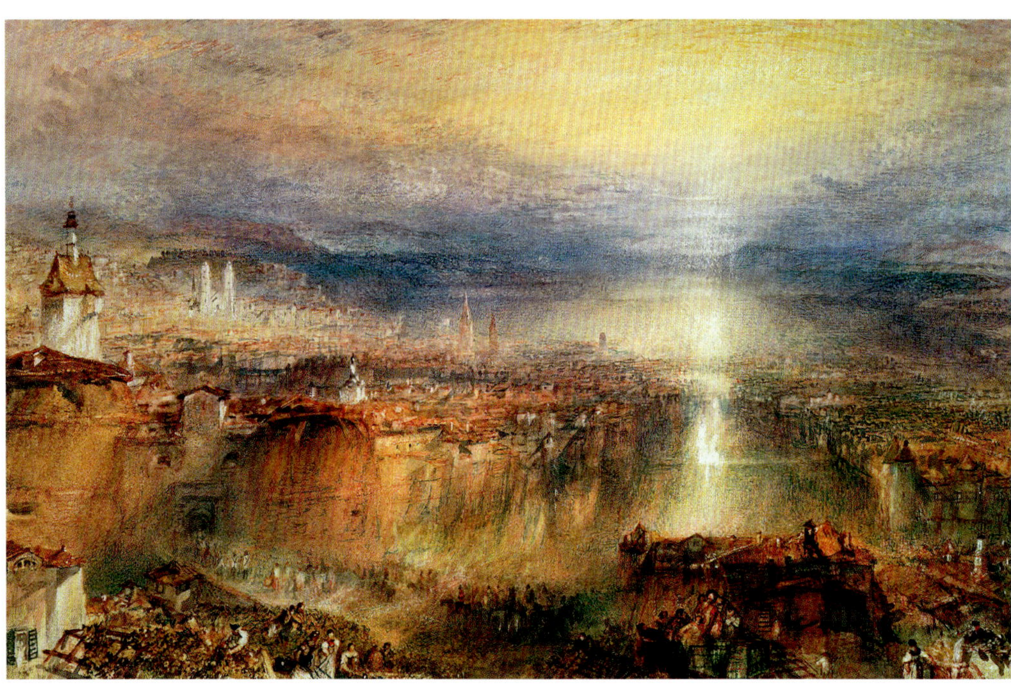

*Snow Storm: Steam Boat off a
Harbour's Mouth Making
Signals in Shallow Water, and
Going by the Lead*, 1842,
oil on canvas,
Tate Britain, London, UK,
92 x 122cm (36 x 48in)

This work, one of the most
talked about and written
about of Turner's paintings,
was not understood at the
Academy exhibition of 1842.
One critic referred to it as a
"mass of soapsuds and
whitewash", vitriol that hurt
the artist. Turner did,
however, perpetuate a myth,
yet to be proven, that he
was inspired to create this
work by lashing himself to a
mast during a storm.

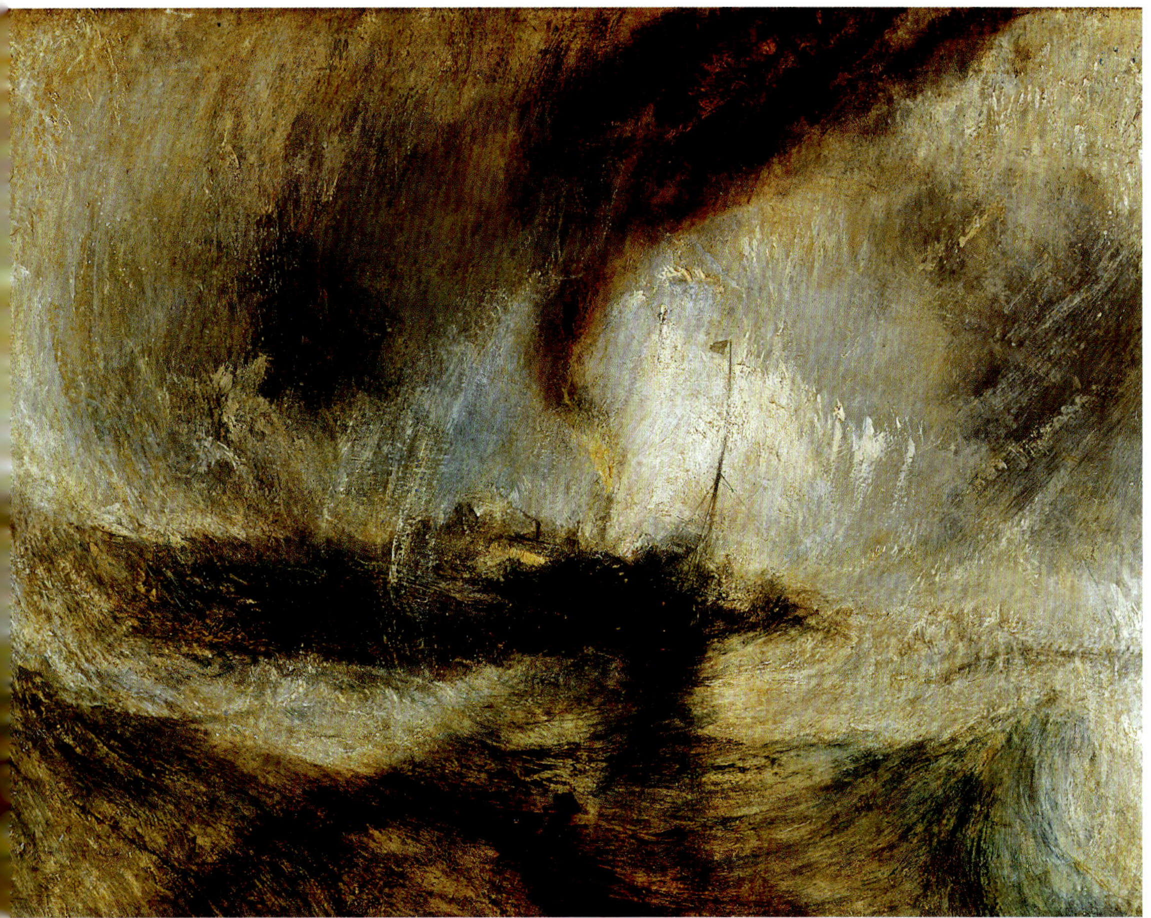

The Dogana and Santa Maria della Salute, Venice, 1843, oil on canvas, National Gallery of Art, Washington, DC, USA, 62 x 93cm (24 x 37in)

Some critics considered that this picture was "divested of all absurdities…content to copy nature as she is". It is a rare example of a portrait-format painting by Turner and it was sold at the 1843 Academy exhibition. Equally unusual was the picture's showing at the Royal Birmingham Society of Artists the same year, probably at the instigation of its owner, who was a resident of the city.

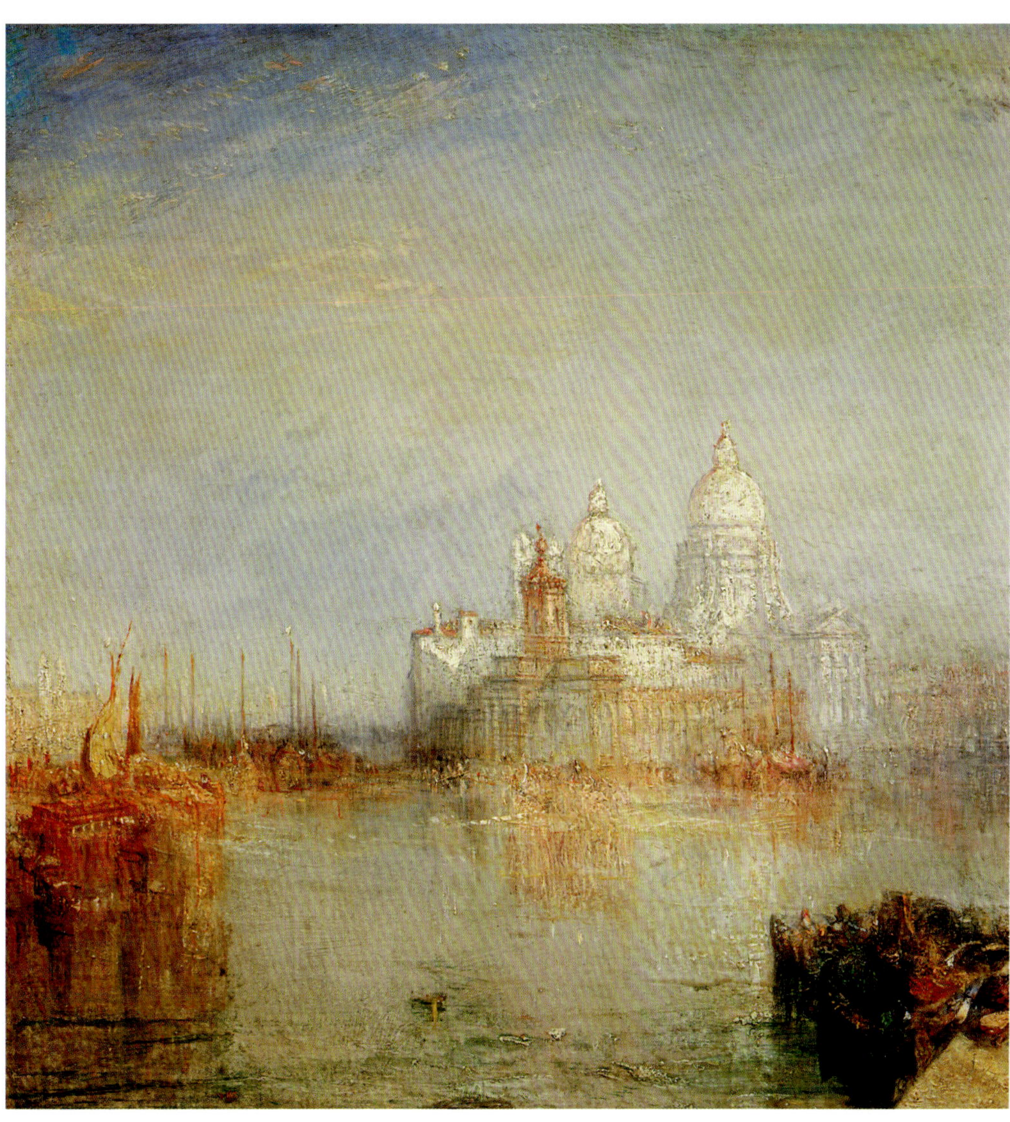

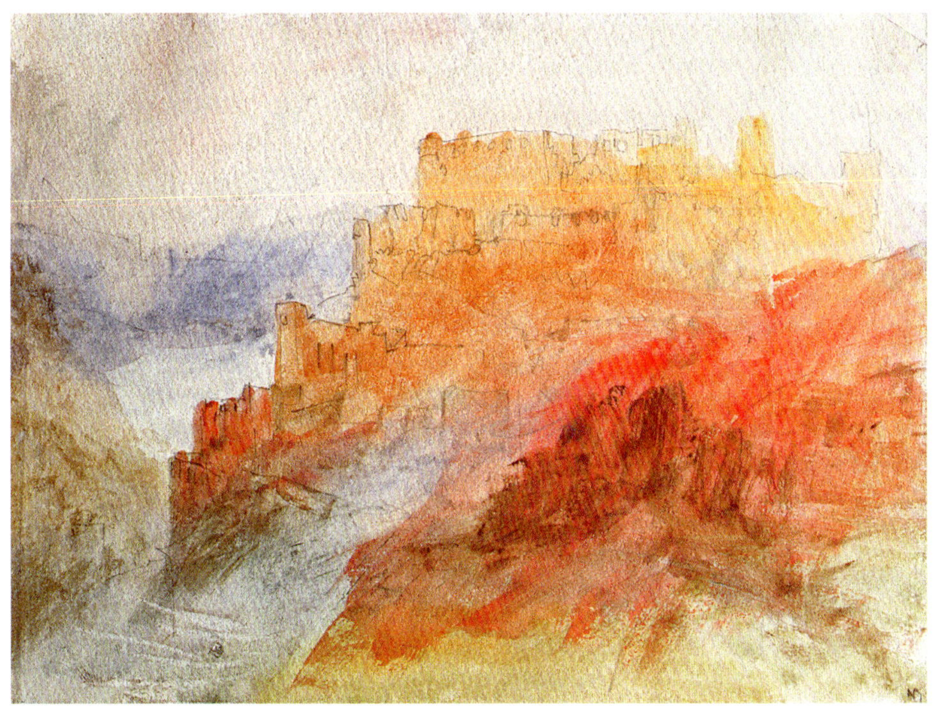

A Castle above a Chasm, c.1841–4, pencil and watercolour, Private Collection, 18 x 24cm (7 x 9in)

The identity of the castle is unknown since for Turner it was no longer a matter of topographical interest, but a vehicle for exploring the use of colour to create spatial awareness. The use of red in the foreground and its echo around the castle has the effect of bringing the castle into the viewer's own space. This is helped by the cooler receding blue and purple in the background.

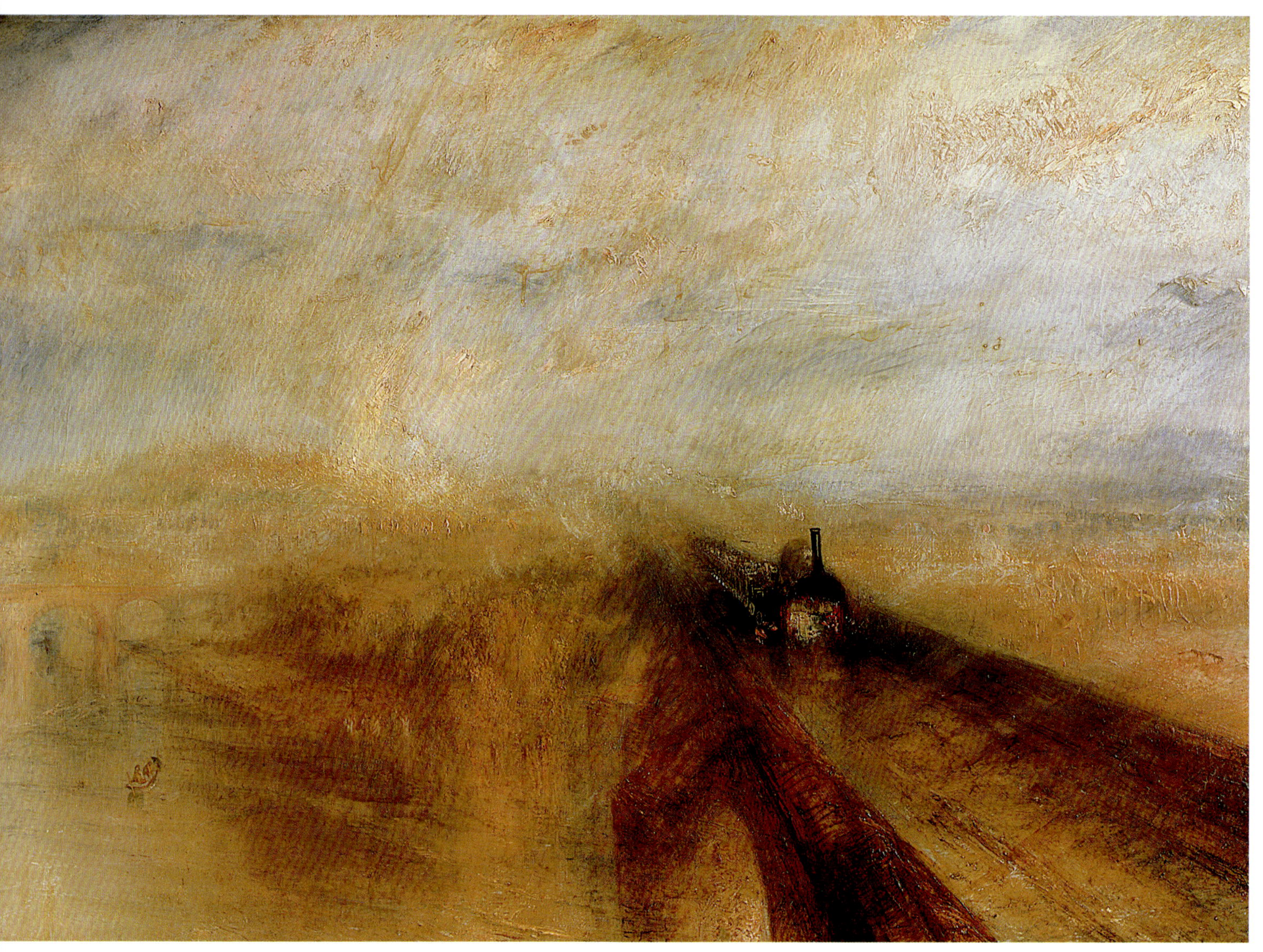

Rain, Steam and Speed – The Great Western Railway, 1844, oil on canvas, National Gallery, London, UK, 91 x 122cm (36 x 48in)

A legend that Turner had put his head out of the window of a moving train, while it was raining, has surrounded this painting ever since it was exhibited at the Academy. A visitor to the exhibition, who had seen the artist do this on the train, had copied his example and immediately recognized the effect in the painting. Whether it is true or not, the picture is legendary for its bravura technique.

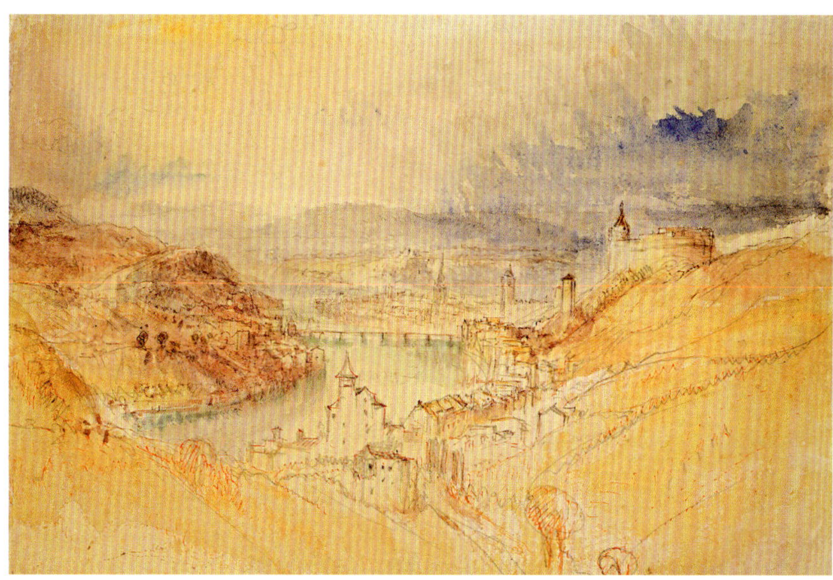

Schaffhausen, 1841–4, watercolour and ink, Fitzwilliam Museum, Cambridge, UK, 24 x 33cm (9 x 13in)

Schaffhausen is in the centre of Switzerland. Turner went there on his trip in 1802 and made notes, which he used for many of the watercolours executed much later, including this one. This one is less about 'the view' and more about the atmosphere of the Swiss Alps, bathed in the summer sunlight.

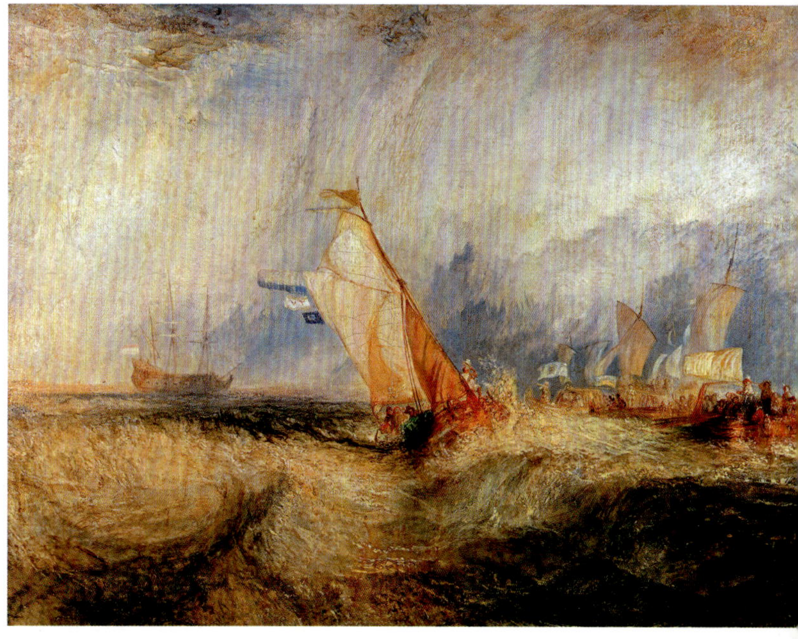

Van Tromp Going about to Please his Masters, Ships at Sea, Getting a Good Wetting, 1844, oil on canvas, Getty Museum, Los Angeles, CA, USA, 91 x 122cm (36 x 48in)

Turner returned to a Dutch influence in this painting, not just in aesthetic but for subject matter too.

The narrative for this picture comes from an admiral of the Dutch fleet who, in the 17th century, refused to obey orders and pursued his own tactics during the Anglo-Dutch wars. Turner's title suggests the subsequent reconciliation between Cornelis van Tromp and his masters.

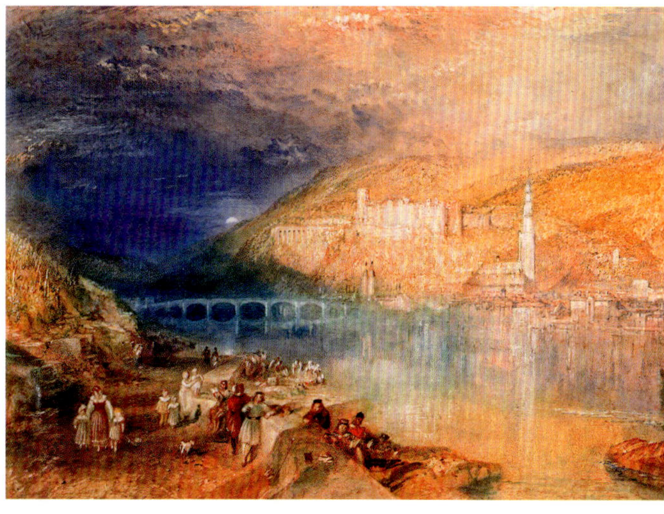

*Heidelberg, c.*1840–2, watercolour, Manchester Art Gallery, UK, 38 x 55cm (15 x 22in)

In the year 1815, the Emperor of Austria, the Tsar of Russia and the King of Prussia formed the so-called 'Holy Alliance' in Heidelberg following the defeat of Napoleon. Turner, however, was more interested in the city's older history and its Romantic connotations as the centre of famous German poets and writers such as Joseph von Eichendorff. The artist has highlighted the medieval ruins of the castle, which had defied recent attempts to rebuild it, and the medieval Church of the Holy Spirit.

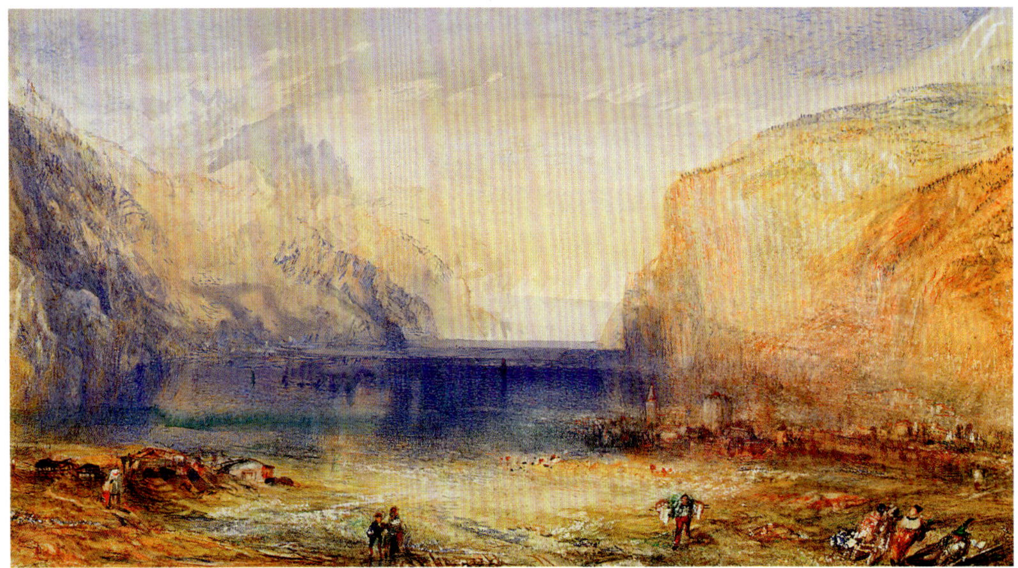

Fluelen: Morning (Looking towards the Lake), 1845, watercolour and bodycolour, Paul Mellon Collection, Yale Center for British Art, CT, USA, 30 x 48cm (12 x 19in)

Fluelen is in the Swiss Canton of Uri on the edge of Lake Lucerne. The valley extends into the St Gotthard Pass, which in Turner's day was impassable in the winter. The town, which suffered during the Napoleonic Wars, is depicted in peacetime.

A Swiss Pass, watercolour, c.1848–50, Victoria and Albert Museum, London, UK, 36 x 51cm (14 x 20in)

In the last decade of his life, Turner managed four visits to Switzerland. The Swiss Alps became his final motif, one that reflected his love of the Sublime. Unlike his first watercolours there is no topographical interest in the work. Instead it is imbued with a sense of isolation and scale that dwarfs human egotism.

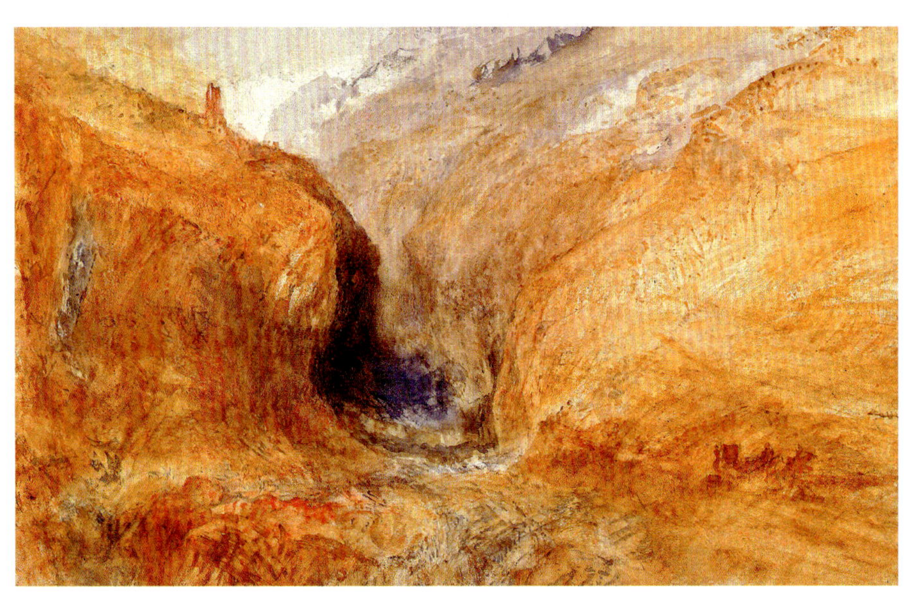

The Day after the Storm, 1840–5, oil on canvas, National Gallery of Wales, Cardiff, UK, 31 x 53cm (12 x 21in)

Turner painted many seascapes at this time: two were companion pieces, this one and *The Storm*, inspired by an event witnessed at Mrs Booth's in Margate. John Pounds, Mrs Booth's son by her first marriage, inherited both pictures. Miss Margaret Davies later purchased both pictures via different sources.

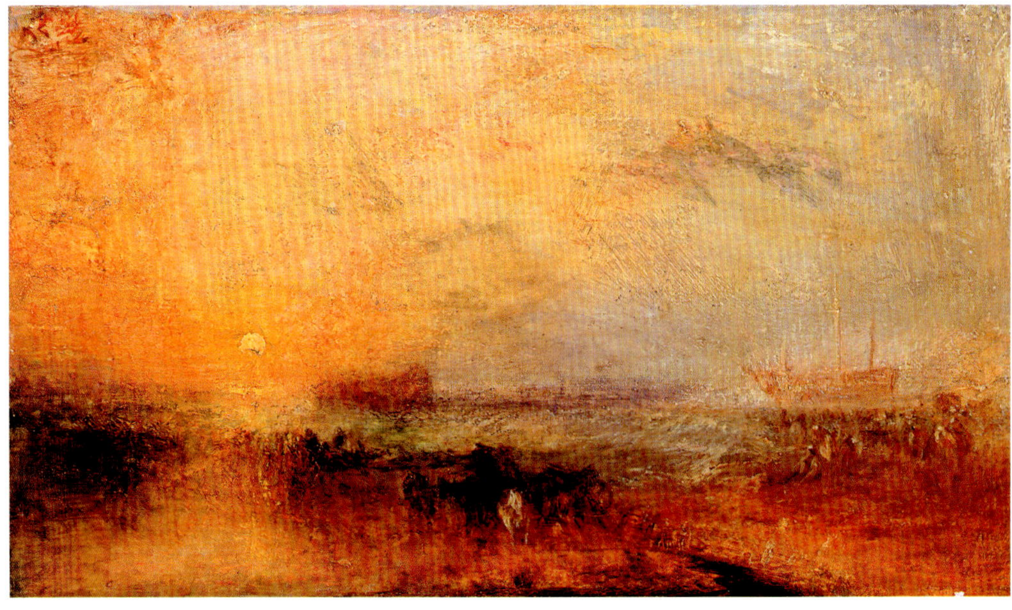

Norham Castle, Sunrise, *c*.1845, oil on canvas, Tate Britain, London, UK, 91 x 122cm (36 x 48in)

Although he painted several views of Norham Castle, the first as early as 1797, this one is the first and only time it had been executed in oil. The composition is similar to the *Liber Studiorum* version that was published in 1816 under 'Pastoral' subjects. The oil painting used many of Turner's watercolour techniques.

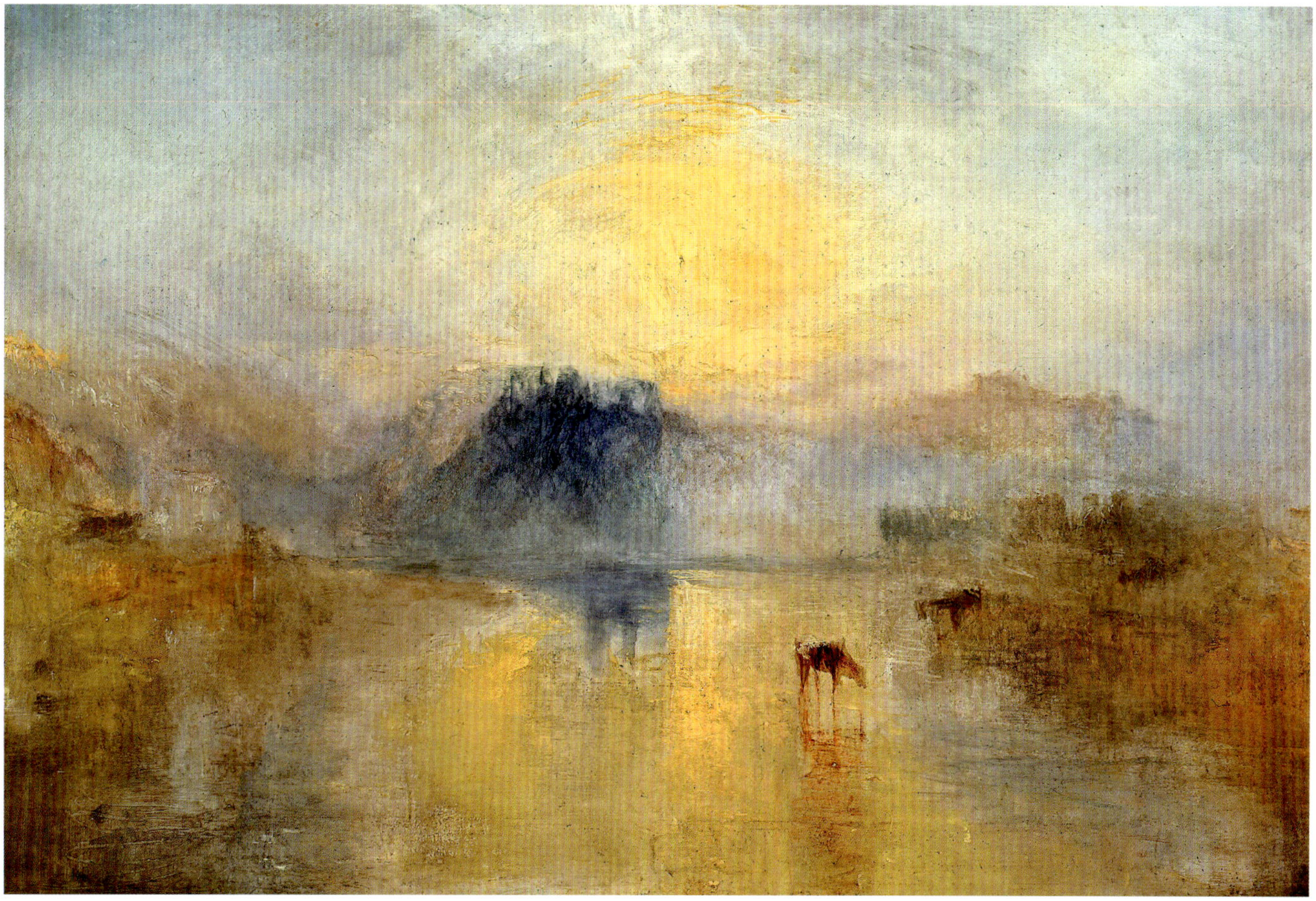

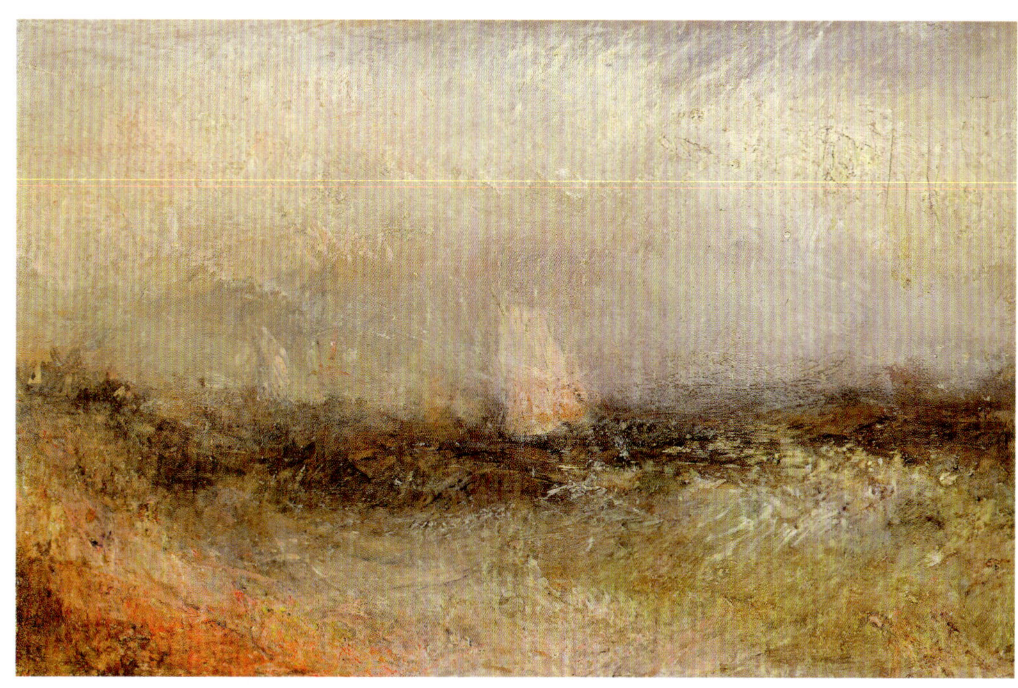

Off the Nore: Wind and Water, *c*.1845, oil on paper, laid down, Paul Mellon Collection, Yale Center for British Art, CT, USA, 31 x 46cm (12 x 18in)

That Turner painted this on paper suggests that it was not intended for exhibition in the first instance. Like many other oil paintings of his late period, this was an experiment in colour and technique. The Nore is a coastal area at the estuary of the River Thames, and the site of a famous naval mutiny in 1797 over pay and conditions.

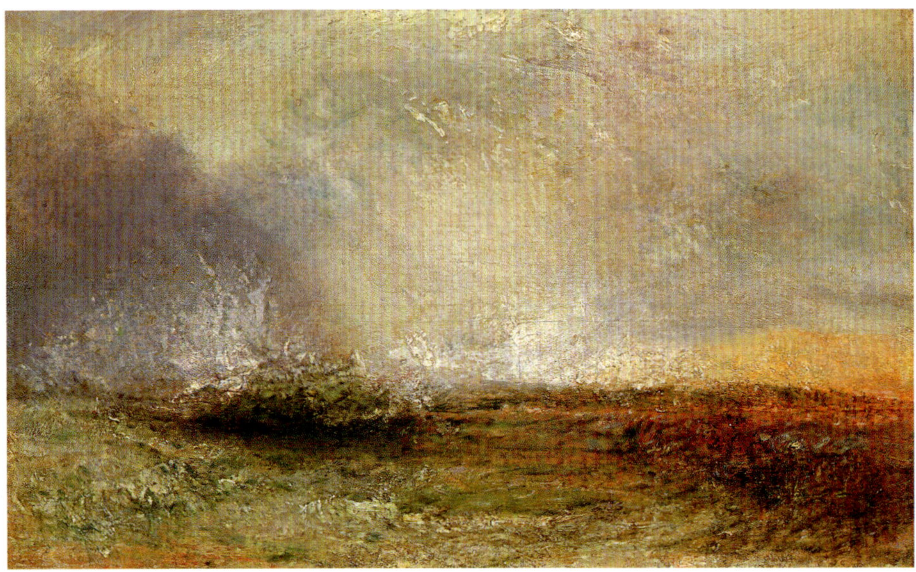

Stormy Sea Breaking on a Shore, c.1840–45, oil on canvas, Paul Mellon Collection, Yale Center for British Art, CT, USA, 45 x 64cm (18 x 25in)

Before its sale to an American collector in 1889, this picture may have belonged to John Pound, the son of Sophia Booth from a previous marriage, who must have disposed of it privately since there are no auction records for it.

Inverary Pier, Loch Fyne, Morning, 1845, oil on canvas, Paul Mellon Collection, Yale Center for British Art, CT, USA, 91 x 122cm (36 x 48in)

Certain motifs that Turner used repeatedly can be used to gauge how his style developed and changed over his long career. The early watercolour version of this picture, translated into an etching for his *Liber Studiorum*, was typical of 18th-century topographical landscape painting. By contrast this oil painting is pure landscape abstraction with no visual markers as to location, anticipating developments in the 20th century.

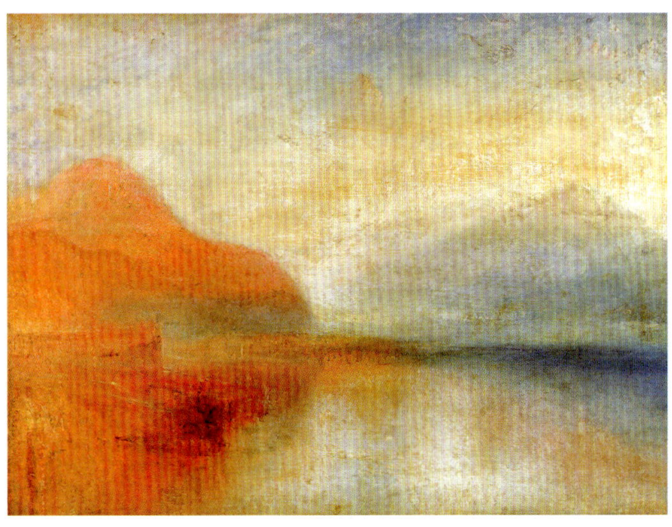

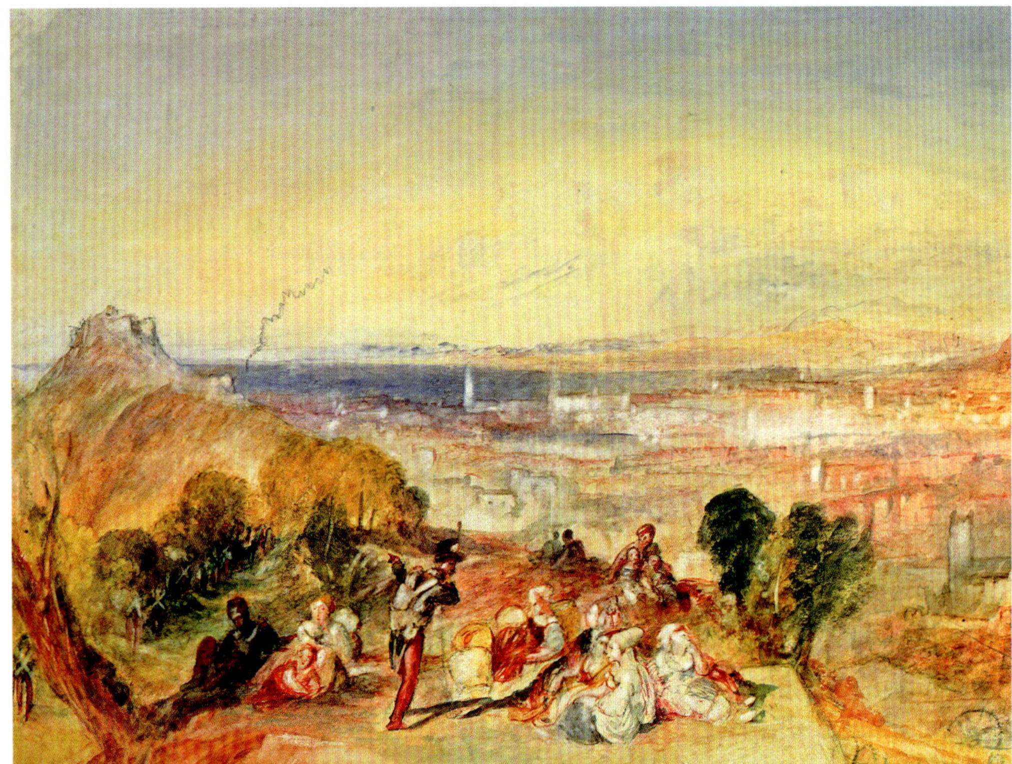

Genoa, 1850–1, pencil and watercolour, Manchester Art Gallery, UK, 37 x 54cm (15 x 21in)

One of the last paintings completed by Turner, this watercolour is a return to the style and subject matter that brought him fame and wealth. Turner was first and foremost a landscape painter and, although his mature style bordered on abstraction and anticipated 20th-century developments, he is revered as the most successful proponent of the genre, before and since.

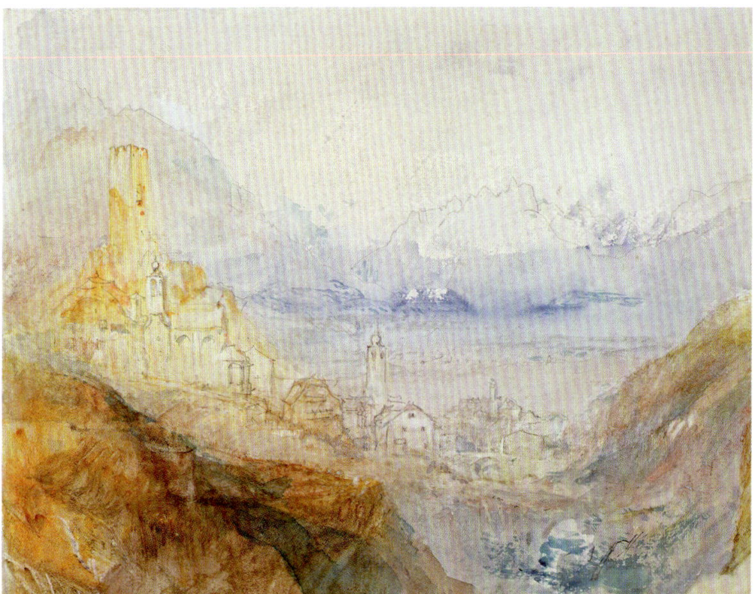

Hospenthal, Fall of St Gotthard, Morning, 1841–2, graphite and watercolour, Fitzwilliam Museum, Cambridge, UK, 23 x 29cm (9 x 11in)

The *hospenthal* or hospice was a refuge for poor travellers. Ever-increasing numbers of tourists came to visit this area, travelling to and from the climb to St Gotthard's Pass. This is one of two paintings of that Hospenthal, which no longer exists.

The Storm, 1840–5, oil on canvas, National Museums and Gallery of Wales, Cardiff, UK, 32 x 55cm (13 x 22in)

A label on the back of this painting states that the artist painted this during the great storm of 21 November 1840. It is, however, more likely that he relied on eyewitness accounts of the storm, since he was in poor health and was capable of using his imagination, having painted so many shipwrecks and storms before.

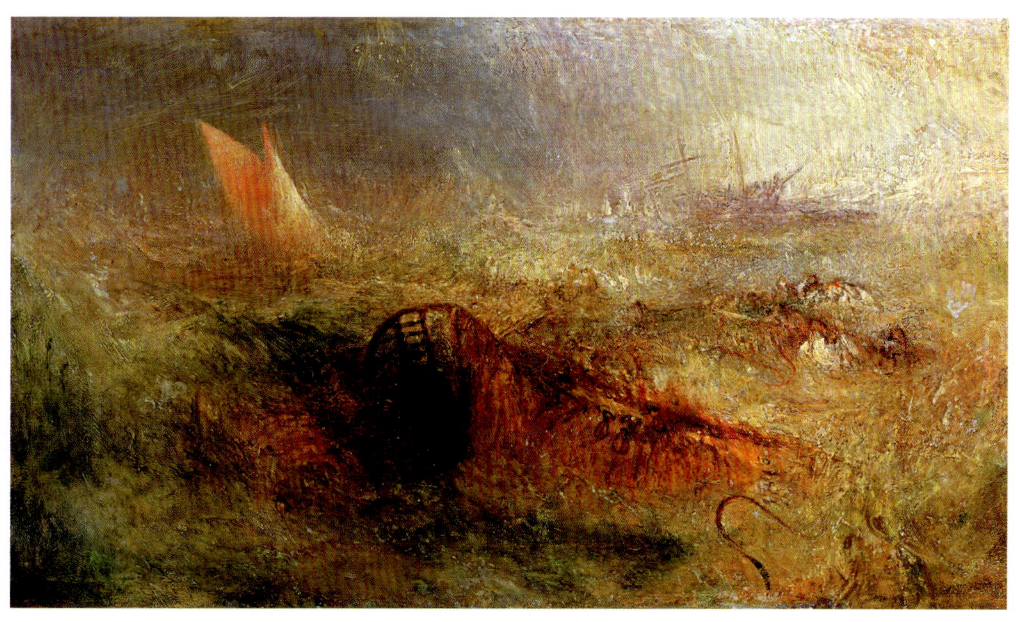

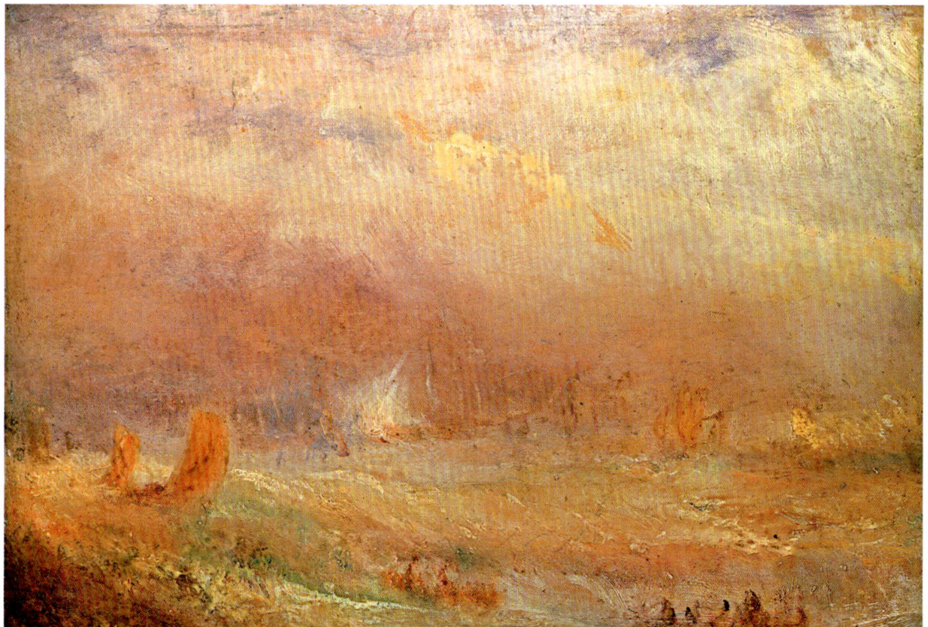

Off Deal, 1835–45, oil on board, Nationalmuseum, Stockholm, Sweden, 25 x 32cm (10 x 13in)

The dating of this painting and its companion piece *A Sailing Boat off Deal* is imprecise because of the provenance. In the 1960s, other oil sketches were unearthed at the British Museum so that works of a similar nature and style could be given approximate dates.

INDEX

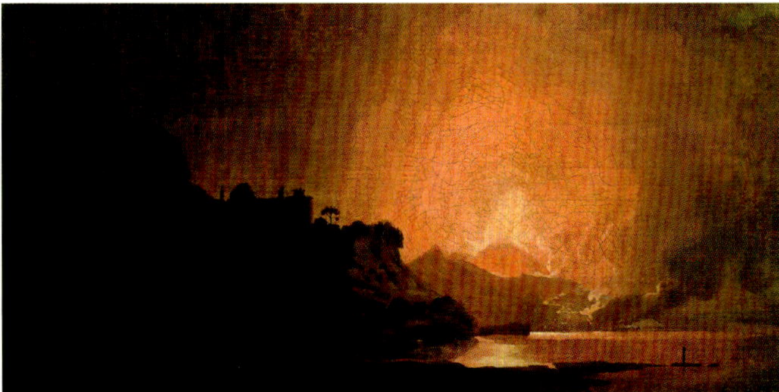

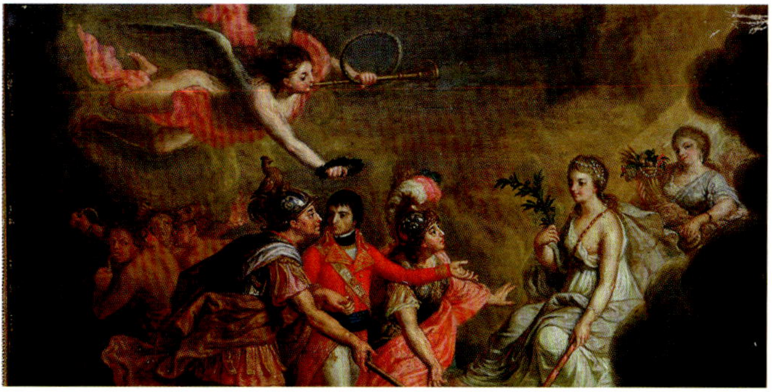

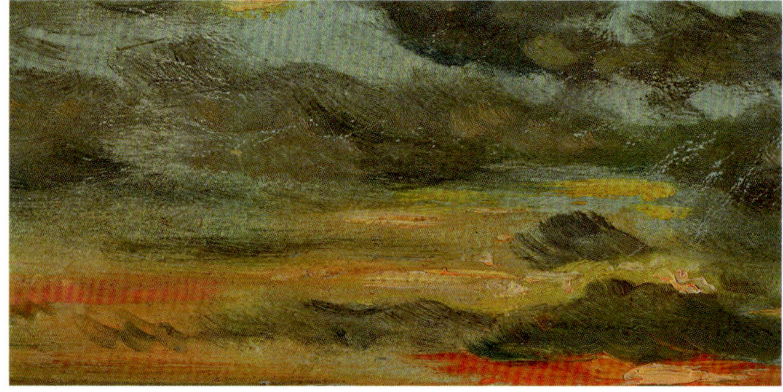

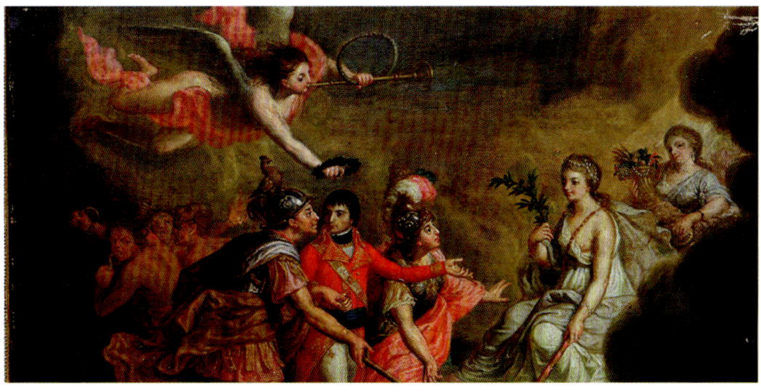

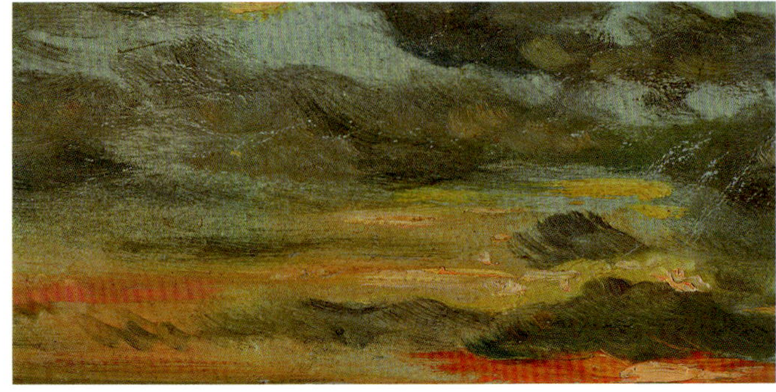

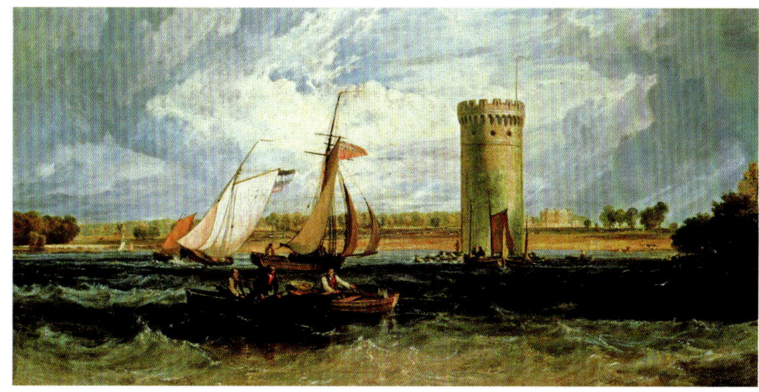

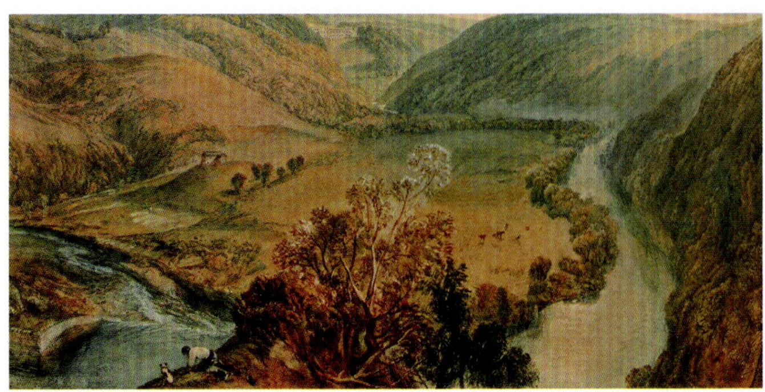

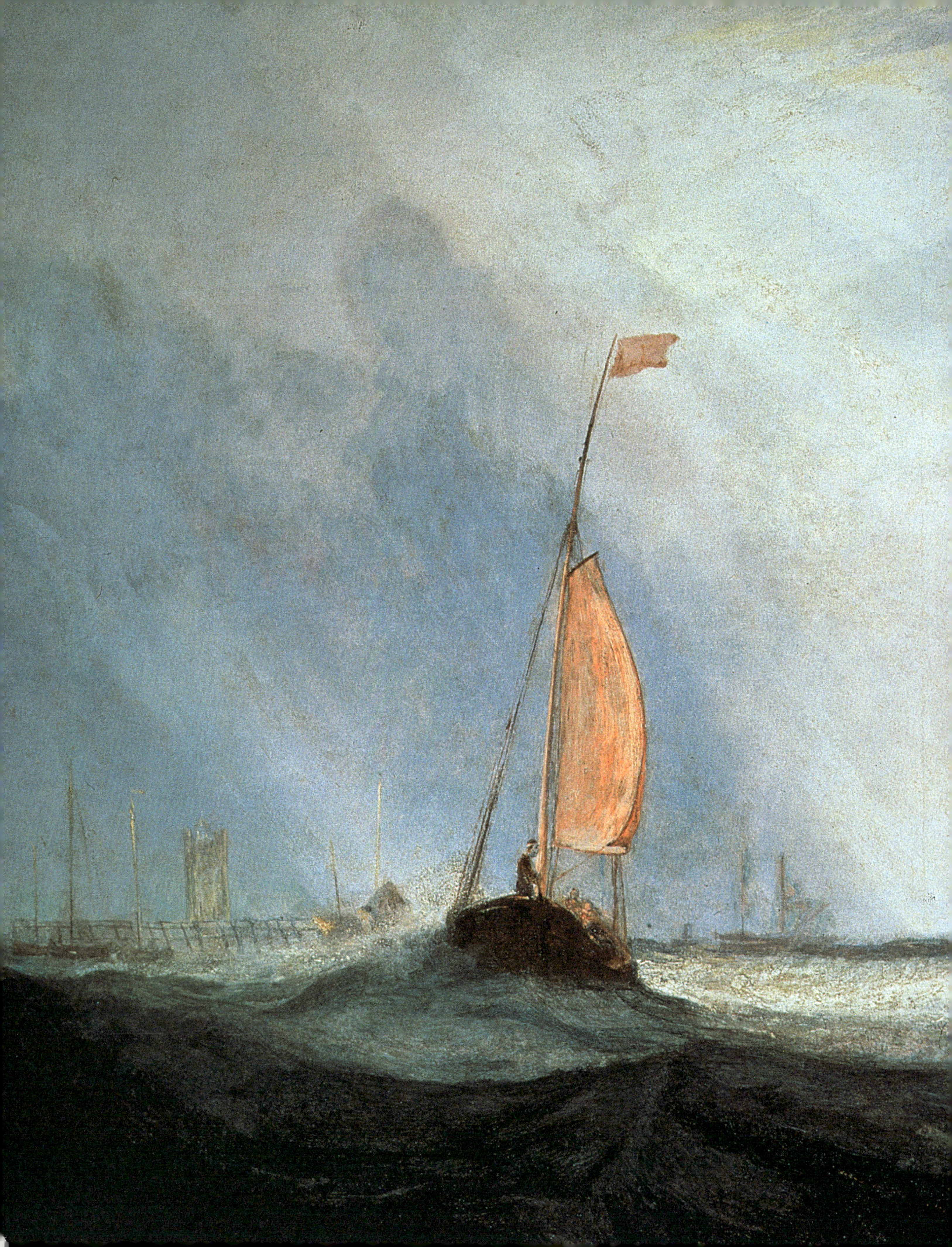